BARRON'S
COOKING GUIDE

Food Lover's Companion

COMPREHENSIVE DEFINITIONS OF OVER 3000 FOOD, WINE AND CULINARY TERMS

By
SHARON TYLER HERBST

BARRON'S

All inquiries should be addressed to:
Barron's Educational Series, Inc.
250 Wireless Boulevard
Hauppauge, New York 11788

International Standard Book No. 0-8120-4156-9

Library of Congress Catalog Card No. 89-140

Library of Congress Cataloging-in-Publication Data

Herbst, Sharon Tyler.
   The food lover's companion/Sharon Tyler Herbst.
      p.   cm.
   Bibliography: p. 574
   ISBN 0-8120-4156-9
   1. Cookery—Dictionaries. I. Title.
TX349.H533   1989
641.5'03'21—dc19   89-140
                                          CIP

PRINTED IN THE UNITED STATES OF AMERICA

34 9770 98

CONTENTS

DEDICATION

Dedicated with love to Ron—my inspiration, my strength and my delight—for the countless hours he spent helping me research this tome, and for his constant support and continual encouragement to become all I can be.

ACKNOWLEDGMENTS

In a book of this scope, you can be sure that there are plenty of people behind the scenes. By all accounts, there are well over 250,000 words in *Food Lover's Companion*, and it took more than one set of eyes to make sure that the information and format were as error-free as possible. So I'm delighted to have the opportunity to acknowledge several special people who were involved in this project. A warm and affectionate thanks to . . .

My parents—Mother for instilling in me a love of words, and Dad for imbuing me with his optimistic outlook on life. Both attributes were called upon continually as I wrote *Food Lover's Companion*.

Veronica (Roni) Durie, my dear friend and the editor of all but one of my books (this one included), for her talent, for her faith in me and for the countless spirit-lifting words of long-distance encouragement at the end of many a 16-hour work day.

Carolyn Horne, Project Editor and my guiding light at Barron's, for her special expertise with this type of book and, just as important to me, for her patience and good humor.

Bev Bennett, my friend and fellow food writer, for sharing with me her incredible knowledge of food in an effort to make this book as accurate as possible.

Grace Freedson, Barron's Publicity Manager, for verbally holding my hand throughout this seemingly endless project.

Pat Connell, who edited *The Joy of Cookies* for me and who was the copy editor on this book, for her skill with words, especially foreign ones.

And all the behind-the-scenes people at Barron's who were involved in the artwork, layout, printing and everything else it took to bring this book together.

INTRODUCTION

"There is no love sincerer than the love of food."

—George Bernard Shaw

Every now and then during the almost three years it took me to research and write *Food Lover's Companion,* one of my friends (often a fellow food writer) would ask, "Why on earth did you ever begin such a huge project?" The answer was simple: I wrote it because I've always wanted such a book . . . and because two major passions in my life are words and food. In short, it was a labor of love.

As will quickly become obvious, this book—unlike my first three—is not a cookbook. There is, in fact, not a single recipe in it. What it is, instead, is an A-to-Z guide to food and drink that's a cross in scope between a dictionary and an encyclopedia. Or as my husband Ron dubbed it, a *dictopedia.*

It's doubtful that any book of this genre could include *all* the information available. If it did, it most certainly would be exorbitantly priced and impossible to lift. I have tried, however, to include everything in *Food Lover's Companion* that I've always wanted in a food reference book . . . namely, lots of data on a broad spectrum of subjects written in a conversational, not esoteric, tone. It's chock-full of food, drink and culinary terms and defines more than 3,300 entries on a broad range of subjects including: foods (ranging from everyday ingredients to those more exotic comestibles used in Middle Eastern, Indian, Greek, Chinese, Japanese, Caribbean, European and South American cuisines); cooking techniques; foreign-food terms; dishes and sauces; cuts of meat; styles of preparation; kitchen equipment; menu terms; potables including wines, liqueurs, beers, liquors and mixed drinks; and much, much more.

In addition, sprinkled throughout this book are hundreds of informative tidbits ranging from facts on how to choose, store and use ingredients . . . to the genesis of various foods and dishes . . . to historical lore on food, drink and gastronomy in general . . . to pronunciations for all but the most basic words. And because I've always been intrigued with the origin of words, etymological background is included in many definitions—a tricky business, since historians will forever argue such issues as how the French soup **billy bi** or the sweet yeast bread **Sally Lunn** came to be named.

And since charts are such a quick and easy reference, I've also included plenty of those on a variety of subjects including equivalents for common measurements, candymaking temperatures, herbs and spices, substitutions for common ingredients, additives, a buying guide for ingredients, altitude adjustments for baking, metric conversions, microwave information, temperature conversions from Fahrenheit to Celsius, and comparative baking pan substitutions. (See the Table of Contents for chart page numbers.

I wrote *Food Lover's Companion* not only for cooks (both amateur and professional), but for *anyone* who loves good food and drink. Whether its a home cook who's curious about **raclette cheese** . . . a professional chef who wants to verify how to garnish an **à la Conti** dish . . . or a bachelor who wants to impress a date with the correct pronunciation of **prix fixe** . . . each one will, I hope, find an answer in *Food Lover's Companion*.

As I researched this book, one fact became patently obvious: there are few definitives in the ever-expanding universe of food and drink. I discovered, for instance, that the word **prawn** is used to describe several different shellfish. And there seems to be immense confusion regarding some terms, one such being **endive**. My aim in writing *Food Lover's Companion* was simple: to be as thorough and accurate as possible, and to deliver the information in a clear, concise manner. And if an ambiguity or two is dispelled along the way, all the better.

In the end, I found that the most difficult part about writing this book was *ending* it. For this fascinating realm of food and drink is in a constant state of evolution. New discoveries seem to occur weekly, changes almost every day . . . how could one possibly conclude such a seemingly infinite subject? I constantly found myself going back to make changes and additions. It was clear that this book could easily grow in size to the culinary equivalent of *War and Peace*.

And so, with more than a modicum of regret, I wrote my last word, flipped the switch on my computer and watched the console fade to black. Now I humbly pass my labor of love on to you, the reader. Hopefully, you'll savor and enjoy it and—in the best of all possible worlds—discover some wonderful bits of information that will delight and inform you. In closing, my simple wish is that the pleasure you receive from reading *Food Lover's Companion* is as great as mine was in writing it.

HOW TO USE THIS BOOK

ENTRIES ARE ARRANGED alphabetically and cross-referenced. Alphabetization is by letter, rather than by word, so that multiple-word entries are treated as single words. For instance, **al dente** is handled as though it were spelled without spacing (*aldente*), and therefore follows **alcohol** and precedes **ale**.

Entries are in lowercase, unless capitals are required for the proper form of the word, as in the case of **Kahlúa** and **Nantua sauce**. All but the most basic words have pronunciations (*see* Pronunciation Guide, page xi). A term with several meanings will list all its definitions in numerical order within the main listing.

Common-usage acronyms and abbreviations appear in their natural alphabetical order. For example, **MSG** follows **mozzarella cheese** and precedes **muddle**.

CROSS-REFERENCES are indicated by SMALL CAPITALS and may appear in the body of a definition, at the end of a definition or in lieu of a definition.

The only time a cross-reference is used within the body of a definition is when the term may not be familiar to the reader. For instance, the listing for **Russian** states. "Dishes that include FOIE GRAS, TRUFFLES and a DEMI-GLACE . . . ." Therefore, though listings for most foods, cooking techniques, kitchen equipment, etc. will be found in *Food Lover's Companion*, common entries (such as **butter, lettuce** or **poach**) are not indicated in small capitals as cross-references in the body of a definition. A word that is cross-referenced will only be capitalized the first time it's used.

Cross-references at the end of a definition refer to entries related to the word being defined.

When a word is fully defined elsewhere, a cross-reference rather than a definition is listed. In the world of food, many terms have more than one name, often depending on the region in which they're used. For example, **alligator pear** is cross-referenced to its more common name, **avocado**. Additionally, subtypes of a species or grouping, such as **alewife**, are cross-referenced to the main listing (in this case, **herring**). Different spellings of a term are also cross-referenced. **Akvavit**, for instance, refers the reader to the more common spelling of **aquavit**.

ITALICS are used in this book for several reasons. One is to point out that the term being defined also goes by another name. **Groats**, for example, are also known as *kasha*. Additionally, italics are used to indicate foreign words and publication titles, and to highlight cross-references at the end of a listing (the end of the **gin** entry states: *See also* SLOE GIN).

BOLDFACE PRINT is used not only for main entry headings, but for sub-entries within a definition as well. For example, the definition for **chocolate** uses boldface to highlight the headings of the various types of this food (**unsweetened chocolate, bittersweet chocolate, milk chocolate,** etc.), which are defined within the body of that entry.

BRACKETS surround an entry's pronunciation, which immediately follows the listing and precedes the definition. *See* Pronunciation Guide, next page for complete information.

PRONUNCIATION GUIDE

All but the most basic words are accompanied by pronunciations, which are enclosed in brackets [—]. I've always thought that the standard phonetic alphabet and diacritical marks such as a tilde (~), diaeresis (¨), breve ( ) and circumflex (∧) slow the reader down because one must often look up the symbol in a chart at the front of a book to see how it affects a word's pronunciation. Ever the advocate of the most direct route, I've chosen to use the "sounding-out" phonetic method, with the accented syllable indicated by capital letters. On a word like **matsutake**, for example, the common dictionary-type of phonetic is *mät sŏŏ tä' kē,* which would force most readers to look up the sounds represented by the diacritics. In this book, however, the word is simply sounded out as *maht-soo-TAH-kee.*

Following is a list of the basic sounds (based on common American usage) employed in this book's pronunciations:

a	as in **can** or **add**	**j**	as in **gin** or **juicy**
ah	as in **father** or **balm**	**k**	as in **cool** or **crisp**
air	as in **rare** or **fair**	**o**	as in **odd** or **bottle**
ay	as in **date** or **face**	**oh**	as in **open** or **boat**
ee	as in **steam** or **bean**	**oo**	as in **food** or **boo**
eh	as in **set** or **check**	**ow**	as in **cow** or **flour**
g	as in **game** or **green**	**uh**	as in **up** or **cup**
i	as in **ice** or **pie**	**zh**	as in **beige** or **vision**
ih	as in **if** or **strip**		

An italicized "*n*" is used in French pronunciations to indicate that the "n" itself is not pronounced and the preceding vowel has a nasal sound.

Two *r*s (rr) indicate the sound of a rolling "r."

balone [a-buh-LOH-nee] A GASTROPOD MOLLUSK (*see both listings*) found along the coastlines of California, Mexico and Japan. The edible portion is the adductor muscle, a broad foot by which the abalone clings to rocks. As with any muscle, the meat is tough and must be pounded to tenderize it before cooking. Abalone, used widely in Chinese and Japanese cooking, can be purchased fresh, canned, dried or salted. Fresh abalone is best sautéed and should be cooked very briefly (20 to 30 seconds a side) or the meat will quickly toughen. Abalone is known as *ormer* in the English Channel, *awabi* in Japan, *muttonfish* in Australia and *paua* in New Zealand. Its iridescent shell is a source of mother-of-pearl. *See also* SHELLFISH.

abbacchio [ah-BAHK-ee-yoh] Italian for a very young lamb.

absinthe [AB-sinth] Reputed to be an aphrodisiac, absinthe is a potent, bitter LIQUEUR distilled from WORMWOOD and flavored with a variety of herbs. It has a distinct ANISE flavor and is 68 percent alcohol (136 PROOF). Absinthe is usually diluted with water, which changes its color from green to milky white. Because it's considered habit-forming and hazardous to health, absinthe is prohibited in many countries and was banned in the United States in the early 1900s.

acetic acid [a-SEE-tihk] Acetic acid is formed when common airborne bacteria interact with the alcohol present in fermented solutions such as wine, beer or cider. It's the constituent of vinegar that makes it sour. *See also* Additives Directory, page 515.

achar [ah-CHAHR] An East Indian word referring to pickled and salted relishes. They can be made sweet or hot, depending on the seasoning added.

achiote seed [ah-chee-OH-tay] The slightly musky-flavored seed of the annatto tree is available whole or ground in East Indian, Spanish and Latin American markets. Buy whole seeds when they're a rusty red color; brown seeds are old and flavorless. Achiote seed is also called ANNATTO which, in its paste and powder form, is used in the U.S. to color butter, margarine, cheese and smoked fish.

acids The word "acid" comes from the Latin *acidus*, meaning "sour." All acids are sour to some degree. Sourness (acidity) is found in many natural ingredients such as vinegar (ACETIC ACID), wine (TARTARIC ACID), lemon juice (CITRIC ACID), sour-milk products (LACTIC ACID), apples (MALIC ACID) and rhubarb leaves (toxic OXALIC ACID). When used in a marinade, acids—such as wine and lemon juice—are natural tenderizers because they break down connective tissue and cell walls.

acidulated water [a-SIHD-yoo-lay-ted] Water to which a small amount of vinegar, lemon or lime juice has been added. It's used as a soak to prevent discoloration of some fruits and vegetables (such as apples and artichokes) that darken quickly when their cut surfaces are exposed to air. It can also be used as a cooking medium.

ackee; akee; achee [ah-KEE] A bright red tropical fruit which, when ripe, bursts open to reveal three large black seeds and a soft, creamy white flesh. The scientific name, *blighia sapida*, comes from Captain Bligh, who brought the fruit from West Africa to Jamaica in 1793. It is extremely popular in one of Jamaica's national dishes, "saltfish and ackee." Because certain parts of the fruit are toxic when underripe, canned ackee is often subject to import restrictions.

acorn Acorns are the fruit of the oak tree. Some varieties are edible and, like chestnuts, may be eaten raw, roasted or baked. They may also be ground and used as a substitute for coffee.

acorn squash A somewhat oval-shaped winter squash with a ribbed, dark green skin and orange flesh. The most common method of preparation is to halve them, remove the seeds and bake. Acorn squash may then be eaten directly from the shell. *See also* SQUASH.

additives, food In the broadest of terms, food additives are substances intentionally added to food either directly or indirectly with one or more of the following purposes: 1. to maintain or improve nutritional quality; 2. to maintain product quality and freshness; 3. to aid in the processing or preparation of food; and 4. to make food more appealing. Some 2,800 substances are currently added to foods for one or more of these uses. During normal processing, packaging and storage, up to 10,000 other compounds can find their way into food. Today more than ever, additives are strictly regulated. Manufacturers must prove the additives they add to food are safe. This process can take several years and includes a battery of chemical studies as well as tests involving animals, the latter to determine whether the substances could have harmful effects such as cancer and birth defects. The results of these comprehensive studies must be presented to the Food and Drug Administration (FDA), who then determines how the additive can be used in food. There are two major categories of food that are exempt from this testing and approval process: 1. a group of 700 substances categorized as GRAS ("generally recognized as safe"), which are so classified because of extensive past use without harmful side effects; and 2. substances approved before 1958 either by the FDA or the USDA. An ongoing review of many of these substances is in effect, however, to make sure they're tested against the most current scientific standards. It's interesting to note that about 98 percent (by weight) of all food additives used in the U.S. are in the form of baking soda, citric acid, corn syrup, mustard, pepper, salt, sugar and vegetable colorings. *For information on specific additives, see* Additives Directory, page 515.

ade [AYD] A drink, such as **lemonade** or **limeade**, made by combining water, sugar and citrus juice.

adjust In cooking, to "adjust flavoring" means to taste before serving, adding seasoning if necessary.

adobo [ah-DOH-boh] A Philippine national dish of braised chicken and pork with coconut milk.

advocaat [ad-voh-CAHT] Reminiscent of eggnog, this Dutch LIQUEUR is made with BRANDY, egg yolks and sugar.

adzuki bean; azuki bean [ah-ZOO-kee; AH-zoo-kee] A small, dried, russet-colored bean with a sweet flavor. Adzuki beans can be purchased whole or powdered at Asian markets. They are particularly popular in Japanese cooking where they're used in confections such as the popular YOKAN, made with adzuki-bean paste and agar. *See also* BEAN.

aerate [AIR-ayt] A term used in cookery as a synonym for SIFT.

agar; agar-agar [AH-gahr; AY-gahr] Also called *kanten* and *Japanese gelatin*, this tasteless dried seaweed acts as a setting agent and is widely used in Asia. It is marketed in the form of blocks, powder or strands and is available at Asian markets and health-food stores. Agar can be substituted for gelatin but has stronger setting properties so less of it is required.

agave [ah-GAH-vee; ah-GAH-vay] Also called *century plant*, this family of succulents grows in the southwestern United States, Mexico and Central America. Though poisonous when raw, agave has a sweet, mild flavor when baked or made into a syrup. Certain varieties are used in making the alcoholic beverages MESCAL, PULQUE and TEQUILA.

age; aged To let food get older under controlled conditions in order to improve flavor or texture or both. 1. **Aged meat** has been stored 3 to 6 weeks at an optimal temperature of 34°F to 38°F and in low humidity. During this time it undergoes an enzymatic change that intensifies flavor, deepens color and tenderizes by softening some of the connective tissue. The longer meat is aged, the more quickly it will cook. The *cryovac* method of aging involves vacuum packing the meat with a vapor- and moistureproof film so the so-called aging takes place in transit from slaughterhouse to the consumer's home. 2. **Aging cheese** refers to storing it in a temperature-controlled area until it develops the desired texture and flavor. 3. **Wine is aged** both in the barrel and in the bottle. White wines generally benefit from about a year of bottle aging; red wines, depending on the grape, improve with 2 to 10 years—or even more—in the bottle.

agneau [an-YOH] The French word for lamb.

aigre-doux [ay-greh-DOO] The French term for the combined flavors of sour (*aigre*) and sweet (*doux*). An *aigre-doux* sauce might contain both vinegar and sugar.

aïoli [ay-OH-lee; i-OH-lee] A strongly flavored garlic MAYONNAISE from the Provence region of southern France. It's a popular accompaniment for fish, meats and vegetables.

aji-no-moto [ah-JEE-no-MO-toh] The Japanese name for MONOSODIUM GLUTAMATE (MSG).

akala [ah-KAH-lah] Hailing from Hawaii, this sweet, juicy berry resembles a very large raspberry. It can range in color from red to almost purple and is good eaten plain or in jams and pies.

akule [ah-KOO-lay] This Hawaiian fish, also known as *bigeye scad*, is usually salted and dried. *See also* FISH.

akvavit *see* AQUAVIT

al [ahl] An Italian word meaning "at the," "to the" or "on the." For example, *al dente* means "to the tooth."

à la [ah-lah] A French idiom meaning "in the manner (or style) of;" the full phrase is *à la mode de*. In cooking, this phrase designates the style of preparation or a particular garnish. *A la bourguignonne*, for example, would mean "as prepared in Burgundy."

à la carte [ah-lah-CAHRT] A menu term signifying that each item is priced separately. *See also* PRIX FIXE; TABLE D'HÔTE.

à la king [ah-lah-KING] A dish of diced food (usually chicken or turkey) in a rich cream sauce containing mushrooms, pimientos, green peppers and sometimes SHERRY.

à la mode [ah-lah-MOHD] French for "in the manner (or mode) [of]," referring to the style in which a dish is prepared. The term has been Americanized to mean pie topped with ice cream.

Alaska cod *see* SABLEFISH

Alaska king crab *see* KING CRAB

albacore [AL-bah-cohr] *see* TUNA

Albert sauce [AL-bert; al-BAIR] Usually served with beef, this is a rich horseradish sauce with a base of butter, flour and cream.

albondiga [ahl-BON-dee-gah] The Mexican word for "meatball." *Albóndigas* is the name of a popular Mexican and Spanish dish of spicy meatballs, usually in a tomato sauce. **Sopa de albóndigas** is a beef-broth soup with meatballs and chopped vegetables.

albumen [al-BYOO-mehn] The old-fashioned word for egg white.

albumin [al-BYOO-mehn] The protein portion of the egg white, comprising about 70 percent of the whole. Albumin is also found in animal blood, milk, plants and seeds.

alcohol The only alcohol suitable for drinking is ethyl alcohol, a liquid produced by distilling the fermented juice of fruits or grains. Pure ethyl alcohol is clear, flammable and caustic. Water is therefore added to reduce its potency. In the United States, the average amount of alcohol in distilled spirits is about 40 percent (80 PROOF). Pure alcohol boils at 173°F, water at 212°F. A mixture of the two will boil somewhere between these two temperatures. When making a sauce containing liquor, the mixture must be boiled at 212°F to make sure the alcohol completely evaporates. Because alcohol freezes at a much lower temperature than water, the amount of alcohol used in a frozen dessert (such as ice cream) must be carefully regulated or the dessert won't freeze.

al dente [al-DEN-tay] An Italian phrase meaning "to the tooth," used to describe pasta or other food that is cooked only until it offers a slight resistance when bitten into, but which is not soft or overdone.

ale [AYL] An alcoholic beverage brewed from MALT and HOPS. It's usually stronger and, because of the hops, more bitter than BEER. The color can vary from light to dark amber.

alewife *see* HERRING

alfalfa [al-FAL-fuh] Though alfalfa is generally grown for fodder, the seeds are also sprouted for human consumption. Alfalfa sprouts are popular in salads and on sandwiches. *See also* SEED SPROUTS.

A

alkali [AL-kah-li] Alkalis counterbalance and neutralize ACIDS. In cooking, the most common alkali used is bicarbonate of soda, commonly known as BAKING SODA. Adding baking soda to the water when cooking green vegetables helps maintain their bright color because it neutralizes the natural acid in the vegetables. Unfortunately, it also destroys some of the vegetable's vitamins. Baking soda is used as a leavener in baked goods where it neutralizes acid ingredients (such as molasses, buttermilk and honey) and produces tender breads, cakes, etc.

alla [ah-lah] The Italian word meaning "as done by, in, for or with." Eggplant *alla parmigiana* refers to eggplant topped with tomato sauce, mozzarella and Parmesan cheese.

allemande sauce [ah-leh-MAHND] A classic VELOUTÉ SAUCE thickened with egg yolks. Also called *Parisienne sauce*.

alligator This lizardlike reptile can grow up to 19 feet in length and is generally found in the swamplands of Louisiana and the Gulf States. Alligator meat is usually only available in its native regions. It comes in three basic types: the tender, white, veallike tail meat; the pinkish body meat, which has a stronger flavor and slightly tougher texture; and the dark tail meat, which is only suitable for braised dishes.

alligator pear *see* AVOCADO

all-purpose flour *see* FLOUR

allspice The pea-size berry of the evergreen pimiento tree, native to the West Indies and South America (though Jamaica provides most of the world's supply). The dried berries are dark brown and can be purchased whole or ground. The spice is so named because it tastes like a combination of cinnamon, nutmeg and cloves. As with all spices, it should be stored in a cool, dark place for no more than 6 months. Allspice is used in both savory and sweet cooking. *See also* SPICES; Herb and Spice Chart, page 538.

allumettes [al-yoo-MEHT] 1. Thin strips of PUFF PASTRY spread or filled with different savory mixtures (such as shrimp butter or grated cheese) and served as an HORS D'OEUVRE. A sweet filling turns this pastry into a dessert. 2. *Allumette*, the French word for "match," also refers to potatoes that have been cut into thin "matchsticks" and fried.

almond The kernel of the fruit of the almond tree, grown extensively in California, the Mediterranean, Australia and South Africa. There are two main types of almonds—sweet and bitter. The flavor of **sweet almonds**

is delicate and slightly sweet. They're readily available in markets and, unless otherwise indicated, are the variety used in recipes. The more strongly flavored **bitter almonds** contain traces of lethal prussic acid when raw. Though the acid's toxicity is destroyed when the nuts are heated, the sale of bitter almonds is illegal in the United States. Processed bitter almonds are used to flavor extracts, LIQUEURS and ORGEAT SYRUP. The kernels of apricot and peach pits have a similar flavor and the same toxic effect (destroyed by heating) as bitter almonds. Almonds are available blanched or not, whole, sliced, chopped, candied, smoked, in paste form and in many flavors. Toasting almonds before using in recipes intensifies their flavor and adds crunch. *See also* ALMOND EXTRACT; ALMOND OIL; ALMOND PASTE; JORDAN ALMOND; NUTS.

almond extract A flavoring produced by combining bitter-ALMOND oil with ethyl ALCOHOL. The flavor is very intense, so the extract should be used with care. *See also* EXTRACTS.

almond oil An oil obtained by pressing sweet almonds. French almond oil, *huile d'amande*, is very expensive and has the delicate flavor and aroma of lightly toasted almonds. The domestic variety is much milder and doesn't compare either in flavor or in price. Almond oil can be found in specialty gourmet markets and many supermarkets.

almond paste Used in a variety of confections, almond paste is made of blanched ground almonds, sugar and GLYCERINE or other liquid. ALMOND EXTRACT is sometimes added to intensify the flavor. Almond paste is less sweet and slightly coarser than MARZIPAN. It should be firm but pliable before use in a recipe. If it becomes hard, it can be softened by heating for 2 or 3 seconds in a microwave oven. Once opened, it should be wrapped tightly and refrigerated. Almond paste is available in most supermarkets in 6- to 8-ounce cans and packages. **Bitter-almond paste** is used to flavor the famous AMARETTI cookies.

alsacienne, à l' [al-zah-SYEHN] A term referring to cooking "in the style of Alsace," a province in northeastern France whose French and German heritage is reflected in its famous cuisine. It usually refers to preparations of meat braised with sauerkraut, potatoes and sausage.

Alsatian wines [al-SAY-shuhn] Wines from the French province of Alsace made from grapes grown in the foothill vineyards of the Vosges Mountains. These white wines are known for their delicate flavor and medium dryness. The APPELLATION CONTRÔLÉE is designated by the type of grape (principally GEWÜRZTRAMINER, PINOT BLANC and SYLVANER), rather than the vineyard.

A

alum [AL-uhm] In cooking, these highly astringent crystals of potassium aluminum sulfate were once widely used as the crisping agent in canning pickles. Alum can cause digestive distress, however, and modern canning methods make its use unnecessary.

aluminum cookware [ah-LOO-mihn-uhm]; Br. **aluminium** [ahl-you-MIHN-ee-uhm] One of the best all-around cooking materials available, aluminum is moderately priced, sturdy and a good heat conductor. It comes in light- and medium-weight cookware and bakeware; the heavier the gauge, the more evenly it cooks. It's available in plain (matte or polished) or anodized (dark gray) finishes. Plain aluminum finishes can darken and pit when exposed to alkaline or mineral-rich foods, and when soaked excessively in soapy water. Likewise, they can discolor some foods containing eggs, wine or other acidic ingredients. (This discoloration, though not harmful, is unattractive.) The anodized finishes are chip-, stain- and scratch-resistant but will spot and fade if cleaned in a dishwasher. Extensive research has proven that the old tales of food being poisoned by aluminum are unequivocally false, and those who claim that some foods take on a metallic taste are counterbalanced by just as many who insist they don't.

aluminum foil Aluminum that has been rolled into a thin, pliable sheet. It's an excellent barrier to moisture, air and odors and can withstand flaming heat and freezing cold. It comes in regular weight (for wrapping food and covering containers) and heavy-duty weight (for freezer storage and lining pans and grills). Because the crinkling of foil creates tiny holes (increasing permeability), it should not be reused for freezer storage. Neither should it be used to wrap acidic foods (such as tomatoes and onions) because the natural acids in the food will eat through the foil. Since metals reflect microwaves, about the only place foil can't always be used is the microwave oven.

amandine [AH-mahn-deen; a-mahn-DEEN] The French term meaning "garnished with almonds." It's often misspelled "almondine."

amaranth [AM-ah-ranth] Once considered a simple weed in the United States, this nutritious annual is finally being acknowledged as the nourishing high-protein food it is. Amaranth greens have a delicious, slightly sweet flavor. The seeds are used as cereal or can be ground into flour for bread. Amaranth seeds and flour can be found in health-food stores, as well as in some Caribbean and Asian markets.

amaretti [am-ah-REHT-tee] Intensely crisp, airy MACAROON cookies that are made either with bitter-ALMOND PASTE or its flavor counterpart, apricot-kernel paste. In the U.S., Italian markets sell pairs of paper-wrapped **Amaretti di Saronno** (made with apricot-kernel paste) under the label of Lazzaroni. **Amarettini** are miniature cookies with the same flavor.

amaretto [am-ah-REHT-toh] A LIQUEUR with the flavor of almonds, though it's often made with the kernels of apricot pits. The original liqueur, *Amaretto di Saronno*, hails from Saronno, Italy. Many American distilleries now produce their own amaretto.

amberjack A lean, mild fish found along the South Atlantic coast. It's hard to find in markets but, when available, is usually sold whole. Amberjack is best baked or sautéed. *See also* FISH.

ambrosia [am-BROH-zhah] According to Greek mythology, ambrosia (meaning "immortality") was the food of the gods on Mt. Olympus. More recently, the word designates a dessert of chilled fruit (usually oranges and bananas) mixed with coconut. Ambrosia is also sometimes served as a salad.

américaine, à l' [a-may-ree-KEHN] A dish (often lobster) prepared with a spicy sauce of tomatoes, olive oil, onions, brandy and wine.

American cheese, processed Any of several types of natural cheese that are PASTEURIZED to lengthen storage life and combined with emulsifiers to aid smoothness. In some cases processed cheeses contain added colorings and preservatives. Products labeled cheese "spreads" or cheese "foods" contain added liquid for a softer, more spreadable mixture. According to U.S. government standards, only 51 percent of the final weight needs to be cheese. Processed cheeses keep well but lack the distinctive flavor and texture of natural cheeses. *See also* CHEESE.

ammonium bicarbonate [ah-MOH-nee-uhm by-CAR-boh-nayt] This LEAVENER is the precursor of today's baking powder and baking soda. It's still used by some Europeans and is called for in some European baking recipes, mainly for cookies. It can be purchased in drugstores but must be ground to a powder before using. Also known as *hartshorn, carbonate of ammonia* and *powdered baking ammonia.*

amontillado [ah-mon-teh-LAH-doh] A Spanish SHERRY made from the palomino grape. It's aged longer and is darker and softer than a FINO. Amontillado should have a distinctively nutty flavor.

anadama bread [a-nuh-DAM-uh] An early American yeast bread flavored with cornmeal and molasses. Legend says this bread was created by a New England farmer plagued by a lazy wife who served him the same cornmeal-molasses gruel every day. One morning, the disgusted farmer grabbed the bowl of gruel, tossed in some flour and yeast, and began stirring like crazy, all the while muttering angrily, "Anna, damn 'er!"

Anaheim chili pepper [AN-uh-hym] Named after the California city, the generally mild Anaheim is one of the most commonly available CHILI PEPPERS in the United States. It is usually medium green in color and has a long, narrow shape. There is also a red strain, commonly called the *New Mexico red chili.* Anaheim chilies can be purchased fresh or canned and have a sweet, simple taste with just a hint of bite. Anaheims are frequently stuffed and commonly used in SALSAS. The dried red variety are those used for the decorative *ristra,* a long string (or wreath) of chili peppers.

ancho chili pepper [AHN-choh] This broad, dried CHILI PEPPER is 3 to 4 inches long and a deep reddish brown; it ranges in flavor from mild to pungent. In its fresh, green state, the ancho is referred to as a *poblano* chili pepper.

anchovy [AN-choh-vee; an-CHOH-vee] Though there are many species of small, silvery fish that are known in their country of origin as "anchovies," the true anchovy comes only from the Mediterranean and southern European coastlines. These tiny fish are generally filleted, salt-cured and canned in oil; they're sold flat and rolled. Because they're so salty, anchovies are used sparingly to flavor or garnish sauces and other preparations. *See also* FISH; ANCHOVY PASTE.

anchovy paste This combination of pounded anchovies, vinegar, spices and water comes in tubes and is convenient for many cooking purposes. It can also be used for CANAPES.

andalouse, à l' [ahn-dah-LOOZ] A French term describing dishes using tomatoes, pimientos and sometimes rice PILAF or sausage. **Andalouse sauce** refers to mayonnaise mixed with tomato puree and pimiento.

andouille sausage [an-DOO-ee; ahn-DWEE] A spicy, heavily smoked sausage made from pork CHITTERLINGS and TRIPE. French in origin, *andouille* is a specialty of CAJUN COOKERY. It's the traditional sausage used in specialties like JAMBALAYA and GUMBO, and makes a spicy addition to any dish that would use smoked sausage. It's also especially good served cold as an HORS D'OEUVRE. *See also* SAUSAGE.

andouillette sausage [ahn-dwee-YET] This smaller version (1 inch or less in diameter) of ANDOUILLE SAUSAGE is a specialty of Normandy. It is sold cooked but not usually smoked. This sausage is traditionally slashed and grilled or fried.

anesone [AN-uh-sohn; an-uh-SOH-nay] A clear anise-flavored LIQUEUR that is drier and of a higher proof than ANISETTE.

angel food cake A light, airy sponge-type cake made with stiffly beaten egg whites but no yolks or other fats. It's traditionally baked in a TUBE PAN and is sometimes referred to simply as angel cake.

angel hair pasta *see* CAPELLI D'ANGELO

angelica [an-JEHL-ih-cah] This sweet "herb of the angels" is a member of the parsley family. Grown extensively in Europe, its pale green, celerylike stalks are most often candied and used as decorations for cakes and other desserts. Angelica is also used to flavor liqueurs and sweet wines.

angels on horseback An HORS D'OEUVRE of bacon-wrapped, shucked oysters that are broiled, baked or grilled and served on buttered toast points. *See also* DEVILS ON HORSEBACK.

anglaise, à l' [ahn-GLEHZ] French for "in the English style," meaning food that is simply poached or boiled. The term can also be used for food that has been coated in breadcrumbs and fried.

angler fish The angler takes its name from the method by which it lures its prey: it lies partially buried on the sea floor and twitches a long filament that grows from its head. The filament resembles a worm and attracts smaller fish that are soon engulfed by the angler's huge mouth. Also known as *monkfish, lotte, bellyfish, frogfish, sea devil* and *goosefish*, this large, extremely ugly fish is low-fat and firm-textured, and has a mild, sweet flavor that has been compared to lobster. Indeed, shellfish are an important part of the angler's diet. The only edible portion of this impressive fish is the tail, which is suitable for almost any method of cooking. *See also* FISH.

angostura bitters [ang-uh-STOOR-ah] *see* BITTERS

animal fat Any fat (such as BUTTER, SUET or LARD) that comes from an animal. Because they are almost entirely saturated, animal fats are not recommended for people on low-fat or low-cholesterol diets. *See also* FATS AND OILS.

anise [AN-ihs] Known as far back as at least 1500 B.C., this small annual plant is a member of the parsley family. Both the leaves and seed have a distinctive, sweet licorice flavor. The greenish brown, comma-shaped **anise seed** perfumes and flavors a variety of confections as well as savory dishes. It's also used to flavor drinks such as PASTIS, ARRACK, ANISETTE and OUZO. Anise seed plays an important role in the cooking of Southeast Asia.

Chinese cooks are more likely to use STAR ANISE than anise seed. *See also* SPICES; Herb and Spice Chart, page 538.

anise seed; aniseed *see* ANISE

anisette [AN-ih-seht; an-ih-SEHT] A clear, very sweet LIQUEUR made with anise seeds and tasting of licorice.

Anjou pear [AHN-zhoo] A large winter pear with firm flesh and a yellowish-green skin that is often blushed with red. It's sweet and succulent and is delicious both cooked and raw. The Anjou is available in most regions from October through mid-winter. *See also* PEAR.

Anna potatoes *see* POMMES ANNA

annatto [uh-NAH-toh] A derivative of ACHIOTE SEED, commercial annatto paste and powder is used to color butter, margarine, cheese and smoked fish. *See also* Additives Directory, page 515.

antipasto [ahn-tee-PAHS-toh; an-tee-PAST-oh] Literally meaning "before the pasta," this Italian term refers to hot or cold HORS D'OEUVRE. An assortment of *antipasti* could include appetizers such as cheese, smoked meats, olives, fish and marinated vegetables. In the U.S., *antipasto* usually refers to a plate of assorted hors d'oeuvre.

apee [AY-pee] Dating back to the 1800s, this soft, sour cream-based sugar cookie takes its name from the initials of its creator, Philadelphia cook Ann Page.

apéritif [ah-pair-uh-TEEF; ay-pair-ee-TEEF] A French term referring to a light alchoholic drink taken before a meal to stimulate the appetite. Popular apéritifs include CHAMPAGNE, LILLET and SHERRY.

à point [ah PWAH] 1. The French term used for food cooked just to the perfect point of doneness. 2. When referring to meat, *à point* means that a steak is cooked rare.

appellation contrôlée [ap-peh-lah-see-OHN kon-troh-LAY] This term is used as a hallmark of quality by the French government to guarantee the place of origin and grape variety of a particular wine. The words *appellation contrôlée* must be printed on the label directly below the name of the wine. The full phrase is *appellation d'origine contrôlée*, sometimes abbreviated as *AC.*

Appenzeller cheese; Appenzell cheese [A-pent-seller] This whole-milk cow's cheese is named for an eastern Swiss canton (a state in the Swiss confederation). It has a golden yellow rind and a firm, straw-colored curd with tiny holes. The flavor is delicate and somewhat fruity owing to the wine or cider wash it receives during curing. *See also* CHEESE.

appetizer Any finger food served before a meal to whet and excite the palate. Used synonymously with the term HORS D'OEUVRE.

apple Grown in temperate zones throughout the world and cultivated for at least 3,000 years, apple varieties now number well into the thousands. Apples range in color from lemony yellow to bright yellow-green to crimson red. Their textures range from tender to crisp, their flavors from sweet to tart and from simple to complex. They're available year-round but are at their best from September through November when newly harvested. Buy firm, well-colored apples with a fresh (never musty) fragrance. The skins should be smooth and free of bruises and gouges. SCALD (a dry, tan- or brown-colored area on the skin of an apple) doesn't usually affect its flavor. Apples come 2 to 4 per pound, depending on size. For cooking and baking, use apples that will remain flavorful and firm, such as Baldwin, Cortland, Northern Spy, Rome Beauty, Winesap and York Imperial. Store apples in a cool, dark place. They do well placed in a plastic bag and stored in the refrigerator. Apples are a good source of vitamins **A** and **C**. *For information on specific apples, see individual listings.*

apple brown betty *see* BETTY

apple butter A thick, dark brown preserve made by slowly cooking apples, sugar, spices and cider together. Used as a spread for breads.

apple corer *see* CORER

apple dumpling *see* DUMPLING

applejack A potent BRANDY made from apple cider and ranging in strength from 80 to 100 PROOF. France is famous for its apple brandy, CALVADOS. In the United States, applejack must spend a minimum of 2 years in wooden casks before being bottled.

apple pandowdy *see* PANDOWDY

applesauce A cooked puree (ranging in texture from smooth to chunky) of apples, sugar and, sometimes, spices.

apple snow A chilled dessert made by combining applesauce, lemon juice, spices, stiffly beaten egg whites and, sometimes, gelatin.

apricot This fruit of ancient lineage has been grown in China for over 4,000 years. It now thrives in most temperate climates, with California producing about 90 percent of the American crop. A relative of the peach, the apricot is smaller and has a smooth, oval pit that falls out easily when the fruit is halved. Throughout the world there are many varieties of apricot, including Riland, Tilton, Blenheim, Royal and Chinese. In color, the skin can range anywhere from pale yellow to deep burnt orange; the flesh from a golden cream color to brilliant orange. Because they're highly perishable and seasonal, 90 percent of the fresh apricots are marketed in June and July. When buying apricots, select plump, reasonably firm fruit with a uniform color. Store in a plastic bag in the refrigerator for 3 to 5 days. Depending on size, there are 8 to 12 apricots per pound. **Dried apricots** are pitted, unpeeled apricot halves that have had a large percentage of the moisture removed. They're usually treated with sulfur dioxide to preserve their color. In addition to being rich in vitamin A, dried apricots are a valuable source of iron and calcium. The kernels of the apricot pits are used in confections and to flavor liqueurs. Like bitter almonds, apricot kernels are poisonous until roasted.

Apry [AP-ree] Another name for apricot BRANDY.

aquavit [AHK-wuh-veet] A strong colorless Scandinavian liquor distilled from grain or potatoes and flavored with caraway seed. It is served icy cold and drunk in a single gulp.

aqua vitae [AHK-wuh VEE-tee; AK-wuh VEE-tee] A term used to describe clear distilled BRANDY; Latin for "water of life." *See also* EAU DE VIE.

Arborio rice [ar-BOH-ree-oh] The high-starch kernels of this Italian-grown grain are shorter and fatter than any other short-grain rice. Arborio is traditionally used for RISOTTO because its increased starch lends this classic dish its requisite creamy texture. *See also* RICE.

Argenteuil [ar-zhawn-TEW-ee] A term describing a dish featuring asparagus, named after the French town that is world renowned for its asparagus.

Armagnac [ar-mahn-YAK] A fine French BRANDY from Gascony, near Condom, a town southeast of Bordeaux. Like COGNAC, Armagnac is aged in oak for up to 40 years.

Armenian cracker bread *see* LAVOSH

aromatic *n.* Any of various plants, herbs and spices (such as bay leaf, ginger or parsley) that impart a lively fragrance and flavor to food and drink.

arrack; arak [AR-rahk; ah-RAK] A name widely used in Asia and the Middle East for a fiery liquor made, depending on the country, from any of several ingredients including rice, sundry-palm sap and dates. In many countries, arrack is strongly flavored with anise seed.

arrowroot   The starchy product of a tropical tuber of the same name. The rootstalks are dried and ground into a very fine powder. Arrowroot is used as a thickening agent for puddings, sauces and other cooked foods, and is more easily digested than wheat flour. Its thickening power is about twice that of wheat flour. Arrowroot is absolutely tasteless and becomes clear when cooked. Unlike cornstarch, it doesn't impart a chalky taste when undercooked. It should be mixed with a cold liquid before being heated or added to hot mixtures. Some English and early American cookie recipes call for *arrowroot flour*, which is the same product. Arrowroot can be found in supermarkets, health-food stores and Asian markets.

arroz   [ah-ROHS]   The Spanish word for "rice."

arroz con pollo   [ah-ROHS con POH-yoh]   Literally "rice with chicken," this Spanish and Mexican dish is made with rice, chicken, tomatoes, green peppers, seasonings and, sometimes, saffron.

artichoke   A name shared by three unrelated plants: the globe artichoke, JERUSALEM ARTICHOKE and CHINESE (or Japanese) ARTICHOKE. Considered the true artichoke, the *globe artichoke* is cultivated mainly in California's mid-coastal region. It's the bud of a large plant from the thistle family and has tough, petal-shaped leaves. To eat a whole cooked artichoke, break off the leaves one by one and draw the base of the leaf through your teeth to remove the soft portion, discarding the remainder of the leaf. The individual leaves may be dipped into melted butter or some other sauce. Once the leaves have been removed, the inedible prickly *choke* is cut or scraped away and discarded. Then the tender artichoke heart and meaty bottom can be eaten. Globe artichokes are available year-round, with the peak season from March through May. Buy deep green, heavy-for-their-size artichokes with a tight leaf formation. They're best used the day of purchase. Artichoke hearts are available frozen and canned; artichoke bottoms are available canned. Artichokes contain small amounts of potassium and vitamin A.

arugula   [ah-ROO-guh-lah]   Also called *rocket, rugula* and *rucola*, arugula is a bitterish, aromatic salad green with a peppery mustard flavor. Though it has long been extremely popular with Italians, American palates generally find its flavor too assertive. It's only in the past few years that arugula (which resembles radish leaves) has been found on restaurant menus and in specialty produce markets. It's sold in small bunches with roots attached. The leaves should be bright green and fresh looking.

Arugula is very perishable and should be tightly wrapped in a plastic bag and refrigerated for no more than 2 days. Its leaves hold a tremendous amount of grit and must be thoroughly washed just before using. Arugula makes a lively addition to salads, soups and sautéed vegetable dishes. It's a rich source of iron as well as vitamins A and C.

asafetida; asafoetida [ah-sah-FEH-teh-dah] A flavoring obtained from a giant fennellike plant that grows mainly in Iran and India. It's used in many Indian dishes and can be found in powdered or lump form in Indian markets. Asafetida has a fetid, garlicky smell and should be used in very small quantities.

ascorbic acid [as-KOHR-bihk] The scientific name for vitamin C.

Asiago cheese [ah-SYAH-goh] A semifirm Italian cheese with a rich, nutty flavor. It's made from whole or part-skim cow's milk and comes in small wheels with glossy rinds. The yellow interior has many small holes. Young Asiago is used as a table cheese; aged over a year, it becomes hard and suitable for grating. *See also* CHEESE.

Asian noodles Though some Asian-style noodles are wheat-based, many others are made from ingredients such as rice flour, potato flour, buckwheat flour, cornstarch and bean, yam or soybean starch. Among the more popular are China's CELLOPHANE NOODLES (made from mung-bean starch), egg noodles (usually wheat-based) and RICE-FLOUR NOODLES, and Japan's harusame (made with cornstarch and potato flour), RAMEN (wheat-based egg noodles) and SOBA (which contain buckwheat flour). Other Asian countries, including Korea, Indonesia, Thailand, Vietnam and the Philippines, have their own versions of the venerable noodle. Asian noodles can be purchased fresh and dried in oriental markets; some dried varieties can be found in supermarkets. Throughout Asian cultures noodles are eaten hot and cold. They can be cooked in a variety of ways including steaming, stir-frying and deep-frying. *See also* NOODLES.

Asian pear There are over 100 varieties (most of them grown in Japan) of this firm, amazingly juicy pear whose season is late summer through early fall. In size and color, they range from huge and golden brown to tiny and yellow-green. In general, ripe Asian pears (also called *Chinese pears*) are quite firm to the touch, crunchy to the bite (unlike the pears we're used to), lightly sweet and drippingly juicy. The most common Asian pear in the United States is the Twentieth Century (also known as *Nijisseiki*), which is large, round, and green to yellow in color. Ripe Asian pears should be stored in the refrigerator. *See also* PEAR.

asparagus This universally popular vegetable is one of the lily family's cultivated forms. The season for fresh asparagus lasts from February through June. The earliest, most tender stalks are a beautiful apple green with purple-tinged tips. Europeans prefer white asparagus (particularly the famous French asparagus of Argenteuil), which is grown underground to prevent it from becoming green. White spears are usually thick and smoother than the green variety. When buying asparagus, choose firm, bright green (or pale ivory) stalks with tight tips. It's best cooked the same day it's purchased but will keep, tightly wrapped in a plastic bag, 3 to 4 days in the refrigerator. Asparagus is grown in sandy soil so thorough washing is necessary to ensure the tips are not gritty. If asparagus stems are tough, remove the outer layer with a vegetable peeler. Canned and frozen asparagus is also available. Asparagus contains a good amount of vitamin A and is a fair source of iron and vitamins B and C.

asparagus bean *see* YARD-LONG BEAN

aspartame [ah-SPAHR-taym; AS-pahr-taym] An artificial sweetener that's 180 times sweeter than sugar. It's synthesized from two amino acids (L-aspartic acid and L-phenylalanine), the building blocks of protein. Aspartame breaks down and loses its sweetness when heated but is excellent for sweetening cold dishes.

aspic [AS-pihk] A savory jelly, usually clear, made of CLARIFIED meat, fish or vegetable stock and GELATIN. Tomato aspic, made with tomato juice and gelatin, is opaque. Clear aspics may be used as a base for molded dishes, or as glazes for cold dishes of fish, poultry, meat and eggs. They may also be cubed and served as a relish with cold meat, fish or fowl.

Asti Spumante [AS-tee spoo-MAHN-tay] A sweet sparkling white wine generally served as a DESSERT WINE but sometimes as an APÉRITIF. Asti Spumante tastes decidedly of the MUSCAT GRAPE from which it's made. It hails from the town of Asti in the Piedmont region of northern Italy.

atemoya [a-teh-MOH-ee-yah] Though it's cultivated in Florida, this cross between CHERIMOYA and SWEETSOP is a native of South America and the West Indies. About the size of a large sweet bell pepper, the atemoya has a tough dusty green skin that has a rough petal configuration. The custardlike pulp is cream-colored and studded with a smattering of large black seeds. Its delicate, sweet flavor tastes like a blend of mango and vanilla. Atemoyas are in season from late summer through late fall. Though they often split slightly at their stem end when ripe, it's best to buy them when they're pale green and tender with unbroken skin. The fruit can continue to ripen at room temperature at home. Refrigerate ripe atemoyas 3 to 5 days. They're best served chilled. Simply halve the fruit, spoon out the pulp and enjoy. Atemoyas are high in potassium and vitamins C and K.

Atlantic croaker *see* DRUM

Atlantic oyster Also called *Eastern oyster,* this species has a thick, elongated shell that ranges from 2 to 5 inches across. It's found along the Atlantic seaboard and the Gulf of Mexico and is considered ideal for serving ON THE HALF SHELL. Atlantic oysters are sold under different names depending on where they're harvested. The most well known is the BLUEPOINT; others include **Apalachicola, Cape Cod, Chesapeake, Chincoteague, Indian River, Kent Island, Malpeque** and **Wellfleet**. *See also* OYSTER.

aubergine [oh-bair-ZHEEN] French for "eggplant."

au bleu [oh-BLEUH] The French term for the method of preparing fish the instant after it's killed. Used especially for trout, as in *truite au bleu*, where the freshly killed fish is plunged into a boiling COURT-BUILLON, which turns the skin a metallic blue color.

au gratin [oh-GRAH-tihn; oh-grah-TAHN] A French phrase referring to food that is topped with breadcrumbs mixed with bits of butter, or with grated cheese, then broiled until brown and crisp.

au jus [oh-ZHOO] A French phrase describing meat served with its own natural juices, commonly used with beef.

au lait [oh-LAY] French for "with milk," referring to foods or beverages served or prepared with milk, as in CAFE AU LAIT.

au naturel [oh-nah-teur-EHL] The French term for food served in its natural state—not cooked or altered in any way.

aurore sauce [oh-ROHR] BÉCHAMEL SAUCE with just enough tomato puree added to tint it pink.

Auslese [OWS-lay-zuh] The German word for "selection," used in the wine trade to describe specially selected, perfectly ripened bunches of grapes that are hand-picked, then pressed separately from other grapes. The superior wine made from these grapes is sweet and expensive. *See also* BEERENAUSLESE; SPÄTLESE; TROCKENBEERENAUSLESE.

avgolemono [ahv-goh-LEH-moh-noh] A Greek soup as well as a sauce, both of which are made from chicken broth, egg yolks and lemon juice.

The main difference is that the soup has rice added to it. The sauce is thicker than the soup.

avocado [a-voh-CAH-doh] Native to the tropics and subtropics, this rich fruit is known for its lush, buttery texture and mild, faintly nutlike flavor. The fruit's name comes from *ahuacatl*, the Nahuatl word for "testicle," which is assumed to be a reference to the avocado's shape. Florida was the site of the first U.S. avocado trees in the 1830s but almost 80 percent of today's crop comes from California. Known early on as *alligator pear*, the many varieties of today's avocado can range from round to pear-shaped. The skin can be thick to thin, green to purplish black, and smooth to corrugated. The flesh is generally a pale yellow-green and softly succulent. The two most widely marketed avocado varieties are the pebbly textured, almost black **Haas** and the green **Fuerte**, which has a thin, smooth skin. Depending on the variety, an avocado can weigh as little as 3 ounces and as much as 4 pounds. There are even tiny Fuerte variety "cocktail avocados" that are the size of a small GHERKIN and weigh about 1 ounce. Like many fruits, avocados ripen best off the tree. Ripe avocados yield to gentle palm pressure, but firm, unripe avocados are what are usually found in the market. Select those that are unblemished and heavy for their size. To speed the ripening process, place several avocados in a paper bag and set aside at room temperature for 2 to 4 days. Ripe avocados can be stored in the refrigerator several days. Once avocado flesh is cut and exposed to the air it tends to discolor rapidly. To minimize this effect it is always advisable to add cubed or sliced avocado to a dish at the last moment. When a dish containing mashed avocado, such as GUACAMOLE, is being prepared, the addition of lemon or lime juice helps to prevent discoloration. (It is not true that burying the avocado pit in the guacamole helps maintain good color.) Though avocados are high in unsaturated fat, the California Avocado Advisory Board states that half of an 8-ounce avocado contains only 138 calories. In addition, avocados contain a fair amount of vitamin C, thiamine and riboflavin.

awabi [ah-WAH-bee] *see* ABALONE

azuki bean *see* ADZUKI BEAN

& B A combination of half BÉNÉDICTINE and half BRANDY; available already mixed and bottled.

baba [BAH-bah] Also called *baba au rhum*, this rich, light, currant- or raisin-studded yeast cake is soaked in a rum or KIRSCH syrup. It's said to have been invented in the 1600s by Polish King Lesczyinski, who soaked his stale KUGELHOPF in rum and named the dessert after the storybook hero Ali Baba. The classic baba is baked in a tall, cylindrical mold but the cake can be made in a variety of shapes, including small individual rounds. When the cake is baked in a large ring mold it's known as a SAVARIN.

baba ghanoush [bah-bah gha-NOOSH] A Middle Eastern puree of eggplant, TAHINI, olive oil, lemon juice and garlic. It's garnished with pomegranate seeds, chopped mint or minced pistachios and used as a spread or dip for PITA or Middle Eastern FLAT BREAD.

babka [BAHB-kah] Hailing from Poland, this rum-scented sweet yeast bread is studded with almonds, raisins and orange peel.

baby corn *see* CORN

bacalao [bah-cah-LAH-oh] The Spanish term for dried salt cod.

baccalà [bah-cah-LAH] The Italian term for dried salt cod.

back bacon *see* CANADIAN BACON

bacon Side pork (the side of a pig) that has been CURED and smoked. Because fat gives bacon its sweet flavor and tender crispness, its proportion should (ideally) be ½ to ⅔ of the total weight. **Sliced bacon** has been trimmed of rind, sliced and packaged. It comes in thin slices (about 35 strips per pound), regular slices (16 to 20 strips per pound) or thick slices (12 to 16 strips per pound). **Slab bacon** comes in one chunk that must be sliced and is somewhat cheaper than presliced bacon. It usually comes complete with rind, which should be removed before cutting. Bits of diced fried rind are called CRACKLINGS. **Bacon grease**, the fat rendered from cooked bacon, is highly prized—particularly in the southern U.S.—as a cooking fat. **Canned bacon** is precooked, needs no refrigeration and is popular with campers. **Bacon bits** are crisp pieces of bacon that are preserved and dried. They must be stored in the refrigerator. There are also vegetable-based imitation "bacon-flavored" bits, which may be kept at room temperature. *See also* CANADIAN BACON; PANCETTA.

bagel [BAY-guhl] A doughnut-shaped yeast roll with a dense, chewy texture and shiny crust. Bagels are boiled in water before they're baked.

B

The water bath reduces starch and creates a chewy crust. The traditional **water bagel** is made without eggs and, because it doesn't contain fat, is chewier than an **egg bagel**. Bagels are the cornerstone of the popular Jewish snack of bagels, lox and cream cheese. Miniature cocktail-size bagels can be split, topped with a spread and served as an HORS D'OEUVRE.

bagna cauda [BAHN-yah COW-dah] This specialty of Piedmont, Italy, is a sauce made of olive oil, butter, garlic and anchovies. It's served warm as an appetizer with raw vegetables for dipping. The term comes from *bagno caldo*, Italian for "hot bath."

baguette [bag-EHT] A FRENCH BREAD that's been formed into a long, narrow, cylindrical loaf. It usually has a crisp brown crust and light, chewy interior.

baguette pan A long metal pan shaped like two half-cylinders joined along one long side. Each compartment is about 3 inches wide and 15 inches long. This pan is used to bake French BAGUETTES.

bahmi goreng [bah-MEE goh-REHNG] *see* NASI GORENG

bain-marie [bahn mah-REE] *see* WATER BATH

bake To cook food in an oven, thereby surrounding it with dry heat. It's imperative to know the accurate temperature of an oven. Because most of them bake either hotter or cooler than their gauges read, an OVEN THERMOMETER is vital for accurate temperature readings.

bake blind An English term for baking a pie shell before it is filled. The shell is usually pricked all over with a fork to prevent it from blistering and rising. Sometimes it's lined with foil or PARCHMENT PAPER, then filled with dried beans or rice, or metal or ceramic PIE WEIGHTS. The French sometimes fill the shell with clean round pebbles. The weights and foil or parchment paper should be removed a few minutes before the baking time is over to allow the crust to brown evenly.

baked Alaska An intriguing dessert consisting of a layer of SPONGECAKE topped by a thick slab of ice cream, all of which is blanketed with MERINGUE. This creation is then baked in a very hot oven for about 5 minutes, or until the surface is golden brown. The meringue layer insulates the ice cream and prevents it from melting.

baker's peel *see* PEEL

baking ammonia, powdered *see* AMMONIUM BICARBONATE

baking powder A LEAVENER containing a combination of baking soda, an acid (such as CREAM OF TARTAR) and a moisture-absorber (such as cornstarch). When mixed with liquid, baking powder releases carbon dioxide gas bubbles that cause a bread or cake to rise. There are three basic kinds of baking powder. The most common is **double-acting**, which releases some gas when it becomes wet and the rest when exposed to oven heat. **Single-acting tartrate** and **phosphate baking powders** (hard to find in most American markets because of the popularity of double-acting baking powder) release their gases as soon as they're moistened. Because it's perishable, baking powder should be kept in a cool, dry place. Always check the date on the bottom of a baking-powder can before purchasing it. To test if a baking powder still packs a punch, combine 1 teaspoon of it with ⅓ cup hot water. If it bubbles enthusiastically, it's fine.

baking sheet A flat, rigid sheet of metal on which cookies, breads, biscuits, etc. are baked. It usually has one or more turned-up sides for ease in handling. Shiny, heavy-gauge aluminum baking sheets are good heat conductors and will produce evenly baked and browned goods. Dark sheets absorb heat and should be used only for items on which a dark, crisp exterior is desired. **Insulated baking sheets** (two sheets of aluminum with an air space sealed between them) are good for soft cookies or bread crusts, but most baked goods will not get crisp on them. Cookies and breadstuffs may burn on lightweight baking sheets. To alleviate this problem, place one lightweight sheet on top of another for added insulation. For even heat circulation, baking sheets should be at least 2 inches smaller all around than the interior of the oven.

baking soda Also known as *bicarbonate of soda*, baking soda is used as a LEAVENER in baked goods. When combined with an acid ingredient such as buttermilk, yogurt or molasses, baking soda produces carbon dioxide gas bubbles, thereby causing a dough or batter to rise. Because it reacts immediately when moistened, it should always be mixed with the other dry ingredients before adding any liquid; the resulting batter should be placed in the oven immediately. At one time, baking soda was used in the cooking water of green vegetables to preserve their color. That practice was discontinued, however, when it was discovered that baking soda destroys the vitamin C content of vegetables.

baking stone A heavy, thick, round or rectangular plate of light brown stone used to duplicate the baking qualities of the brick floors of some commercial bread and pizza ovens. A baking stone should be placed on the lowest oven shelf and preheated with the oven. The item to be baked is then placed directly on the baking stone in the oven. Dough-filled pans or baking sheets may be placed on the stone for a crisper, browner crust. When not in use, the stone can be left in the oven. **Baking tiles,** which are usually less expensive than baking stones, are thick, unglazed quarry tiles 8 to 12 inches square. Look for high-fired tiles, which do not crack as readily as low-fired tiles. Also available are sets of eight small, 8- by 4-inch clay tiles that come on an aluminum tray for ease in handling.

baklava [BAHK-lah-vah; bahk-lah-VAH] Popular in Greece and Turkey, this sweet dessert consists of many layers of butter-drenched PHYLLO pastry, spices and chopped nuts. A spiced honey-lemon syrup is poured over the warm pastry after it's baked and allowed to soak into the layers. Before serving, the dessert is cut into triangles and sometimes sprinkled with coarsely ground nuts.

balachan; blachan A popular flavoring in the cuisines of Southeast Asian countries such as Malaysia, Burma and Indonesia. It is made from shrimp, sardines and other small fish that have been allowed to ferment in the sun until very pungent and odorous. It's then salted, mashed and in some cases dried. Balachan is available in paste, powder or cake form in Asian markets.

Baldwin apple Hailing from the New York region, this all-purpose red-skinned apple is mottled and streaked with yellow. It has a mildly sweet-tart flavor and fairly crisp texture and is available from October to April. *See also* APPLE.

ballotine; ballottine [bal-loh-TEEN] Meat, fish or fowl that has been boned, stuffed, rolled and tied in the shape of a bundle. It is then braised or roasted and is normally served hot but can be served cold. Often confused with GALANTINE, which is poached and served cold.

balm *see* LEMON BALM

balsamella [bal-sah-MEHL-ah] *see* BÉCHAMEL SAUCE

balsamic vinegar [bal-SAH-mihk] *see* VINEGAR

Balthazar [bal-THAY-zuhr] *see* WINE BOTTLES

bamboo shoot The tender-crisp, ivory-colored shoot of a particular edible species of bamboo plant. Bamboo shoots are cut as soon as they appear above ground while they're still young and tender. Fresh shoots are sometimes available in Asian markets; canned shoots can be found in the oriental or gourmet section of most supermarkets.

banana Grown in the warm, humid tropics, bananas are picked and shipped green; contrary to nature's norm, they are one fruit that develops better flavor when ripened off the bush. Banana bushes mature in about

15 months and produce one 50-pound bunch of bananas a piece. Each bunch includes several "hands" of a dozen or so bananas (fingers). There are hundreds of banana species but the yellow Cavendish is America's favorite. Choose plump, evenly colored, yellow bananas flecked with tiny brown specks (a sign of ripeness.) Avoid those with blemishes, which usually indicate bruising. Bananas that are still greenish at the tips and along the ridges will need further ripening at home. To ripen, keep uncovered at room temperature (about 70°F). For speedy ripening, enclose bananas in a perforated brown paper bag. Ripe bananas can be stored in the refrigerator for several days. The peel will turn brown but the flesh will remain unchanged. Once exposed to air, a peeled banana will begin to darken. To avoid discoloration, sprinkle with lemon juice or ACIDULATED WATER. Now available in some markets are the short, chunky **red banana** and the **dwarf** or **finger banana**, both of which are sweeter than the Cavendish. The **plantain**, a very large, firm variety, is also referred to as a "cooking banana" and is extremely popular in Latin American countries. It has a mild, almost squashlike flavor and is used very much as a potato would be in the United States. **Banana leaves** are used in the cooking of Mexico, Central and South America, the Caribbean and Southeast Asia to wrap foods for steaming. They can be found in Latin markets. **Banana flour** is a nutritious and easily digestible powder made from specially selected bananas that have been dried and ground. Bananas are high in carbohydrates and low in protein and fats; they're also rich in potassium and vitamin C.

bananas Foster Created at New Orleans's Brennan's Restaurant in the 1950s, this dessert consists of lengthwise-sliced bananas quickly sautéed in a mixture of rum, brown sugar and banana liqueur and served with vanilla ice cream. It was named for Richard Foster, a regular Brennan's customer.

banana split A decadent dessert made of a banana cut in half lengthwise and placed in an individual-size bowl (preferably oblong). The banana is topped with three scoops of ice cream (traditionally chocolate, vanilla and strawberry), over which sweet syrups are poured (usually chocolate, butterscotch and marshmallow). The entire concoction is topped with rosettes of whipped cream and a maraschino cherry.

Banbury cake Originating in Banbury, Oxfordshire, in England, this oval "cake" is made of a flaky pastry filled with mixed dried fruit.

banger British slang for a number of English sausages originally made of ground pork and breadcrumbs. Beef bangers are also available nowadays.

banneton [BAN-tahn] A French, cloth-lined woven basket in which bread is allowed to rise before being baked.

bannock [BAN-nuhk] Baked on a griddle, this traditional Scottish cake is usually made of barleymeal and oatmeal. Bannocks are sometimes flavored with almonds and orange peel and are particularly popular at breakfast or HIGH TEA.

banon cheese; le banon [ba-NON; ba-NOHN] A French goat's-milk cheese that is cured in chestnut leaves and sometimes washed in MARC or COGNAC. It has a soft to semisoft texture and a mild lemony flavor, and is best from late spring to early fall. *See also* CHEESE.

bap A soft yeast roll with a characteristic floury finish. Baps are popular in Scotland as hot breakfast rolls.

barack Made of apricots, this Hungarian EAU DE VIE has a distinctive flavor somewhere between apricots and SLIVOVITZ.

Barbados sugar *see* SUGAR

barbecue; barbeque *n.* 1. Generally a brazier fitted with a grill and sometimes a spit. The brazier can range anywhere from a simple firebowl, which uses hot coals as heat, to an elaborate electric barbecue. 2. Food (usually meat) that has been cooked using a barbecue method. 3. A term used in the United States for an informal style of outdoor entertaining where barbecued food is served. **barbecue** *v.* A method of cooking by which meat, poultry or fish (either whole or in pieces) or other food is covered and slowly cooked in a pit or on a spit, using hot coals or hardwood as a heat source. The food is basted, usually with a highly seasoned sauce, to keep it moist. South Carolina and Texas boast two of the most famous American regional barbecue styles.

barbecue sauce A sauce used to BASTE barbecued meat; also used as an accompaniment to the meat after it's cooked. It's traditionally made with tomatoes, onion, mustard, garlic, brown sugar and vinegar; beer or wine is also a popular ingredient.

barberry Native throughout most of Europe and also grown in New England, the barberry has elongated bright red berries which, because of their high acidity, are seldom eaten raw. Some varieties produce white or yellow fruit. Ripe barberries are used in pies, preserves and syrups; they can also be candied. Green berries are sometimes pickled and used as a relish.

bar cookie A cookie made by spooning a batter or soft dough into a baking pan. The mixture is baked, cooled in the pan and then cut into bars, squares or diamonds. *See also* COOKIE.

bard To tie fat, such as bacon or fatback, around lean meats or fowl to prevent their drying out during roasting. Barding is necessary only when natural fat is absent. The barding fat bastes the meat while it cooks, thereby keeping it moist and adding flavor. The fat is removed a few minutes before the meat is done to allow the meat to brown.

Bardolino [bar-doh-LEE-noh] A light, fruity red wine from northern Italy. Bardolino is best drunk young.

Bar-le-Duc [bar-luh-DOOK] A choice currant preserve that originally came from the French town of Bar-le-Duc in Lorraine. At one time, the preserve was made from white currants whose tiny seeds were removed manually. Today it's made with red and white currants as well as other berry fruits, and the seeds are not generally removed by hand.

barley This hardy grain dates back to the Stone Age and has been used throughout the eons in dishes ranging from cereals to breads to soups (such as the famous SCOTCH BROTH). Most of the barley grown in the Western world is used either for animal fodder or, when malted, to make beer and whiskey. **Hulled** (also called *whole-grain*) **barley** has only the outer husk removed and is the most nutritious form of the grain. **Scotch barley** is husked and coarsely ground. Both hulled and Scotch barley are generally found in health-food stores. **Pearl barley** has also had the bran removed and has been steamed and polished. It comes in three sizes— coarse, medium and fine—and is good in soups and stews. When combined with water and lemon, pearl barley is used to make **barley water**, an old-fashioned restorative for invalids.

barley sugar A hard, lemon-flavored candy that was originally made from barley water to which sugar had been added. It's now more often made with plain water, with TARTARIC ACID added to achieve a similar flavor and texture.

barm brack; barmbrack [BAHRM-brak] An Irish bread with raisins or currants and candied fruit peel. It's generally slathered with butter and served as a tea accompaniment. Literally translated it means "yeast bread," although it's not always made with yeast.

Barolo [bahr-OH-loh] From the Piedmont region, this exceptional Italian red wine, made from Nebbiolo grapes, is known for its lush bouquet and robust body.

baron In England, a large cut of beef (50 to 100 pounds, depending on the size of the animal) usually consisting of a double SIRLOIN. A baron of beef is generally roasted only for traditional or ceremonial occasions. In France, a baron refers to the saddle and two legs of lamb or mutton.

barquette [bahr-KEHT] A boat-shaped pastry shell that can contain a savory filling (when served as an appetizer) or a sweet filling (for a dessert).

barracuda [bair-ah-COO-dah] The type most commonly found in American markets is the **Pacific barracuda** (also called **California barracuda**), which usually ranges from 4 to 8 pounds. It's a firm-textured fish with a moderate fat content and is best grilled or broiled. Barracuda can be substituted for WAHOO or MAHI MAHI. The **great barracuda**, whose flesh is often toxic, can weigh over 100 pounds and can exceed 6 feet in length. *See also* FISH.

Bartlett pear This large bell-shaped fruit has a smooth, yellow-green skin that is sometimes blushed with red. The Bartlett's flesh is sweet and juicy. It's generally available from late July through October and is delicious either cooked or raw. Developed in 18th-century England, it was introduced to America by Dorchester, Massachusetts, resident Enoch Bartlett. *See also* PEAR.

basil [BAY-zihl; BA-zihl] Called the "royal herb" by ancient Greeks, this annual is a member of the mint family. Fresh basil has a pungent flavor that some describe as a cross between licorice and cloves. It's a key herb in Mediterranean cooking, essential to the delicious Italian PESTO, and is becoming more and more popular in American cuisine. Most varieties of basil have green leaves, but one—**opal basil**—is a beautiful purple color. Basil is a summer herb but can be grown successfully inside during the winter in a sunny window. It's plentiful during summer months, and available year-round in many markets. Choose evenly colored leaves with no sign of wilting. Refrigerate basil, wrapped in barely damp paper towels and then in a plastic bag, for up to 4 days. Or store a bunch of basil, stems down, in a glass of water with a plastic bag over the leaves. Refrigerate in this manner for up to a week, changing the water every 2 days. To preserve fresh basil, wash and dry the leaves and place layers of leaves, then coarse salt in a container that can be tightly sealed. Alternatively, finely chop the cleaned basil and combine it with a small amount of olive oil. Freeze in tiny portions to flavor sauces, salad dressings, etc. Dried basil, though it bears little resemblance in either flavor or aroma to the fresh herb, can be purchased in the spice section of most supermarkets. Store dried basil airtight in a cool, dark place for up to 6 months. *See also* HERB; Herb and Spice Chart, page 538.

B

basmati rice   [bahs-MAH-tee]   Literally translated as "queen of fragrance," basmati has been grown in the foothills of the Himalayas for thousands of years. Its perfumy, nutlike flavor and aroma can be attributed to the fact that the grain is aged to decrease its moisture content. Basmati is a long-grained rice with a fine texture. It can be found in Indian and Middle Eastern markets and some supermarkets. *See also* RICE.

bass   A general term for any of numerous (often unrelated) freshwater or saltwater fish, many of which are characterized by spiny fins. In fact, though many of these different species are often sold simply as bass, the only fish with the single name "bass" is a European species (unavailable in the U.S.), which in France is known as *bar* or *loup*. True basses include the GROUPERS, BLACK SEA BASS and STRIPED BASS. Among other fish that are commonly referred to as bass are the **largemouth**, **redeye**, **rock**, **smallmouth** and **spotted bass**, all of which are really members of the SUNFISH family. *See also* SEA BASS; FISH.

bastard saffron   *see* SAFFLOWER OIL

baste   To spoon or brush food as it cooks with melted butter or other fat, meat drippings or liquid such as stock. A BULB BASTER can also be used to drizzle the liquid over the food. In addition to adding flavor and color, basting keeps meats and other foods from drying out. Fatty roasts, when cooked fat side up, do not need basting.

bastela; bastila   *see* B'STEEYA

baster   *see* BULB BASTER

Bath bun   Said to have originated in the English town of Bath in the 18th century, this sugar-coated yeast bun is studded with candied fruit and currants or golden raisins.

Bath chap   The lower portion of a pig's cheek that has been CURED somewhat like bacon. Chaps must come from a long-jawed pig rather than the flat-headed species. Though quite fatty, Bath chap is served cold in the same way as ham.

batter   An uncooked, semiliquid mixture (thick or thin) that can be spooned or poured, as for cakes, muffins, pancakes or waffles. Batters are usually mixtures based on flour, eggs and milk. They can also be used to coat food before frying, as in batter-fried chicken.

batter bread   A yeast bread that is formed without KNEADING. It begins with a very thick batter that often requires extra yeast and, in order to stretch the GLUTEN so the bread will rise effectively, always demands vigorous beating (which can be accomplished with an electric mixer). The mixture should be stiff enough for a spoon to stand up in. A batter bread's texture won't be as refined as that of a bread that has been kneaded but the results are equally delicious.

batterie de cuisine [bat-TREE duh-kwih-ZEEN] The French term for the cooking equipment and utensils necessary to equip a kitchen.

bauerwurst [BOW-er-wurst; BOW-er-vursht]   A coarse-textured German sausage that is SMOKED and highly seasoned. It's usually steamed or sautéed. *See also* SAUSAGE.

Bavarian cream   A cold dessert composed of a rich CUSTARD, whipped cream, various flavorings (fruit puree, chocolate, liqueurs, etc.) and GELATIN. The mixture may be spooned into stemmed glasses or into a decorative mold to be unmolded when set.

bavarois [bah-vah-RWAH] French for "BAVARIAN CREAM."

bay leaf   Also called *laurel leaf* or *bay laurel*, this aromatic herb comes from the evergreen bay laurel tree, native to the Mediterranean. Early Greeks and Romans attributed magical properties to the laurel leaf and it has long been a symbol of honor, celebration and triumph, as in "winning your laurels." The two main varieties of bay leaf are Turkish (which has 1- to 2-inch-long oval leaves) and Californian (with narrow, 2- to 3-inch-long leaves). The Turkish bay leaves have a more subtle flavor than do the California variety. Bay leaves are used to flavor soups, stews, vegetables and meats. They're generally removed before serving. Overuse of this herb can make a dish bitter. Fresh bay leaves are seldom available in markets. Dried bay leaves, which have a fraction of the flavor of fresh, can be found in supermarkets. Store dried bay leaves airtight in a cool, dark place for up to 6 months. *See also* HERB; Herb and Spice Chart, page 538.

Bayonne ham [bay-YOHN] A mildly smoked ham that has been cured in a wine mixture. It's produced in a small town near Bayonne, France. *See also* HAM.

beach plum   A wild, dark purple plum found growing in sandy soil along the Atlantic coast. Its flavor is reminiscent of a grape-plum cross but because it's quite tart and bitter, the beach plum is not good for out-of-hand eating. It makes superior jams and jellies, however, as well as a delicious condiment for meats.

beans   These seeded pods of various LEGUMES are among the oldest foods known to humanity, dating back at least 4,000 years. They come in two broad categories—fresh and dried. Some beans, such as BLACK-EYED PEAS, LIMA BEANS and CRANBERRY BEANS, can be found in both fresh and dried forms. **Fresh beans** are those that are commercially available in their fresh form and are generally sold in their pods. The three most commonly available fresh-bean varieties are GREEN BEANS (eaten with their shell or pod) and lima beans and FAVA (or broad) BEANS, which are eaten shelled. Store fresh beans in a tightly covered container in the refrigerator up to 5 days; after that, both color and flavor begin to diminish. If cooked properly, fresh beans contain a fair amount of vitamins A and C; lima beans are also a good source of protein. **Dried beans** are available prepackaged or in bulk. Some of the more popular dried beans are BLACK BEANS, CHICKPEAS, KIDNEY BEANS, PINK BEANS and PINTO BEANS. Dried beans must usually be soaked in water for several hours or overnight to rehydrate them before cooking. Beans labeled "quick-cooking" have been presoaked and redried before packaging.; they require no presoaking and take considerably less time to prepare. The texture of these "quick" beans, however, is not as firm to the bite as regular dried beans. Store dried beans in an airtight container for up to a year. Dried beans are rich in protein, calcium, phosphorus and iron. Their high protein content, along with the fact that they're easily grown and stored, make them a staple throughout many parts of the world where animal protein is scarce or expensive. *For information on specific beans, see individual listings.*

bean curd *see* TOFU

bean paste *see* MISO

bean sprouts The crisp, tender sprouts of various germinated beans and seeds. **Mung bean sprouts**, used often in Chinese cooking, are the most popular. However, other seeds and beans—such as **alfalfa** seeds, **soybeans** and **wheat berries**—may also be sprouted. For optimum crispness, sprouts are best eaten raw. They may also be stir-fried or sautéed, but should only be cooked for 30 seconds or less; longer cooking will wilt the sprouts. Though you may grow your own fresh sprouts (refer to a general cookbook), they're now available in most large supermarkets. Choose crisp-looking sprouts with the buds attached; avoid musty-smelling, dark or slimy-looking sprouts. Mung-bean sprouts should be refrigerated in a plastic bag for no more than 3 days. More delicate sprouts—like alfalfa sprouts—should be refrigerated in the ventilated plastic container in which they're usually sold and kept for no more than 2 days. Canned mung-bean sprouts—available in most supermarkets-do not have either the texture or flavor of fresh.

bean threads *see* CELLOPHANE NOODLES

béarnaise sauce [bair-NAYZ] A classic French sauce made with a REDUCTION of vinegar, wine, tarragon and shallots and finished with egg yolks and butter. Béarnaise is served with meat, fish, eggs and vegetables.

B

beat To stir rapidly in a circular motion. Generally, 100 strokes by hand equals about 1 minute by electric mixer.

beaten biscuit A traditional Southern biscuit that dates back to the 1800s. Whereas most biscuits are soft and light, beaten biscuits are hard and crisp. The classic texture is obtained by beating the dough for 30 to 45 minutes until it becomes blistered, elastic and smooth. The beating may be done with a mallet, rolling pin, the flat side of a cleaver . . . any heavy object that will pound the dough into submission. One can also use an old-fashioned beaten-biscuit machine, a contraption with wooden or metal rollers reminiscent of an old-time clothes wringer. The dough is passed through the rollers, which are operated by a hand crank. This method takes no less time but saves on the wear and tear of the baker. After the dough is beaten, it is rolled out, cut into small circles and pricked with the tines of a fork before baking.

Beaujolais [boh-zhoh-LAY] Light and dry, this fruity red wine comes from a hilly region in southern Burgundy. **Beaujolais Nouveau** is new wine, bottled right after fermentation without aging. It's very light and fruity and should be drunk within a few months.

béchamel sauce [bay-shah-MEHL; BEH-shah-mehl] Also called by its Italian name, *balsamella*, this basic French white sauce is made by stirring milk into a butter-flour ROUX. Béchamel, the base of many other sauces, was named after its inventor, Louis XIV's steward Louis de Béchamel.

beef Beef, the meat of an adult (over 1 year) bovine, wasn't always as popular as it is today. America has had cattle since the mid-1500s, but most immigrants preferred either pork or chicken. Shortages of those two meats during the Civil War, however, suddenly made beef attractive and very much in demand. Today's beef comes from cows (females that have borne at least one calf), steers (males castrated when very young), heifers (females that have never borne a calf) and bulls under 2 years old. **Baby beef** is the lean, tender but not too flavorful meat of a 7- to 10-month-old calf. Meat packers can request and pay for their meat to be graded by the U.S. Department of Agriculture (USDA). The grading is based on three factors: conformation (the proportion of meat to bone), finish (proportion of fat to lean) and overall quality. Beginning with the best quality, the eight USDA grades for beef are Prime, Choice, Select, Standard, Commercial, Utility, Cutter and Canner. The meat's grade is stamped within a purple shield (a harmless vegetable dye is used for the ink) at regular intervals on the outside of each carcass. USDA Prime and the last three grades are rarely seen in retail outlets. Prime is usually reserved for fine restaurants and specialty butcher shops; the lower- quality grades are generally only used for sausages and in cured and canned meats. Ideally, beef is at its best— both in flavor and texture—at 18 to 24 months. The meat at that age is an even rosy-red color. If the animal is over 2½ years old it is usually classified as "well-matured beef" and, though more full-flavored, the meat begins to toughen and darken to a purplish red. Slow, moist-heat cooking, however, will make it perfectly delicious. *To store fresh beef:* If the meat will be cooked within 6 hours of purchase, it may be left in its plastic-wrapped package. Otherwise, remove the packaging and either store unwrapped in the refrigerator's meat compartment or wrap loosely with waxed paper and keep in the coldest part of the refrigerator for up to 2 days for GROUND BEEF, 3 days for other cuts. The object is to let the air circulate and keep the meat's surface somewhat dry, thereby inhibiting rapid bacterial growth. Cooked meat should be wrapped airtight and stored in the refrigerator. Ground beef can be frozen, wrapped airtight, for up to 3 months, solid cuts up to 6 months. *See also* KOBE BEEF; VEAL; Beef Chart, page 573. *For information on specific meat cuts, see individual listings.*

beefalo [BEEF-ah-loh] A cross between the American bison (commonly called BUFFALO) and cattle, the beef strain being dominant. The dark red meat of beefalo is very lean and has a somewhat stronger flavor than beef. It may be cooked in any manner suitable for beef and is currently available only in specialty meat markets.

beef jerky *see* JERKY

beefsteak tomato *see* TOMATO

beef Stroganoff *see* STROGANOFF

beef tartare [tar-TAR] A dish of coarsely ground or finely chopped high-quality, raw, lean beef that has been seasoned with salt, pepper and herbs. It's thought to have originated in the Baltic provinces of Russia where, in medieval times, the Tartars shredded red meat with a knife and ate it raw. Today the seasoned raw meat is usually shaped into a mound with an indentation in the top, into which is placed a raw egg yolk. Beef tartare (also referred to as *steak tartare*) is usually served with capers, chopped parsley and onions.

beef Wellington A FILLET of beef that has been covered with PÂTÉ DE FOIE GRAS or DUXELLES, wrapped in pastry and baked.

beer A low-alcohol (usually a maximum of 5 percent alcohol by weight) beverage brewed from MALTED barley and other cereals (such as corn or rye) mixed with cultured YEAST for FERMENTATION and flavored with HOPS. Since about nine-tenths of beer's volume is water, the quality of the water is of utmost importance. Beers from different regions of America and other countries take their character from the water used in the brewing. There are many varieties of beer including ALE, STOUT, PORTER and America's favorite, LAGER. Beer adds character and flavor to many foods from breads to stews.

Beerenauslese [BAIR-uhn-OWS-lay-zuh] Any of several fine, sweet German wines made from superior, slightly overripe grapes that have been individually picked or cut from their bunches. Some Beerenausleses are made from grapes that have been infected with BOTRYTIS CINEREA (noble rot). Because of their special selection and picking, these wines are very choice and expensive. *See also* AUSLESE; SPÄTLESE; TROCKENBEERENAUSLESE.

beet Commonly known as the *garden beet*, this firm, round root vegetable has leafy green tops, which are also edible and highly nutritious. The most common color for beets (called "beetroots" in the British Isles) is a garnet red. However, they can range in color from deep red to white, the most intriguing being the **Chioggia** (also called "candy cane"), with its concentric rings of red and white. Beets are available year-round and should be chosen by their firmness and smooth skins. Small or medium beets are generally more tender than large ones. If the beet greens are attached they should be crisp and bright. Because they leach moisture from the bulb, greens should be removed as soon as you get them home. Leave about 1 inch of the stem attached to prevent loss of nutrients and color during cooking. Store beets in a plastic bag in the refrigerator for up to 3 weeks. Just before cooking, wash beets gently so as not to pierce the thin skin, which could cause nutrient and color loss. Peel beets after they've been cooked. In addition to the garden beet are the **spinach** or **leaf beet** (better known as Swiss chard), the **sugar beet** (a major source of sugar) and the **mangold** (used as fodder).

beignet [ben-YAY] A traditional New Orleans yeast pastry that is deep-fried and served hot with a generous dusting of confectioners' sugar. The name comes from the French word for "fritter." Savory beignets, such as herb or crab, are also very popular.

Belgian endive *see* ENDIVE

Bellelay cheese [BEL-luh-lay] Also called *Tête de Moine* ("monk's head"), this rich, semisoft cheese is made in Switzerland and has a flavor similar to that of GRUYÈRE. It is named after the monastery where it originated, the Abbey of Bellelay in the canton of Bern. *See also* CHEESE.

Bellini [behl-LEE-nee] An APÉRITIF made with peach nectar and CHAMPAGNE.

bell pepper *see* SWEET PEPPERS

bellyfish *see* ANGLER

belon oyster Though indigenous to France, this tender, sweet oyster is now being aquacultured in California, Maine and Washington. The belon is small, ranging from 1½ to 3½ inches across, and has a slightly metallic flavor. It's considered superior, especially for eating ON THE HALF SHELL. *See also* OYSTER.

Bel Paese cheese [BELL pah-AY-zay] Translated as "beautiful country," this popular semisoft Italian cheese has a mild, buttery flavor that is delicious with fruity wines. Though originally and still made in a small town outside Milan, Bel Paese is now also produced in the United States. It can be served as a dessert cheese or for snacks and melts beautifully for use in casseroles or on pizza. See also CHEESE.

Beluga caviar [buh-LOO-guh] *see* CAVIAR

Bénédict, à la *see* EGGS BENEDICT

Bénédictine [ben-eh-DIHK-teen] This sweet LIQUEUR was named after the Benedictine monks of the Abbey of Fecamp, Normandy, who first began making it in the 16th century. Though the recipe is a closely guarded secret, it is known that Bénédictine is cognac-based and flavored with various AROMATICS, fruit peels and herbs.

benne seed [BEHN-ee] *see* SESAME SEED

benne wafers [BEHN-ee] A traditional recipe from the Old South, benne wafers are thin, crisp cookies made with brown sugar, pecans and sesame seed.

berbere An Ethiopian spice blend containing garlic, red pepper, cardamom, coriander, fenugreek and various other spices. It's often used in stews and soups.

Bercy [bair-SEE; BUR-see] Bercy is a section of Paris after which two sauces are named. **Bercy butter** is a sauce made with a REDUCTION of white wine with shallots, butter, MARROW, lemon juice, parsley, salt and pepper.

It's served with broiled or grilled meat or fish. **Bercy sauce** is a fish stock–based VELOUTÉ with SHALLOTS—a reduction of white wine, and fish stock and seasonings. It's served with fish.

bergamot [BER-gah-mot] A small acidic orange with a peel that yields an essential oil—called *essence* of bergamot—which is used for perfumes and confections. The peel is used in EARL GRAY TEA. It's also candied and used in the same way as other candied fruit peels.

betty Dating back to colonial America, betties are baked puddings made of layers of sugared and spiced fruit and buttered bread crumbs. Though many fruits can be used, the most popular is **Apple Brown Betty**, made with sliced apples and brown sugar.

beurre [burr] The French word for "butter."

beurre blanc [burr BLAH*N*; burr BLAH*N*GK] Meaning "white butter," this classic French sauce is composed of a wine, vinegar and SHALLOT REDUCTION into which chunks of cold butter are whisked until the sauce is thick and smooth. It's excellent with poultry, seafood, vegetables and eggs.

beurre composé [BURR com-poh-ZAY] The French term for "COMPOUND BUTTER."

beurre manié [burr mahn-YAY] French for "kneaded butter," beurre manié is a paste made of softened butter and flour (usually in equal parts) that is used to thicken sauces.

beurre noir [burr NWAR] A French term meaning "black butter," referring to butter cooked over low heat until dark brown (not black). Beurre noir is usually flavored with vinegar or lemon juice, capers and parsley and served with eggs, fish, brains and some vegetables.

beurre noisette [burr nwah-ZEHT] The French term for "brown butter," referring to butter cooked to a light hazelnut (noisette) color. It's prepared in the same manner as BEURRE NOIR.

bialy [bee-AH-lee] Jewish-American in origin, this large very chewy yeast roll is round and flat with a depression in the center. The bialy is sprinkled with sautéed chopped onion before baking. The name comes from the Polish city of Bialystok.

Bibb lettuce *see* BUTTERHEAD LETTUCE

bicarbonate of soda *see* BAKING SODA

bierkäse [BEER-kay-seh] Literally translated as "beer cheese," this soft, ripened German cheese has a sharp, pungent flavor similar to LIMBURGER. It goes well with dark bread and dark beer. *See also* CHEESE.

bierwurst; beerwurst [BEER-wurst; BEER-vursht] A German cooked sausage with a garlicky flavor and dark red color. It's usually sold as sandwich meat. *See also* SAUSAGE.

bigarade sauce [bee-gah-RAHD] A classic French brown sauce flavored with oranges and served with duck. Bigarade sauce combines beef stock, duck drippings, orange and lemon juice, blanched orange peel, and if desired, CURAÇAO. The original French recipe used bitter Seville oranges (*bigarade* is French for "bitter orange"). Today's cooks should avoid using overly sweet citrus in this sauce.

bigeye scad *see* AKULE

bigos [BEE-gohs] A Polish dish consisting of layers of sauerkraut, onions and apples with cooked meats such as venison, chicken, duck, ham or sausages. The layers are buttered, stock is poured over all and the casserole is baked slowly to allow the flavors to mingle. Tradition says that *bigos* should be made several days in advance because it is best when reheated.

bilberry Also called *whortleberry*, this indigo-blue berry grows wild in Great Britain and other parts of Europe from July to September, depending on the area. Bilberries are smaller and tarter than their cousin the American blueberry, and make delicious jams, syrups and tarts.

billy bi; billi-bi [BILL-ee BEE] An elegant French soup made with mussels, onions, wine, cream and seasonings. The mussels are strained out of a classic billy bi, leaving a smooth and silky soup. However, today it is often served with the mussels. Though there are several stories of the soup's origin, the most popular is that Maxim's chef Louis Barthe named it after a regular patron who particularly loved the soup, American tin tycoon William B. (Billy B.) Leeds.

biltong [BILL-tong] Developed in South Africa and a staple in many African countries, biltong consists of strips of CURED, air-dried beef or game. Though its keeping properties are the same, it is a finer form of jerked meat than American JERKY. The best biltong has been compared to the PROSCIUTTO of Italy.

bind To stir any of a variety of ingredients (eggs, flour and butter, cheese, cream, etc.) into a hot liquid, causing it to thicken.

Bing cherry A very large, delicious cherry that ranges in color from a deep garnet to almost black. The skin is smooth and glossy and the flesh firm and sweet. Bing cherries are good for cooking as well as out-of-hand eating. *See also* CHERRY.

birch beer Dating back to the late 1800s, this American carbonated drink (usually non-alcoholic) is flavored with an extract from birch bark. It's sweet and similar in flavor to root beer.

bird *see* ROULADE

bird's nest soup A classic Chinese specialty made from the nest of an Asian bird similar to the swift. These birds attach their nests to cavern walls in Southeast Asia by using a gelatinous spit. Because of their hazardous location, the nests are dangerous to collect and therefore very expensive. White nests and black nests are the two types used. The more desirable of the two are the white nests, composed mainly of the weblike strands of saliva and containing few foreign particles. Black nests contain feathers, twigs and insects and are labor-intensive to clean. Both types must be cleaned and soaked overnight before using. They're available in Chinese markets.

biscotte *see* RUSK

biscotto; *pl.* biscotti [bee-SKAWT-toh; bee-SKAWT-tee] A twice-baked Italian biscuit (cookie) that's made by first baking it in a loaf, then slicing the loaf and baking the slices. The result is an intensely crunchy cookie that is perfect for dipping into DESSERT WINE or coffee. Biscotti can be variously flavored; the most popular additions are anise seed, hazelnuts or almonds.

biscuit [BIHS-kiht] In America, biscuits refer to small QUICK BREADS, which often use LEAVENERS like baking powder or baking soda. Biscuits are generally savory (but can be sweet), and the texture should be tender and light. In the British Isles, the term "biscuit" usually refers to a flat, thin cookie or cracker.

bishop; bischof This traditional northern European drink, similar to MULLED WINE, consists of wine or PORT that is heated with spices and orange peel and served hot.

Bismark herring *see* HERRING

bisque [bihsk] A thick, rich soup usually consisting of pureed seafood (sometimes fowl or vegetables) and cream.

bisteeya *see* B'STEEYA

bitter almond *see* ALMOND

bitter melon Also referred to as a *balsam pear*, this fruit resembles a cucumber with a bumpy skin and is used as a vegetable in Chinese cooking. When first picked, the bitter melon is yellow-green and has a delicate, sour flavor. As it ripens it turns yellow-orange and becomes bitter and acrid, which is how many people prefer it. Bitter melon is available fresh from April through September in most Asian markets. It can also be purchased canned or dried.

bitter orange *see* SEVILLE ORANGE

bitters Made from the DISTILLATION of aromatic herbs, barks, roots and plants, bitters are a liquid used to flavor cocktails, APÉRITIFS or foods. They are also used as a digestive aid and appetite stimulant. Bitters generally have a high alcohol content and are bitter or bittersweet to the taste. **Angostura bitters**, called for by name in many recipes, is simply the trade name for a brand of bitters. Other popular brands include CAMPARI, Fernet-Branca and Peychaud's.

bivalve Any soft-bodied MOLLUSK, such as a clam, scallop, oyster or mussel, that has two shells hinged together by a strong muscle.

black beans Also called *turtle beans*, these dried beans have long been popular in Mexico, Central and South America, the Caribbean and the southern United States. They have a black skin, cream-colored flesh and a sweet flavor, and form the base for the famous black-bean soup. They are commonly available in supermarkets. *See also* BEAN.

black beans, fermented *see* FERMENTED BLACK BEANS

blackberry Also called a *bramble* because it grows on thorny bushes (brambles), the blackberry is the largest of the wild berries. Purplish-black in color, it ranges from ½ to 1 inch long when mature. Blackberries are widely cultivated in the United States and are available, depending on the region, from May through August. Look for plump, deep-colored berries sans hull. If the hulls are still attached, the berries are immature and were picked too early; the flavor will be tart. Fresh blackberries are best used immediately but they may be refrigerated, lightly covered and preferably in a single layer, for 1 to 2 days. They are wonderful both for cooking and for out-of-hand eating. In Britain, blackberries and apples are a traditional duo for pies.

black bottom pie A rich pie with a layer of dark chocolate CUSTARD, topped with a layer of rum custard. The top is garnished with sweetened whipped cream and chocolate shavings.

black bread Almost black in color, this European peasant bread gets its hue from a variety of ingredients including dark rye flour, toasted dark breadcrumbs, molasses, cocoa powder, dark beer and coffee. It's a hearty, full-flavored loaf that, depending on the baker, can be lightly sweet.

black bun Not a bun in the sense of bread, the Scottish black bun is a spicy mixture of nuts with dried and candied fruit enclosed in a rich pastry crust. Traditionally, Scots serve it at Hogmanay (the New Year). It's best prepared several weeks in advance so the fruit mixture can ripen and develop flavor.

black butter *see* BEURRE NOIR

black cod *see* SABLEFISH

black currant *see* CURRANT

black-eyed pea Originating in Asia, the black-eyed pea is thought to have been introduced to the United States through the African slave trade. This small beige bean has a black circular "eye" at its inner curve. It can be purchased fresh or dried. Though originally cultivated for animal fodder, black-eyed peas are now a popular LEGUME (particularly in the South) and are essential in the traditional dish HOPPIN' JOHN. Also called *cowpea* and, if the "eye" is yellow, *yellow-eyed pea.*

blackfish Also called *Chinese steelhead* and *black trout*, this lean Pacific fish is a favorite in Chinese communities. It has a delicious, delicate flavor but can be troublesome because of its network of tiny fine bones. It is suitable for most methods of cooking. *See also* FISH.

Black Forest torte The famous *Schwarzwälder Kirschtorte* hails from Swabia in Germany's Black Forest region. This exquisite dessert is created by layering KIRSCH-scented chocolate cake, sour cherries and kirsch-laced whipped cream. A generous coating of whipped cream garnished with chocolate curls and cherries completes the cake.

black pepper; black peppercorn *see* PEPPERCORN

black pudding *see* BLOOD SAUSAGE

black Russian A cocktail made with two parts vodka and one part coffee-flavored liqueur served over ice. *See also* white russian.

black sea bass A true bass, this Atlantic coast fish can be found from Cape Cod to Florida, though it's more abundant from New York to North Carolina. A bestselling fish, it can vary in color from brown to dark gray. It has a firm, moderately fat flesh which has a delicate flavor, due largely to its diet of crabs and shrimp. Black sea bass is sold whole, and in steaks and fillets. It's suitable for almost any method of preparation. *See also* sea bass; striped bass; fish.

blackstrap *see* molasses

black tea *see* tea

black trout *see* blackfish

black velvet A drink made with equal parts champagne and stout. A *brown velvet* substitutes port for stout.

black walnut This native American nut has an extraordinarily hard shell, which makes it extremely difficult to crack and therefore not as popular as the more widely known English walnut. Its strong, slightly bitter flavor is highly valued by black-walnut devotees, but its high fat content makes it turn rancid quickly. *See also* nuts.

blanc de blancs [BLAHN deh BLAHN; BLAHNGK deh BLAHNGK] A term used to describe champagnes made exclusively from the white Chardonnay grape. It also refers to white wines made entirely from white grapes, rather than from a blend using some red grapes.

blanc de noirs [BLAHN deh NWAHR; BLAHNGK deh NWAHR] A description for champagne made with a blend of Pinot Noir and Chardonnay grapes. The flavor has slightly more fruit than a blanc de blancs.

blanch 1. To plunge food (usually vegetables and fruits) into boiling water briefly, then into cold water to stop the cooking process. Blanching is used to firm the flesh, to loosen skins (as with peaches and tomatoes) and to heighten and set color and flavor (as with vegetables before freezing). 2. This term also refers to the horticultural technique whereby the leaves of plants are whitened or prevented from becoming green by growing them in complete darkness. It's this labor-intensive process that makes Belgian endive so expensive.

blancmange [bluh-MAHNZH] A simple cooked pudding made of milk, cornstarch, sugar and vanilla. Gelatin may be substituted for the cornstarch. The hot mixture is poured into a mold, chilled, unmolded and served with a sweet sauce or fresh fruit. The original blancmange used pulverized almonds in lieu of cornstarch.

blanquette [blahn-KEHT] A rich, creamy stew made with veal, chicken or lamb, button mushrooms and small white onions. The name comes from the French word *blanc*, meaning "white."

blend *n.* A mixture of two or more flavors combined to obtain a particular character and quality, as in wines, teas and blended whiskey. **blend** *v.* To mix two or more ingredients together with a spoon, beater or electric blender until combined.

blender A small electrical appliance that uses short rotating blades to chop, blend, puree and liquefy foods. Because blender containers are tall and narrow, air is not incorporated into the food so this appliance will not "whip" foods such as egg whites and cream. Blenders can be used for making soups, purees, sauces, milkshakes and other drinks, as well as for chopping small amounts of foods such as breadcrumbs and herbs. *See also* IMMERSION BLENDER.

blenny [BLEN-ee] A genus of small (4- to 6-inch-long) freshwater and saltwater fish characterized by its lack of scales; instead, its body is covered by a mucous membrane. The blenny has a mild, white, flavorful flesh and is best served fried. *See also* FISH.

bleu [BLUEH] A French term used for a steak cooked so rare that it is barely warmed through. À POINT is the next step, which means the steak is cooked rare.

bleu cheese *see* BLUE CHEESE

blind baking *see* BAKE BLIND

blini [BLEE-nee] Hailing from Russia, blini (sing. blin) are small, yeast-raised buckwheat pancakes that are classically served with sour cream and caviar or smoked salmon.

blintz [BLIHNTS] A tender, ultra-thin pancake which can be made with any number of flours. The blintz is rolled to enclose a sweet or savory filling including cottage or ricotta cheese, fruit or meat mixtures. It's then sautéed until golden brown and served with sour cream.

bloaters *see* HERRING

blood orange A sweet-tart orange with a bright red or red-streaked white flesh. Most blood oranges are best eaten fresh, but the more acidic varieties like the **Maltese** work well in cooked sauces like the HOLLANDAISE-based MALTAISE SAUCE. *See also* ORANGE.

blood pudding *see* BLOOD SAUSAGE

blood sausage Also known as *blood pudding* and in Ireland as *black pudding*, this large link sausage is made of pig's blood, suet, breadcrumbs and oatmeal. Almost black in color, blood sausage is generally sold precooked. It's traditionally sautéed and served with mashed potatoes. *See also* SAUSAGE.

Bloody Mary A popular COCKTAIL made with tomato juice, vodka, Worcestershire sauce, Tabasco and other seasonings.

blueberry Round and smooth-skinned, these blue-black berries are juicy and sweet. There are two main types of blueberries (often confused with HUCKLEBERRIES). The high-bush variety can grow up to 15 feet in height; the hardy low-bush blueberry plants are only about 1 foot high and thrive in Canada and the northern United States. Cultivated blueberries comprise the majority of those that reach the market and the season can span from the end of May to early October. Large New Zealand blueberries are in markets in the winter at a premium price. Choose blueberries that are firm, uniform in size and indigo blue with a silvery frost. Discard shriveled or moldy berries. Do not wash until ready to use, and store (preferably in a single layer) in a moistureproof container in the refrigerator for 2 to 3 days. Use blueberries in baked goods, jams, pies, pancakes, salads or, best of all, with a simple splash of sweet cream.

blue cheese This genre of cheese has been treated with molds that form blue or green veins throughout and give the cheese its characteristic flavor. Some of the more popular of the blues include DANABLU, GORGONZOLA, ROQUEFORT and STILTON. Blue cheeses tend to be strong in flavor and aroma, both of which intensify with aging. *See also* CHEESE.

blue crab Named because of its blue claws and oval, dark blue-green shell, the blue crab is found along the Gulf and Atlantic coasts. It's marketed in both its hard- and soft-shell stages. *See also* CRAB.

bluefish Found along the Atlantic and Gulf coasts, the bluefish is nicknamed "bulldog of the ocean" because of its tenacity. It ranges from 3 to 10 pounds and has a fatty, fine-textured flesh that ranges in color from white to silver gray. Removing the dark, oily strip that runs down its center is important to prevent the flesh from absorbing a strong fishy flavor. Bluefish is best when baked or broiled. *See also* FISH.

Blue Hawaii A sweet COCKTAIL composed of two parts each rum and cream to one part each of COINTREAU and blue CURAÇAO.

bluepoint oyster Though originally named for Blue Point, Long Island, where this oyster is said to have been first found, "bluepoint oyster" is now used as a general term referring to any of many small Atlantic oysters from 2 to 4 inches long. They are considered the best for eating ON THE HALF SHELL. *See also* OYSTER.

blush wines In the U.S., the phrase "blush wine" has almost replaced that of *rosé*, which is considered terribly passé. Initially, the term applied to very pale-colored ROSE WINES. Today, however, it's used to encompass a full spectrum of wines that, like rosés, are made with red grapes. The juice has had only brief (2 to 3 days') contact with the stems and skins—the reason for the wines' pale color. The term "blush," however, is broadly used to describe wines that can range in color from various shades of pink to pale orange to light red. Unlike the common rosé, blush wines can range from DRY to sweet and may be be light- to medium-bodied. They should be served chilled—but not icy—and may accompany a variety of lightly flavored foods.

bobwhite *see* QUAIL

bock beer A German beer that is full-bodied, slightly sweet and usually dark. It's brewed in the fall, aged through winter and celebrated in the spring at traditional Bavarian bock beer festivals.

bockwurst [BAHK-wurst; BAHK-vursht] Delicately flavored with chopped parsley and chives, this ground-veal sausage is of German origin. It's generally sold raw and must be well cooked before serving. Bockwurst is traditionally served with BOCK BEER, particularly during springtime. *See also* SAUSAGE.

body A word used with food and wine to describe a full, rich flavor and texture. For instance, a full-bodied wine, beer or coffee has a complex, well-rounded flavor that lingers in the mouth.

boeuf [beuf] The French word for "beef."

boeuf bourguignon [BEUF boor-gee-NYON] *see* BOURGUIGNONNE

boil "Bring to a boil" refers to heating a liquid until bubbles break the surface (212°F for water at sea level). The term also means to cook food in a boiling liquid. A "full rolling boil" is one that cannot be dissipated by stirring.

boiled dinner *see* NEW ENGLAND BOILED DINNER

boiled icing A fluffy cake FROSTING made by gradually pouring a hot SUGAR SYRUP over stiffly beaten egg whites, beating constantly until the mixture is smooth and satiny. An Italian MERINGUE is made in the same manner.

boilermaker A shot of whiskey followed by a chaser of beer.

boiling firepot *see* MONGOLIAN HOT POT

boiling-water bath *see* CANNING

bok choy [bahk CHOY] Also called *Chinese white cabbage* and *white mustard cabbage*, bok choy is a mild, versatile vegetable with crunchy white stalks and tender, dark green leaves. It resembles a bunch of wide-stalked celery with long, full leaves. Bok choy is available year-round in most supermarkets and should be refrigerated airtight for no more than 3 to 4 days. It can be used raw in salads, in a STIR-FRY or as a cooked vegetable. Bok choy is related to but not the same as CHINESE CABBAGE.

bolete; boletus [BOH-leet; boh-LEE-tuhs] *see* CÈPES

bologna; baloney [bah-LOW-nyah; bah-LOW-nee] Precooked and highly seasoned, this popular sausage is usually sliced and served as a sandwich meat or cold cut. The word comes from Italy's city of Bologna, though true Italian bologna sausage is called *mortadella*. *See also* SAUSAGE.

Bombay duck Not a duck at all, this pungent, flavorful food is actually dried salted fish. It can be found in East Indian markets and some specialty markets. Bombay duck is most often used to flavor curried dishes. When cooked until crisp, it can also be eaten as a snack.

bombe [BAHM] A frozen dessert consisting of layers of ice cream or sherbet. The ice cream is softened and spread, one layer at a time, in a mold. Each layer is hardened before the next one is added. The center of a bombe is often custard laced with fruit. After it's frozen solid, the bombe is unmolded and often served with a dessert sauce. The original bombe molds were spherical; however, any shape mold may be used today.

bonbel cheese [bahn-BEHL] The brand name of a popular semisoft cheese sold in small paraffin-coated rounds. It's pale cream in color and has a mild flavor and smooth, buttery texture that's a perfect complement for fruit; it's also used in sandwiches and salads. *See also* CHEESE.

bonbon [BAHN-bahn] A piece of chocolate-dipped candy, usually with a center of FONDANT that is sometimes mixed with fruits or nuts.

bone To remove the bones from meat, fish or fowl.

bonito *see* TUNA

bonne femme, à la [bohn FEHM; bohn FAM] Literally translated as "good wife," the term *bonne femme* describes food prepared in an uncomplicated, homey manner. Sole *bonne femme* is a simply poached fish served with a sauce of white wine and lemon juice, and often garnished with small onions and mushrooms.

borage [BOHR-ihj; BAHR-ihj] Bright flowers and hairy leaves distinguish this European herb whose flavor is reminiscent of cucumber. Both the flowers and leaves are used in salads, but the leaves must be chopped finely so their hirsute texture isn't offputting. The leaves are also used to flavor teas and vegetables.

Bordeaux wines [bohr-DOH] Bordeaux wines take their name from their region of origin in southwest France and are known for their elegant richness and fragrance. Bordeaux is the largest fine-wine district in the world. Some of the best red Bordeaux (also known as *clarets*) include **Medoc, Saint-Emilion** and **Pomerol**; fine white Bordeaux include **Sauternes, Barsac** and **Graves.** *Château* is the word for a wine estate in Bordeaux; three of the best are **Château Latour, Chateau Mouton-Rothschild** and **Chateau Lafite-Rothschild**.

bordelaise, à la [bohr-dl-AYZ; bohr-dl-EHZ] A French term meaning "of or from Bordeaux" and referring to dishes served with BORDELAISE sauce.

bordelaise sauce [bohr-dl-AYZ; bohr-dl-EHZ] A French sauce made with red or white wine, brown stock, bone MARROW, shallots, parsley and herbs. It's usually served with broiled meats.

borek; bourek; burek [BOOR-ehk] Though thought of as Turkish, these thin packets of pastry (ranging from PHYLLO to PUFF PASTRY) are found throughout the Middle East. They can contain a variety of fillings, including cheese, spinach or ground meat, and may be baked or fried. Borek are served hot as an HORS D'OEUVRE or with a salad as a main course.

borscht; borsch [BOHR-sht; BOHR-sh] Originally from Russia and Poland, borscht is a soup made with fresh beets. It can be prepared using an assortment of vegetables, or with meat and meat stock, or with a combination of both. Borscht can be served hot or cold; it should always be garnished with a dollop of sour cream.

Bosc pear [BAWSK] A large winter pear with a slender neck and a russeted yellow skin. Bosc pears are available from October through April.

They have an agreeably sweet-tart flavor and are delicious fresh or cooked. The Bosc holds its shape well when baked or poached.. *See also* PEAR.

Boston baked beans A melange of NAVY BEANS or PEA BEANS (the latter a favorite with New Englanders), SALT PORK, molasses and brown sugar, baked in a casserole for hours until tender. The dish is so named because it was made by Puritan Bostonian women on Saturday, to be served for dinner that night. Because cooking was forbidden on the Sabbath, leftover beans were served with BOSTON BROWN BREAD for Sunday breakfast . . . and, ofttimes, lunch.

Boston brown bread Rye and wheat flour, cornmeal and molasses flavor this dark, sweet STEAMED BREAD. It often contains raisins and is the traditional accompaniment for BOSTON BAKED BEANS.

Boston cream pie Not a pie at all, this dessert consists of two layers of SPONGECAKE with a thick custard filling, topped either by a dusting of confectioners' sugar or chocolate glaze.

Boston lettuce *see* BUTTERHEAD LETTUCE

botrytis cinerea [boh-TRY-tihs sihn-AIR-ee-uh] Also called *noble rot*, this beneficial mold develops on grapes under certain environmental conditions. The mold causes the grape to shrivel, concentrating and intensifying both sugar and flavor. Most winemakers are exhilarated when noble rot descends on their grapes because it gives them fruit from which to make very elegant, intensely flavored DESSERT WINES. In California these wines are usually referred to as LATE HARVEST wines and in France, where noble rot is called *pourriture noble*, they're known as SAUTERNES. In Germany noble rot is called *Edelfäule*, and German winemakers are experts at producing a large variety of elegant botrytis-infected wines such as TROCKENBEERENAUSLESE and some BEERENAUSLESES.

bottled in bond A phrase used on whiskey labels indicating that the contents are 100 PROOF, at least 4 years old, and that the whiskey was produced by a single distiller and stored in a bonded warehouse under government supervision until taxed and shipped to the retailer.

bouchée [boo-SHAY] The French word for "mouthful," a *bouchee* is a small PUFF PASTRY shell filled with various savory preparations such as creamed seafood.

boudin blanc [boo-DAHN BLAH*N*; boo-DAHN BLAHNGK] A delicate sausage, similar to a QUENELLE in texture, made with pork, chicken, fat, eggs, cream, breadcrumbs and seasonings. It is most often gently sautéed and served hot. The term is French for "white pudding." *See also* SAUSAGE.

boudin noir [boo-DAHN NWAHR] The French term for "black pudding" (*see* BLOOD SAUSAGE).

bouillabaisse [BOOL-yuh-BAYZ; BOOL-yuh-BEHZ] A celebrated seafood stew from Provence, made with an assortment of fish and shellfish, onions, tomatoes, white wine, olive oil, garlic, saffron and herbs. The stew is ladled over thick slices of French bread.

bouillon [BOOL-yahn] Any broth made by cooking vegetables, poultry, meat or fish in water. The liquid that is strained off after cooking is the bouillon, which can form the base for soups and sauces.

bouillon cube A compressed, flavor-concentrated cube of dehydrated beef, chicken or vegetable stock. **Bouillon granules** are the granular form of the dehydrated concentrate. Both the cubes and granules must be dissolved in a hot liquid before using.

bounce A popular beverage in Colonial days, bounce is made by combining rum or brandy with fruit, sugar and spices and allowing the mixture to ferment for 1 to 3 weeks.

bounceberry Another name for CRANBERRY.

bouquet [boo-KAY] A term referring to a wine's characteristic aroma.

bouquet garni [boo-KAY gahr-NEE] A bunch of herbs (the classic trio being parsley, thyme and bay leaf) that are either tied together or placed in a CHEESECLOTH bag and used to flavor soups, stews and broths. Tying or bagging the herbs allows for their easy removal before the dish is served.

bourbon Named for Bourbon County, Kentucky, this all-American LIQUOR is distilled from fermented grain. **Straight bourbon** is distilled from a MASH of at least 51 percent corn; **blended bourbon** must contain not less than 51 percent straight bourbon. **Sour mash bourbon** is made by adding a portion of the old mash to help ferment each new batch in the same way as a portion of SOURDOUGH STARTER is the genesis of each new batch of sourdough bread.

bourguignonne, à la [boor-gee-NYON] The French term for "as prepared in Burgundy," one of France's most famous gastronomic regions. Meat (usually beef, as in *boeuf bourguignonne*) is braised in red wine and usually garnished with small mushrooms and white onions. *For information on fondue bourguignonne see listing for* FONDUE.

bourride [boo-REED] Similar to BOUILLABAISSE, this Mediterranean fish soup is pungent with garlic, onions, orange peel and sometimes saffron.

It's usually thickened with egg yolks and flavored with AÏOLI. Bourride is traditionally served EN CROÛTE.

boursault cheese [boor-SOH] A soft, snowy rind surrounds this rich TRIPLE-CREAM CHEESE that has the consistency of thick sour cream. It comes in small paper-wrapped cylinders; avoid any with discolored paper. *See also* CHEESE.

Boursin cheese [boor-SAHN] White and smooth with a buttery texture, this TRIPLE-CREAM CHEESE is often flavored with herbs, garlic or cracked pepper. It's wonderful with dry white and fruity red wines. *See also* CHEESE.

boxty [BOX-tee] Said to have originated during the Irish famine, boxty is rather like a thick pancake composed of mashed and shredded potatoes, flour and baking soda or baking powder. Like a SCONE, the dough is shaped into a circle, cut into quarters and baked on a griddle. Boxty is usually served as a side dish with meat.

boysenberry Horticulturist Rudolph Boysen created this hybrid berry in 1923 by crossing a RASPBERRY, BLACKBERRY and LOGANBERRY. It's shaped like a large raspberry, has a purple-red hue and a rich sweet-tart flavor. Choose boysenberries that are firm and uniform in size. Discard shriveled or moldy berries. Do not wash until ready to use, and store (preferably in a single layer) in a moistureproof container in the refrigerator for 2 to 3 days.

braciola [brah-chee-OH-lah] The Italian name for ROULADE.

brains Beef, pork and lamb brains are available in many supermarkets and most specialty meat markets. Purchase brains that are a bright pinkish-white color, plump and firm. They are very perishable and should be used the day of purchase. Brains must be well washed, then BLANCHED in ACIDULATED WATER. They can then be poached, fried, baked or broiled, and are particularly delicious when served with BEURRE NOIR.

braise [BRAYZ] A cooking method by which food (usually meat or vegetables) is first browned in fat, then cooked, tightly covered, in a small amount of liquid at low heat for a lengthy period of time. The long, slow cooking develops flavor and tenderizes foods by gently breaking down their fibers. Braising can be done on top of the range or in the oven. A tight-fitting lid is very important to prevent the liquid from evaporating.

bramble *see* BLACKBERRY

bran The outer layer of grains (such as wheat or oats) that is removed during milling. Bran is a good source of carbohydrates, calcium, phosphorus and fiber. It's found in cereals and baked goods and can be purchased at health-food stores and most supermarkets.

branch water　A term first used in the 1800s referring to pure, clean water from a tiny stream called a "branch." An order for "bourbon and branch" is a nostalgic request for bourbon and water.

brandade　[brahn-DAHD]　The famous *brandade de morue* of Provence is a pounded mixture of salt COD, olive oil, garlic, milk and cream. This flavorful puree is served with CROÛTES and often garnished with chopped black truffles. Other salted or smoked fish can also be used to make brandade.

brandy　A liquor distilled from wine (such as ARMAGNAC) or other fermented fruit juice (such as the apple-based CALVADOS). Brandies are aged in wood, which contributes flavor and color. The finest of all brandies is COGNAC. The name "brandy" comes from the Dutch *brandewijn*, meaning "burned (distilled) wine."

brandy Alexander　A sweet COCKTAIL which is usually served after dinner. It's made with brandy, chocolate liqueur and cream.

brasserie　[BRAHS-uhr-ee]　An informal French café that serves beer, wine and simple, hearty food.

bratwurst　[BRAHT-wurst; BRAHT-vursht]　A German sausage made of pork and veal seasoned with a variety of spices including ginger, nutmeg and coriander or caraway. Though it is now available precooked, bratwurst is generally found fresh and must be well grilled or sauteed before eating. *See also* SAUSAGE.

braunschweiger　[BROWN-shwi-ger; BROWN-shvi-ger]　Named after the German town of Braunschweig, this smoked liver sausage enriched with eggs and milk is the most famous of the LIVERWURSTS. It's soft enough to be spreadable and is usually served at room temperature. *See also* SAUSAGE.

brazil nut　Actually the seed of a giant tree that grows in South America's Amazon jungle. These seeds come in clusters of 8 to 24 inside a hard, 4- to 6-inch globular pod that resembles a coconut. The extremely hard shell of each seed, or "nut," is dark brown and triangular in shape. The kernel is white, rich and high in fat. *See also* NUTS.

bread　*n*. A staple since prehistoric times, bread is made from flour, water (or other liquid) and usually a LEAVENER. It can be baked (in an oven or, as with pancakes, on a griddle), fried or steamed. Yeast is the leavener in

yeast bread, which requires KNEADING to stretch the flour's GLUTEN. A yeast **batter bread** uses strenuous beating instead of kneading to the same end. **quick breads** are so called because they require no kneading and use baking soda, baking powder or eggs to leaven the bread. As the name implies, **unleavened bread** (such as MATZO) uses no leavening and therefore is quite flat. Grains, seeds, nuts and fruit are often added to bread for flavor and texture. *For information on specific breads, see individual listings.* **bread** *v.* To coat food with bread, cracker or other crumbs, usually by dipping it first into a liquid (beaten eggs, milk, beer, etc.), then into the crumbs, which may be seasoned with various herbs. The breaded food is then fried or baked. Breading helps retain a food's moisture and forms a crisp crust after cooking.

bread-and-butter pickles   Sweet pickles made from thin slices of unpeeled cucumber; usually pickled with onion and sweet green bell pepper, and flavored with mustard and celery seeds, cloves and turmeric.

breadcrumbs   There are dry and fresh (or soft) breadcrumbs, and the two should not be used interchangeably. **Fresh crumbs** are made by placing bread slices (trimmed of crusts or not) in a food processor or blender and processing until the desired size of crumb is reached. They can be stored, tightly sealed, in the refrigerator for a week or frozen for at least 6 months. Fresh breadcrumbs give more texture to breaded dishes. **Dry breadcrumbs**—either plain or flavored—can be purchased in any supermarket. Homemade dry crumbs are made by placing a single layer of bread slices on a baking sheet and baking at 300°F until completely dry and lightly browned. The slices are cooled before processing in a blender or food processor until very fine.

bread flour   *see* FLOUR

breadfruit   Native to the Pacific, breadfruit is large (8 to 10 inches in diameter), has a bumpy green skin and a rather bland-tasting cream-colored center. It is picked and eaten before it ripens and becomes too sweet. Like squash, breadfruit can be baked, grilled, fried or boiled and served as a sweet or savory dish. It's available fresh in some Latin and specialty produce markets and may also be purchased canned.

bread pudding   A simple, delicious baked dessert made with cubes or slices of bread saturated with a mixture of milk, eggs, sugar, vanilla and spices. Chopped fruit or nuts also can be added. **Bread and butter pudding** is made by buttering the bread slices before adding the liquid mixture. Both may be served hot or cold with cream or a dessert sauce.

breakfast tea   *see* ENGLISH BREAKFAST TEA; IRISH BREAKFAST TEA

bream [BREEM] The name applied to any of several freshwater or saltwater fish such as the American *porgy*, the Japanese *sea bream* and the French *daurade*. In general, bream can be grilled, baked or fried. *See also* FISH.

brek; brik [BREHK] From Tunisia, this savory, deep-fried turnover usually contains a spicy meat or fish filling and often an egg. Though the fillings may vary, brek is traditionally served with HARISSA SAUCE.

bresaola [brehsh-ay-OH-lah] Dried, salted beef FILLET that has been aged about 2 months. Bresaola is usually thinly sliced, drizzled with olive oil and lemon juice and served as an ANTIPASTO.

brick cheese The name of this all-American Wisconsin cheese is said to have come from the fact that bricks were once used to weight the CURD and press out the WHEY; it's also brick shaped. Pale yellow and semisoft, brick cheese has a mild, earthy flavor when young. As it ripens, however, it becomes almost as strong as LIMBURGER. *See also* CHEESE.

Brie cheese [BREE] Acclaimed as one of the world's great cheeses, Brie is characterized by an edible, downy white rind and a cream-colored, buttery-soft interior that should "ooze" when at the peak of ripeness. Though several countries (including the United States) make this popular cheese, Brie from France is considered the best and French *Brie de Meaux* dates back to the 8th century. Brie can be made from raw or PASTEURIZED, whole or skim milk. Because Brie must be perfectly ripe for the best flavor, it's important to select one that is plump and resilient to the touch; the rind might show some pale brown edges. Once ripe, Brie has a short shelf life and should be used within a few days. *See also* CHEESE.

brik *see* BREK

brill An excellent European saltwater FLATFISH closely related to the TURBOT. It has a delicate, light flesh that can be broiled, fried, baked, grilled or poached. *See also* FISH.

brine A strong solution of water and salt used for pickling or preserving foods. A sweetener such as sugar or molasses is sometimes added to brine.

brioche [BREE-ohsh; bree-AHSH] This French creation is a light yeast bread rich with butter and eggs. The classic shape, called *brioche à tête*, has a fluted base and a jaunty topknot. It comes in the form of small buns or a large round loaf. Special fluted brioche molds, available in metal, glass or ceramic, are necessary for the *brioche à tête*. Brioche comes in many shapes, however, and is also used to enclose foods such as sausage or cheese.

brisket [BRIHS-kiht] A cut of beef taken from the breast section under the first five ribs. Brisket is usually sold without the bone and is divided into two sections. The **flat cut** has minimal fat and is usually more expensive than the more flavorful **point cut**, which has more fat. Brisket requires long, slow cooking and is best when braised. Corned beef is made from brisket. *See also* BEEF.

brisling [BRIHZ-ling] *see* SPRAT

broad bean *see* FAVA BEAN

broccoli The name comes from the Italian word for "cabbage sprout" and indeed, broccoli is a relative of cabbage, Brussels sprouts and cauliflower. This deep emerald-green vegetable (which sometimes has a purple tinge) comes in tight clusters of tiny buds that sit on stout, edible stems. It's available year-round, with a peak season from October through April. Look for broccoli with a deep, strong color—green, or green with purple; the buds should be tightly closed and the leaves crisp. Refrigerate unwashed, in an airtight bag, for up to 4 days. If the stalks are tough, peel before cooking. Broccoli is an excellent source of vitamins C and A, as well as riboflavin, calcium and iron.

broccoli raab *see* RAPE

brochette [broh-SHEHT] The French word for "skewer." *En brochette* refers to food cooked on a skewer.

brodo [BROH-doh] The Italian word for "broth."

broil To cook food directly under or above the heat source. Food can be broiled in an oven, directly under the gas or electric heat source, or on a barbecue grill, directly over charcoal or other heat source.

broiler-fryer *see* CHICKEN

brook trout *see* TROUT

broth A liquid resulting from cooking vegetables, meat or fish in water. The term is used synonymously with *bouillon*.

brown To cook quickly over high heat, causing the surface of the food to turn brown while the interior stays moist. This method not only gives food an appetizing color, but also a rich flavor. Browning is usually done on top of the stove, but may also be achieved under a broiling unit.

brown betty *see* BETTY

brown butter *see* BEURRE NOISETTE

brownie A dense, chewy, cakelike cookie that is generally chocolate-flavored (hence the name), but can also be a variety of other flavors including butterscotch and vanilla.

brown rice *see* RICE

brown sauce Also known as *espagnole sauce*, brown sauce is used as a base for dozens of other sauces. It's traditionally made of a rich meat stock, a MIREPOIX of browned vegetables, a brown ROUX, herbs and sometimes tomato paste. *See also* SAUCE.

brown sugar *see* SUGAR

brown velvet *see* BLACK VELVET

bruise [BROOZ] In cooking, to partially crush an ingredient in order to release its flavor. Bruising a garlic clove with the flat side of a knife crushes without cutting it.

brûlé [broo-LAY] The French word for "burned," as in CRÈME BRÛLÉE.

brunch A combination of breakfast and lunch, usually eaten sometime between 11 a.m. and 3 p.m. Sunday brunch has become quite popular both for home entertaining and in restaurants. Though brunch is thought of as an American tradition, H. L. Mencken tells us that it was popular in England around 1900 . . . long before it reached the U.S.

brunoise [broo-NWAHZ] A mixture of vegetables that have been finely diced or shredded, then cooked slowly in butter. The brunoise is then used to flavor soups and sauces.

bruschetta [broo-SHEH-tah; broo-SKEH-tah] From the Italian *bruscare* meaning "to roast over coals," this traditional garlic bread is made by rubbing slices of toasted bread with garlic cloves, then drizzling the bread with extra-virgin olive oil. The bread is salted and peppered, then served while warm.

brush To apply a liquid (such as melted butter or glaze) with a pastry (or basting) brush to the surface of food such as meat or bread.

Brunswick stew Brunswick County, Virginia, was the birthplace in 1828 of this hearty squirrel-meat and onion stew. Today, it is generally made with rabbit or chicken and often contains a variety of vegetables including okra, lima beans, tomatoes and corn.

Brussels sprouts Said to have been cultivated in 16th-century Belgium, Brussels sprouts are a member of the cabbage family and, indeed, resemble tiny cabbage heads. Many rows of sprouts grow on a single long stalk. They range from 1 to 1½ inches in diameter; the smaller sprouts are more tender. Brussels sprouts are available from late August through March. Buy small bright green sprouts with compact heads. Store unwashed sprouts in an airtight plastic bag in the refrigerator up to 3 days; longer than that and sprouts will develop a strong flavor. Brussels sprouts are high in vitamins A and C, and are a fair source of iron.

brut [BROOT] A term applied to the driest CHAMPAGNE (*see* DRY). Brut champagnes are drier than those labeled "extra dry."

Bryndza cheese; Brinza [BRIHN-zah] Of Romanian origin, this sheep's-milk cheese is cured in brine. It's creamy, rich and salty, and ranges from soft and spreadable to semidry and crumbly. *See also* CHEESE.

b'steeya [bs-TEE-yah] A Moroccan dish of PHYLLO dough surrounding a melange of shredded pigeon (or chicken), ground almonds and spices. The "pie" is baked until a crisp golden brown, then sprinkled with confectioners' sugar and cinnamon. Also spelled *bastela, bastila, bisteeya* and *pastilla.*

bubble and squeak An English dish of equal parts mashed potatoes and chopped cooked cabbage mixed together and fried until well browned. Originally, the dish included chopped boiled beef. The name is said to come from the sounds the potato-cabbage mixture makes as it cooks (some say it's from the sounds one's stomach makes after eating bubble and squeak).

bûche de Noël [BOOSH duh noh-EHL] Literally translated as "yule log," this traditional French Christmas cake is shaped and decorated to resemble a log. It's made of a sheet of GÉNOISE that is spread with mocha or chocolate BUTTERCREAM, rolled into a log shape and covered with more buttercream. The surface is ridged to resemble the bark of a log, and sometimes garnished with MERINGUE "mushrooms" and with "moss" made from chopped pistachio nuts.

Bucheron cheese [BOOSH-raw*n*] A tangy yet mild CHÈVRE (goat cheese) that is usually soft and spreadable. Bûcheron comes in logs either with white rinds or covered with black ash. *See also* CHEESE.

buckwheat A native of Russia, buckwheat is thought of as a cereal, but is actually an herb of the genus *Fagopyrum*. The triangular seeds of this plant are used to make **buckwheat flour**, which has an assertive flavor and is used for pancakes and as an addition to some baked goods. The famous Russian BLINI are made with buckwheat flour. **Buckwheat groats,**

also referred to as KASHA, are the hulled, crushed kernels. They're usually cooked in a manner similar to rice. Groats come in coarse, medium and fine grinds.

buffalo The American buffalo, now being raised on game farms, is really a bison—a shaggy, humped member of the cattle family. Buffalo meat is surprisingly tender and tastes somewhat like lean beef. It has no pronounced gamey flavor. It can be found on some restaurant menus and is available in some specialty meat markets. The cuts are similar to beef and, likewise, similarly prepared.

Buffalo chicken wings Buffalo, New York's, Anchor Bar originated this dish of deep-fried chicken wings served in a spicy hot sauce and accompanied by blue-cheese dressing.

buffalo fish Similar to CARP, this freshwater fish is a member of the sucker family. It has a coarse but sweet, lean flesh that can be baked, poached, sautéed or grilled. Buffalo fish can be purchased whole or in FILLETS or STEAKS. It's especially good in its smoked form. *See also* FISH.

bulghur wheat; bulgar [BUHL-guhr] Also called *burghul*. A nutritious staple in the Middle East, bulghur wheat consists of wheat kernels that have been steamed, dried and crushed. It is often confused with but is not exactly the same as CRACKED WHEAT. Bulghur has a tender, chewy texture and comes in coarse, medium and fine grinds. It makes an excellent wheat PILAF and is delicious in salads (*see* TABBOULEH), and in meat or vegetable dishes.

bullhead *see* CATFISH

bullshot A drink composed of two parts beef bouillon and one part vodka, plus dashes of WORCESTERSHIRE SAUCE, BITTERS and TABASCO sauce.

Bundnerfleisch [BOOND-ner-flysh] A Swiss salt-CURED, air-dried beef similar to (but considered superior to) Africa's BILTONG. It's available only in specialty gourmet markets.

Bundt pan [BUNT] Originally the trademark name of a TUBE PAN with fluted sides, "Bundt pan" is now the general name of any of that style of cake pan. To prevent a cake from sticking to this pan, it's extremely important that all the creases of the fluted sides are well greased before pouring in a batter.

buñuelo [boo-NWAY-loh] A thin, deep-fried Mexican pastry sprinkled with cinnamon-sugar.

burbot [BUR-buht] This freshwater COD has a fairly lean, white flesh with a delicate flavor. It can be poached, baked, broiled or sautéed. *See also* FISH.

burdock Known in Japan as *gobo*, burdock is a slender root vegetable with a rusty brown skin and grayish-white flesh. Cultivated primarily in Japan, it grows wild throughout much of Europe and the United States. Burdock has a sweet, earthy flavor and tender-crisp texture. It's important to choose firm, young burdock, preferably no more than 1 inch in diameter; they will be about 18 inches long. Do not wash the earth-covered roots until ready to use. Store, tightly wrapped in a plastic bag, in the refrigerator for up to 4 days. Scrub before cooking; peeling isn't necessary. Burdock can be thinly sliced or shredded and used in soups as well as with vegetables and meats.

burghul *see* BULGHUR WHEAT

burgoo [bur-GOO] Also called *Kentucky burgoo*, this thick stew is full of meats (usually pork, veal, beef, lamb and poultry) and vegetables (including potatoes, onions, cabbage, carrots, sweet green peppers, corn, okra, lima beans and celery). Early renditions were more often made with small game such as rabbit and squirrel. Burgoo is popular for large gatherings in America's southern states. Originally, the word "burgoo" was used to describe an oatmeal porridge served to English sailors as early as 1750.

Burgundy wines The Burgundy region in eastern France produces a group of superb red and white wines, though four times as much red is bottled as white. Burgundies are more robust and full-bodied than BORDEAUX WINES. Some of the better known wines of Burgundy include BEAUJOLAIS, Pommard, Beaune, Meursault, CHABLIS, Pouilly-Fuissé and Echézeaux.

burnet [BUR-niht] Native to Europe, burnet includes any of several herbs, the most common being **salad burnet**. Its leaves are used in salads and with vegetables. Like BORAGE, burnet leaves are also used to flavor drinks, such as tea. When crushed, they have a fragrance similar to cucumber.

burnt sugar *see* CARMELIZE

burrito [bur-EE-toh] A flour TORTILLA folded and rolled to completely enclose any of several savory fillings including shredded or chopped meat, refried beans, grated cheese, sour cream, lettuce, etc.

butcher's steel *see* SHARPENING STEEL

butter Made by churning cream until it reaches a semisolid state, butter must by U.S. law be at least 80 percent BUTTERFAT. The remaining 20 percent consists of water and milk solids. The U.S. Department of Agriculture (USDA) grades butter quality based on flavor, body, texture, color and salt. Butter packages bear a shield surrounding the letter grade (and occasionally the numerical score equivalent) indicating the quality of the contents. The grades, beginning with the finest, are AA (93 score), A (92 score), B (90 score) and C (89 score.) AA and A grades are those most commonly found at the retail level. Butter may be artificially colored (with natural ANNATTO); it may also be salted or unsalted. **Unsalted butter** is usually labeled as such and contains absolutely no salt. It's sometimes erroneously referred to as "sweet" butter—a misnomer because any butter made with sweet instead of sour cream is sweet butter. Therefore, expect packages labeled "sweet cream butter" to contain salted butter. Unsalted butter is preferred by many for everyday eating and baking. Because it contains no salt (which acts as a preservative), it is more perishable than salted butter and therefore stored in the freezer section of some markets. **Whipped butter** has had air beaten into it, thereby increasing volume and creating a softer, more spreadable consistency when cold. It comes in salted and unsalted forms. **Butter-flavor granules** are made by a process that removes the fat and water from a butter extract (a blend of modified butter oil and spray-dried butter). The granules are 6 (compared to butter's 100) calories per tablespoon and contain no cholesterol. They may either be reconstituted by blending with a liquid, or sprinkled directly on the food involved. Butter-flavor granules cannot be used as a butter substitute for baking, frying or greasing pans. *See also* CLARIFIED BUTTER; GHEE.

butter bean *see* LIMA BEAN

butter clam A small, sweet, hard-shell clam from Puget Sound. Butter clams can be cooked in a variety of ways, including steaming, stewing and frying. *See also* CLAM.

buttercream A light, creamy frosting made with softened butter, confectioners' sugar, egg yolks and milk or light cream. This uncooked frosting is beaten until light and creamy. It can be flavored in many ways and is used both as a filling and frosting for a variety of cakes and pastries.

buttercup squash A variety of TURBAN SQUASH that ranges from 4 to 8 inches in diameter and 2 to 3 inches high. It has a light blue-gray turban with a dark green shell flecked with gray. The flesh is orange and the flavor reminiscent of sweet potato. It can be baked, steamed or simmered. *See also* SQUASH.

butter curler A small (6- to 7-inch-long) utensil with a serrated hook at one end. The hook is drawn down the length of a stick of butter to make butter curls. The curls are then dropped into ice water to set their shape.

butterfat The fatty particles in whole milk that are separated out to make cream and subsequently butter. The higher the butterfat content in milk, cream, ice cream, etc., the creamier, richer and more caloric the product.

butterfish Found off the Atlantic and Gulf coasts, the small (average 8 ounces), high-fat butterfish has a tender texture and a rich, sweet flavor. It is usually sold whole and is sometimes smoked. Butterfish can be broiled, baked, grilled or sautéed. Depending on the region, they're also known as *dollarfish, Pacific pompano* and *pomfret. See also* FISH; SABLEFISH.

butterfly In cooking, to split a food (such as shrimp) down the center, cutting almost but not completely through. The two halves are then opened flat to resemble a butterfly shape.

butterhead lettuce One of two varieties of head lettuce (the other being CRISPHEAD). Butterhead lettuces have small, round, loosely formed heads with soft, buttery-textured leaves ranging from pale green on the outer leaves to pale yellow-green on the inner leaves. The flavor is sweet and succulent. Because the leaves are quite tender, they require gentle washing and handling. **Boston** and **Bibb** (also called **limestone**) lettuce are the two most well known of the butterhead family. The smaller Bibb is highly prized by gourmets. Both Boston and Bibb lettuce are sometimes referred to simply as "butterhead" or "butter" lettuce. *See also* LETTUCE.

buttermilk *see* MILK

butter mold These decorative molds are used to form butter into fancy shapes. They come in ceramic, metal, wood and plastic; their sizes range from small, individual portions to large 8-ounce or more family-style molds. The molds are filled with softened butter and leveled off. After chilling, the solidified butter is removed from the mold and refrigerated until ready to serve.

butternut This native American nut grows in New England and is also known as the *white walnut.* It has a rich, oily meat which is generally used in candies and baked goods. Because of the high oil content, butternuts become rancid quickly. *See also* NUTS; WALNUTS.

butternut squash This large, cylindrical winter squash looks rather like a pear-shaped bat. It's 8 to 12 inches long, 3 to 5 inches at its widest point and can weigh from 2 to 3 pounds. The color of the smooth shell ranges from yellow to camel; the flesh is sweet and orange. It can be baked, steamed or simmered. *See also* SQUASH.

butterscotch The flavor of butterscotch is a blend of butter and brown sugar. It is popular for cookies, ice-cream toppings, frostings and candies.

Byrrh [bihr] A French APÉRITIF wine that is a blend of red wine and quinine.

abbage The word cabbage is a derivation of the French word *caboche*, a colloquial term for "head." The cabbage family—of which Brussels sprouts, broccoli, cauliflower and kale are all members—is wide and varied. Cabbage itself comes in many forms—the shapes can be flat, conical or round, the heads compact or loose, and the leaves curly or plain. In the United States, the most widely used cabbage comes in compact heads of waxy, tightly wrapped leaves that range in color from almost white to green to red. SAVOY CABBAGE and CHINESE CABBAGE are considered culinarily superior but are less readily available. Choose a cabbage with fresh, crisp-looking leaves that are firmly packed; the head should be heavy for its size. Cabbage may be refrigerated, tightly wrapped, for about a week. It can be cooked in a variety of ways or eaten raw, as in SLAW. Cabbage contains a good amount of vitamin C and some vitamin A.

cabbage turnip *see* KOHLRABI

Cabernet [cab-air-NAY] The Cabernet grape creates some of the world's best red wines (notably in Europe, California, Australia and South America). It's used to produce full-bodied, fruity Cabernet wines, as well as the red BORDEAUX WINES (also known as CLARETS). California Cabernets are usually rich, complex and intensely flavorful. At their very best, they have nuances of raspberries and CASSIS. They often require considerable bottle aging to achieve their full potential. **Cabernet Sauvignon** grapes are smaller and produce longer-lived wines that are slightly higher in TANNIN. The juice from the prolific **Cabernet Franc** grape is generally used as a blending agent.

cabinet pudding This classic English dessert is made with layers of bread, cake or LADYFINGERS (which may be soaked with LIQUEUR), dried fruit and custard. The pudding is baked, unmolded and usually served with CRÈME ANGLAISE. Another version of cabinet pudding uses gelatin and whipped cream; rather than being baked, it's simply chilled until set.

cacao [kah-KAY-oh; kah-KAH-oh] The tropical, evergreen cacao tree is cultivated for its seeds (also called beans), from which COCOA BUTTER, CHOCOLATE and COCOA POWDER are produced.

cacciatore [kah-chuh-TOR-ee] Italian for "hunter," this American-Italian term refers to food prepared "hunter-style," with mushrooms, onions, tomatoes, various herbs and sometimes wine. Chicken *cacciatore* is the most popular dish prepared in this style.

caciocavallo cheese [kah-choh-kuh-VAH-loh] From southern Italy, *caciocavallo* (meaning "cheese on horseback") is said to date back to the

14th century, and believed by some to have originally been made from mare's milk. Today's *caciocavallo* comes from cow's milk and has a mild, slightly salty flavor and firm, smooth texture when young (about 2 months.) As it ages, the flavor becomes more pungent and the texture more granular, making it ideal for grating. Caciocavallo is one of the *pasta filata* types of cheeses (like PROVOLONE and MOZZARELLA), which means it has been stretched and shaped by hand. It may be purchased plain or smoked and comes in string-tied gourd or spindle shapes. *See also* CHEESE.

cactus pear   *see* PRICKLY PEAR

Caerphilly cheese   [kar-FIHL-ee]   This mild yet tangy cow's-milk cheese has a moist, semifirm texture and is generally sold in cylinders or blocks. It's best eaten fresh (the English prefer it only a few weeks old) and is delicious with dark breads and ALE. Though now produced in England, Caerphilly gets its name from the village in Wales where it was first made; it was the traditional lunch of Welsh miners. *See also* CHEESE.

Caesar salad   [SEE-zer]   A salad consisting of greens (classically, ROMAINE LETTUCE) tossed with a garlic VINAIGRETTE dressing (made with WORCESTERSHIRE SAUCE and lemon juice), grated Parmesan cheese, croutons, a CODDLED egg and sometimes anchovies. It is said to have been created in 1924 by Italian chef Caesar Cardini, who owned a restaurant in Tijuana, Mexico.

café; cafe   [ka-FAY]   1. The French word for "coffee." 2. A small, unpretentious restaurant.

café au lait   [ka-FAY oh-LΛY]   French for "coffee with milk." It usually consists of equal portions of scalded milk and coffee.

café brûlot   [ka-FAY broo-LOW]   A traditional New Orleans flaming brew consisting of coffee blended with spices, orange and lemon peel and brandy. *Café brûlot* is generally made in a flameproof bowl and ladled into cups. In French, *brûlot* means "burnt brandy."

Cajun cooking   [KAY-juhn]   Today's Cajuns are the descendants of 1,600 French Acadians whom the British forced from their Nova Scotian homeland in 1785. The local Indians transmuted the word *Acadians* to *Cagians* and, eventually, to *Cajuns*. Many confuse Cajun cooking with CREOLE COOKING but though there are many points of similarity, there are also distinct differences. Cajun cooking, a combination of French and Southern cuisines, is robust, country-style cookery that uses a dark ROUX and plenty of animal (usually pork) fat. Creole cooking places its emphasis on butter and cream. Some maintain that Creole cooking uses more tomatoes and the Cajuns more spices. Both cuisines make generous use of FILÉ POWDER and the culinary "holy trinity" of chopped green peppers, onions and celery. Two of the more traditional Cajun dishes include JAMBALAYA and coush-coush (a thick cornmeal breakfast dish).

cake A sweet, baked confection usually containing flour, sugar, flavoring ingredients and eggs or other LEAVENER such as baking powder or baking soda.

cake comb A flat, small (usually 5- by 5- by 4- inch), triangle-shape tool, generally made of stainless steel. Each of the three edges has serrated teeth of a different size. This tool is used to make decorative designs and swirls in the frosting on a cake.

cake flour *see* FLOUR

calamari [kal-uh-MAHR-ee] *see* SQUID

calamata olive *see* KALAMATA OLIVE

cala [kah-LAH] The word "cala" comes from an African word for "rice," and refers to a deep-fried pastry made with rice, yeast, sugar and spices. Calas resemble small, round doughnuts without a hole and are usually sprinkled with confectioners' sugar.

caldo verde [KAHL-doh VAIR-deh] *Caldo verde* ("green soup") is a Portuguese favorite that combines shredded KALE, sliced potatoes, LINGUIÇA sausage and olive oil for a deliciously satisfying soup.

calf's foot jelly An ASPIC made by boiling calves' feet until the natural GELATIN is extracted. The liquid is strained, then combined with wine, lemon juice and spices and refrigerated until set. If sugar is added, it can be eaten as a dessert. Calf's-foot jelly was once thought to be a restorative for invalids.

calico bean *see* LIMA BEAN

California Jack cheese *see* MONTEREY JACK CHEESE

California corbina *see* DRUM

Calvados [KAL-vah-dohs] A dry apple BRANDY made in Calvados, in the Normandy region of northern France. It's often used for cooking, particularly in chicken, pork and veal dishes.

calzone [kal-ZOH-nay; kahl-SOH-neh] Originating in Naples, calzone is a stuffed PIZZA that resembles a large turnover. It is usually made as an individual serving. The fillings can be various meats, vegetables or cheese; mozzarella is the cheese used most frequently. Calzones can be deep-fried or brushed with olive oil and baked.

cambric tea [KAYM-brihk] An American term used to describe a hot drink of milk, water, sugar and, if desired, a dash of tea. It was a favorite of children and the elderly in the late 19th and early 20th century. The name is taken from a fabric called cambric, which is white and thin . . . just like the "tea."

Camembert cheese [KAM-uhm-bair] Napoleon is said to have christened this cheese with the appellation "Camembert," naming it after the Norman village where a farmer's wife first served it to him. Now world famous, this cow's-milk cheese has a white, downy rind and a smooth, creamy interior. When perfectly ripe, the cheese should ooze thickly. When overripe, it becomes runny, bitter and rank. Choose Camembert that is plump and soft to the touch. Avoid those with hardened edges, which may forecast overripeness. *See also* CHEESE.

camomile; chamomile [KAM-uh-meel; KAM-uh-myl] Resembling a daisy, this aromatic flower is dried and used to flavor camomile tea, reputed to be a soothing drink. The flowers are also used as a fragrance in shampoos and other hair preparations.

Campari [kahm-PAH-ree] A popular Italian BITTERS, often mixed with soda for an APÉRTITIF. It's also consumed without a mixer and used in some COCKTAILS. Regular Campari has an astringent, bittersweet flavor; sweet Campari is also available.

can; canning A method of preserving food by hermetically sealing it in glass containers. The use of special canning jars and lids is essential for successful canning. The canning process involves quickly heating jars of food to high temperatures, thereby retaining maximum color, flavor and nutrients while destroying the microorganisms that cause spoilage. During processing, the food reaches temperatures of 212°F (with the boiling-water-bath method) to 240°F (using a pressure canner). Any air in the container is forced out between the jar and lid. A vacuum is created as the food cools and contracts, sucking the lid tightly to the jar. This airtight seal is vital to prevent invasion by microorganisms. Refer to a general cookbook for specific instructions on canning foods.

Canadian bacon Called *back bacon* in Canada, this lean smoked meat is a closer kin to HAM than it is to regular bacon. It's taken from the lean, tender eye of the LOIN, which is located in the middle of the back. Canadian bacon comes in cylindrical chunks that can be sliced or cut in any manner desired. It costs more than regular bacon, but it's leaner and pre-cooked (meaning less shrinkage) and therefore provides more servings per pound. It can be fried, baked, barbecued or used cold as it comes from the package in sandwiches and salads.

C

Canadian whisky Dropping the "*e*" from WHISKEY is traditionally British and is used in the spelling of Canadian whisky. Made only in Canada, this distilled blend of rye, corn, wheat and barley is smoother and lighter than its cousins, rye and bourbon.

canapé [KAN-uh-pay; KAN-uh-pee] Small, decorative pieces of bread (toasted or untoasted) that are topped with a savory garnish such as anchovy, cheese or some type of spread. Crackers or pastry may also be used as a base. Canapés may be simple or elaborate, hot or cold. They're usually served as an appetizer with COCKTAILS. The word "canapé" is French for "couch." *See also* HORS D'OEUVRE.

canard [kah-NARD; kah-NAR] The French word for "duck."

candied fruit; candied flowers Fruit or flowers that have been boiled or dipped in SUGAR SYRUP, then sometimes into granulated sugar after being dried. Candied fruits (also called *glacé fruits*) are generally used in cakes, breads and other sweets. Candied flowers are generally reserved for decorating desserts; candied fruits can also be used in this manner. The most common fruits that are candied are cherries, pineapple and citrus rinds. ANGELICA and GINGER are also candied favorites. Among the crystallized flowers, violets and miniature rosebuds and rose petals are the most common. Candied fruit and flowers can be found at gourmet markets and specialty shops. They should be stored airtight in a cool, dry place.

candy *n.* Any of a number of various confections—soft and hard—composed mainly of sugar with the addition of flavoring ingredients and fillings such as chocolate, nuts, peanut butter, NOUGAT, fruits, etc. Candy may come in tiny bits, small one- or two-bite pieces, or in the form of a candy "bar," containing several bites. Candy bars usually have a chocolate coating. So-called "nutritious" candy bars usually contain honey instead of sugar, and often substitute CAROB for chocolate. **candy** *v.* To sugar-coat various fruits, flowers and plants such as cherries, pineapple, citrus rinds, ANGELICA, GINGER, CHESTNUTS, violets, miniature rose petals and mint leaves. Candying food not only preserves it, but also retains its color, shape and flavor. The candying process usually includes dipping or cooking the food in several boiling SUGAR SYRUPS of increasing degrees of density. After the candied fruit air-dries, it is sometimes dipped in granulated sugar.

candy thermometer A kitchen thermometer used for testing the temperature during the preparation of candy, syrups, jams, jellies and deep fat. It should register from 100° to 400°F. Choose a thermometer that is easy to handle in hot mixtures, such as one with a plastic handle. Many have adjustable hooks or clips so the thermometer can be attached to a pan. There are dual-purpose thermometers with readings both for candy and deep fat. *See also* Candy-Making Temperatures and Cold Water Tests Chart, page 537.

cane syrup Made from sugar cane, this thick, extremely sweet syrup is used in Caribbean and Creole cookery and is available in shops specializing in those cuisines.

cannellini bean [kan-eh-LEE-nee] Large, white Italian kidney beans, available both in dry and canned forms. Cannellini beans are particularly popular in salads and soups. *See also* BEANS.

cannelloni [kan-eh-LOH-nee] Large PASTA tubes (or squares of pasta that have been rolled into tubes) that are boiled, then stuffed with a meat or cheese filling and baked with a sauce.

cannoli [kan-OH-lee] An Italian dessert consisting of tubular or horn-shaped pastry shells that have been deep-fried, then filled with a sweetened filling of whipped RICOTTA (and often whipped cream) mixed with bits of chocolate, candied citron and sometimes nuts.

canola oil [kan-OH-luh] The market name for *rapeseed oil* which, as might be assumed from the name, is expressed from rape seeds. For obvious reasons, the name was changed to canola by the Canadian seed-oil industry. Canola is, in fact, Canada's most widely used oil. It's commonly referred to there as *lear oil*, for "low erucic acid rapeseed" oil. The popularity of canola oil is rising fast in the U.S., probably because it's been discovered to be lower in saturated fat (about 6 percent) than any other oil. This compares to the saturated fat content of peanut oil (about 18 percent) and palm oil (at an incredibly high 79 percent). Another canola oil selling point is that it contains more cholesterol-balancing monounsaturated fat than any oil except olive oil. It also has the distinction of containing Omega-3 fatty acids, the wonder polyunsaturated fat reputed to not only lower both cholesterol and triglycerides, but to contribute to brain growth and development as well. The bland-tasting canola oil is suitable both for cooking and for salad dressings. *See also* FATS AND OILS.

cantaloupe [KAN-teh-lohp] Named for a castle in Italy, the true cantaloupe is a European melon that is not exported. American "cantaloupes" are actually MUSKMELONS. When perfectly ripe, these cantaloupes have a raised netting on a smooth greyish-beige skin. The pale orange flesh is extremely juicy and sweet. Choose cantaloupes that are heavy for their size, have a sweet, fruity fragrance, a thick, well-raised netting and yield slightly to pressure at the blossom end. Avoid melons with soft spots or an overly strong odor. Store unripe cantaloupes at room temperature, ripe melons in the refrigerator. Cantaloupes easily absorb other food odors so if refrigerating for more than a day or two, wrap the melon in plastic wrap. Just before serving, cut melon in half and remove the seeds. Cantaloupe is an excellent source of vitamins A and C. *See also* MELON.

cape gooseberry Though this intriguing berry grows wild in many locations throughout the continental United States, it's generally cultivated in tropical zones such as Hawaii, Australia, New Zealand, South Africa, India and China. At first glance the cape gooseberry (also called golden berry), with its inflated, papery skin (calyx), looks somewhat like a Chinese lantern. The bittersweet, juicy berries that hide inside the calyx are opaque and golden in color. To use the berries, peel back the parchmentlike husk and rinse. Because of their piquant aftertaste, cape gooseberries go nicely with meats and other savory foods. They're wonderful in pies, jams and all by themselves. Imported cape gooseberries are available from March to July. Look for those with a bright golden color; green berries are not ripe. Cape gooseberries are high in vitamin C.

capelli d'angelo [ka-PELL-ee DAN-zheh-low] Italian for "angel hair" (which this PASTA is also called), this term describes a long, delicate, extremely thin noodle. Because they are so fine, *capelli d'angelo* must be served either in a very light sauce or in a simple broth.

caper [KAY-per] The flower bud of a bush native to the Mediterranean and parts of Asia. The small buds are picked, sun-dried and then pickled in a vinegar brine. Capers range in size from the petite nonpareil variety from southern France (considered the finest), to those from Italy, which can be as large as the tip of your little finger. They generally come in brine but can also be found salted and sold in bulk. Either way, capers should be rinsed before using to remove excess salt. The pungent flavor of capers lends piquancy to many sauces and condiments; they're also used as a garnish for meat and vegetable dishes.

capon [KAY-pahn] *see* CHICKEN

caponata [kap-oh-NAH-tah] A Sicilian dish that is generally served as a salad, side dish or relish. *Caponata* is composed of eggplant, onions, tomatoes, anchovies, olives, pine nuts, capers and vinegar, all cooked together in olive oil. It's most often served at room temperature.

cappelletti [kap-eh-LEHT-tee] Small, stuffed squares of PASTA, similar to ravioli. The stuffing is usually ground meat, but can also be made from cheese or vegetables. The name is taken from the plural of the Italian word *cappelletto*, which means "little hat."

cappuccino [kap-poo-CHEE-noh] An Italian coffee made by topping ESPRESSO with the creamy foam from steamed milk. Some of the steamed milk is also added to the mix. The foam's surface may be dusted with sweetened cocoa powder or cinnamon.

capsicum [KAP-sih-cuhm] Any of hundreds of varieties of plant-bearing fruits called peppers, all of which belong to the nightshade family. Capsicums fall into two categories—CHILI PEPPERS and SWEET PEPPERS.

carafe [kuh-RAF] A decorative beverage container, usually narrow-necked and fitted with a stopper. Carafes are generally made of glass and used for cold beverages.

carambola [kair-ahm-BOH-lah] When cut crosswise, this showy fruit has a striking star shape, which is why it's also called *star fruit*. It favors tropical climates and thrives in the Caribbean countries, Hawaii, Central and South America, and parts of Asia. The carambola ranges from 3 to 5 inches long and is easy to identify by the five definitive ribs which traverse its length. Its thin skin is a glossy golden-yellow, its matching flesh beautifully translucent and dotted occasionally with a dark seed. When ripe, the carambola is exceedingly juicy and fragrant. Its flavor, depending on the variety, can range from exotically sweet to refreshingly tart. In general, the broader set the ribs, the sweeter the fruit. Carambolas are available from summer's end to mid-winter. Choose firm fruit that has a bright, even color. Those with greening on the ribs may be ripened at room temperature. Use ripe carambolas within a few days or store, wrapped tightly in a plastic bag, in the refrigerator for up to a week. Carambolas, which do not require peeling, are delicious eaten out-of-hand, or used in salads, desserts or as a garnish.

caramel [KAIR-ah-mehl; KAR-ah-mehl] A mixture produced when sugar has been cooked (caramelized) until it melts and becomes a thick, clear liquid that can range in color from golden to deep brown (from 320° to 350°F on a candy thermometer). Water can be added to thin the mixture. Caramel is used to flavor soups, stocks and sauces—sweet and savory. It's also used in desserts. When it cools and hardens, caramel cracks easily and is the base for nut brittles. Crushed caramel is used as a topping for ice cream and other desserts. A **soft caramel** is a candy made with caramelized sugar, butter and milk.

caramelize [KAIR-ah-meh-lyz; KAR-ah-meh-lyz] To heat sugar until it liquefies and becomes a clear syrup ranging in color from golden to dark brown (from 320° to 350°F on a candy thermometer). Granulated or brown sugar can also be sprinkled on top of food and placed under a heat source, such as a broiler, until the sugar melts and caramelizes. A popular custard dessert finished in this fashion is CRÈME BRÛLÉE. Caramelized sugar is also referred to as *burnt sugar.*

caraway seed [KAIR-uh-way] These aromatic seeds come from an herb in the parsley family. They have a nutty, delicate anise flavor and are widely used in German, Austrian and Hungarian cuisine. Caraway seeds flavor many foods including cheese, breads, cakes, stews, meats, vegetables and the liqueur KÜMMEL. They should be stored airtight in a cool, dark place for no more than 6 months. *See also* SPICES; Herb and Spice Chart, page 538.

carbonara, alla [kar-boh-NAH-rah] The Italian term describing a PASTA dish of spaghetti (or other noodles) with a sauce composed of cream, eggs, Parmesan cheese and bits of bacon. The sauce is heated only until it begins to thicken (2 to 3 minutes). It's important that the pasta be very hot so that when the sauce is poured over it, the eggs will briefly continue to cook. Fresh green peas are sometimes added for flavor and color.

carbonate of ammonia *see* AMMONIUM BICARBONATE

carbonnade à la flamande [kar-bohn-AHD ah-lah flah-MAHND] Beer, bacon, onions and brown sugar flavor this thick Belgian beef stew from Flanders. Also referred to as *carbonnade of beef.* The word *carbonnade* is French for "meat cooked over hot coals."

cardamom [KAR-duh-muhm] A member of the GINGER family, this aromatic spice is native to India and grows in many other tropical areas including Asia, South America and the Pacific Islands. Cardamom seeds are encapsulated in small pods about the size of a cranberry. Each pod contains 17 to 20 tiny seeds. Cardamom has a pungent aroma and a warm, spicy-sweet flavor. It's widely used in Scandinavian and East Indian cooking. Cardamom can be purchased either in the pod or ground. The latter, though more convenient, is not as full-flavored because cardamom seeds begin to lose their essential oils as soon as they're ground. The seeds may be removed from the pods and ground, or the entire pod may be ground. A MORTAR AND PESTLE make quick work of the grinding. If using cardamom to flavor dishes such as stews and curries, lightly crush the shell of the pod and add the pod and seeds to the mixture. The shell will disintegrate while the dish cooks. Be frugal when using cardamom—a little goes a long way. *See also* SPICES; Herb and Spice Chart, page 538.

cardoon [kahr-DOON] Tasting like a cross between artichoke, celery and SALSIFY, this delicious vegetable is very popular in France, Italy and Spain. The cardoon resembles a giant bunch of wide, flat celery. Cardoons can be found from mid-winter to early spring. Look for stalks that are firm and have a silvery gray-green color. Refrigerate in a plastic bag up to 2 weeks. To prepare, remove tough outer ribs. Cut the inner ribs into the size indicated in the recipe and soak in ACIDULATED WATER to prevent browning. Cardoons can be boiled, braised or baked. Precooking about 30 minutes in boiling water is suggested in many recipes. Though high in sodium, cardoons are a good source of potassium, calcium and iron.

caribou [KAR-uh-boo] *see* GAME ANIMALS

carob [KAIR-uhb] The long, leathery pods from the tropical carob tree contain a sweet, edible pulp (which can be eaten fresh) and a few hard, inedible seeds. After drying, the pulp is roasted and ground into a powder. It is then used to flavor baked goods and candies. Both fresh and dried carob pods, as well as carob powder, may be found in health-food and specialty food stores. Because carob is sweet and tastes vaguely of chocolate, it's often used as a chocolate substitute. Carob is also known as *St. John's bread* and *locust bean.*

Carolina rice This is the long-grain rice that is most popular in the U.S. It was originally planted in North Carolina in the late 17th century from East African rice brought back by a sea captain. Carolina rice is now cultivated mainly in Calfornia, Texas, Louisiana and Arkansas. *See also* RICE.

carotene [KAIR-uh-teen] A fat-soluble pigment, ranging in color from yellow to orange, found in many fruits and vegetables (carrots, for one). It converts to vitamin A in the liver and is essential for normal human growth and eyesight.

carp The principal ingredient in the Jewish dish GEFILTE FISH, carp is a freshwater fish native to Asia but found throughout the world. It ranges in size from 2 to 7 pounds and favors muddy waters, which often give a mossy flavor to the lean, white flesh. This musky nuance is least evident from November to April. Carp is best baked, fried or poached. *See also* FISH.

carpaccio [kahr-PAH-chee-oh] Italian in origin, carpaccio consists of thin shavings of raw beef FILLET which may be drizzled with olive oil and lemon juice or served with a mayonnaise or mustard sauce. The dish is often topped with capers and sometimes onions. It's generally served as an appetizer.

carpetbag steak Although claimed by many to be of Australian origin, an Australian cookbook, *The Captain Cook Book: Two Hundred Years of Australian Cooking*, declares that the carpetbag steak came from the United States. It is a thick-cut steak with a pocket cut into it. The pocket is stuffed with seasoned fresh oysters (sometimes with the addition of breadcrumbs), skewered shut, then the steak is grilled.

carrageen; carragheen [KAIR-ah-geen] Also called *Irish moss*, carrageen is a stubby, purplish seaweed found along the west coast of Ireland, as well as America's Atlantic coast. When dried, carrageen is used in cosmetics and medicines and is greatly valued as a thickening agent for foods such as puddings, ice cream and soups.

carrot This member of the parsley family has lacy green foliage and long, slender, edible orange roots. Carrots have been renowned for over 2,000 years for their health-giving properties and high vitamin A content. They're available year-round, making them a highly popular vegetable. If buying carrots with their greenery, make sure the leaves are moist and bright green; the carrots should be firm and smooth. Avoid those with cracks or any that have begun to soften and wither. The best carrots are young and slender. Tiny **baby carrots** are very tender but, because of their lack of maturity, not as flavorful as their full-grown siblings. Remove carrot greenery as soon as possible because it robs the roots of moisture and vitamins. Store carrots in a plastic bag in the refrigerator's vegetable bin. Avoid storing them near apples, which emit ethylene gas that can give carrots a bitter taste. A light rinsing is all that's necessary for young carrots and tiny baby carrots; older carrots should be peeled. If carrots have become limp, recrisp them in a bowl of ice water. The coarse core of older carrots should be removed. Carrots may be eaten raw or cooked in almost any manner imaginable.

casaba melon [kah-SAH-bah] Though it was first cultivated in Persia thousands of years ago, the casaba melon wasn't introduced to the U.S. until the late 19th century when it was imported from Kasaba, Turkey. A member of the MUSKMELON family, this large, round melon has a thick yellow rind with deep, rough furrows. The creamy-colored flesh is extremely juicy and has a distinctive yet mild cucumberlike flavor. Casabas are now grown in California and are most readily available from September through November. Choose a melon with an even-colored yellow rind; it should give slightly when gently pressed at the blossom end. **Avoid**

casabas with soft spots or mold. Store at room temperature until completely ripe, then refrigerate. *See also* MELON.

cashew apple Native to Brazil, India and the West Indies, this pear-shaped apple has a yellow-orange skin that is often blushed with touches of red. The flesh is tart and astringent and though not favored for out-of-hand eating, is used to make wine, liqueur and vinegar. The cashew apple's biggest gift to the world is the CASHEW NUT which grows on the outside of the apple at its base. Cashew apples are not imported to the U.S.

cashew nut A kidney-shaped nut that grows out from the bottom of the cashew apple. The shell is highly toxic so great care is taken in shelling and cleaning the nut. Cashew nuts have a sweet, buttery flavor and contain about 48 percent fat. Because of their high fat content, they should be stored, tightly wrapped, in the refrigerator to retard rancidity. As with most nuts, roasting cashews brings out their nutty flavor. *See also* NUTS.

casing A thin, tubular intestinal membrane that has been cleaned and stuffed with processed meat, such as for salami and other sausages. The membrane may come from the intestines of sheep, hogs or cattle. Casings can be purchased—thoroughly cleaned and packed in salt—from specialty butchers. Today, most commercial sausages have casings of formed collagen.

cassareep [KAS-sah-reep] Used primarily in West Indian cookery, cassareep is a bittersweet condiment made by cooking the juice of bitter CASSAVA with brown sugar and spices until it reduces to a syrup. Bottled cassareep can be found in Caribbean markets.

cassata [kah-SAH-tah] A traditional Italian dessert served at celebrations such as weddings. The word *cassata* means "in a case (or chest)." One version of this dessert has a rich filling of RICOTTA, candied fruit and grated chocolate encased by thin slices of liqueur-sprinkled spongecake. The cake and cheese mixture may also be layered. The dessert is chilled, then decorated with whipped cream, ricotta cheese or chocolate frosting. Another version, **cassata gelata**, is made by lining a mold with layers of ice cream of contrasting colors, then filling the center with a ricotta-whipped cream-candied fruit mixture. The mold is frozen completely before serving.

cassava [kuh-SAH-vuh] Though native to South America, the majority of cassava now comes from Africa, where it's an important staple. Also called *manioc* and *yuca*, the cassava is a root that ranges from 6 to 12 inches in length and from 2 to 3 inches in diameter. It has a tough brown skin which, when peeled, reveals a crisp, white flesh. There are many varieties of cassava but only two main categories, sweet and bitter. The bitter cassava is poisonous unless cooked. Cassava is available year-round in Caribbean and Latin American markets. It should be stored in the refrigerator for no more than 4 days. Grated, sun-dried cassava is called **cassava meal**. Cassava is also used to make CASSAREEP and TAPIOCA.

cassava flour *see* TAPIOCA

casserole This term refers to both a baking dish and the ingredients it contains. Casserole cookery is extremely convenient because the ingredients are cooked and served in the same dish. A "casserole dish" usually refers to a deep, round, ovenproof container with handles and a tight-fitting lid. It can be glass, metal, ceramic or any other heatproof material. A casserole's ingredients can include meat, vegetables, beans, rice and anything else that might seem appropriate. Often a topping such as cheese or breadcrumbs is added for texture and flavor.

cassia [KAH-see-uh; KASH-uh] *see* CINNAMON

cassis [kah-SEES] A European black currant used mainly to make CRÈME DE CASSIS liqueur and black currant syrup. *See also* LIQUEUR.

cassoulet [ka-soo-LAY] A classic dish from France's Languedoc region consisting of white beans and various meats (such as sausages, pork and preserved duck or goose). The combination varies according to regional preference. A *cassoulet* is covered and cooked very slowly to harmonize the flavors.

castor sugar; caster sugar *see* SUGAR

Catawba grape [kuh-TAH-buh] Grown on the East Coast, this purplish-red grape is medium-size and oval in shape. It has seeds and an intense, sweet flavor. The Catawba grape is available from September to November but is mainly used commercially (for jams, jellies and white wines), and is rarely found in the market. *See also* GRAPE.

catchup *see* KETCHUP

catfish This fish gets its name from its long, whiskerlike barbels (feelers), which hang down from around the mouth. Most catfish are freshwater fish, though there is also a saltwater variety sometimes referred to as **hogfish**. The majority of the catfish in today's market are farmed. The **channel catfish**, weighing from 1 to 10 pounds, is considered the best eating. The **bullhead** is smaller and usually weighs no more than a pound. Catfish have a tough, inedible skin that must be removed before cooking. The flesh is firm, low in fat and mild in flavor. Catfish can be fried, poached, steamed, baked or grilled. They are also well suited to soups and stews. *See also* FISH.

cats' tongues Also known as *langues-de-chat* (French for "cats' tongues"), these long, thin cookies resemble their namesakes in shape. They are light, dry and slightly sweet. Cats' tongues may be flavored with citrus ZEST, chocolate or flavoring EXTRACTS. Two are sometimes sandwiched together with jam or another sweet filling; they may also be frosted. Cats' tongues are commonly made by pressing a thick batter through a pastry bag. A special *langues-de-chat* pan is also available in cookware shops.

catsup *see* KETCHUP

caudle [KAW-dl] A hot drink once popular in England and Scotland, especially with the elderly and infirm because of its purported restorative powers. Caudle was generally a blend of wine or ALE, GRUEL, eggs, sugar and spices.

caul [KAWL] A thin, fatty membrane that lines the abdominal cavity, usually taken from pigs or sheep; pork caul is considered superior. The caul resembles a lacy net and is used to wrap and contain PÂTÉS, CRÉPINETTES, FORCEMEATS and the like. The fatty membrane melts during the baking or cooking process. Caul may be ordered and purchased through your local butcher. To prevent tearing, it may be necessary to soak the membrane in warm salted water to loosen the layers before using.

cauliflower [KAWL-ih-flow-uhr] In Mark Twain's words, "cauliflower is nothing but cabbage with a college education." The name of this elegant member of the cabbage family comes from the Latin *caulis* ("stalk") and *floris* ("flower"). Cauliflower is composed of bunches of tiny creamy white flowerets on clusters of stalks the same color. Some varieties have a purple or greenish tinge. The entire white portion (called the "curd") is edible. The bright green leaves at the base are also edible, but take longer to cook and have a stronger flavor than the curd. Choose a firm cauliflower with compact flowerets; the leaves should be crisp and green with no sign of yellowing. The size of the head doesn't affect the quality. Refrigerate raw cauliflower, tightly wrapped, for 3 to 5 days; cooked for 1 to 3 days. To use, separate cauliflower head into flowerets and wash. Cauliflower can be eaten raw or cooked in a number of ways including boiling, baking and sautéing. Whole cauliflower heads may also be cooked in one piece. Adding a tablespoon of lemon juice or ¼ cup milk to the cooking water will prevent discoloration. Cauliflower is high in vitamin C and is a fair source of iron.

caviar [KA-vee-ahr; KAH-vee-ahr] This elegant and expensive appetizer is simply sieved and lightly salted fish ROE (eggs). Sturgeon roe is premium and considered the "true" caviar. The three main types of caviar are **beluga**, **osetra** and **sevruga**. The best (and costliest) is from the beluga sturgeon that swim in the Caspian Sea, which is bordered by Russia and Iran. Caviar production is a major industry for both countries. Beluga caviar is prized for its soft, extremely large (pea-size) eggs. It can range in color from pale silver-gray to black. Next in quality is the medium-sized, gray to gray-green osetra, and the smaller, gray sevruga caviar. The small, golden **sterlet** caviar is so rare that it was once reserved for Russian czars, Iranian shahs and Austrian emperors. Other popular (and much less expensive) types include **lumpfish caviar** (tiny, hard, black eggs), **whitefish caviar** (also called *American Golden*) with its small yellow-gold eggs, and **salmon** or **red caviar** (medium-size, pale orange to deep red eggs.) The word *malossol* on the label doesn't describe the type of caviar but rather the fact that the roe is preserved with a minimum amount of salt; *malossol* is Russian for "little salt." Caviar is extremely perishable and must be refrigerated from the moment it's taken from the fish to the time it's consumed. **pasteurized caviar** is roe that has been partially cooked, thereby giving the eggs a slightly different texture. It's less perishable and may not require refrigeration before opening. **Pressed caviar** is composed of damaged or fragile eggs and can be a combination of several different roes. It's specially treated, salted and pressed, and can in no way be compared to fresh caviar. Be sure to read the label for information on how to handle the caviar you purchase. Serve caviar very cold, preferably in a bowl that has been set into another container of ice. It should be presented simply, with toast points and lemon wedges. If desired, it may be garnished with sour cream, minced onion, and hard-cooked egg whites and yolks. Two classic caviar accompaniments are iced vodka and champagne.

cayenne pepper [KI-yen; KAY-yen] A hot, pungent powder made from several of various tropical CHILI PEPPERS that originated in French Guiana. The term cayenne pepper is gradually being phased out by the spice industry in favor of the more general term **red pepper**.

ceci bean [CHEH-chee] *see* CHICKPEA

celeriac [seh-LER-ee-ak] This rather ugly, knobby, brown vegetable is actually the root of a special celery cultivated specifically for its root. It's also called *celery root* and *celery knob*. Celeriac tastes like a cross between a strong celery and parsley. It's available from September through May and can range anywhere from the size of an apple to that of a small cantaloupe. Choose a relatively small, firm celeriac with a minimum of rootlets and knobs. Avoid those with soft spots, which signal decay. The inedible green leaves are usually detached by the time you buy celeriac. Refrigerate the root in a plastic bag for 7 to 10 days. Celeriac can be eaten raw or cooked. Before using, peel and soak briefly in ACIDULATED WATER to prevent discoloration. To eat raw, grate or shred celeriac and use in salads. Cooked, it's wonderful in soups, stews and purees. It can also be boiled, braised, sautéed and baked. Celeriac contains small amounts of vitamin B, calcium and iron.

céleri bâtard *see* LOVAGE

celery Before the 16th century, celery was used exclusively as a medicinal herb. Now it's become one of the most popular vegetables of the Western world. Celery grows in bunches that consist of leaved ribs surrounding the tender, choice heart. There are two main varieties of celery grown today. The most common is the pale green **Pascal celery. Golden celery** is grown under a layer of soil or paper to prevent chlorophyll from developing and turning it green. Celery is available year-round. Choose firm bunches that are tightly formed; the leaves should be green and crisp. Store celery in a plastic bag in the refrigerator. Leave the ribs attached to the stalk until ready to use. Celery should be well washed and trimmed of leaves and at the base. Reserve the leaves for soups and salads. Celery is usually eaten raw, but is delicious cooked in soups, stews and casseroles.

celery knob *see* CELERIAC

celery root *see* CELERIAC

celery salt A seasoning that is a blend of ground CELERY SEED and salt.

celery seed The seed of a wild celery called LOVAGE, most of which comes from India. Celery seed has a strong flavor and should therefore be used sparingly. It's used in pickling and to flavor soups, salads and various meat dishes. *See also* Herb and Spice Chart, page 538.

cellophane noodles [SEHL-uh-fayn] Also called **bean threads**, these gossamer, translucent threads are not really noodles in the traditional sense, but are made from the starch of green MUNG BEANS. Sold dried, cellophane noodles must be soaked briefly in hot water before using in most dishes. Presoaking isn't necessary when they're added to soups. They can also be deep-fried. Cellophane noodles can be found in the ethnic section of many supermarkets and in oriental grocery stores.

Celsius [SEHL-see-uhs] A temperature scale (also called *centigrade*) in which 0° represents freezing and 100° represents the boiling point. The scale was devised by the Swedish astronomer Anders Celsius. To convert Celsius temperatures to FAHRENHEIT, multiply the Celsius figure by 9, divide by 5 and add 32. *See also* Temperature Equivalents Chart, page 533.

centigrade [SIHN-tih-grayd] *see* CELSIUS

century egg *see* HUNDRED-YEAR EGG

cèpes [SEHP] Known in Italy as *porcini*, these delicious, earthy treasures are members of the *Boletus edulis* species of wild mushroom. They're pale brown in color and can weigh from an ounce or two up to a pound. Their caps can range from 1 to 10 inches in diameter. Cèpes have a smooth, meaty texture and pungent, woodsy flavor that is much regaled, especially by the French and Italians. You'll seldom find them fresh in the U.S. but you might try looking for them in specialty produce markets in late spring or in the autumn. If you get lucky, choose fresh cèpes with firm, large (about 6-inch) caps and pale undersides. The dried form of this mushroom is more readily available. Choose those that are a tan to pale brown in color; avoid those that are crumbly. Dried cèpes must be softened in hot water for about 20 minutes before using. They can be substituted for cultivated mushrooms in most recipes. One ounce of dried cèpes will serve about 4 people in soups, stuffings, stews and the like. Cèpes are also known as *Boletes* and *Steinpilze*. *See also* MUSHROOM.

cephalopod [SEHF-uh-luh-pod] A class of MOLLUSK that includes the OCTOPUS, SQUID and CUTTLEFISH. It's the most biologically advanced of the mollusks. All cephalopods share two common characteristics—tentacles attached to the head, and ink sacs, which they use to evade their predators. Though cephalopods have never been broadly accepted in the U.S., they're quite popular with many southern Europeans, Japanese and Chinese.

cereal [SEER-ee-uhl] Breakfast cereals are processed foods (usually ready-to-eat) made from cereal grains. W. H. Kellogg and C. W. Post were the first to begin mass-producing these foods, which have become a morning meal staple in the U.S. *See also* CEREAL GRAINS.

cereal grains The word "cereal" comes from Ceres, a pre-Roman goddess of agriculture. Cereal includes any plant from the grass family that yields an edible grain (seed). The most popular grains are BARLEY, CORN, MILLET, OATS, QUINOA, RICE, RYE, SORGHUM, TRITICALE, WHEAT and WILD RICE. Because cereals are inexpensive, are a readily available source of protein and have more carbohydrates than any other food, they're a staple throughout the world.

ceriman [SEHR-uh-muhn] *see* MONSTERA

cervelat [SIR-vuh-lat] A style of sausage that combines chopped pork and/or beef with various mixtures of herbs, spices and other flavorings like garlic or mustard. Cervelats are uncooked but perfectly safe to eat without cooking because they have been preserved by curing, drying and smoking. They can range from semidry to moist and soft. Many countries make cervelats; two of the more well known are Germany's THURINGER and Italy's MORTADELLA. These sausages can be sliced and served with bread or cut into pieces and used in a variety of other dishes. *See also* SAUSAGE.

ceviche *see* SEVICHE

Ceylon tea One of the world's most popular teas, Ceylon is a black PEKOE tea whose leaves have been fermented before drying. A two-temperature drying process seals in essential oils that give this tea its special flavor. This superior tea originated in Ceylon (now Sri Lanka), but is now grown in other countries such as India and China. *See also* TEA.

Chablis [sha-BLEE; *pl.* sha-BLEEZ] Though the United States, Australia and South Africa all make a wine labeled *Chablis*, only France creates a *true* Chablis, made entirely from CHARDONNAY grapes. Considered one of the world's great white wines, French Chablis has a crisp, dry flavor with a decided FLINTY quality. It comes from a small (2,600-acre) area surrounding the town of Chablis, France. The very best French Chablis comes from one of seven *grand cru* ("great growth") vineyards that lie in a single block facing south and west toward the village. The term *grand cru* will appear on the labels of these special wines, followed by the name of the vineyard from which it came. Next in excellence are the Chablis labeled *premier cru* (meaning "first growth"). Others are considered "plain" Chablis and have no special designation on the label.

chafing dish [CHAYF-ing] Chafing dishes found in the ruins of Pompeii prove that this style of cookery is nothing new. Used to warm or cook food, a chafing dish consists of a container (today, usually metal) with a heat source directly beneath it. The heat can be provided by a candle, electricity or solid fuel (such as Sterno). There's often a larger dish that is used as a water basin (like the bottom of a double boiler) into which the dish containing the food is placed. This prevents food from burning.

chalazae [kuh-LAY-zee] Thick, cordlike strands of egg white which are attached to 2 sides of the yolk, thereby anchoring it in the center of the egg. The more prominent the chalazae, the fresher the egg. Chalazae don't affect the egg in any way, though some custard recipes call for straining to remove them for a smoother texture.

challah; hallah; challa [KHAH-lah; HAH-lah] Served on the Sabbath, holidays, other ceremonial occasions and for everyday consumption, challah is a traditional Jewish yeast bread. It's rich with eggs and has a light, airy texture. Though it can be formed into many shapes, braided challah is the most classic form.

chalupa [chah-LOO-pah] Spanish for "boat" or "launch," a chalupa is a corn tortilla dough formed into a small boat shape and fried until crisp. It's then usually filled with shredded beef, pork or chicken, vegetables, cheese or a combination of these, and served as an appetizer.

champ A traditional Irish dish made by combining mashed potatoes and green onions with plenty of butter.

champagne [sham-PAYN] This most celebrated sparkling wine always seems to signal "special occasion." Though bubbling wines under various appellations abound throughout the world, true champagne comes only from the Champagne region in northeast France. Most countries bow to this tradition by calling their sparkling wines by other names such as *spumante* in Italy, *Sekt* in Germany and *vin mousseux* in other regions of France. Only in America do some wineries refer to their bubbling wine as "champagne." Dom Perignon, 17th-century cellarmaster of the Abbey of Hautvillers, is celebrated for developing the art of blending wines to create champagnes with superior flavor. He's also credited for his work in preventing champagne bottles and corks from exploding by using thicker bottles and tying the corks down with string. Even then, it's said that the venerable Dom Perignon lost half his champagne through the bottles bursting. French champagne is usually made from a blend of CHARDONNAY and PINOT NOIR or PINOT BLANC grapes. California "champagnes" generally use the same varieties, while those from New York more often are from the pressings of CATAWBA and DELAWARE GRAPES. Good champagne is expensive not only because it's made with premium grapes, but because it's made by the *méthode champenoise*. This traditional method requires a second fermentation in the bottle as well as some 100 manual operations (some of which are mechanized today). Champagnes can range in color from pale gold to apricot blush. Their flavors can range from toasty to yeasty and from dry (no sugar added) to sweet. A sugar-wine mixture called a DOSAGE added just before final corking determines how sweet a champagne will be. The label indicates the level of sweetness: **brut** (bone dry—less than 2 percent sugar); **extra sec** or **extra dry** (dry—up to 2.5 percent sugar); **sec** (slightly sweet—up to 4 percent sugar); **demi-sec** (sweet—up to 6 percent sugar); and **doux** (very sweet—over 6 percent sugar). The last two are considered DESSERT WINES.

champignon [sham-pee-NYOHN] The French word for an edible "mushroom," generally the button variety.

chanterelle [shan-tuh-REHL] A trumpet-shaped wild mushroom with a color that ranges from bright yellow to orange. The chanterelle mushroom has a delicate, nutty (sometimes fruity) flavor and a somewhat chewy texture. Chanterelles are usually imported from Europe and can be found dried or canned in many large supermarkets. Although they're not widely cultivated, chanterelles are found growing in parts of the Pacific Northwest and along the East Coast. They are occasionally found fresh in some markets during summer and winter months. Choose those that are plump and spongy; avoid ones with broken or shriveled caps. Chanterelles can be cooked as a separate side dish or as an addition to other foods. Because they tend to toughen when overcooked, it's best to add them to the dish toward the end of the cooking time. *See also* MUSHROOM.

chantilly [shan-TIHL-lee; shahn-tee-YEE] A French term referring to sweet or savory dishes that are prepared or served with whipped cream. **Crème chantilly** is lightly sweetened whipped cream—sometimes flavored with vanilla or LIQUEUR—used as a dessert topping.

Chaource cheese [shah-OORS] Similar to CAMEMBERT, Chaource cheese takes its name from a town in France's Champagne region. It has a white, downy rind with an ivory-colored center. The fruity, rich flavor intensifies and becomes saltier as it matures. Chaource makes a pleasant after-dinner cheese and pairs well with full-bodied white wines. *See also* CHEESE.

chapati; chapatti [chah-PAH-tee] An unleavened pancakelike bread from India, usually made from a simple mixture of whole-wheat flour and water. The dough is rolled into thin rounds and baked on a griddle. Pieces of chapati are torn off and used as a scoop or pusher for many East Indian dishes.

chapon [shah-POHN] A slice or cube of bread that has either been rubbed with garlic or dipped in garlic-flavored oil. The bread is then used to rub the inside of a salad bowl to impart the barest hint of garlic to the greens. The chapon may either be removed or—for a more intense garlic flavor—left in the bowl to toss with the salad.

charcuterie [shahr-COO-tuhr-ee; shar-coo-tuhr-EE] Taken from the term *cuiseur de chair*, meaning "cooker of meat," charcuterie has been considered a French culinary art at least since the 15th century. It refers to the products, particularly (but not limited to) pork specialties such as PÂTÉS, RILLETTES, GALANTINES, CRÉPINETTES, etc., which are made and sold in a delicatessen-style shop, also called a *charcuterie*.

chard Also referred to as *Swiss chard*, this member of the beet family is grown for its crinkly green leaves and silvery, celerylike stalks. The variety with dark green leaves and reddish stalks (sometimes referred to as *rhubarb chard*) has a stronger flavor than that with lighter leaves and stalks. Chard is only available during the summer. Choose it for its tender greens and crisp stalks. Store, wrapped in a plastic bag, in the refrigerator for up to 3 days. The greens can be prepared like spinach, the stalks like asparagus. Chard is a good source of vitamins A and C, as well as iron.

Chardonnay [shar-duh-NAY] The Chardonnay grape, grown mainly in France and California, produces superior white wines. It's one of the grapes used in making fine French CHAMPAGNES and white Burgundies. In California, the wine produced from this grape is referred to simply as "Chardonnay." These complex wines are generally rich, buttery, fruity and on the dry side. Some will age up to 10 years. Chardonnay grapes are also grown in parts of Australia, New Zealand, Bulgaria, Italy and Spain. *See also* BURGUNDY WINES.

charlotte [SHAR-luht] This classic molded dessert begins with a mold lined with SPONGE CAKE, LADYFINGERS or buttered bread. The traditional charlotte container is pail-shaped, but almost any mold is acceptable. The lined mold is then filled with layers (or a mixture) of fruit and CUSTARD or whipped cream that has been fortified with gelatin. The dessert is chilled thoroughly and unmolded before serving. **Charlotte russe**, said to have been created for the Russian Czar Alexander, is a ladyfinger shell filled with the ethereal BAVARIAN CREAM, and decorated elaborately with whipped-cream rosettes. The classic **apple charlotte** is a buttered-bread shell filled with spiced, sautéed apples. Unlike other charlottes, this one is baked and served hot.

charlotte russe *see* CHARLOTTE

Chartreuse [shar-TROOZ] Originally made by the Carthusian monks in France's La Grande Chartreuse monastery, this aromatic LIQUEUR comes in green and yellow varieties. The yellow, colored with saffron, is lighter and sweeter in flavor. Green Chartreuse—colored with chlorophyll—is drier, has a sharper, more aromatic flavor and is higher in alcohol (110 PROOF).

chasoba [chah-SOH-bah] *see* SOBA

chasseur sauce [shah-SUR] French for "hunter," chasseur is a hunter-style brown sauce consisting of mushrooms, shallots and white wine (sometimes tomatoes and parsley). It's most often served with game and other meats.

château-bottled [sha-TOH] This designation on a wine label indicates that the wine was bottled on the property where the grapes were grown and the wine made. Other wines are often made from grapes grown throughout a region and brought to a winery for wine production. *Estate-bottled* means the same as *château-bottled*. Both usually designate a wine of superior quality and character.

Châteaubriand [sha-toh-bree-AHN] Contrary to popular belief, Châteaubriand is actually a recipe, not a cut of beef. This method of preparation is said to be named for the 19th-century French statesman and author, François Châteaubriand. It's a succulent, thick cut of beef (usually taken from the center of the tenderloin) that's large enough for two people. The Châteaubriand is usually grilled or broiled and served with BÉARNAISE SAUCE and château potatoes (potatoes trimmed into olive shapes and sautéed in butter). *See also* SHORT LOIN.

Châteauneuf-du-Pape [sha-toh-NOEF deu PAHP] Literally translated as "new castle of the Pope," this famous wine comes from a village of the same name near Avignon, France. Each château creates its own special blend from the classic 13 grape varieties permitted for this wine. Most Châteauneuf-du-Papes are dry, full-bodied red wines; a small number are white. They're best when aged 5 to 10 years.

chaud-froid [shoh-FRWAH] *Chaud* (French for "hot") and *froid* (French for "cold") combine in this term to explain food (usually meat, poultry or game) that is first cooked, then chilled before serving. The distinguishing feature of a chaud-froid is that the food is glazed with an ASPIC, which is allowed to set before serving. Decorative vegetable cutouts are often set into the aspic for a colorful garnish.

chayote [chy-OH-tay] Once the principal food of the Aztecs and Mayas, this gourdlike fruit is about the size and shape of a very large pear. Beneath its furrowed, pale green skin is a white, rather bland-tasting flesh surrounding one soft seed. In the United States, chayote is grown in several states including California, Florida and Louisiana (where it's known as *mirliton*). Chayote are widely available during winter months, but can be found in some supermarkets throughout the year. Look for those that are small, firm and unblemished. Refrigerate in a plastic bag up to a month. Chayotes can be prepared in any way suitable for summer squash. It can also be split, stuffed and baked like acorn squash, or used raw in salad. Because of its mild flavor it requires assertive seasoning. Chayote, known in France as *christophene*, is a good source of potassium.

checkerberry *see* WINTERGREEN

cheddar cheese This popular cheese originated in the village of Cheddar in the Somerset region of England. It's a firm, cow's-milk cheese that ranges in flavor from mild to sharp, and in color from natural white to pumpkin orange. Orange cheddars are colored with a natural dye called ANNATTO. Cheddar is used to eat out of hand, as well as in a panoply of cooked dishes including casseroles, sauces, soups, etc. *See also* CHEESE.

cheese Author Clifton Fadiman said it best when he described cheese as "milk's leap toward immortality." Almost everyone loves one type of cheese or another, whether it's delectably mild, creamy and soft or pungent, hard and crumbly. To begin with, cheese can be broken down into two very broad categories—*fresh* and *ripened*. Within these basic categories, however, are a multitude of subdivisions, usually classified according to the texture of the cheese and how it was made. Naturally, many of these categories overlap because a cheese can have an entirely different character when young than it does when aged. Most cheese begins as milk (usually cow's, goat's or sheep's) that is allowed to thicken (sometimes with the addition of RENNET or special bacteria) until it separates into a liquid (WHEY) and semisolids (CURD). The whey is drained off and the curds are either allowed to drain or pressed into different shapes, depending on the variety. At this stage it is called **fresh** (or **unripened**) **cheese**. Among the most popular fresh cheeses on the market today are COTTAGE CHEESE, CREAM CHEESE, POT CHEESE and RICOTTA. In order to become a **ripened** (or **aged**) **cheese**, the drained curds are CURED by a variety of processes including being subjected to heat, bacteria, soaking, etc. The curds are also sometimes flavored with salt, spices or herbs and some, like many cheddars, are colored with a natural dye. After curing, natural cheese begins a ripening process during which it's stored, usually uncovered, at a controlled temperature and humidity until the desired texture and character is obtained. It can be covered with wax or other protective coating before or after this ripening process. Ripened cheeses are further classified according to texture. **Firm cheeses** are cooked, pressed and aged for long periods (usually at least 2 years) until hard and dry, and are generally used for grating. Among the more well known of this genre are PARMESAN and PECORINO. **Semifirm cheeses** such as CHEDDAR, EDAM and JARLSBERG are firm but not usually crumbly. They have been cooked and pressed but not aged as long as those in the firm-cheese category. **Semisoft cheeses** are pressed but can be either cooked or uncooked. Their texture is sliceable but soft. Among the more popular semisoft cheeses are GOUDA, MONTEREY JACK and TILSIT. **Soft-ripened** (or **surface-ripened**) **cheeses** are neither cooked nor pressed. They are, however, subjected to various bacteria (either by spraying or dipping), which ripens the cheese from the outside in. Such cheeses develop a rind that is either powdery white (as in BRIE) or golden orange (like PONT L'ÉVÊQUE). The consistency of soft-ripened cheese can range from semisoft to creamy and spreadable. Some cheeses are further categorized by process. **Blue-veined cheeses,** for example, are inoculated or sprayed with spores of the molds *Penicillium roqueforti* or *penicillium glaucum.* Some of these cheeses are punctured with holes to ensure that the mold will penetrate during the aging period. The result of these painstaking efforts are cheeses with veins or pockets of flavorful blue or green mold. Another special-process category is **pasta filata** ("spun paste"), Italy's famous stretched-curd cheeses. They're made using a special technique whereby the curd is given a hot-whey bath, then kneaded and stretched to the desired pliable consistency. Among the *pasta filata* cheeses are MOZZARELLA, PROVOLONE and CACIOCAVALLO. **Whey cheeses** are another special category. Instead of beginning with milk, they're made from the whey drained from the making of other cheeses. The whey is reheated (usually with rennet) until it coagulates. Probably the best known of this cheese type are GJETOST and Italian RICOTTA. *For additional information on specific cheeses, see individual listings. See also* BLUE CHEESE; DOUBLE-CREAM CHEESES; PROCESSED CHEESE.

cheesecake Though a cheesecake can be savory (and served with crackers as an appetizer), most of us think of the term as describing a luscious, rich dessert. The texture of any cheesecake can vary greatly—from light and airy to dense and rich to smooth and creamy. All cheesecakes begin with cheese—usually cream cheese, ricotta cheese, cottage cheese or sometimes Swiss or cheddar cheese. A cheesecake may or may not have a crust, which can be a light dusting of breadcrumbs, a cookie crust or a pastry crust. The filling is made by creaming the cheese and mixing it with eggs, sugar (for desserts) and other flavorings. The mixture is then poured into a special SPRINGFORM PAN and baked. After baking, the cheesecake is thoroughly chilled and generally topped by sour cream, whipped cream, fruit or some other embellishment.

cheesecloth Long a versatile kitchen helper, this lightweight natural cotton cloth won't fall apart when wet and will not flavor the food it touches. Cheesecloth has a multitude of culinary uses including straining liquids, forming a packet for herbs and spices (as with BOUQUET GARNI) that can be dropped into a soup or stock pot, and lining molds (such as for COEUR À LA CRÈME. It comes in both fine and coarse weaves and is available in gourmet shops, supermarkets and the kitchen section of many department stores. In Britain it's sometimes called *butter muslin.*

cheese steak Also called *Philadelphia cheese steak* after the illustrious city that's said to have originated this sandwich in the 1930s. It consists of an Italian or French roll topped by thin slices of beef, cheese (usually American) and sometimes sautéed onions.

cheese straws Strips of cheese pastry or plain pastry sprinkled with cheese, baked until crisp and golden brown. The pastry strips are sometimes twisted before baking. Cheese straws are served as an appetizer or an accompaniment to soups or salads.

cheese wire A long, thin wire with wooden handles at each end, used to cut large rounds or wedges of cheese.

chef garde manger *see* GARDE MANGER

chef's salad An entree salad of tossed greens topped by cold JULIENNED cheeses and meats (such as chicken and ham), thinly sliced vegetables and slices of hard-cooked egg. The salad may be topped with any one of a variety of dressings.

Chenin Blanc [SHEN-ihn BLAH*N*; SHEN-ihn BLAHNGK] Grown in California and France's Loire Valley, the Chenin Blanc grape makes intense, spicy, slightly sweet wine that often displays a grassy or herbaceous character. Chenin Blancs have a strong acidity that modulates the sweetness and promotes good aging. This well-balanced grape is responsible for France's famed Vouvray, Côteaux du Layon and Saumur. It's also used to produce several of California's sparkling wines.

cherimoya [chair-uh-MOY-ah] Also called *custard apple*, this large tropical fruit tastes like a delicate combination of pineapple, mango and strawberry. Irregularly oval in shape, the cherimoya has a leathery green skin that has a scaly pattern not unlike large, overlapping thumbprint indentations. The flesh, peppered with large, shiny black seeds, is cream-colored and the texture of firm custard. Now grown in California, cherimoyas are available from November through May. Purchase fruit that's firm, heavy for its size and without skin blemishes; avoid those with brown splotches. Store at room temperature until ripe (they will give slightly with soft pressure), then refrigerate, well wrapped, up to 4 days. Serve cherimoyas well chilled. Simply halve, remove the seeds and scoop out the flesh with a spoon. Cherimoyas contain a fair amount of niacin, iron and vitamin C.

Chéri-Suisse A Swiss LIQUEUR with a cherry-chocolate flavor.

cherries jubilee A dessert of pitted Bing or other dark red cherries, sugar and KIRSCH or BRANDY, which are combined, flambéed and spooned over vanilla ice cream. The cherries are usually prepared in a CHAFING DISH at the table and flamed with great flourish.

cherry   Said to date as far back as 300 B.C., cherries were named after the Turkish town of Cerasus. Throughout the centuries, cherry trees have been lauded for their deliciously succulent fruit as well as for their beauty. Tourists flock to Washington, D.C., every year to see the cherry blossoms on the ornamental cherry trees that were originally presented to America's capital in 1912 by Tokyo's governor. There are two main groups of cherries—sweet and sour. The larger of the two are the firm, heart-shaped **sweet cherries**. They're delicious for eating out of hand and can also be cooked. The most popular varieties range from the dark red to purplish black **Bing**, **Lambert** and **Tartarian** to the golden, red-blushed **Royal Ann**. MARASCHINO CHERRIES are usually made from Royal Ann cherries. **Sour cherries** are smaller, softer and more globular than the sweet varieties. Most are too tart to eat raw, but make excellent pies, preserves and the like. The bestselling sour cherry varieties are the bright red **Early Richmond** (the first cherry available in the late spring) and **Montmorency**, and the dark mahogany red **English Morello**. Most fresh cherries are available from May (June for sour cherries) through August. Choose brightly colored, shiny, plump fruit. Sweet cherries should be quite firm, but not hard; sour varieties should be medium-firm. Stemmed cherries are a better buy, but those with stems last longer. Store unwashed cherries in a plastic bag in the refrigerator. Fresh cherries contain minor amounts of vitamins and minerals. *For information on specific cherries, see individual listings.*

Cherry Heering   [HEER-ing] A dark red, cherry-flavored LIQUEUR from Denmark.

cherry plum   *see* MIRABELLE

cherrystone clam   This East Coast medium-sized clam (shell diameter of about 2½ inches) is of the hard-shell variety. Cherrystones are good both raw and cooked, steaming and baking being the most popular cooking methods. *See also* CLAM.

cherry tomato   *see* TOMATO

chervil   [CHER-vuhl] A mild-flavored member of the parsley family, this aromatic herb has curly, dark green leaves with an elusive anise flavor. Chervil is one of the main ingredients in FINES HERBES. Though most chervil is cultivated for its leaves alone, the root is edible and was, in fact, enjoyed by early Greeks and Romans. Today it's available dried but has the best flavor when fresh. Both forms can be found in most supermarkets. It can be used like parsley but its delicate flavor is diminished when boiled. *See also* HERB; Herb and Spice Chart, page 538.

Cheshire cheese   [CHESH-ur] Hailing from the county of Cheshire, this rich, cow's-milk cheese comes in three varieties—white, red and blue—and has a reputation as one of England's most famous cheeses. The white (actually pale yellow) and red (apricot-colored) Cheshires are very similar, differing mainly in the fact that the red variety has been dyed with ANNATTO. They're young cheeses, having an average age of 8 weeks, with a semifirm texture and a mild, tangy, cheddarlike flavor. **Farmhouse Cheshire**, rarely exported, is usually aged about 9 months and has a richer, fuller flavor for the effort. **Blue Cheshire**, boasting a beautiful golden interior veined with blue, is just as rich as STILTON but milder in flavor. Cheshire cheese has long been a favorite for WELSH RAREBIT. *See also* CHEESE;BLUECHEESE.

chess pie This is one of the South's favorite pies, with a simple filling of eggs, sugar, butter and a small amount of flour. Chess pie can be varied by adding flavorings such as lemon juice or vanilla, or substituting brown sugar for granulated sugar.

chestnut Mount Olympus, home of the gods, was said to have had an abundance of chestnut trees producing this sweet, edible nut. There are many varieties of chestnuts and the trees are common throughout Europe, Asia and the United States. Once peeled of their hard, dark brown outer shells and bitter inner skin, chestnuts can be enjoyed in a variety of ways including roasted, boiled, pureed, preserved and candied. They can be used in desserts or as a savory main-dish accompaniment. Fresh chestnuts, most of which are imported, are available from September through February. Choose firm, plump nuts without shell blemishes. Store unshelled nuts in a cool, dry place; refrigerate shelled nuts in a covered container. Chestnuts can also be found canned whole, in pieces or as a puree. They can be unsweetened, or sweetened as in MARRONS GLACÉS. Dried chestnuts, as well as chestnut flour (dried nuts that have been ground to a powder), are often found in ethnic markets.

chèvre cheese [SHEHV-ruh; SHEHV] French for "goat," chèvre is a pure white goat's-milk cheese with a delightfully tart flavor that easily distinguishes it from other cheeses. Some of the better known chèvres include BANON, BÙCHERON and MONTRACHET. "*Pur chèvre*" on the label ensures that the cheese is made entirely from goat's milk; others may have the addition of cow's milk. *Chèvres* can range in texture from moist and creamy to dry and semifirm. They come in a variety of shapes including cylinders, discs, cones and pyramids, and are often coated in edible ash or leaves, herbs or pepper. Store, tightly wrapped, in the refrigerator up to 2 weeks. Old chèvre takes on a sour taste and should be discarded. *For information on specific chèvres, see individual listings. See also* CHEESE.

Chianti [kee-AHN-tee] Named for the Chianti region in Tuscany, Italy, this sturdy, dry red wine was once instantly recognizable by its squat, straw-covered bottles (*fiaschi*). However, Chianti—particularly the better brands—is now more often found in the traditional Bordeaux-type bottle. Only a few vintners use the straw-based bottle, which today usually designates a cheaper (and often inferior) product. Though the original (and reputed to be best) Chianti comes from Italy, California and Argentina also make this wine. In Italy, Chianti has long been made from four or five grape varieties, Trebbiano and Malvasia being two of them. Today, however, the CABERNET SAUVIGNON grape is being added to some Chianti blends. The word *Riserva* on the label indicates that the wine is of superior quality and has been aged in oak for at least 3 years before being bottled. Labels indicating "Chianti Classico" refer to the central and original (dating back to the 14th century) growing area from which the grapes came. Chianti's bold flavor is particularly suited to highly seasoned foods.

chicharrón [chee-chah-RROHN] This crispy rich snack is made from pork skin that has been deep-fried twice, once in 325°F oil, then again in 375°F oil, making it balloon into a honeycombed puff. It is available in Latin American markets.

chicken History tells us that today's chickens are descendants of wild fowl that roamed the dense jungles of primeval Asia. Thousands of years later, France's King Henry IV stated in his coronation speech that he hoped each peasant in his realm would have "a chicken in his pot every Sunday" (a quote later paraphrased by President Herbert Hoover). It surprises many people that chicken wasn't always the reasonably priced meat it is today. Until after World War II, only the affluent (and chicken farmers) could manage even the proverbial Sunday chicken. Today, thanks to modern production methods, almost anyone can afford this versatile fowl, which provides not only meat and eggs but feathers as well. Chickens fall into several classifications. The **broiler-fryer** can weigh up to 3½ pounds and is usually around 2½ months old. These chickens, as the name implies, are best when broiled or fried. The more flavorful **roasters** have a higher fat content and therefore are perfect for roasting and rotisserie cooking. They usually range between 2½ and 5 pounds and can be up to 8 months old. **Stewing chickens** (also called *hens, boiling fowl* and just plain *fowl*) usually range in age from 10 to 18 months and can weigh from 3 to 6 pounds. Their age makes them more flavorful but also less tender, so they're best cooked with moist heat, such as in stewing or braising. A **capon** is a rooster that is castrated when quite young (usually before 8 weeks), fed a fattening diet and brought to market before it's 10 months old. Ranging from 4 to 10 pounds, capons are full-breasted with tender, juicy, flavorful meat that is particularly suited to roasting. **Rock Cornish hen**, also called *Rock Cornish game hen*, is a hybrid of Cornish and White Rock chickens. These miniature chickens weigh up to 2½ pounds and are 4 to 6 weeks old. Because of the relatively small amount of meat to bone, each hen is usually just enough for one serving. Rock Cornish hens are best broiled or roasted. **Squab Chicken** (*poussin* in French), different from the true SQUAB, is a very small, 4- to 6-week-old chicken that weighs no more than 1½ pounds. These tiny birds are best broiled, grilled or roasted. The **cock** or **rooster** is an older bird and therefore rather tough. It's best used in soups or to make broths. **Range chickens** (also called *free-range*) are the elite of the poultry world in that, instead of the mass-produced birds' allotted 1 square foot of space, each range chicken has double that area indoors plus the occasional freedom to roam outdoors. They're fed a special vegetarian diet free (according to most range chicken breeders) of antibiotics, animal byproducts, hormones and growth enhancers. The special diet and freedom of movement is thought by some to give this fowl a fuller, more "chickeny" flavor, but the added amenities make these birds much more expensive than mass-produced chickens. Range chickens average 4½ pounds and are usually around 10 to 12 weeks old. **Chicken grades:** The government grades chicken quality with USDA classifications A, B and C. The highest grade is A, and is generally what is found in markets. Grade B chickens are less meaty and well finished; grade C is usually reserved for scrawny turkeys. The grade stamp can be found within a shield on the package wrapping, or sometimes on a tag attached to the bird's wing. Chicken is available in markets throughout the year either fresh or frozen, and whole or cut into parts. The neck and GIBLETS (liver, gizzard and heart) are either packaged separately and placed in a whole bird's body cavity, or sold individually. Choose a meaty, full-breasted chicken with plump, short legs. The skin—which can range from cream-colored to yellow, depending on the breed and the chicken's diet—should be smooth and soft. Avoid chickens with an off odor, or with skin that's bruised or torn. Store chicken in the coldest part of the refrigerator. If packaged tightly in cellophane, loosen packaging or remove and loosely rewrap chicken in waxed paper. Remove and store separately any giblets in body cavity. Refrigerate raw chicken up to 2 days, cooked chicken up to 3 days. For maximum flavor, freeze raw chicken no longer than 2 months, cooked chicken up to a month. Salmonella bacteria are present on most poultry (though only about 4 percent of salmonella poisonings are chicken-related). To avoid any chance of bacterial contamination, it's important to handle raw chicken with care. The first rule is never to eat chicken in its raw state. After cutting or working with raw chicken, thoroughly wash utensils, cutting tools, cutting board and your hands.

Cooking chicken to 170°F (the juices will be yellow and the meat opaque) will kill any lurking bacteria. Don't let any raw juice come in contact with cooked chicken. The versatile chicken can be prepared in almost any way imaginable, including baking, broiling, boiling, roasting, frying, braising, barbecuing and stewing. Boning chicken will shorten any cooking time but will also slightly diminish the flavor. Chicken is an excellent source of protein, and a good to fair source of niacin and iron. White meat and chicken without skin have fewer calories.

chicken à la king *see* À LA KING

chicken cacciatore *see* CACCIATORE

chicken-fried steak Particularly popular in the South and Midwest, this dish is said to have been created to use inexpensive beef. It refers to a thin cut of steak that has been tenderized by pounding. It's dipped into a milk-egg mixture and seasoned flour, then fried like chicken until crisp and brown, and served with COUNTRY GRAVY.

chicken Kiev [kee-EHV] A boned chicken breast rolled around a chilled chunk of herbed butter, with the edges fastened so the butter won't escape during cooking. The breast is dipped in egg and then breadcrumbs and fried until crisp. When pierced with a fork or cut into, the chicken emits a jet of the fragrant melted butter.

chicken Marengo *see* MARENGO

chicken paprikash *see* PAPRIKÁS CSIRKE

chicken Tetrazzini [teh-trah-ZEE-nee] Said to have been named for the opera singer Luisa Tetrazzini, this rich dish combines cooked spaghetti and strips of chicken with a sherry-Parmesan cheese cream sauce. Parmesan or breadcrumbs are sprinkled over the surface and the dish is baked until bubbly and golden brown. Turkey is sometimes substituted for chicken in this dish.

chickpea; chick-pea Slightly larger than the average pea, these round, irregular-shaped, buff-colored LEGUMES have a firm texture and mild, nutlike flavor. Chickpeas (also called *garbanzo beans* and *ceci*) are used extensively in the Mediterranean, India and the Middle East for dishes such as COUSCOUS and HUMMUS. They've also found their way into Spanish stews, Italian MINESTRONE and various Mexican dishes, and are fast becoming popular in many parts of the Western and Southwestern United States. Chickpeas are available canned, dried and in some areas, fresh. They're most commonly used in salads, soups and stews. *See also* BEAN.

chicory [CHIHK-uh-ree] This relative of the ENDIVE has curly, bitter-tasting leaves that are often used as part of a salad or cooked as greens. In the U.S., early endive is sometimes erroneously called chicory. Chicory is available year-round. Choose leaves that are brightly colored and crisp. Store unwashed greens in an airtight container in the refrigerator up to 3 days. Today's trendy **radicchio** is a red-leafed Italian chicory. **Roasted chicory** (also called *succory*) comes from the roasted, ground roots of some varieties of chicory. It's used as a coffee substitute, and added to some coffees for body and aroma and as an "extender." This coffee-chicory blend is often referred to as "New Orleans" or "Creole" coffee and is a popular beverage in Louisiana.

chiffon [shih-FAHN] An airy, fluffy mixture, usually a filling for pie. The lightness is achieved with stiffly beaten egg whites and sometimes gelatin.

chiffonade [shihf-uh-NAHD; shihf-uh-NAYD] Literally translated, this French phrase means "made of rags." Culinarily, it refers to thin strips or shreds of vegetables (classically, sorrel and lettuce), either lightly sautéed or used raw to garnish soups. **Chiffonade salad dressing** is a classic FRENCH DRESSING with the addition of finely chopped or shredded hard-cooked egg, green pepper, chives, parsley, beet and onion.

chiffon cake Said to have been created in the late 1940s by a professional baker, chiffon cake is distinguished from others of its genre by the fact that oil, rather than solid shortening, is used. It contains LEAVENING, such as baking powder, and stiffly beaten egg whites, which contribute to its rather spongecakelike texture.

chilaca chili pepper [chihl-AH-kah] *see* PASILLA CHILI PEPPER

chilaquiles [chee-lah-KEE-lehs] Because it was invented to use leftovers, this Mexican entree is sometimes called "poor man's dish." It consists of corn TORTILLA strips sautéed with other foods such as mild green chilies, cheese, CHORIZO and shredded chicken or beef. The dish may also be layered like LASAGNA and baked.

chiles rellenos [CHEE-lehs rreh-YEH-nohs] Literally translated as "stuffed peppers," this Mexican specialty consists of cheese-stuffed mild green chilies, cloaked with an egg batter and fried until the outside is crisp and the cheese inside is melted.

chili con carne [CHIHL-ee kon KAHR-nay; CHIHL-ee kon KAHR-nee] Spanish for "chili with meat," this dish is a melange of diced or ground beef and chili peppers or chili powder (or both). It originated in the Lone Star State and Texans, who commonly refer to it as "a bowl of red," consider it a crime to add beans to the mixture. In many parts of the country, however, beans are requisite and the dish is called "chili con carne with beans."

chili oil Vegetable oil in which hot red chili peppers have been steeped to release their heat and flavor. This spicy-hot oil is red-colored (from the chilies) and is a mainstay of Chinese cookery. It will keep 6 months at room temperature, but will retain its potency longer if refrigerated.

chili paste Widely used in Chinese cooking, this paste is made of fermented FAVA BEANS, flour, red chili peppers and sometimes garlic. It's available in Chinese markets and many large supermarkets.

chili pepper; chili; chile; hot pepper One of the wonders that Christopher Columbus brought back from the New World was a member of the *Capsicum* genus, the chili pepper. Now this pungent pod plays an important role in the cuisines of many countries including Africa, China (Szechuan region), India, Mexico, South America, Spain and Thailand. There are more than 200 varieties of chili pepper, over 100 of which are indigenous to Mexico. They vary in length from a huge 12 inches to a ¼-inch peewee. Some are long, narrow and no thicker than a pencil while others are plump and globular. Their heat quotient varies from mildly warm to mouth-blistering hot. A chili pepper's color can be anywhere from yellow to green to red to black. Dried chili peppers are available year-round. The availability of fresh chilies varies according to the variety and season. Choose those with deep, vivid colors; avoid chilies with any sign of shriveling or soft spots. Fresh chilies can be stored in the vegetable drawer of the refrigerator. Most of a chili pepper's heat is centered in its seeds and membrane, so removing those will make at least small amounts of even the hottest specimen tolerable. After working with chilies, it's extremely important to wash your hands thoroughly; failure to do so can result in painful burning of the eyes or skin (wearing rubber gloves will remedy this problem). Chili peppers are used to make a plethora of byproducts including CHILI PASTE, TABASCO SAUCE, ground red pepper and the dried red pepper flakes commonly found in pizzerias. *For information on specific chili peppers, see individual listings. See also* SWEET PEPPERS.

chili powder A powdered seasoning mixture of dried chilies, garlic, oregano, cumin, coriander and cloves. *See also* Herb and Spice Chart, page 538.

chili sauce A spicy blend of tomatoes, chili peppers or chili powder, onions, green peppers, vinegar, sugar and spices. This ketchuplike sauce is used as a condiment.

chimichanga [chee-mee-CHAN-gah] This specialty of Sonora, Mexico, is actually a BURRITO that is fried or deep-fried. It can contain any number of fillings including shredded chicken, beef or pork, grated cheese, refried beans and rice. To prevent the filling from spilling out during frying, the flour TORTILLA must be rolled around it, with the ends tucked in. Chimichangas are often garnished with SALSA, GUACAMOLE, sour cream and shredded cheese.

chine *n.* [CHYN] This term refers to the backbone of an animal. It can also describe a cut of meat including the backbone with some adjoining flesh. The chine is removed from the rib bones in cuts such as rack of lamb. **chine** *v.* A butchering term meaning to sever the backbone.

Chinese artichoke Also known as *Japanese artichoke, knotroot* and *chorogi*, this hairy plant is a native of China and Japan. It has small white tubers that have a sweet, nutty taste similar to a JERUSALEM ARTICHOKE. They can seldom be found in the United States but, if available, should be purchased when firm and white. Refrigerate in a plastic bag up to a week. Chinese artichokes can be eaten raw, or boiled, baked or steamed. *See also* ARTICHOKE.

Chinese cabbage The heading "Chinese cabbage" is confusing, at best. This variety, *Brassica pekinensis*, is also called *Napa cabbage, Chinese celery cabbage, wong bok* and *Peking cabbage*, just to name a few. Another *Brassica* subspecies—*chinensis*—is better known as BOK CHOY and is also called *Chinese white cabbage* and *white mustard cabbage*. It's clear that the confusion is warranted. The predominant variety of the *pekinensis* sub-species of Chinese cabbage has crinkly, thickly veined leaves that are cream-colored with celadon green tips. Unlike the strong-flavored waxy leaves on round heads of cabbage, these are thin, crisp and delicately mild. Chinese cabbage is generally available year-round. Choose firm, tightly packed heads with crisp, green-tipped leaves. Refrigerate, tightly wrapped, up to 3 days. Use raw, or sauté, bake or braise. Chinese cabbage is a good source of vitamin A, folic acid and potassium.

Chinese cuisine The combined cuisines of China have often been compared to French cuisine as having made the greatest contribution to the world of food. Chinese cooking styles have been divided into five main regions: Southeastern (Canton), East Coast (Fukien), Northeastern (Peking-Shantung), Central (Honan) and Western (Szechwan-Hunan). **Cantonese** cuisine is famous for its meat roasting and grilling, fried rice, and BIRD'S NEST and SHARK FIN SOUP. The province of **Fukien** is noted for its multitudinous selection of soups and for its seafood dishes. The light, elegant **Peking-Shantung** style originated the famous PEKING DUCK, and is highly acclaimed for its subtle and artful use of seasonings. China's **Honan** province is the home of SWEET-AND-SOUR cooking, and the **Szechwan-Hunan** school is known for its hot, spicy dishes. **Mandarin** cooking and **Shanghai** cooking are not regional designations, but terms used to describe cooking styles. The word *mandarin* means "Chinese official," and mandarin cooking suggests an aristocratic cuisine that gleans the very finest elements from all the regions. *Shanghai* cooking refers to a cosmopolitan combination of many Chinese cooking styles.

Chinese date Also called *Chinese jujube* and *red date*, this olive-sized fruit has a leathery skin which, depending on the variety, can be red (most common), off-white or almost black. The flavor of the rather dry, yellowish flesh is prunelike. The Chinese date is generally imported from China, though some are being grown on the West Coast. Some fresh fruit is available (mainly in the West), but those found most often (usually in Chinese markets) are dried and must be soaked in water before using. Chinese cooks use this fruit in both savory and sweet dishes.

Chinese firepot *see* MONGOLIAN HOT POT

Chinese five-spice powder *see* FIVE SPICE POWDER

Chinese gooseberry *see* KIWI

Chinese jujube *see* CHINESE DATE

Chinese parsley *see* CORIANDER

Chinese pear *see* ASIAN PEAR

Chinese pepper *see* SZECHWAN PEPPER

Chinese pickle *see* TEA MELON

Chinese sausage Texturally similar to pepperoni, this dry, rather hard sausage is usually made from pork meat and a goodly amount of fat. It's smoked, slightly sweet and highly seasoned. Probably the most popular Chinese sausage in this country is **lop chong**. It and others like it are available in specialty meat shops and Chinese markets. Store up to 1 month in the refrigerator. Chinese sausage makes an excellent addition to STIR-FRY dishes. *See also* SAUSAGE.

Chinese snow pea *see* SNOW PEA

Chinese steel *see* BLACKFISH

Chinese white cabbage *see* BOK CHOY

chinois [sheen-WAH] A conical sieve with an *extremely* fine mesh, used for pureeing or straining. The mesh is so fine that a spoon or pestle must be used to press the food through it.

chinook salmon [shih-NUHK] *see* SALMON

chinquapin [CHING-kuh-pihn] *see* CRAPPIE

chipolata sausage [chee-poh-LAH-tah; chih-poh-LAH-tah] Sometimes called "little fingers," these tiny (2- to 3-inch-long), coarse-textured pork sausages are highly spiced with thyme, chives, coriander, cloves and sometimes hot red-pepper flakes. The French term *à la chipolata* refers to a garnish of chipolata, chestnuts and glazed vegetables used to accompany roasts. *See also* SAUSAGE.

chipotle chili pepper [chih-POHT-lay] This hot chili pepper can be found dried, canned and pickled. It's dried by smoking and has a wrinkled, dark red skin. Chipotles are generally added to stews and sauces; the pickled variety are often eaten as appetizers. *See also* CHILI PEPPER.

chipped beef These wafer-thin slices of salted and smoked, dried beef are usually packed in small jars and were once an American staple. Chipped beef is also referred to simply as *dried beef*. "Shit on a shingle," known in polite society as *SOS*, is military slang used for creamed chipped beef served on toast.

chips The British word for what Americans call "FRENCH FRIES." Their potato chips are called "crisps."

chitlins; chitlings [CHIHT-lihnz] *see* CHITTERLINGS

chitterlings [CHIHT-lihnz; CHIHT-lingz] Popular in Southern cooking, chitterlings are the small intestines of animals, usually freshly slaughtered pigs. Once cleaned, chitterlings must be simmered until tender. They can then be served with a sauce, added to soups, battered and fried or used as a sausage CASING.

chive Related to the onion and leek, this fragrant HERB has slender, vivid green, hollow stems. Chives have a mild onion flavor and are available fresh year-round. Look for those with a uniform green color and no signs of wilting or browning. Store in a plastic bag in the refrigerator up to a week. Fresh chives can be snipped with scissors to the desired length. They're delicious in many cooked dishes but should be added toward the end of the cooking time to retain their flavor. Both chives and their edible lavender flowers are a tasty and colorful addition to salads. Frozen and freeze-dried chives are also available in most supermarkets. Chives are a good source of vitamin A and also contain a fair amount of potassium and calcium.

chlodnik [CHLAHD-nihk] Of Polish origin, this BORSCHT-like soup is made of beets, onions, cucumbers, herbs and sometimes veal. It's served cold, garnished with sour cream.

chocolate The word "chocolate" comes from the Aztec *xocolatl*, meaning "bitter water." Indeed, the unsweetened drink the Aztecs made of pounded cocoa beans and spices was probably extremely bitter. Bitterness notwithstanding, the Aztec king Montezuma so believed that chocolate was an aphrodisiac that he purportedly drank 50 golden goblets of it each day. Chocolate comes from the tropical cocoa bean, *Theobroma* ("food of the gods") *cacao*. After the beans are removed from their pods they're fermented, dried, roasted and cracked, separating the nibs (which contain an average of 54 percent cocoa butter) from the shells. The nibs are ground to extract some of the COCOA BUTTER (a natural vegetable fat), leaving a thick, dark brown paste called chocolate liquor. Next, the chocolate liquor receives an initial refining. If additional cocoa butter is extracted from the chocolate liquor, the solid result is ground to produce unsweetened COCOA POWDER. If other ingredients are added (such as milk powder, sugar, etc.), the chocolate is refined again. The final step for most chocolate is conching, a process by which huge machines with rotating blades slowly blend the heated chocolate liquor, ridding it of residual moisture and volatile acids. The conching continues for 12 to 72 hours (depending on the type and quality of chocolate) while small amounts of cocoa butter and sometimes LECITHIN are added to give chocolate its voluptuously smooth texture. Unadulterated chocolate is marketed as **unsweetened chocolate**, also called **baking** or **bitter chocolate**. U.S. standards require that unsweetened chocolate contain between 50 and 58 percent cocoa butter. The addition of sugar, lecithin and vanilla (or vanillin) creates, depending on the amount of sugar added, **bittersweet**, **semisweet** or **sweet chocolate**. Bittersweet chocolate must contain at least 35 percent chocolate liquor; semisweet and sweet can contain from 15 to 35 percent. Adding dry milk to sweetened chocolate creates **milk chocolate**, which must contain at least 12 percent milk solids and 10 percent chocolate liquor. Though bittersweet, semisweet and sweet chocolate may often be used interchangeably in *some* recipes with little textural change, milk chocolate—because of the milk protein—cannot. **Liquid chocolate**, developed especially for baking, is found on the supermarket shelf alongside other chocolates. It's unsweetened, comes in individual 1-ounce packages, and is convenient because it requires no melting. However, because it's made with vegetable oil rather than cocoa butter, it doesn't deliver either the same texture or flavor as regular unsweetened chocolate. **Couverture** is a term describing professional-quality coating chocolate that is extremely glossy. It usually contains a minimum of 32 percent cocoa butter, which enables it to form a much thinner shell than ordinary CONFECTIONERY COATING. Couverture is usually only found in specialty candymaking shops. **White chocolate** is not true chocolate because it contains no chocolate liquor and, likewise, very little chocolate flavor. Instead, it's usually a mixture of sugar, cocoa butter, milk solids, lecithin and vanilla. Read the label: if cocoa butter isn't mentioned, the product is confectionery (or summer) coating, not white chocolate. Beware of products labeled **artificial chocolate** or **chocolate-flavored**. They are, just as the label states, not the real thing and both flavor and texture confirm that fact. Chocolate comes in many forms, from **1-ounce squares** to **½-inch chunks** to **chips** ranging in size from ½ to ⅛ inch in diameter. Many chocolate chunks and chips come in flavors including milk, semisweet, mint-flavored and white chocolate. Chocolate should be stored, tightly wrapped, in a cool (60° to 70°F), dry place. If stored at warm temperatures, chocolate will develop a pale gray "bloom" (surface streaks and blotches), caused when the cocoa butter rises to the surface. In damp conditions, chocolate can form tiny gray sugar crystals on the surface. In either case, the chocolate can still be used, with flavor and texture affected only slightly. Under ideal conditions, dark chocolate can be stored 10 years. However, because of the milk solids in both milk chocolate and white chocolate, they shouldn't be stored for longer than 9 months. Because all chocolate scorches easily—which completely ruins the flavor—it should be melted slowly over low heat. One method is to place the chocolate in the top of a double boiler over simmering water. Remove the top of the pan from the heat when the chocolate is a little more than halfway melted and stir until completely smooth. Another method is to place the chocolate in a microwave-safe bowl and, in a 650- to 700-watt microwave oven, heat at 50 percent power. Four ounces of chocolate will take about 3 minutes, but the timing will vary depending on the oven and the type and amount of chocolate. Though chocolate can be melted *with* liquid (at least ¼ cup liquid per 6 ounces chocolate), a single drop of moisture in melted chocolate will cause it to seize (clump and harden). This problem can sometimes be corrected if vegetable oil is immediately stirred into the chocolate at a ratio of about 1 tablespoon oil to 6 ounces chocolate. Slowly remelt the mixture and stir until once again smooth. *See also* CHOCOLATE SYRUP; MEXICAN CHOCOLATE.

chocolate syrup A ready-to-use syrup, usually a combination of unsweetened cocoa powder, sugar or corn syrup and various other flavorings. Chocolate syrup is usually quite sweet and is most often used to flavor milk or as a dessert sauce. It cannot be substituted for melted chocolate in recipes.

chokecherry Any of several varieties of wild cherries native to North America. These small cherries turn from red to almost black when mature. They're very astringent and, though not good for out-of-hand eating, make excellent jams and jellies. *Chokeberries* are the inedible fruit of an ornamental shrub.

cholent [CHAW-lent; CHUH-lent] Of Central European origin, cholent is a traditional Jewish food served on the Sabbath. It varies greatly from family to family, but generally consists of some kind of meat (such as brisket, short ribs or chuck), lima or navy beans, potatoes, barley, onions, garlic and other seasonings. The ingredients are combined in one pot and simmered on stovetop or baked at a very low heat for many hours. Since cooking is forbidden on the Sabbath, many Jewish families prepare and combine the ingredients and place the cholent in a low oven at sundown on Friday, to be ready the following day, which is the Sabbath.

chop *n.* A small cut of meat taken from the rib section and including part of the rib. Pork, veal and lamb chops are the most popular. **chop** *v.* Using quick, heavy blows of a knife or cleaver to cut food into bite-size (or smaller) pieces. A food processor may also be used to "chop" food. Chopped food is more coarsely cut than MINCED food.

chop suey [chop SOO-ee] Thought to date back at least to the mid 19th century, this Chinese-American dish includes small pieces of meat (usually chicken) or shrimp, mushrooms, bean sprouts, water chestnuts, bamboo shoots and onions. These ingredients are cooked together and served over rice. Chop suey doesn't exist as a dish in China.

chorizo [chor-EE-zoh; chor-EE-soh] A highly seasoned, coarsely ground pork sausage flavored with garlic, chili powder and other spices. It's widely used in both Mexican and Spanish cookery. Mexican chorizo is made with fresh pork, while the Spanish version uses smoked pork. The CASING should be removed and the sausage crumbled before cooking. Chorizo makes a tasty addition to many dishes including casseroles, soups, stews and ENCHILADAS. *See also* SAUSAGE.

chorogi [CHAWR-oh-gee] *see* CHINESE ARTICHOKE

Choron sauce [show-RAWHN] Named for the French chef who created it, Choron sauce is a HOLLANDAISE or BÉARNAISE SAUCE that has been tinted pink by the additon of tomato puree. It can be served with poultry, meat or fish.

choucroute [shoo-CROOT] This French word for "sauerkraut" describes it when cooked with goose fat, onions, juniper berries and white wine. It can be served as a side or main dish. *Choucroute garni* is sauerkraut garnished with potatoes and a variety of meats such as sausages, pork, ham or goose.

choux pastry [shoo] Also called *choux paste, pâte à choux* and *cream-puff pastry*, this special pastry is made by an entirely different method from other pastries. The dough, created by combining flour with boiling water and butter, then beating eggs into the mixture, is very sticky and pastelike. During baking, the eggs make the pastry puff into irregular domes (as with CREAM PUFFS). After baking, the puffs are split, hollowed out and filled with a custard, whipped cream, etc. Besides cream puffs, *choux* pastry is used to make such delights as ÉCLAIRS, GOUGÈRE and PROFITEROLES.

chow-chow; chowchow Thought to have been brought to America by the Chinese railroad laborers, chow-chow is a mustard-flavored mixed-vegetable-and-pickle relish. Originally, the term was used to describe a Chinese condiment of orange peel and ginger in a heavy syrup.

chowder A thick, chunky seafood soup, of which clam chowder is the most well known. The name comes from the French *chaudière*, a caldron in which fishermen made their stews fresh from the sea. **New England-style chowder** is made with milk or cream, **Manhattan-style** with tomatoes. Chowder can contain any of several varieties of seafood and vegetables. The term is also used to describe any thick, rich soup containing chunks of food (for instance, corn chowder).

chowder clam The largest of the East Coast hard-shell clams, the chowder clam (also called *quahog* or *large clam*) has a shell diameter of at least 3 inches. As their name implies, these clams are often cut up to use in chowders. They're also excellent stuffed and as clam fritters. *See also* CLAM.

chow mein [chow MAYN] A Chinese-American dish that consists of small pieces of meat (usually chicken) or shrimp and vegetables such as bean sprouts, water chestnuts, bamboo shoots, mushrooms and onions. The ingredients are usually fried separately, then combined at the last minute and served over crisp noodles.

Christmas melon *see* SANTA CLAUS MELON

christophene [KRIHS-tuh-feen] *see* CHAYOTE

chuck An inexpensive beef cut taken from between the neck and shoulder blade. The most popular cuts of chuck are roasts and steaks. Chuck roasts usually include a portion of the blade bone, which is why they're sometimes referred to as *blade pot roasts*. For maximum tenderness, chuck cuts must be cooked slowly, as in stewing or braising. *See also* BEEF; Beef Chart, page 573.

churn To agitate cream briskly so that the fat separates from the liquid, thereby forming a solid (butter). The old-fashioned butter churn consisted of a container fitted with wooden blades which, when a crank was rotated, would whirl the cream inside until it turned to butter. The modern household substitute for a butter churn is the food processor.

chutney [CHUHT-nee] From the East Indian word *chatni*, this spicy condiment contains fruit, vinegar, sugar and spices. It can range in texture from chunky to smooth and in degrees of spiciness from mild to hot. Chutney is a delicious accompaniment to curried dishes. The sweeter chutneys also make interesting bread spreads and are delicious served with cheese.

cider Apple cider was a highly popular early American beverage. Cider is made by pressing the juice from fruit (usually apples). It can be drunk straight or diluted with water. Before FERMENTATION, it's referred to as "sweet" cider. It becomes "hard" cider after fermentation, and can range widely in alcohol content. Apple cider is also used to make vinegar and brandy.

cider vinegar VINEGAR made from CIDER, usually apple.

cilantro [sih-LAHN-troh; see-LAHN-troh] *see* CORIANDER

cinnamon [SIH-nuh-muhn] Once used in love potions and to perfume wealthy Romans, this age-old spice comes in two varieties— *Cinnamomum zeylancum* (Ceylon cinnamon) and *Cinnamomum cassia* (cassia). Cinnamon is the inner bark of a tropical evergreen tree. The bark is harvested during the rainy season when it's more pliable. When dried, it curls into long quills, which are either cut into lengths and sold as cinnamon sticks, or ground into powder. **Ceylon cinnamon** is buff-colored and mildly sweet in flavor; **cassia cinnamon** is a dark, reddish brown color and has a more pungent, slightly bittersweet flavor. Cassia cinnamon is used and sold simply as "cinnamon" in many countries (including the U.S.). Cinnamon is widely used in sweet dishes, but also makes an intriguing addition to savory dishes such as stews and curries. **Oil of cinnamon** comes from the pods of the cinnamon tree and is used as a flavoring, as well as a medicinal. *See also* SPICES; Herb and Spice Chart, page 538.

cioppino [chuh-PEE-noh] San Francisco's Italian immigrants are credited with creating this delicious fish stew made with tomatoes and a variety of fish and shellfish.

cipollini [chihp-oh-LEE-nee] These bittersweet bulbs of the grape hyacinth taste and look like small onions. They're hard to find in the U.S. but do make an appearance in some Italian markets during the fall. For peak flavor, *cipollini* should be slowly simmered or braised. They can be served as an appetizer or vegetable.

citric acid [SIHT-rihk] A white powder extracted from the juice of citrus and other acidic fruits (such as pineapples and gooseberries). It's also produced by the FERMENTATION of glucose. Citric acid has a strong, tart taste and is used as a flavoring agent for foods and beverages. Small bottles of crystallized **sour salt** (also called *citric salt*) are often found in the kosher-foods section of supermarkets. Sour salt is used to impart a tart flavor to traditional dishes such as BORSCHT.

citron [SIHT-ron] This semitropical citrus fruit looks like a huge (6 to 9 inches long), yellow-green, lumpy lemon. Citron pulp is very sour and not suitable for eating raw. This fruit is grown instead for its extremely thick peel, which is candied and used in baking. Before candying, the peel is processed in brine and pressed to extract citron oil, used to flavor liqueurs and to scent cosmetics. Candied citron can be purchased fresh in specialty markets, or with preservatives (necessary for the expected long shelf life) in supermarkets. Either should be stored in the freezer for maximum freshness. Candied citron halves are sometimes available, but it will more likely be found chopped or in strips.

citrus fruits This large family of fruit includes among its members the CITRON, GRAPEFRUIT, KUMQUAT, LEMON, LIME, ORANGE, SHADDOCK, TANGELO, TANGERINE and UGLI FRUIT. Native to Asia, citrus fruits prefer tropical to temperate climates and thrive in many Central and South American countries, as well as the states of Arizona, California, Florida, Louisiana and Texas. All fresh citrus fruits share some degree of tartness and are rich in vitamin C.

citrus stripper A special tool with a stainless-steel notched edge that cuts ¼ inch-wide strips from the rind of citrus fruits as well as other fruits and vegetables. It's commonly used to make lemon or lime strips which are used to flavor drinks or garnish dishes such as salads and desserts. The strips can be cut long or short, depending on whether the stripper is pulled from top to bottom (short strips) or in a long spiral around the fruit (long strips). A citrus stripper can also be used to cut decorative designs in vegetables such as cucumbers and zucchini.

citrus zester The stainless-steel cutting edge of this kitchen tool has five tiny cutting holes which, when the zester is pulled across the surface of a lemon or orange, create threadlike strips of peel. The zester removes only the colored outer portion (ZEST) of the peel, leaving the pale bitter pith.

civet [SIHV-iht] Culinarily, civet is a well-seasoned stew of furred game—usually rabbit—flavored with onions, mushrooms and red wine.

clabber A popular dish of the Old South, clabber is unpasteurized milk that has soured and thickened naturally. Depending on its thickness, icy-cold clabbered milk was (and sometimes still is) enjoyed as a drink. It may also be eaten with fruit, or topped with black pepper and cream, or simply sprinkled with sugar.

clafouti [kla-foo-TEE] Originally from the Limousin region, this country-French dessert is made by topping a layer of fresh fruit with batter. After baking it's served hot, sometimes with cream. Some clafoutis have a cakelike topping while others are more like a pudding. Though cherries are traditional, any fruit such as plums, peaches or pears can be used.

clam American Indians used parts of the shell from these BIVALVE MOLLUSKS to make wampum—beads used for barter, ornamental, ceremonial and spiritual purposes. The two main varieties of clams are hard-shell and soft-shell. The **hard-shell clams** found on the East Coast (where they're also called by the Indian name, *quahog*) come in three sizes. The smallest are **littleneck clams**, which have a shell diameter less than 2 inches. Next comes the medium-sized **cherrystone clam**, about 2½ inches across. The largest of this trio is the **chowder clam** (also called simply "large" clam), with a shell diameter of at least 3 inches. Among the West Coast hard-shell varieties are the **Pacific littleneck clam**, the **pismo** and the small, sweet **butter clams** from Puget Sound. **Soft-shell clams**, also called *soft clams*, actually have thin, brittle shells. They can't completely close their shells because of a long, rubbery neck (or siphon) that extends beyond its edge. The most common East Coast soft-shell is the **steamer clam**. The most famous West Cost soft-shells are the **razor clam** (so named because its shell resembles a folded, old-fashioned straight razor) and the **geoduck clam** (pronounced *goo-ee-duck*). The geoduck is a comical-looking, 6-inch-long clam with a neck that can reach up to about

1½ feet long. On the East Coast and in the Pacific Northwest, clams are available year-round. In California, the season is November through April. Clams are sold live in the shell, fresh or frozen shucked, and canned. When buying hard-shell clams in the shell, make sure the shells are tightly closed. If a shell is slightly open, tap it lightly. If it doesn't snap shut, the clam is dead and should be discarded. To test a soft-shell clam, lightly touch its neck; if it moves, it's alive. The guideline for buying shucked clams is plumpness and clear liquid. Store live clams up to 2 days in a 40°F refrigerator; refrigerate shucked clams up to 4 days. Clams can be cooked in a variety of ways, including steaming and baking. All clams should be cooked gently to prevent toughening. Clams are high in protein and contain fair amounts of calcium and iron. *For information on specific clams, see individual listings. See also* SHELLFISH.

Clamart, à la [kla-MAHR] A French term referring to dishes garnished with peas. It can also refer to a garnish of potato balls.

clam chowder *see* CHOWDER

clam knife A small, sturdy, round-tipped knife used for opening live clams.

claret [KLAR-iht] A term used in Britain to refer to any red BORDEAUX WINE.

clarified butter [KLAIR-ih-fyd] Also called *drawn butter*, this is unsalted butter that has been slowly melted, thereby evaporating most of the water and separating the milk solids (which sink to the bottom of the pan) from the golden liquid on the surface. After any foam is skimmed off the top, the clear (clarified) butter is poured or skimmed off the milky residue and used in cooking. Because the milk solids (which make butter burn when used for frying) have been removed, clarified butter has a higher SMOKE POINT than regular butter and therefore may be used to cook at higher temperatures. Additionally, the lack of milk solids prevents clarified butter from becoming rancid as quickly as regular butter. It also means that the butter won't have as rich a flavor. GHEE is an East Indian form of highly clarified butter.

clarify [KLAIR-ih-fy] To clear a cloudy liquid by removing the sediment. The most common method is to add egg whites and/or eggshells to a liquid (such as a stock) and simmer for 10 to 15 minutes. The egg whites attract any particles in the liquid like a magnet. After cooling for about an hour, the mixture is poured through a cloth-lined SIEVE to strain out all residue. Rendered fat can be clarified by adding hot water and boiling for about 15 minutes. The mixture is then strained through several layers of

CHEESECLOTH and chilled. The resulting top layer of fat should be almost entirely clear of residue.

cleaver Used mainly by butchers and Chinese cooks, a cleaver is an axlike cutting tool. Its flat sides can be used for pounding, as in tenderizing meat. Cleavers are usually heavy for their size, but evenly weighted. A good cleaver can cut through bone just as easily as it can chop vegetables. The butt end can be used as a PESTLE to pulverize seeds or other food items; the flat side is also great for crushing garlic.

clementine [KLEHM-uhn-tyn] *see* MANADARIN ORANGE

clingstone A term used to describe fruit that has a pit to which the flesh clings tenaciously, one of the most well known being the *cling* or *clingstone peach. See also* FREESTONE.

clotted cream This specialty of Devonshire, England (which is why it's also known as *Devonshire* or *Devon cream*) is made by gently heating rich, unpasteurized milk until a semisolid layer of cream forms on the surface. After cooling, the thickened cream is removed. Clotted cream can be spread on bread or spooned atop fresh fruit or desserts. The traditional English "cream tea" consists of clotted cream and jam served with SCONES and tea. Clotted cream can be refrigerated, tightly covered, for up to 4 days.

cloudberry Found in northern climes such as New England, Canada and Scandinavia, the cloudberry looks like an amber-colored version of the raspberry to which it's related. The berries are too tart for out-of-hand eating but make excellent jam. Cloudberries are usually wild and therefore hard to find in markets. Other names for this delicious fruit include *bake-apple berry, yellow berry* and *mountain berry*.

cloud ear *see* WOOD EAR

clove 1. Considered one of the world's most important spices, cloves are the dried, unopened flower bud of the tropical evergreen clove tree. Reddish brown and nail-shaped, their name comes from *clavus*, the Latin word for nail. Cloves are sold whole or ground and can be used to flavor a multitude of dishes ranging from sweet to savory. *See also* SPICES; Herb and Spice Chart, page 538. 2. The term "clove" also refers to a segment of a bulb, such as in garlic clove.

club sandwich; clubhouse sandwich A double-decker sandwich consisting of 3 slices of toast or bread between which are layers of chicken or turkey, bacon, lettuce, tomato and whatever else pleases the sandwich maker.

club soda *see* SODA WATER

club steak This tender, flavorful beef cut comes from the small end of the SHORT LOIN next to the rib. It has a bone along one side, but includes no portion of the TENDERLOIN. *See also* BEEF; Beef Chart, page 573.

coat In cooking, this term refers to covering food with an outer "coating." It can mean dipping or rolling food (such as chicken) in seasoned breadcrumbs or flour. The food can be dipped into beaten eggs before being coated with the dry mixture. Coating food in this manner usually precedes frying. A semiliquid, such as mayonnaise or sauce, can also be used to coat food.

coat a spoon A cooking technique used to test the doneness of cooked, egg-based custards and sauces. The mixture is done when it leaves an even film (thin to thick, depending on the recipe instructions) on the spoon. This film can be tested by drawing your finger across the coating on the spoon. If it doesn't run and leaves a clear path, it's ready.

cobbler 1. A baked, deep-dish fruit dessert topped with a thick biscuit crust sprinkled with sugar. 2. An old-fashioned punch made by mixing liquor (usually rum or whiskey) or wine with fruit juice and sugar. The punch is usually garnished with mint and slices of citrus.

cobb salad Hollywood's Brown Derby Restaurant made this salad famous. It consists of finely chopped chicken or turkey, bacon, hard-cooked eggs, tomatoes, avocado, scallions, watercress, cheddar cheese and lettuce tossed with a VINAIGRETTE dressing and topped with an ample portion of crumbled Roquefort or other blue cheese.

cobnut *see* HAZELNUT

cock-a-leekie [KAHK-uh-LEE-kee] A Scottish soup made with chicken broth, chicken, leeks and, sometimes, oatmeal or cream.

cockle [KAHK-uhl] Any of various BIVALVES of the genus *Cardium* with a heart-shaped, radially ribbed "cockleshell." They have a tendency to be quite gritty and must be washed thoroughly to rid them of sand. Cockles, which have always been more popular in Europe than the United States, can be eaten raw or cooked, as with clams or oysters.

cocktail 1. A beverage that combines an alcohol (such as bourbon, gin, rum, scotch or vodka) with a mixer (such as fruit juice, soda or liqueur). Popular cocktails include MARTINI, OLD-FASHIONED and TOM COLLINS. 2. This term also applies to an appetizer served before a meal such as a "seafood" or "fruit" cocktail, which would be a dish of mixed seafood or mixed fruit respectively.

cocktail sauce A combination of ketchup or chili sauce with prepared horseradish, lemon juice and Tabasco sauce or other hot red pepper seasoning. Cocktail sauce is used with seafood and as a condiment for HORS D'OEUVRE, etc.

cocoa butter [KOH-koh] The natural, cream-colored vegetable fat extracted from cocoa beans during the process of making CHOCOLATE and COCOA POWDER. It's used to add smoothness and flavor in some foods (including chocolate) and in making cosmetics and soaps.

cocoa mix [KOH-koh] Also called *instant cocoa,* this mixture of cocoa powder, dry milk and sugar is combined with cold or boiling water to make a cold or hot, chocolate-flavored beverage.

cocoa powder [KOH-koh] Both CHOCOLATE and cocoa powder come from cocoa beans that grow in pods on the tropical *Theobroma cacao* tree, prominent in Southeast Asia, Africa, Brazil and other South American countries. Once cocoa beans are fermented, dried, roasted and cracked, the nibs are ground to extract about half of the cocoa butter, leaving a dark brown paste called chocolate liquor. After drying again, the hardened mass is ground into the powder known as unsweetened cocoa. The richer, darker **Dutch cocoa** has been treated with an ALKALI, which helps neutralize cocoa's natural acidity. Cocoa powder is sold plain or mixed with other ingredients such as milk powder and sugar, forming an instant cocoa mix. Cocoa mixes should not be substituted for cocoa powder in recipes.

coconut Malaysia is the motherland of the coconut palm, which now grows in parts of South America, India, Hawaii and throughout the Pacific Islands. This prolific tree yields thousands of coconuts over its approximately 70-year lifespan. Each coconut has several layers: a smooth, deep tan outer covering; a hard, dark brown, hairy husk with three indented "eyes" at one end; a thin brown skin; the creamy white coconut meat; and, at the center, a thin, opaque coconut juice. The smooth outer shell is usually removed before the coconut is exported. The coconut palm maximizes its potential by producing several products including food (coconut meat and buds) and drink (coconut juice, vinegar and toddy— the latter a potent fermented drink made from the tree's sap). Dried coconut meat, called *copra,* is pressed and used to make **coconut oil**, which is used in commercial frying and as a component in many packaged goods such as candies, margarines, soap and cosmetics. Coconut oil—one of the few non-animal saturated fats—is used widely in the manufacture of baked goods such as commercial cookies. Certain major manufacturers have replaced it with the more expensive unsaturated fats with an eye toward cholesterol consciousness. The coconut palm's hard shells can be used for bowls, the fiber for ropes and nets, the wood for building, the roots for fuel and the leaves for baskets, hats, mats and thatching. The flesh of *unripe* coconut (usually not exported) has a jellylike consistency and can be eaten from the shell with a spoon. Upon ripening, the flesh becomes white and firm. **Fresh coconuts** are available year-round, with the peak season being October through December. Choose one that's heavy for its size and that sounds full of liquid when shaken; avoid those with damp "eyes." Whole, unopened coconuts can be stored at room temperature for up to 6 months, depending on the degree of ripeness. The liquid in a coconut is drained by piercing two of the three eyes with an ice pick. This thin juice can be used as a beverage, though it shouldn't be confused with coconut "milk" (*see below*). Then the meat is removed and the inner skin scraped off. Chunks of coconut meat can be grated or chopped, either in the food processor or by hand. One medium coconut will yield 3 to 4 cups grated. Grated fresh coconut should be tightly covered and can be refrigerated up to 4 days, frozen up to 6 months. **Packaged coconut** is available in cans or plastic bags, sweetened or unsweetened, shredded or flaked, and dried, moist or frozen. It can sometimes also be found toasted. Unopened canned coconut can be stored at room temperature up to 18 months; coconut in plastic bags up to six months. Refrigerate both after opening. Coconut is high in saturated fat and is a good source of potassium. Coconut milk and coconut cream are sometimes called for in recipes, particularly in curried dishes. **Coconut milk** is made by combining equal parts water and shredded fresh or desiccated coconut meat and simmering until foamy. The mixture is then strained through CHEESECLOTH, squeezing as much of the liquid as possible from the coconut meat. The coconut meat can be combined with water again for a second, diluted batch of coconut milk. **Coconut cream** is made in the same manner, but enriches the mix by using 1 part water to 4 parts coconut. Milk can be substituted for water for an even richer result. Discard the coconut meat after making these mixtures. Coconut milk and cream also come canned and may sometimes be found frozen in Asian markets and some supermarkets. Do not confuse sweetened "cream of coconut"—used mainly for desserts and mixed drinks—with unsweetened coconut milk or cream.

coconut cream *see* COCONUT

coconut milk *see* COCONUT

coconut oil *see* COCONUT

cocotte [koh-KOT] This French word for "casserole" refers to a round or oval casserole with a tight-fitting lid. It can be either individual-size or large and is traditionally made of EARTHERNWARE. The phrase *en cocotte* means "cooked in a casserole."

cod This popular saltwater fish can range from 1½ to 100 pounds and comes from the Pacific and North Atlantic Oceans. Cod's mild-flavored meat is white, lean and firm. It's available year-round and comes whole (the smaller specimens) or in large pieces. Cod can baked, poached, braised, broiled and fried. Whole cod are often stuffed before baking. Cod can be preserved by smoking, salting or drying. **Salt cod**, an important staple in many tropical countries because of its storage properties, has been salted and dried. It's used to make the popular French dish BRANDADE. **Cod cheeks** and **tongues** are considered a delicacy. So are **scrod**, which are young cod (and haddock) weighing under 2½ pounds. HADDOCK, HAKE and POLLOCK are all close relatives of cod. *See also* FISH.

coddle A cooking method most often used with eggs, though other foods can be coddled as well. There are special containers with tight-fitting lids called "egg coddlers" made specifically for this purpose. Coddling is usually done by placing the food in an individual-size container that is covered, set in a larger pan of simmering water and placed either on stovetop or in the oven at very low heat. The gentle warmth of this WATER BATH slowly cooks the food. Coddling can also be done by gently lowering the food into water that's come to a boil and removed from the heat.

coeur à la crème [KEWR-ah-la-KREHM] French for "heart with cream," this classic dessert is made in a special heart-shaped wicker basket or mold with holes in it. Cream cheese is mixed with sour cream or whipping cream (and sometimes sugar) and placed into the special mold or CHEESECLOTH-lined basket. The dessert is then refrigerated overnight, during which time the WHEY (liquid) drains out through the basket or perforated mold. To serve, the dessert is unmolded and garnished with fresh berries or other fruit.

coffee Ethiopia is thought to be the motherland of the first coffee beans which, throughout the ages, found their way to Brazil and Colombia—the two largest coffee producers today. Coffee plantations abound throughout other South and Central American countries, Cuba, Hawaii, Indonesia, Jamaica and many African nations. The coffee plant is actually a small tree that bears a fruit called the "coffee cherry." Growing and tending these coffee trees is a labor-intensive process because blossoms, unripe (green) and ripe red cherries can occupy a tree simultaneously, necessitating hand-picking the fruit. The coffee cherry's skin and pulp surround two beans enclosed in a parchmentlike covering. Once these layers are discarded, the beans are cleaned, dried, graded and hand-inspected for color and quality.

The "green" beans (which can range in color from pale green to muddy yellow) are then exported, leaving the roasting, blending and grinding to be done at their destination. Coffee can be composed of a single type of coffee bean or a blend of several types. Blended coffee produces a richer, more complex flavor than single-bean coffees. The length of time coffee beans are roasted will affect the color and flavor of the brew. Among the most popular roasts are American, French, Italian, European and Viennese. **American roast** (also called **regular roast**) beans are medium-roasted, which results in a moderate brew—not too light or too heavy in flavor. The heavy-roasted beans are **French roast** and **dark French roast**, which are a deep chocolate brown and produce a stronger coffee, and the glossy, brown-black, strongly flavored **Italian roast,** used for espresso. **European roast** contains two-thirds heavy-roast beans blended with one-third regular-roast; **Viennese roast** reverses those proportions. **Instant coffee powder** is a powdered coffee made by heat-drying freshly brewed coffee. **Freeze-dried coffee granules** (or **crystals**) are derived from brewed coffee that has been frozen into a slush before the water is evaporated. Freeze-dried coffee is slightly more expensive than regular instant coffee, but is also reputed to be superior in flavor. Coffee, tea and cocoa all contain caffeine, a stimulant that affects many parts of the body including the nervous system, kidneys, heart and gastric secretions. **Decaffeinated coffee** has had the caffeine removed by one of two methods, either of which is executed before the beans are roasted. In the first method, the caffeine is chemically extracted with the use of a solvent, which must be completely washed out before the beans are dried. The second method—called *Swiss water process*—first steams the beans, then scrapes away the caffeine-rich outer layers. Though there was once concern about the safety of solvent residues, research has found that the volatile solvents disappear entirely when the beans are roasted. Coffee, whether ground or whole-bean, loses its flavor quickly. To assure the freshest, most flavorful brew, buy fresh coffee beans and grind only as many as needed to brew each pot of coffee. Inexpensive grinders are available at most department and discount stores. Store whole roasted beans in an airtight container in a cool, dry place for up to 2 weeks. For longer storage, freeze whole beans, freezer-wrapped, up to 3 months. Since room-temperature ground coffee begins to go stale within a couple of days after it's ground, it should be refrigerated in an airtight container and can be stored up to 2 weeks. *See also* CAFÉ AU LAIT; CAFÉ BRÛLOT; CAPPUCCINO; ESPRESSO; IRISH COFFEE; TURKISH COFFEE; VIENNESE COFFEE.

coffeecake This rich, sweet, cakelike bread is usually eaten for breakfast or brunch. Coffeecakes can be made with yeast, but those using baking soda or baking powder take less time and are also delicious.

Coffeecakes often contain fruit, nuts and sometimes a cream-cheese filling. They can be frosted or not and are usually best served slightly warm.

cognac [KON-yak] Hailing from in and around the town of Cognac in western France, this potent potable is the finest of all BRANDIES. Cognac is double-distilled immediately after FERMENTATION. It then begins its minimum 3-year aging in Limousin oak. Stars on a cognac label denote the following oak-aging: 1 star—aged 3 years; 2 stars—aged at least 4 years; 3 stars—aged at least 5 years. Older cognacs are labeled **V.S.** (very superior), **V.S.O.P.** (very superior old pale) and **V.V.S.O.P.** (very, very, superior old pale). A cognac label can no longer legally claim over 7 years aging. *Fine champagne* on the label indicates that 60 percent of the grapes came from a superior grape-growing section of Cognac called *Grande Champagne*. One designating *grande fine champagne* proclaims that all the grapes for that cognac came from that eminent area.

coho salmon [KOH-hoh] *see* SALMON

Cointreau [KWAHN-troh; kwahn-TROH] A fine French LIQUEUR that's clear, colorless and orange-flavored.

colander [KAWL-an-der; KUHL-en-der] Used for draining liquid from solids, the colander is a perforated, bowl-shaped container. It can be metal, plastic or ceramic.

cola [KOH-lah] A sweet carbonated beverage containing COLA-NUT extract and other flavorings.

cola nut; kola nut [KOH-lah] Caffeine and theobromine, used in the manufacture of some soft drinks, are derivatives of the cola nut, offspring of the cola tree that grows in Africa, South America and the West Indies. Chewing this nut is a favorite pastime of natives who claim it diminishes fatigue and thirst and (for some) has aphrodisiac properties.

Colbert sauce [kohl-BAIR; KOHL-bair] Named after the chief minister of King Louis XIV, this sauce combines meat glaze, butter, wine, shallots, tarragon and lemon juice. It's served with grilled meats and game.

colby cheese [KOHL-bee] A mild, whole-milk CHEDDAR CHEESE that has a softer, more open texture than regular cheddar. Because it's a high-moisture cheese, it doesn't keep as well as other cheddars. Colby is popular for eating out of hand, in sandwiches and for cooking. *See also* CHEESE.

colcannon [kuhl-CAN-uhn] A delicious Irish peasant dish of milk- and butter-moistened mashed potatoes mixed with finely chopped cooked onions and kale or cabbage.

cold duck Originating in Germany, this pink sparkling wine is a mixture of champagne, sparkling Burgundy and sugar. The wines used to make cold duck are often of inferior quality. The resulting potation is quite sweet with few other distinguishable characteristics.

cold-pressed oils *see* FATS AND OILS

cole slaw From the Dutch *koolsla*, meaning "cool cabbage," cole slaw is a salad of shredded red or white cabbage mixed with a MAYONNAISE, VINAIGRETTE or other type of dressing. Other ingredients such as chopped onion, celery, sweet green or red pepper, pickles, bacon or herbs may be added. There are probably as many variations of cole slaw as there are cooks.

collard; collard greens; collards [KAHL-uhrd] Long a staple of SOUL FOOD, collard (also called *collard greens* and just plain *collards*) is a variety of cabbage that doesn't form a head, but grows instead in a loose rosette at the top of a tall stem. It's often confused with its close relative KALE and, in fact, tastes like a cross between cabbage and kale. Collard's peak season is January through April, but it's available year-round in most markets. Look for crisp green leaves with no evidence of yellowing, wilting or insect damage. Refrigerate collard in a plastic bag 3 to 5 days. The Southern style of cooking the greens is to boil them with a chunk of bacon or salt pork. They can be prepared in any manner suitable for spinach or cabbage. Collard is an excellent source of vitamins A and C, calcium and iron.

collins A tall, iced cocktail made with liquor (gin, rum, vodka, whiskey or brandy), lemon juice, sugar and soda water, and garnished with a lemon slice. The drink is served in a 10- to 12-ounce "collins" glass. The most popular of this genre is the **Tom Collins**, which is made with gin and is said to have been named for its creator.

comal [koh-MAHL] A round, flat griddle on which TORTILLAS are cooked. In Mexico, comals used over open fires are usually made of unglazed EARTHENWARE. Those intended for use with electric and gas heat are more often made of a light metal, such as tin. The earthenware and thin metal allow fast heat penetration, thereby cooking the tortillas quickly—important so they don't become dry and brittle.

combine To mix two or more ingredients together until they do not separate.

Comice pear [cuh-MEES] This large, exquisite pear has a meltingly smooth, sweet flesh and fruit-filled fragrance. It ranges in color from greenish-yellow to yellow blushed with red. It's available from October to January and is best eaten uncooked. *See also* PEAR.

comino [koh-MEE-noh] *see* CUMIN

compote [KAHM-poht] 1. A chilled dish of fresh or dried fruit that has been slowly cooked in a SUGAR SYRUP (which may contain liquor or liqueur and sometimes spices). Slow cooking is important for the fruit to retain its shape. 2. Also called *compotier,* a deep, stemmed dish (usually of silver or glass) used to hold fruit, nuts or candy.

compound butter Butter creamed with other ingredients such as herbs, garlic, wine, shallots, etc. The French term for compound butter is *beurre composé.*

compressed yeast *see* YEAST

conch [KONGK] This GASTROPOD MOLLUSK (*see both listings*) is encased in a beautiful, brightly colored spiral shell. Conch is found in southern waters and is particularly popular with Floridians and Caribbeans. Summer is the peak season for fresh conch, which will most likely be available in Chinese or Italian markets or specialty fish stores. Store fresh conch, tightly wrapped, in the refrigerator up to 2 days. Conch can also be purchased canned or frozen. The footlike muscle can be eaten raw in salads, or tenderized by pounding, then quickly sautéed like ABALONE. It's also often chopped and used in chowders. Conch is sometimes erroneously referred to as *whelk* which, though related, is a different species.

conching [KONCH-ing] A manufacturing technique used to give chocolate a smooth texture. *See* CHOCOLATE *for a more complete description of this process.*

conchiglie [kon-KEE-lyay] Italian for "seashells," this shell-shaped PASTA is formed to resemble a CONCH shell.

Concord grape Grown mainly on the East Coast, the Concord is a beautiful blue-black grape that often appears to have been powdered with silver. This mild-flavored grape has seeds and a slip-off skin. It's available in September and October and is used mainly for juice, jams and for out-of-hand eating. *See also* GRAPE.

condensed milk *see* SWEETENED CONDENSED MILK

condiment [KON-duh-muhnt] A savory, piquant, spicy or salty accompaniment to food, such as a relish, sauce, mixture of spices, etc. Ketchup and mustard are two of the most popular condiments.

confection [kuhn-FEHK-shuhn] A piece of candy or sweetmeat; also a sweet dish. A *confectionery* is a candy shop.

confectioners' sugar; powdered sugar [kuhn-FEHK-shuh-nuhrs] *see* SUGAR

confectionery coating [kuhn-FEHK-shuh-nair-ee] Used as a dip for candies, a confectionery or *summer coating* is a blend of sugar, milk powder, hardened vegetable fat and various flavorings. It comes in a variety of pastel colors. Some have lowfat cocoa powder added, but they do not contain cocoa butter.

confit [kohn-FEE; kon-FEE] This specialty of Gascony, France, is derived from an ancient method of preserving meat (usually goose, duck or pork) wherby it is salted and slowly cooked in its own fat. The cooked meat is then packed into a crock or pot and covered with its cooking fat, which acts as a seal and preservative. *Confit* can be refrigerated up to 6 months. **Confit d'oie** and **confit de canard** are preserved goose and preserved duck, respectively.

confiture [kon-fih-TYOOR] Fruit jam or preserves.

conger eel [KONG-gur] *see* EEL

Congo pea *see* PIGEON PEA

conserve [kuhn-SURV; KON-surv] A mixture of fruits, nuts and sugar, cooked together until thick, often used to spread on biscuits, crumpets, etc.

consommé [KON-suh-may; kon-suh-MAY] A clarified meat or fish broth. Consommé can be served hot or cold, and is variously used as a soup or sauce base. A **double consommé** has been reduced until it is half the volume (and has twice the flavor) of regular (or single) consommé.

Conti, à la [KON-tee] A French term referring to dishes made or garnished with lentils (usually pureed) and sometimes bacon.

continental breakfast A light breakfast that usually consists of a breadstuff (such as toast, croissants, pastries, etc.) and coffee, tea or other liquid. The continental breakfast is the antithesis of the hearty ENGLISH BREAKFAST.

convection oven A special gas or electric oven equipped with a fan that provides continuous circulation of hot air around the food, thereby cooking it not only more evenly, but also up to 25 percent faster. For most foods, the oven temperature can be reduced 25°F as well. Because convection ovens heat up so fast, there's usually no need for preheating.

Convection ovens, unlike microwave ovens, do not require special cookware or major adjustments in cooking time or technique. There are also microwave-convection oven combinations, which combine the even cooking of convection with the speed of microwaving.

converted rice A term created by the brand name Uncle Ben's, used to describe parboiled rice. *See also* RICE.

cookie A cookie can be any of various hand-held, flour-based sweet cakes—either crisp or soft. The word *cookie* comes from the Dutch *koekje*, meaning "little cake." The earliest cookie-style cakes are thought to date back to 7th-century Persia, one of the first countries to cultivate sugar. There are six basic cookie styles, any of which can range from tender-crisp to soft. A **drop cookie** is made by dropping spoonfuls of dough onto a baking sheet. **Bar cookies** are created when a batter or soft dough is spooned into a shallow pan, then baked, cooled and cut into bars. **Hand-formed** (or **molded**) **cookies** are made by shaping dough by hand into small balls, logs, crescents and other shapes. **Pressed cookies** are formed by pressing dough through a COOKIE PRESS (or PASTRY BAG) to form fancy shapes and designs. **Refrigerator** (or **icebox**) **cookies** are made by shaping the dough into a log, which is refrigerated until firm, then sliced and baked. **Rolled cookies** begin by using a rolling pin to roll the dough out flat; then it is cut into decorative shapes with COOKIE CUTTERS or a pointed knife. Other cookies, such as the German SPRINGERLE, are formed by imprinting designs on the dough, either by rolling a special decoratively carved rolling pin over it or by pressing the dough into a carved COOKIE MOLD. In England, cookies are called *biscuits*, in Spain they're *galletas*, Germans call them *keks*, in Italy they're *biscotti* and so on.

cookie cutter A metal or plastic device used to cut decorative shapes out of dough that has been rolled flat. Cookie cutters are available singly or in sets. Dipping a cookie cutter into flour or granulated sugar will prevent it from sticking to soft doughs. A **rolling cookie cutter** has a wooden handle at the end of which is a metal or plastic cylinder marked with raised designs. When the cutter is rolled across the dough, it cuts a jigsaw-puzzle pattern of differently shaped cookies without any wasted dough.

cookie gun *see* COOKIE PRESS

cookie mold Most often made of wood, these decorative molds are used to create designs in some European cookies. The cookie dough is pressed into a floured mold, leveled off with a knife, then inverted onto a baking sheet. Cookie molds come in all sizes and shapes and are available at specialty kitchenware shops.

cookie press Also called a *cookie gun*, this tool consists of a hollow tube fitted at one end with a decorative template or nozzle, and at the other with a plunger. The tube is filled with a soft cookie dough that the plunger forces out through the decorative tip to form professional-looking pressed cookies. Cookie presses come with a selection of interchangeable templates and other tips. SPRITZ are one of the best-known cookies formed by this tool.

cookie stamp A small, decorative, round or square cookie imprinter, usually made of glass, ceramic or wood. When the stamp is pressed into a ball of cookie dough, it not only flattens it, but imprints a relief design on the surface. Cookie stamps come in many designs and are available at specialty kitchenware shops.

cooking wine A wine labeled "cooking wine" is generally an inferior wine that would not be drunk on its own. It lacks distinction and flavor and in times past has often been adulterated with salt. The rule of thumb when cooking with wine is only to use one you'd drink and to be sure the wine's flavor complements the food with which it's paired.

cooling rack Used to cool baked goods such as cakes and breads, a cooling rack is made of a network of closely arranged wires, set on short legs to raise it above the level of the countertop. The raised surface provides air circulation so the baked goods won't get soggy on the bottom. It's important that the rack have thick, strong wires so it won't sag in the center. Cooling racks can be round, square or rectangular and can range from small to large.

coq au vin [kohk-oh-VAHN; kohk-oh-VAHM] This classic French dish is composed of pieces of chicken, mushrooms, onions, bacon or salt pork and various herbs cooked together with red wine.

coquilles St. Jacques [koh-KEEL sah*n*-ZHAHK; koh-KEE sah*n*-ZHAK] Classically served in a SCALLOP shell, this special dish consists of scallops in a creamy wine sauce, topped with breadcrumbs or cheese and browned under a broiler. *Coquille* is French for "shell"; it can also mean "scallop."

coral Eaten plain or used in a sauce or COMPOUND BUTTER, coral is simply the ROE (eggs) of a CRUSTACEAN such as lobster or scallop. When cooked, it turns a beautiful coral-red color.

cordial *see* LIQUEUR

cordon bleu [kor-doh*n*-BLUH] 1. A French term (literally translated as "blue ribbon") that referred originally to an award given to women chefs for culinary excellence. The term now can apply to any superior cook. 2. The term also refers to a dish—chicken (or veal) *cordon bleu*—in which a thin scallop of veal or chicken is topped with a thin slice each of prosciutto or other ham and Gruyère or other Swiss cheese, then another meat scallop. The stacked meats and cheese are then breaded and sautéed until golden.

core *n.* The center of a fruit such as an apple, pear or pineapple. Cores may contain small seeds, or they may be tough and woody. **core** *v.* As a verb, the word refers to removing the core from the fruit.

corer A utensil designed to remove the core (or center) from fruit or vegetables. Corers are usually made of stainless steel and come in different shapes for different uses. An all-purpose corer, used for apples, pears and the like, has a medium-length shaft with a circular cutting ring at the end. The core can be cut and removed with this tool. Another kind of apple corer is shaped like a spoked wheel with handles and not only cores the apple, but cuts it into wedges as well. A **zucchini corer** has a long, pointed, trough-shaped blade that, when inserted at one end of the zucchini and rotated, will remove the center, leaving a hollow tube for stuffing. A **pineapple corer** is a tall, arch-handled utensil with two serrated, concentric cutting rings at the base. After the top and bottom of the pineapple are sliced off, the corer is inserted from the top and twisted downward. The tool not only removes the core, but also the outer shell, leaving pineapple rings.

coriander [KOR-ee-an-der] Native to the Mediterranean and the Orient, coriander is related to the parsley family. It's known for both its seeds (actually the dried, ripe fruit of the plant) and for its dark green, lacy leaves. The flavors of the seeds and leaves bear absolutely no resemblance to each other. Mention of **coriander seeds** was found in early Sanskrit writings and the seeds themselves have been discovered in Egyptian tombs dating to 960 B.C. The tiny (⅛-inch), yellow-tan seeds are lightly ridged. They are mildly fragrant and have an aromatic flavor akin to a combination of lemon, sage and caraway. Whole coriander seeds are used in pickling and for special drinks, such as mulled wine. Ground seed is used in many baked goods (particularly Scandinavian), curry blends, soups, etc. (*See* Herb and Spice Chart, page 538.) Both forms are commonly available in supermarkets. **Coriander leaves** are also commonly known as *cilantro* and *Chinese parsley*. Fresh coriander leaves have an extremely pungent (some say fetid) odor and flavor that lends itself well to highly seasoned food. Though it's purported to be the world's most widely used herb, many Americans and Europeans find that fresh coriander is definitely an acquired taste. Choose leaves with an even green color and no sign of wilting. Store a bunch of coriander, stems down, in a glass of water with a plastic bag over the leaves. Refrigerate in this manner for up to a week, changing the water every 2 days. Use only the leaves in cooking. Coriander leaves are used widely in the cuisines of India, Mexico, the Orient and the Caribbean.

corkage [KORK-ihj] A fee charged by some restaurants to open and serve a bottle of wine brought in by the patron.

corkscrew A tool used to withdraw corks from bottles. Typically, a corkscrew has a pointed metal spiral with a transverse handle at one end. There are many varieties of corkscrews, however, including one that holds the bottle while a crank handle drives the screw into the cork and then extracts it.

corn Throughout Europe, "corn" has always been the generic name for any of the cereal grains; Europeans call corn *maize*, a derivative of the early American Indian word *mahiz*. In fact, before settlers came to the New World Europeans had never seen this food—called *Indian corn* by colonists. What a wonderfully versatile and useful gift the Indians gave the world. Everything on the corn plant can be used: the husks for TAMALES, the silk for medicinal tea, the kernels for food and the stalks for fodder. Corn is not only a popular food, but the foundation of many byproducts including BOURBON, CORN FLOUR, CORNMEAL, CORN OIL, CORNSTARCH, CORN SYRUP, CORN WHISKEY and laundry starch. The multicolored Indian corn—used today mainly for decoration—has red, blue, brown and purple kernels. Horticulturists developed the two most popular varieties today—white (**Country Gentleman**) and yellow (**Golden Bantam**) corn. **Yellow corn** has larger, fuller-flavored kernels; **white corn** kernels are smaller and sweeter. The hybrid **butter and sugar corn** produces ears of yellow and white kernels. The peak season for fresh corn is May through September. As soon as it's picked, the corn's sugar immediately begins its gradual conversion to starch which, in turn, lessens the corn's natural sweetness. Therefore, it's important to buy corn as soon after it's picked as possible. Look for ears with bright green, snugly fitting husks and golden brown silk. The kernels should be plump and milky, and come all the way to the ear's tip; the rows should be tightly spaced. Fresh corn should be cooked and served the day it's purchased, but it can be refrigerated up to a day. Strip off the husks and silk just before cooking. Corn can also be purchased canned or frozen. Tiny **baby corn**, particularly popular with Thai and Chinese cooks, can be purchased in cans or jars. Unfortunately, its flavor bears little resemblance to the fresh (or even frozen) vegetable. HOMINY is specially processed kernels of corn.

cornbread An all-American QUICK BREAD that substitutes cornmeal for most (or sometimes all) of the flour. It can include various flavorings such as cheese, scallions, molasses and bacon. Cornbread can be thin and crisp or thick and light. It can be baked Southern style in a skillet or in a shallow square, round or rectangular baking pan. Some of the more popular cornbreads are HUSH PUPPIES, JOHNNYCAKES and SPOON BREAD.

corn dog Created in 1942 by Texan Neil Fletcher for the State Fair, a corn dog is a frankfurter or other sausage dipped in a heavy cornbread batter and fried or baked. Corn dogs are often served on a stick for easy eating.

corned beef Beef (usually BRISKET, but also ROUND) CURED in a seasoned BRINE. Sometimes the brine is pumped through the arterial system. The term "corned" beef comes from the English use of the word "corn," meaning any small particle (such as a grain of salt). Two types of corned beef are available, depending on the butcher and the region. Old-fashioned corned beef is grayish-pink in color and very salty; the newer style has less salt and is a bright rosy red. Much corned beef is now being made without nitrites, which are reputed to be carcinogenic.

Cornell bread The Cornell formula to enrich bread was developed in the 1930s at New York's Cornell University. It consists of 1 tablespoon each soy flour and nonfat milk powder plus 1 teaspoon wheat germ for each cup of flour used in a bread recipe. These enrichments are placed in the bottom of the measuring cup before the flour is spooned in.

cornet [cor-NAY; cor-NEHT] French for "horn," a cornet can be any of several horn- or cone-shaped items including pastry (filled with whipped cream), a thin slice of ham (filled with cheese), or a paper cone (filled with candy or nuts).

corn flour Finely ground cornmeal, corn flour comes in yellow and white and is used for breading and in combination with other flours in baked goods. Corn flour is milled from the whole kernel, while CORNSTARCH is obtained from the endosperm portion of the kernel. In British recipes the term "cornflour" is used synonymously with the U.S. word cornstarch. MASA HARINA is a special corn flour that's the basic ingredient for corn tortillas.

cornichon [KOR-nih-shohn; kor-nee-SHOHM] French for "gherkin," cornichons are crisp, tart pickles made from tiny gherkin cucumbers. They're a traditional accompaniment to PÂTÉS as well as smoked meats and fish.

Cornish game hen *see* CHICKEN

Cornish pasty [PASS-tee] Named after Cornwall, England, these savory TURNOVERS consist of a short-crust pastry enfolding a chopped meat-and-potato filling. Other vegetables and sometimes fish are also used. In the 18th and 19th centuries, pasties were the standard lunch of Cornwall's tin miners. It was common to place a savory mixture in one end and an apple mixture in the other so both meat and dessert could be enjoyed in the same pasty.

cornmeal Dried corn kernels that have been ground in one of three textures—fine, medium or coarse. There are two methods of grinding. The old-fashioned water-ground (also called stone-ground) method—so named because water power is used to turn the mill wheels—retains some of the hull and germ of the corn. Because of the fat in the germ, water-ground cornmeal is more nutritious, but won't keep as long and should be stored (up to 4 months) in the refrigerator. Water-ground cornmeal is available at health-food stores and some supermarkets. The newer style of milling is done by huge steel rollers that remove the husk and germ almost completely. The product can be stored almost indefinitely in an airtight container in a cool, dry place. Water-ground or stone-ground cornmeal is usually so labeled; steel-ground cornmeal rarely carries any designation on the package. Cornmeal is either yellow, white or blue, depending on the type of corn used. Yellow cornmeal has slightly more vitamin A than white. Blue cornmeal is usually available only in specialty markets or the gourmet section of some supermarkets. However, there are an increasing number of blue-corn products available such as blue-cornmeal flakes and chips. *See also* CORN FLOUR.

corn oil High in polyunsaturates, this odorless, almost tasteless oil is obtained from the endosperm of corn kernels. It has a high SMOKE POINT, and is therefore good for frying. It's also used in baking, for salad dressings and to make margarine. *See also* FATS AND OILS.

corn pone [pohn] Extremely popular in the southern U.S., corn pone is an eggless CORNBREAD that is shaped into small ovals and fried or baked.

corn salad Native to Europe, corn salad has nothing to do with corn . . . but it is used in salads. The narrow, dark green leaves of this plant are tender and have a tangy, nutlike flavor. In addition to being used as a salad green, corn salad can also be steamed and served as a vegetable. Though it's often found growing wild in American cornfields, it's considered a "gourmet" green and is therefore expensive and hard to find. It doesn't keep well and should be used within a day or two of purchase. Corn salad should be washed and drained completely of any excess moisture before being stored airtight in a plastic bag. It's also called *field salad, lamb's lettuce* and *mâche*.

cornstarch A dense, powdery "flour" obtained from the endosperm portion of the corn kernel. Cornstarch is most commonly used as a thickening agent for puddings, sauces, soups, etc. Because it tends to form lumps, cornstarch is generally mixed with a small amount of cold liquid to form a thin paste before being stirred into a hot mixture. Mixing it with a granular solid like granulated sugar will also help it disperse into a liquid. Sauces thickened with cornstarch will be clear, rather than opaque, as with flour-based sauces. However, they will thin if cooked too long or stirred too vigorously. Cornstarch is also used in combination with flour in many European cake and cookie recipes; it produces a finer-textured, more compact product than flour alone. In British recipes, cornstarch is referred to as *cornflour*.

corn sugar *see* DEXTROSE

corn syrup A thick, sweet syrup created by processing cornstarch with acids or enzymes. Corn syrup comes in light or dark forms. **Dark corn syrup** has a stronger flavor and a darker color than **light corn syrup**, which has been clarified to remove all color and cloudiness. Because it inhibits crystallization, corn syrup is particularly popular as an ingredient in frosting, candy, jams and jellies. It's also used as a pancake syrup, either maple-flavored or plain.

corn whiskey Still called *moonshine* and *white lightning* in some rural areas of the South, corn whiskey is distilled from a fermented mash of not less than 80 percent corn. It's distilled at less than 160 PROOF (80 percent alcohol). *See also* WHISKEY.

Cortland apple A popular apple in the Northeast and northern Midwest, the Cortland has a smooth, shiny red skin. Its flesh is crisp, juicy, sweet-tart and resists browning. It's an all-purpose apple good for cooking as well as out-of-hand eating. *See also* APPLE.

cos lettuce [KOS] *see* ROMAINE LETTUCE

cotechino [coh-teh-KEE-noh] A specialty of several of Italy's Emilian provinces, this fresh pork sausage is quite large—usually about 3 inches in diameter and 8 to 9 inches long. It's made from pork rind and meat from the cheek, neck and shoulder, and is usually seasoned with nutmeg, cloves, salt and pepper. The best cotechino is delicately flavored and has a soft, almost creamy texture. It's a traditional ingredient in *bollito misto*, a classic Italian dish of mixed boiled meats accompanied by a savory broth and a piquant green sauce. *See also* SAUSAGE.

Côtes du Rhône [kot deuh ROHN] The generic appellation given to red, white and rosé wines grown in an area covering 83,000 acres in France's Rhône Valley. The majority of Rhône wines are red. Some of these are a deep ruby-black color, with full-bodied, concentrated flavors that benefit from at least 5 years' aging, while others are lighter and fruitier. The white Rhônes are fruity and dry and can be quite heady; the rosés can also be rather dry. Rhône wines are not made from one grape variety, but from a blend of from 2 to 13. Some of the more well-known Rhône wines are *Côte Rôtie, Hermitage* and *Syrah.*

cotriade [koh-tree-AHD] From Brittany, France, *cotriade* is a fish soup made with potatoes and without shellfish. It's usually ladled over thick slices of bread.

cottage cheese A fresh cheese made from whole, part-skimmed or skimmed PASTEURIZED cow's milk. "Sweet curd" cottage cheese—by far the most popular—has a rather mild (sometimes bland) flavor because the curds are washed to remove most of the cheese's natural acidity. The texture of cottage cheese is usually quite moist. If the curds are allowed to drain longer, pot cheese is formed; longer yet and the firm farmer's cheese is created. Cottage cheese comes in three forms: **small-curd**, **medium-curd** and **large-curd** (sometimes called "popcorn" cottage cheese). **Creamed** cottage cheese has had 4 to 8 percent cream added to it. Cottage cheese is sold plain and flavored, the most popular additions being chives and pineapple (but not together). Because it's more perishable than other cheeses, cartons of cottage cheese are stamped on the bottom with the date they should be pulled from the shelves. *See also* CHEESE.

cottage fried potatoes *see* HOME FRIED POTATOES

cottage pudding A dessert composed of a plain but rich cake smothered with a sweet sauce, such as lemon or chocolate.

cotto sausage The word *cotto* is Italian for "cooked," and is used to describe this soft Italian salami. It can be found whole in some specialty shops, but is more often sold sliced. Cotto sausage is excellent for sandwiches and cold-cut platters. *See also* SAUSAGE.

cottonseed oil A viscous oil obtained from the seed of the cotton plant. Most of the cottonseed oil produced is used in combination with other oils to create vegetable oil products. It's used in some margarines and salad dressings, and for many commercially fried products. *See also* FATS AND OILS.

coulibiac [koo-lee-BYAHK] This French adaptation of the Russian original (*kulebiaka*) consists of a creamy melange of fresh salmon, rice, hard-cooked eggs, mushrooms, shallots and dill enclosed in a hot pastry envelope. The pastry is usually made with BRIOCHE dough. Coulibiacs can be large or small but are classically oval in shape. They can be served as a first or main course.

coulis [koo-LEE] 1. A general term referring to a thick puree or sauce, such as a tomato *coulis*. 2. The word can also refer to thick, pureed shellfish soups. 3. Originally, the term *coulis* was used to describe the juices from cooked meat.

country captain Now an American classic, country captain is said to have taken its name from a British army officer who brought the recipe back from his station in India. It consists of chicken, onion, tomatoes, green pepper, celery, currants, parsley, curry powder and other seasonings, all slowly cooked together over low heat in a covered skillet. The finished dish is sprinkled with toasted almonds and usually served with rice.

country-cured ham Ham that has been dry-CURED in a mixture of salt, sodium nitrate, sugar and other seasonings for a period of days (depending on the weight of the ham). The salt is then rinsed off and the ham is slowly smoked over hardwood fires before being aged 6 to 12 months. Most are sold uncooked, though fully cooked hams are now becoming more readily available. Country-cured ham is distinguished by its salty, well-seasoned, firm flesh. America's most famous country-cured hams come from Georgia, Kentucky, Tennessee and Virginia. *See also* HAM.

country gravy A gravy made from pan drippings, flour and milk. It can be thick to thin, depending on the amount of milk added. Country gravy is a popular accompaniment to CHICKEN FRIED STEAK.

coupe [KOOP] Ice cream or sherbet with a topping of fruit, whipped cream and, traditionally, glazed chestnuts (MARRONS GLACÉS). Classically, the dessert is served in a *coupe* dish, which is stemmed, and has a wide, deep bowl.

court-bouillon [koor bwee-YAWN] Traditionally used for poaching fish, seafood or vegetables, a *court-bouillon* is a broth made by cooking various vegetables and herbs (usually an onion studded with a few whole cloves, celery, carrots and a BOUQUET GARNI) in water for about 30 minutes. Wine, lemon juice or vinegar may be added. The broth is allowed to cool before the vegetables are removed.

couscous [KOOS-koos] A staple of North African cuisine, couscous is granular SEMOLINA. Cooked, **it** may be served with milk as porridge, with a dressing as a salad or sweetened and mixed with fruits for dessert. Packaged precooked couscous is available in Middle-Eastern markets and large supermarkets. The name couscous also refers to the famous Maghreb dish in which semolina or cracked WHEAT is steamed in the perforated top part of a special pot called a *couscoussière*, while chunks of meat (usually lamb or chicken), various vegetables, chickpeas and raisins simmer in the bottom part. In lieu of a *couscoussière*, a colander set over a large pot will do. The cooked semolina is heaped onto a platter, with the meats and vegetables placed on top. All diners use chunks of bread to scoop the couscous from this central platter. Couscous varies from country to country—Moroccans include saffron, Algerians like to add tomatoes and Tunisians spice theirs up with the hot-pepper-based HARISSA SAUCE.

couverture [koo-vair-TYOOR] *see* CHOCOLATE

cowberry Often found growing in pastures, the tart, red cowberry is a member of the cranberry family. It grows in northern Europe, Canada and Maine, and is used for sauces and jams. Also called *mountain cranberry*.

cowpee *see* BLACK-EYED PEA

crab Any of a large variety of CRUSTACEANS (animals with a shell) with 10 legs, the front two of which have pincers. Crabs are noted for their sweet, succulent meat and are the second most popular shellfish (after shrimp) in the U.S. There are fresh- and saltwater crabs, the latter being the most plentiful. The major catch on the Pacific coast is DUNGENESS CRAB, from the North Pacific come the KING CRAB and SNOW CRAB, along the Atlantic and Gulf coasts it's BLUE CRAB, and Florida waters give us the STONE CRAB. Hard-shell crabs are available year-round in coastal areas. They're sold whole (cooked or live), and in the form of cooked lump meat (whole pieces of the white body meat) or flaked meat (small bits of light and dark meat from the body and claws). Always sold whole, SOFT-SHELL CRABS—in season from April to mid-September (with a peak in June and July)—are blue crabs that have shed their hard shells. All live crabs should be used on the day they're purchased. Refrigerate them until just before cooking. Cook raw crabmeat within 24 hours after the crab dies. Crabmeat is also available frozen, canned or pasteurized (heated in cans at a temperature high enough to kill bacteria, but lower than that used in canning). Pasteurized crabmeat should be stored unopened in the refrigerator for up to 6 months and used within 4 days of opening. Whole crabs and crabmeat can be cooked in a variety of ways including frying, steaming, broiling or in soups, GUMBOS or CRAB CAKES. Crab ROE, available only in the spring, is a prized addition to the South Carolina specialty, SHE-CRAB SOUP. *For information on specific crabs, see individual listings. See also* SHELLFISH.

crabapple A small, rosy red apple with a rather hard, extremely tart flesh. Crabapples, available during the fall months, are too sour for out-of-hand eating but make outstanding jellies and jams. Spiced and canned whole, they're a delicious accompaniment for meats such as pork and poultry. *See also* APPLE.

crab boil Sold packaged in supermarkets and specialty markets, crab boil (also called *shrimp boil*) is a mixture of herbs and spices added to water in which crab, shrimp or lobster is cooked. The blend can include mustard seeds, peppercorns, bay leaves, whole allspice and cloves, dried ginger pieces and red chilies.

crab cake A mixture of lump crabmeat, breadcrumbs, milk, egg, scallions and various seasonings, formed into small cakes and fried until crisp and golden brown.

crab imperial A classic American dish of crabmeat combined with mayonnaise or a sherried WHITE SAUCE, spooned into blue-crab or scallop shells, sprinkled with Parmesan cheese or breadcrumbs and baked until golden brown.

crab Louis [LOO-ee] San Francisco is said to be the origin of this cold dish in which lump crabmeat on a bed of shredded lettuce is topped with a dressing of mayonnaise, chili sauce, cream, scallions, green pepper, lemon juice and seasonings. The crab can be garnished with a quartered tomato and hard-cooked egg.

cracked wheat *see* WHEAT

crackling Delicious, crunchy pieces of either pork or poultry fat after it has been RENDERED, or the crisp, brown skin of fried or roasted pork. Cracklings are sold packaged in some supermarkets and specialty markets. "Cracklin' bread" is cornbread with bits of cracklings scattered throughout.

cranberry These shiny scarlet berries are grown in huge, sandy bogs on low, trailing vines. They're also called *bounceberries*, because ripe ones bounce, and *craneberries*, after the shape of the shrub's pale pink blossoms, which resemble the heads of the cranes often seen wading through the cranberry bogs. Cranberries grow wild in northern Europe and in the northern climes of North America, where they are also extensively cultivated—mainly in Massachusetts, Wisconsin, Washington and Oregon. Harvested between Labor Day and Halloween, the peak market period for cranberries is from October through December. They're usually packaged in 12-ounce plastic bags. Any cranberries that are discolored or shriveled should be discarded. Cranberries can be refrigerated, tightly wrapped, for at least 2 months or frozen up to a year. Besides the traditional cranberry sauce, this fruit also makes delicious CHUTNEYS, pies, COBBLERS and other desserts. Because of their extreme tartness, cramberries are best combined with other fruits, such as apples or dried apricots. Canned cranberry sauce—jelled and whole-berry—is available year-round, as are frozen cranberries in some markets. Sweetened dried cranberries, which can be used like raisins in baked goods or as snacks, are also available in many supermarkets. Fresh cranberries are very high in vitamin C.

cranberry bean Also called *shell beans* or *shellouts*, these beautiful beans have large, knobby beige pods splotched with red. The beans inside are cream-colored with red streaks and have a delicious nutlike flavor. Cranberry beans must be shelled before cooking, and lose their red color during the cooking process. They're available fresh in the summer and dried throughout the year. *See also* BEANS

Cranshaw melon *see* CRENSHAW MELON

crappie Found mainly in the Great Lakes and Mississippi regions, crappies are large, freshwater sunfish that are about 12 inches long and range from 1 to 2 pounds. There are both black and white crappies; the latter is also called *chinquapin*. Crappies have lean flesh that is particularly suited to broiling or sautéing. *See also* FISH.

crawdads *see* CRAYFISH

crawfish *see* CRAYFISH

crayfish Any of various freshwater CRUSTACEANS that resemble tiny lobsters, complete with claws. Other coastal crustaceans (such as spiny or rock lobster) are sometimes mistakenly called *saltwater crayfish*. They are not, however, of the same species. Crayfish range from 3 to 6 inches long and weigh from 2 to 8 ounces. They're very popular in France (where they're called *écrevisses*), New Zealand, Scandinavia and parts of the U.S.— particularly Louisiana, where they're known as *crawfish* and *crawdads*. The great majority of the U.S. harvest comes from the waters of the Mississippi basin, and many Louisianans call their state the "crawfish capital of the world." Crayfish can be prepared in most manners appropriate for lobster and, like lobster, turn bright red when cooked. They're usually eaten with the fingers, and the sweet, succulent meat must be picked or sucked out of the tiny shells. *See also* SHELLFISH.

cream *n*. Upon standing, unhomogenized milk naturally separates into two layers—a BUTTERFAT-rich cream on top and almost fat-free (or skimmed) milk on the bottom. Commercially, the cream is separated from the milk by centrifugal force. Almost all cream that reaches the market today has been pasteurized. There are many varieties of cream, all categorized according to the amount of butterfat in the mixture. **Light cream**, also called **coffee** or **table cream**, can contain anywhere from 18 to 30 percent fat, but commonly contains 20 percent. **Light whipping cream**, the form most commonly available, contains 30 to 36 percent butterfat and sometimes stabilizers and emulsifiers. **Heavy cream**, also called **heavy whipping cream**, is whipping cream with a butterfat content of between 36 and 40 percent. It's usually only available in specialty or gourmet markets. Whipping cream will double in volume when whipped. **Half-and-half** is a mixture of equal parts milk and cream, and is 10 to 12 percent butterfat. Neither half-and-half nor light cream can be whipped. Commercial **sour cream** contains from 18 to 20 percent fat, and has been treated with a lactic acid culture to add its characteristic tang. Sour cream often contains additional ingredients such as GELATIN, RENNET and vegetable enzymes. **Light sour cream** contains about 40 percent less fat than regular sour cream because it's made from half-and-half. **Ultrapasteurized cream**, seen more and more in markets today, has been briefly heated at temperatures up to 300°F to kill microorganisms that cause milk products to sour. It has a longer shelf life than regular cream, but it doesn't whip as well and it has a slight "cooked" flavor. All other cream is highly perishable and should be kept in the coldest part of the refrigerator. **Pressurized whipped cream**, contained in cans under pressure, is a mixture of cream, sugar, stabilizers, emulsifiers and gas, such as nitrous oxide. It's not really "whipped" but, more aptly, expanded by the gas into a puffy form. Aerosol "dessert toppings," which are usually made with hydrogenated vegetable oils, have absolutely no cream in them . . . and taste like it. Read the label—the fat content of real cream mixtures must be indicated on the product label. *See also* CLOTTED CREAM; CRÈME FRAÎCHE. **cream** *v.* To beat an ingredient or combination of ingredients until the mixture is soft, smooth and "creamy." Often a recipe calls for creaming a fat, such as butter, or creaming a mixture of butter and sugar. When creaming two or more ingredients together, the result should be a smooth, homogeneous mixture that shows neither separation nor evidence of any particles (such as sugar). Electric mixers and food processors make quick work of what used to be a laborious, time-consuming process.

cream cheese Thanks to American ingenuity, cream cheese—the most popular ingredient for cheesecake—was developed in 1872. The appellation comes from the smooth, creamy texture of this mildly tangy, spreadable cheese. The soft, unripened cheese is made from cow's milk and by law must contain at least 33 percent BUTTERFAT and not more than 55 percent moisture. GUM ARABIC is added to some cream cheese to increase firmness and shelf life. American NEUFCHATEL CHEESE is slightly lower in calories because of a lower butterfat content (about 23 percent). It also contains slightly more moisture. Cream cheese and Neufchatel are sometimes sold mixed with other ingredients such as herbs, spices or fruit. *See also* CHEESE.

cream of tartar A fine white powder derived from a crystalline acid deposited on the inside of wine barrels. Cream of tartar is added to candy and frosting mixtures for a creamier consistency, and to egg whites before beating to improve stability and volume. It's also used as the acid ingredient in some baking powders.

cream puff A small, hollow puff made from CHOUX PASTRY (cream-puff pastry) filled with sweetened whipped cream or custard.

cream-puff paste; cream-puff pastry *see* CHOUX PASTRY

cream sauce A classic BÉCHAMEL (white) SAUCE made with milk and sometimes cream. The sauce's thickness depends on the proportion of flour to liquid. Cream sauces are used as a base for many dishes, such as chicken À LA KING.

cream sherry *see* SHERRY

Crécy, à la [KREH-see; kray-SEE] A French term referring to dishes cooked or garnished with carrots. The name comes from Crécy, France, where the finest French carrots are cultivated.

crema caramella *see* CRÈME CARAMEL

Crema Dania cheese; Crema Danica cheese [KREHM-uh DAHN-yuh; KREHM-uh DAHN-uh-kuh] Denmark gives us this exquisitely rich gift in the form of small cheese rectangles with a white downy rind and soft ivory interior. Crema Dania is a rich double-cream cheese that, at 72 percent butterfat, almost qualifies as a triple-cream. It's a wonderful cheese for after dinner. *See also* CHEESE; DOUBLE-CREAM CHEESES.

crème [KREHM] The French word for "cream."

crème anglaise [krehm ahn-GLEHZ; krehm ahn-GLAYZ] The French term for a rich custard sauce that can be served hot or cold over cake, fruit or other dessert.

crème brûlée [krehm broo-LAY] The literal translation of this rich dessert is "burnt cream." It describes a chilled, stirred CUSTARD which, just before serving, is sprinkled with brown or granulated sugar. The sugar topping is quickly caramelized under a broiler or with a SALAMANDER. The caramelized topping becomes brittle, creating a delicious flavor and textural contrast to the smooth, creamy custard beneath.

crème caramel [krehm kair-ah-MEHL; krem CAR-uh-mehl] Also known in France as *crème renversée*, crème caramel is a CUSTARD that has been baked in a CARAMEL-coated mold. When the chilled custard is turned out onto a serving plate it is automatically glazed and sauced with the caramel in the mold. In Italy it's known as *crema caramella,* and in Spain as *flan.*

crème chantilly *see* CHANTILLY

crème d'abricots [krehm dah-bree-KOH] A sweet apricot LIQUEUR.

crème d'ananas [krehm dah-nah-NAHS] Pineapple-flavored LIQUEUR.

crème d'amande [krehm dah-MAHND] A pink, almond-flavored LIQUEUR.

crème de [KREHM deuh] A French phrase meaning "cream of," and used to describe an intensely sweet LIQUEUR.

crème de banane [krehm deuh bah-NAHN] A sweet LIQUEUR with a full, ripe banana flavor.

crème de cacao [krehm deuh kah-KAH-oh] A dark, chocolate-flavored LIQUEUR with a hint of vanilla. **White crème de cacao** is a clear form of the same liqueur.

crème de cassis [krehm deuh kah-SEES] Black currant-flavored LIQUEUR; an integral ingredient in KIR.

crème de cerise [krehm deuh sair-EEZ] A French cherry-flavored LIQUEUR.

crème de menthe [krehm deuh MENTH; MAHNT] Tasting of cool summer mint, this LIQUEUR comes clear (called white) or green-colored.

crème de noyaux [krehm deuh nwah-YOH] The word *noyaux* is French for "fruit pits," and this sweet pink LIQUEUR is flavored with the pits of various fruits. The resulting flavor is of almonds.

crème de rose [krehm deuh ROSE] An exotically scented LIQUEUR flavored with rose petals, vanilla and various spices.

crème de violette [krehm deuh VEE-oh-leht; vyo-LEHT] Dutch LIQUEUR, amethyst in color, perfumed and flavored with essence of violets.

crème fraîche [krehm FRESH] This matured, thickened cream has a slightly tangy, nutty flavor and velvety rich texture. The thickness of crème fraîche can range from that of commercial sour cream to almost as solid as room-temperature margarine. In France, where crème fraîche is a specialty, the cream is unpasteurized and therefore contains the bacteria necessary to thicken it naturally. In America, where all commercial cream is PASTEURIZED, the fermenting agents necessary for crème fraîche can be obtained by adding buttermilk or sour cream. A very expensive American facsimile of crème fraîche is sold in some gourmet markets. The expense seems frivolous, however, when it's so easy to make an equally delicious version at home. To do so, combine 1 cup whipping cream and 2 tablespoons buttermilk in a glass container. Cover and let stand at room temperature from 8 to 24 hours, or until very thick. Stir well before covering and refrigerate up to 10 days. Crème fraîche is the ideal addition for sauces or soups because it can be boiled without curdling. It's delicious spooned over fresh fruit or other desserts such as warm cobblers or puddings.

crème pâtissière [KREHM pah-tee-see-AIR] The French term for "pastry cream," a thick, flour-based egg CUSTARD used for tarts, cakes, and to fill CREAM PUFFS, ÉCLAIRS and NAPOLEONS.

crème pralinée [KREHM prah-lee-NAY] CRÈME PÂTISSIÈRE flavored with PRALINE powder and used to fill various French pastries.

crème renversée [KREHM rahn-vair-SAY] Another name for CRÈME CARAMEL.

Crenshaw melon; Cranshaw melon Considered one of the most sweetly succulent members of the melon family, the Crenshaw is a hybrid MUSKMELON. It has a golden-green, lightly ribbed rind and a beautiful salmon-orange flesh. The fragrance of a ripe Crenshaw melon is seductively spicy. These melons are large (5 to 9 pounds) with an oval shape that's rounded at the blossom end and slightly pointed at the stem end. They're available from July to October, with the peak season from August to mid-September. *See also* MELON.

Creole cooking [KREE-ohl] In the 18th century, the Spaniards governing New Orleans named all residents of European heritage *Criollo*. The name, which later became *Creole*, soon began to imply one of refined cultural background with an appreciation for an elegant lifestyle. Today, Creole cookery reflects the full-flavored combination of the best of French, Spanish and African cuisines. Its style, with an emphasis on butter and cream, is more sophisticated than CAJUN COOKING (which uses prodigious amounts of pork fat). Another difference between the two cuisines is that Creole uses more tomatoes and the Cajuns more spices. Both cuisines rely on the culinary "holy trinity" of chopped green peppers, onions and celery, and make generous use of FILE POWDER. Probably the most famous dish of Creole heritage is GUMBO.

Creole cream cheese [KREE-ohl] This New Orleans specialty has the texture of very thick sour cream and a slightly more tart flavor. It's used as a topping or, especially by southern Louisianans, eaten for breakfast with salt and pepper or sugar and fruit. Creole cream cheese may be carried in some gourmet markets but is generally available outside Louisiana only through mail order.

Creole mustard [KREE-ohl] A specialty of Louisiana's German Creoles made from vinegar-marinated brown mustard seeds with a hint of horseradish. This hot, spicy mustard is available in gourmet markets or the gourmet section of some supermarkets.

crêpe [KREHP; KRAYP] The French word for "pancake," which is exactly what these light, paper-thin creations are. They can be made from plain or sweetened batters with various flours, and used for savory or dessert dishes. Dessert crêpes may be spread with a jam or fruit mixture, rolled or folded and sometimes flamed with brandy or liqueur. Savory crêpes are filled with various meat, cheese or vegetable mixtures—sometimes topped with a complementary sauce—and served as a first or main course.

crêpes suzette [KREHP soo-ZEHT] Prepared in a CHAFING DISH, this illustrious dessert consists of an orange-butter sauce in which CRÊPES are warmed, then doused with GRAND MARNIER (or other orange liqueur) and ignited to flaming glory.

crépinette [kray-pih-NEHT; kray-pee-NEHT] French in origin, this small, slightly flattened sausage is made of minced pork, lamb, veal or chicken and sometimes truffles. *Crépine* is the French word for "pig's caul," in which a crépinette is wrapped instead of a casing. Crépinettes are usually cooked by coating them in melted butter and breadcrumbs before sautéing, grilling or broiling. *See also* SAUSAGE.

crespelle [krehs-PEHL-lay] Thin Italian pancakes that are either stacked with different fillings between the layers or filled and rolled like CRÊPES.

crevette [kruh-VEHT] The French word for "shrimp."

crimp 1. To pinch or press two pastry edges together, thereby sealing the dough while forming a decorative edge with fingers, fork or other utensil. The pastry for a single-crust pie is crimped by turning it under to form a ridge, then shaping (or *fluting*) the raised edge into a fancy pattern. A raised crimped edge not only seals the pastry but acts like a dam to contain the filling during cooking. 2. To cut gashes at 1- or 2-inch intervals along both sides of a freshly caught fish. The fish is then soaked in ice water for up to an hour. Crimping a fish creates a firmer-textured flesh and skin that quickly becomes crisp when cooked.

crisp *v.* To refresh vegetables such as celery and carrots by soaking them in ice water until they once again become crisp. Other foods, such as crackers that have lost their snap, may be heated in a moderate oven until their crispness returns.

crisphead lettuce One of two varieties of head lettuce (the other being BUTTERHEAD). It's commonly known as **iceberg** which, in truth, is a variety of crisphead. Other varieties include **Great Lakes**, **Imperial**, **Vanguard** and **Western**. Crisphead lettuce comes in large, round, tightly packed heads of pale green leaves. Though crisp, succulent and wilt-resistant, all crispheads have a rather bland flavor. Choose those that are heavy for their size with no signs of browning at the edges. *See also* LETTUCE.

croaker *see* DRUM

croissant [kwah-SAHN; KWAH-sawhn; kruh-SAHNT] The origin of this flaky, buttery-rich yeast roll dates back to 1686, when Austria was at war with Turkey. In the dead of night a group of bakers, hearing Turks tunneling under their kitchens, spread the alarm that subsequently led to the Turkish defeat. In turn, the vigilant bakers were awarded the privilege of creating a commemorative pastry in the shape of the crescent on the Turkish flag. *Croissant* is the French word for "crescent." Originally, the croissant was made from a rich bread dough. It wasn't until the early 1900s that a creative French baker had the inspiration to make it with a dough similar to puff pastry . . . and so a classic was born. Croissants can be made with buttered layers of yeast dough or puff pastry. They're sometimes stuffed (such as with a stick of chocolate or cheese) before being rolled into a crescent shape and baked. Croissants are generally thought of as breakfast pastries but can also be used for sandwiches and meal accompaniments.

crookneck squash Any of several varieties of summer squash with a long, curved neck that is slightly more slender than the bulbous base. Crookneck squash have a light to deep yellow skin that can range in texture from almost smooth when quite young to slightly bumpy as the squash matures. The creamy-yellow flesh has a mild, delicate flavor. Crooknecks average from 8 to 10 inches long, but are best when a youthful 6 inches. Choose firm squash with no sign of shriveling; the skin should be easily pierced with a fingernail. *See also* SQUASH.

croque madame [KROHK mah-DAHM] In France, this is a CROQUE MONSIEUR (toasted ham and cheese sandwich) with the addition of a fried egg. In Britain and America, a croque madame simply substitutes sliced chicken for the ham, with no sign of an egg.

croquembouche [kroh-kuhm-BOOSH] French for "crisp in mouth," this elaborate dessert is classically made with PROFITEROLES (tiny, custard-filled cream puffs), coated with CARAMEL and stacked into a tall pyramid shape. As the caramel hardens, it becomes crisp. For added glamour, the croquembouche can be wreathed or draped with SPUN SUGAR.

croque monsieur [KROHK muhs-YUR] A French-style grilled ham and cheese sandwich that is dipped into beaten egg before being sautéed in butter. Croque monsieur is sometimes made in a special sandwich-grilling iron consisting of two hinged metal plates, each with two shell-shaped indentations. *See also* CROQUE MADAME.

croquette [kroh-KEHT] A mixture of minced meat or vegetables, a thick white sauce and seasonings that is formed into small cylinders, ovals or rounds, dipped in beaten egg and then breadcrumbs, and deep-fried until crisp and brown.

croustade [kroo-STAHD] An edible container used to hold a thick stew, creamed meat or vegetable mixture, puree, etc. A croustade can be made from pastry, a hollowed-out bread loaf, or pureed potatoes or pasta that have been shaped to form a casing for food. Before filling it with food, the container is deep-fried or toasted until golden-brown and crisp. Small filled croustades can be served as an appetizer or first course.

croûte [KROO'T] French for "crust," *croûte* generally describes a thick, hollowed-out slice of bread (usually toasted) that is filled with food. It can also refer to a pastry case used for the same purpose. For example, *croûte landaise* is fried bread with FOIE GRAS topped with a cheese sauce. **En croute** describes a food (usually partially cooked) that is wrapped in pastry and baked.

crouton [KROO-tawn] A small piece or cube of bread that has been browned, either by sautéing or baking. Croutons are used to garnish soups, salads and other dishes. They're available packaged either plain or seasoned with herbs, cheese, garlic, etc.

crown roast This special-occasion roast is formed from the rib section of pork or lamb LOIN by tying it into a circle, ribs up. After it's cooked, the tips of the bones are often decorated with paper FRILLS. The roast's hollow center section is usually filled with mixed vegetables or other stuffing.

crudités [kroo-dee-TAY] Often served as an appetizer, crudités are raw seasonal vegetables, frequently accompanied with a dipping sauce, such as BAGNA CAUDA.

cruller [KRUHL-uhr] A doughnut-style dough (usually LEAVENED with baking powder) that's shaped into a long twist, fried and sprinkled with granulated sugar or brushed with a sweet glaze. The extremely light **French cruller** is made with CHOUX PASTRY (cream-puff dough). The word "cruller" comes from the Dutch *krulle,* meaning "twisted cake."

crumble *n.* A British dessert in which raw fruit is topped with a crumbly pastry mixture and baked. **crumble** *v.* To break food up (usually with the fingers) into small pieces, such as "crumbled" bacon.

crumpet [KRUHM-piht] Hailing from the British Isles, crumpets are small, yeast-raised breads about the size of an English muffin. The unsweetened batter is poured into special *crumpet rings* (which have been arranged on a griddle), then "baked" on stovetop. The finished crumpet has a smooth, brown bottom and a top riddled with tiny holes. Crumpets are toasted and spread with butter and jam, as desired.

crush To reduce a food to its finest form, such as crumbs, paste or powder. Crushing is often accomplished with a MORTAR AND PESTLE, or with a rolling pin.

crust This multipurpose word has many meanings, including the hardened outer layer of a cooked food such as bread; a thin layer of pastry covering a pie, pâté, etc.; and the sediment of organic salts deposited in a bottle of aged red wine.

crustacean [kruh-STAY-shuhn] One of two main classifications of SHELLFISH (the other being MOLLUSK), crustaceans have elongated bodies and jointed, soft (crustlike) shells. The crustacean family includes CRABS, CRAYFISH, LOBSTER and SHRIMP. *For information on specific crustaceans, see individual listings.*

crystallized flowers *see* CANDIED FRUIT; CANDIED FLOWERS

crystallized fruit *see* CANDIED FRUIT; CANDIED FLOWERS

Cuba libre [KYOO-buh LEE-bruh; KYOO-buh LEE-bray] An iced COCKTAIL made with rum, lime juice and cola.

cube 1. To cut food (such as meat or cheese) into ½-inch cubes. Cubes of food are larger than diced or mirepoix. 2. A term also used to describe tenderizing meat with an instrument that leaves cube-shaped imprints on the surface (*see* CUBE STEAK).

cube steak A flavorful cut of beef taken from the top or bottom ROUND and tenderized (or cubed) by running it through a butcher's tenderizing machine once or twice. Cube steak would be too tough to eat without being tenderized. *See also* BEEF; Beef Chart page 573.

cucumber Believed to have originated in either India or Thailand, the cucumber has been cultivated for thousands of years. This long, cylindrical, green-skinned fruit of the gourd family has edible seeds surrounded by a mild, crisp flesh. The thin skin, unless waxed, does not require peeling. Cucumbers are usually eaten raw, as in salads. The smaller cucumber varieties are used for pickles. As a cucumber matures, the seeds grow larger and more bitter. Therefore, the seeds of an older cucumber should be removed before it's used. The more expensive **English** (or **hothouse) cucumber** can grow up to 2 feet long and is virtually seedless. Cucumbers are available year-round, with the peak crop from May to August. Choose firm fruit with smooth, brightly colored skins; avoid those with shriveled or soft spots. Store whole cucumbers, unwashed, in a plastic bag in the refrigerator up to 10 days. Wash thoroughly just before using. Cut cucumbers can be refrigerated, tightly wrapped, for up to 5 days.

cuisine [kwih-ZEEN; kwee-ZEEN] A French term pertaining to a specific style of cooking (as in Chinese cuisine), or a country's food in general. **Haute cuisine** refers to food prepared in a gourmet or elaborate manner.

cuisine minceur [kwee-ZEEN man-SEUR] Developed by French chef Michel Guérard in the 1970s, *cuisine minceur* is light-style, healthful cooking that avoids fat and cream.

culatello [koo-lah-TEHL-oh] A lean, rosy red, raw Italian ham that has been cured and soaked in wine during aging. Considered superior, culatello has a clean, delicate flavor. It's often served as part of an ANTIPASTO platter. *See also* HAM.

Cumberland sauce A favorite with the English, this full-flavored sauce is a combination of red currant jelly, PORT, orange and lemon ZESTS, mustard and seasonings. It's excellent served with venison, duck and other game.

cumin [KUH-mihn; KYOO-mihn; KOO-mihn] Also called *comino*, this ancient spice dates back to the Old Testament. Shaped like a caraway seed, cumin is the dried fruit of a plant in the parsley family. Its aromatic, nutty-flavored seeds come in three colors: amber (the most widely available), white and black (both found in Asian markets). White cumin seed is interchangeable with amber, but the black seed has a more complex, peppery flavor. Cumin is available in seed and ground forms. As with all seeds, herbs and spices, it should be stored in a cool, dark place for no more than 6 months. Cumin is particularly popular in Middle-Eastern, Asian and Mediterranean cooking. Among other things, it's used to make curries, chili powders and KÜMMEL LIQUEUR. *See also* SPICE; Herb and Spice Chart page 538.

curaçao [KYEUR-uh-soh; KOO-rah-soh] An orange-flavored LIQUEUR made from the dried peel of bitter oranges found on the Caribbean island of Curaçao.

curd When it coagulates, milk separates into a semisolid portion (curd) and a watery liquid (WHEY). CHEESE is made from the curd.

curdle To coagulate, or separate into curds and whey. Soured milk curdles, as do some egg- and milk-based sauces when exposed to prolonged or high heat. Acids such as lemon juice also cause curdling in some mixtures.

cure To treat food (such as meat, cheese or fish) by one of several methods in order to preserve it. **Smoke-curing** is generally done in one of two ways. The cold-smoking method (which can take up to a month) smokes the food at about 90°F. Hot-smoking partially or totally cooks the food by treating it at temperatures ranging from 100° to 190°F. **Pickled foods** are soaked in variously flavored acid-based BRINES. **Corned products** (such as corned beef) have also been soaked in brine—usually one made with water, salt and various seasonings. **Salt-cured foods** have been dried and packed in salt preparations. **Cheese curing** can be done by several methods, including injecting or spraying the cheese with specific bacteria or by wrapping the cheese in various flavored materials. Some of the more common cured foods are **smoked ham, pickled herring** and **salted fish.**

curly endive *see* ENDIVE

currant [KUR-uhnt] There are two distinctly different fruits called currant. 1. The first—resembling a tiny, dark raisin—is the seedless, dried ZANTE GRAPE. Its name comes from its place of origin—Corinth, Greece. In cooking, this type of currant (like raisins) is used mainly in baked goods. 2. The second type of currant is a tiny berry related to the gooseberry. There are black, red and white currants. The black ones are generally used for preserves, syrups and liqueurs (such as CASSIS), while the red and white berries are good for out-of-hand eating and such preparations as the famous French preserve BAR-LE-DUC and (using the red currants) CUMBERLAND SAUCE. Fresh currants are in season June through August. Choose those that are plump and without hulls. They can be refrigerated, tightly covered, up to 4 days. Currants are delicious in jams, jellies, sauces and simply served with sugar and cream.

curry From the southern Indian word *kari*, meaning "sauce," comes this catch-all term that is used to refer to any number of hot, spicy, gravy-based dishes of East Indian origin. CURRY POWDER is an integral ingredient in all curries.

curry leaf From a plant native to southern Asia, this fragrant herb looks like a small, shiny lemon leaf and has a pungent curry fragrance. Its flavor is essential in a substantial percentage of East Indian fare. Most Indian markets sell fresh curry leaves. Choose those that are bright green, with no sign of yellowing or wilting. They can be refrigerated in an airtight container up to 2 weeks. Packaged, dried curry leaves—also available in Indian markets—can be substituted for fresh but lack their snappy flavor.

curry paste Available in East Indian markets and the gourmet section of some supermarkets, curry paste is a blend of GHEE (clarified butter), CURRY POWDER, vinegar and other seasonings. It's used in lieu of curry powder for many curried dishes.

curry powder Widely used in Indian cooking, authentic Indian curry powder is freshly ground each day and can vary dramatically depending on the region and the cook. Curry powder is actually a pulverized blend of up to 20 spices, herbs and seeds. Among those most commonly used are cardamom, chilies, cinnamon, cloves, coriander, cumin, fennel seed, fenugreek, mace, nutmeg, red and black pepper, poppy and sesame seeds, saffron, tamarind and turmeric (the latter is what gives curried dishes their characteristic yellow color). Commercial curry powder (which bears little resemblance to the freshly ground blends of southern India) comes in two styles—standard, and the hotter of the two, "Madras." Since curry powder quickly loses its pungency, it should be stored, airtight, no longer than 2 months. *For information on specific spices used in this blend, see individual listings. See also* Herb and Spice Chart, page 538.

cush [KOOSH; KUHSH] 1. A sweetened, mushlike cornmeal mixture, fried in lard and served as a cereal with cream or CLABBER and sugar or cane syrup. 2. A Southern cornmeal pancake. 3. A Southern soup of cornmeal, milk, onion and seasonings.

cusk [KUHSK] Related to the cod, this large saltwater fish has a firm, lean flesh. It ranges from 1½ to 5 pounds and can be purchased whole or in fillets. Cusk can be prepared in a variety of ways including baking, broiling, poaching and sautéing. *See also* FISH.

custard A puddinglike dessert (made with a sweetened mixture of milk and eggs) that can either be baked or stirred on stovetop. Custards require slow cooking and gentle heat in order to prevent separation (curdling). For this reason, stirred custards are generally made in a DOUBLE BOILER; baked custards in a WATER BATH. A safeguard when making custard is to remove it from the heat when it reaches 170° to 175°F on a CANDY THERMOMETER. Custards may be enhanced with various flavorings such as chocolate, vanilla, fruit, etc. Stirred custards are softer than baked custards and are often used as a sauce or as an ice cream base.

custard apple *see* CHERIMOYA

cut in To mix a solid, cold fat (such as butter or shortening) with dry ingredients (such as a flour mixture) until the combination is in the form of small particles. This technique can be achieved by using a PASTRY BLENDER, two knives, a fork or fingers (which must be cool so as not to melt the fat). A FOOD PROCESSOR fitted with a metal blade does an excellent job of cutting fat into dry ingredients, providing the mixture is not overworked into a paste.

cutlet 1. A thin, tender cut of meat (usually from lamb, pork or veal) taken from the leg or rib section. Cutlets are best when quickly cooked, such as sautéed or grilled. 2. A mixture of finely chopped meat, fish or poultry that's bound with a sauce or egg mixture and formed into the shape of a cutlet. This type of formed cutlet is often dipped into beaten egg and then into breadcrumbs before being fried.

cuttlefish Resembling a rather large SQUID, the cuttlefish has 10 appendages and can reach up to 16 inches in length. It can be prepared like its less tender relatives, the squid and octopus, but must still be tenderized before cooking in order not to be exceedingly chewy. Cuttlefish are most popular in Japan, India and many Mediterranean countries. Dried cuttlefish is available in some oriental markets. It should be reconstituted before cooking. **Sarume**, also available in ethnic markets, is cuttlefish that has been seasoned and roasted.

D **ab** Any of several varieties of FLOUNDER, the dab is a small FLATFISH with a sweet, lean, firm flesh. It can be prepared in any manner suitable for flounder. *See also* FISH; PLAICE.

dacquoise [da-KWAHZ] A dessert of disc-shaped, nut-flavored MERINGUES stacked and filled with sweetened whipped cream or BUTTERCREAM. It's served chilled, often with fruit. *See also* MARJOLAINE.

Dagwood sandwich Named after Dagwood Bumstead, a character in the "Blondie" comic strip, this extremely thick sandwich is piled high with a variety of meats, cheeses, condiments and lettuce.

daikon [DI-kuhn; DI-kon] From the Japanese words *dai* (large) and *kon* (root), this vegetable is in fact a large oriental radish with a sweet, fresh flavor. The daikon's flesh is crisp, juicy and white, while the skin can be either creamy white or black. It can range from 6 to 15 inches in length with an average diameter of 2 to 3 inches. Some exceptional daikon are as fat as a football. Choose those that are firm and unwrinkled. Refrigerate, wrapped in a plastic bag, up to a week. Daikon radishes are used raw in salads, shredded as a garnish or cooked in a variety of ways, such as in a STIR-FRY.

daiquiri [DAK-uh-ree] A cocktail made with rum, lime juice and sugar. Some daiquiris are made with fruit, the mixture being pureed in a blender. Frozen daiquiris are made either with crushed ice or frozen fruit chunks, all processed until smooth in a blender.

dal; dhal, dhall [DAHL] A spicy dish made with lentils (or other PULSES), tomatoes, onions and various seasonings. *Dal* is often pureed and served with curried dishes. In India, the term "dal" refers to any of almost 60 varieties of dried pulses, including peas, mung beans and lentils.

damson plum This small, oval-shaped plum has an indigo skin and yellow-green flesh. Because the damson is extremely tart, it makes excellent pies and jams. *See also* PLUM.

Danablu cheese [DAN-uh-bloo] Also called *Danish blue cheese*, this rich cow's-milk cheese is milder and less complex than ROQUEFORT, but has a zest all its own. Known as one of the world's best blues, the versatile, semisoft Danablu can be sliced, spread and crumbled with equal ease. It's excellent with fruit, dark breads and red wines. *See also* BLUE CHEESE; CHEESE.

Danbo cheese [DAN-boh] A Swiss-style cheese from Denmark with a red or yellow wax rind and pale yellow interior dotted with holes. Danbo has a firm texture and mildly sweet, nutlike flavor. Regular Danbo has about 45 percent butterfat; the lowfat variety contains only 20 percent fat. *See also* CHEESE.

dancy orange *see* MANADARIN ORANGE

dandelion greens [DAN-dl-i-uhn] The name dandelion comes from the French *dent de lion*, meaning "lion's tooth," a reference to the jagged-edged leaves of this noteworthy weed that grows both wild and cultivated. The bright green leaves have a slightly bitter, tangy flavor that adds interest to salads. They can also be cooked like spinach. The roots can be eaten as vegetables or roasted and ground to make root "coffee." Though they're available until winter in some states, the best, most tender dandelion greens are found in early spring, before the plant begins to flower. Look for bright-green, tender-crisp leaves; avoid those with yellowed or wilted tips. Refrigerate, tightly wrapped in a plastic bag, up to 5 days. Wash thoroughly before using. Dandelion greens are an excellent source of vitamin A, iron and calcium.

Danish blue cheese *see* DANABLU CHEESE

Danish lobster *see* PRAWN

Danish pastry This butter-rich pastry begins as a yeast dough that is rolled out, dotted with butter, then folded and rolled again several times, as for PUFF PASTRY. The dough may be lightly sweetened and is usually flavored with vanilla or cardamom. Baked Danish pastries (often referred to simply as "Danish") contain a variety of fillings including fruit, cream cheese, almond paste and spiced nuts.

Danziger Goldwasser *see* GOLDWASSER

dariole [DAIR-ee-ohl; dah-ree-OHL] A French term referring to a small, cylindrical mold, as well as to the dessert baked in it. Classically, the dessert is made by lining the mold with puff pastry, filling it with an almond cream and baking until golden brown. Today there are also savory darioles, usually made with vegetable custards.

Darjeeling tea [dahr-JEE-ling] This full-bodied BLACK TEA comes from India's province of Darjeeling, in the foothills of the Himalayas. Darjeeling tea leaves are grown at about 7,000 feet and are considered one of India's finest. *See also* TEA.

dash A measuring term referring to a very small amount of seasoning added to food with a quick, downward stroke of the hand, such as "a dash of Tabasco." In general, a dash can be considered to be somewhere between 1/16 and a scant 1/8 teaspoon. *See also* PINCH.

dasheen [da-SHEEN] *see* TARO

dashi [DA-shee] Used extensively in Japanese cooking, dashi is a soup stock made with dried bonito tuna flakes (KATSUOBUSHI), dried kelp and water. **Dashi-no-moto** is this stock in instant form; it comes granulated, powdered and in a concentrate.

date With a history stretching back over over 5,000 years, this venerable fruit grows in thick clusters on the giant date palm, native to the Middle East. The name is thought to come from the Greek *daktulos*, meaning "finger," after the shape of the fruit. Dates require a hot, dry climate and—besides Africa and the Middle East—flourish in California and Arizona. Most varieties range from 1 to 2 inches long and are oval in shape (though some are so chunky they're almost round). All dates have a single, long, narrow seed. The skin is thin and papery, the flesh cloyingly sweet. Dates are green when unripe and turn yellow, golden brown, black or mahogany red—depending on the variety—as they ripen. They're generally picked green and ripened off the tree before drying. When fresh, dates contain about 55 percent sugar, a percentage that increases dramatically as the date dries and the sugar becomes concentrated. Fresh dates are available in some specialty markets from late summer through mid-fall. Dried dates are available year-round and are sold packaged—pitted and unpitted—and in bulk, unpitted. Chopped dried dates are also available in packages. Choose plump, soft dates with a smooth, shiny skin. Avoid very shriveled dates or those with mold or sugar crystals on the skin. Store fresh dates, wrapped in a plastic bag, in the refrigerator up to 2 weeks. Dried dates can be stored, airtight, at room temperature in a cool, dry place for up to 6 months or up to a year in the refrigerator. Dates are a good source of protein and iron.

daube [DOHB] A classic French dish made with beef, red wine, vegetables and seasonings, all slowly braised for several hours. Every region in France has its own version of daube, sometimes made in a special, very deep, covered pottery casserole called a *daubière*.

dauphine [doh-FEEN] 1. *Pommes dauphine* (dauphine potatoes) are CROQUETTES made by combining potato puree with CHOUX PASTRY (cream-puff pastry dough) and forming the mixture into balls, which are then rolled in breadcrumbs and deep-fried. 2. *Sole dauphine* is an elaborate preparation of deep-fried sole fillets garnished with mushrooms, crayfish, truffles and QUENELLES.

decant To pour a liquid (typically wine) from its bottle to another container, usually a carafe or decanter. This is generally done to separate the wine from any sediment deposited in the bottom of the bottle during the aging process. Decanting is also done to allow a wine to "breathe," which thereby enhances its flavor.

decanter A narrow-necked, stoppered container—usually made of glass—used to hold wine, liqueur or other spirits.

decorating sugar *see* SUGAR

deep-dish A term usually referring to a sweet or savory pie made either in a deep pie dish or shallow casserole, and having only a top crust.

deep-fat thermometer *see* CANDY THERMOMETER

deep-fry To cook food in hot fat deep enough to completely cover the item being fried. The oil or fat used for deep-frying should have a high SMOKE POINT (the point to which it can be heated without smoking). For that reason, butter and margarine are not good candidates for frying; shortening, lard and most oils are. The temperature of the fat is all-important and can mean the difference between success and disaster. Fat at the right temperature will produce a crisp exterior and succulent interior. If it's not hot enough, food will absorb fat and be greasy; too hot, and it will burn. An average fat temperature for deep-frying is 375°F, but recipes differ according to the characteristics of each food. To avoid ruined food, a special DEEP-FAT THERMOMETER should be used. Most thermometers used for deep-fat are dual-purpose and also used as CANDY THERMOMETERS. Though special deep-fat fryers fitted with wire baskets are available, food can be deep-fried in any large, heavy pot spacious enough to fry it without crowding. To allow for bubbling up and splattering, the container should be filled no more than halfway full with oil. Fat or oil used for deep-frying may be reused. Let it cool, then strain it through CHEESECLOTH and funnel into a bottle or other tightly sealed container before refrigerating.

deer *see* GAME ANIMALS

deglaze [dee-GLAYZ] After food (usually meat) has been sautéed and the food and excess fat removed from the pan, deglazing is done by heating a small amount of liquid in the pan and stirring to loosen browned bits of food on the bottom. The liquid used is most often wine or stock. The resultant mixture often becomes a base for a sauce to accompany the food cooked in the pan.

degrease [dee-GREES] Using a spoon to skim fat from the surface of a hot liquid, such as soup, stock or gravy. Another way to degrease is to chill the mixture until the fat becomes solid and can be easily lifted off the surface.

dehydrate [dee-HY-drayt] To remove the natural moisture from food by slowly drying it. Considered the original form of food preservation, dehydration prevents moisture spoilage such as mold or fermentation. Food can be dehydrated manually by placing thin slices on racks and allowing them to dry assisted only by sun or air. It can also be done with an *electric dehydrator*, which resembles a large three-sided toaster oven with anywhere from 5 to 10 wire-grid racks. The food placed on these racks dries with the aid of fan-circulated air. Dried foods are convenient to store and transport because of their greatly reduced volume and weight.

déjeuner [day-zhoo-NAY] The French word for "lunch."

Delaware grape Grown in the eastern U.S., this small, pale red grape has a tender skin and juicy, sweet flesh. It's used as a table grape, as well as for some wines. *See also* GRAPE.

delicata squash [dehl-ih-CAH-tah] Also called *sweet potato squash*, the delicata squash has a pale yellow skin with medium green striations. Inside, the succulent yellow flesh tastes like a cross between sweet potatoes and butternut squash. The oblong delicata can range from 5 to 9 inches in length and 1½ to 3 inches in diameter. It's in season from late summer through late fall. Choose squash that are heavy for their size; avoid those with soft spots. Delicata squash can be stored up to 3 weeks at an average room temperature. As with other winter squash, the delicata is best baked or steamed. It's a good source of potassium, iron and vitamins A and C. *See also* SQUASH.

Delicious apple *see* GOLDEN DELICIOUS APPLE; RED DELICIOUS APPLE

Delmonico potatoes [dehl-MAHN-ih-coh] Named after the 19th-century New York restaurant of the same name whose owner-chef created this dish. It consists of cooked and creamed diced (or mashed) potatoes topped with grated cheese and buttered breadcrumbs, then baked until golden brown.

Delmonico steak Another specialty made famous at Delmonico's (*see* DELMONICO POTATOES), this tender, flavorful steak is a boneless beef cut from the SHORT LOIN. Depending on the region, butcher, etc., it's also referred to as a NEW YORK STEAK. The Delmonico steak can be broiled, grilled or fried. *See also* BEEF; Beef chart, page 573.

Demerara sugar [dehm-uh-RAIR-ah] *see* SUGAR

demi-glace [DEHM-ee glahs] A rich brown sauce that begins with a basic ESPAGNOLE SAUCE, which is combined with beef stock and MADEIRA or

SHERRY and slowly cooked until it's reduced by half to a thick glaze that coats a spoon. This intense flavor is used as a base for many other sauces.

demi-sec [DEHM-ee sehk] A French term meaning "half dry" used to describe wine that is sweet (up to 6 percent sugar). *See listing for* CHAMPAGNE *for information on other wine classifications.*

demitasse [DEHM-ee-tahs; DEHM-ee-tass] Literally French for "half cup," the term "demitasse" can refer to either a tiny coffee cup or the very strong black coffee served in the cup.

Denver sandwich Also called a *Western sandwich*, this classic consists of an egg scrambled with chopped ham, onion and green pepper, sandwiched with two slices of bread and garnished with lettuce.

Derby cheese; Derbyshire cheese [DER-bee; DAHR-bee-sheer] This mild, semifirm, cow's-milk cheese is similar to CHEDDAR. It has a pale, golden orange interior with a natural or waxed rind. **Sage Derby** is generously flavored with the herb, which also lends color interest. Both are good for snack or sandwich cheese. *See also* CHEESE.

dessert wine Any of a wide variety of sweet wines—sometimes fortified with BRANDY, all of which are compatible with dessert. Some of the more popular dessert wines are LATE HARVEST RIESLING, MADEIRA, PORT, SAUTERNES, SHERRY and some sparkling wines, such as ASTI SPUMANTE.

devein [dee-VAYN] To remove the gray-black vein from the back of a shrimp. This can be done with the tip of a sharp knife or a special tool called a deveiner. On small and medium shrimp, this technique need be done only for cosmetic purposes. However, because the intestinal vein of large shrimp contains grit, it should always be removed.

devil To combine a food with various hot or spicy seasonings such as red pepper, mustard or Tabasco sauce, thereby creating a "deviled" dish.

devilfish *see* OCTOPUS

devil's food A dark, dense baked chocolate item (such as a cake or cookie). On the opposite end of the spectrum is the airy, white ANGEL FOOD CAKE.

devils on horseback 1. A "hot" version of ANGELS ON HORSEBACK (oysters wrapped in bacon strips), enlivened by the additon of red pepper or Tabasco sauce. 2. The British rendition of this appetizer consists of wine-poached prunes stuffed with a whole almond and mango chutney, then wrapped in bacon and broiled. Like the American version, these devils on horseback are also served on toast points.

Devon cream [DEHV-uhn] *see* CLOTTED CREAM

Devonshire cheese [DEHV-uhn-sheer; DEHV-uhn-shuhr] A soft, creamy-rich cheese made by draining all the whey from Devonshire cream, also known as CLOTTED CREAM. *See also* CHEESE.

Devonshire cream *see* CLOTTED CREAM

dewberry [DOO-beh-ree] Any of several varieties of the trailing-vine form of the BLACKBERRY.

dextrose [DEHK-strohs] Also called *corn sugar* and *grape sugar*, dextrose is a naturally occurring form of GLUCOSE.

dhal *see* DAL

diable sauce; à la diable [dee-AH-bl] 1. A basic brown sauce with the addition of wine, vinegar, shallots and red or black pepper. It's usually served with broiled meat or poultry. 2. *A la diable* refers to a French method of preparing poultry by grilling a split bird, which is then sprinkled with breadcrumbs and broiled until brown. The bird is served with diable sauce.

dice To cut food into tiny (about ⅛- to ¼-inch) cubes.

Dijon mustard [dee-ZHOHN] Hailing originally from Dijon, France, this pale, grayish-yellow mustard is known for its clean, sharp flavor, which can range from mild to hot. Dijon mustard is made from brown mustard seeds, white wine, unfermented grape juice (MUST) and various seasonings. The best-known maker of Dijon mustard is the house of Poupon, particularly famous in the U.S. for their Grey Poupon mustard. *See also* MUSTARD.

dill Thought by first-century Romans to be a good luck symbol, dill has been around for thousands of years. This annual herb grows up to a height of about 3 feet and has feathery green leaves called **dill weed**, marketed in both fresh and dried forms. The distinctive flavor of fresh dill weed in no way translates to its dried form. Fresh dill does, however, quickly lose its fragrance during heating, so should be added toward the end of the cooking time. Dill weed is used to flavor many dishes such as salads, vegetables, meats and sauces. The tan, flat **dill seed** is actually the dried fruit of the herb. Heating brings out the flavor of dill seed, which is stronger and more pungent than that of the leaves. It's most often used in the U.S. for the brine in which dill pickles are cured. *See also* HERB; Herb and Spice Chart, page 538.

dilute [dih-LOOT] To reduce a mixture's strength by adding liquid (usually water).

dim sum; dem sum [DIHM SUHM] Cantonese for "heart's delight," dim sum includes a variety of small, mouthwatering snacks such as steamed or fried dumplings, shrimp balls, SPRING ROLLS, steamed buns and Chinese pastries. Dim sum—standard fare in tea houses—can be enjoyed any time of the day.

diplomat pudding This cold, molded dessert consists of alternating layers of LIQUEUR-soaked ladyfingers (or spongecake), jam, chopped candied fruit and custard (sometimes combined with whipped cream). Diplomat pudding is usually garnished with whipped-cream rosettes and candied fruit.

diplomat sauce A fish stock-based VELOUTÉ SAUCE enriched with cream, brandy, LOBSTER BUTTER and truffles. It's generally served with fish and shellfish.

dirty rice A Cajun specialty of cooked rice combined with ground chicken or turkey livers and gizzards, onions, chicken broth, bacon drippings, green pepper and garlic. The name comes from the fact that the ground giblets give the rice a "dirty" look . . . but delicious flavor.

disjoint To separate meat at the joint, such as cutting the chicken leg from the thigh.

dissolve To incorporate a dry ingredient (such as sugar, salt, yeast or gelatin) into a liquid so thoroughly that no grains of the dry ingredient are evident, either by touch or sight.

distillation The process of separating the components in a liquid by heating it to the point of vaporization, then cooling the mixture so it condenses into a purified and/or concentrated form. In the making of liquor, this distilled product is called "neutral spirits" because it has little flavor, color or aroma.

distilled water Water from which all minerals and other impurities have been removed by the process of DISTILLATION.

ditalini [diht-ah-LEE-nee] Tiny, very short tubes of macaroni. *See also* PASTA.

divinity [dih-VIHN-ih-tee] A fluffy yet creamy candy made with granulated sugar, corn syrup and stiffly beaten egg whites. Nuts, chocolate, coconut or various other flavorings are often added to the basic mixture. When brown sugar is subsituted for granulated sugar, the candy is called **seafoam**.

Dobos torte [DOH-bohs; DOH-bohsh] Created by Austrian pastry chef Josef Dobos, this rich torte is made by stacking 9 extra-thin layers of GÉNOISE (or spongecake) spread with chocolate buttercream. The top is covered with a hard caramel glaze.

dock *see* SORREL

Dolcelatte cheese [dol-chay-LAHT-tay] Also called *Gorgonzola dolce*, this soft, mild, blue-veined cheese can be served as either an appetizer or dessert. It's difficult to find but is sometimes available in specialty cheese shops. *See also* CHEESE.

dollarfish *see* BUTTERFISH

dollop [DOLL-uhp] A small glob of soft food, such as whipped cream or mashed potatoes. When referring to a liquid, dollop refers to a dash or "splash" of soda water, water, etc.

Dolly Varden *see* TROUT

dolma [DOHL-mah] From the Arabic word for "something stuffed," referring to grape leaves, vegetables or fruits stuffed with a savory, well-seasoned filling. Among the most popular dolmas are grape leaves stuffed with a filling of ground lamb, rice, onion, currants, pine nuts and various seasonings. Other foods used as casings include squash, eggplant, sweet peppers, cabbage leaves, quinces and apples. Dolmas are usually braised or baked. They may be eaten hot, cold or at room temperature, and served as an appetizer or entree.

dolphin; dolphinfish [DAHL-fihn] *see* MAHI MAHI

dorado *see* MAHI MAHI

dosage [doh-SAHJ] A mixture of sugar and spirits (often brandy) that is added to champagne and other sparkling wine immediately prior to final bottling. The percentage of sugar in the syrup determines the degree of sweetness in the final wine.

dot To scatter small bits (dots) of an ingredient (usually butter) over another food or mixture. Distributing bits of butter over the fruit in an apple pie, for example, allows the butter to melt evenly over the pie as it bakes.

double-acting baking powder *see* BAKING POWDER

double boiler A double-pan arrangement whereby two pots are formed to fit together, with one sitting partway inside the other. A single lid fits both pans. The lower pot is used to hold simmering water, which gently heats the mixture in the upper pot. Double boilers are used to warm or cook heat-sensitive food such as custards, delicate sauces and chocolate.

double-cream cheeses; double crème   Any of various cow's-milk cheeses that have been enriched with cream so that they contain a minimum of 60 percent butterfat. **Triple-cream cheeses** must have at least 75 percent butterfat. Both double- and triple-creams can be fresh or ripened. They share the distinction of being seductively soft and creamy in texture with a mild, slightly sweet flavor. **Boursin** is an example of a triple-cream cheese, whereas **Crema Dania** is a double-cream. Because of their natural sweetness, these cheeses are perfect when served with fruit for dessert. *See also* CHEESE.

double Gloucester cheese   *see* GLOUCESTER CHEESE

dough   [DOH]   A mixture of flour, liquid and other ingredients (often including a leavening) that's stiff but pliable enough to work with the hands. Unlike a batter, dough is too stiff to pour.

doughnut; donut   A small, typically ring-shaped pastry that is usually leavened with yeast or baking powder, and which can be baked but is generally fried. The traditional doughnut shape is formed by using a special doughnut cutter that cuts out the center hole in the dough. It can also be made with two biscuit cutters, large and small (for the hole). Fried doughnut holes are favorites with children. There are two main styles of doughnuts. **Raised doughnuts** are leavened with yeast and allowed to rise at least once before being fried. Besides the traditional ring-shape, raised doughnuts also come in squares and twists. Additionally, the dough is used to make oblong and round jelly-filled doughnuts—commonly called **jelly doughnuts**. **Cake doughnuts** receive their leavening power from baking powder and are chilled before frying to prevent the dough from absorbing too much oil in the process. The dough for cake doughnuts is often flavored with spices, orange or lemon zest or chocolate. **Crullers** are made from cake-doughnut dough. They're formed by twisting two (about 5-inch) strips of dough together before frying. Both types are usually either dusted with granulated sugar (cake doughnuts often with confectioners' sugar) or topped with a flavored glaze (such as chocolate or butterscotch). **French doughnuts**, though not as readily available as the other two types, are made with CHOUX PASTRY (cream-puff pastry dough). They're very tender and light.

Dover sole   *see* SOLE

draft beer Beer served straight from the keg by means of a spigot. Unlike the bottled or canned varieties, draft beer hasn't been subjected to the PASTEURIZATION process. Also spelled *draught*.

dragée [dra-ZHAY] 1. Tiny, round, hard candies used for decorating cakes, cookies and other baked goods. Dragées come in a variety of sizes (from pinhead to ¼-inch) and colors, including silver. 2. Almonds with a hard sugar coating.

dragon's eye *see* LONGAN

drain To pour off a liquid or fat from food, often with the use of a COLANDER. "Drain" can also mean to blot greasy food (such as bacon) on paper towels.

Drambuie [dram-BOO-ee] A golden, Scotch-based LIQUEUR sweetened with heather honey and flavored with herbs.

draught beer [draft] *see* DRAFT BEER

draw 1. In cooking, to eviscerate; to remove the entrails, as from poultry or fish. 2. To CLARIFY a mixture, as in drawn butter.

drawn butter *see* CLARIFIED BUTTER

dredge [DREHJ] To lightly coat food to be fried, as with flour, cornmeal or breadcrumbs. This coating helps brown the food. Chicken, for example, might be dredged with flour before frying.

dress 1. To prepare game, fowl, fish, etc. for cooking by plucking, scaling, eviscerating, and so on. 2. To "dress a salad" simply means adding a DRESSING.

dressing 1. A sauce—usually cold—used to coat or top salads and some cold vegetable, fish and meat dishes. 2. A mixture used to stuff poultry, fish, meat and some vegetables. It can be cooked separately or in the food in which it is stuffed. Dressings (also called *stuffings*) are usually well seasoned and based on breadcrumbs or cubes—though rice, potatoes and other foods are also used.

dried beef *see* CHIPPED BEEF

dried fruit Fruit from which the majority of the moisture has been dehydrated. The final moisture content of dried fruit usually ranges from 15 to 25 percent. Drying fruit greatly concentrates both sweetness and flavor, and the taste is much changed, as from grape to raisin or from plum to prune. Fruit can be dried in the sun or by machine. Machine-drying usually takes no more than 24 hours. Sun-drying can take three to four times as long, causing additional loss of nutrients through heat and time. Vitamins A and C are the most susceptible to depletion during the drying process, but a wealth of other vitamins and minerals remains in great force. Before drying, fruits are often sprayed with sulfur dioxide gas, which helps preserve the fruit's natural color and nutrients. Though decried by some, clinical research has shown no negative effects from sulfur intake. Imported dried fruit, however, is fumigated with chemical pesticides, which have been proven toxic to humans. Dried fruit is available year-round and comes in five basic designations: **extra fancy, fancy, extra choice**, **choice** and **standard**. These grades are based on size, color, condition and moisture content. Most dried fruit can be stored at room temperature, tightly wrapped in a plastic bag, for up to a year. Though dried fruits can be stored longer and take less space, they contain 4 to 5 times the calories by weight of fresh fruit. Dried fruit can be used as is or reconstituted in water. It may be eaten out of hand or put to a variety of uses such as in baked goods, fruit compotes, stuffings, conserves, etc.

drippings The melted fat and juices that gather in the bottom of a pan in which meat or other food is cooked. Drippings are used as a base for gravies and sauces and to cook other foods in (such as YORKSHIRE PUDDING).

drizzle To slowly pour a liquid mixture in a very fine stream over food (such as a sweet glaze over cake or bread, or melted butter over food before baking).

drop cookie A cookie made by dropping spoonfuls of dough onto a baking sheet. *See also* COOKIE.

drum Any of a large and diverse family of fish, so named for the odd drumming or deep croaking noise it makes, particularly during the mating season. Drum, also known as *croaker*, is a firm, lowfat fish found in temperate waters. **Croakers**, averaging 1 pound, are the small fry of the drum family and are usually sold whole. However, many drum can weigh up to 30 pounds and are generally sold in fillets and steaks. Drum can be baked, broiled or fried. Other members of the drum family include **Atlantic and black croaker, black drum, California corbina, hardhead, kingfish, redfish (red drum), kingfish, spot and white seabass.** *See also* FISH.

dry *adj.* A term used to describe a wine that isn't sweet; also referred to as SEC (*see listing*). **dry** *v. see* DEHYDRATE.

dry ice Dry ice is really crystallized carbon dioxide. It doesn't produce water when it melts and is generally used only for long-term refrigeration. Touching dry ice with bare hands can result in burns.

dry yeast *see* YEAST

Dubarry, à la; du Barry [doo-BAIR-ee] Said to have been named after the Comtesse du Barry, mistress of Louis XV, this term denotes a dish using cauliflower—particularly cooked cauliflower served with cheese sauce. **Crème Dubarry** is a creamy cauliflower soup.

Dublin Bay prawn *see* PRAWN

Dubonnet [doo-boh-NAY] A bittersweet, fortified wine-based APÉRITIF flavored with herbs and quinine. Dubonnet comes in red and white versions, the white being the drier (*see* DRY) of the two.

duchess potatoes Cooked potatoes that are pureed with egg yolks and butter, then formed into small shapes or piped as a garnish and baked until golden brown.

duck; duckling Any of many species of wild or domestic web-footed birds that live in or near water. As with so many things culinary, the Chinese are credited with being the first to raise ducks for food. Today's domestic ducks are all descendants of either of two species—the mallard or the muscovy duck. Comprising about half the domesticated ducks in the U.S. are the white-feathered, full-breasted **Long Island ducks**, known for their dark, succulent flesh. These direct descendents of the **Peking duck** (a variety of mallard) are all the progeny of three ducks and a drake brought from Peking on a clipper ship in 1873. Besides Long Island, the locations most widely known for the cultivation of superior ducks are Peking and Rouen, France. Since most ducks are marketed while still quite young and tender, the words "duck" and "duckling" are interchangeable. **Broilers** and **fryers** are less than 8 weeks old, **roasters** no more than 16 weeks old. Domestic ducks can weigh between 3 and 5½ pounds; the older ducks are generally larger. Fresh duck is available from late spring through early winter, but generally only in regions where ducks are raised. Almost 90 percent of ducks that reach market are frozen and available year-round. The government grades duck quality with USDA classifications A, B and C. The highest grade is A, and is usually what is found in markets. Grade B ducks are less meaty and well finished; grade C ducks are usually used for commercial purposes. The grade stamp can be found within a shield on the package wrapping or sometimes on a tag attached to the bird's wing. When buying fresh duck, choose one with a broad, fairly plump breast; the skin should be elastic, not saggy. For frozen birds, make sure the packaging is tight and unbroken. Fresh duck can be stored, loosely covered, in the coldest section of the refrigerator for 2 to 3 days. Remove any giblets from the body cavity and store separately. Frozen duck should be thawed in the refrigerator; it can take from 24 to 36 hours, depending on the size of the bird. Do not refreeze duck once it's been thawed. Duck can be prepared in a variety of manners including roasting, braising, broiling, etc. Though higher in fat than other domestic birds, it is a good source of protein and iron. *For information about wild duck, see* GAME BIRDS.

duck press A kitchen device used to extract the juices from a cooked duck carcass. This step is necessary for some gourmet duck recipes, specifically PRESSED DUCK.

duck sauce Also called *plum sauce*, this thick, sweet-and-sour condiment is made with plums, apricots, sugar and seasonings. Duck sauce is most often served with duck, pork or spareribs.

dulce [DOOL-say] Spanish for "sweet," *dulce* generally refers to an intensely sweet confection made with sugar and cream.

dumpling Savory dumplings are small or large mounds of dough that are usually dropped into a liquid mixture (such as soup or stew) and cooked until done. Some are stuffed with meat or cheese mixtures. Dessert dumplings most often consist of a fruit mixture encased in a sweet pastry dough and baked. They're usually served with a sauce. Some sweet dumplings are poached in a sweet sauce and served with cream.

Dundee cake [duhn-DEE; DUHN-dee] A classic Scottish fruitcake made with candied citron, orange and lemon peels, almonds and various spices. The top of a Dundee cake is traditionally covered completely with blanched whole almonds.

Dungeness crab [DUHN-juh-nehs] The pride of the Pacific coast, Dungeness crab can be found all the way from Alaska to Mexico. This large crab can range from 1 to almost 4 pounds; its pink flesh is succulent and sweet. *See also* CRAB.

Dunlop cheese Hailing from Scotland, this cow's-milk cheese is quite mild when young, sharpening slightly as it ages. The ivory-colored Dunlop resembles a soft CHEDDAR in texture. It's delicious with breads and melts beautifully. *See also* CHEESE.

durian [DOOR-ee-uhn] This larger-than-life fruit of the Malaysian tree can weigh up to 10 pounds, has a brownish-green, semihard shell covered with thick spikes, and is slightly larger than a football. To all but its Southeast Asian fans, the durian has a nauseating smell—a truth attested to by the fact that it's been outlawed by many airlines. The creamy, slightly sweet flesh, however, has an exquisitely rich, custardy texture. This fruit is not generally available in the U.S.

durum wheat [DOOR-uhm; DYOOR-uhm] *see* WHEAT

dust 1. In cooking, this term refers to lightly coating a food with a powdery ingredient such as flour or confectioners' sugar. 2. A term used to describe inferior, coarsely crushed tea leaves.

Dutch oven A large pot or kettle, usually made of cast iron, with a tight-fitting lid so steam cannot readily escape. It's used for moist-cooking methods, such as braising and stewing. Dutch ovens are said to be of Pennsylvania Dutch heritage, dating back to the 1700s.

duxelles [dook-SEHL; deu-SEHL] A mixture of finely chopped mushrooms, shallots and herbs slowly cooked in butter until it forms a thick paste. It's used to flavor sauces, soups and other mixtures, as well as for a garnish.

arl Grey tea This popular BLACK TEA was named for Charles Grey, the second earl in his line, who was also prime minister to King William IV in the early 19th century. An amalgamation of Indian and Sri Lankan teas, Earl Grey gets its elusive flavor from oil of BERGAMOT. The Earl is said to have been given the recipe by a Chinese mandarin with whom he was friends. *See also* TEA.

Early Richmond cherry So named because it's the first sour cherry available in the late spring, the bright red Early Richmond is excellent for cooking purposes. *See also* CHERRY.

earthenware Clay bakeware that is glazed with a hard, nonporous coating. If high-fired, the earthenware is hard; lowfiring produces soft, fragile ware. Because of its inherent ability to release heat slowly, earthenware is favored for dishes requiring lengthy cooking such as baked beans and stews. Care must be taken to cool earthenware slowly and completely before washing in order to prevent the glaze from cracking. Once the glaze cracks, the exposed surfaces can adversely affect the flavor of foods cooked in the container.

earth nut *see* PEANUT

Eastern oyster *see* ATLANTIC OYSTER

eau de vie [oh-deuh-VEE] French for "water of life," this term describes any colorless, potent BRANDY or other spirit distilled from fermented fruit juice. KIRSCH (made from cherries) and FRAMBOISE (from raspberries) are the two most popular *eaux de vie. See also* AQUA VITAE; LIQUEUR.

Eccles cake [EHK-uhls] Named for the Lancashire, England, town of Eccles, this small domed confection has a filling of CURRANTS and other dried fruit mixed with sugar and butter and encased in a PUFF PASTRY shell.

éclair [ay-KLAIR] A small, oblong, cream-filled pastry made with CHOUX PASTRY (cream-puff pastry dough). Unlike CREAM PUFFS, éclairs are usually topped with a sweet icing.

Edam cheese [EE-duhm] Hailing from Holland, this mellow, savory cheese has a pale yellow interior with a red or yellow paraffin coating (the yellow is more common in Holland). It's made from part-skimmed milk (40 percent butterfat) and comes in spheres that can weigh anywhere from 1 to 4 pounds. Edam is second only to Gouda as Holland's most exported cheese. It's a great all-purpose cheese, especially good when served with dark beer. *See also* CHEESE.

eel The legends of eels have colored folklore throughout the ages. Some Philippine tribes say that eels are the souls of the dead, while in parts of

Europe it's believed that rubbing the skin with eel oil will cause a person to see fairies. Whatever their origin or exterior application, eels are widely popular in Europe and Japan, where many consider their rich, sweet, firm meat a delicacy. This rather long, snakelike fish—of which there are both freshwater and saltwater varieties—has a smooth, scaleless skin. It spawns at sea and dies shortly thereafter. The European and American eel breed deep in Atlantic waters near Bermuda. The minuscule, transparent eel larvae drift on ocean currents for enormous distances—their journey to Europe taking about 3 years—until they reach coastal areas. There they transform into tiny, wormlike *elvers* (baby eel) and begin wriggling up inland waterways and crossing boggy grounds to reach small ponds and streams. After about 10 years of living in this freshwater habitat, the eel begins its migration back to Atlantic waters where it spawns and dies. The *conger eel*, a scaleless, saltwater "monster" fish that can reach up to 10 feet long and weigh over 170 pounds, is a relative of the common eel. Fresh eels, depending on the region, are available year-round, the fall being the peak season. Those under 2 pounds will be more tender. Before cooking, the thick, tough skin and outer layer of fat must be removed—a task usually handled by the fish dealer. Fresh eel should be refrigerated and used within a day or two. It's excellent baked, stewed or grilled. Because conger eel meat is very tough, it is most often used in soups and stews. Eel is also available jellied in cans or smoked. Though considered a fatty fish, the eel is high in vitamins A and D, as well as being a good source of protein. *See also* FISH.

egg *see* EGGS

egg cream This favorite New York City soda fountain drink has been popular since the 1930s. Egg creams don't contain a speck of egg but are so named because of the froth (resembling beaten egg whites) that crowns the drink. They're made with a mixture of milk and CHOCOLATE SYRUP into which SELTZER WATER is spritzed, causing the mixture to foam enthusiastically.

egg foo yong [foo YUHNG] A Chinese-American dish made by combining eggs with various foods such as bean sprouts, water chestnuts, scallions, ham, chicken or pork. Small, pancake-size portions are poured into a skillet and fried until golden brown. Egg foo yong can also be made in one large round. It is sometimes topped with a sauce of chicken broth, soy sauce and various seasonings.

eggnog This chilled Christmas beverage consists of a homogeneous blend of milk or cream, beaten eggs, sugar, nutmeg and usually liquor of some kind. Rum was the spirit noted in early references to the drink, but brandy and whiskey are also common additions. Liquor-free eggnog has long been served to convalescents and growing children. Some eggnogs are made by separating the eggs and stiffly beating the whites before adding them to the milk mixture; this produces an airier brew. Commercial eggnog is sans liquor and must contain 1 percent egg-yolk solids by weight. It's available in cartons beginning around mid-October. Canned eggnog can be found year-round in some locations, though some think its flavor takes on a metallic quality.

egg piercer   A kitchen tool with a sharp steel pin, usually spring-mounted, which pokes a tiny hole in the large end of an egg. This hole prevents the egg from cracking because the air inside (which expands during boiling) can gradually escape.

eggplant   Because the eggplant is a member of the nightshade family, it's related to the potato and tomato. Though commonly thought of as a vegetable, eggplant is actually a fruit . . . specifically a berry. There are many varieties of this delicious food, ranging in color from rich purple to white, in length from 2 to 12 inches and in shape from oblong to round. In the U.S., the most common eggplant is the large, cylindrical- or pear-shape variety with a smooth, glossy, dark purple skin. It's available year-round, with the peak season during August and September. Choose a firm, smooth-skinned eggplant heavy for its size; avoid those with soft or brown spots. Eggplants become bitter with age and are very perishable. They should be stored in a cool, dry place and used within a day or two of purchase. If longer storage is necessary, place the eggplant in the refrigerator vegetable drawer. When young, the skin of most eggplants is deliciously edible; older eggplants should be peeled. Since the flesh discolors rapidly, an eggplant should be cut just before using. Bitter, overripe fruit can benefit by the ancient method of salting both halves and weighting them for 20 minutes before rinsing; the salt helps eliminate some of the acrid taste. Eggplant can be prepared in a variety of ways including baking, broiling and frying. It does, however, have spongelike capacity to soak up oil so it should be well coated with a batter or crumb mixture to inhibit fat absorption. Eggplant is a good source of folic acid and potassium. Many other varieties of this versatile fruit are now finding their way into some markets. The very narrow, straight **Japanese** or **oriental eggplant** ranges in color from solid purple to striated shades and has tender, slightly sweet flesh. The **Italian or baby eggplant** looks like a miniature version of the common large variety, but has a more delicate skin and flesh. The appearance of the egg-shaped **white eggplant** makes it clear how this fruit was named. It has a tougher skin, but firmer, smoother flesh. In general, these varieties can be cooked in many of the same methods as the large eggplant. They rarely require salting, however, and usually benefit from a short cooking time.

egg roll A small, stuffed Chinese pastry usually served as an appetizer. Paper-thin pastry wrappers are folded around a savory filling of minced or shredded vegetables and sometimes meat, then folded and rolled before being deep-fried. Egg roll skins (the pastry wrappers) are available in the refrigerator section of oriental markets and most supermarkets. **Spring rolls,** so named because they're traditionally served on the first day of the Chinese New Year (in early spring), are smaller, more delicate versions of the egg roll.

egg roll skins *see* WON TON SKINS

E

eggs Legends about eggs have abounded throughout the eons. Early Phoenicians thought that a primeval egg split open to form heaven and earth; Egyptians believed that their god Ptah created the egg from the sun and the moon; and American Indians thought that the Great Spirit burst forth from a giant golden egg to create the world. In all of the early legends the chicken is never mentioned, making the answer to the question of which came first—the chicken or the egg—seem obvious. The most common egg used for food today is the hen's egg, though those from other fowl—including duck, goose and quail—are sold in many areas. Hens' eggs have long been bedeviled by their high cholesterol content (about 213 milligrams for a large egg), which is contained entirely in the yolk. Since the American Heart Association recommends that adults limit their cholesterol consumption to no more than 300 milligrams of cholesterol a day, strict cholesterol watchers had to either drastically reduce their egg consumption or eat the whites only. However, modern feeding techniques have now produced some **low-cholesterol eggs** with 150 to 200 milligrams of cholesterol (depending on the chicken's breeding and feed, as well as the method of cholesterol analysis) and 55 milligrams of sodium (compared to 70 milligrams in a regular egg). Unfortunately, these low-cholesterol eggs are presently available only on a limited basis, mainly on the West Coast. Most hens' eggs on the market today have been classified according to quality and size under USDA standards. In descending order, egg grades are AA, A, B and C, the classification being determined by both exterior and interior quality. C-grade eggs have cracked or abnormal shells and never reach the consumer market. The factors determining exterior quality include the soundness, cleanliness, shape and texture of the shell. Interior quality is judged by "candling," so named because in days gone by an egg was held up in front of a candle to see inside. Today, candling is more likely to be accomplished electrically, with the eggs moving and rotating on rollers over high-intensity lights. The interior quality is determined by the size of the air cell (the empty space between the white and shell at the large end of the egg—smaller in high-quality eggs), the proportion and density of the white, and whether or not the yolk is firm and free of defects. In high-quality eggs, both the white and yolk stand higher, and the white spreads less than in lower-grade eggs. Eggs come in the following sizes based on their minimum weight per dozen: jumbo (30 oz. per dozen), extra large (27 oz.), large (24 oz.), medium (21 oz.), small (18 oz.) and peewee (15 oz.). Large eggs are those on which most recipes are based. An egg shell's color—white or brown—is determined by the breed of hen that laid it and has nothing to do with either taste or nutritive value. The egg white is an excellent source of protein and riboflavin. Egg yolks contain all of the fat in an egg and are a good source of protein, iron, vitamins A and D, choline and phosphorus. The color of the yolk depends entirely on the hen's diet. Hens fed on alfalfa, grass and yellow corn lay eggs with darker yolks than wheat-fed hens. CHALAZAE are the thick, cordlike strands of egg white attached to 2 sides of the yolk that serve to anchor it in the center of the egg. The more prominent the chalazae, the fresher the egg. Blood spots on egg yolks are the result of a natural occurrence, such as a blood vessel rupturing on the surface. They do not indicate that the egg is fertile, nor do they affect flavor. Contrary to popular belief, fertile eggs—expensive because of high production costs—are no more nutritious than nonfertile ones. They do contain a small amount of male hormone and do not keep as well as other eggs. Eggs must always be refrigerated. When stored at room temperature, they lose more quality in 1 day than in a week in the refrigerator. Eggs should be stored in the carton in which they came; transferring them to the egg container in the refrigerator door exposes them to odors and damage. They should always be stored large-end-up and should never be placed near odoriferous foods (such as onions) because they easily absorb odors. The best flavor and cooking quality will be realized in eggs used within a week. They can, however, be refrigerated up to a month, providing the shells are intact. Eggs with cracked shells should be used as soon as possible and only in foods that are to be well cooked. Leftover yolks can be covered with cold water and refrigerated, tightly covered, for up to 3 days. They can be frozen only with the addition of ⅛ teaspoon salt or 1½ teaspoons sugar or corn syrup per ¼ cup egg yolks. Tightly covered egg whites can be refrigerated up to a week. They can be frozen as is up to 6 months. An easy way to freeze whites is to place one in each section of an ice cube tray. Freeze, then pop the egg-white squares out into a freezer-weight plastic bag. Both frozen egg yolks and whites should be thawed overnight in the refrigerator before being used. Hard-cooked eggs should be refrigerated no more than a week. Eggs are available in other forms including powdered and frozen (whole or separated). Commercially frozen egg products are generally pasteurized and some contain stabilizing ingredients. A liquid product labeled "**imitation eggs**" is sold in cartons. This product is usually a blend of egg whites, food starch, corn oil, skim-milk powder, artificial coloring and a plethora of additives. It contains no cholesterol but each serving is almost as high in sodium as a real egg. Imitation eggs can be scrambled and also used in many baking and cooking recipes calling for whole eggs. The multi-talented egg is delicious not only as a food in its own right but has numerous other uses as a LEAVENER in cakes, breads and soufflés; a base for dressings such as mayonnaise; a thickener in sauces and custards; a clarifying agent for stocks; and a coating for breaded or battered foods.

E

eggs Benedict A breakfast or brunch specialty consisting of two toasted English muffin halves, each topped with a slice of ham or Canadian bacon, a poached egg and a dollop of HOLLANDAISE SAUCE. The most popular legend of the dish's origin says that it originated at Manhattan's famous Delmonico's Restaurant when regular patrons, Mr. and Mrs. LeGrand Benedict, complained that there was nothing new on the lunch menu. Delmonico's maitre d' and Mrs. Benedict began discussing possibilities and eggs Benedict was the result.

egg slicer A kitchen tool with a slatted, egg-shaped hollow on the bottom and a hinged top consisting of 10 fine steel wires. When the upper portion is brought down onto a hard-cooked egg sitting in the base, it cuts the egg into even slices.

eggs Sardou [sahr-DOO] Named for Victorien Sardou, a famous French dramatist, this specialty of Antoine's restaurant in New Orleans consists of poached eggs topped with artichoke hearts, ham, anchovies, truffles and HOLLANDAISE SAUCE.

egg timer A tiny "hourglass" that holds just enough sand to run from top to bottom in 3 minutes, the time it takes to soft-boil an egg.

egg wash Egg yolk or egg white mixed with a small amount of water or milk. It's brushed over breads, pastry and other baked goods before baking to give them color and gloss.

Elberta peach [ehl-BUR-tuh] A large FREESTONE peach with a sweet, succulent flesh and red-blushed, yellow skin. It's good both for eating out of hand and for cooking. *See also* PEACH.

elbow pasta Any of a wide variety of short, curved tubular PASTAS, such as MACARONI.

elderberry The purple-black, tart fruit of the elder tree, elderberries can be eaten raw (though they are quite sour) but are better used to make jams, pies and homemade wine. The creamy white **elderberry flowers** can be added to salads or batter-dipped and fried like fritters.

election cake This rich, yeast-raised cake is replete with nuts, candied fruit and sherry-soaked raisins. It was created in the 18th century to celebrate election day.

elk *see* GAME ANIMALS

elver *see* EEL

Emmentaler cheese; Emmental; Emmenthaler [EM-en-tahl-er] Switzerland's oldest and most important cheese, Emmentaler has a distinctively nutty-sweet, mellow flavor that makes it perfect for almost any use—from snacks to an après-dinner fruit-and-cheese plate. This cow's-milk cheese is light gold in color, with marble-size holes and a natural light brown rind. It was named for Switzerland's Emmental valley and is exported in giant wheels weighing from 150 to 220 pounds each. *See also* CHEESE.

empanada [em-pah-NAH-dah; em-pah-NAH-thah] *Empanar* is Spanish for "to bake in pastry," and these Mexican and Spanish specialties are usually single-serving turnovers with a pastry crust and savory meat-and-vegetable filling. They can also be filled with fruit and served as dessert. Empanadas range in size from the huge *empanada gallega*, large enough to feed an entire family, to *empanaditas*—tiny, ravioli-size pastries.

emperor grape In season from November to May, the large emperor grape comes from California and has an elongated oval shape. The thin, pale red to purple-red skin covers a mild-flavored flesh with scattered seeds. *See also* GRAPE.

emulsion [ih-MUHL-shuhn] A mixture of one liquid with another with which it cannot normally combine smoothly—oil and water being the classic example. Emulsifying is done by slowly (sometimes drop-by-drop) adding one ingredient to another while at the same time mixing rapidly. This disperses and suspends minute droplets of one liquid throughout the other. Emulsified mixtures are usually thick and satiny in texture. Mayonnaise (an uncooked combination of oil, egg yolks and vinegar or lemon juice) and HOLLANDAISE SAUCE (a cooked mixture of butter, egg yolks and vinegar or lemon juice) are two of the best-known emulsions.

enamelware Cast-iron or steel pots and pans that have been completely coated with thin layers of brightly colored enamel. Enamelware is a good heat conductor, easy to clean and doesn't interact with food to impart off-flavors. Light-colored enameled surfaces do not brown food well; they will also discolor over a long period of use. Overheating enamelware may cause the surface to crack. Care must be taken not to use abrasives to clean enamel as it easily scratches.

enchilada [en-chuh-LAH-dah; en-chee-LAH-thah]   This Mexican specialty is made by rolling a softened corn tortilla around a meat or cheese filling. It's served hot, usually topped with a tomato-based salsa and sprinkled with cheese.

en croûte   *see* CROÛTE

endive [EN-dyv; AHN-deev; ahn-DEEV] Endive is closely related to and often confused with its cousin, CHICORY. They're both part of the same botanical family, *Cichorium*. There are three main varieties of endive: Belgian endive, curly endive and escarole. **Belgian endive**, also known as *French endive* and *witloof* (white leaf), is a small (about 6-inch-long), cigar-shaped head of cream-colored, tightly packed, slightly bitter leaves. It's grown in complete darkness to prevent it from turning green, using a labor-intensive growing technique known as BLANCHING. Belgian endive is available from September through May, with a peak season from November through April. Buy crisp, firmly packed heads with pale, yellow-green tips. Belgian endives become bitter when exposed to light. They should be refrigerated, wrapped in a paper towel inside a plastic bag, for no more than a day. They can be served cold as part of a salad, or cooked by braising or baking. **Curly endive**, often mistakenly called *chicory* in the U.S., grows in loose heads of lacy, green-rimmed outer leaves that curl at the tips. The off-white center leaves form a compact heart. The leaves of the curly endive have a prickly texture and slightly bitter taste. **Escarole** has broad, slightly curved, pale green leaves with a milder flavor than either Belgian or curly endive. Both curly endive and escarole are available year-round, with the peak season from June through October. They should be selected for their fresh, crisp texture; avoid heads with discoloration or insect damage. Store curly endive and escarole, tightly wrapped, in the refrigerator for up to 3 days. They're both used mainly in salads, but can also be briefly cooked and eaten as a vegetable or in soups.

English breakfast A large, hearty breakfast that can include fruit or juice, eggs, ham or other meat, fish, cereal, baked goods, jam and tea. Compare to CONTINENTAL BREAKFAST.

English breakfast tea A hearty blend of several of various black teas. English breakfast tea is more full-flavored than a single black tea. *See also* TEA.

English Morello cherry   *see* MORELLO CHERRY

English muffin   This round, rather flat (about 3 inches in diameter by 1 inch high) "muffin" is made from a soft yeast dough which, after being formed into rounds, is baked on a griddle. It can be made at home but is readily available commercially in an assortment of flavors including sourdough, whole wheat, raisin, cinnamon and cornmeal. English muffins are halved before toasting. In order to produce a surface with the proper peaks and craters (which adds to their crunchy texture and provides plentiful pockets for butter and jam), English muffins must be fork-split and gently pulled apart. Using a knife to cut them in half will not produce the desired result.

English mustard   An extremely hot powdered mustard containing ground mustard seeds (both black or brown and yellow-white), wheat flour and turmeric. The most well-known brand of powdered mustard today is Colman's, named for its 19th-century British developer, Jeremiah Colman. *See also* MUSTARD.

English pea   This is the common *garden pea*, also known simply as *green pea*. But there's nothing common about its flavor, particularly during the peak months of March, April and May and again from August to November. The French are famous for their tiny, young green peas known as *petits pois*. Choose fresh peas that have plump, unblemished, bright green pods. The peas inside should be glossy, crunchy and sweet. Because peas begin the sugar-to-starch conversion process the moment they're picked, it's important to buy them as fresh as possible. Refrigerate peas in their pods in a plastic bag for no more than 2 to 3 days. Shell just before using. Both English peas and the French petits pois are available frozen and canned. Peas are a fair source of vitamins A and C, as well as niacin and iron. *See also* PEA; LEGUME.

English sole   Also called *lemon sole* in the U.S., this species of FLOUNDER is low in fat and finely textured. It ranges from ¼ to 2 pounds and can be purchased whole or in fillets. It's often labeled simply as "fillet of SOLE." English sole can be prepared in a variety of ways including baking, broiling, poaching and sautéing. *See also* FISH.

English walnut   The U.S. (mainly California) is the world's leading producer of the English walnut (also called *Persian walnut*). It's grown in several other countries including China, France, India, Iran, Turkey and Yugoslavia. The English walnut has a wrinkled, tan-colored shell that encloses two large, double-lobed halves. Its sweet flavor makes it a delicious choice for out-of-hand eating, as well as a popular addition for all manner of foods sweet and savory. English walnuts are used to produce walnut oil; they also come in candied and pickled forms. They're available prepackaged or in bulk. *See also* NUTS; WALNUTS.

enoki mushrooms *see* ENOKITAKE

enokitake; enokidake; enoki mushrooms [en-oh-kee-TAH-kee] The cultivated variety of these crisply delicate mushrooms comes in clumps of long, spaghettilike stems topped with tiny, snowy white caps. (In contrast, the wild form has orangy-brown, very shiny caps.) Enokitake have an appealingly crunchy texture and mild—almost fruity—taste, unlike the bosky flavor of most mushrooms. They're available fresh year-round (depending on the region) in oriental markets and some supermarkets. They can also be purchased canned. Choose fresh mushrooms that are firm and white. Refrigerate, tightly wrapped in a plastic bag, up to 5 days. Before using, they should be cut away from the mass at the base of the stems. Enokitake are particularly good raw in salads. They may also be used to garnish soups or other hot dishes. If used as part of a cooked dish, they should be added at the last minute, as heat tends to make them tough. These tiny mushrooms provide a good source of vitamin D, as well as small amounts of the B-complex vitamins. *See also* MUSHROOMS.

en papillote *see* PAPILLOTE

enriched; enrich 1. A term usually applied to flour which, after the milling has stripped it of the wheat germ and other nutritious elements, has niacin, riboflavin and thiamin added back into it. U.S. law requires that flours not containing wheat germ must have these nutrients replenished. 2. The term can also apply to enriching and thickening a sauce with the last-minute addition of an ingredient such as butter, cream or egg yolks.

entrecôte [ahn-treh-KOHT] Literally meaning "between the ribs," this French term refers to a steak cut from between the ninth and eleventh ribs of beef. It's a very tender cut and is usually cooked by quickly broiling or sautéing.

entree [AHN-tray] 1. In America, the term "entree" refers to the main course of a meal. 2. In parts of Europe, it refers to the dish served between the fish and meat courses during formal dinners.

epazote [eh-pah-ZOH-teh] A pungent, wild herb whose strong flavor is, like that of fresh coriander, an acquired taste. It has flat, pointed leaves and is available dried (and infrequently fresh) in Latin markets. Epazote is popular in many bean dishes because it's a carminative, which means it reduces gas. It's also used as a tea. *See also* HERB.

épices fines [ay-PEES feen] Literally meaning "fine spices," this complex blend of herbs and spices is usually marketed under the name SPICE PARISIENNE.

epicure [EHP-ih-kyoor] One who cultivates the knowledge and appreciation of fine food and wine.

épinard [ay-pee-NAHR] French for "spinach."

escabèche [es-keh-BEHSH] Of Spanish origin, escabèche is a dish of poached or fried fish, covered with a spicy MARINADE and refrigerated for at least 24 hours. It's a popular dish in Spain and the Provençal region of France, and is usually served cold as an appetizer.

escalope [eh-SKAL-ohp; eh-skah-LAWP] The French term for a very thin, usually flattened, slice of meat or fish. The tender escalope requires only a few seconds of sautéing on both sides. In the U.S., this cut is known as "scallop."

escargot [ehs-kahr-GOH] The French word for "SNAIL."

escarole [EHS-kuh-rohl] *see* ENDIVE

espagnole sauce [ehs-pah-NYOLE] *see* BROWN SAUCE

espresso [ehs-PREHS-oh] A dark, strong coffee made by forcing steam (or hot water) through finely ground, Italian-roast coffee especially blended for making espresso. This form of brewing produces a thin layer of creamy, dark beige froth on the coffee's surface. When topped with foam made from steamed milk, espresso becomes CAPPUCCINO.

Esrom cheese [EHS-rom] Named for its town of origin, Esrom, Denmark, this semisoft cheese has a mildly pungent flavor that's well complemented by dark beer or bold red wines. As it ages, its flavor intensifies until strong and earthy. Esrom has a thin, yellow-brown rind and a pale yellow interior studded with irregular holes. *See also* CHEESE.

essences Concentrated, usually oily substances extracted from food such as fish, mint leaves or vegetables and used in small amounts to flavor various dishes. Like EXTRACTS, essences will keep indefinitely if stored in a cook, dark place.

ethyl alcohol *see* ALCOHOL

evaporated milk   This canned, unsweetened milk is fresh, homogenized milk from which 60 percent of the water has been removed. Vitamin D is added for extra nutritional value. It comes in whole and skim forms; the whole-milk version must contain at least 7.9 percent butterfat, the skim version ½ percent or less. As it comes from the can, evaporated milk is used to enrich custards or add a creamy texture to many dishes. When mixed with an equal amount of water, it can be substituted for fresh milk in recipes. Evaporated milk is less expensive than fresh milk and is therefore popular for many cooked dishes. It has a slightly caramelized, "canned" flavor that is not appreciated by all who taste it. Canned milk can be stored at room temperature until opened, after which it must be tightly covered and refrigerated for no more than a week. When slightly frozen, evaporated milk can be whipped and used as an inexpensive substitute for whipped cream.

eviscerate   [eh-VIHS-uh-rayt]   *see* DRAW

Explorateur cheese   This sensuously rich TRIPLE-CREAM CHEESE is made from cow's milk and contains 75 percent fat. It comes in chunky cylinders with white rinds. When ripe, the ivory interior has a delicately piquant flavor. Explorateur is wonderful as a snack or after-dinner cheese served with a dry, fruity white wine. *See also* CHEESE.

extracts   Concentrated flavorings derived from various foods or plants, usually through evaporation or DISTILLATION. Extracts can come in several forms including solid (as in a bouillon cube), liquid (such as vanilla extract) or jellylike (as with a DEMI-GLACE). They deliver a powerful flavor impact to foods without adding excess volume or changing the consistency. Liquid extracts will keep indefinitely if stored in a cool, dark place. *See also* ESSENCES.

F **agioli** [fa-ZHOH-lee] The Italian word for "beans," usually white kidney beans. String beans are called *fagiolini*. *See also* BEAN.

Fahrenheit [FAIR-uhn-hyt] A temperature scale in which 32° represents freezing and 212° represents the steam point. The scale was devised by Gabriel Daniel Fahrenheit, an 18th-century German physicist. To convert Fahrenheit temperatures to CELSIUS, subtract 32 from the Fahrenheit reading, multiply by 5 and divide by 9. *See also* Temperature Equivalents Chart, page 533.

fajitas [fah-HEE-tuhs] SKIRT STEAK that has been marinated in a mixture of oil, lime juice, red pepper, and garlic for at least 24 hours before being grilled. The cooked meat is cut into strips which are then usually wrapped (BURRITO-style) in warm TORTILLAS, accompanied by a variety of garnishes including grilled onions and sweet peppers, GUACAMOLE, REFRIED BEANS and SALSA.

falafel; felafel [feh-LAH-fehl] A Middle Eastern specialty consisting of small, deep-fried CROQUETTES or balls made of highly spiced, ground CHICK-PEAS. They're generally tucked inside PITA bread, sandwich-style, but can also be served as appetizers. A yogurt- or TAHINI-based sauce is often served with falafel.

farce [FAHRS] The French word for "stuffing." *Farci* [fahr-SEE] means "stuffed."

farfalle [fahr-FAH-lay] PASTA shaped like small butterflies or bow ties.

farfel [FAHR-fuhl] 1. An egg-noodle dough that is grated or minced and used in soups. 2. In Jewish cookery, *farfel* refers to food—such as dried noodles—broken into small pieces.

farina [fuh-REE-nuh] Made from CEREAL grains, farina is a bland-tasting flour or meal that, when cooked in boiling water, makes a hot breakfast cereal. It's very easily digested and rich in protein.

farmer cheese This fresh cheese is a form of COTTAGE CHEESE from which most of the liquid has been pressed. The very dry farmer cheese is sold in a solid loaf. It has a mild, slightly tangy flavor and is firm enough to slice or crumble. It's an all-purpose cheese that can be eaten as is or used in cooking. *See also* CHEESE.

fasnacht; fastnacht [FAHS-nahkt] A yeast-raised potato pastry that's deep-fried like a doughnut. *Fasnachts* were originally made and served on

Shrove Tuesday to use up the fat that was forbidden during Lent. They're diamond-shaped and often have a slit cut down the center before frying. They first appeared in Pennsylvania, though there is some argument whether the actual origin is German or Dutch.

fatback Often confused with SALT PORK (which comes from the sides and belly of a pig), fatback is the fresh (unsmoked and unsalted) layer of fat that runs along the animal's back. It is used to make LARD and CRACKLINGS and for cooking—especially in many Southern recipes. Salt-cured fatback is also sometimes available. All fatback should be refrigerated: fresh up to a week, cured up to a month.

fats and oils In cooking, any of a wide variety of edible, greasy, solid or liquid substances that are a byproduct of animal or plant cells. All forms of fat are made up of a combination of fatty acids, which are the building blocks of fats much as amino acids are the building blocks of proteins. Fats and oils are either **saturated** or **unsaturated**, the latter classification being broken down into **monounsaturated** and **polyunsaturated** fats. For a simple example of the difference between the terms saturated and unsaturated, picture a fat molecule as a train of passenger cars (carbon atoms). In layman's terms, if every seat on the train is filled by a passenger (hydrogen atom) and no one else can board, then this is a molecule of saturated fat. If there is one seat open in each car where a hydrogen-atom "passenger" could sit, the molecule is monounsaturated and, if there are several seats available, it's polyunsaturated. In general, saturated fats come from animals (with the exception of fish) and are solid enough to hold their shape at room temperature (about 70°F), while unsaturated fats come mainly from plants and are liquid (in the form of an oil) at room temperature. (The chief exception to this rule is coconut oil which, though of plant origin, is solid at room temperature and highly saturated.) An oil is extracted from its source by one of two methods. In the **solvent-extraction method**, the ground ingredient is soaked in a chemical solvent that is later removed by boiling. The second method produces **cold-pressed oils**, a misnomer because the mixture is heated to temperatures up to 160°F before being pressed to extract the oil. After the oil is extracted, it's either left in its crude state or refined. **Refined oils**—those found on most supermarket shelves—have been treated until they're transparent, have a delicate to bland flavor and an increased SMOKE POINT and shelf life. **Unrefined (or crude) oils** are usually cloudy and have an intense flavor and odor that clearly signals their origin. Because they turn rancid quickly, unrefined oils should always be refrigerated. Generally speaking, oils are composed of **monounsaturated** and **polyunsaturated fats** (in varying degrees), both of which are believed by some scientists to lower the amount of cholesterol in the blood. The three most widely used oils that are high in monounsaturates are OLIVE OIL, PEANUT OIL and COTTONSEED OIL, the latter containing the highest percentage of saturated fat. In the polyunsaturated oil category, ranked in order according to proportion of polyunsaturates—most to least—are SAFFLOWER OIL, SOYBEAN OIL, CORN OIL and SESAME OIL. **Omega-3 oils** are a particular classification of fatty acids found in the tissues of all sea creatures. These special polyunsaturated oils have been found to be particularly beneficial to coronary health as well as to brain growth and development. Among the popular fish that are particularly good sources of Omega-3 oil (in order of importance) are sardines, herring, mackerel, bluefish, tuna, salmon, pilchard, butterfish and pompano. High cooking temperatures can destroy almost half the Omega-3 in fish, whereas microwave cooking doesn't appear to have an adverse effect on it. Canned tuna packed in water is a quick and easy way for many people to get their Omega-3 oil, but it's worth noting that combining it with the fat in mayonnaise offsets any positive effects. The most commonly used **saturated fats** are BUTTER, COCONUT OIL, LARD, PLAM OIL, SUET and hydrogenated vegetable oils such as MARGARINE and VEGETABLE SHORTENING. The term **hydrogenated** refers to the process of hardening unsaturated oil into a semisolid. This transforms it into a saturated fat, obliterating any benefits it had as a polyunsaturate. Research has shown that hydrogenated oils may actually be more damaging than regular saturated fats for those limiting cholesterol in their diets. Fats and oils are used in cooking to add richness and flavor to foods, to tenderize baked goods and for frying. Saturated fats such as butter, margarine and lard should be tightly wrapped and refrigerated. They can usually be stored this way for up to 2 weeks. Hydrogenated vegetable shortening can be stored, tightly covered, at room temperature for up to 3 months. Refined oils, sealed airtight, can be stored on the kitchen shelf up to 2 months. Oils with a high proportion of monounsaturates—such as olive oil and peanut oil—are more perishable and should be refrigerated if kept longer than a month. *For information on specific fats and oils, see individual listings.*

fatty acids *see* FATS AND OILS

fava bean [FAH-vuh] This tan, rather flat bean resembles a very large LIMA BEAN. It comes in a large pod which, unless *very* young, is inedible. Fava beans can be purchased dried, cooked in cans and, infrequently, fresh. If you find fresh fava beans, choose those with pods that aren't bulging with beans, which indicates age. Fava beans have a very tough skin, which should be removed by BLANCHING before cooking. They're very popular in Mediterranean and Middle Eastern dishes, can be cooked in a variety of ways and are often used in soups. Also called *faba bean, broad bean* and *horse bean. See also* BEAN.

feijoa [fay-YOH-ah; fay-JOH-ah] This small, egg-shaped fruit is native to South America, though New Zealand is now a major exporter and California cultivates a small crop. It's also referred to as a *pineapple guava*, and is often mislabeled in produce sections as GUAVA. A thin, bright green skin surrounds the feijoa's exceedingly fragrant, cream-colored flesh that encases a jellylike center. The flavor is complex, with sweet notes of quince, pineapple and eucalyptus. New Zealand feijoas are available from spring to early summer; those from California reach the market in the fall. Choose fruit that has a rich, perfumy fragrance and gives slightly to the touch. Ripen by placing it in a paper bag with an apple for several days at room temperature. Ripe feijoas can be refrigerated 3 to 5 days. Before using, remove the slightly bitter peel. Feijoas are naturals in fruit salads, desserts and as garnishes. They contain a fair amount of vitamin C.

feijoada [fay-ZHWAH-duh] Brazil's most famous regional dish, feijoada is an assorted platter of thinly sliced meats (such as sausages, pig's feet and ears, beef and smoked tongue) accompanied by side dishes of rice, black beans, shredded KALE or COLLARD greens, HEARTS OF PALM, orange slices and hot peppers.

fennel [FEHN-uhl] There are two main types of this aromatic plant, both with pale green, celerylike stems and bright green, feathery foliage. **Florence fennel**, also called finocchio, is cultivated throughout the Mediterranean and in the United States. It has a broad, bulbous base that's treated like a vegetable. Both the base and stems can be eaten raw in salads or cooked in a variety of methods such as braising, sautéing, or in soups. The fragrant, graceful greenery can be used as a garnish or snipped like dill and used for a last-minute flavor enhancer. This type of fennel is often mislabeled "sweet anise," causing those who don't like the flavor of licorice to avoid it. The flavor of fennel, however, is sweeter and more delicate than anise and ,when cooked, becomes even lighter and more elusive than in its raw state. **Common fennel** is the variety from which the oval, greenish-brown **fennel seeds** come. The seeds are available whole and ground and are used in both sweet and savory foods, as well as to flavor many LIQUEURS. As with most seeds, they should be stored in a cool, dark place for no more than 6 months. Though common fennel is bulbless, its stems and greenery are used in the same ways as those of Florence fennel. Fennel is available from fall through spring. Choose clean, crisp bulbs with no sign of browning. Any attached greenery should be a fresh green color. Refrigerate, tightly wrapped in a plastic bag, up to 5 days. Fennel is rich in vitamin A and contains a fair amount of calcium, phosphorus and potassium. *See also* Herb and Spice Chart, page 538.

fennel seeds *see* FENNEL

fenugreek [FEHN-yoo-greek] Native to Asia and southern Europe, this aromatic plant is known for its pleasantly bitter, slightly sweet seeds. Its leaves (not generally available in the U.S.) can be used in salads. Fenugreek seeds, which come whole and ground, are used to flavor many foods including curry powders, spice blends and teas. Fenugreek seeds should be stored in a cool, dark place for no more than 6 months.

fermentation A process by which a food goes through a chemical change caused by enzymes produced from bacteria, microorganisms or yeasts. Fermentation alters the appearance and/or flavor of foods and beverages such as beer, buttermilk, cheese, wine, vinegar and yogurt.

fermented black beans Also called *salty black beans*, this Chinese specialty consists of small black soybeans that have been preserved in salt before being packed into cans or plastic bags. They have an extremely pungent, salty flavor and must be soaked in warm water for about 30 minutes before using. Fermented black beans are usually finely chopped before being added to fish or meat dishes as a flavoring. They can be stored, tightly covered, in the refrigerator for up to a year. If the beans begin to dry out, a few drops of peanut oil will refresh them.

feta cheese [FEHT-uh] This classic Greek cheese is traditionally made of sheep's or goat's milk, though today large commercial producers often make it with cow's milk. Because it's cured and stored in its own salty WHEY BRINE (*see both listings*), feta is often referred to as "pickled" cheese. White, crumbly and rindless, feta is usually pressed into square cakes. It has a rich, tangy flavor, contains from 45 to 60 percent butterfat and can range in texture from soft to semidry. Feta makes a zesty addition to salads and many cooked dishes. *See also* CHEESE.

fettuccine; fettuccini [feht-tuh-CHEE-nee] Egg noodles cut into flat, narrow (about ⅜-inch) strips. *See also* PASTA.

fettuccine Alfredo [feht-tuh-CHEE-nee al-FRAY-doh] Roman restaurateur Alfredo di Lello is credited with creating this dish in the 1920s. The FETTUCCINE is enrobed in a rich sauce of butter, grated PARMESAN CHEESE, heavy cream and plentiful grindings of black pepper. Other noodles may be substituted for the fettuccine.

feuilletage [fuh-yuh-TAHZH] French for "flaky" or "puff pastry." Also called pâte feuilletée. *See also* PUFF PASTRY.

fiddlehead fern A young, edible, tightly coiled fern frond that resembles the spiral end of a violin (fiddle). Also referred to as *ostrich fern*. The shoots are in their coiled form for only about 2 weeks before they unfurl into graceful greenery. Fiddlehead ferns are a rich, deep green color and are about 2 inches long and 1½ inches in diameter. They have a flavor akin to an asparagus-green bean cross and a texture that's appealingly chewy. Fiddleheads can be found throughout the eastern half of the United States, ranging from as far south as Virginia north to Canada. They're available in specialty produce markets from April through July, depending on the region. Choose small, firm, brightly colored ferns with no sign of softness or yellowing. Refrigerate, tightly wrapped, for no more than 2 days. Fiddleheads should be washed and the ends trimmed before being briefly cooked by steaming, simmering or sautéing. They may be served cooked as a first course or side dish or used raw in salads. Fiddlehead ferns are a good source of vitamins A and C.

fideos [fih-DAY-ohs] Very thin, VERMICELLI-type noodles. In Spain, they're often tossed with vegetables; in Mexico, they're used to make one version of SOPA SECA (dry soup).

field pea A variety of yellow or green pea grown specifically for drying. These peas are dried and usually split along a natural seam, in which case they're called *split peas*. Whole and split dried field peas are available packaged in supermarkets and in bulk in health-food stores. Field peas do not usually require presoaking before cooking. *See also* PEA; LEGUME.

field salad *see* CORN SALAD

fig Originally hailing from southern Europe, Asia and Africa, figs were thought to be sacred by the ancients; they were also an early symbol of peace and prosperity. Figs were brought to North America by the Spanish Franciscan missionaries who came to set up Catholic missions in southern California . . . hence the now-popular *Mission* fig. There are hundreds of varieties of figs, all having in common a soft flesh with a plenitude of tiny edible seeds. They range in color from purple-black to almost white and in shape from round to oval. The most well-known varieties today include the green-skinned, white-fleshed **Adriatic;** the pear-shaped, violet- to brown-skinned **Brown Turkey;** the large, squat white-fleshed, green-skinned **Calimyrna** (when grown in California) or **Smyrna** (when from Turkey); the **Celeste,** medium and pear-shaped, with a purple skin and pinkish pulp; the **Kadota,** a small, thick-skinned, yellow-green fruit; the **Magnolia** (also called *Brunswick*), large, with a pinkish-yellow flesh and amber skin; and the purple-black **Mission** (or **Black Mission**), with its extremely small seeds. Fresh figs are available from June through October. They're extremely perishable and should be used soon after they're purchased. Figs may be stored in the refrigerator for 2 to 3 days. They're also sold candied, dried or canned in sugar syrup or water. All figs are a good source of iron, calcium and phosphorus.

figaro sauce [FIHG-uh-roh] Tomato puree and minced parsley are added to HOLLANDAISE SAUCE for this rich accompaniment to fish or poultry.

filbert *see* HAZELNUT

filé powder [fih-LAY; FEE-lay] Choctaw Indians from the Louisiana bayou country are said to have been the first users of this seasoning made from the ground, dried leaves of the sassafras tree. It's since become an integral part of CREOLE COOKING and is used to thicken and flavor GUMBOS and other Creole dishes. Filé has a woodsy flavor reminiscent of root beer. It must be stirred into a dish after it's removed from the heat because undue cooking makes filé tough and stringy. Filé powder is available in the spice or gourmet section of most large supermarkets. As with all spices, it should be stored in a cool, dark place for no more than 6 months.

filet mignon [fih-LAY mihn-YON] This expensive, boneless cut of beef comes from the small end of the tenderloin. The filet mignon is usually 1 to 2 inches thick and 1½ to 3 inches in diameter. It's extremely tender but lacks the flavor of beef with the bone attached. Cook filet mignon quickly by broiling, grilling or sautéing. *See also* BEEF; SHORT LOIN.

fillet *n*. [fih-LAY; FILL-iht] A boneless piece of meat or fish. *Filet* is the French spelling. **fillet** *v*. To cut the bones from a piece of meat or fish, thereby creating a meat or fish fillet.

filo *see* PHYLLO

filter To strain through a paper filter or several layers of CHEESECLOTH.

fines herbes [FEEN erb; FEENZ airb] A mixture of very finely chopped herbs. The classic quartet is chervil, chives, parsley and tarragon, though burnet, marjoram, savory or watercress are often used as part of the blend. Because they quickly lose their flavor, fines herbes should be added to a cooked mixture shortly before serving. Unlike BOUQUET GARNI, they're not removed from the dish before serving. *For information on specific herbs used in this blend, see individual listings.*

fining [FYN-ing] A term usually referring to the process of removing minute floating particles that prevent wines and beers from being clear (*see* CLARIFY). Besides egg whites and eggshells, other substances used to fine these liquids include GELATIN, ISINGLASS and diatomaceous earth.

finnan haddie; finnan haddock [FIHN-uhn HAD-ee] Named after Findon, Scotland, a fishing village near Aberdeen, finnan haddie is partially boned, lightly salted and smoked HADDOCK. It was originally smoked over peat fires, a rarity now in wide commercial production. In the British Isles, finnan haddie has long been a favorite breakfast dish. Though once exclusively from Scotland, it's now being produced in New England and other eastern coastal states. It's available whole or in fillets and can be refrigerated, tightly wrapped, for up to a month. Finnan haddie is best baked, broiled or poached. It's generally served with a cream sauce. *See also* FISH.

fino [FEE-noh] This pale, delicate, very dry Spanish wine is considered by many to be the world's finest SHERRY. Finos are excellent when young, but also have the distinction of aging well. They are often served chilled as an APÉRITIF.

finocchio [fih-NOH-kee-oh] *see* FENNEL

firm-ball stage A test for SUGAR SYRUP describing the point at which a drop of boiling syrup immersed in cold water forms a firm but pliable ball. On a CANDY THERMOMETER, the firm-ball stage is between 244° and 248°F. *See* Candy-making Temperatures and Cold Water Tests Chart, page 537.

fish All fish are broken down into two very broad categories—fish and shellfish. In the most basic terms, **fish** are equipped with fins, backbones and gills, while **shellfish** have shells of one form or another. (*For details on* SHELLFISH, *see that listing*.) Fish without shells are separated into two groups—freshwater fish and saltwater fish. Because salt water provides more buoyancy than fresh water, **saltwater fish**—such as COD FLOUNDER and TUNA—can afford to have thicker bones. **Freshwater fish**—like CATFISH, PERCH and TROUT—can't be weighted with a heavy skeletal framework. Instead, their structure is based on hundreds of minuscule bones, a source of frustration to many diners. Additionally, fish are separated into two more categories: FLATFISH and ROUNDFISH. **Flatfish**, which swim horizontally along the bottom of the sea, are shaped like an oval platter, the top side being dark and the bottom white. Both eyes are on the side of the body facing upward. **Roundfish** have a rounder body, with eyes on both sides of the head. Further, fish are divided into three categories based on their fat content—lean, moderate-fat and high-fat. The oil in **lean fish** is concentrated in the liver, rather than being distributed through the flesh. Their fat content is less than 2½ percent and the flesh is mild and lightly colored. Fish in the lean category include BLACK SEA BASS, brook TROUT, COD, CROAKER, FLOUNDER, HADDOCK, HAKE, HALIBUT, POLLACK, OCEAN PERCH, RED SNAPPER, ROCKFISH, SMELTS, STURGEON, and TILEFISH. **Moderate-fat fish** usually have less than 6 percent fat and include BARRACUDA, BLUEFISH, STRIPED BASS, SWORDFISH, TUNA and WHITING. The fat content of **high-fat fish** can reach as high as 30 percent (as with EEL), but the average is closer to 12 percent. Some of the more popular high-fat fish are Atlantic HERRING, BUTTERFISH, MACKEREL, rainbow TROUT, SALMON, SHAD and YELLOWTAIL. The wider distribution of fat in moderate- and high-fat fish gives their flesh a darker color, firmer texture and more distinctive flavor. When buying fresh, whole fish, look for the following characteristics: bright, clear, full eyes (cloudy or sunken eyes denote stale fish); shiny, brightly colored skin; a fresh, mild odor; firm flesh that clings tightly to the bones and springs back when pressed with your finger; and red to bright pink gills, free from any slime or residue. Whole fish comes either ungutted or DRAWN, meaning its entrails and sometimes its gills have been removed. A fish that has been DRESSED has, in addition to being drawn, had the scales removed. *Whole-dressed* usually refers to the whole fish; *pan-dressed* to a fish with head, tail and fins removed. **Fish fillets and steaks** should have a fresh odor, firm texture and moist appearance. Fillets are a boneless, lengthwise cut from the sides of a fish. They are usually single pieces, though *butterfly fillets* (both sides of the fish connected by the uncut strip of skin on the belly) are also available. Fish steaks are cross-section cuts from large, dressed fish. They're usually ⅝ to 1 inch thick and contain a small section of the backbone. Fresh fish should immediately be refrigerated, tightly wrapped, and used within a day—2 days at most. Never store ungutted fish, as the entrails decay much more rapidly than the flesh. When purchasing **raw frozen fish,** make sure it's solidly frozen. It should be tightly wrapped in an undamaged, moisture- and vaporproof material and should have no odor. Any white, dark, icy or dry spots indicate damage through drying or deterioration. Avoid fish that is suspected of having been thawed and refrozen, a process that reduces the overall quality of both texture and flavor. Frozen fish should be stored in a moisture- and vaporproof wrapping in the freezer for up to 6 months. Thaw in the refrigerator 24 hours (for a 1-pound package) before cooking. Quick-thawing can be accomplished by placing the wrapped, frozen fish in cold water, allowing 1 hour to thaw a 1-pound package. Never refreeze fish. **Canned fish**, such as tuna, salmon and sardines, will generally keep for about a year stored at 65°F or less. However, since the consumer doesn't know under what conditions canned goods have been stored in warehouses, the best idea is to buy only what will be used within a few months. Fish are an excellent source of protein, B complex vitamins and minerals including calcium, iron, potassium and phosporus. Both saltwater and freshwater fish are low in sodium content and, compared to meat, also low in calories. *For information on specific fish, see individual listings.*

fish and chips A traditional British dish of deep-fried fish FILLETS and FRENCH FRIES, most often served with malt VINEGAR.

five-spice powder Used extensively in CHINESE COOKING, this pungent mixture of five ground spices usually consists of equal parts of cinnamon, cloves, fennel seed, star anise and szechuan peppercorns. Prepackaged five-spice powder is available in oriental markets and many supermarkets. *For information on specific spices used in this blend, see individual listings.*

fizz Gin fizz is the most popular of this genre of drinks made with liquor, lemon juice, sugar and soda, and served over ice. An egg white is added to some fizzes, in which case a gin fizz becomes a **silver fizz**.

flageolet [fla-zhoh-LAY] These tiny, tender French kidney beans range in color from pale green to creamy white. They're rarely available fresh in the United States but can be purchased dried, canned and occasionally frozen. Flageolets are usually prepared simply in order to showcase their delicate flavor. They're a classic accompaniment to lamb. *See also* BEANS.

flaky *adj.* A term describing a food, such as pie crust, with a dry texture that easily breaks off into flat, flakelike pieces. **flake** *v.* The verb form of this term refers to using a utensil (usually a fork) to break off small pieces or layers of food.

flamande, á la [flah-MAHND] *Á la flamande* is French for "in the Flemish style," indicating a garnish of braised cabbage, carrots, turnips, potatoes and sometimes pork or sausages. It's a classic accompaniment for meat or poultry.

flambé [flahm-BAY] French for "flamed" or "flaming," this dramatic method of food presentation consists of sprinkling certain foods with liquor which, after warming, is ignited with a match just before serving.

flamed The American word for FLAMBÉ.

Flame Tokay grape *see* TOKAY GRAPE

flan [FLAHN] 1. A round pastry tart that can have a sweet filling (such as CUSTARD or fruit) or savory filling (vegetable, meat or savory custard). The pastry is usually formed and baked in a special **flan ring**, a bottomless metal ring with straight (about 1½-inch-high) sides. The flan ring is set on a baking sheet before the dough is baked. 2. A famous Spanish baked custard coated with caramel. *See also* CRÈME CARAMEL.

flank steak Long, thin and fibrous, this boneless cut of beef comes from the animal's lower hindquarters. It's usually tenderized by marinating, then broiled or grilled whole. In the case of *London broil*, the flank steak is cut and cooked in large pieces, then thinly sliced across the grain. *See also* BEEF; Beef Chart, page 573.

flapjack *see* PANCAKE

flat bread; flatbread; flatbrod These traditional Scandinavian crisps are thin, crackerlike breads usually made with rye flour. Many are also based on combinations of flours including wheat, barley or potato. Flat breads (*flatbrod* in Norwegian) are most often served with soups, salads or cheeses.

flatfish A species of fish (including FLOUNDER, HALIBUT and SOLE) characterized by a rather flat body, with both eyes located on the upper side. Flatfish swim on one side only; the side facing downwards is always very pale. *For information on specific flatfish, see individual listings. See also* FISH.

flauta [FLAUW-tah] Meaning "flute," a flauta is a corn TORTILLA rolled around a savory (usually shredded meat or poultry) filling, then fried until crisp.

flavoring extracts *see* EXTRACTS

fleuron [FLUR-awn; FLOOR-ahn] A tiny, crescent-shaped piece of puff pastry used as a garnish, usually atop hot food.

flinty [FLIHN-tee] A wine-tasting term describing a slightly metallic taste and bouquet characteristic of certain dry, white wines from grapes grown in particular soils. SAUVIGNON BLANC is one wine often associated with the "flinty" quality.

flip A cold drink made with liquor or wine mixed with sugar and egg, then shaken or blended until frothy. Early flips made in England and Colonial America were warmed by plunging a red-hot poker into the brew just before serving.

floating islands 1. A light dessert of stiffly beaten, sweetened egg white mounds that have been poached in milk. These puffs are then floated in a thin CUSTARD sauce. The dessert is also known as *oeufs à la neige*, "snow eggs." 2. In France, *île flottante* ("floating island") is LIQUEUR-sprinkled spongecake spread with jam, sprinkled with nuts, topped with whipped cream and surrounded by a pool of custard.

florentine [FLOHR-uhn-teen; FLAWR-uhn-teen] Though Austrian bakers are credited with inventing these cookies, their name implies an Italian heritage. They're a mixture of butter, sugar, cream, honey, candied fruit (and sometimes nuts) that is cooked in a saucepan before being dropped into mounds on a cookie sheet and baked. The chewy, candylike florentines often have a chocolate coating on one side.

Florentine, à la Meaning "in the style of Florence (Italy)," and referring to dishes (usually of eggs or fish) that are presented on a bed of spinach and topped with MORNAY SAUCE. A "Florentine" dish is sometimes sprinkled with cheese and browned lightly in the oven.

flounder Members of this large species of FLATFISH are prized for their fine texture and delicate flavor. Some of the better known members of the flounder family are DAB, ENGLISH SOLE and PLAICE. In America, flounder is often mislabeled as *fillet of sole*— a misnomer because all of the fish called "sole" (except for imported European DOVER SOLE) are actually varieties of flounder. Flounder is available whole or in fillets. It can be baked, broiled, poached, steamed or sautéed. *See also* FISH.

flour *n.* The finely ground and sifted meal of any of various edible grains. Giant steel or stone rollers are used to break and grind the grain. Most supermarkets carry **steel-ground flour**, meaning it's crushed with huge, high-speed steel rollers or hammers. The heat that is generated with these high-velocity machines strips away the WHEAT GERM and destroys valuable vitamins and enzymes. The more naturally nutritious **stone-ground flour** is produced by grinding the grain between two slowly-moving stones. This process crushes the grain without generating excess heat and separating the germ. Stone-ground flours must usually be purchased in health-food stores, though some large supermarkets also carry them. A flour can range in texture from coarse to extremely soft and powdery, depending on the degree of bolting (sifting) it receives at the mill. Wheat is the most common source of the multitude of flours used in cooking. It contains gluten, a protein which forms an elastic network that helps contain the gases that make mixtures (such as doughs and batters) rise as they bake. **All-purpose flour** is made from a blend of high-gluten hard wheat and low-gluten soft wheat. It's a fine-textured flour milled from the inner part of the wheat kernel and contains neither the **germ** (the sprouting part) nor the **bran** (the outer coating). U.S. law requires that all flours not containing wheat germ must have niacin, riboflavin, thiamin and iron added. (Individual millers sometimes also add vitamins A and D.) These flours are labeled "ENRICHED." All-purpose flour comes in two basic forms—**bleached** and **unbleached**—that can be used interchangeably. Flour can be bleached either naturally, as it ages, or chemically. Most flour on the market today is presifted, requiring only that it be stirred, then spooned into a measuring cup and leveled off. **Bread flour** is a specially formulated, high-gluten blend of 99.8 percent hard-wheat flour, a small amount of malted barley flour (to improve yeast activity) and vitamin C or potassium bromate (to increase the gluten's elasticity and the dough's gas retention). Bread flour, available bleached and unbleached, is ideally suited for YEAST BREADS. The fuller-flavored **whole-wheat flour** contains the wheat germ, which means that it also has a higher fiber, nutritional and fat content. Because of the latter, it should be stored in the refrigerator to prevent rancidity. **Cake or pastry flour** is a fine-textured, soft-wheat flour with a high starch content. It makes particularly tender cakes and pastries. **Self-rising flour** is an all-purpose flour to which baking powder and salt have been added. It can be substituted for all-purpose flour in yeast breads by omitting the salt and in QUICK BREADS by omitting both baking powder and salt. **Instant flour** is a granular flour especially formulated to dissolve quickly in hot or cold liquids. It's used mainly as a thickener in sauces, gravies and other cooked mixtures. **Gluten flour** is high-protein, hard-wheat flour treated to remove most of the starch (which leaves a high gluten content). It's used mainly as an additive to doughs made with low-gluten flour (such as RYE FLOUR), and to make low-calorie "gluten" breads. All flour should be stored in an airtight container. All-purpose and bread flour can be stored up to 6 months at room temperature (about 70°F). Temperatures higher than that invite bugs and mold. Flours containing part of the grain's germ (such as whole wheat) turn rancid quickly because of the oil in the germ. Refrigerate or freeze these flours tightly wrapped and use as soon as possible. Other grains—such as BARLEY, BUCKWHEAT, CORN, OATS, RICE, RYE and TRITICALE—are also milled into flours. **flour** *v.* To lightly coat a food, utensil or baking container with flour. Flouring food to be fried facilitates browning, and coating foods that tend to stick together (such as chopped dried apricots) helps separate the pieces. Flouring a pie, pastry or cookie dough will prevent it from sticking to a work surface; flouring your hands, rolling pin or work surface prevents dough from sticking. Dusting greased baking pans with flour provides for easy removal of cakes, breads and other baked goods.

flowers, crystallized *see* CRYSTALLIZED FLOWERS

flowers, edible Flowers that are used as a garnish or as an integral part of a dish, such as a salad. Not all flowers are edible. Those that are must usually be purchased from specialty produce markets or supermarkets that carry gourmet produce. They can be stored, tightly wrapped, in the refrigerator up to a week. Flowers that have been sprayed with pesticides (such as those found at florists') should never be eaten. Some of the more popular edible flowers are: the peppery-flavored **nasturtiums**; **chive blossoms**, which taste like a mild, sweet onion; **pansies** and **violas**, both with a flavor reminiscent of grapes; and perfumy, sweet **roses**. Other edible flowers include: **almond, apple, borage, chamomile, lavender, lemon, lovage, mimosa, orange, peach, plum** and **squash blossoms, chrysanthemums, daisies, geraniums, jasmine, lilacs, marigolds,**

and **violets.** Edible flowers may be used culinarily in a variety of ways. They make colorful, striking garnishes for drinks as well as food—for everything from salads to soups to desserts. Some of the larger flowers such as squash blossoms can be stuffed and deep-fried.

flummery [FLUHM-muh-ree] A sweet soft pudding made of stewed fruit (usually berries) thickened with CORNSTARCH. British flummeries are usually made by cooking oatmeal until smooth and gelatinous. A sweetener and milk are sometimes added.

flute [FLOOT] 1. To press a decorative pattern into the raised edge of a pie crust (*See also* CRIMP). 2. To carve slashes, grooves and other decorative markings in vegetables (such as mushrooms) and fruits. 3. A thin, lightly sweet, flute-shaped cookie served with ice cream, pudding, etc. 4. A stemmed champagne glass with a tall, slender, cone-shaped bowl.

focaccia [foh-CAH-chee-ah] This Italian bread begins by being shaped into a large, flat round that is liberally brushed or drizzled with olive oil and sprinkled with salt. Slits cut into the dough's surface may be stuffed with fresh ROSEMARY before the bread is baked. Focaccia can be eaten as a snack, or served as an accompaniment to soups or salads.

foie gras [FWAH GRAH] Although the literal translation from French is "fat liver," *foie gras* is the term generally used for *goose liver*. This specialty of Alsace and Perigord, is in fact, the enlarged liver from a goose or duck that has been force-fed and fattened over a period of 4 to 5 months. These specially bred fowl are not permitted to exercise—which, combined with the overeating, creates a huge (up to 3 pounds), fatty liver. After the bird is killed, the liver is soaked overnight in milk, water or port. It's drained, then marinated in a mixture usually consisting of ARMAGNAC, PORT or MADEIRA and various seasonings. The livers are then cooked, usually by baking. The preparation, of course, depends on the cook. In general, goose liver is considered superior to duck liver; all foie gras is very expensive. At its best, it is a delicate rosy color with mottlings of beige. The flavor is extraordinarily rich and the texture silky smooth. **Pâté de foie gras** is pureed goose liver (by law, 80 percent) that usually contains other foods such as pork liver, TRUFFLES and eggs. **Mousse** or **purée de foie gras** must contain at least 55 percent goose liver. Foie gras should be served chilled with thin, buttered toast slices. A SAUTERNES is the perfect accompaniment.

fold A technique used to gently combine a light, airy mixture (such as beaten egg whites) with a heavier mixture (such as whipped cream or custard). The lighter mixture is placed on top of the heavier one in a large bowl. Starting at the back of the bowl, a rubber spatula is used to cut down vertically through the two mixtures, across the bottom of the bowl and up the nearest side. The bowl is rotated a quarter turn with each series of strokes. This down-across-up-and-over motion gently turns the mixtures over on top of each other, combining them in the process.

fondant [FAHN-duhnt] Used as both candy and icing, fondant is a simple sugar-water-CREAM OF TARTAR mixture cooked to the SOFT-BALL STAGE. After cooling, the mixture is beaten and kneaded until extremely pliable. It can be formed into decorations or candy, which can be dipped in chocolate. Heating fondant makes it soft enough to be used as an icing to coat large and small cakes. FOOD COLORING and a variety of flavorings can be added to fondant for visual and taste appeal. It can be refrigerated, tightly wrapped, for up to 3 months.

fondue [fahn-DOO] From *fondre*, the French word for "melt," the term "fondue" has several meanings. The first three definitions pertain to food cooked in a central pot at the table. 1. **Fondue au fromage** is a classic dish of Swiss heritage consisting of cheese (usually EMMENTALER and GRUYÈRE) melted and combined with white wine, KIRSCH and seasonings. Bite-size chunks of French bread are dipped into the hot, savory mixture. 2. **Fondue bourguignonne** is a variation whereby cubes of raw beef are cooked in a pot of hot oil, then dipped into various savory sauces. 3. Another version is **chocolate fondue**, a combination of melted chocolate, cream and sometimes LIQUEUR into which fruit or cake may be dipped. 4. In French cooking, the term "fondue" refers to finely chopped vegetables that have been reduced to a pulp by lengthy and slow cooking. This mixture is often used as a garnish, usually with meats or fish.

fontina cheese [fahn-TEE-nah] Also called *Fontina Val d'Aosta* after the Italian valley from which it comes, this is one of Italy's great cheeses. Semifirm yet creamy, fontina is a cow's-milk cheese with about 45 percent butterfat. It has a dark golden brown rind with a pale yellow interior dotted with tiny holes. The mild, nutty flavor, and the fact that it melts easily and smoothly, make fontina perfect for almost any use. Besides Italy, fontinas are made in other countries including Denmark, France and the United States. Many of these fontinas, especially when young, tend to be blander and softer than the Italian original. *See also* CHEESE.

food additives *see* ADDITIVES

food coloring Dyes of various colors (most commonly blue, green, red and yellow) used to tint foods such as frostings and candies. The most familiar form of food coloring is liquid, which comes in little bottles available at any supermarket. **Food coloring paste**, which comes in a wider variety of colors, can usually only be found in specialty stores such as cake-decorating shops. It's particularly suitable for mixtures that do not combine readily with liquid, such as WHITE CHOCOLATE. A little of any food coloring goes a long way, so it's best to begin with only a drop or two, blending it into the mixture being tinted before adding more.

food mill A kitchen utensil that can be best described as a mechanical SIEVE. It has a hand-turned paddle that forces food through a strainer plate at the bottom, thereby removing skin, seeds and fiber. Some food mills come equipped with several interchangeable plates with small, medium and large holes.

food processor This kitchen appliance was brought to the U.S. from France in the 1970s and has since revolutionized a majority of home kitchens. It consists of a sturdy plastic work bowl that sits on a motorized drive-shaft. The cover of the bowl has a feed tube through which foods can be added. An expanded feed tube—large enough for some whole items such as a tomato or onion—is available with some machines. The food processor is efficient and speedy and can easily chop, dice, slice, shred, grind and puree most food. Many of the larger machines can also knead dough. Most processors come with a standard set of attachments including an S-shaped chopping blade and several discs for slicing and shredding. There are special attachments including juicers and pasta makers, as well as accessories such as French-fry cutters and julienne discs. Food processors range from large to small in motor size and bowl capacity.

fool England is the home of this old-fashioned but delicious dessert made of cooked, pureed fruit that is strained, chilled and folded into whipped cream. The fruit mixture may be sweetened or not. Fool is traditionally made from gooseberries, though today any fruit may be substituted.

foo yong *see* EGGFOOYONG

forcemeat A mixture of finely ground, raw or cooked meat, poultry, fish, vegetables or fruit mixed with breadcrumbs and various seasonings. The ingredients are usually ground several times to obtain a very smooth texture. A forcemeat can be used to stuff other foods or by itself, such as to make QUENELLES.

formaggio [for-MAH-jhee-oh; for-MAH-zhoh] The Italian word for "cheese."

fortified wine A wine to which BRANDY (or other spirit) has been added in order to increase alcoholic content. Such wines include PORT, SHERRY and many DESSERTWINES.

fortune cookie This Chinese-American invention consists of a plain, griddle-baked wafer cookie which, while warm, is folded around a small strip of paper with a fortune printed on it. The cooled cookie becomes crisp and must be broken in order to retrieve the fortune.

fouet [foo-AY] French for "WHISK."

fowl The term fowl is used generally to refer to any edible, mature, wild or domestic bird. Specifically, a fowl (also called *hen* or *stewing chicken*) is a female chicken over 10 months old and usually weighing 3 to 6 pounds. Because of its age, a fowl is best when cooked with moist heat, as in braising.

fraise [FREHZ] The French word for "strawberry."

fraise des bois [frehz day BWAH] 1. Intensely sweet, tiny wild strawberries from France. 2. A colorless, strawberry-flavored EAU DE VIE.

framboise [frahm-BWAHZ] 1. The French word for "raspberry." 2. A colorless, potent EAU DE VIE made from raspberries.

frangipane [FRAM-juh-payn] 1. A type of pastry made with egg yolks, flour, butter and milk that is very similar to CHOUX PASTRY. Baked frangipane puffs are often filled with FORCEMEAT. 2. A rich CRÈME PÂTISSIÈRE flavored with ground almonds and used as a filling or topping for various pastries and cakes. Also called *frangipani*.

frankfurter This smoked, seasoned, precooked sausage—also known as *hot dog, wiener* and *frank*—is America's favorite. Frankfurters can be made from beef, pork, veal, chicken or turkey. They may have casings or not and can contain up to 30 percent fat and 10 percent added water. They range in size from the tiny "cocktail frank" to the famous foot-long giants. The most common size is about 6 inches long. Frankfurters labeled **"beef"** or **"all-beef"** must, by law, contain only beef; fillers like soybean protein and dry milk solids are forbidden. **Kosher** frankfurters are all-beef sausages, usually liberally seasoned with garlic. Those labeled **"meat"** can't contain fillers either, but can be made with a combination of pork and beef. A typical proportion would be 40 percent pork to 60 percent beef. Sausages simply labeled **"frankfurters"** can contain up to 3½ percent fillers and are usually made from a combination of meats. Almost all frankfurters contain sodium nitrate and sodium nitrite, chemical salts that are reported to be carcinogenic. To store frankfurters, refrigerate in original package up until the manufacturer's pull date. Although precooked, frankfurters benefit from heating and may be prepared in a variety of ways including grilling, frying, steaming and braising. *See also* SAUSAGE.

frappé [fra-PAY] 1. A mixture made of fruit juice or other flavored liquid that has been frozen to a slushy consistency. It can be sweet or savory and served as a drink, appetizer or dessert. 2. An after-dinner drink of LIQUEUR poured over shaved or crushed ice.

free-range chicken *see* CHICKEN

freestone A term used to describe fruit that has a pit to which the flesh does not cling, as in a *freestone peach*. *See also* CLINGSTONE.

freezer burn Frozen food that has been either improperly wrapped or frozen can suffer from freezer burn—a loss of moisture that affects both texture and flavor. Freezer burn is indicated by a dry surface, which may also have white or gray spots on it.

French bean Any young, green string bean, all of which (including the pod) can be eaten. **Frenched** or **French green beans** are those that have been cut lengthwise into very thin strips. *See also* BEANS.

French bread A light, crusty, yeast-raised bread made with water instead of milk. The dark brown, intensely crisp crust is created by brushing or spraying the loaf's exterior with water during the baking process. French bread comes in many shapes, including the classic long, thin BAGUETTE, rounds and fat ovals.

French Colombard One of California's top two white-wine grapes, French Colombard is used extensively in blending as well as for a VARIETAL WINE. It produces a crisp, moderately dry, spicy wine that goes well with lightly seasoned dishes. It should be drunk young (under 4 years) and always served chilled.

French dressing 1. A simple oil-and-vinegar combination, usually seasoned with salt, pepper and various herbs. This classic dressing is also referred to as VINAIGRETTE. 2. A commercial American dressing that is creamy, tartly sweet and red-orange in color.

French endive *see* ENDIVE

French fries Potatoes that have been cut into thick to thin strips, soaked in cold water, blotted dry, then DEEP-FRIED until crisp and golden brown. They are called *pommes frites* in France and *chips* in Britain. The name does not come from the fact that their origin is French, but because the potatoes are "Frenched"—cut into lengthwise strips. Other versions of French-fried potatoes are *shoestring potatoes* (matchstick-wide) and *steak fries* (very thick strips).

French fry *see* DEEP-FRY

French 75 Named after the powerful French 75-millimeter howitzer cannon, this potent COCKTAIL is made by combining gin or brandy, lemon juice and cracked ice in a glass and filling it with champagne.

French toast A breakfast dish made by dipping bread into a milk-egg mixture, then frying it until golden brown on both sides. It's usually served with syrup, jam or powdered sugar. In England, French toast is called "poor knights of Windsor." The French call it "*pain perdu*" (lost bread) because it is a way of reviving French bread, which becomes dry after only a day or two.

Fresno chili pepper [FREHS-noh] Short and cone-shaped, the Fresno is as hot as the more well-known JALAPEÑO CHILI PEPPER. It ranges in color from light green to bright red when fully mature. Because of its heat, the Fresno is best used in small amounts as a seasoning. *See also* CHILI PEPPER.

fricassee [FRIHK-uh-see; frihk-uh-SEE] A dish of meat (usually chicken) that has been sautéed in butter before being stewed with vegetables. The end result is a thick, chunky stew, often flavored with wine.

fried rice An oriental dish of rice that has been cooked and refrigerated for a day before being fried with other ingredients, such as small pieces of meat and vegetables, and seasonings such as SOY SAUCE. An egg is also often added to the mix. The name of the rice depends on the main ingredient (besides rice), such as "chicken" fried rice, "shrimp" fried rice, etc.

frijoles [free-HOH-lehs] The Mexican word for "beans."

frijoles refritos [free-HOH-lehs reh-FREE-tohs] *see* REFRIED BEANS

frill A decorative, fluted paper "sock" that is slipped over a protruding meat bone, such as in a CROWN ROAST.

frittata [frih-TAH-tuh] An Italian OMELET that usually has the ingredients mixed with the eggs rather than being folded inside, as with a French omelet. It can be flipped or the top can be finished under a broiling unit. An omelet is cooked quickly over moderately high heat and, after folding, has a flat-sided oval shape. A frittata is firmer because it's cooked very slowly over low heat, and round because it isn't folded.

fritter A small, sweet or savory, deep-fried cake made either by combining chopped food with a thick batter or by dipping pieces of food into a similar batter. Some of the more popular foods used for fritters are apples, corn and crab.

fritto misto [FREE-toh MEES-toh] Italian for "mixed fried (food)" or "mixed fry," fritto misto is a selection of small, bite-size pieces of meat, fish or vegetables, dipped in a batter and deep-fried.

frizzes [FRIHZ-ihs] A dry Italian pork or beef SALAMI flavored with garlic and anise. Its name comes from its squiggly, contorted shape. The hot style is corded with red string and the mild (or "sweet") is corded with blue string. Frizzes are most often used as a garnish, as on pizza or in pasta. *See also* SAUSAGE.

frizzle To fry thinly sliced meat (such as bacon) over high heat until crisp and slightly curly in shape.

frogfish *see* ANGLER

frogs' legs The only edible part of a frog is its hind legs. The delicate meat is tender and lightly sweet and can be most closely compared to the white meat of a very young chicken. Fresh frogs' legs can be found from spring through summer in the fish section of many gourmet markets. They're usually sold in connected pairs ranging from 2 to 8 ounces. Look for those that are plump and slightly pink. Store, loosely wrapped, in the refrigerator for up to 2 days. Frozen frogs' legs can usually be purchased year-round, though the flavor doesn't compare to fresh. Thaw in the refrigerator overnight before cooking. Because their flavor is so subtle, frogs' legs should be cooked simply and briefly. A quick dusting of seasoned flour before sautéing in butter or olive oil will gild the lily perfectly. Overcooking frogs' legs will cause them to toughen.

froid [FRWAH] The French word for "cold" or "chilled."

fromage [froh-MAHZH] French for "cheese."

fromage blanc [froh-MAHZH BLAHN; froh-MAHZH BLAHNGK] An extremely soft, fresh cream cheese that has the consistency of sour cream. Fromage blanc is usually eaten with fruit and sugar as dessert, but can also be used in cooking. *See also* CHEESE.

frost 1. In cooking, frost means to cover and decorate a cake with a FROSTING or icing. 2. To chill a glass in the freezer until it's frosted with a thin coating of ice crystals.

frosting Also called *icing*, this sweet, sugar-based mixture is used to fill and coat cakes, pastries, cookies, etc. In addition to sugar, frosting can contain a combination of other ingredients including butter, milk, water, eggs and various flavorings. It can be cooked (as with BOILED ICING) or uncooked (as with BUTTERCREAM), and can range from thick to thin. The main requirement for frosting is that it be thick enough to adhere to the item being coated, yet soft enough to spread easily.

frothy A descriptive cooking term referring to mixtures that are foamy, having a formation of tiny, light bubbles.

frozen daiquiri *see* DAIQUIRI

frozen yogurt *see* YOGURT

fructose [FRUHK-tohs; FROOK-tohs] Also called *fruit sugar* and *levulose*, this extremely sweet substance is a natural byproduct of fruits and honey. It's more water-soluble than GLUCOSE and sweeter than SUCROSE (though it contains half the calories). Unlike glucose, it can be used by diabetics. Fructose comes in granulated and syrup forms. Except in the case of some liquids, such as a sauce or beverage, it should not be substituted for regular sugar (sucrose) unless a recipe gives specific substitution. When heated, fructose loses some of its sweetening power.

fruit butter A sweet spread for bread made by stewing fresh fruit with sugar and spices until it becomes thick and smooth. *See* APPLE BUTTER.

fruitcake Traditional winter holiday cakes made with an assortment of CANDIED FRUIT and fruit rind, nuts, spices and usually liquor or BRANDY. Fruitcakes can have a moderate amount of cake surrounding the chunky ingredients, or only enough to hold the fruits and nuts together. **Dark fruitcakes** are generally made with molasses or brown sugar and dark liquor such as bourbon. Dark-colored fruits and nuts, such as prunes, dates, raisins and walnuts, may also contribute to the blend. **Light fruitcakes** are generally made with granulated sugar or light corn syrup and light ingredients such as almonds, dried apricots, golden raisins, etc. Fruitcakes are baked slowly and, after cooling, usually covered in CHEESECLOTH moistened with liquor or brandy and tightly wrapped in foil. Stored in this manner, they have tremendous staying power and, providing they are occasionally remoistened, can be kept for years.

fruit cocktail A mixture of various chopped fruits, served chilled as an appetizer. Any combination of fruit can be used, though a mixture of tart fruit (such as oranges and pineapples) and sweet fruit (peaches, melons or berries) is most appealing. The fruit may be spiced or drizzled with CHAMPAGNE or LIQUEUR for added flavor. Canned fruit cocktail is available, although the flavors of the individual fruits are barely discernible.

fruit leather Pureed fruit that is spread in a thin layer and dried. The puree sometimes has sugar or honey added to it. After drying, the sheet of fruit is often cut into strips or rolled into cylinders for easy snacking. Rolls of fruit leather in a variety of flavors are available in health-food stores and most supermarkets. It can also be made at home.

fruits de mer [frwee duh MAIR] The French term translating as "fruits of the sea," referring to a combination of seafood.

fruit soup A Scandinavian specialty of cooked, pureed fruit combined with water, wine, milk or cream, spices and other flavorings. Danish apple soup is made, for example, with apples, cloves, lemon juice, wine, cream, sugar and curry powder. Though sugar is added to most fruit soups, they are not generally overly sweet. They may be served hot or cold.

fruit sugar *see* FRUCTOSE

fry 1. To cook food in hot fat over moderate to high heat. DEEP-FRIED food is submerged in hot, liquid fat. Frying (also called *pan frying*) or SAUTÉING refers to cooking food in a lesser amount of fat, which doesn't cover the food. There is little difference in these two terms, though sautéing is often thought of as using less fat and being the faster of the two methods. 2. The term also describes a special (usually outdoor) occasion at which fried foods are served, such as a *fish fry*.

fry bread This specialty of many Southwest Indians (mainly Navajo and Hopi) is made of flour, water or milk and salt. It's formed into very thin rounds, deep-fried and served hot. It can be eaten with savory foods or drizzled with honey and enjoyed as a sweet.

frying pan Also called a *skillet*, this long-handled , usually round pan has low, gently sloping sides so steam doesn't collect within the pan. It's used for frying foods over high heat, so it should be thick enough not to warp and should be able to conduct heat evenly. Frying pans come in various sizes, usually 8, 10 and 12 inches in diameter. **Electric frying pans or skillets** are often square or oblong in shape. Their heat is controlled by an adjustable thermostat unit that can be detached when the skillet is washed.

fudge A creamy, semisoft candy most often made with sugar, butter or cream, corn syrup and various flavorings. The most popular fudge flavor is chocolate, though maple (made with maple syrup), butterscotch (made with brown sugar or dark corn syrup) and vanilla are also favorites. Fudge can be plain and perfectly smooth or it may contain other ingredients such as nuts, chocolate chips, candied or dried fruit, etc. It may be cooked or uncooked, but both styles must be allowed to set before cutting.

Fumé Blanc [fyoo-may BLAN] *see* SAUVIGNON BLANC

fumet [fyoo-MAY; foo-MAY] A concentrated STOCK made from fish, poultry or game and used as a base for sauces.

funnel cake This pastry is a Pennsylvania Dutch specialty made by pouring batter through a funnel into hot, deep fat and frying the resulting spirals until crisp and brown. Funnel cakes are served hot, often with sugar or maple syrup.

Furmint grape *see* TOKAY GRAPE

fusille; fusilli [fyoo-SEE-lay; fyoo-SEE-lee] A spiraled SPAGHETTI that can range from about 1½ to 12 inches long. *See also* PASTA.

futomaki [foo-toh-MAH-kee] *see* SUSHI

fuzzy melon Of Chinese origin, this cylindrical (6 to 10 inches long, 2 to 3 inches thick) melon has a medium green skin covered with fine, hairlike fuzz. Its creamy-colored, medium-firm flesh is mildly flavored and has a tendency to take on the flavor of whatever food it's cooked with. Fuzzy melons—also called *hairy melons* and *fuzzy squash*—can be purchased in oriental markets and some specialty produce markets. Choose those that are fairly heavy for their size with wrinkle-free skins. Store ripe melons in a plastic bag in the refrigerator for up to 10 days. Fuzzy melons must be peeled before using. They're a popular addition to Chinese soups and STIR-FRIES.

ado gado; gado-gado [GAH-doh GAH-doh]   This Indonesian favorite consists of a mixture of raw and slightly cooked vegetables served with a spicy peanut sauce made with hot chili peppers and COCONUT MILK. Sometimes the term "gado gado" refers only to the spicy sauce, which is used as a condiment with rice and various vegetable dishes.

galantine [GAL-uhn-teen; gal-ahn-TEEN] A classic French dish that resembles a meat-wrapped PÂTÉ. It's made from poultry, meat or fish that is boned and stuffed with a FORCEMEAT, which is often studded with flavor- and eye-enhancers such as pistachio nuts, olives and TRUFFLES. The stuffed meat roll is formed into a symmetrical loaf, wrapped in CHEESECLOTH and gently cooked in stock. It's then chilled, glazed with aspic made from its own jellied stock and garnished with items (such as pistachios, olives and truffles) that have been included in the filling. Galantines are normally served cold, cut in slices.

galette [gah-LEHT] Hailing from France, a galette is a round, rather flat cake made of flaky-pastry dough, yeast dough or sometimes unleavened dough. The term also applies to a variety of tarts, both savory and sweet, and there are as many variations as there are French regions. They may be topped with fruit, jam, nuts, meat, cheese, etc. *Galette des Rois,* the traditional cake served during Twelfth Night festivities, often contains a bean or other token, which is guaranteed to bring the recipient good luck.

Galliano [gal-LYAH-noh] A sweet, anise-flavored, golden yellow LIQUEUR made in Italy.

game animals A term applied to wild animals that are deemed suitable for human consumption. Some species are now domesticated and because their diets and activity levels are changed, their meat has a different flavor than that of field animals. Game animals are categorized as large game and small game. The most common **large game** meat is venison which, though commonly thought of as deer, is a term that broadly includes the meat from elk, moose, reindeer, caribou and antelope. Other popular large game animals include BUFFALO, wild boar and, to a lesser degree, bear. Additionally, there are even rarer varieties eaten around the world such as camel, elephant, kangaroo, zebra and wild sheep and goats. The most common **small game** animal is RABBIT. Squirrel is also quite popular, followed distantly by beaver, muskrat, opossum, raccoon, armadillo and even porcupine. Any game found in commercial markets is Federally inspected. Whether purchased commercially or obtained directly from the hunter, the factors that determine the meat's quality include the age of the animal (younger animals are more tender), the animal's diet and the time of year the animal was killed (best is fall, after plentiful spring and summer feeding). Equally important is how the dead animal was handled in the field. The meat of many otherwise excellent animals is damaged (and sometimes ruined) because of the manner in which it is dressed and transported after the kill. The tenderness of a particular cut of meat from large game animals is similar to the corresponding cut of beef and pork. In general, wild game is less tender than meat from domestic animals because the wild animals get more exercise and are therefore leaner. What fat there is is generally rank-tasting and should be removed. For maximum tenderness, most game meat should be cooked slowly and not overdone. It can be cooked with moist heat by braising, or with dry heat by roasting (with an effort to ensure maximum moistness through BASTING, LARDING or BARDING).

game birds Any wild bird suitable for food, including the larger species (such as wild turkey and goose), medium-sized birds (including PHEASANT and wild duck) and smaller game birds (such as the coot, dove, grouse, hazel hen, lark, mud hen, PARTRIDGE, pigeon, PLOVER, QUAIL, rail, snipe, thrush and woodcock). Except for the few raised on game farms (which are usually expensive), game birds are not readily available. Those that are found in markets are usually of good quality. Most game birds are sold frozen; some of the smaller birds are canned. Factors affecting quality include the age of the bird and the manner in which it was treated after it was killed. Quality birds should have no off odor; the skin should be fresh-looking, not dull or dry. Young birds are best and can be identified by their pliable breastbone, feet and legs; their claws will be sharp. Wild birds are much leaner than the domesticated variety. Because of a lack of natural fat—particularly in younger birds—they must be BASTED, BARDED or LARDED before roasting. Older birds are best cooked with slow, moist heat such as braising, or used in soups or stews.

ganache [gahn-AHSH] A rich chocolate icing made of semisweet chocolate and whipping cream that are heated and stirred together until the chocolate has melted. The mixture is cooled until lukewarm and poured over a cake or torte. **Ganache soufflé** is made from the same base but often includes a tablespoon or so of rum or cognac. When cooled to room temperature, the mixture is whipped to approximately twice its original volume. Whereas ganache is used to glaze cakes, pastries and tortes, ganache soufflé is generally used to fill them.

garam masala [gah-RAHM mah-SAH-lah] *Garam* is the Indian word for "warm" or "hot," and this blend of dry-roasted, ground spices from the colder climes of northern India adds a sense of "warmth" to both palate and spirit. There are as many variations of garam masala (which may contain up to 12 spices) as there are Indian cooks. It can include black pepper, cinnamon, cloves, coriander, cumin, cardamom, dried chilies, fennel, mace, nutmeg and other spices. Garam masala may be purchased in Indian markets and in the gourmet section of some supermarkets. It's also easily prepared at home, but should be made in small batches to retain its freshness. As with all spices, it should be stored in a cool, dry place for no more than 6 months. Garam masala is usually either added to a dish toward the end of cooking or sprinkled over the surface just before serving. *For information on specific spices, see individual listings.*

garbanzo bean *see* CHICKPEA

garbure [gar-BOOR] A vegetable or meat soup so thick it could be considered a stew or casserole dish. Garbure has many variations, but most commonly contains cabbage, beans, potatoes and bits of pork, bacon or preserved goose. It's usually served with roasted or fried bread. Garbure is immensely popular with Basques and the most famous version comes from Béarn, France.

garde manger [gahrd mahn-ZHAY] A French term for the cool, well-ventilated pantry area (usually in hotels and large restaurants) where cold buffet dishes are prepared and other foods are stored in refrigerated units. Some of the items prepared in a garde manger are salads, PÂTÉS, CHAUD-FROIDS and other decorative dishes. The person in charge of this area is known as *chef garde manger.*

garden pea *see* ENGLISH PEA

garlic Garlic has long been credited with providing and prolonging physical strength and was fed to Egyptian slaves building the giant pyramids. Throughout the centuries, its medicinal claims have included cures for toothaches, consumption, open wounds and evil demons. A member of the lily family, garlic is a cousin to leeks, chives, onions and shallots. The edible bulb or "head" grows beneath the ground. This bulb is made up of sections called cloves, each encased in its own parchmentlike membrane. Today's major garlic suppliers include the U.S. (mainly California, Texas and Louisiana), France, Spain, Italy and Mexico. There are three major types of garlic available in the U.S.: the white-skinned, strongly flavored **American garlic;** the **Mexican** and **Italian garlic,** both of which have mauve-colored skins and a somewhat milder flavor; and the Paul Bunyanesque, white-skinned **elephant garlic,** the most mildly flavored of the three. Depending on the variety, cloves of American, Mexican and Italian garlic can range from ½ to 1½ inches in length. Elephant garlic (grown mainly in California) has bulbs the size of a small grapefruit, with huge cloves averaging 1 ounce each. It can be purchased through mail order and in some gourmet markets. **Green garlic**, available occasionally in specialty produce markets, is young garlic before it begins to form cloves. It resembles a baby LEEK, with a long green top and white bulb, sometimes tinged with pink. The flavor of a baby plant is much softer than that of mature garlic. Fresh garlic is available year-round. Purchase firm, plump bulbs with dry skins. Avoid heads with soft or shriveled cloves, and those stored in the refrigerated section of the produce department. Store fresh garlic in an open container (away from other foods) in a cool, dark place. Properly stored, unbroken bulbs can be kept up to 8 weeks, though they will begin to dry out toward the end of that time. Once broken from the bulb, individual cloves will keep from 3 to 10 days. Garlic is usually peeled before use in recipes. Among the exceptions are roasted garlic bulbs and the famous dish, "chicken with 40 cloves of garlic," in which unpeeled garlic cloves are baked with chicken in a broth until they become sweet and butter-soft. Crushing, chopping, pressing or pureeing garlic releases more of its essential oils and provides a sharper, more assertive flavor than slicing or leaving it whole. Garlic is readily available in forms other than fresh. Dehydrated **garlic flakes** (sometimes referred to as **instant garlic**) are slices or bits of garlic that must be reconstituted before using (unless added to a liquid-based dish, such as soup or stew). When dehydrated garlic flakes are ground, the result is **garlic powder**. **Garlic salt** is garlic powder blended with salt and a moisture-absorbing agent. **Garlic extract** and **garlic juice** are derived from pressed garlic cloves. Though all of these products are convenient, they're a poor flavor substitute for the less expensive, readily available and easy-to-store fresh garlic. One unfortunate side effect of garlic is that, because its essential oils permeate the lung tissue, it remains with the body long after it's been consumed, affecting breath and even skin odor. Chewing chlorophyll tablets or fresh parsley is helpful but, unfortunately, modern-day science has yet to find the perfect antidote for residual garlic odor.

garlic bread   Said to have been invented during the late 1940s boom of Italian-American restaurants, garlic bread consists of Italian or French bread slices, spread on both sides with GARLIC BUTTER and heated in the oven. There are many variations, including bread brushed with olive oil and sprinkled with minced garlic and herbs. It can also be broiled or grilled.

garlic butter   Softened butter blended with crushed or minced garlic. The intensity of the garlic flavor is governed by the amount of garlic used and the length of time the mixture is allowed to stand. Garlic butter is used on a broad range of foods including GARLIC BREAD, ESCARGOTS, meats, poultry, fish and vegetables.

garlic flakes *see* GARLIC

garlic powder *see* GARLIC

garlic press A kitchen tool used to press a garlic clove through small holes, thereby extracting both pulp and juice. Leaving the skin on the clove facilitates cleaning, which should be done immediately after pressing, before any garlic left in the press dries. The press can also be set in a cup of warm water until cleaning time. Some presses contain teeth that push garlic fragments back out through the holes, making cleaning much easier. Garlic presses can be made of aluminum, stainless steel and strong plastics.

garlic salt *see* GARLIC

garni [gahr-NEE] The French word for "garnish" when used as an adjective describing a food. For example, "steak garni" usually means it's accompanied by vegetables and potatoes.

garnish *n.* A decorative, edible accompaniment to finished dishes, from appetizers to desserts. Garnishes can be placed under, around or on food, depending on the dish. They vary from simple sprigs of parsley or exotically carved vegetables on plated food, to CROUTONS in soup, to chocolate leaves on top of chocolate mousse. Garnishes should not only be appealing to the eye, but should also echo or complement the flavor of the dish. **garnish** *v.* To decorate or accompany a dish with a garnish.

garniture [gahr-nih-TEUR] The French word for "garnish," used as a noun.

garum [GAR-uhm] The ancient Romans used garum as a flavoring much like salt. This extremely pungent sauce was made by fermenting fish in a brine solution for several days in the sun. The resulting liquid was combined with various other flavorings such as oil, pepper, wine and spices. The modern-day counterpart to garum is Thailand's NAM PLA.

gastronome [GAS-truh-nohm] A connoisseur of good food—someone with a refined palate.

gastronomy [gas-TRON-uh-mee] The art of fine dining; the science of gourmet food and drink.

gastropod [GAS-truh-pod] Often referred to as a *univalve*, a gastropod can be any of several MOLLUSKS with a single (univalve) shell and single muscle. Among the more common gastropods are the ABALONE, LIMPET,

PERIWINKLE, SNAIL and WHELK. With a few exceptions (such as the abalone), gastropods are not as highly regarded culinarily as BIVALVE mollusks such as the CLAM and OYSTER.

gâteau [ga-TOH] The French word for "cake," which can refer to those both plain and fancy.

gâteau Saint-Honoré *see* SAINT-HONORÉ

gaufrette [goh-FREHT] 1. Thin, lightly sweet, fan-shaped wafers usually served with ice cream, mousse and other such desserts. When baked on a special gaufrette iron (similar to a waffle iron), the wafer's surface is waffled. Before cooling and crisping, gaufrettes are sometimes curled to form an ice cream cone. 2. *Gaufrettes pommes de terre* are crisp, latticed potato wafers.

gazpacho [gahz-PAH-choh] A refreshingly cold, summertime soup hailing from the Andalusia region in southern Spain. This uncooked soup is usually made from a pureed mixture of fresh tomatoes, sweet bell peppers, onions, celery, cucumber, breadcrumbs, garlic, olive oil, vinegar and sometimes lemon juice. Gazpacho can be a meal in itself, particularly when extra fresh vegetables such as sliced celery, green onion, cucumber and green pepper are added. Popular garnishes include croutons and diced hard-cooked eggs.

gefilte fish [geh-FIHL-teh] This popular Jewish dish consists of ground fish (usually CARP, PIKE or WHITEFISH) mixed with eggs, MATZO MEAL and seasonings. The mixture is formed into balls or patties that are then simmered in vegetable or fish stock. After chilling, the gefilte fish is served in its own jellied stock and often garnished with grated horseradish, vegetable relishes or dill pickles. The name comes from the Yiddish term for "stuffed (gefüllte) fish;" in the past the mixture was stuffed back into the fish skin before cooking.

gelatin [JEHL-uh-tihn] An odorless, tasteless and colorless thickening agent which when dissolved in hot water and then cooled, forms a jelly. It's useful for many purposes such as jelling molded desserts and salads, thickening cold soups and glazing CHAUD-FROID preparations. Gelatin is pure protein derived from beef and veal bones, cartilage, tendons and other tissue. Much of the commercial gelatin today is a byproduct of pig skin. Until the advent of commercial gelatin in the late 19th century, jelled dishes were not very popular because housewives had to make their own jelling agent by laboriously boiling calves' feet or knuckles. Their only alternative was to use either the hard-to-obtain ISINGLASS (gelatin from fish air bladders) or CARRAGEEN (a dried seaweed product). **Granulated gelatin**

is the most common form of unsweetened commercial gelatin on the market. It's packaged in boxes of ¼-ounce envelopes and is also available in bulk. Generally, 1 envelope of gelatin will jell 2 cups of liquid. It's important to soak gelatin in cold liquid (whatever the recipe directs) for 3 to 5 minutes before dissolving it. This softens and swells the gelatin granules so they will dissolve smoothly when heated. Not as readily available as granulated gelatin is **leaf** (or **sheet**) **gelatin,** which comes in packages of paper-thin sheets. Leaf gelatin must be soaked longer than granulated gelatin and is therefore not as popular. This product is often called for in jelled European dessert recipes. It can be found in some gourmet and bakery supply shops. Sweetened gelatin dessert mix is also available in various artificial fruit flavors.

gelato [jehl-LAH-toh] The Italian word for "ice cream," gelato doesn't contain as much air as its American counterpart and therefore has a denser texture. An Italian ice cream parlor is called a *gelateria*.

gem pan; mini muffin pan A miniature muffin pan designed (depending on the pan) to make 12 to 24 tiny muffins about 1½ inches in diameter. "Gem" is an old-fashioned reference to a small (non-yeast) bread or cake.

génoise [zhayn-WAHZ; zhehn-WAHZ] This rich, light cake is made with flour, sugar, eggs, butter and vanilla. It's similar in texture to a moist SPONGE CAKE. It was developed in Genoa, Italy, adapted by the French and is now baked by gourmet cooks throughout Europe and the U.S. Génoise is an extremely versatile cake and is used for many elegant presentations such as PETITS FOURS, CAKE ROLLS and BAKED ALASKA.

geoduck; gweduck [GOO-ee duhk] This huge, funny-looking SOFT-SHELL CLAM hails from the Pacific Northwest. It averages 3 pounds in weight and is distinguished by a long (up to 18-inch) neck (siphon) that extends from its 6-inch shell. The neck can be cut or ground and used in chowders. The body meat, when sliced, pounded and sautéed, resembles ABALONE. *See also* CLAMS; SHELLFISH.

German potato salad A bacon-studded potato salad made with a dressing of bacon fat, vinegar, seasonings and sometimes sugar. German potato salad can be served hot, cold or at room temperature. Favorite additions include minced onion, celery and green pepper.

Gervais cheese [zhair-VAY] The most well-known brand of PETIT SUISSE, made in Normandy and named for Jules Gervais, a famous French cheesemaker. *See also* CHEESE.

Gewürztraminer [geh-VOORTS-truh-mee-nuhr] The German word *Gewürz* means "spicy," and this white wine is known for its crisp, spicy characteristics. It's a specialty of Alsace—the area that buffers Germany and France—and is also produced in Germany and California. Gewürztraminer has a distinctively pungent, perfumy, yet clean flavor. It's available in varying degrees of sweetness; the drier versions complement fish and poultry, the slightly sweeter styles are perfect for summer SPRITZERS, and the sweet LATE-HARVEST versions make excellent DESSERT WINES. Gewürztraminer is best when drunk fairly young because even the vintage versions won't usually age well over 5 years.

ghee [GEE] Butter that has been slowly melted, thereby separating the milk solids (which sink to the bottom of the pan) from the golden liquid on the surface. This form of CLARIFIED BUTTER is taken a step further by simmering it until all of the moisture evaporates and the milk solids begin to brown, giving the resulting butter a nutty, caramellike flavor and aroma. This extra step also gives ghee a longer life and much higher SMOKE POINT than regular clarified butter. Because the smoke point is raised to almost 375°F, ghee is practical for a variety of sautéing and frying uses. Although it originated in India, the best commercially available ghee comes from Holland, followed closely by products from Scandinavia and Australia. It's quite expensive, but can be purchased in Middle Eastern, Indian and some gourmet markets. Whereas ghee was once made only with butter derived from water buffalo milk, today it can be made with any unsalted butter. Making it at home is not a difficult task, and flavored ghees are created by simply adding ingredients such as ginger, peppercorns or cumin at the beginning of the clarifying process. Tightly wrapped ghee can be refrigerated for up to 6 months and frozen up to a year.

gherkin [GER-kihn] The young fruit of a variety of small, dark green cucumbers especially grown to make pickles. Gherkins are usually sold in jars, packed in pickling brine. CORNICHONS are the French version of this pickle.

giant garlic *see* ROCAMBOLE

giant sea bass *see* BASS

giblets [JIHB-liht] Generally, the term "giblets" refers to the heart, liver and gizzard of domesticated fowl and game birds. Sometimes the neck is also included in this grouping. All but the liver are used for flavoring stocks and soups. The liver is usually cooked separately and, in the case of ducks and geese, is considered a delicacy.

Gibson [GIHB-suhn] Named for the famous American "Gibson Girl" illustrator, Charles Dana Gibson, this COCKTAIL is identical to the MARTINI (gin and dry VERMOUTH), differing only in that it is served garnished with a tiny white onion instead of an olive.

gigot [zhee-GOH] French for "leg of mutton." The term is also used to refer to a leg of lamb, in which case the French call it *gigot d'agneau*.

gimlet [GIHM-liht] A COCKTAIL made with SUGAR SYRUP, lime juice, vodka or gin and sometimes soda water. According to the British, the secret of a good gimlet is thorough stirring.

gin [JIHN] An unaged LIQUOR made by distilling grains such as barley, corn or rye with JUNIPER BERRIES. **London dry gin** is any colorless gin, the majority of which is made in England and America. **Hollands gin**, also known as *genever gin*, is a Dutch product that tastes very different from other gins because it's made with a large proportion of barley malt. The first Dutch gin was used as medicine. *See also* SLOE GIN.

gin fizz A COCKTAIL made with gin, lemon juice, sugar and soda, served in a tall glass over ice. When an egg white is added, the drink is called a **silver fizz**. Adding ORANGE-FLOWER WATER and cream or milk to a silver fizz transforms it into a **Ramos gin fizz**, a New Orleans favorite.

ginger; ginger root A plant from tropical and subtropical regions that's grown for its gnarled and bumpy root. Most ginger comes from Jamaica, followed by India, Africa and China. Ginger root's name comes from the Sanskrit word for "horn root," undoubtedly referring to its knobby appearance. It has a tan skin and a flesh that ranges in color from pale greenish yellow to ivory. The flavor is peppery and slightly sweet, while the aroma is pungent and spicy. This extremely versatile root has long been a mainstay in oriental and Indian cooking and found its way early on into European foods as well. The Chinese, Japanese and East Indians use fresh ginger root in a variety of forms—grated, ground and slivered—in many savory dishes. Europeans and most Americans, however, are more likely to use the dried ground form of ginger, usually in baked goods. **Fresh ginger** is available in two forms—young and mature. Young ginger, sometimes called spring ginger, has a pale, thin skin that requires no peeling. It's very tender and has a milder flavor than its mature form. Young ginger can be found in most oriental markets during the springtime. Mature ginger has a tough skin that must be carefully peeled away to preserve the delicate, most desirable flesh just under the surface. Look for mature ginger with smooth skin (wrinkled skin indicates that the root is dry and past its prime). It should have a fresh, spicy fragrance. Fresh unpeeled ginger root, tightly wrapped, can be refrigerated for up to a week and frozen for up to 2 months. To use frozen ginger, slice off a piece of the unthawed root and return the rest to the freezer. Place peeled ginger root in a screw-top glass jar, cover with dry SHERRY or MADEIRA and refrigerate up to 3 weeks. The wine will impart some of its flavor to the ginger—a minor disadvantage to weigh against having peeled ginger ready and waiting. On the plus side, the delicious, ginger-flavored wine can be reused for cooking. The flavor of **dried ground ginger** is very different from that of its fresh form and is not an appropriate substitute for dishes specifying fresh ginger. It is, however, delicious in many savory dishes such as soups, curries and meats, a sprightly addition to fruit compotes, and indispensable in sweets like GINGERBREAD, GINGERSNAPS and many spice cookies. Ginger is the flavor that has long given the popular beverages GINGER ALE and GINGER BEER their claim to fame. In addition to its fresh and dried ground forms, ginger comes in several other guises. **Crystallized** or **candied ginger** has been cooked in a sugar syrup and coated with coarse sugar. Another form called **preserved ginger** has been preserved in a sugar-salt mixture. These types of ginger can be found in oriental markets and many supermarkets. They are generally used as a confection or added to desserts. Melon and preserved ginger are a classic combination. **Pickled ginger**, available in oriental markets, has been preserved in sweet vinegar. It's most often used as a garnish for Asian dishes. The sweet **red candied ginger** is packed in a red sugar syrup. It's used to flavor dishes both sweet and savory. *See also* Herb and Spice Chart, page 538.

ginger ale　A carbonated, ginger-flavored SOFT DRINK.

ginger beer　Made in both non-alcoholic and alcoholic forms, this carbonated beverage tastes like GINGER ALE with a stronger ginger flavor. It's an integral ingredient in the mixed drink, MOSCOW MULE.

gingerbread　This sweet dates back to the Middle Ages, when fair ladies presented the rather hard, honey-spice bread as a favor to dashing knights going into tournament battle. In those days, gingerbread was intricately shaped and decorated, sometimes with gold leaf. Today, gingerbread generally refers to one of two desserts. It can be a dense, ginger-spiced cookie flavored with molasses or honey and cut into fanciful shapes (such as the popular gingerbread man). Or, particularly in the U.S., it can describe a dark, moist cake flavored with molasses, ginger and other spices. This gingerbread "cake" is usually baked in a square pan and often topped with lemon sauce or whipped cream.

ginger root　*see* GINGER

gingersnap　A small, very crisp ginger cookie flavored with molasses.

ginkgo nut　[GING-koh; JING-koh] This buff-colored, delicately sweet nut comes from the center of the inedible fruit of the maidenhair tree, a native of China. Fresh ginkgo nuts are available during fall and winter and can be found in many oriental and gourmet markets. Their hard shells must be removed with a nutcracker and the nutmeats soaked in hot water to loosen their skins. Ginkgo nuts are also available dried or canned in brine. The canned nuts must be rinsed of brine before using. Ginkgo nuts, which turn bright green when cooked, are particularly popular in Japanese cooking. *See also* NUT.

ginseng [JIHN-sing] The Chinese name for this sweet licorice-flavored root is "human-shaped root" and indeed some have extraordinarily human shapes. This rather amazing plant has been credited for centuries with being everything from an aphrodisiac to a restorative. Recent scientific discoveries have linked ginseng to the treatment of high blood pressure. It's referred to as **white ginseng** when simply sun-dried. When steamed and dried over a fire or with other heat, it takes on a reddish tinge and is called **red ginseng**. Ginseng is used in soups, for tea and as a medicinal. It's available in oriental markets and some health-food stores.

gizzard Found in the lower stomach of fowl, this muscular pouch grinds the bird's food, often with the aid of stones or grit swallowed for this purpose. The portion that actually does the work is in the center of the pouch and is usually removed before the gizzard reaches the market. Gizzards can be very tough unless cooked slowly with moist heat, such as braising.

gjetost cheese [YEHT-ohst] Made from a combination of goat's- and cow's-milk WHEY, this Norwegian cheese is faintly sweet and caramel-colored. The texture can range from semifirm like fudge to the consistency of stiff peanut butter. The brown color and sweetness result from slowly cooking the milk until its sugars caramelize. Gjetost is particularly good spread on dark bread. Scandinavia's *mysost* cheese (also called *primost*) is made exclusively from cow's milk in exactly the same way and tastes almost identical to gjetost. *See also* CHEESE.

glacé [glah-SAY] French for "glazed" or "frozen," such as MARRONS GLACÉS (candied chestnuts). It can also refer to the frosting on a cake.

glace [GLAHS] The French word for "ice cream."

glacé fruit [glah-SAY] *see* CANDIED FRUIT

glace de viande [glahs duh vee-AHND] French for "meat glaze," *glace de viande* is made by boiling meat juices until they are reduced to a thick syrup. It's used to add flavor and color to sauces

glassword *see* SAMPHIRE

Glayva [gla-VAH] This Scottish LIQUEUR is made with SCOTCH WHISKY, honey and a well-guarded herbal formula.

glaze *n.* A thin, glossy coating for both hot and cold foods. A savory glaze might be a reduced meat stock or ASPIC, whereas a sweet glaze could be anything from melted jelly to a chocolate coating. An EGG WASH brushed on pastry before baking to add color and shine is also called a glaze. **glaze** *v.* To coat food with a thin, liquid, sweet or savory mixture that will be smooth and shiny after setting.

globe artichoke *see* ARTICHOKE

glögg [GLUHG; GLOEG] Especially popular during Advent, this Swedish spiced-wine punch gets its *punch* from the addition of AQUAVIT or BRANDY. To take the chill off cold winter nights, it's served hot in cups with several almonds and raisins added to each serving.

Gloucester cheese [GLOSS-tuhr] Also called *double Gloucester,* this dense, satiny, golden yellow cheese is one of England's finest. It was once made only with the milk from Gloucester cows (now almost extinct) and until the end of World War II single (smaller) Gloucester rounds were also available. The mellow, full-flavored double Gloucester comes in large, flat rounds or tall cylinders—both with a natural rind. It's a fine, multi-purpose cheese equally as good with a meal or after it. *See also* CHEESE.

glucose [GLOO-kohs] The most common form of this sugar is **dextroglucose**, a naturally occurring form commonly referred to as DEXTROSE (also called *corn sugar* and *grape sugar*). This form of glucose has many sources including grape juice, certain vegetables and honey. It has about half the sweetening power of regular sugar. Because it doesn't crystallize easily, it's used to make commercial candies and frostings, as well as in baked goods, soft drinks and other processed foods. Corn syrup is a form of glucose made from cornstarch.

gluten [GLOO-tihn] Wheat and other cereals that are made into flour contain proteins, one of which is glutenin, commonly known as *gluten.* Viewed alone, gluten is a tough, elastic, grayish substance resembling chewing gum. It's the gluten in flour which, when a dough is kneaded, helps hold in the gas bubbles formed by the leavening agent (*see* LEAVENER). Gas contained within a dough or batter helps a bread or other baked good rise, creating a light structure. Most (but not all) flours contain gluten in varying amounts. Bread (or hard wheat) flour has a high gluten content and is therefore good for yeast breads, which require an elastic framework. On the other hand, low-protein (and therefore low-gluten) cake flour has a softer, less elastic quality and is better suited for cakes. *See also* BREAD; FLOUR.

gluten flour *see* FLOUR

glycerin; glycerine [GLIH-ser-ihn] The commercial name for *glycerol*, a colorless, odorless, syrupy liquid—chemically, an alcohol— obtained from fats and oils and used to retain moisture and add sweetness to foods. It also helps prevent sugar crystallization in foods like candy. Outside the world of food, glycerin is used in cosmetics, inks and certain glues.

gnocchi [NYOH-kee; NOH-kee] Italian for "dumplings," gnocchi can be made from potatoes, flour or FARINA. Eggs or cheese can be added to the dough, and finely chopped spinach is also a popular addition. Gnocchi are generally shaped into little balls, cooked in boiling water and served with butter and Parmesan or a savory sauce. The dough can also be chilled, sliced and either baked or fried. Gnocchi are usually served as a side dish and make excellent accompaniments for meat or poultry.

goa bean [GOH-uh] *see* WINGED BEAN

goat Though goat meat has been enjoyed in southern Europe, Latin America and many Mediterranean countries for centuries, it has never really caught on in the U.S. The meat of mature goats is extremely tough and strong-flavored. Most goat meat consumed comes from a kid, a baby goat that is usually not more than 6 months old. Kid meat is as tender and delicate as that of young lamb, and it can be prepared in any manner suitable for lamb. It can sometimes be found in specialty meat markets. Goats also provide milk, which is usually made into goat cheese, better known as CHÈVRE. Fresh goat's milk can sometimes be purchased in health-food stores; canned goat's milk is carried in many supermarkets.

goat cheese *see* CHÈVRE CHEESE

goatfish Found in temperate to tropical seas, the goatfish is so named because of its two long chin barbels which resemble a goat's whiskers. Probably the most famous member of this fish family is the superior RED MULLET, which is not a mullet at all. Depending on the species, goatfish can range in color from brilliant yellow to rose red. The meat is firm and lean and can be cooked in almost any manner including broiling, frying and baking. In the U.S., goatfish is usually only available on the East Coast and throughout the Florida Keys. *See also* FISH.

goat's milk *see* GOAT

gobo *see* BURDOCK

golden Cadillac Named for its luxurious creamy texture and golden color, this COCKTAIL is made with GALLIANO, white CRÈME DE CACAO and heavy cream.

Golden Delicious apple   This yellow to yellow-green apple has a sweet, rather bland flavor and juicy, crisp flesh that resists browning. Golden Delicious apples have a long season, usually from September to early June. They're a fairly good all-purpose apple though they do tend to lose some flavor when cooked. *See also* APPLE; RED DELICIOUS APPLE.

golden needles   *see* TIGER LILY BUDS

golden nugget squash   A small (3 to 4 inches in diameter), pumpkin-shaped winter squash with a bright orange skin. The flesh, which is also orange, is sweet and slightly bland. Golden nugget squash is available from late summer through winter. Choose a squash that's heavy for its size. The skin should be colorful but have a dull finish (the latter indicates maturity). If the surface is shiny, the flesh will be flavorless. Golden nugget squash can be stored at room temperature for up to a month. It can be baked or steamed, either whole or halved. *See also* SQUASH.

golden oak   *see* SHIITAKE

golden syrup   Particularly popular in England (where it's also known as *light* TREACLE), this liquid sweetener has the consistency of CORN SYRUP and a clear golden color. It's made from evaporated sugar cane juice and has a rich, toasty flavor unmatched by any other sweetener. Golden syrup, the most readily available brand being *Lyle's*, can be found in some supermarkets and many gourmet markets. It can be used as a substitute for corn syrup in cooking and baking, and for everything from pancake syrup to ice cream topping.

Goldwasser   [GOLT-vahs-sehr; GOLD-vahs-sehr] Also called *Danziger Goldwasser*, this full-bodied LIQUEUR is flavored with caraway seed, orange peel and spices. Its name, which translates from German as "gold water," comes from the fact that it has minuscule flecks of gold leaf suspended in it. The gold leaf is harmless to drink.

goober   A derivative of the African word *nguba*, "goober" is a southern U.S. name for peanut. It's also referred to as a "goober pea."

goose   Any of many species of large, web-footed, wild or domestic birds. Geese are much larger than ducks, weighing from 5 to 18 pounds, compared to 3 to 5½ pounds for a duck. The female of the species is simply known as a *goose*, a male as a *gander*, and a young goose—of whichever sex—as a *gosling*. Geese were bred in ancient Egypt, China and India. The Romans revered them because it was a noisy gaggle of geese that alerted 4th-century B.C. Romans that the enemy Gauls were about to attack. Geese are immensely popular in Europe, where they're traditional Christmas holiday fare in many countries. They're also renowned for two French specialties—FOIE GRAS, the creamy-rich enlarged liver from force-fed geese, and CONFIT, goose cooked and preserved in its own fat. Because geese are so fatty, they have not achieved the same popularity in America and therefore, though they're domesticated, have never been mass-marketed. The U.S. government grades the quality of geese with USDA classifications A, B and C. The highest grade is A, and is generally what is found in markets. Grade B geese are less meaty and well finished; those that are grade C are not usually available to the consumer. The grade stamp can usually be found within a shield on the package wrapping. Most geese marketed in the U.S. are frozen and can be purchased throughout the year. A frozen bird's packaging should be tight and unbroken. The goose should be thawed in the refrigerator and can take up to 2 days to defrost, depending on the size of the bird. Do not refreeze goose once it's been thawed. Fresh geese can be found in some specialty markets and are available from early summer through December. When available, buy goslings (the smaller the better) because they are the most tender. One way to determine age is to check the goose's bill; if it's pliable, the bird is still young. Choose a goose that is plump, with a good fatty layer and skin that is clean and unblemished. Store loosely covered in the coldest section of the refrigerator 2 to 3 days. Remove and store separately any giblets in the body cavity. Because geese have so much fat, they are best roasted. Larger, older birds are tougher and therefore should be cooked using a moist-heat method, such as braising. The fat derived from roasting a goose is prized by many cooks as a cooking fat. Goose benefits from being served with a tart fruit sauce, which helps offset any fatty taste. Geese are high in calories but are a good source of protein and iron. *See also* GAME BIRDS.

gooseberry These large, tart berries grow on bushes and come in many varieties including green, white, yellow and red; their skins can be smooth or fuzzy. Though they're rather rare in the U.S., they flourish in northern Europe. Gooseberries are in season during the summer months. If you can find them fresh, choose those that are fairly firm and evenly colored. Canned gooseberries (usually the green variety) are available year-round. Gooseberries make excellent jams, jellies, pies and the dessert for which they're duly famous, FOOL.

goosefish *see* ANGLER

goose liver *see* FOIE GRAS

Gorgonzola cheese [gohr-guhn-ZOH-lah] Named for a town outside Milan where it was originally made, Gorgonzola is one of Italy's great cheeses. It has an ivory-colored interior that can be lightly or thickly streaked with bluish-green veins. This cow's-milk cheese is rich and creamy with a savory, slightly pungent flavor. When aged over 6 months, the flavor and aroma can be quite strong—sometimes downright stinky. The cheese usually comes in foil-wrapped wedges cut from medium-size wheels. Gorgonzola is a perfect accompaniment for pears, apples and peaches, and pairs nicely with hearty red wines. It's delicious when melted over potatoes or crumbled in salads. *See also* CHEESE.

Gorgonzola dolce   *see* DOLCELATTE CHEESE

gorp Eaten as a snack, this dry mixture consists of a combination of foods, usually nuts, seeds, raisins or other dried fruit and oats. It's particularly favored by hikers and campers as an energy booster.

Gouda cheese [GOO-dah] Holland's most famous exported cheese is Gouda, with its characteristic yellow interior dotted with a few tiny holes. It has a mild, nutlike flavor that is very similar to EDAM, but its texture is slightly creamier due to its higher butterfat content (about 48 percent compared to Edam's 40 percent). Gouda can be made from whole or part-skim cow's milk, and aged anywhere from a few weeks to over a year. The younger the Gouda, the milder the flavor. When aged over a year, it takes on almost a cheddarlike flavor. It comes in large wheels ranging from 10 to 25 pounds, and usually has a yellow wax rind. **Baby Gouda**, which comes in rounds weighing no more than a pound, usually has a red wax coating. Some Goudas are flavored with CUMIN or herbs. Though Gouda is also made in the U.S., the domestic version is rarely aged and is extremely mild-flavored. Gouda is particularly good with beer, red wines and dark bread. The Dutch make a dish called *kaasdoop*, a Gouda FONDUE served with potatoes and rye bread. *See also* CHEESE.

gougère [goo-ZHAIR] GRUYÈRE-flavored CHOUX PASTRY that is piped into a ring shape before being baked. A gougère can be served hot or cold as an HORS D'OEUVRE or snack.

goulash [GOO-lahsh] Known as *gulyás* in its native Hungary, goulash is a stew made with beef or other meat and vegetables and flavored with Hungarian PAPRIKA. It's sometimes garnished with dollops of sour cream and often served with buttered noodles.

gourd [GOHRD] The inedible fruit of any of various plants with an extremely hard, tough shell. When all the flesh is removed, the shell can be dried and used as a container, utensil or for decorative purposes.

gourmand [goor-MAHND] A gourmand is one who appreciates fine food . . . often to indiscriminate excess. *See also* GOURMET.

Gourmandise cheese [goor-mahn-DEEZ] Flavored with cherry juice, this soft, creamy processed cheese has a mild, sweet flavor. It's usually sold in small cakes or wedges, sometimes with a chopped-nut coating. Gourmandise is delicious with fruit and as a snack with crackers. *See also* CHEESE.

gourmet [goor-MAY] 1. One of discriminating palate; a connoisseur of fine food and drink. 2. Gourmet food is that which is of the highest quality, perfectly prepared and artfully presented. 3. A gourmet restaurant is one that serves well-prepared, high-quality food.

graham cracker A rectangular-shaped, whole-wheat cracker that has been sweetened, usually with honey. **Graham-cracker crust** is made from a mixture of finely crushed graham crackers, sugar and butter that is pressed into a pie pan. It's usually baked, but can simply be chilled before being filled.

graham flour Whole-wheat flour that is slightly coarser than regular grind. *See also* FLOUR.

grain *see* CEREAL GRAINS

grana [GRAH-nuh] The Italian word for "grain," referring to any of various very hard cheeses with a granular texture. Such cheeses, like PARMIGIANO REGGIANO, are particularly suited for grating. This special texture is the result of long aging, which is usually anywhere from 2 to 7 years, though some (rare) cheeses are ripened up to 20 years. *See also* CHEESE.

granadilla [gran-DEE-yuh] *see* PASSION FRUIT

Grand Marnier [GRAN mahr-NYAY] A clear, dark golden, brandy-based French LIQUEUR flavored with orange peel.

granité (*Fr.*); **granità** (*It.*) [grah-nee-TAY; grah-nee-TAH] *see* ICE

Granny Smith apple Most of these crisp, juicy apples are imported from New Zealand and Australia, though the U.S. now produces some principally in California and Arizona. The Granny Smith's freckled green skin covers a sweetly tart flesh that's excellent for both out-of-hand eating and cooking. The imported crop arrives during summer, while those from the U.S. are available through the winter months, making the popular Granny Smith a year-round, all-purpose apple. *See also* APPLE.

granola [gruh-NOH-luh] A breakfast food consisting of various combinations of grains (mainly oats), nuts and dried fruits. Some manufacturers toast their granola with oil and honey, giving it a crisp texture, sweet glaze and more calories. *See also* MUESLI.

granulated sugar *see* SUGAR

grape These edible berries grow in clusters on small shrubs or climbing vines in temperate zones throughout the world including Africa, Asia, Australia, Europe and North and South America. California is the largest U.S. producer of grapes—both for wine and for the table. There are thousands of grape varieties, each with its own particular use and charm. In general, grapes are smooth-skinned and juicy; they may have several seeds in the center or they may be seedless. There are "slip-skin" varieties, which have skins that slip easily off the berry—like a mitten being pulled off a hand—and those with skins that cling stubbornly to the flesh. Grapes are divided into color categories of white or black (also referred to as "red"). White grape varieties range in color from pale yellow-green to light green, and black grapes from light red to purple-black. They're also classified by the way they're used—whether for wine (such as CABERNET or RIESLING), table (like THOMPSON SEEDLESS or RIBIER) or commercial food production, such as MUSCAT grapes for raisins, ZANTE grapes for CURRANTS and CONCORD grapes for grape juice, jams and jellies. Wine grapes, for instance, have high acidity and are therefore too tart for general eating. Table grapes, with their low acid, would make dull, bland-tasting wines. The availability of table grapes depends on the variety. Buy grapes that are plump, full-colored and firmly attached to their stems. White (or green) grapes should have a slight pale yellow hue, a sign of ripeness. Dark grapes should be deeply colored, with no sign of green. In general, grapes should be stored, unwashed and in a plastic bag, in the refrigerator. They will keep for up to a week, though quality will diminish with time. Because most supermarket grapes have been sprayed with insecticide, they should be thoroughly washed and blotted dry with a paper towel just before eating or using. Ideally, grapes should be served at about 60°F, so it's best to remove them from the refrigerator about 30 minutes before serving. Table grapes can be used in salads, for pies and other desserts and of course for out-of-hand eating. Whole grapes are also available canned. Grape juice comes in cans or bottles; grape jelly, jam and preserves in jars. Fresh grapes contain small amounts of vitamin A and a variety of minerals. *For information on specific grapes, see individual listings.*

grapefruit This tropical citrus fruit grows in great abundance in Arizona, California, Florida and Texas. Its name comes from the fact that the grapefruit grows in grapelike clusters. There are two main categories of grapefruit—seeded and seedless. They're also broken into color classifications—white, which has a yellowish-white flesh, and pink, the flesh of which can range from pale yellow-pink to brilliant ruby red. Pink grapefruit has a higher amount of vitamin A than does the white. The skins of all varieties of grapefruit are yellow, some with a pink blush. Fresh grapefruit is available year-round—those from Arizona and California are in the market from about January through August; Florida and Texas grapefruits usually arrive around October and last through June. Choose grapefruit that have thin, fine-textured, brightly colored skin. They should be firm yet springy when held in the palm and pressed. The heavier they are for their size, the juicier they'll be. Do not store grapefruit at room temperature for more than a day or two. They keep best (up to 2 weeks) when wrapped in a plastic bag and placed in the vegetable drawer of the refrigerator. Grapefruit is usually eaten fresh, either halved or segmented and used in salads. It can also be sprinkled with brown sugar and broiled. Canned and frozen forms of grapefruit are available in segments or juice. Grapefruit is a good source of vitamin C.

grapefruit knife   A small knife with a curved, flexible blade that is serrated on both sides. It is used to free grapefruit flesh from both rind and membrane.

grape leaves   The large green leaves of the grapevine are often used by Greek and Middle Eastern cooks to wrap foods for cooking, as with DOLMAS. Grape leaves are not usually commercially available fresh so, unless you have a grapevine in your backyard, you'll probably have to buy canned grape leaves packed in brine. They should be rinsed before using to remove some of the salty flavor. Fresh grape leaves must be simmered in water for about 10 minutes to soften them enough to be pliable. In addition to wrapping foods, grape leaves can be used as decorations or garnishes, or in salads. Also called *vine leaves.*

grapeseed oil   Extracted from grape seeds, most of this oil comes from France, Italy or Switzerland, with a few sources now in the U.S. Some grapeseed oils have a light "grapey" flavor and fragrance but most imported into the U.S. are on the bland side. Grapeseed oil can be used for salad dressings and, because it has a relatively high SMOKE POINT, it's also good for sautéing. It may be stored at room temperature (70°F or under) or in the refrigerator. Grapeseed oil is available in gourmet food stores and some supermarkets. *See also* FATS AND OILS.

grape sugar   *see* DEXTROSE

grappa   [GRAHP-pah] A colorless Italian EAU DE VIE distilled from the residue (grape skins and seeds) left in the wine press after the juice is removed for wine.

grasshopper A COCKTAIL made with cream, CRÈME DE MENTHE and white CRÈME DE CACAO. Because it's very sweet, a grasshopper is usually served after dinner.

grasshopper pie Like the drink of the same name, this light, airy and rich pie is flavored with CRÈME DE MENTHE and white CRÈME DE CACAO. The richness comes from whipped cream and the lightness from beaten egg whites. Grasshopper pie usually has a Graham cracker- or cookie-crumb crust. It must be refrigerated several hours to set, and is served chilled.

grate To reduce a large piece of food to small particles or thin shreds by rubbing it against a coarse, serrated surface, usually on a kitchen utensil called a GRATER. A FOOD PROCESSOR fitted with the metal blade can also be used to reduce food to small bits or, fitted with the shredding disc, to long, thin strips. The food to be grated should be firm, which in the case of cheese can usually be accomplished by refrigeration. Grating food makes it easier to incorporate with other foods.

grater Graters come in several shapes—the most popular styles are flat, cylindrical and box-shape. They're used to reduce hard foods to small particles or long, thin strips. Most graters are made of metal or plastic that has been perforated with sharp-edged, small or medium-size holes or slits. Many have handles at the top for a sure grip. Graters made of stainless steel will not rust, whereas those of tinned steel will. *See also* MOULI GRATER; NUTMEG GRATER.

Gravenstein apple [GRA-vuhn-steen] This crisp, juicy, sweetly tart apple has a beautiful green skin streaked with red. It's in season from August to late September and available mainly on the West Coast. Although the Gravenstein is considered an all-purpose apple and makes delicious pies and applesauce, it does not do well when baked whole. *See also* APPLE.

Graves [GRAHV] Any of several notable wines from the region of Graves, southwest of Bordeaux, France. Although the name *Graves* is generally associated with several fine, dry white wines, the reds are also quite distinctive. They are, however, generally bottled under the name of their château of origin, though the Graves designation is usually in fine print somewhere on the label.

gravlax [GRAHV-lahks] This Swedish specialty of raw salmon cured in a salt-sugar-dill mixture is prized around the world. It's sliced paper-thin and served on dark bread as an appetizer, on an open-faced sandwich or as part of a smorgasbord, often accompanied by a dill-mustard sauce. Gravlax can usually be found in gourmet markets or specialty fish markets. It can be stored, tightly wrapped, in the refrigerator for up to a week.

gravy A sauce made from meat juices, usually combined with a liquid such as chicken or beef broth, wine or milk and thickened with flour, cornstarch or some other thickening agent. A gravy may also be the simple juices left in the pan after meat, poultry or fish has been cooked.

gravy boat An elongated, boat-shaped pitcher used to serve gravy. A gravy boat usually sits on a matching plate, which is used to catch gravy drips. Sometimes the plate is permanently attached to the pitcher. A matching ladle often accompanies a gravy boat. Also called *sauceboat*.

grease *n.* Any RENDERED animal fat, such as bacon, beef or chicken fat.
grease *v.* To rub the surface of a pan—such as a griddle, muffin pan or cake pan—with grease or SHORTENING in order to prevent the food prepared in it from sticking. **Grease and flour** refers to rubbing the pan with grease or shortening before lightly dusting it with flour. The flour coating is applied by sprinkling the pan with flour, then inverting it and tapping the bottom of the pan to remove any excess flour.

great Northern bean Large white beans that resemble LIMA BEANS in shape but that have a delicate, distinctive flavor. They're grown in the Midwest and are generally available dried. As with other dried beans, they must be soaked before cooking. Great Northern beans are particularly popular in baked bean dishes and can be substituted for any white beans in most recipes. *See also* BEAN.

grecque, à la [ah lah GREHK] French for "in the Greek style," usually referring to vegetables (such as mushrooms and artichokes) and herbs cooked in olive oil and lemon juice and served cold as an appetizer.

green bean The green bean has a long, slender green pod with small seeds inside. The entire pod is edible. It's also called *string bean* (because of the fibrous string—now bred out of the species—that used to run down the pod's seam) and *snap bean* (for the sound the bean makes when broken in half). The *wax bean* is a pale yellow variety of green bean. Green beans are available year-round, with a peak season of May to October. Choose slender beans that are crisp, bright-colored and free of blemishes. Store in the refrigerator, tightly wrapped in a plastic bag, for up to 5 days. Cook gently by steaming or simmering just until tender-crisp. Green beans have a fair amount of vitamins A and C. *See also* BEAN.

greengage plum A small, round, tangy-sweet plum with a greenish-yellow skin and flesh. It's good for both out-of-hand eating and cooking. *See also* PLUM.

green goddess dressing This dressing was created in the 1920s by the chef at San Francisco's Palace Hotel in honor of actor George Arliss, who was appearing locally in a play called "Green Goddess." The classic green goddess dressing is a blend of mayonnaise, tarragon vinegar, anchovies, parsley, chives, tarragon, scallions and garlic. In addition to dressing salads, it's often used as a sauce for fish and shellfish.

greenling Found along the Pacific coast of the U.S., this rather ugly fish has a huge mouth and sharp teeth. There are nine greenling species but only one, the LINGCOD (*see listing*), is generally sold commercially. *See also* FISH.

green onion *see* SCALLION

green pepper *see* SWEET BELL PEPPER

green peppercorn *see* PEPPERCORN

greens Edible leaves of certain plants such as the BEET, COLLARD, DANDELION and TURNIP. Greens are usually steamed or quickly cooked in some other manner. *For information on specific greens, see individual listings.*

green tea *see* TEA

gremolada; gremolata [greh-moh-LAH-dah] A garnish made of minced parsley, lemon peel and garlic. It's sprinkled over OSSO BUCO and other dishes to add a fresh, sprightly flavor.

grenadine [grehn-uh-DEEN; GREHN-uh-deen] A sweet, deep red, pomegranate-flavored syrup used to color and flavor drinks and desserts. At one time, grenadine was made exclusively from pomegranates grown on the island of Grenada in the Caribbean. Now other fruit-juice concentrates are also used to make the syrup. Grenadine sometimes contains alcohol, so be sure and check the label.

griddle A special flat, customarily rimless pan designed to cook food (such as pancakes) with a minimal amount of fat or oil. Griddles are usually made of thick, heavy metals that are good heat conductors, such as cast aluminum or cast iron. Some griddles have a nonstick coating. Like a frying pan, they usually have a long handle; some have handgrips on opposite sides.

griddle cake Another name for PANCAKE.

grill *n.* 1. A heavy metal grate that is set over hot coals or other heat source and used to cook foods such as steak, hamburgers, etc. 2. A dish of food (usually meat, such as MIXED GRILL) cooked on a grill. **grill** *v.* To prepare food on a grill over hot coals or other heat source.

grillade [gruh-LAHD; gree-YAHD] 1. French for "grilled (or broiled) food," usually meat. 2. A CREOLE dish of pieces of pounded round steak seared in hot fat, then braised in a rich sauce with vegetables and tomatoes. Grillade is customarily served with GRITS.

grind To reduce food to small particles. Coffee beans can be ground in a coffee GRINDER, while meats such as beef must be run through a meat grinder. A FOOD PROCESSOR fitted with a metal blade can also grind some foods. Food can be ground to various degrees—fine, medium and coarse.

grinder 1. Any of various hand-driven or electric devices used to reduce food to small particles of varying degrees. **Coffee grinders** are electric and usually have an exposed, disc-style blade inside the unit's container. The grind can be adjusted from *fine* to *coarse*. Some nuts and spices can also be ground in a coffee grinder. **Meat grinders** can be either manual (operated by a hand crank) or electric; the housing made of cast iron or tough plastic. Hand-operated meat grinders are attached to a countertop by a clamp-and-screw mechanism, whereas electric models are freestanding. They both work on the same principle, by forcing chunks of meat through a rotating blade, then through a perforated cutting disc. *See also* NUT MILL. 2. In some regions, "grinder" also refers to a huge sandwich; see HERO SANDWICH.

grissini [gruh-SEE-nee] Italian for "breadsticks" (the singular form is *grissino*), referring to thin, crisp breadsticks that originated in Turin, Italy. They're available commercially in many supermarkets.

grits Though it's now commonly used to mean "HOMINY grits," the term "grits" actually refers to any coarsely ground grain such as corn, oats or rice. Most grits come in a choice of grinds—coarse, medium and fine. Grits can be cooked with water or milk—usually by boiling or baking—and eaten as hot cereal or served as a side dish. *See also* GROATS.

groats Hulled crushed grain, such as barley, buckwheat or oats. The most widely used are BUCKWHEAT GROATS (also known as *kasha*), which are usually cooked in a manner similar to rice. Though groats are generally thought to be more coarsely ground than GRITS, they come in a variety of grinds including coarse, medium and fine. The two names—grits and groats—are often used synonymously. Groats are widely used in cereals, as a side dish with vegetables or as a thickener and enricher for soup.

grog A hot drink made with rum, a sweetener such as sugar or honey and boiling water. Grog is served in a ceramic or glass mug and often garnished with a slice of lemon and a few whole cloves. It has long been considered a curative for colds but is generally consumed simply for its pleasure- and warmth-giving properties.

ground beef Also referred to as *hamburger*, ground beef is simply beef that has been ground or finely chopped. The price of ground beef is determined by the cut of meat from which it was made and the amount of fat incorporated into the mix. High-fat mixtures are less costly but will shrink more when cooked. The least expensive product is sold as **regular ground beef** or **regular hamburger**. It's usually made with trimmings of the less expensive cuts such as BRISKET and SHANK, and can contain up to 30 percent fat. The moderately priced **ground chuck** is the next level of ground beef. Because it contains enough fat (about 15 to 20 percent) to give it flavor and make it juicy, yet not enough to cause excess shrinkage, ground chuck is the best meat for hamburgers. The leanest (around 11 percent fat) and most expensive of the ground meats are **ground round** and **ground sirloin**. Though they're great for calorie watchers, they become quite dry when cooked beyond medium-rare. Ground beef is sold fresh and frozen, prepackaged in bulk (usually 1 to 5 pounds) or in pre-formed patties. It may also be ground to order. The way it is used determines how the beef should be ground. In general, the finer the beef is ground, the more compact it will be when cooked. For instance, firm-textured combinations such as Meatloaf or Meatballs should be made with beef that has been ground at least 2 or 3 times. For hamburgers, however, where a light, juicy texture is preferable, the beef should be coarsely ground. Ground beef should be lightly wrapped before storing in the coldest section of the refrigerator for up to 2 days. To freeze, shape into individual patties or a large, flat disc and wrap with freezer-proof packaging. It can be frozen up to 6 months. *See also* BEEF; HAMBURGER.

ground cherry *see* CAPE GOOSEBERRY

groundnut *see* PEANUT

grouper [GROO-puhr] Although some weigh ⅓ ton, the average size of this fish is from 5 to 15 pounds. Groupers are found in the waters of the Gulf of Mexico and the North and South Atlantic. They're marketed whole as well as in fillets and steaks. They have a lean, firm flesh which is suitable for baking, broiling, frying, poaching or steaming. The grouper's skin, which is very strongly flavored, should always be removed before cooking. The most popular members of this sea bass family are the **black grouper, Nassau grouper, red grouper** and **yellowmouth** (also called *yellowfin*) **grouper**. *See also* FISH.

grouse *see* GAME BIRDS

gruel [GROO-uhl] A cereal (usually oatmeal) cooked with water or milk and generally of a very thin consistency.

grunion [GRUHN-yuhn] Tiny (3- to 6-ounce) fish found along the Southern California coast, known for their spawning habits. The "running of the grunion" occurs by the light of the full moon as these silvery fish wriggle their way above high tide to spawn in the wet sand. Legally, grunion can only be caught by hand, though many people snare them with nets or scoops. The moderately fat grunion are best broiled, deep-fried or sautéed. *See also* FISH.

grunt 1. Named after the grunting noise it makes, this rich, sweet-flavored fish can be found mainly in Florida's coastal waters. It's generally available only in its region, and is best either broiled or sautéed. *See also* FISH. 2. An old-fashioned dessert of fruit topped with biscuit dough and stewed. Also called *slump*.

Gruviera cheese; Groviera [groo-vee-YAIR-uh] This Italian version of the Swiss GRUYÈRE has a sweet, nutlike flavor that is very like the original. It can be used in any manner suitable for Gruyère. *See also* CHEESE.

Gruyère cheese [groo-YAIR; gree-YAIR] Swiss Gruyère is named for the valley of the same name in the canton of Fribourg. This moderate-fat, cow's-milk cheese has a rich, sweet, nutty flavor that is highly prized both for out-of-hand eating and cooking. It's usually aged for 10 to 12 months and has a golden brown rind and a firm, pale yellow interior with well-spaced, medium-size holes. It's made in 100-pound wheels that are cut into wedges for the market. Gruyère is also produced in France and several other countries. A processed Gruyère is also marketed in small, foil-wrapped wedges but, as with all PROCESSED CHEESE, it in no way compares to the real thing. *See also* CHEESE.

guacamole [gwah-kah-MOH-lee; gwah-kah-MOH-leh] A popular Mexican specialty of mashed avocado mixed with lemon or lime juice and various seasonings (usually chili powder and red pepper). Sometimes finely chopped tomato, green onion and CILANTRO are added. Guacamole can be used as a dip, sauce, topping or side dish. It must be covered closely and tightly to prevent discoloration.

guajillo chili pepper [gwah-HEE-yoh] The skin of this dried CHILI PEPPER is shiny-smooth and a deep, burnished red. The chili is very tough and must be soaked longer than most dried chilis. The flavorful guajillo chili is pointed, long and narrow (about 4 inches by 1 inch). Because it's so extremely hot, the guajillo is also sometimes called the *travieso* ("mischievous") *chili*, in reference to its not-so-playful sting. It's used in both sauces and cooked dishes.

guava [GWAH-vah] This sweet, fragrant tropical fruit grows in its native South America as well as in California, Florida and Hawaii. There are many varieties of guavas, which can range in size from a small egg to a medium apple. Typically, the fruit is oval in shape and about 2 inches in diameter. The color of the guava's thin skin can range from yellow to red to purple-black, the flesh from pale yellow to bright red. Guavas are usually only available fresh in the region where they're grown. Choose those that give to gentle palm pressure but that have not yet begun to show spots. To be eaten raw, guavas should be very ripe. Ripen green ones at room temperature. Store ripe guavas in the vegetable drawer of the refrigerator for up to 4 days. Guavas make excellent jams, preserves and sauces. Canned whole guavas as well as juice, jams, jellies, preserves and sauce are available in many supermarkets. Fresh guavas are a good source of vitamins A and C.

gugelhopf *see* KUGELHOPF

guinea fowl [GIHN-ee] Thought to have originated in Guinea, West Africa, this small bird is a relative of the chicken and partridge. The meat of the guinea fowl is dark, somewhat dry and has a pleasantly gamey flavor. Guinea hens are more tender than the male of the species. The hens range in size from ¾ pound (called *guinea squab*) to about 4 pounds. Guinea fowl are available fresh and frozen. If fresh, loosen package wrapping slightly and remove any giblets from the body cavity before storing in the refrigerator for up to 2 days. Frozen guinea fowl should be thawed overnight in the refrigerator and used within 2 days. Never refreeze fowl once it's thawed. Guinea fowl may be prepared in any way suitable for chicken, keeping in mind that because the meat is drier, moist cooking methods will produce a more satisfactory end result. Any fowl over 2½ pounds should probably be BARDED with fat before cooking to ensure moistness.

gulyás *see* GOULASH

gum arabic A natural additive obtained from the bark of certain varieties of acacia tree. Gum arabic is colorless, tasteless and odorless and is used in commercial food processing to thicken, emulsify and stabilize foods such as candy, ice cream and sweet syrups. *See also* Additives Directory, page 515.

gumbo [GUHM-boh] This CREOLE specialty is a mainstay of New Orleans cuisine. It's a thick, stewlike dish that can have any of many ingredients, including vegetables such as okra, tomatoes and onions, and one or several meats or shellfish such as chicken, sausage, ham, shrimp, crab or oysters. The one thing all good gumbos begin with is a dark ROUX, which adds an unmistakable, incomparably rich flavor. Okra serves to thicken the mixture, as does FILÉ POWDER, which must be stirred in just before serving after the pot's off the fire. The famous *gumbo z'herbes* ("with herbs") was once traditionally served on Good Friday and contains at least seven greens (for good luck) such as spinach, mustard greens, collard greens, etc. The name gumbo is a derivation of the African word for "okra."

gum tragacanth [TRAG-uh-kanth] A substance obtained from an Asian shrub, *Astragalus gummifer*, and used in the same way as GUM ARABIC. *See also* Additives Directory, page 515.

gunpowder tea This fine Chinese tea is considered the highest grade of green tea and is noted for both its form and its flavor. The small, young tea leaves are rolled into minuscule balls, giving the tea a granular appearance. Gunpowder tea is light in color, with a distinctively sharp flavor. *See also* TEA.

gur [GOOR] *see* JAGGERY

gweduck *see* GEODUCK

gyro [JEER-oh; ZHEER-oh; Gk. YEE-roh] A Greek specialty consisting of minced lamb that is molded around a spit and vertically roasted. The meat is usually sliced, enfolded in a PITA and topped with grilled onions, sweet peppers and a cucumber-yogurt sauce.

abañero chili pepper [ah-bah-NEH-roh] This distinctively flavored, extremely hot CHILI PEPPER is small and lantern-shaped. It's native to the Caribbean, the Yucatan and the north coast of South America. The habañero ranges from light green to bright orange when ripe. It's generally used for sauces in both its fresh and roasted form.

haddock [HAD-uhk] A saltwater fish that is closely related to but smaller than COD. The low-fat haddock has a firm texture and mild flavor. It can weigh anywhere from 2 to 6 pounds and is available fresh either whole or in fillets and steaks, and frozen in fillets and steaks. Haddock is suitable for any style of preparation including baking, poaching, sautéing and grilling. Smoked haddock is called FINNAN HADDIE. *See also* FISH.

haggis [HAG-ihs] This Scottish specialty is made by stuffing a sheep's (or other animal's) stomach lining with a minced mixture of the animal's organs (heart, liver, lungs, etc.), onion, SUET, oatmeal and seasonings, then simmering the sausage in water for about 4 hours. **Haggamuggie** is a simplified version of haggis made with fish liver.

 hairy melon *see* FUZZY MELON

hake [HAYK] Related to the COD, hake is a saltwater fish that makes its home in the Atlantic and northern Pacific Oceans. It's low in fat and has white, delicately flavored meat. Ranging in size from 1 to 8 pounds, hake is marketed whole or in fillets and steaks. It comes in fresh, frozen, smoked and salted forms. Hake may be prepared in any way suitable for cod. *See also* FISH.

half-and-half; half & half *see* CREAM

halibut [HAL-uh-buht] Abundant in northern Pacific and Atlantic waters, this large member of the FLATFISH family can weigh up to half a ton. The norm, however, ranges between 50 and 100 pounds. Considered the finest are the young **chicken halibut**, which can weigh anywhere from 2 to 10 pounds. Halibut meat is low-fat, white, firm and mild-flavored. Fresh halibut is available year-round but most abundant from March to September. Both fresh and frozen halibut is usually marketed in fillets and steaks. It's suitable for almost any manner of preparation. Halibut cheeks are sometimes available in specialty fish markets. *See also* FISH.

hallacas [ay-YAH-kahs] Hailing from Colombia and Venezuela, hallacas are South America's version of the TAMALE. They consist of ground beef, pork or chicken mixed with other foods such as cheese, olives or raisins, surrounded by a ground-corn dough, wrapped in banana leaves and gently boiled. Hallacas are served as both an appetizer and main dish.

hallah *see* CHALLAH

halvah; halva [hahl-VAH; HAHL-vah] Hailing from the Middle East, this confection is made from ground SESAME SEED and honey, sometimes with the addition of chopped dried fruit and pistachio nuts. It's available in most supermarkets in wrapped bars, and in Jewish delicatessens in long slabs from which individual slices can be cut.

ham The cut of meat from a hog's hind leg, generally from the middle of the shank bone to the aitch (hip) bone. The actual length of the cut varies according to the producer. The unprocessed meat is referred to as **fresh ham**, but most ham goes through a curing process after which it's referred to as **cured ham**. The final flavor of a ham can be attributed to a combination of many factors. Before the animal is slaughtered, those factors include its breed, the type of feed on which it was raised and the age at which it was slaughtered. Most hogs are fed corn, but animals headed for the gourmet market may have treats such as acorns, beechnuts, chestnuts or peanuts added to their diets. After the hog is slaughtered, the meat is usually cured in one of three ways—dry curing, sweet-pickle curing or injection curing. **Dry curing** involves salting the surface of the ham thoroughly, then storing it until the salt saturates the meat. This procedure may be repeated several times. **Sweet-pickle curing** involves immersing the ham in a sweet BRINE with added seasonings (usually a secret recipe of the producer). If sugar is added to the curing mix the ham may be labeled *sugar-cured*. Most mass producers of ham use the **injection-curing** method whereby the ham is injected with brine. This method is sometimes combined with one of the other curing methods. The length of time a ham is cured will affect the final flavor. Most hams for American consumers have a light or mild cure. After curing, a ham may go through a smoking process that adds both flavor and aging capability. The length of time a ham is smoked varies widely depending on the desired result. Those being prepared for the mass market are usually smoked lightly or not at all. Hams for the gourmet palate are more heavily smoked, the process lasting a month or more. The smoked flavor will vary depending on the substance used. Hickory and maple are the woods of preference, and some producers add exotic ingredients such as JUNIPER BERRIES, sage or peat. Once curing and smoking are completed, gourmet hams are usually aged to further develop flavors; most mass-produced hams are not. In some cases, aging can take up to 2 years. Hams are sold in several forms including **boneless** (with the hip, thigh and shank bones removed), **partially boned** (with the hip and/or shank bones removed) and **bone-in**. Since bone contributes flavor to the meat during cooking, most gourmet-ham producers leave some bone in. Hams are marketed in several sizes, the most popular being whole, halves (shank or butt, ends only), shank, butt and center-cut slices or steaks ranging in thickness from ½ to ¾ inch. Whole hams usually weigh from 8 to 18 pounds. Canned hams are "formed" from bits and pieces of meat held together with a gelatin mixture. Hams are available fully cooked, partially cooked or uncooked. Those that are **fully-cooked** are heated to an internal temperature of 148°F or above, **partially cooked** hams to at least 137°F (which kills the trichina parasite). **Uncooked and partially cooked** hams must be cooked prior to serving. Fully cooked hams, sometimes labled "heat-and-serve" or "ready-to-eat," do not require additional cooking and may be eaten cold or heated until warm. Carefully check the label for instructions. Most hams sold today are of the mass-produced variety sometimes referred to as "city "or "urban" hams. Higher-quality American hams are generally labeled "COUNTRY-CURED" (or "country-style"). The majority of these "country" hams come from Georgia, Kentucky, Tennessee and Virginia; each region adds its own distinctive style to the ham it produces. Probably the most famous country-cured ham is the SMITHFIELD HAM from the Virginia town of the same name. A wide selection of specially cured hams are also imported from many European countries. The most well known are PROSCIUTTO from Italy, Germany's WESTPHALIAN, France's BAYONNE and the York ham from England. Prosciutto and Westphalian are generally sold in paper-thin slices. When buying a fresh ham, look for one with a firm white layer of fat, with well-marbled lean portion. In younger animals, the meat should be a grayish-pink color; older pork should be a delicate shade of rose. Loosen any packaging material and store the fresh ham in the coldest part of the refrigerator for up to 5 days. When purchasing a cured ham, choose one that's firm and plump. The meat should be finely grained and rosy pink. Refrigerate in the ham's original wrapping or container. Some country-style hams can be stored in a cool place for 1 to 2 months. Longer storage is possible, but moisture evaporation causes the ham to shrink and toughen. Canned hams should be stored according to label directions. Some require refrigeration; others have been sterilized and do not need to be refrigerated until after they've been opened. Ham can be baked, grilled, sautéed, broiled or simmered. Precooked hams can be eaten without additional cooking. Heavily cured country-style hams, depending on how salty they are, may require scrubbing, then soaking up to 24 hours before cooking. *For information on specific hams, see individual listings.*

Haman's hats *see* HAMANTASCHEN

hamantaschen [HAH-mahn-tah-shuhn] These small triangular pastries hold a sweet filling, either of honey-poppy seed, prune or apricot. They're one of the traditional sweets of Purim, a festive Jewish holiday. Also called *Haman's hats* after Haman, the wicked prime minister of Persia who plotted the extermination of Persian Jews. Haman's plot was foiled at the last minute and the joyous festival of Purim was proclaimed in celebration.

hamburger 1. Said to have made its first appearance at the St. Louis Louisiana Purchase Exposition in 1904, the hamburger is one of America's favorite foods. It consists of a cooked patty of ground beef sandwiched between two bread halves, usually in the form of a HAMBURGER BUN. The meat can be mixed with various flavorings including finely chopped onions and herbs, and is sometimes topped with a slice of cheese, in which case it becomes a **cheeseburger**. It's also commonly referred to as a *burger* and *hamburger steak*. The name "hamburger" comes from the seaport town of Hamburg, Germany, where it is thought that 19th-century sailors brought back the idea of raw shredded beef (known today as BEEF TARTARE) after trading with the Baltic provinces of Russia. Some anonymous German chef decided to cook the beef . . . and the rest is history. 2. Ground, shredded or finely chopped beef. *See also* GROUND BEEF.

hamburger bun A soft, round yeast roll 3½ to 4 inches in diameter, made to fit the size of a HAMBURGER. It may be made with regular or wholewheat flour and variously topped with flavorings such as sesame seed, poppy seed or toasted chopped onion.

hamburger press A plastic or cast-aluminum utensil that forms perfectly round, flat hamburger patties. It comes in two separate round pieces, the top part having a plunger. The hamburger meat is placed in the bottom half, which is shaped like a disc with ½- to 1-inch sides. The top of the utensil is set over the base and, by pushing the plunger, the hamburger meat inside is pressed into a perfect disc.

Hamburg parsley *see* PARSLEY ROOT

ham hock The hock is the lower portion of a hog's hind leg, made up of meat, fat, bone, gristle and connective tissue. In the market, ham hocks are often cut into 2- to 3-inch lengths. Most have been cured, smoked or both, but fresh hocks can sometimes also be found. Ham hocks are generally used to flavor dishes such as soups, beans and stews that require lengthy, slow cooking. *See also* HAM.

hand cheese *see* HANDKÄSE CHEESE

handkäse cheese [HAHND-kay-zeh] The name of this German specialty means "hand cheese," referring to the fact that it's hand-shaped into irregular rounds, cylinders or other forms. It's made from skimmed, sour cow's milk, which gives the cheese a sharp, pungent flavor and very strong (some say overpowering) smell. The rind is gray and the interior off-white and soft. Handkäse is usually eaten as a snack. *See also* CHEESE.

hand-formed cookie; hand-shaped cookie Also called *molded* cookie, this style is made by shaping dough by hand into small balls, logs, crescents and other shapes. *See also* COOKIE.

Hangtown Fry This dish is said to have been created during the California Gold Rush in a rowdy burg called Hangtown (now Placerville) because of the town's frequent hangings. It consists of fried breaded oysters cooked together with eggs and fried bacon, rather like an omelet or scramble.

hard-ball stage A test for SUGAR SYRUP desribing the point at which a drop of boiling syrup immersed in cold water forms a rigid ball. Though the ball is hard, it will still be somewhat pliable. On a CANDY THERMOMETER, the hard-ball stage is between 250° and 265°F. *See* Candymaking Temperatures and Cold Water Tests Chart, page 537.

hard cider *see* CIDER

hard-crack stage A test for SUGAR SYRUP describing the point at which a drop of boiling syrup immersed in cold water separates into hard, brittle threads. On a CANDY THERMOMETER, the hard-crack stage is between 300° and 310°F. *See* Candymaking Temperatures and Cold Water Tests Chart, page 537.

hardhead *see* DRUM

hard sauce The traditional accompaniment for PLUM PUDDING, hard sauce is made by beating butter, sugar and flavoring together until smooth and creamy. The sugar can be confectioners', granulated or brown. The flavoring is generally brandy, rum or whiskey, though vanilla or other extracts may also be used. This mixture is refrigerated until "hard" (the texture of butter). It's often spooned into a decorative mold before chilling and unmolded before serving. Hard sauce is known in England as *brandy butter*.

hard-shell clam One of the two varieties of clam, the other being **soft-shell clam**. On the East Coast, hard-shell clams, also called by their Indian name, *quahog*, come in three sizes. The smallest are LITTLENECK CLAMS, which have a shell diameter less than 2 inches. Next comes the medium-sized CHERRYSTONE CLAM, about 2½ inches across. The largest of this trio is the CHOWDER CLAM, (also simply called *large clam*), with a shell diameter of at least 3 inches. Among the West Coast hard-shell varieties are the

PACIFIC LITTLENECK CLAM, the PISMO and the small, sweet BUTTER CLAMS from the Puget Sound. *For information on specific clams, see individual listings. See also* CLAM.

hardtack   Also called *ship biscuit* and *sea bread*, this large, hard biscuit is made with an unsalted, unleavened flour-and-water dough. After it's baked, hardtack is dried to lengthen shelf life. It's been used at least since the 1800s as a staple for sailors on long voyages.

hard wheat   *see* WHEAT

haricot vert   [ah-ree-koh VAIR]   The French term for "green bean," *haricot* meaning "bean" and *vert* translating as "green."

harissa sauce   [hah-REE-suh]   From Tunisia, this fiery-hot sauce is usually made with hot chili peppers, garlic, cumin, coriander and caraway. It's the traditional accompaniment for COUSCOUS but is also used to flavor soups, stews and other dishes. Harissa can be found in cans and jars in Middle Eastern markets.

hartshorn   *see* AMMONIUM BICARBONATE

harusame   *see* ASIAN NOODLES

Harvard beets   Sliced beets cooked in a thickened sweet-and-sour sauce composed of vinegar, sugar, water, butter, cornstarch and seasonings. Harvard beets are served hot as a side dish.

Harvey Wallbanger   A sweet COCKTAIL made of vodka, orange juice and GALLIANO (an anise-flavored LIQUEUR).

hasenpfeffer   [HAH-zuhn-fehf-uhr]   Literally translated from German as "hare pepper," this dish is a thick, highly seasoned stew of rabbit meat. Before stewing, the meat is soaked in a wine-vinegar marinade for 1 to 3 days. Hasenpfeffer is often served garnished with sour cream and accompanied by noodles or dumplings.

hash   *n.* A dish of finely chopped meat (roast beef and corned beef are the most common), potatoes and seasonings, usually fried together until lightly browned. Other chopped vegetables, such as green pepper, celery and onion, can also be added. Hash is sometimes served with gravy or sauce. **hash**   *v.* To chop food into small pieces.

hash browns; hash-brown potatoes   Finely chopped, cooked potatoes that are fried (often in bacon fat) until well browned. The mixture is usually pressed down into a flat cake in the pan and browned on one side, then turned and browned on the other. It's sometimes only browned on one side. Other ingredients such as chopped onion and green pepper are often added for flavor excitement.

hasty pudding This easy, versatile dish was enjoyed by our Colonial ancestors both in the morning for breakfast and after dinner for dessert. It's a simple cornmeal mush made with water or milk and sometimes sweetened with molasses, maple syrup or honey. If the dish isn't sweetened during cooking, a syrup or sweet sauce usually accompanies a hasty pudding. It's served hot, sometimes with milk or cream.

haute cuisine [OHT kwih-ZEEN] Food that is prepared in an elegant or elaborate manner; the very finest food, prepared perfectly.

Havarti cheese [hah-VAHR-tee] Named after the Danish experimental farm where it was developed, Havarti is often referred to as the Danish TILSIT because of its similarity to that cheese. It's semisoft and pale yellow with small irregular holes. The flavor of young Havarti is mild yet tangy. As the cheese ages, its flavor intensifies and sharpens. Havarti comes in loaves or blocks and is often wrapped in foil. *See also* CHEESE.

hazelnut These wild nuts grow in clusters on the hazel tree in temperate zones around the world. The fuzzy outer husk opens as the nut ripens, revealing a hard, smooth shell. Italy, Spain, France and Turkey lead the way in hazelnut production. Until the 1940s, the U.S. imported most hazelnuts; however, they're now grown in Oregon and Washington. Also called *filberts* and *cobnuts*, particularly when cultivated, these sweet, rich, grape-size nuts are used chopped, ground and whole in all manner of sweets. They also add flavor and texture to savory items such as salads and main dishes. Hazelnuts are usually packaged whole, though some producers are now also offering them chopped—a real timesaver. Hazelnuts have a bitter brown skin that is best removed, usually by heating them at 350°F for 10 to 15 minutes, until the skins begin to flake. By placing a handful of nuts at a time in a dish towel, then folding the towel over the warm nuts and rubbing vigorously, most of the skin will be removed. *See also* HAZELNUT OIL; NUTS.

hazelnut oil A fragrant, full-flavored oil pressed from hazelnuts and tasting like the roasted nut. Most hazelnut oil is imported from France and is therefore expensive. It can be purchased in cans or bottles in gourmet markets and many supermarkets. Hazelnut oil can be stored in a cool (under 65°F) place for up to 3 months. To prevent rancidity, it's safer to store it in the refrigerator. Because it's so strong-flavored, hazelnut oil is generally combined with lighter oils. It can be used in dressings, to flavor sauces and main dishes and in baked goods. *See also* FATS AND OILS.

head cheese Not a cheese at all, but a sausage made from the meaty bits of the head of a calf or pig (sometimes a sheep or cow) that are seasoned, combined with a gelatinous meat broth and cooked in a mold. When cool, the sausage is unmolded and thinly sliced. It's usually eaten at room temperature. Head cheese can be purchased in delicatessens and many supermarkets. In England this sausage is referred to as *brawn,* and in France it's called *fromage de tête*—"cheese of head." *See also* SAUSAGE.

head lettuce Generally, the term *head lettuce* describes those varieties on which the leaves grow in a dense rosette. There are two subcategories— CRISPHEAD (commonly known as *iceberg*) and BUTTERHEAD (the *Bibb* and *Boston* varieties). *See also* LETTUCE.

heart Since heart consists almost entirely of muscle, it tends to be quite tough. In general, the younger the animal, the more tender the heart. Beef heart is the largest of those commonly available, followed by those of calves, lambs and chickens. Choose hearts that are fresh-smelling, plump and red, avoiding those with a brown or gray hue. Refrigerate, loosely wrapped, for no more than a day or two. Before using, remove any excess fat and wash thoroughly. Heart can be braised, stewed or chopped and added to cooked dishes such as stews. Small hearts, such as those from young lambs and pigs, are often stuffed and sautéed or roasted and served one per person. Chicken hearts from a young bird can also be sautéed.

hearts of palm The edible inner portion of the stem of the cabbage palm tree, which grows in many tropical climates and is Florida's official state tree. Hearts of palm are slender, ivory-colored, delicately flavored and expensive. They resemble white asparagus, sans tips, and the flavor is reminiscent of an artichoke. Each stalk is about 4 inches long and can range in diameter from pencil-thin to 1 to 1½ inches. The hearts of palm we get in the U.S. are either from Florida or imported from Brazil. They're available fresh only in Florida and in other countries where they're grown. Canned hearts of palm are packed in water, and can be found in gourmet markets and many large supermarkets. Once opened, they should be transferred to a nonmetal container with an airtight cover. They can be refrigerated in their own liquid for up to a week. Hearts of palm can be used in salads and in main dishes, or deep-fried.

heavy cream *see* CREAM

hen *see* FOWL

herbs [ERB; Brit. HERB] The fragrant leaves of any of various annual or perennial plants that grow in temperate zones and do not have a woody stem. Herbs can be purchased in dried or fresh forms. Some, like CHIVES, are also sold frozen. Some of the more commonly available **fresh herbs** are BASIL, BAY LEAF, CHERVIL, CORIANDER, MARJORAM, MINT, OREGANO, PARSLEY, ROSEMARY, SAGE, SAVORY, TARRAGON and THYME. They can be found at various times of year, depending on the herb. Choose herbs that have a clean, fresh fragrance and a bright color without any sign of wilting or browning. They can be stored in the refrigerator, wrapped in barely damp paper towel and sealed airtight in a plastic bag for up to 5 days. For storage up to 10 days (depending on the herb), place the bouquet of herbs, stem end down, in a tall glass and fill with cold water until the ends are covered by 1 inch. Cover the top of the bouquet with a plastic bag, securing it to the glass with a rubber band. Alternatively, the herb bouquet may be placed in a screw-top jar in the same manner and sealed tightly. Either way, the water should be changed every 2 days. Just before using, wash the herbs and blot dry with a paper towel. **Dried herbs** are available year-round in metal or cardboard boxes, bottles, cellophane packages and unglazed ceramic pots. They have a stronger, more concentrated flavor than fresh herbs, but quickly lose their pungency. Crushed or ground herbs become lackluster more quickly than whole herbs. The more airtight the storage container, the longer the herbs will last. Transfer those in cardboard, tin, unglazed ceramic or cellophane to small glass bottles or jars with screw-top lids. Each time you use the herb, make sure the lid is tightly resealed. Store dried herbs in a cool, dark place for a maximum of 6 months. After 3 months, it is best to refrigerate them. Herbs are used to flavor all manner of food and drink. Most should be used judiciously because many of them can be quite pungent. *For information on specific herbs, see individual listings. See also* SPICES; Herb and Spice Chart, page 538.

herbes de Provence [AIRB duh proh-VAWNS] An assortment of dried herbs said to reflect those most commonly used in southern France. The blend can be found packed in tiny clay crocks in the spice section of large supermarkets. The mixture commonly contains basil, fennel seed, lavender, marjoram, rosemary, sage, summer savory and thyme. The blend can be used to season dishes of meat, poultry and vegetables. *For information on specific herbs, see individual listings.*

herb tea *see* TISANE

herb vinegar *see* VINEGAR

Herkimer cheese [HER-kuh-mer] A famous CHEDDAR made in Herkimer County, New York. *See also* CHEESE.

hermit An old-fashioned favorite said to have originated in Colonial New England, this spicy, chewy cookie is full of chopped fruits and nuts. It's usually sweetened with molasses or brown sugar. It's said that hermits were named for their long keeping qualities—they're better when hidden away like a hermit for several days.

hero sandwich This huge sandwich goes by many names, depending on where it's made. Among its aliases are *submarine, grinder, hoagie* and *poor boy* (or *po' boy*). Generally, the hero sandwich consists of a small loaf of Italian or French bread (or a large oblong roll), the bottom half of which is heaped with layers of any of various thinly sliced meats, cheeses, tomatoes, pickles, lettuce, peppers—anything the cook is in the mood for.

herring This huge family of saltwater fish has over a hundred varieties. The popular herring swims in gigantic schools and can be found in the cold waters of the North Atlantic and Pacific oceans. In the U.S., two of the most popular members of this family are the American **shad** and the **alewife,** both of which are anadromous, meaning that they migrate from their saltwater habitat to spawn in fresh water. Herring are generally small (ranging between ¼ and 1 pound) and silvery. The major exception to that rule is the American shad, which averages 3 to 5 pounds and is prized for its eggs—the delicacy known as *shad roe*. Young herring are frequently labeled and sold as SARDINES. Fresh herring are available during the spring on both the Pacific and Atlantic coasts. When fresh, the high-fat herring has a fine, soft texture that is suited for baking, sautéing and grilling. The herring's flesh becomes firm when cured by either pickling, salting, smoking or a combination of those techniques. There are many variations of cured herring. **Bismarck herring** are unskinned fillets that have been cured in a mixture of vinegar, sugar, salt and onions. **Rollmops** are Bismarck herring fillets wrapped around a piece of pickle or onion and preserved in spiced vinegar. **Pickled herring** (also called **marinated herring**) have been marinated in vinegar and spices before being bottled in either a sour-cream sauce or a wine sauce. The term can also refer to herring that have been dry-salted before being cured in brine. **Kippered herring** (also called **kippers**) are split, then cured by salting, drying and cold-smoking. **Bloaters** are larger than kippers but treated in a similar manner. They have a slightly milder flavor due to a lighter salting and shorter smoking period. Their name comes from their swollen appearance. **Schmaltz herring** are mature, higher-fat herring that are filleted and preserved in brine. The reddish **Matjes herring** are skinned and filleted before being cured in a spiced sugar-vinegar brine. *See also* FISH.

Hervé cheese [air-VAY] From the Belgian town of the same name, this cow's-milk, LIMBURGERlike cheese is pungent soft and very strong-smelling. It is sometimes flavored with herbs. Hervé has a pale yellow interior with a reddish-brown coating created by the bacteria that grow during its 3-month aging. Because it's so strong, Hervé is best eaten with dark breads and beers. *See also* CHEESE.

hibachi [hih-BAH-chee] Japanese for "fire bowl," a hibachi is just that—a small (generally cast-iron) container made for holding fuel (usually charcoal). A grill that sits on top of the bowl is used to cook various foods. Hibachis come in square, oblong and round models. Because of their compact size, they're completely portable.

hickory nut There are 17 varieties of hickory trees, 13 of which are native to the U.S. The extremely hard hickory wood is widely used to smoke American hams. All varieties of the hickory tree bear nuts, the most popular being the PECAN, partially due to its thin shell. The common "hickory nut" has an extraordinarily hard shell, the cracking of which usually requires a hammer swung with a great deal of muscle. Hickory nuts have an excellent, rich flavor with a buttery quality due to their high fat content. They're available only in certain parts of the country and are generally sold unshelled. Hickory nuts can be used in a variety of baked goods and in almost any recipe as a substitute for pecans. *See also* NUTS.

high-altitude cooking and baking Simply put, the weight of air on any surface it comes in contact with is called *air* (or *atmospheric*) *pressure*. There's less (or lower) air pressure at high altitudes because the blanket of air above is thinner than it would be at sea level. As a result, at sea level water boils at 212°F; at an altitude of 7,500 feet, however, it boils at about 198°F because there's not as much air pressure to inhibit the boiling action. This also means that because at high altitudes boiling water is 14°cooler than at sea level, foods will take longer to cook because they're heating at a lower temperature. Lower air pressure also causes boiling water to evaporate more quickly in a high altitude. This decreased air pressure means that adjustments in some ingredients and cooking time and temperature will have to be made for high-altitude baking, as well as some cooking techniques such as candy making, deep-fat frying and canning. Consult a general cookbook for details on high-altitude cooking and baking adjustments. *See charts on* High Altitude Adjustments for Baking, page 535, and Approximate Boiling Temperature of Water at Various Altitudes, page 535.

highball A COCKTAIL served in a tall glass over ice. Usually a simple concoction of whiskey mixed with SODA WATER or plain water.

high tea This British tradition is a late-afternoon or early evening meal, usually quite substantial. It originated in the 19th century as a simple, early workingman's supper. High tea can be served buffet-style or set on a table.

It includes a variety of dishes such as CORNISH PASTIES, WELSH RAREBIT, SCOTCH WOODCOCK and various other meat and fish dishes. Also included are plenty of buns, CRUMPETS, biscuits and jams, as well as an elaborate array of cakes and pastries and, of course, steaming pots of hot tea.

hoagie [HOH-gee] *see* HERO SANDWICH

hock 1. The lower portion of an animal's leg, generally corresponding to the ankle in a human. *See* HAM HOCK. 2. A term used in England for any RHINE WINE.

hoe cake; hoecake *see* JOHNNY CAKE

hogfish *see* CATFISH

hog jowl The cheek of a hog, which is usually cut into squares before being cured and smoked. Hog jowl is generally only available in the South. Tightly wrapped, it can be refrigerated for up to a week. It's fattier than bacon but can be cut into strips and fried in the same manner. It's also used to flavor stews, bean dishes and the like.

hog maw A pig's stomach, commonly stuffed with a sausage mixture, simmered until done, then baked until brown. It's usually available only by special order and should be stored in the refrigerator for no more than 2 days. Before using, the stomach should be cleaned of all membrane, rinsed thoroughly, then patted dry.

hoisin sauce [HOY-sihn; hoy-SIHN] Also called *Peking sauce*, this thick, reddish-brown sauce is sweet and spicy, and widely used in Chinese cooking. It's a mixture of soybeans, garlic, chili peppers and various spices. Hoisin sauce is mainly used as a table condiment and as a flavoring agent for many meat, poultry and shellfish dishes. It can be found in oriental markets and many large supermarkets. Once opened, canned hoisin should be transferred to a nonmetal container, tightly sealed and refrigerated. Bottled hoisin can be refrigerated as is. Both will keep indefinitely when stored in this manner.

hollandaise sauce [HOL-uhn-dayz] This smooth, rich, creamy sauce is generally used to embellish vegetables, fish and egg dishes, such as the classic EGGS BENEDICT. It's made with butter, egg yolks and lemon juice, usually in a DOUBLE BOILER to prevent overheating, and served warm.

homard [oh-MAHR] French for "lobster."

home-fried potatoes Potatoes that are sliced and fried, often with finely chopped onions or green peppers. The potatoes can either be raw or boiled before slicing. Also called *cottage-fried potatoes*.

hominy One of the first food gifts the American Indians gave to the colonists, hominy is dried white or yellow corn kernels from which the hull and germ have been removed. This process is done either mechanically or chemically by soaking the corn in slaked lime or lye. Hominy is sold canned, ready-to-eat or dried (which must be reconstituted before using). It's commonly served as a side dish or as part of a casserole. When dried hominy is broken or very coarsely ground it's called **samp**. When ground, it's called **hominy grits**—or simply *grits*—and usually comes in three grinds—fine, medium and coarse. Hominy grits are generally simmered with water or milk until very thick. The mixture can be served in this mushlike form or chilled, cut into squares and fried. In the South, grits are served as a side dish for breakfast or dinner.

homogenize [huh-MAHJ-uh-nyz] To create an EMULSION by reducing all the particles to the same size. In homogenized milk, for instance, the fat globules are broken down mechanically until they are evenly and imperceptibly distributed throughout the liquid. Commercial salad dressings are also often homogenized.

honey A thick, sweet liquid made by bees from flower nectar. Contrary to what many people think, a honey's color and flavor does not derive from the bee, but from the flower from which the nectar comes. In general, the darker the color the stronger the flavor. There are hundreds of different honeys throughout the world, most of them named for the flower from which they originate. The flowers that produce some of America's most popular honeys are clover, orange blossom and sage. Other honeys, some of which are only available in limited quantities in the region from which they originate, come from the following blossoms: alfalfa, buckwheat, dandelion, heather, linden, raspberry, spearmint and thyme, just to name a few. When using honey in cooking, it's important to know its source—buckwheat honey, for example, has far too strong a flavor to be used in a recipe that calls for orange blossom honey, which has a light, delicate fragrance and flavor. Honey comes in three basic forms: **comb honey** with the liquid still in the chewy comb, both of which are edible; **chunk-style honey**, which is honey with pieces of the honeycomb included in the jar; and regular **liquid honey** that has been extracted from the comb, much of which has been PASTEURIZED to help prevent crystallization. Other honey products such as **honey butters** and **honey spreads** are available at most supermarkets. Store tightly sealed honey in a cool, dry place. When refrigerated, honey crystallizes, forming a gooey, grainy mass. It can easily be reliquefied by placing the opened jar either in a microwave oven at 100 percent power for about 30 seconds (depending on the amount), or in a pan of hot water over low heat for 10 to 15 minutes. Honey is widely used as a bread spread and as a sweetener and flavoring agent for baked goods, liquids (such as tea), desserts and in some cases savory dishes like honey-glazed ham or carrots.

honeydew melon   This sweet, succulent member of the MUSKMELON family was prized by ancient Egyptians thousands of years ago, and ages before that in Persia, where the muskmelon is thought to have originated. Luckily for American honeydew enthusiasts, the melons are now grown in California and parts of the Southwest. The slightly oval honeydew is distinguished by a smooth, creamy-yellow rind and pastel green flesh that's extraordinarily juicy and sweet. It ranges in weight from 4 to 8 pounds. Honeydews are available year-round, though the peak months are generally July through September. Perfectly ripe honeydews will have an almost indistinguishable wrinkling on the skin's surface, often detectable only by touch. Choose one that's very heavy for its size. Underripe melons can be ripened at room temperature. Wrap ripe melons in a plastic bag and refrigerate up to 5 days. Honeydew melons can be used in salads, desserts, as a garnish and in FRUIT SOUPS. They are a good source of vitamin C. *See also* MELON.

hoppin' John; hopping John   Said to have originated with African slaves on Southern plantations, hoppin' John is a dish of BLACK-EYED PEAS cooked with SALT PORK and seasonings and served with cooked rice. Tradition says that if hoppin' John is eaten on New Year's day, it will bring good luck.

hops   A hardy, vining plant that produces conelike flowers. The dried flowers are used to impart a pleasantly bitter flavor to beers and ales. This same plant produces **hop shoots**, which are widely available commercially only in Europe and can be cooked like asparagus and served as a vegetable.

horehound   A member of the mint family, this downy-leaved plant yields a juice that, culinarily, is generally only used to make horehound candy—a brittle, sugar-drop confection with a slightly bitter undertaste. Extract of horehound is also used to make cough syrup and lozenges.

hors d'oeuvre   [or DERV]   Small savory appetizers served before the meal, customarily with APÉRITIFS or COCKTAILS. They are usually one- or two-bite size and can be cold or hot. Hors d'oeuvre may be in the form of a fancy CANAPÉ or as simple as a selection of CRUDITÉS. The word "hors d'oeuvre" is used for both the singular and plural forms and should not be written as *hors d'oeuvres*. The reason is that the term translates literally as (dishes) "outside the work (meal)" and no matter how many dishes there are, there is only one "work."

horseradish This ancient herb (one of the five bitter herbs of the Jewish Passover festival) is a native of eastern Europe but now grows in other parts of Europe as well as the U.S. Though it has spiky green leaves that can be used in salads, horseradish is grown mainly for its large, white, pungently spicy roots. Fresh horseradish is available in many supermarkets. It should be refrigerated, wrapped in a plastic bag, and peeled before using. It's most often grated and used in sauces or as a condiment with fish or meat. Bottled horseradish is available white (preserved in vinegar), and red (in beet juice). Also available is dried horseradish, which must be reconstituted before using. *See also* WASABI.

hosomaki [hoh-soh-MAH-kee] *see* SUSHI

hot cake *see* PANCAKE

hotchpotch [HAHCH-pahch] Each country has its own version of this rich, layered, vegetable-and-meat stew. Scots usually add barley and the meat is mutton or beef or sometimes grouse and rabbit. The English call it **hot pot** and their famous **Lancashire hot pot** contains mutton, sheep's kidneys and, when available, oysters, all covered with a layer of potatoes. The Dutch **hutspot** uses beef, whereas in France and Belgium the dish is referred to as **hochepot** and the ingredients include pig's ears and feet.

hot cross buns Traditionally served on Good Friday, these small, lightly sweet yeast buns contain raisins or currants and sometimes chopped candied fruit. Before baking, a cross is slashed in the top of the bun. After baking, a confectioner's sugar icing is used to fill the cross.

hot dog *see* FRANKFURTER

hot pepper *see* CHILI PEPPER

hot pot *see* HOTCHPOTCH

hubbard squash A very large winter squash with a thick, bumpy, hard shell ranging in color from dark green to bright orange. Hubbards are available from early September to March, either whole or, if extraordinarily large, cut into pieces. Look for those with clean-colored rinds free from blemishes. Store unwrapped in a cool (under 50°F) place (or in the refrigerator) up to 6 months. Hubbard squash is best boiled or baked. Because of its rather grainy texture, the yellow-orange flesh is often mashed or pureed and mixed with butter and seasonings before serving. Hubbard squash is an excellent source of vitamin A and contains a fair amount of iron and riboflavin. *See also* SQUASH.

huckleberry A wild, blue-black berry that closely resembles (and is often mistaken for) the BLUEBERRY. The huckleberry, however, has 10 small, hard seeds in the center, whereas the blueberry has many seeds, so tiny and soft that they're barely noticeable. Additionally, the huckleberry has a thicker skin and a flavor that is slightly less sweet and more astringent. Unless you pick them yourself, or have a friend who does, it's unlikely that you'll find fresh huckleberries because they're not cultivated. They're in season from June through August and are good eaten plain or in baked goods such as muffins or pies.

hull *n.*1. The outer (usually fibrous) covering of a fruit or seed—also called *husk* or *shell.* 2. The attached, leafy calyx of some fruits, such as the strawberry. **hull** *v.* To prepare a food for eating by removing the outer covering or, as in the case of strawberries, the leafy portion at the top. *See also* SCHUCK.

humble pie A 17th century English dish, in which the heart, liver, kidney and other innards of a deer were combined with apples, currants, sugar and spices and baked as a pie. The servants ate this inexpensive but filling repast while the gentry dined on the VENISON. The name comes from the old-English word *numble*, meaning a deer's innards. "A numble pie" became "an umble pie," which eventually worked it's way to "a humble pie."

hummus [HOOM-uhs] This thick Middle Eastern sauce is made from mashed CHICKPEAS seasoned with lemon juice, garlic and olive or sesame oil. It's usually served as a dip with pieces of PITA, or as a sauce. When TAHINI (sesame-seed paste) is added, it becomes **hummus bi tahina**. Middle Eastern markets carry both forms in cans or jars or sometimes fresh.

hundred-year egg Also called *century egg, thousand-year egg* and *Ming Dynasty egg*, all of which are eggs that have been preserved by being covered with a coating of lime, ashes and salt before being shallowly buried for 100 days. The lime "petrifies" the egg, making it look like it's been buried for at least a century. The black outer coating and shell are removed to reveal a firm, amber-colored white and creamy, dark green yolk. The flavor is pungent and cheeselike. Eggs from chickens are generally used, though duck and goose eggs are also preserved in this manner. Hundred-year eggs are sold individually and can be found in Chinese markets. They will keep at room temperature (under 70°F) for up to 2 weeks or in the refrigerator up to a month. These preserved eggs are usually eaten uncooked, either for breakfast or served as an appetizer, often with accompaniments such as soy sauce or minced ginger.

hushpuppy This Southern specialty is a small cornmeal DUMPLING, flavored with chopped scallions, deep-fried and served hot. Hushpuppies are a traditional accompaniment for fried catfish. Their name is said to have come from the fact that, to keep hungry dogs from begging for food while the rest of the dinner was being prepared, cooks used to toss scraps of the fried batter to the pets with the admonition, "Hush, puppy!"

husk *see* HULL

hutspot *see* HOTCHPOTCH

hydrogenated oil *see* FATS AND OILS

hyssop [HIHS-up] Any of various herbs belonging to the mint family with aromatic, dark green leaves that have a slightly bitter, minty flavor. Hyssop adds intrigue to salads, fruit dishes (it particularly complements cranberries), soups and stews. It's also used to flavor certain LIQUEURS, such as CHARTREUSE.

ce *n.* Called *granité* in France and *granità* in Italy, an ice is a frozen mixture of water, sugar and liquid flavoring such as fruit juice, wine or coffee. The proportion is usually 4 parts liquid to 1 part sugar. During the freezing process, ices are generally stirred frequently to produce a slightly granular final texture. **ice** *v.* 1. To chill a food, glass or serving dish in order to get it icy cold and sometimes coated with frost. 2. To spread frosting over the surface of a cake.

ice, dry *see* DRY ICE

iceberg lettuce *see* CRISPHEAD LETTUCE

icebox cookie *see* REFRIGERATOR COOKIE

ice cream America's favorite dessert is thought to have originated in the mountains of ancient China, with snow probably used as the base. Today's ice cream is made with a combination of milk products (usually cream combined with fresh, condensed or dry milk), a sweetening agent (sugar, honey, corn syrup or artificial sweetener) and sometimes solid additions such as pieces of chocolate, nuts, fruit, etc. According to USDA regulations, ice creams with solid additions must contain a minimum of 8 percent butterfat, while plain ice creams must have at least 10 percent butterfat. **French ice cream** has a cooked egg-custard base. **Ice milk** is made in much the same way as ice cream, except for the fact that it contains less butterfat and milk solids. The result, other than a lowered calorie count, is a lighter, less creamy texture. Commercial ice creams usually contain stabilizers to improve both texture and body, and to help make them melt resistant. Many also contain artificial coloring. Those made with natural flavorings (for instance, chocolate) will be labeled simply "Chocolate Ice Cream." If the majority of the flavoring is natural with a boost from an artificial-flavor source, the label will read "Chocolate-Flavored Ice Cream"; if over 50 percent of the flavoring is artificial it will read "Artificial Chocolate Ice Cream." All commercial ice creams have "overrun," a term applied to the amount of air they contain. The percentage of overrun ranges from 0 (no air) to 200, a theoretical figure that would be all air. The legal overrun limit for ice cream is 100 percent, which would amount to half air. Ice cream needs some air or it would be rock-hard. But one with 100 percent overrun would have so little body that it would feel mushy in the mouth; it would also melt extremely fast. An ice cream with the more desirable proportion of 20 to 50 percent overrun (10 to 25 percent air) would be denser, creamier and eminently more satisfying. Since the overrun is not listed on the package, the only way to be absolutely sure is to weigh the carton. Ice cream with a 50 percent overrun (25 percent air) will weigh about 18 ounces per pint (subtract about 1½ ounces for the weight of the container). The weight of the ice cream will be proportionately higher with a lower percentage of overrun. During storage, ice cream has a tendency to absorb other food odors and to form ice crystals. For that reason, it's best not to freeze it for more than 2 to 3 days. Sealing the carton airtight in a plastic bag will extend storage life up to a week. Ice cream is used for a plethora of delicious treats including BAKED ALASKAS, BANANA SPLITS and ice-cream bars, sandwiches and cakes (cake layered with ice cream and frozen). *See also* GELATO; GRANITÀ; ICE; SHERBERT.

ice-cream makers Generally speaking, there are two basic styles of ice-cream maker—manual and electric. They can be simple or fancy and can cost from $25 to almost $1,000. In addition to ice cream, they can be used to make ice milk, frozen yogurt and frozen drinks. All of them work on the same principle—a canister with a central, vertical paddle (called a dasher) is placed inside a container that holds the freezing agent—either ice and salt, a chemical coolant or an electric refrigeration unit. The inner canister is filled with an ice-cream mixture that the dasher stirs (gently scraping the sides of the canister) when rotated. This stirring action aerates the mixture and keeps it smooth by preventing ice crystals from forming while it freezes. There are several different kinds of ice-cream freezers. Among the **manual-style ice-cream makers** are the old-fashioned, wooden buckets with a metal inner container for the ice-cream mixture. They require ice, ROCK SALT (which lowers the temperature of the ice) and plenty of physical stamina to turn the crank that rotates the dasher. They usually take 30 to 40 minutes to make 4 to 6 quarts of ice cream. Some of these wooden bucket-style makers have an electric motor that sits on top of the unit, saving manpower. A newer form of manual ice-cream maker is the *prechilled chamber freezer*, which ranges in size from 1 pint to 1½ quarts. The container is placed in the freezer for 24 to 48 hours to freeze the coolant sealed between the walls lining this unit. The ice-cream mixture is poured into the center cavity; a crank-and-dasher assembly and lid covers the entire unit. The hand-rotated crank is turned once every 2 to 3 minutes for 15 to 30 minutes, depending on the amount of ice cream being made. **Electric ice-cream machines** are all equipped with electric motors that rotate either the ice-cream canister or the dasher. There are several different styles and sizes of electric ice-cream machines. The most common is the *self-contained countertop unit* that uses refrigerator ice cubes and table salt, and in which the motor turns the canister. This type can make up to 2 quarts of ice cream. There is also a *small freezer unit* (averaging 1 quart) that doesn't require salt or ice but instead is placed in the freezer compartment of the refrigerator with the electric cord exiting between the freezer's seal and the closed door. In this type, the dasher is motor-turned, while the canister is stationary. The Rolls-Royce of electric ice-cream freezers is the large, *self-contained countertop machine* that has the freezing unit built into it. All that's required for this expensive pleaser is to pour the ice-cream mixture into the canister and flick a button.

ice-cream salt   *see* ROCK SALT

ice-cream scoop   A utensil used to remove ice cream from a carton or other container while forming the ice cream into a ball or oval shape. Ice-cream scoops come in several styles and sizes. The simplest is a plain metal scoop- or spade-shaped utensil. Next comes one shaped like a half-globe with a spring-action lever in the handle. When squeezed, the lever moves an arc-shaped blade across the scoop's interior and ejects the ice-cream ball. The nonstick-style scoop has antifreeze sealed inside. This model is especially helpful for extremely hard ice cream. Scoops come in many sizes, from tiny to large (about 1 to almost 3 inches in diameter).

ice milk   *see* ICE CREAM

icing   *see* FROSTING

icing sugar   *see* CONFECTIONERS' SUGAR

Idaho potato   The Idaho is considered by many to be the best variety of America's most popular potato for baking, the russet. Though some russets are commonly called *Idaho potatoes*, many government officials of that state are pushing to make the name exclusive to spuds grown in local soil. *See also* POTATO.

île flottante   [eel floh-TANT]   *see* FLOATING ISLANDS

immersion blender   This handheld BLENDER is tall, narrow and has a rotary blade at one end. It has variable speeds, is entirely portable and may be immersed right into a pot of soup (or other mixture) to puree or chop the contents. Many immersion blenders come with a whisk attachment (good for whipping cream), and other accouterments such as strainers or beakers for mixing individual drinks. Some also come with wall mounts.

impératrice, à l'   *see* RIZ À L'IMPÉRATRICE

Indian date   *see* TAMARIND

Indian pudding   This hearty, old-fashioned dessert originated in New England. It's a spicy, cornmeal-molasses baked pudding that can sometimes include sliced apples. Indian pudding is usually served with whipped cream, HARD SAUCE or ice cream.

Indian nut   *see* PINE NUT

indienne, à l' [ah lahn-DYEHN] A French term describing Indian-style dishes flavored with curry and served with rice.

infusion [ihn-FYOO-zhuhn] An infusion is the flavor that's extracted from an ingredient such as tea leaves, herbs or fruit by STEEPING them in a liquid (usually hot), such as water, for tea.

insalata [ihn-sah-LAH-tah] The Italian word for "salad."

instant cocoa   *see* COCOA MIX

instant flour   *see* FLOUR

invert sugar Invert sugar is created by combining a SUGAR SYRUP with a small amount of acid (such as CREAM OF TARTAR or lemon juice) and heating. This inverts, or breaks down, the SUCROSE into its two components, GLUCOSE and FRUCTOSE, thereby reducing the size of the sugar crystals. Because of its fine crystal structure, invert sugar produces a smoother product and is used in making candies such as fondant, and some syrups. The process of making jams and jellies automatically produces invert sugar by combining the natural acid in the fruit with granulated sugar and heating the mixture. Invert sugar can usually be found in jars in cake-decorating supply shops.

Irish breakfast tea A strong, robust black-tea blend that includes the superior CEYLON TEA. *See also* TEA.

Irish coffee Guaranteed to warm the cockles of anyone's heart, this hot beverage blends strong coffee, IRISH WHISKEY and a small amount of sugar. It's usually served in a glass mug and topped by a dollop of whipped cream.

Irish mist A LIQUEUR made from a blend of IRISH WHISKEY and heather honey.

Irish moss   *see* CARRAGEEN

Irish potato A round, white, thin-skinned potato whose origin is actually South America. It's good for boiling, frying and pan-roasting. *See also* POTATO.

Irish soda bread This classic Irish QUICK BREAD uses baking soda (as the name implies) as its LEAVENER. It's usually made with buttermilk and is speckled with currants and caraway seed. Before baking, a cross is slashed in the top of the loaf. The purpose of the cross, legend says, is to scare away the devil.

Irish stew A traditional layered dish of equal parts seasoned lamb or mutton chops, potatoes and onions. Water or stock is poured over all, the pot is covered tightly and the stew is cooked slowly for 2 to 3 hours. It's best made the day before to allow the flavors to blend.

Irish whiskey Made in Ireland, this light, dry WHISKEY is distilled from a mash of fermented barley and other grains.

ironware Pots and pans made from iron or cast iron, both known for excellent heat conductivity. Modern-day ironware is either preseasoned or coated with a thick enamel glaze. The advantage of the enamel coating is the ease with which it cleans. Old-fashioned unseasoned iron pots and pans must be seasoned before using. *See also* SEASON.

irradiation An FDA-approved process by which food is bombarded with low doses of gamma rays. The purpose for this radiation is to extend shelf life by inhibiting maturation and decay through the elimination of microorganisms and insect invasion. Most foods processed with irradiation will last weeks instead of days. All irradiated foods must bear an international symbol—a plant within a broken circle. Exceptions to this rule are irradiated foods—such as spices and herbs—that are used as an ingredient in other food products. The jury is still out on the safety of irradiated foods. Of concern are potentially toxic elements that irradiation may produce in foods, as well as the possible long-term side effects of eating these treated products. Proponents suggest that irradiation serves as a substitute for many questionable chemicals and preservatives now used in food processing. Those foods currently approved by the FDA for irradiation treatment are: fruits, vegetables, dried spices, herbs, seasonings and teas, pork, white potatoes, wheat and wheat flours. Most food producers, however, have not taken advantage of that approval.

isinglass [I-zuhn-glas; I-zing-glas] Transparent and pure, this form of GELATIN comes from the air bladders of certain fish, especially the STURGEON. It was popular 100 years ago, particularly for making jellies and to CLARIFY wine. With the convenience of today's modern gelatin, isinglass is rarely used.

Italian bread Almost identical to FRENCH BREAD, with the exception of its shape, which is shorter and plumper than the French BAGUETTE. The top of Italian bread is sometimes sprinkled with sesame seed.

Italian eggplant *see* EGGPLANT

Italian meringue A creamy MERINGUE made by slowly beating hot SUGAR SYRUP into stiffly beaten egg whites. Because the sugar syrup is cooked to the SOFT-BALL STAGE, the resulting meringue becomes very dense, glossy and smooth. The same method is used to make BOILED ICING. Italian meringue is used in soufflés, to frost cakes and pastries and to top pies (in the last case it's usually lightly browned in the oven before serving).

Italian parsley *see* PARSLEY

Italian sausage This favorite pizza topping is a coarse pork sausage, generally sold in plump links. Italian sausage is usually flavored with garlic and fennel seed or anise seed. It comes in two styles—**hot** (flavored with hot, red peppers) and **sweet** (without the added heat). It must be well cooked before serving, and is suitable for frying, grilling or braising. *See also* SAUSAGE.

I

ack cheese *see* MONTEREY JACK CHEESE

jackfruit This huge relative of the BREADFRUIT and fig can weigh up to 100 pounds. Spiny and oval or oblong-shaped, the tropical jackfruit grows in parts of Africa, Brazil and Southeast Asia. When green, both its flesh and edible seeds are included in curried dishes. Ripe jackfruit has a bland, sweet flavor and is generally used for desserts. In the U.S., jackfruit is only available canned.

jaggery [JAG-uh-ree] This dark, coarse, unrefined sugar (sometimes referred to as *palm sugar*) can be made either from the sap of various palm trees or from sugar-cane juice. It is primarily used in India, where many categorize sugar made from sugar cane as **jaggery** and that processed from palm trees as **gur**. It comes in several forms, the two most popular being a soft, honeybutter texture and a solid cakelike form. The former is used to spread on breads and confections, while the solid version serves to make candies, and when crushed, to sprinkle on cereal, etc. Jaggery has a sweet, winey fragrance and flavor that lends distinction to whatever food it embellishes. It can be purchased in East Indian markets. *See also* SUGAR.

jagging wheel *see* PASTRY WHEEL

jalapeño chili pepper [hah-lah-PEH-nyoh] Named after Jalapa, the capital of Veracruz, Mexico, these smooth, dark green CHILI PEPPERS range from hot to very hot. They have a rounded tip and are about 2 inches long and ¾ to 1 inch in diameter. Besides their flavor, jalapeños are quite popular because they're so easily seeded. The seeds and veins are extremely hot. They're available fresh and canned and are used in a variety of sauces, sometimes stuffed with cheese, fish or meat, and in a multitude of dishes.

jalousie [JAL-huh-see; ZHAH-loo-zee; zhah-loo-ZEE] A small cake made with flaky pastry, filled with a layer of ALMOND PASTE topped with jam. A latticed pastry topping allows the colorful jam filling to peek through.

jam A thick, mixture of fruit, sugar (and sometimes PECTIN) that is cooked until the pieces of fruit are very soft and almost formless. It is used as a bread spread, a filling for pastries and cookies and an ingredient for various desserts. *See also* JELLY; PRESERVES.

jambalaya [juhm-buh-LI-yah; jam-buh-LI-yah] One of CREOLE cookery's hallmarks, jambalaya is a versatile dish that combines cooked rice with a variety of ingredients including tomatoes, onion, green peppers and almost any kind of meat, poultry or shellfish. The dish varies widely from cook to cook. It's thought that the name derives from the French *jambon*, meaning "ham," the main ingredient in many of the first jambalayas.

jambon persillé [zham-BOHN pair-see-YAY] A molded dish of strips or cubes of cooked ham and chopped parsley held together with a meat-wine gelatin. It is served chilled and, when cut into slices, resembles a colorful red-and-green mosaic.

Japanese artichoke *see* CHINESE ARTICHOKE

Japanese gelatin *see* AGAR

Japanese king crab *see* KING CRAB

Japanese eggplant *see* EGGPLANT

Japanese medlar *see* LOQUAT

Japanese oyster *see* PACIFIC OYSTER

Japanese plum *see* LOQUAT

jardinière, à la [jahr-duh-NIHR; zhahr-dee-NYAIR] The French term referring to a dish garnished with vegetables.

Jarlsberg cheese [YAHRLZ-berg] This mild Swiss-style cheese has large irregular holes. It hails from Norway and has a yellow-wax rind and semifirm yellow interior. The texture is buttery rich and the flavor mild and slightly sweet. It's an all-purpose cheese that's good both for cooking and for eating as a snack. *See also* CHEESE.

jell To congeal a food substance, often with the aid of GELATIN.

jelly 1. A clear, bright mixture made from fruit juice, sugar and sometimes PECTIN. The texture is tender but will be firm enough to hold its shape when turned out of its container. Jelly is used as a bread spread and as a filling for some cakes and cookies. 2. In Britain, jelly is the term used for gelatin dessert. *See also* JAM; PRESERVES.

jelly bag Used to strain and CLARIFY the juice from fruit in order to prepare jelly. A jelly bag is made from a porous yet closely woven fabric like unbleached muslin. Jelly bags are hung over a bowl with the aid of loops at the top. The crushed fruit is placed in the bowl and left to drain for several hours, preferably overnight. Before use, the jelly bag is rinsed in water and wrung dry. This prevents too much juice from being absorbed into the fabric.

jelly bean This small, brightly colored, egg-shaped candy has a chewy, gelatinous texture and a hard candy coating. Jelly beans come in many flavors including lime, orange, licorice, cherry, chocolate, banana, etc. **Jelly Bellies** is a brand name that is now used generically to describe a miniature (about ½-inch-long) jelly bean. They come in many more exotic flavors such as piña colada, pink lemonade, chocolate fudge-mint, etc.

jelly roll Known since the mid 1800s, jelly rolls are cakes made of a thin sheet of SPONGE CAKE, spread with jam or jelly (and sometimes whipped cream or frosting) and rolled up. This type of cake is traditionally sprinkled with confectioners' sugar, rather than being frosted. When cut, jelly rolls have an attractive pinwheel design. The British term for jelly roll is *Swiss roll.*

jelly-roll pan A rectangular baking pan with about 1-inch-deep sides used to make sheet cakes or SPONGE CAKES used for JELLY ROLLS. These pans are usually 15½ × 10½ × 1 inch; however there is a smaller pan measuring 12 × 7 × ¾ inch and a larger one measuring 17 × 11 × 1 inch.

jerky Also called *jerked meat,* jerky is meat (usually beef) that is cut into long, thin strips and dried (traditionally by the sun). Jerky was a popular staple with early trappers, just as it is with today's backpackers because it keeps almost indefinitely and is light and easy to transport. It's quite tough and salty but is very flavorful and high in protein. *See also* BILTONG.

Jeroboam [jehr-uh-BOH-uhm] *see* WINE BOTTLES

Jerusalem artichoke This vegetable is not truly an artichoke but a variety of sunflower with a lumpy, brown-skinned tuber that often resembles a ginger root. Contrary to what the name implies, this vegetable has nothing to do with Jerusalem but is derived instead from the Italian word for sunflower, *girasole.* Because of its confusing moniker, modern-day growers have begun to call Jerusalem artichokes *sunchokes,* which is how they're often labeled in the produce section of many markets. The white flesh of this vegetable is nutty, sweet and crunchy. Jerusalem artichokes are available from about October to March. Select those that are firm and fresh-looking and not soft or wrinkled. Store in a cool, dry place for up to 5 days. After that, they will begin to wither because of moisture loss. They may be peeled or, because the skin is very thin and quite nutritious, simply washed well before being used. Jerusalem artichokes can be eaten raw in salad or cooked by boiling or steaming and served as a side dish. They also make a delicious soup. Jerusalem artichokes are a good source of iron.

jewfish Found off the coast of Florida and in the Gulf of Mexico, the true jewfish is a member of the GROUPER family and can weigh up to 750 pounds. (Giant SEA BASS are also sometimes referred to as jewfish.) Its firm, white meat is usually sold in steaks and fillets. Jewfish can be cooked in any manner suitable for GROUPER. *See also* FISH.

Jícama [HEE-kah-mah] Often referred to as the *Mexican potato*, this large, bulbous root vegetable has a thin brown skin and white crunchy flesh. Its sweet, nutty flavor is good both raw and cooked. Jícama is available from November through May and can be purchased in Mexican markets and most large supermarkets. It should be stored in the refrigerator and will last up to 5 days. The thin skin should be peeled just before using. When cooked, jícama retains its crisp, water chestnut–type texture. It's a fair source of vitamin C and potassium.

Jigger Also called a *shot* or *shot glass*, a jigger is a small glass-shaped container that usually holds about 1½ ounces, but can also be a 1- or 2-ounce size. It's generally used to measure liquor. *See also* PONY.

Johannisberg Riesling [yoh-HAH-nihs-boerg REEZ-ling; joh-HAN-ihs-burg] Also called *White Riesling*, this wine comes from the classic German Riesling grape, which is said to produce some of Germany's greatest wine. California and Australia also produce the grape and wine. Riesling grapes can be vinified either sweet, which makes a delicious APÉRITIF, or dry, in which case the wine can be served with meals. Johannisberg Riesling is characterized by its delicate, flower-scented bouquet and spicy, fruity flavor.

John Dory Found in European waters, this incredibly odd-looking fish has an oval, flat body and a large, spiny head. The John Dory's flesh is delicate and mild and can be cooked in a variety of ways including grilling, sautéing and poaching. It's rarely exported to the U.S., but PORGY may be substituted for any recipe calling for John Dory. *See also* FISH.

johnnycake; johnny cake, jonnycake Thought to be the precursor of the pancake, the johnnycake dates back to the early 1700s. It's a rather flat griddlecake made of cornmeal, salt and either boiling water or cold milk; there are strong advocates of both versions. Today's johnnycakes often have eggs, oil or melted butter and leavening (such as baking powder) added. Some renditions are baked in the oven, more like traditional cornbread. Also called *hoe cake* or *hoecake*.

Jonathan apple The spicy fragrance of this bright red apple is to some just as seductive as its juicy, sweet-tart flavor. The Jonathan is in season from September through February. This all-purpose apple is great for out-of-hand eating, and for pies, applesauce and other cooked dishes. It doesn't fare well, however, when used as a baking apple. *See also* APPLE.

Jordan almond This large, plump almond is imported from Spain and sold plain as well as encased in hard pastel candy coatings of various colors. *See also* ALMOND; NUTS.

juicer A manual or electric kitchen device used to extract the juice from fruit, and with some models, vegetables. Most of those used strictly for juicing citrus fruits have a ridged cone onto which a halved fruit is pressed. An old-fashioned form of this tool is the *reamer*, a ridged, teardrop-shaped tool with a handle.

jujube 1. [JOO-joo-bee] A tiny fruit-flavored candy with a hard, gelatinous texture. 2. [JOO-joob] *see* CHINESE DATE.

julienne [joo-lee-EHN; zhoo-LYEHN] Foods that have been cut into thin, matchstick strips. The food (such as a potato) is first cut into ⅛-inch-thick slices. The slices are stacked, then cut into ⅛-inch-thick strips. The strips may then be cut into whatever length is desired. If the object is round, cut a thin slice from the bottom so it will sit firmly and not roll on the work surface. Julienne is most often used as a garnish.

jumble; jumbal Dating back to early America, this delicate, crisp, ring-shaped cookie was particularly popular in the 1800s. It's like a thin, rich sugar cookie, often made with sour cream and formerly, scented with ROSE WATER. Jumbles can also be made with other flavorings such as orange zest or grated coconut.

juniper berry These astringent blue-black berries are native to both Europe and America. Juniper berries are too bitter to eat raw and are usually sold dried and used to flavor meats, sauces, stuffings, etc. They're generally crushed before using to release their flavor. These pungent berries are the hallmark flavoring of GIN. In fact, the name is derived from the French word for juniper berry—*genièvre*, which is the name for gin in France.

junket [JUHNG-kiht] This sweet, mild-flavored dessert is made with milk, sugar, various flavorings and RENNET. The rennet coagulates the mixture into a soft puddinglike texture. Junket is served chilled, sometimes accompanied by fruit.

jus *see* AU JUS

abob *see* KEBAB

kabocha squash [kah-BOH-chah] New to the U.S. market, this winter squash has a beautiful jade green rind with celadon green streaks. When cooked, its pale orange flesh is tender-smooth and sweet. An average kabocha ranges from 2 to 3 pounds, though they have been known to weigh as much as 8 pounds. Choose squash that are heavy for their size. The rind should be dull and firm; avoid any with soft spots. Kabochas can be cooked in any way suitable for ACORN SQUASH, such as baking or steaming. Before cooking, they must be halved and seeded. *See also* SQUASH.

Kahlúa [kah-LOO-ah] A coffee-flavored LIQUEUR made in Mexico.

kalamata olive [kahl-uh-MAH-tuh] *see* OLIVE

kale This attractive, nonheading member of the cabbage family has been cultivated for over 2,000 years. Though it grows in warm climates, it's happiest in colder climes where for centuries its high vitamin content has made it particularly popular with northern Europeans. Kale has a mild, cabbagey flavor and comes in many varieties and colors. Most kale is easily identified by its frilly leaves arranged in a loose bouquet formation. The color of the leaves of the varieties most commonly available in the U.S. is deep green variously tinged with shades of blue or purple. There are ornamental varieties in gorgeous shades of lavender, purple and celadon green. Kale's best during the winter months, though it's available year-round in most parts of the country. Choose richly colored, relatively small bunches of kale, avoiding any with limp or yellowing leaves. Store in the coldest section of the refrigerator no longer than 2 or 3 days. After that, the flavor of kale becomes quite strong and the leaves limp. Because the center stalk is tough, it should be removed before the kale is used. It may be prepared in any way suitable for spinach and small amounts make a nice addition to salads. Kale provides ample amounts of vitamins A and C, folic acid, calcium and iron.

kamut [kah-MOOT] The name "kamut" comes from the ancient Egyptian word for "wheat." Considered by some to be the great-great grandfather of grains, kamut is a variety of high-protein wheat that has never been hybridized. Thirty-six kernels were brought to Montana in the late 1940s and, at this writing, the grain is grown commercially only in that state. Kamut's kernels are two to three times the size of most wheat. Not only does this grain have a deliciously nutty flavor, but it also has a higher nutritional value than its modern-day counterparts. In the United States, kamut is available only in processed foods. It's used mainly for pastas, puffed cereal and crackers. Because cultivation is limited, kamut products are hard to find, and are generally only available in health-food stores. *See also* WHEAT.

kanten [kan-TEHN] *see* AGAR

kasha [KAH-shuh] *see* BUCKWHEAT

kasseri cheese [kuh-SAIR-ee] This Greek cheese is made from sheep's or goat's milk. It has a sharp, salty flavor and hard cheddarlike texture that's perfect for grating. An American version is made with cow's milk. The creamy gold-colored kasseri has a natural rind and is usually sold in blocks. It's delicious plain, grated over hot foods or used in cooking. Kasseri is the cheese used in the famous Greek dish SAGANAKI, where it's sautéed in butter, sprinkled with lemon juice and sometimes flamed with brandy. *See also* CHEESE.

katsuobushi; katsuo-bushi [KAH-tsuh-oh-boo-shee] Pink flakes of dried bonito (TUNA) which are used in Japanese cooking as a garnish and in some cooked preparations, principally DASHI. The tuna is boiled, smoked, then sun-dried. A special tool is used to flake the extremely hard chunks. Katsuobushi can be purchased in oriental markets and the specialty section of some large supermarkets. Depending on how fresh it is when purchased, it can be stored in a cool, dry place up to a year.

kebab; kabob [kuh-BOB] Small chunks of meat, fish or shellfish that are usually marinated before being threaded on a skewer and grilled over coals. Pieces of vegetables can also accompany the meat on the skewer. Also called *shish kebab* and *shashlik*.

kedgeree; kegeree [kehj-uh-REE; KEHJ-uh-ree] A spiced East Indian dish of rice, lentils and onions, Anglicized in the 18th century when the English added flaked smoked fish, hard-cooked eggs and a rich cream sauce. Kedgeree is a popular English breakfast dish.

K

kefir [keh-FEER] Originally made from camel's milk, kefir comes from high in the Caucasus—a 700-mile-long mountain range in the U.S.S.R. between the Caspian and Black seas. Today, however, it's more commonly produced from cow's milk. It's a slightly sour brew of fermented milk, most of which contains about 2½ percent alcohol. Kefir is reminiscent in both taste and texture of a liquid YOGURT. It's available in cartons or bottles in health-food stores. *See also* KUMISS.

kelp Also called *kombu* or *konbu*, kelp is particularly popular in Japanese cookery and is one of the two basic ingredients used for DASHI (soup stock). It's a long dark brown to greyish-black algae which, after harvesting, is sun-dried and folded into sheets. Kelp is sold in Japanese and health-food markets and when stored unopened in a dry place it will keep indefinitely. After opening, store in a cool, dry place for up to 6 months. Kelp has a natural white-powder covering that delivers considerable flavor. For that reason, the surface should be lightly wiped off, not washed. Kelp is used to flavor cooked foods as well as for SUSHI. It's sometimes pickled and used as a CONDIMENT.

ketchup [KEHCH-uhp; KACH-uhp] *Ke-tsiap*—a spicy pickled-fish condiment popular in 17th-century China—is said to be the origin of the name "ketchup." British seamen brought the *ke-tsiap* home and throughout the years the formula was changed to contain anything from nuts to mushrooms. It wasn't until the late 1700s that canny New Englanders added tomatoes to the blend and it became what we know today as ketchup. Also called *catsup* and *catchup*, this thick, spicy sauce is a traditional American accompaniment for French-fried potatoes, hamburgers and many other foods. Ketchup usually has a tomato foundation, though gourmet markets often carry condiments with similar appellations that might have a base of anything from walnuts to mangoes to mushrooms. Vinegar gives ketchup its tang, while sugar, salt and spices contribute to the blend. In addition to being used as a condiment, ketchup is used as an ingredient in many dishes.

Key lime *see* LIME

Key lime pie A custard pie very similar to a lemon meringue pie, except that it's made with the yellowish, very tart Key lime from Florida.

kibbe; kibbee [KIH-bee] *see* BULGHUR WHEAT

kidney One of the VARIETY MEATS, the kidney is a glandular organ. The most popular kidneys for cooking are beef, veal, lamb and pork. They're easily distinguishable because beef and veal kidneys are multi-lobed while lamb and pork are single-lobed. In general, the texture is more tender and the flavor more delicate in younger animals. The kidneys from younger animals are pale while those from older animals become deep reddish-brown; they're also tougher and stronger-flavored. Look for kidneys that are firm, with a rich, even color. Avoid those with dry spots or a dull surface. Kidneys should be used the day they're purchased, or store loosely wrapped in the refrigerator for up to 1 day. Before cooking, remove skin and any excess fat. Soaking helps reduce the strong odor in kidneys from more mature animals. See a general cookbook for details pertaining to the particular type of kidney you wish to cook. Kidneys may be braised, broiled, simmered or cooked in casseroles, stews and dishes like the famous STEAK AND KIDNEY PIE. All kidneys are a good source of protein, iron, phosphorus, vitamin A, thiamine and riboflavin.

kidney bean Particularly popular for CHILI CON CARNE, this firm, medium-size bean has a dark red skin and cream-colored flesh. Its popularity can be attributed to its full-bodied flavor. On the downside, it's an enthusiastic producer of flatulence. Unless you live in an area that grows kidney beans, you won't find them fresh but will have to settle for the dried or canned forms. White kidney beans—referred to as CANNELLINI BEANS—aren't favored with the robust flavor of their red cousins, and are only available dried or canned. *See also* BEANS.

kielbasa [kihl-BAH-sah; keel-BAH-sah] Also called *kielbasy* or *Polish sausage*, this smoked sausage is usually made of pork, though beef can also be added. It comes in chunky (about 2 inches in diameter) links and is usually sold precooked, though an occasional butcher will sell it fresh. Kielbasa can be served separately or cut into pieces as part of a dish. Even the precooked kielbasa tastes better when heated. *See also* SAUSAGE.

Kiev, chicken   *see* CHICKEN KIEV

kimchi [KIHM-chee] This spicy-hot, extraordinarily pungent CONDIMENT is served at almost every Korean meal. It's made of fermented vegetables—such as cabbage or turnips—that have been pickled before being stored in tightly sealed pots or jars and buried in the ground. It's dug up and used as needed. Commercial kimchi can be purchased in Korean markets. It will keep indefinitely in the refrigerator.

king crab This delicious giant can measure up to 10 feet, claw to claw, and it isn't unusual for it to weigh 10 to 15 pounds. The delicately flavored meat is snowy white and edged with a beautiful bright red. It's found in the northern Pacific and because it's most abundant around Alaska and Japan, is also referred to as Alaska king crab and Japanese king crab. Because the species is rapidly dwindling, the catch of king crab is rigidly quota-controlled. *See also* CRAB; SHELLFISH.

kingfish There are two distinct types of fish known as kingfish. The first is actually the regional name for a king MACKEREL. The name of the second type, found along the Atlantic coast, applies to any of several species of DRUM.

king mackerel   *see* MACKEREL

king orange This large Florida-grown orange has a rather flattened shape and loose rough skin. It has a juicy, sweetly tart flesh and is in season from December to April. *See also* ORANGE.

king salmon *see* SALMON

kinome [kih-noh-MEH] These young leaves of the prickly ash tree have a fresh, subtle mint flavor and a tender texture. They're occasionally available fresh in Japanese markets during the spring. Kinome is used as a garnish for many Japanese dishes. Store the fresh leaves in a plastic bag in your refrigerator's vegetable drawer. They should be used within 3 to 4 days. Though watercress or mint can be used as a substitute for color, nothing can duplicate the flavor of kinome.

kipfel; kipferln [KIHP-fuhl; KIHP-ferln] 1. A small, crescent-shaped yeast pastry with a filling of chopped nuts and brown sugar. Also known as RUGALACH. 2. A crescent-shaped, butter-rich cookie with either a jam filling or a filling similar to that of the pastry.

kippered herring; kippers *see* HERRING

kir [KEER] White wine that is flavored with a soupçon of CASSIS, usually served as an APÉRITIF. When made with champagne, it's referred to as a **kir royale**.

kirsch; kirschwasser [KEERSH; KEERSH-vah-ser] From the German *kirsch* ("cherry") and *wasser* ("water"), this clear BRANDY is distilled from cherry juice and pits. In cookery, it's most prominently known as a flavorful addition to FONDUE and CHERRIES JUBILEE.

kishke; kishka [KIHSH-keh] A Jewish-American sausage made with flour, MATZO MEAL, fat, onions and the cook's choice of ground meat. The mixture is stuffed into a beef CASING before being steamed, then roasted. *See also* SAUSAGE.

kiss 1. A small, mound-shape, baked MERINGUE, which often contains chopped nuts, cherries or coconut. The texture of a kiss is light and chewy. 2. The term also applies to small one-bite candies, usually commercially produced.

kissel [kee-SUHL] Next to ice cream, Russians claim kissel as their favorite dessert. It's a sweetened fruit puree thickened with either CORNSTARCH or POTATO FLOUR, which gives it a soft-custard texture. Kissel can be served hot or cold, usually topped with cream or a custard sauce.

kiwi fruit; kiwifruit [KEE-wee] Also known as the *Chinese gooseberry*, this odd-looking fruit received its moniker from the flightless bird of the same name from New Zealand. It looks like a large brown egg with a covering of fine downy hair. But this rather unusual exterior hides a beautiful brilliant green flesh, spattered with tiny edible black seeds. The kiwi's flavor is elusive. Some say it's reminiscent of pineapple . . . others say strawberry . . . but all agree that it has a sweet-tart flavor unlike any other fruit. The kiwi is cultivated in both New Zealand and California. Since New Zealand's seasons are the opposite of ours, this delectable fruit is pretty much available year-round. Ripe kiwis can be stored in the refrigerator up to 3 weeks. They can be halved and scooped out like a melon or peeled, sliced and used in salads, desserts or as a garnish. New Zealand's popular PAVLOVA dessert is a favorite local way to feature this fruit's beauty and flavor. Kiwis are a good source of vitamin C.

knackwurst; knockwurst [NAK-wurst; NAHK-vursht] Short, thick links of precooked beef and/or pork sausage that is well-flavored with garlic. Knackwurst is usually boiled or grilled before serving, often with sauerkraut. The name comes from the German *knack* ("crack") and *wurst* ("sausage"). It was so named from the crackling sound the sausage makes when bitten into. *See also* SAUSAGE.

knaidel, *pl.* **knaidlach** [KNAYD-l; KNAYD-luhkh] Also called a *matzo ball*, this small, round dumpling is made with MATZO MEAL, eggs, chicken fat and seasonings. Knaidlach are usually cooked and served in chicken soup.

knead A technique used to mix and work a dough in order to form it into a cohesive, pliable mass. During kneading, the network of GLUTEN strands stretches and expands, thereby enabling a dough to hold in the gas bubbles formed by a LEAVENER (which allows it to rise). Kneading is accomplished either manually or by machine—usually a large mixer equipped with a dough hook (some machines have two dough hooks) or a FOOD PROCESSOR with a plastic blade. By hand, kneading is done with a pressing-folding-turning action performed by pressing down into the dough with the heels of both hands, then pushing away from the body. The dough is folded in half and given a quarter turn, and the process is repeated. Depending on the dough, the manual kneading time can range anywhere from 5 to 15 minutes (or more). Well-kneaded dough is smooth and elastic.

knife A sharp-edged instrument used for cutting, peeling, slicing, spreading, etc. Most knife blades are made of steel, but a material called *ceramic zirconia* is now also being used. It reportedly won't rust, corrode or interact with food and is reputed to be second only to the diamond in hardness. Knife handles can be one of many materials including wood, plastic-impregnated wood, plastic, horn and metal. The blade should be forged carbon or high-carbon steel that resists stains and rust and gives an excellent cutting edge. A good knife should be sturdy and well balanced.

In the best knives, the end of the blade (called the tang) extends all the way to the end of the handle, where it's anchored by several rivets. Knives come in a variety of different sizes and shapes—each with its own specific use. **A French knife**, with its broad, tapered shape and fine edge is perfect for chopping vegetables, while the **slicing knife** cuts cleanly through cooked meat with its long, thin, narrow blade. Knives with **serrated or scalloped** edges make neat work of slicing softer foods such as bread, tomatoes and cake. The pointed, short-bladed **paring knife** is easy to handle and makes quick work of peeling, removing cores, etc. Knives used for table service are usually named after their use, such as dinner, luncheon, fish, butter and steak knives.

Knorr® [nor] Superior quality products including sauce and gravy mixes, bases, dessert mixes, soup mixes, bouillons, consommes and specialty items that help chefs add exceptional flavor, value and style to foodservice menus.

knotroot *see* CHINESE ARTICHOKE

Kobe beef [KOH-bee] An exclusive grade of beef from cattle raised in Kobe, Japan. These pampered cattle are massaged with SAKE and fed a special diet that includes plentiful amounts of beer. This specialized treatment results in beef that is extraordinarily tender and full-flavored. It also makes the beef extravagantly expensive, which is why it's rarely available in the U.S. *See also* BEEF.

kohlrabi [kohl-RAH-bee] This vegetable is a member of the turnip family and, for that reason, is also called *cabbage turnip*. Like the turnip, both its purple-tinged, white bulblike stem and its greens are edible. The kohlrabi bulb tastes like a mild, sweet turnip. It's available from mid-spring to mid-fall. Those under 3 inches in diameter are the most tender. Choose a kohlrabi that is heavy for its size with firm, deeply colored green leaves. Avoid any with soft spots on the bulb or signs of yellowing on leaf tips. Store tightly wrapped up to 4 days in the refrigerator. Kohlrabi's best steamed, but can also be added to soups and stews as well as used in STIR-FRIES. It's rich in potassium and vitamin C.

kolacky; kolachke [koh-LAH-chee; koh-LAH-kee] Claimed by both Poles and Czechs, these sweet yeast buns are filled with poppy seeds, nuts, jam or a mashed fruit mixture.

kombu; konbu [KOHM-boo] *see* KELP

korma [KOR-mah] Popular in India and Pakistan, korma is a spicy curried dish of mutton, lamb or chicken, usually with the addition of onions and sometimes other vegetables.

kosher [KOH-sher] Food that conforms to strict Jewish biblical laws pertaining not only to the type of food that may be eaten, but to the kinds of food that can be combined at one meal. In addition to the kinds of animals considered kosher (pigs and rabbits are among the non-kosher group), the laws also determine how an animal is killed. The word "kosher" is a derivation of the Hebrew *kasher*, meaning "proper" or "pure." Kosher foods can be purchased in most supermarkets throughout the U.S.

kosher salt *see* SALT

kourabiedes [koo-rah-bee-YAY-dehs] These popular melt-in-the-mouth Greek cookies are served on festive occasions such as christenings, weddings and holiday celebrations. They're buttery-rich and can contain nuts or not, but are always rolled in confectioners' sugar after baking. Kourabiedes come in various forms from balls to ovals to S-shapes. At Christmastime, a clove inserted in the top symbolizes the rare spices brought to Christ by the Magi.

kreplach [KREHP-luhkh; KREHP-lahk] Of Jewish origin, these small noodle dumplings are filled with chopped meat or cheese, simmered in broth or as part of a soup. Kreplach resembe the Italian RAVIOLI.

kuchen [KOO-khehn] A fruit- or cheese-filled yeast-raised cake, usually served for breakfast but also enjoyed as a dessert. It originated in Germany but is now enjoyed in many variations throughout much of Europe and the U.S.

kugel [KOO-guhl] Traditionally served on the Jewish Sabbath, kugel is a baked pudding usually made with potatoes or noodles, though meat, vegetables and other ingredients are sometimes included. It's generally served as a side dish, though a sweet version with raisins and spices is equally delicious as dessert.

kugelhopf; kugelhupf [KOO-guhl-hopf] Though generally thought of as Austrian, bakers from Alsace, Germany and Poland also claim credit for this light yeast cake. It's filled with raisins, candied fruits and nuts, and generally embellished with a simple dusting of confectioners' sugar. It's traditionally baked in a special fluted kugelhopf ring mold. Also called *gugelhopf.*

kulebiaka; koulibiaka [koo-lee-BYAH-kah] *see* COULIBIAC

kulich [koo-LIHCH] A tall cylindrical Russian Easter cake that's traditionally served with PASHKA (a creamy cheese mold). Kulich is yeast-raised and flavored with raisins, candied fruit and saffron. It's usually crowned with a white confectioners' sugar icing and sprinkled with chopped candied fruits and almonds.

kuminost cheese [KOO-mihn-ohst] Also called *nökkelost*, this Danish cheese can be made from whole or skimmed cow's milk. It can have either a natural or waxed rind and its interior is pale yellow and semifirm. Kuminost is flavored with cumin, caraway seed and clove and is popular for snacks and sandwiches, as well as melted in dishes such as casseroles and quiches. *See also* CHEESE.

kumiss; koumiss [KOO-mihs] Thought to have originated with the Mongols, this acrid, slightly alcoholic beverage is made from fermented mare's or camel's milk. Like KEFIR, today's kumiss is more likely produced from cow's milk. It's often used as a digestive aid.

kümmel [KIHM-uhl; KOO-muhl] A sweet, colorless LIQUEUR flavored with caraway seed, cumin and fennel.

kumquat [KUHM-kwaht] This pigmy of the citrus family looks like a tiny oval or round orange. It's cultivated in China, Japan and the U.S. The edible golden orange rind is sweet, while the rather dry flesh is very tart. The entire fruit—skin and flesh—is eaten, and very ripe fruit can be sliced and served raw in salads or as a garnish. The kumquat is more likely to be found cooked, however, either candied or pickled whole or in preserves or marmalades. Fresh kumquats are available from November to March. Look for firm fruit without blemishes. Refrigerate wrapped in a plastic bag for up to a month. Kumquats contain good amounts of potassium, vitamins A and C.

kuzu; kudzu [KOO-zoo] A traditional Japanese thickener made from the root of the kuzu vine. Like ARROWROOT, it produces light, translucent sauces. It's usually mixed with water to form a thin paste before being added to another mixture. Kuzu is also used to coat food before frying for a crisp crust. It's available in both Japanese and health-food markets.

actic acid [LAK-tihk] A bitter-tasting acid that forms when certain bacteria combine with LACTOSE (milk sugar). Lactic acid is used to impart a tart flavor, as well as in the preservation of some foods. It occurs naturally in the souring of milk and can be found in foods such as cheese and yogurt. It's also used in the production of acid-fermented foods such as pickles and SAUERKRAUT.

lactose [LAK-tohs] This sugar occurs naturally in milk and is also called *milk sugar*. It's the least sweet of all the natural sugars and is used commercially in foods such as baby formulas and candies.

lady apple A tiny apple that can range in color from brilliant red to yellow with generous red blushing. Its flesh is sweet-tart and it can be eaten raw or cooked. Fresh lady apples are available during the winter months. They're also available canned, and are widely used for garnishing purposes. *See also* APPLE.

Lady Baltimore cake A moist, three-layered white cake with a succulent filling of raisins, nuts and sometimes other fruit such as figs. The cake is covered with a fluffy white frosting such as BOILED ICING. It was first mentioned by novelist Owen Wister in his 1906 novel, *Lady Baltimore*. Legend has it that a young woman gave Wister such a cake, which he later chronicled in his novel.

ladyfinger A light, delicate sponge cake roughly shaped like a rather large, fat finger. It's used as an accompaniment to ice cream, puddings and other desserts. Ladyfingers are also employed as an integral part of some desserts, such as CHARLOTTES. Ladyfingers can be made at home or purchased in bakeries or supermarkets.

lager [LAH-guhr] Beer that is stored in its cask or vat until free of sediment and crystal clear. It's a light, bubbly, golden brew that ranks as America's most popular. *See also* BEER.

lahvosh; lavash [LAH-vohsh] A round, thin, crisp bread that's also known as *Armenian cracker bread*. It comes in various sizes, ranging from about 6 to 14 inches in diameter. Lahvosh is available in Middle Eastern markets and most supermarkets.

lamb A sheep less than 1 year old, known for its tender meat. Baby lamb and spring lamb are both milk fed. **Baby lamb** is customarily slaughtered at between 6 and 8 weeks old. **Spring lamb** is usually 3 to 5 months old and must be killed between March and the first full week in October. **Regular lamb** is slaughtered under a year of age. Lamb over 1 year old is referred to as **mutton** and has a much stronger flavor and less tender flesh. There are five USDA grades for lamb based on proportion of fat to lean. Beginning with the best, they are *Prime, Choice, Good, Utility* and *Cull.* When purchasing lamb, let color be the guide. In general, the darker the color, the older the animal. Baby lamb will be pale pink, while regular lamb is pinkish-red. Lamb can be purchased ground and in STEAKS, CHOPS and ROASTS. Lamb VARIETY MEATS can also be purchased. Refrigerate ground and small lamb cuts loosely wrapped for up to 3 days. Roasts can be stored up to 5 days. Ground lamb can be freezer-wrapped and frozen up to 3 months, solid cuts up to 6 months. *See also* Lamb Chart, page 570.

Lambert cherry A sweet cherry variety that's large, round and a deep ruby red. The flesh is sweet, firm and meaty. A superior cherry for out-of-hand eating as well as cooking. *See also* CHERRY.

lambrusco [lam-BROO-skoh] From Italy, this semisweet, slightly effervescent wine is America's most popular imported red wine. This fruity potable is best served young (under 2 years) and chilled. It goes well with lightly spiced foods.

lamb's lettuce *see* CORN SALAD

lamprey [LAM-pree] Varieties of this long (about 21 inches), EEL-shaped fish are found in both fresh and marine waters. It has a delicately flavored but extremely fatty flesh, which makes it indigestible for many people. Lamprey can be cooked whole (if small to medium) or in pieces. It's usually braised in wine, but is suitable for other manners of cooking such as baking or sautéing. *See also* FISH.

Lancashire cheese [LANG-kuh-sheer; LANG-kuh-shuhr] Made in Lancashire, England, this white cheese can range from soft to semifirm depending on how long it's aged. When young, the flavor is mild yet tangy. It becomes stronger and richer in flavor as it matures. Lancashire melts beautifully and is a favorite cheese for WELSH RAREBIT. *See also* CHEESE.

Lancashire hot pot *see* HOTCHPOTCH

Lane cake Particularly popular throughout the South, this white or yellow cake is layered with a mixture of coconut, nuts and dried fruits and covered with a fluffy white frosting. Lane cake is said to have originated in Clayton, Alabama, when its creator, Emma Rylander Lane, won a prize for it in the state fair.

langostino [lahn-goh-STEEN-oh] The Spanish word for "PRAWN."

langouste [lahn-GOOST] The French word for "spiny LOBSTER."

langoustine [lahn-goo-STEEN] The French word for "PRAWN."

langues-de-chat [law*ng*-duh-CHAH] *see* CATS' TONGUES

lapin [la-PAH] The French word for "RABBIT."

lard *n.* RENDERED and CLARIFIED pork fat, the quality of which depends on the area the fat came from and the method of rendering. The very best is **leaf lard**, which comes from the fat around the animal's kidneys. Unprocessed lard has quite a strong flavor and a soft texture. Lard can be processed in many ways including filtering, bleaching, hydrogenation and emulsification. In general, processed lard is firmer (about the consistency of VEGETABLE SHORTENING), has a milder, more nutlike flavor and a longer shelf life. Lard is richer than many other fats and therefore makes extremely tender, flaky biscuits and pastries. It's a flavorful fat for frying and is widely used throughout South America and many European countries. When substituting lard for butter in baking, reduce the amount by 20 to 25 percent. All lard should be tightly wrapped to prevent absorption of other flavors. It may be stored at room temperature or in the refrigerator, depending on how it has been processed. Always check the label for storage directions. **lard** *v.* To insert long, thin strips of fat (usually pork) or bacon into a dry cut of meat. The purpose of larding is to make the cooked meat more succulent, tender and flavorful. These strips are commonly referred to as LARDONS and are inserted with a special tool called a LARDING NEEDLE. *See also* BARD.

larding needle A special tool used to LARD meats. There are many styles, but the most common is one that has a sharp, pointed tip and a hollow body. A long, thin strip of the larding agent (usually pork fat or bacon) is inserted into the tool's hollow cavity and the needle is then used to thread the fat through the meat. *See also* LARD v.

lardons; lardoons [LAHR-don; lar-DOON] 1. Narrow strips of fat used to LARD meats. 2. The French also use the term *lardon* to refer to bacon that has been diced, blanched and fried.

lasagna; lasagne [luh-ZAHN-yuh] 1. A wide (about 2 inches), flat noodle, sometimes with ruffled edges. The plural form is *lasagne*. 2. A dish made by layering boiled lasagna noodles with various cheeses (usually including mozzarella) with the cook's choice of sauce, the most common being tomato, meat or BÉCHAMEL. This dish is then baked until bubbly and golden brown.

late harvest An American wine term referring to wines made from grapes picked toward the end of the harvest (usually late fall), preferably those with BOTRYTIS, a fungus that shrivels the grape thereby concentrating its sugar. Late-harvest wines are very sweet and usually have a high alcohol content. The most popular grapes used for these DESSERT WINES are RIESLING, GEWÜRZTRAMINER and SAUVIGNON BLANC.

latke [LAHT-kuh] Traditionally served at Hanukkah, the latke is a pancake usually made from grated potatoes mixed with eggs, onions, MATZO MEAL and seasonings. It's fried and served hot as a side dish.

laurel leaf; bay laurel *see* BAY LEAF

lavender A relative of mint, this aromatic plant has violet flowers and green or pale gray leaves, both of which lend their bitter pungency to salads. The leaves may also be used to make herb tea or, more accurately, TISANE.

laver [LAY-vuhr] This highly nutritious dried seaweed comes in tissue-thin sheets about 7½ inches square. It has a fresh, tangy-sweet flavor and a dark purple color, which is why it's also called *purple laver*. Before using, laver must be soaked in cold water. After an hour of soaking, it doubles in size. Laver is often used in soups. Strips of it can also be deep-fried and served as an appetizer.

leaf gelatin *see* GELATIN

leaf lard *see* LARD

leaf lettuce Any of several varieties of lettuce with leaves that branch from a single stalk in a loose bunch rather than forming a tight head. The leaves are crisper and more full-flavored than those of the HEAD LETTUCE varieties. Depending on the variety, leaf lettuce (also called *looseleaf* and *Simpson lettuce*) can range in color from medium to dark green; some have red-tipped leaves. Among the more popular leaf lettuces are **Oakleaf, Salad Bowl**, frilly **Red Leaf** and crinkly **Green Leaf**. In general, leaf lettuce is more perishable than head lettuce. Choose bunches with crisp, evenly colored leaves with no sign of wilting or yellowing at the edges. As with all greens, leaf lettuce should be washed and either drained completely or blotted with a paper towel to remove any excess moisture before being refrigerated in a plastic bag. It will keep this way up to about 3 days. *See also* LETTUCE.

leather *see* FRUIT LEATHER

leavener; leavening agent *n.* [LEHV-uhn-er] Agents that are used to lighten the texture and increase the volume of baked goods such as breads, cakes and cookies. baking powder, baking soda and yeast are the most common leaveners used today. When mixed with a liquid they form carbon dioxide gas bubbles which cause a batter or dough to rise during (and sometimes before) the baking process. Some foods, such as ANGEL FOOD CAKE and SPONGE CAKE, are leavened by the air beaten into egg whites. When heated, the egg whites cook and set, trapping the air inside and creating a light, airy cake. **leaven** *v.* To add a leavening agent to a mixture such as a batter or dough in order to make it rise. *For information on specific leaveners, see individual listings.*

leberkäse sausage [LAY-buhr-kah-suh] This smooth, delicate pork PÂTÉ is made with onion, garlic and eggs. The tubular sausage is cut into thick slices and either steamed or gently sautéed. *Leberkäse* (German for "liver cheese") is served warm or at room temperature. It's delicious with rye bread and mustard. *See also* SAUSAGE.

lebkuchen [LAYB-koo-kuhn] This thick, cakelike cookie is a specialty of Nuremberg and one of the most popular in Germany. It's honey-sweetened, full of spices, CITRON and almonds and often topped with a hard confectioners' sugar glaze. Lebkuchen has been made for centuries and is often baked in decorative molds to shape the cookie into intricate designs. *See also* COOKIE.

lecithin [LEHS-uh-thihn] A fatty substance obtained from egg yolks and LEGUMES, used to preserve, emulsify and moisturize food. Lecithin–vegetable oil sprays (available in every supermarket) can be used instead of high-calorie oils for greasing pans and sautéing foods.

leckerle [LEH-kehr-lee] This popular Swiss cookie comes in two versions—one made with honey, one with ground almonds. Both are chewy and delicious. The dough is traditionally pressed into special wooden molds, which imprint designs on the surface of the cookies.

leek Native to the Mediterranean countries, the leek has been prized by gourmets for thousands of years. Nero believed leeks would improve his singing voice and is said to have eaten prodigious quantities to that end. In the sixth century A.D., the Welsh made leeks their national symbol because they were convinced that the leeks they wore on their helmets to distinguish them from their enemies strengthened them and helped them win wars. Leeks still hold a flavorful spotlight in today's cuisine. Looking like a giant SCALLION, the leek is related to both the garlic and the onion, though its flavor and fragrance are milder and more subtle. It has a thick, white stalk that's cylindrical in shape and has a slightly bulbous root end. The broad, flat, dark green leaves wrap tightly around each other like a rolled newspaper. Leeks are available year-round in most regions. Choose those with crisp, brightly colored leaves and an unblemished white portion. Avoid any with withered or yellow-spotted leaves. The smaller the leek, the more tender it will be. Refrigerate leeks in a plastic bag up to 5 days. Before using, trim rootlets and leaf ends. Slit the leeks from top to bottom and wash thoroughly to remove all the dirt trapped between the leaf layers. Leeks can be cooked whole as a vegetable or chopped and used in salads, soups and a multitude of other dishes.

lees [LEEZ] The sediment (dregs) of wine or liquor after fermenting.

legume [lehg-YOOM] Any of thousands of plant species that have seed pods that split along both sides when ripe. Some of the more common legumes used for human consumption are BEANS, LENTILS, PEANUTS, PEAS and SOYBEANS. Others, such as clover and alfalfa, are used as animal fodder. When the seeds of a legume are dried, they're referred to as PULSES. The high-protein legumes are a staple throughout the world. They contain some vitamin B, carbohydrates, fats and minerals. *For information on specific legumes, see individual listings.*

Leicester cheese [LESS-ter] This orangy-red, cow's-milk cheese resembles CHEDDAR but has a higher moisture content. Its crumbly texture makes slicing difficult but facilitates grating. The flavor is mellow with a tangy aftertaste. Leicester melts beautifully, which makes it perfect for dishes such as WELSH RAREBIT. It's also good for snacks and makes a mild accompaniment for fruit. *See also* CHEESE.

lekvar [LEHK-vahr] A thick, soft spread made of fruit (usually prunes or apricots) cooked with sugar. This Hungarian specialty is used to fill a variety of pastries and cookies. Lekvar can be purchased in cans or jars in most supermarkets.

lemon Throughout the eons, lemons have been used for a multitude of nonculinary purposes —as an epilepsy remedy, a toothpaste, an invisible ink and a bleaching agent as well as in witchcraft. Though it originated in Southeast Asia, the lemon is now cultivated in tropical and temperate climates around the world, with California leading production in the U.S. This bright yellow citrus fruit is oval in shape, with a pronounced bulge on the blossom end. The flesh is juicy and acidic. The lemon can range in size from that of a large egg to that of a small grapefruit. Some have thin skins while others have very thick rinds which are used to make candied lemon peel. Lemons are available year-round with a peak during the summer months. Choose fruit with smooth, brightly colored skin with no tinge of green (which signals underripeness). Lemons should be firm, plump and heavy for their size. Depending on their condition when purchased, they can be refrigerated in a plastic bag for up to 10 days. The lemon has a multitude of culinary uses for dishes sweet to savory, as well as a flavoring in many drinks. Few foods add such flavor magic as the simple lemon. **Bottled** and **frozen lemon juice** are also available in most supermarkets. The frozen juice is a passable substitute but the bottled product bears little resemblance to the real thing. Though the lemon is an excellent source of vitamin C (one provides 40 to 70 percent of the minimum daily requirement), it begins to lose its vitamin power soon after it's squeezed. There's a 20 percent loss of vitamin C after only 8 hours at room temperature or 24 hours in the refrigerator.

lemonade   *see* ADE

lemon balm   Widely available in Europe, this herb has lemon-scented, mintlike leaves that are often used to brew an aromatic tea (TISANE). Its slightly tart flavor is used to flavor salads as well as meats and poultry. Also called simply *balm*.

lemon curd   Used to fill pastries and as a bread spread, this creamy concoction is made from lemon juice, sugar, butter and egg yolks. It's cooked in a double boiler and strained before using. Commercial lemon curd is available in specialty gourmet shops and most large supermarkets.

lemon grass   One of the most important flavorings in Thai cooking, this herb has long, thin, gray-green leaves and a scallionlike base. Citral, an essential oil also found in lemon peel, gives lemon grass its sour-lemon flavor and fragrance. Lemon grass is available fresh or dried in oriental (particularly Thai) markets. It's used to make tea and to flavor soups and other dishes.

lemon verbena   [ver-BEE-nuh]   Native to South America, the long, slender leaves of this potent herb have an overpowering lemonlike flavor. For that reason, a light touch is necessary when adding lemon verbena (also called simply *verbena*) to food. It's available dried and sometimes fresh in specialty produce markets. It's used to flavor fruit salads and some sweet dishes, and for tea (TISANE).

lentil   Popular in parts of Europe and a staple throughout much of the Middle East and India, this tiny, lens-shaped PULSE has long been used as a meat substitute. There are two varieties of lentils. The **French** or **European lentil**, sold with the seed coat on, has a grayish-brown exterior and a creamy yellow interior. The reddish orange **Egyptian** or **red lentil** is smaller, rounder and sans seed coat. Neither variety is used fresh but they are dried as soon as they're ripe. The regular brown lentils are commonly found in supermarkets whereas the red lentil, though available in some supermarkets, must usually be purchased in Middle Eastern or East Indian markets. Lentils should be stored airtight at room temperature and will keep about 6 months. They can be used as a side dish (pureed, whole and combined with vegetables), in salads, soups and stews. One of the most notable showcases for the lentil is the spicy East Indian DAL. Lentils have a fair amount of calcium and vitamins A and B, and are a good source of iron and phosphorus.

lettuce There are hundreds of varieties of lettuce grown throughout the world and, because they peak at different times of year, there's always a plenitude of this universal salad favorite. Of the lettuce used in this country, there are four general classifications—BUTTERHEAD, CRISPHEAD, LEAF and ROMAINE, most of which comprise many varieties. When shopping for any kind of lettuce a general rule of thumb is to choose those that are crisp and free of blemishes. As with all greens, lettuce should be washed and either drained completely or blotted with a paper towel to remove any excess moisture. A SALAD SPINNER, which uses centrifugal force to remove water from leafy greens, is a real timesaver for this process. Never allow lettuce to soak, as the water tends to soften some leaves. Refrigerate washed-and-dried greens airtight in a plastic bag for 3 to 5 days, depending on the variety. All lettuce is low-calorie and most of it is rich in calcium, iron and vitamins A and C. Keep in mind that the darker green leaves contain the most nutrients. *For information on specific varieties of lettuce, see individual listings.*

levulose [LEHV-yuh-lohs] *see* FRUCTOSE

Leyden cheese [LY-dn] Flavored with CARAWAY or CUMIN seeds, this Dutch cheese is made from a combination of partially skimmed cow's milk and buttermilk. It's spicy and semisoft and delicious as a snack, especially when served with dark bread and dark beer. *See also* CHEESE.

liaison [lee-ay-ZON; lee-AY-zon] In cooking, a liaison is a thickening agent for soups, sauces and other mixtures. BEURRE MANIÉ, ROUX, egg yolks or starches such as FLOUR, CORNSTARCH and ARROWROOT are among those agents used for thickening.

lichee; lichi *see* LITCHI

licorice [LIHK-uh-rihsh; LIHK-uh-rihs] 1. This feathery-leaved plant grows wild throughout southern and parts of central Europe. It's favored for the extract taken from its root—as well as for the root itself when dried—and has long been used to flavor confections and medicine. 2. A candy flavored with licorice extract.

Liebfraumilch [LEEB-frow-mihlk; LEEP-frow-mihlkh] This, lightly sweet German white wine is made from a blend that often includes

Riesling, Silvaner or Müller-Thurgau grapes. Its quality varies greatly depending on the shipper. *Liebfraumilch* is German for "the milk of the Blessed Mother," and was so named because it originally came from the vineyards of a church of the same name.

Liederkranz cheese [LEE-duhr-krahntz] This American original was created in 1882 by Emil Frey, a New York cheesemaker. He named it after a New York singing society of the same name, whose members were great fans of the cheese. Made from cow's milk, Liederkranz has an edible, pale yellow crust and semisoft, ivory interior. The flavor is mildly pungent and the aroma distinctive. As it matures, the crust turns golden brown and the cheese a deep honey color; both flavor and aroma become much stronger. Liederkranz makes a full-flavored snack cheese and is particularly well complemented by dark bread and dark beer. *See also* CHEESE.

light cream *see* CREAM

lights The lungs of an animal such as a calf or pig, sometimes used in various preparations like PÂTÉS. Lights can also be sliced and sautéed or used in a stew such as CIVET. Though readily available in Europe, lights are rarely seen in U.S. markets.

Lillet [lee-LAY] A French APÉRITIF made from a blend of wine, BRANDY, fruits and herbs. It originated in the French village of Podensac and has been made since the late 1800s. **Lillet Blanc** is made from white wine and is drier than **Lillet Rouge**, its red-wine counterpart. Both are classically served over ice with an orange twist.

lily buds *see* TIGER LILY BUDS

lima bean [LY-muh] This New World bean was named for Lima, Peru, where it was found as early as 1500. There are two distinct varieties of lima—the **Fordhook** and the **baby lima** (and Fordhooks are not adult baby limas). Both are pale green, plump-bodied and have a slight kidney-shape curve. The Fordhook is larger and plumper than the baby lima. It also has a fuller flavor than its smaller relative. Fresh limas are available from June to September. They're usually sold in their pods, which should be plump, firm and dark green. The pods can be refrigerated in a plastic bag for up to a week. They should be shelled just before using. Frozen lima beans are available year-round and are labeled according to variety (Fordhook or baby). Canned and dried limas are usually labeled "jumbo," "large" or "small," a designation that relates to size and not variety. In the South, dried limas are frequently referred to as *butter beans*. When mottled with purple they're called *calico* or *speckled butter beans*. A traditional way to serve limas is with corn in SUCCOTASH. They're also used alone as a side dish, in soups and sometimes in salads. Lima beans contain a good amount of protein, phosphorus, potassium and iron. The lima is also called the *Madagascar bean. See also* BEAN.

Limburger cheese [LIHM-buhr-guhr] Undoubtedly the stinkiest of the strong-smelling cheeses, limburger has a rind that ranges in color from yellow to reddish-brown and a yellow, pasty interior. This strong, pungently flavored cheese is made from cow's milk and is soft-ripened for about 3 months. Though it originated in Belgium and is now also made in the U.S., most limburger comes from Germany. The imports continue to ripen during transit, however, and often arrive devastatingly odorous. Though it's definitely categorized among those foods that are an "acquired taste," limburger has legions of fans. It's best served with full-flavored food and drink such as onions, dark breads and dark beer. *See also* CHEESE.

lime This small, lemon-shaped citrus fruit has a thin green skin and a juicy, pale green pulp. Limes grow in tropical and subtropical climes such as Mexico, California, Florida and the Caribbean. Because they're an excellent source of vitamin C, limes were fed to British sailors as a scurvy preventative (the fact that was the springboard for the pejorative nickname "limey"). The two main varieties are the **Persian lime** (the most widely available in the U.S.) and the **Key lime** from Florida. The latter is smaller, rounder and has a color more yellow than green. Outside of Florida, the Key lime is usually found only in specialty produce markets and some supermarkets that carry gourmet produce. Though Persian limes are available year-round, their peak season is from May through August. Look for brightly colored, smooth-skinned limes that are heavy for their size. Small brown areas (SCALD) on the skin won't affect flavor or succulence but a hard or shriveled skin will. Refrigerate uncut limes in a plastic bag for up to 10 days. Cut limes can be stored in the same way up to 5 days. Sweetened or unsweetened **bottled lime juice**, as well as **frozen lime juice** and LIMEADE, are some of the more popular lime products and are available in most supermarkets. The versatile lime has a multitude of uses, from a sprightly addition to mixed drinks (like MARGARITAS), to a marinade for raw fish dishes (such as SEVICHE), to the famous KEY LIME PIE.

limeade *see* ADE

limestone lettuce *see* BUTTERHEAD LETTUCE

limpa bread [LIHM-puh] Also called *Swedish limpa*, this moist rye bread is flavored with FENNEL or ANISE, CUMIN and orange peel. The result is an immensely flavorful, fragrant loaf of bread.

limpet [LIHM-piht] Easily identified by its coolie hat-shaped shell, this GASTROPOD can be seen clinging to rocks along the seashore. Its meat, which is flavorful but tough, can be consumed raw—either plain or tossed with a VINAIGRETTE dressing. More often, it's tenderized by pounding before being sautéed for a few seconds on each side. Lengthy cooking will toughen the meat. Limpets are usually only available in coastal areas and then only from specialty fish markets. *See also* SHELLFISH.

line *v.* A pan is lined for many reasons—to prevent the mixture in it from sticking, to provide structure to a soft mixture or to add texture and/or flavor. The lining can be a non-edible material such as PARCHMENT PAPER, thin slices of cake (for structure, as in a CHARLOTTE), slices of bacon (as with a PÂTÉ), or a simple coating of bread or cookie crumbs.

lingcod Found on the North American Pacific coast, lingcod is not really a cod but a GREENLING. This fish won't win any beauty contests, but its mildly sweet flavor and firm, low-fat texture makes up for its appearance. Lingcod ranges from 3 to 20 pounds and is available whole or as steaks or fillets. It can be prepared in almost any manner including baking, broiling, frying or grilling. Lingcod also does nicely in soups and stews. *See also* FISH.

lingonberry This tiny COWBERRY (a member of the CRANBERRY family) grows wild in the mountainous regions of Scandinavia, Russia, Canada and—in the U.S.—Maine. The tart red berries are available fresh only in the regions where they're grown. They can be purchased as sweet sauces or preserves, however, and make excellent accompaniments for pancakes, crepes, puddings, etc.

linguiça [lihng-GWEE-suh] Heavily flavored with garlic, this slim (about ½ inch in diameter) Portuguese sausage can be found in Latin American markets and many supermarkets. It's used in many Latin dishes such as Brazil's FEIJOADA and Portugal's CALDO VERDE. *See also* SAUSAGE.

linguine [lihn-GWEE-nee] Italian for "little tongues," linguine are long, narrow, flat noodles sometimes referred to as "flat spaghetti." *See also* PASTA.

linzertorte [LIHN-zuhr-tort] Though it's now famous around the world, the motherland of this elegant, rich tart is Linz, Austria. Ground almonds, grated lemon rind and spices add their magic to the buttery crust, which is spread with jam (usually raspberry) before being topped with a lattice of crust. After baking, the tart is served at room temperature.

Liptauer cheese [LIHP-tower] Hailing from and named after a province in Hungary, liptauer contains about 45 percent fat and is made from sheep's milk. This soft, fresh cheese has a mild flavor which is commonly seasoned with herbs, onions, garlic and paprika (which turns it red). It's a delicious snack cheese which, depending on the flavoring, can go nicely with anything from beer to white wine. Though in Hungary the cheese itself is referred to as "liptauer," those in German-speaking countries use the same word to describe the cheese when mixed with flavorings. *See also* CHEESE.

liqueur [lih-KUHR; lih-KYOOR] A sweet alcoholic beverage made from an INFUSION of flavoring ingredients (such as seeds, fruits, herbs, flowers, nuts or spices) and a spirit (such as BRANDY, RUM or WHISKEY). Essential oils and EXTRACTS are used to flavor many of today's liqueurs. Artificial flavorings make a lackluster contribution to the less expensive brands. Most commercial liqueurs are made with closely guarded secret formulas. Also called *cordials* and *ratafias*, liqueurs are usually high in alcohol and range from 49 PROOF for CHERRY HEERING to 110 proof for green CHARTREUSE. The **crème liqueurs** (such as CRÈME DE MENTHE) are distinguished by being sweeter and more syrupy. Liqueurs were originally used (and some still are) as a digestive. They are now usually served after dinner but also play an important role in many cocktails. Liqueurs can also be used in cooking, particularly for desserts. *For information on specific liqueurs, see individual listings. See also* EAU DE VIE.

liquor [LIH-kuhr] 1. A distilled, alcoholic beverage made from a fermented MASH of various ingredients including grains or other plants. WHISKEY, GIN, VODKA and RUM are among the most popular. *For information on specific liquors, see individual listings.* 2. An oyster's natural juices are referred to as its "liquor." 3. Pot liquor or POT LIKKER refers to the liquid resulting from cooking meats or vegetables.

litchi [LEE-chee] One of China's cherished fruits for over 2,000 years, the small (1 to 2 inches in diameter) litchi has a rough, bright red shell. The creamy white flesh is juicy, smooth and delicately sweet. It surrounds a single seed. Native to Southeast Asia, the litchi is cultivated in subtropical regions including California, Florida and Hawaii. Fresh litchis are available from June to about mid-July. Choose those with brightly colored skins free of blemishes. Place in a plastic bag and refrigerate unshelled for up to a week. Shell, seed and eat plain or as part of a fruit salad or dessert. Canned and dried litchis are available year-round. When dried they're often referred to as *litchi nuts* because they resemble a nut—the shell turns a dark reddish brown and the flesh becomes brown and crisp. They're eaten as a snack, much in the same way as nuts or candy.

littleneck clam Called *littlenecks* on the East Coast and *Pacific littlenecks* on the West Coast, these small, hard-shell clams have a shell diameter of less than 2 inches. They're usually reserved for eating ON THE HALF SHELL. *See also* CLAM.

liver The largest and one of the most important organs, liver has immense nutritional value . . . providing, that is, that it comes from a fairly young animal. Because liver acts as a clearing house for substances that enter the body, it tends to store and absorb unwanted chemicals, medicines and hormones that an animal might be fed. Naturally, the older the animal the greater the accumulation of these unwanted substances which, according to some, offset liver's nutritional value. For this very reason, many people choose the more expensive calf's liver over beef liver. There are several ways to distinguish between the two. The color of beef liver is reddish-brown, compared to the paler pinkish-brown of calf's liver. Liver from a mature animal also has a stronger odor and flavor than that from a youngster. Additionally, it will be less tender. Besides beef and calf's, the most common animal livers used in cookery are lamb, pork, poultry and goose, the latter used mainly to produce PÂTÉ DE FOIE GRAS. The strongest-flavored and least tender of the livers is pork, while poultry livers are the most mild and tender of the lot. All livers are usually available fresh—beef and chicken livers may also be purchased frozen (though the quality of frozen liver is considerably lower than that of fresh). While chicken livers are sold whole, most of those from other animals are marketed sliced. Look for liver that has a bright color and moist (not slick) surface. It should have a fresh, clean smell. Refrigerate loosely wrapped for no more than a day. Liver can be prepared in a variety of ways though quick sautéing is the most popular. It toughens quickly with overcooking. Liver is rich in iron, protein and vitamin A.

liverwurst [LIHV-uhr-wurst; LIHV-uhr-vursht] A broad term for "liver sausage" referring to well-seasoned, ready-to-eat sausage made from at least 30 percent pork liver mixed with pork or other meat. The texture of liverwurst can range from firm enough to slice to creamy-smooth and spreadable. It can be smoked or plain and comes in large links, loaves and slices. It's generally used for snacks and sandwiches and is especially suited to rye bread and crackers. *See also* SAUSAGE; BRAUNSCHWEIGER—the most popular of the liverwursts.

L

lobster Up until the end of the 19th century lobster was so plentiful that it was used for fish bait. Alas, with lobster's ever-increasing popularity (and price), those days are gone forever. This king of the CRUSTACEAN family has a jointed body and limbs covered with a hard shell. The most popular variety in the U.S. is the **Maine lobster,** also called *American lobster.* It has 5 pairs of legs, the first of which is in the form of large, heavy claws (which contain a good amount of meat). Maine lobsters are found off the Atlantic coast of the northern U.S. and Canada. They have a closely related European cousin that lives in Mediterranean and South African waters and along Europe's Atlantic coast. **Spiny lobsters** (commonly called *rock lobsters*) are found in waters off Florida, Southern California, Mexico, Australia, New Zealand and South Africa. They're easily distinguished from the Maine lobster by the fact that all 10 of their legs are about the same size. Almost all of the meat is in the tail because the spiny lobster has no claws. That meat is firmer, stringier and not quite as sweet as that of the Maine lobster. Outside California and Florida, most of the spiny lobster meat sold in this country is in the form of frozen tails, usually labeled "rock lobster tails." Live lobsters have a mottled shell splotched with various colors, generally greenish blue and reddish brown. Their shell turns vivid red only after the lobster is cooked. Fresh lobsters are available year-round and are most economical during spring and summer. **Female lobsters** are prized by many for their delectable CORAL (eggs). Because bacteria form quickly in a dead lobster, it's important that it be alive when you buy it. To make sure, pick up the lobster—if the tail curls under the body it's alive. This test is especially important with lobsters that have been stored on ice because they're so sluggish that it's sometimes hard to see movement. Lobsters come in various sizes and are categorized as follows: **jumbo**, over 2 pounds; **large**, from 1½ to 2 pounds; **quarters**, from 1¼ to 1½ pounds; **eighths**, from 1⅛ to 1¼ pounds; and **chicken lobsters**, which average about a pound. Lobsters must be purchased the day they're to be cooked. They will die in fresh water, so must either be kept in seawater or wrapped in a wet cloth and stored for no more than a few hours on a bed of ice in the refrigerator. All lobsters must either be cooked live or killed immediately prior to cooking. They may be cleaned before or after cooking, depending on the cooking method and the way in which they are to be used. Though whole lobsters are best simply boiled or broiled, lobster meat may be prepared in a variety of ways. Consult a general cookbook for cleaning and cooking instructions. Whole lobsters and chunk lobster meat are also sold precooked. One caveat when buying whole cooked lobster: be sure the tail is curled, a sign that it was alive when cooked. Frozen and canned cooked lobster meat, as well as raw spiny (or rock) lobster tails, are also available. *See also* SHELLFISH.

lobster butter A COMPOUND BUTTER made by heating ground lobster shells together with butter. Sometimes lobster meat and CORAL are also included. The mixture is then strained into ice water, which hardens the butter. Lobster butter has a multitude of uses including flavoring sauces or soups or as a spread.

lobsterette *see* PRAWN

lobster Newburg *see* NEWBURG

lobster pick Generally made of stainless steel, this long, narrow utensil is used to pull every shred of meat from the hard-to-reach cavities (such as the legs) of lobsters and crabs. The tip of a lobster pick can either be pointed or in the shape of a tiny, two-prong fork.

lobster Thermidor [THUHR-mih-dohr] A dish composed of lobster tails from which the cooked meat is removed, chopped and combined with a BÉCHAMEL SAUCE flavored with white wine, shallots, tarragon and mustard. The sauced lobster is spooned back into the shells, sprinkled with Parmesan cheese and broiled until golden brown. Crab and shrimp are also sometimes prepared in this manner. The dish is thought to have been named by Napoleon after the month in which he first tasted it (the 11th month, July 19th to August 17th, according to the French Revolutionary calendar).

locust bean *see* CAROB

loganberry There's disagreement as to the origin of this beautiful ruby red, BLACKBERRY-shaped berry. Some botanists think it's a separate species while others consider it a raspberry-blackberry hybrid. All agree that it was discovered by California Judge J. H. Logan in the late 1800s. Available in June and July, the loganberry is juicy and sweetly tart, and turns purple-red when very ripe. Choose plump, brightly colored berries that are uniform in size. Avoid soft, shriveled or moldy fruit. Do not wash until ready to use, and store (preferably in a single layer) in a moistureproof container in the refrigerator for 2 to 3 days. Loganberries are delicious both cooked and fresh. They make wonderful jams and preserves.

loin Depending on the animal, the loin comes from the area on both sides of the backbone extending from the shoulder to the leg (for pork) or from the rib to the leg (in beef, lamb and veal). Beef loin is divided into SHORT LOIN and SIRLOIN. In general, the loin is a tender cut that can be butchered into chops, steaks and roasts.

London broil A FLANK STEAK that has been cut into large pieces, tenderized by marinating, broiled or grilled, then thinly sliced across the grain.

longan [LONG-uhn] Also called *dragon's eye*, this native Southeast Asian fruit is small (about 1 inch in diameter) and round and has a thin brown shell. Inside is a translucent white, juicy-soft pulp that surrounds a large black seed. The perfumy flavor is delicate and sweet. Fresh longans can occasionally be found in oriental markets during July and August. They may be refrigerated in a plastic bag for up to 3 weeks. The easy-to-peel shell must be removed before eating. Dried and canned longans are available year-round. Longans are eaten as a snack and used in some oriental soups, SWEET-AND-SOUR dishes and desserts.

long bean *see* YARD-LONG BEAN

longhorn cheese Named after the longhorn cow, this cheese is a mild form of CHEDDAR. It comes in cylinders and rectangles. *See also* CHEESE.

Long Island duck *see* DUCK

Long Island tea A potent mixed drink composed of gin, vodka, cola and lemon. It's served in a tall glass over ice. Sometimes tequila is also added to the mix.

long-neck clam *see* SOFT-SHELL CLAM

looseleaf lettuce *see* LEAF LETTUCE

lop chong sausage; lop cheong *see* CHINESE SAUSAGE

loquat [LOH-kwaht] Though it originated in China, the loquat is also called *Japanese medlar* and *Japanese plum*. This slightly pear-shaped fruit resembles an apricot in size and color. The juicy, crisp flesh is pale yellow and has a delicate, sweetly tart flavor. It surrounds 1 to 3 rather large seeds. Besides China, the loquat grows in Japan, India, Central and part of South America, California, Florida and throughout the Mediterranean. Loquats bruise easily so they're not good travelers. For that reason, fresh loquats are usually found only in the regions in which they're grown. Choose large fruit with no sign of bruising. Store at room temperature or, if very ripe, refrigerate in a plastic bag. Loquats can be eaten as a snack, added to salads or used in chicken or duck dishes. They're also available dried or canned in oriental markets.

Lord Baltimore cake A three-layered yellow cake with a filling of chopped pecans or almonds, MARASCHINO cherries and MACAROON crumbs. The cake is covered with a fluffy white frosting such as BOILED ICING. *See also* LADY BALTIMORE CAKE.

lotte [LOT] *see* ANGLER

lotus A water lily whose leaves, root and seeds are frequently used in oriental cooking. The huge **lotus leaves** have a diameter of from 11 to 15 inches. They can be found fresh and dried in oriental markets. These leaves are used both as a flavoring and to wrap sweet and savory mixtures (rice, meat, fruit, etc.) for steaming. The underwater **lotus root** can be up to 4 feet long. It looks like a solid-link chain with 8-inch lengths, each about 3 inches in diameter. It has a reddish-brown skin that must be peeled before using. The lotus root's creamy-white flesh has the crisp texture of a raw potato and a flavor akin to fresh coconut. Besides the fresh form, it's also available canned, dried and candied. Lotus root is used as a vegetable as well as in sweet dishes. The oval, delicately flavored **lotus seeds** are eaten out of hand both in their fresh and dried forms. Dried lotus seeds are also candied and used in desserts and pastry fillings. They can be purchased canned or in bulk in oriental markets.

lotus leaves　*see* LOTUS

lotus root　*see* LOTUS

lotus seeds　*see* LOTUS

loukanika sausage　[loo-KAH-nih-kah]　Seasoned with orange rind, this Greek sausage is made with both lamb and pork. Loukanika is a fresh sausage and must therefore be cooked before eating. It's usually cut into chunks and sautéed. *See also* SAUSAGE.

lovage　[LUHV-ihj]　The French call lovage *céleri bâtard*, "false celery," because of its strong resemblance to that plant. Lovage has been used since Greek and Roman times for everything from a seasoning, to a curative for maladies ranging from indigestion to freckles, to a love potion. It grows up to 7 feet high and has large, dark green, celerylike leaves. The flavor of the pale stalks is that of very strong celery. The leaves, seeds and stalks can be used (in small amounts because of their potent flavor) in salads, stews and other dishes such as fowl and game. The stalks can be cooked as a vegetable. Dried lovage leaves and chopped or powdered stalks can be found in health-food stores and gourmet markets. The seeds are commonly called CELERY SEED. Lovage is also called *smallage* and *smellage*.

love apple　A tomato moniker that originated in the 16th century when tomatoes from North Africa were known in Italy as *pomo dei Mori*, "apples of the Moors." That was transliterated to the French *pomme d'amour* . . . "love apple."

lox　*see* SMOKED SALMON

luau　[LOO-ow]　A traditional Hawaiian feast, the highlight of which is usually roast pig. This celebration is almost always accompanied by Hawaiian music, singing and dancing.

lumpia　[LOOM-pee-ah]　This Philippine version of the EGG ROLL consists of a lumpia wrapper (a thin "skin" made of flour or cornstarch, eggs and water) wrapped around a filling and fried. Sometimes a lettuce leaf is used to enfold the filling mixture, in which case lumpia is not fried. The filling can be made of chopped raw or cooked vegetables, meat or a combination of the two. Lumpia can be served as an appetizer or side dish.

lychee *see* LITCHI

lyonnaise, à la [ly-uh-NAYZ; lee-oh-NEHZ] A French term for "in the manner of Lyons," a city in central France known for its excellent food. It refers to dishes prepared or garnished with onions, such as *pommes lyonnaise*, which are sliced potatoes fried with onions.

Lyonnaise sauce A classic French sauce made with white wine, sautéed onions and DEMI-GLACE. The sauce is strained before being served with meats and sometimes poultry.

atjes herring *see* HERRING

macadamia nut [mak-uh-DAY-mee-uh] As hard as it is to believe, the macadamia tree was first grown only for ornamental purposes. Thankfully, the buttery-rich, slightly sweet nature of the tree's nut was eventually discovered and has been prized ever since. The macadamia tree is native to Australia and was named for John McAdam, the Scottish-born chemist who cultivated it. In the 1890s the macadamia journeyed from Tasmania to be cultivated in Hawaii (now its largest exporter) and, eventually, California. Because of its extremely hard shell, this marble-size, golden brown nut is usually sold shelled, either roasted or raw. It has a high fat content and should be stored in the refrigerator or freezer to prevent rancidity. Macadamias are widely used in a variety of sweet and savory dishes. *See also* NUTS.

macaroni [mak-uh-ROH-nee] Legend has it that upon being served a dish of this food, an early Italian sovereign exclaimed "*Ma caroni!*" meaning "how very dear." This semolina-and-water PASTA does not traditionally contain eggs. Most macaronis are tube-shape, but there are other forms including **shells, twists** and **ribbons**. Among the best-known tube shapes are: **elbow** (a short, curved tube); **ditalini** (tiny, very short tubes); **mostaccioli** (large, 2-inch-long tubes cut on the diagonal, with a ridged or plain surface); **penne** (large, straight tubes cut on the diagonal); **rigatoni** (short, grooved tubes); and **ziti** (long, thin tubes). Most macaronis almost double in size during cooking. The Italian spelling of the word is *maccheroni.*

macaroon [mak-uh-ROON] A small cookie classically made of almond paste or ground almonds (or both) mixed with sugar and egg whites. Almond macaroons can be chewy, crunchy or a combined texture with the outside crisp and the inside chewy. There is also a **coconut macaroon**, which substitutes coconut for the almonds. Macaroons can be flavored with various ingredients such as chocolate, maraschino cherries or orange peel.

mace [MAYS] This spice tastes and smells like a pungent version of NUTMEG, and for a very good reason . . . mace is the bright red membrane that covers the nutmeg seed. After the membrane is removed and dried it becomes a yellow-orange color. It's sold ground and, less frequently, whole (in which case it's called a "blade"). Mace is used to flavor all manner of foods, sweet to savory. *See also* SPICES; Herb and Spice Chart, page 538.

macédoine [mas-eh-DWAHN] A dish of colorful, attractively cut fresh fruits or, less commonly, vegetables, either of which may be raw or cooked.

The fruits are customarily either briefly soaked or drizzled with a mixture of SUGAR SYRUP and LIQUEUR. A fruit macédoine is served for dessert, either cold or FLAMBÉED. For a savory macédoine, each vegetable is cooked separately, then artfully arranged together on a plate and dressed with seasoned melted butter. It can be served as a side dish or a first course.

macerate [MAS-uh-rayt] To soak a food (usually fruit) in a liquid in order to infuse it with the liquid's flavor. A spirit such as brandy, rum or a LIQUEUR is usually the macerating liquid. *See also* MARINATE.

mâche [MAHSH] *see* CORN SALAD

mackerel [MAK-uhr-uhl] Any of several species of fish found in the Atlantic Ocean off both the North American and European coasts. The **king mackerel** (also called *kingfish*) is probably the most well known of this family of fish. The mackerel has a firm, high-fat flesh with a pleasant savory flavor. When small (about 1 pound), it's sold whole. Larger fish are cut into fillets and steaks. Mackerel is also available smoked or salted. The latter must be soaked overnight before using to leach excess salt. Mackerel can be cooked in almost any manner including broiling, baking and sautéing. *See also* FISH.

Macoun apple [muh-KOON] This favorite East Coast apple is small to medium-size and wine red in color. It's crisp, juicy and sweetly tart. The Macoun is considered an all-purpose apple, but is especially good for eating out of hand. *See also* APPLE.

Madagascar bean [mad-uh-GAS-cahr] Another name for lima bean.

Madeira [muh-DEER-uh] Named after the Portuguese-owned island where it's made, Madeira is a distinctive FORTIFIED WINE that's subjected to a lengthy heating process during maturation. It can range in color from pale blond to deep tawny and runs the gamut from quite dry to very sweet. The pale golden **Sercial** is the lightest, driest Madeira, while the rich, dark **Malmsey** is the sweetest. **Bual** and **Verdelho** are both medium-sweet wines. The flavor of American-made Madeiras cannot compare with that of the Portuguese originals . . . but then they're a fraction of the price. The lighter Madeiras are often served as APÉRITIFS, while the richer, darker Malmsey is perfect for after-dinner sipping. Madeira is also an excellent cooking wine and can be used in both sweet and savory preparations.

Madeira cake A traditional English favorite that's like a simple POUND CAKE, the top of which is sprinkled with candied lemon peel halfway through baking. The name comes from the fact that it is usually served with a glass of MADEIRA. Some cooks also sprinkle the baked cake with Madeira before it cools.

madeleine [MAD-l-ihn; mad-LEHN] A small, feather-light, spongy cake which is eaten like a cookie, often dipped in coffee or tea. Madeleines are baked in a special pan with scallop-shell indentations; the finished cakes take the form of the shell. In his landmark novel *Remembrance of Things Past*, French novelist Marcel Proust immortalized the madeleine when he wrote, "I raised to my lips a spoonful of the cake . . . a shudder ran through my whole body and I stopped, intent upon the extraordinary changes that were taking place." Sounds as though he rather liked it.

madrilène [MAD-ruh-lehn; mad-rih-LAYN] 1. A CONSOMMÉ flavored with fresh tomato juice. Madrilène may be served hot or cold; in the latter instance it's usually jellied. A lemon slice or wedge is the traditional accompaniment. Canned madrilène is available in most supermarkets. It should be shaken well before being refrigerated to set. 2. *À la madrilène* is French for "in the manner of Madrid" and refers to many foods that are cooked or flavored with tomatoes or tomato juice.

mafalda [mahl-FAHL-duh] A broad, flat noodle that resembles a narrow, ripple-edged LASAGNA noodle; *pl.* mafalde. *See also* PASTA.

magnum [MAG-nuhm] *see* WINE BOTTLES

mahi mahi; mahi-mahi [MAH-hee MAH-hee] Though this is actually a type of DOLPHIN, it shouldn't be confused with the dolphin that is a mammal. To avoid this misunderstanding, the Hawaiian name *mahi mahi* is becoming more widespread. Also called *dolphinfish* and *dorado*, mahi mahi is found in warm waters throughout the world. It's a moderately fat fish with firm, flavorful flesh. It ranges in weight from 3 to 45 pounds and can be purchased in steaks or fillets. Mahi mahi is best prepared simply, as in grilling or broiling. *See also* FISH.

mahleb; mahlab [MAH-lehb] Used in the Middle East as a flavoring in baked goods, mahleb is ground black-cherry pits. It can be purchased in Greek or Middle Eastern markets, either prepackaged or ground to order.

Maibowle [MAY-bohl] *see* MAY WINE

mai tai [MY-ty] A potent, complex mixed drink made with light and dark rums, ORGEAT SYRUP, CURAÇAO, orange and lime juices and any other touches the bartender might add. It's served over ice and garnished with a skewer of fresh fruit. The mai tai is said to have been created by Victor Bergeron, the original owner of Trader Vic's restaurant, who said he created it for a couple of Tahitian friends. On tasting it, they reportedly exclaimed, "Mai Tai!" meaning "out of this world."

maison [may-ZOHN] The French word for "house." On a menu, such a designation—like *pâté maison*—refers to a specialty of the house or to the fact that the dish was made by the house chef.

maître d'hôtel; maître d' [MAY-truh (MAY-tehr) doh-TELL; may-truh DEE] 1. A headwaiter or house steward, sometimes informally referred to simply as *maître d'*. 2. In cookery, the term refers to melted butter cooked with lemon juice or vinegar, chopped parsley and seasonings. It is served as an accompaniment to fish and poultry.

maize [MAYZ] *see* CORN

malic acid [MAL-ihk; MAH-lihk] A natural acid found in sour apples and other fruits. In winemaking, when certain bacteria convert malic acid to LACTIC ACID (which is much less strong and sour), a process called "malolactic fermentation" occurs. This reduces the wine's tartness, adds complexity to the flavor and sometimes contributes a slight sparkle. Malic acid is used as an acidulant as well as a flavoring agent in the processing of some foods.

malossol caviar [MAHL-oh-sahl] *see* CAVIAR

malt [MAWLT] A grain (usually barley) that is sprouted, kiln-dried and ground into a mellow, slightly sweet-flavored powder. This powdered malt has many uses including making vinegar, brewing beer, distilling liquor and as a nutritious additive to many foods. **Malted-milk powder** and **malt vinegar** are two of the most popular malt products available today. **Malt extract** is a heavy syrup used as a sugar substitute for special diets as well as in some baked goods. The average consumer can find it in health-food stores.

malted milk 1. A delicious, nourishing and distinctively flavored beverage made by mixing milk with either plain or chocolate-flavored MALTED MILK POWDER. 2. Also simply called *malted*, this soda-fountain drink is a thick, rich mixture made by combining malted-milk powder, milk, ice cream and a flavoring such as chocolate or vanilla. *See also* MILK SHAKE.

malted milk powder *see* MALT

Maltese sauce; Maltaise sauce [mahl-TEEZ] HOLLANDAISE SAUCE blended with orange juice and grated orange rind, used to top cooked vegetables, particularly asparagus and green beans.

malt extract *see* MALT

malt liquor A beer that has a relatively high alcohol content by weight—usually from 5 to 8 percent, with several varieties reaching as high as 9 percent. *See also* BEER.

maltose [MAHL-tohs] Also called *malt sugar*, this disaccharide plays an important role in the fermentation of alcohol by converting starch to sugar. It also occurs when enzymes react with starches (such as wheat flour) to produce carbon dioxide gas (which is what makes most bread doughs rise).

malt sugar *see* MALTOSE

malt vinegar *see* MALT; VINEGAR

manchego cheese [mahn-CHAY-goh] Spain's most famous cheese, so named because it was originally made only from the milk of Manchego sheep that grazed the famous plains of La Mancha. Manchego is a rich, golden, semifirm cheese that has a full, mellow flavor. The two that are most commonly exported are **curado**, aged between 3 and 4 months, and **viejo**, aged longer. Manchego is a wonderful snack cheese and melts beautifully in heated dishes. *See also* CHEESE.

Mandarine liqueur [man-duh-RIHN] An orange-flavored LIQUEUR made with COGNAC and the juice and peel of mandarin oranges.

mandarin orange [MAN-duh-rihn] A loose-skinned orange category that includes several varieties that can be sweet or tart, seedless or not and can range in size from as small as an egg to as large as a medium grapefruit. They all, however, have skins that slip easily off the fruit. Among the more well-known mandarin-orange family members are clementine, dancy, satsuma and tangerine. The tiny **clementine** has a thin peel and a tangy-sweet red-orange flesh that's usually seedless. It's cultivated in Spain and North Africa and can usually be found only in specialty produce markets. **Dancy oranges** are similar in size and color (and equally rich-flavored) to clementines but have a plenitude of seeds. The small Japanese **satsuma oranges** are almost seedless. Most of the canned mandarin oranges on the market are satsumas. The most common mandarin found in the U.S. is the **tangerine**, which has a thick, rough skin and sweet flesh. It was named for the city of Tangier, Morocco. Mandarin oranges can, depending on the variety, be found in the market from November through June. *See also* ORANGE; TANGELO.

mandelbrot [MAHN-duhl-broht] From the German words *mandel* ("almond") and *brot* ("bread"), this Jewish favorite is a crisp almond bread which is eaten as a cookie.

mandoline [MAHN-duh-lihn; mahn-duh-LEEN] A compact, hand-operated machine with various adjustable blades for thin to thick slicing and for JULIENNE and FRENCH-FRY cutting. Mandolines have folding legs and come in both wood- or stainless steel-frame models. They're used to cut firm vegetables and fruits (such as potatoes and apples) with uniformity and precision. On most machines, the food is held in a metal carriage on guides so that fingers aren't in danger.

mango [MANG-goh] The mango tree is considered sacred in India, the land of the fruit's origin. Now this delectable fruit is cultivated in temperate climates around the world, including California and Florida. Mangoes grow in a wide variety of shapes (oblong, kidney and round) and sizes (from about 6 ounces to 4 pounds). Their thin, tough skin is green and, as the fruit ripens, becomes yellow with beautiful red mottling. The fragrant flesh is a brilliant golden orange, exceedingly juicy and exotically sweet and tart. Perhaps the only negative to the mango is the huge, flat seed that traverses its length. The fruit must be carefully carved away from the seed with a sharp knife. Mangoes are in season from May to September, though imported fruit is in the stores sporadically throughout the remainder of the year. Look for fruit with an unblemished, yellow skin blushed with red. Because the seed is so oversized, the larger the mango the higher the fruit-to-seed ratio. Underripe fruit can be placed in a paper bag at room temperature. Ripe mangoes can be placed in a plastic bag and held in the refrigerater for a couple of days. Mangoes need no embellishment and are delicious simply peeled and eaten plain. They're also wonderful in fruit salads and have long been made into chutney. Canned mangoes and mango nectar are available in many supermarkets. Fresh mangoes are rich in vitamins A, C and D.

mangosteen [MANG-uh-steen] Widely cultivated in the Asian tropics, the mangosteen is no relation to the mango. In size and structure, it's much like a tangerine, having 5 to 8 fruit segments. The segmented flesh is soft, cream-colored and juicy. It has a tantalizingly sweet-tart flavor that is extremely refreshing. The hard skin of the mangosteen is a dark purple-brown. Unfortunately, the mangosteen is rarely imported to the U.S.

Manhattan A COCKTAIL made with bourbon or blended whiskey mixed with sweet vermouth. It's served over ice and garnished with a maraschino cherry. A **perfect Manhattan** uses equal parts sweet and dry vermouth, while a **dry Manhattan** uses all dry vermouth.

manicotti [man-uh-KOT-tee] Tube-shaped noodles about 4 inches long and 1 inch in diameter. They're available packaged in supermarkets. Manicotti are boiled, then stuffed with a meat or cheese mixture, covered with a sauce and baked. *See also* PASTA.

manioc [MAN-ee-ok] *see* CASSAVA

mannitol [MAN-ih-tahl] A white, crystalline sweetener added to processed foods for the purpose of thickening, stabilizing and sweetening.

manzanilla [mahn-suh-NEE-yuh; mahn-suh-NEEL-yuh] A favorite APÉRITIF in its native Spain, manzanilla is a light, extremely dry SHERRY. It's served cold, often to accompany seafood, and is commonly used in savory sauces.

maple sugar; maple syrup The American Indians taught the Colonists how to tap the maple tree for its sap and boil it down to what the Indians called "sweetwater." Canada, New York and Vermont are all known for their superior maple products. The maple-tapping season (called "sugar season") usually begins sometime around mid-February and can last anywhere from 4 to 6 weeks. The "sugarmakers" insert spouts into the maple trees (a grove of which is called a "sugarbush") and hang buckets from them to catch the sap. Some companies connect plastic tubing to the spout, running it from tree to tree and eventually directly to a large holding tank where it's stored until ready to be processed. The sap is then taken to the "sugarhouse," where it's boiled until evaporated to the desired degree. Quite simply, **maple syrup** is sap that has been boiled until much of the water has evaporated and the sap is thick and syrupy. At the beginning of the sugar season, when the sap is concentrated, it only takes about 20 gallons of it to make a gallon of syrup, whereas toward the end of the season it may take up to 50 gallons of sap. **Maple sugar,** which is about twice as sweet as granulated white sugar, is the result of continuing to boil the sap until the liquid has almost entirely evaporated. In between those two stages at least two other products are made: **maple honey** (thicker than syrup) and **maple cream or butter** (thick and spreadable). Maple syrup is graded according to color and flavor. Generally, U.S. grades are: **Fancy** or **Grade AA,** a light amber colored syrup with a mild flavor; **Grade A** is medium amber and mellow-flavored; **Grade B** is dark amber and hearty flavored; and **Grade C** is very dark with a robust, molasseslike flavor. Since the processing of maple syrup is labor-intensive, pure maple syrup is quite expensive. A less costly product labeled **maple-flavored syrup** is a combination of less expensive syrup (such as CORN SYRUP) and a small amount of pure maple syrup. **Pancake syrups** are usually nothing more than corn syrup flavored with artificial maple extract. Pure maple syrup should be refrigerated after opening. Warm to room temperature before serving.

maraschino cherry [mar-uh-SKEE-noh; mar-uh-SHEE-noh] This specially treated fruit can be made from any variety of cherry, though the ROYAL ANN is most often used. The cherries are pitted and then MACERATED in a flavored SUGAR SYRUP (usually almond flavor for red cherries, mint for green). At one time they were traditionally flavored with MARASCHINO LIQUEUR, though such an extravagance is now rare. The cherries are then dyed red or green. The Federal government has now banned the use of the harmful dyes that were used until recently. Maraschino cherries can be purchased with or without stems. They're used as a garnish for desserts and cocktails, as well as in baked goods and fruit salads.

maraschino liqueur [mar-uh-SKEE-noh; mar-uh-SHEE-noh] An Italian LIQUEUR made from wild *marasca* cherries (and their crushed pits) grown in the area of Trieste.

marbling Flecks or thin streaks of fat that run throughout a piece of meat, enhancing its flavor, tenderness and juiciness. Very lean cuts of meat are sometimes artificially marbled (*see* LARD *v.*).

marc [MARK] 1. The residue (skins, pits, seeds, etc.) remaining after the juice has been pressed from a fruit, usually grapes. 2. A potent EAU DE VIE distilled from this mixture. It's the French counterpart to GRAPPA.

Marengo, à la [muh-RENG-goh] A veal or chicken dish in which the meat is sautéed in olive oil, then braised with tomatoes, onions, olives, garlic, white wine or brandy and seasonings. Sometimes scrambled eggs accompany the dish. It's said to have been created by Napoleon's chef after the 1800 Battle of Marengo.

margarine [MAHR-juh-rihn; MAHRJ-rihn] Developed in the late 1800s as a butter substitute, margarine (which is less expensive but not as flavorful as butter) is made with vegetable oils. Those margarines lowest in cholesterol are made from a high percentage of polyunsaturated safflower or corn oil. To make this butter substitute taste and look more like the real thing, cream or milk is often added. Food coloring, preservatives, emulsifiers and vitamins A and D are also common additives. Careful label scrutiny is advised because the ingredients affect everything from flavor to texture to nutritive value. **Regular margarine** must contain 80 percent fat. The remaining 20 percent consists of liquid, coloring, flavoring and other additives. Margarine is available salted and unsalted. So are **butter-margarine blends**, which are usually proportioned 40 to 60 percent respectively. **Soft margarine** is made with all vegetable oils (no animal fats) and remains soft and spreadable when cold. **Whipped margarine** has had air (which sometimes can equal half the volume) beaten into it, making it fluffy and easy to spread. Because of the added air, it cannot be substituted of regular margarine in baked goods. So-called **liquid margarine** is soft enough to be squeezable when cold and comes in pliable bottles made specifically for that purpose. It's convenient for basting and for foods such as corn on the cob and waffles. **Diet spreads** only contain 40 percent fat and approximately half the calories of regular margarine. Because they contain so little fat, they can't be substituted for regular margarine in baked goods. Margarine comes in 1-pound packages—either in 4 (4-ounce) sticks or in 2 (8-ounce) tubs. It's also available in 1-pound tubs. All margarine should be refrigerated. *See also* BUTTER; FATS AND OILS.

margarita [mahr-gah-REE-tah] A COCKTAIL made with tequila, an orange-flavored liqueur (usually TRIPLE SEC) and lime juice. The rim of the glass is traditionally dipped in lime juice, then salt. A margarita may be served STRAIGHT UP or ON THE ROCKS. It can also be blended with ice into a slushy consistency.

marigold This bright yellow flower is used culinarily to flavor and add color to salads, soups and other dishes. The petals are sometimes dried, powdered and used as a coloring agent. *See also* FLOWERS, EDIBLE.

marinade [MAIR-ih-nayd] A seasoned liquid in which foods such as meat, fish and vegetables are soaked (marinated) in order to absorb flavor and, in some instances, to be tenderized. Most marinades contain an acid (lemon juice, vinegar or wine) and herbs or spices. The acid ingredient is especially important for tough cuts of meat because it serves as a tenderizer. Because most marinades contain acid ingredients, the marinating should be done in a glass, ceramic or stainless-steel container—never in aluminum. *See also* MARINATE.

marinara sauce [mah-ree-NAHR-uh] A highly seasoned Italian tomato sauce made with onions, garlic and oregano. It's used with pasta and some meats.

marinate [MAIR-ih-nayt] To soak a food such as meat, fish or vegetables in a seasoned liquid mixture called a MARINADE. The purpose of marinating is for the food to absorb the flavors of the marinade or, as in the case of a tough cut of meat, to tenderize. Because most marinades contain acid ingredients, the marinating should be done in a glass, ceramic or stainless-steel container—never in aluminum. Foods should be covered and refrigerated while they're marinating. When fruits are similarly soaked, the term used is MACERATE.

marinière [mah-reen-YAIR] 1. *À la marinière* is a French phrase meaning "mariner's style." It refers to the preparation of SHELLFISH with white wine and herbs. It can also refer to a fish dish garnished with mussels. 2. *Marinière* sauce is a mussel stock-based BERCY sauce enriched with butter or egg yolks.

marjolaine [mahr-juh-LAYN; mahr-juh-LEHN] 1. A long, rectangular DACQUOISE made with ground almonds and hazelnuts and layered with chocolate BUTTERCREAM. 2. The French word for the herb marjoram.

marjoram [MAHR-juhr-uhm] Early Greeks wove marjoram into funeral wreaths and planted it on graves to symbolize their loved one's happiness both in life and beyond. There are many species of this ancient herb, which is a member of the mint family. The most widely available is **sweet marjoram**, usually simply called "marjoram." It has oval, inch-long, pale green leaves and a mild, sweet, oreganolike flavor. In fact, **wild marjoram** is another name for OREGANO. Marjoram is available fresh in some produce markets and supermarkets with large fresh-herb sections. More often, it is found dried in small bottles or cans. There's also a very hardy species called **pot marjoram**, which has a stronger, slightly bitter flavor. It's found throughout Mediterranean countries but rarely seen in the U.S. Marjoram can be used to flavor a variety of foods, particularly meats (especially lamb and veal) and vegetables. Because marjoram's flavor is so delicate, it's best added toward the end of the cooking time so its essence doesn't completely dissipate. *See also* HERBS; Herb and Spice Chart, page 538.

Marlborough pie [MARHL-bur-oh] This Massachusetts specialty is a single-crust pie with a custardlike filling of applesauce, eggs, cream and sometimes SHERRY. Many Massachusetts families serve it as a traditional Thanksgiving dessert.

marmalade [MAHR-muh-layd] A preserve containing pieces of fruit rind, especially CITRUS FRUIT. The original marmalades were made from quince—the Portuguese word *marmelada* means "quince jam." Now, however, Seville oranges are the most popular fruit for marmalades.

marmite [mahr-MEET] A tall, covered, straight-sided cooking pot from France, used for long-cooking stews and dishes such as CASSOULET and POT-AU-FEU. It's usually made of EARTHENWARE. *Petites marmites* are identically shaped miniature covered pots used as soup bowls.

marron; marron glacé [ma-ROHN glah-SAY] *Marron* is the French word for "chestnut." *Marrons glacés* are chestnuts that have been preserved in a sweet syrup. They can be found in jars or cans in the gourmet section of most supermarkets and are quite expensive. They're eaten as a confection, chopped and used to top desserts such as ice cream and mixed fruit, or used to make desserts such as the rich MONT BLANC.

marrow A soft, fatty tissue found in the hollow center of an animal's leg bones and, though not as plentiful, in the spinal bones. It isn't widely consumed in the U.S., but marrow is considered a delicacy by many Europeans and is the highlight of the famous Milanese specialty OSSO BUCO. Marrowbones (those that contain marrow) can be purchased at meat markets and most supermarkets (though special ordering may be necessary). They should be wrapped, refrigerated and used within a day or two of purchase. Marrow is extremely light and digestible. It can be cooked in the bone (and removed afterwards) or it may be removed first and cooked separately. The common methods of preparation are baking or poaching, after which the marrow is often spread on toast and served as an appetizer. A special long, narrow utensil called a marrow spoon or scoop can be used to extract the marrow from the bone. Marrow is also added to soups for body and flavor. It has the same calorie count as beef fat and contains a small amount of protein.

marrow beans Grown chiefly in the East, these are the largest and roundest of the WHITE BEANS. They're usually found fresh only in the region where they're grown, but are available dried year-round in most supermarkets. Marrow beans are customarily served sauced as a side dish, in the manner of a pasta. *See also* BEAN.

marrowbone A bone, usually from the thigh and upper legs of beef, containing MARROW. The long bones are usually cut into 2- to 3-inch lengths.

marrow spoon *see* MARROW

marrow squash *see* VEGETABLE MARROW

Marsala [mahr-SAH-lah] Imported from Sicily and made from local grapes, Marsala is Italy's most famous FORTIFIED WINE. It has a rich, smoky flavor that can range from sweet to DRY. Sweet Marsala is used as a DESSERT WINE, as well as to flavor such desserts as the famous ZABAGLIONE. Dry Marsala makes an excellent APÉRITIF. There are also special Marsala blends with added ingredients such as cream, eggs and almonds.

marshmallow [MAHRSH-mehl-oh] Once created from the sweetened extract of the roots of the marshmallow plant, this sweet is now commercially made from corn syrup, gelatin, GUM ARABIC and flavorings. Light, fluffy marshmallows come packaged in regular size (about 1½ inches in diameter) and miniature (½ inch in diameter). They may be white or pastel colors. Marshmallows are used variously to top hot chocolate and dishes such as sweet potatoes. **Marshmallow creme** is a thick, whipped mixture available in jars. It's used in fudge, as an ice-cream topping and as a filling for cakes and candies.

martini [mahr-TEE-nee] Said to have been named after the company of Martini & Rossi (famous for their VERMOUTH), this COCKTAIL is made with gin and vermouth, garnished with either a green olive or a lemon twist. The less vermouth it contains, the "drier" it is. A martini may be served STRAIGHT

UP or ON THE ROCKS. It may also be made with vodka, in which case it's called a **vodka martini**. A GIBSON is a martini garnished with a tiny white onion.

marzipan [MAHR-zih-pan] A sweet, pliable mixture of almond paste, sugar and unbeaten egg whites. It's often tinted with FOOD COLORING and molded into a variety of forms including fruits, animals and holiday shapes. Some fancy commercial marzipan fruit is colored so convincingly that it can almost be mistaken for the real thing. Marzipan is also rolled into thin sheets and used either to cover cakes or to cut into strips to form ribbons, bows and a variety of other shapes. Marzipan is available in most supermarkets, packaged in cans or plastic-wrapped logs.

masa; masa harina [MAH-sah ah-REE-nah] The Mexican word for "dough," *masa* is the traditional dough used to make corn TORTILLAS. It's made with sun- or fire-dried corn kernels which have been cooked in limewater (water mixed with calcium oxide). After having been cooked, then soaked in the limewater overnight, the wet corn is ground into masa. **Masa harina** (literally "dough flour") is flour made from dried masa.

mascarpone cheese [mas-cahr-POHN-ay] Hailing from Italy's Lombardy region, mascarpone is a buttery-rich DOUBLE-CREAM to TRIPLE-CREAM CHEESE made from cow's milk. It's ivory-colored, soft and delicate, and ranges in texture from that of a light CLOTTED CREAM to that of room-temperature butter. It's versatile enough to be blended with other flavors and is sometimes sold sweetened with fruit. In Italy's Friuli region a favorite blend is mascarpone mixed with anchovies, mustard and spices. But in truth, this delicately flavored cheese needs little embellishment other than being topped with fruit. *See also* CHEESE.

mash *n.* Grain or malt that is ground or crushed before being steeped in hot water. Mash is used in brewing beer and in the fermentation of whiskey. **Sour mash** is made by adding a portion of the old mash to help ferment each new batch in the same way as a portion of SOURDOUGH STARTER is the genesis of each new batch of sourdough bread. **mash** *v.* To crush a food (such as cooked potatoes) into a smooth, evenly textured mixture.

matsutake mushroom [maht-soo-TAH-kay; maht-soo-TAH-kee] This dark brown Japanese wild mushroom has a dense, meaty texture and nutty, fragrant flavor. It's available fresh from late fall to mid-winter, usually only in Japanese markets or specialty produce stores. Canned *matsutake* are also marketed. These mushrooms can be cooked by a variety of methods including braising, grilling, steaming and frying. *See also* MUSHROOM.

matzo; matzoh [MAHT-suh] A thin, brittle, unLEAVENED bread traditionally eaten during the Jewish Passover holiday. Tradition states that matzo is made only with water and flour but some modern-day versions include flavorings like onion. Matzo can be found in Jewish markets as well as most supermarkets. *See also* MATZO MEAL.

matzo ball *see* KNAIDEL

matzo meal Ground MATZO, generally available in two textures—fine and medium. Matzo meal is used in a variety of foods including GELFITE FISH, KNAIDELS (matzo balls) and pancakes. It's also used to thicken soups and for breading foods to be fried. Matzo meal is available in Jewish markets and most supermarkets.

May apple Though poisonous when green, the yellow, egg-shaped May apple can be safely eaten after ripening. This member of the barberry family is about the size of a large cherry. It's lightly sweet and acidic and makes very good preserves. The May apple is found in the East but is rarely available in markets. *See also* APPLE.

mayonnaise [MAY-uh-nayz; may-uh-NAYZ] A thick, creamy dressing that's an EMULSION of vegetable oil, egg yolks, lemon juice or vinegar and seasonings. If egg yolks aren't used, the product is called salad dressing, which is also sweeter than mayonnaise. Commercial mayonnaise (which must contain at least 65 percent oil by weight) sometimes contains other additions including emulsifiers and sweeteners. **Reduced-calorie** or **light-style mayonnaise** contains much less oil and has thickeners and emulsifiers added to give it the proper consistency. It has about half the calories of the regular style. Electric mixers, blenders and food processors make homemade mayonnaise a cinch. All mayonnaise should be refrigerated once made or opened. Unfortunately, the homemade style—which is far superior in taste and texture—lasts only 3 to 4 days. The commercial product can be stored up to 6 months. Mayonnaise is widely used as a spread, a dressing and a sauce. It's also used as the base for a plethora of other mixtures including TARTAR SAUCE, THOUSAND ISLAND DRESSING, AÏOLI and REMOULADE.

May wine A German white-wine punch flavored with WOODRUFF. Also called *Maibowle*, May wine is sold bottled and can be found in some gourmet liquor and wine stores.

McIntosh apple [MAK-ihn-tahsh] Discovered in the late 1700s by Canadian John McIntosh, this medium-crisp, tart-sweet apple has a bright red skin that is sometimes tinged with green. It's available from late September through March. Though the McIntosh is considered an all-purpose apple, it doesn't hold up well when subjected to lengthy cooking. *See also* APPLE.

mead Dating back to Biblical times, mead is a beverage made by fermenting honey, water and yeast or HOPS with flavorings such as herbs, spices or flowers. Mead was popular in early England and, though not widely distributed today, is still bottled.

meal 1. The coarsely ground seeds of any edible grain such as oats or corn. 2. Any dry, ground substance such as bone or dried fish meal.

mealy 1. Having a dry or powdery texture that resembles MEAL. 2. A term used to describe the texture of a baked potato as slightly dry and almost crumbly.

measuring cup A cup that comes in graduated sizes, used to measure amounts of food. **Dry measuring cups** come in nested sets that can include 2-cup, 1-cup, ½-cup, ⅓-cup, ¼-cup and ⅛-cup (2-tablespoon) sizes. The dry ingredient can either be stirred first (as with flour and confectioners' sugar) or simply spooned lightly into the cup, then leveled off with the straight edge of a knife. Brown sugar and shortening should be packed tightly into the cup before being leveled off. For foods such as coconut, nuts and chocolate chips, the cups should be filled, then leveled off with your fingers. **Liquid measuring cups** range in size from 1 to 4 cups. To use, simply pour in liquid and read measurement at eye level.

meat tenderizers Hanging and aging is how many meat processors tenderize meat, but the home cook can easily do so by simple mechanical or chemical methods. **Tenderizing meat mechanically** is accomplished by breaking down the meat's tough fibers through pounding. *Meat pounders* (also called *meat bats, mallets* and *tenderizers*) come in metal or wood and in a plethora of sizes and shapes. They can be large or small, have horizontal or vertical handles and be round-, square- or mallet-shaped. Some have smooth surfaces while others are ridged. **Tenderizing meat chemically** refers to softening the meat fibers by long, slow cooking, by MARINATING it in an acid-based MARINADE, or by using a commercial meat tenderizer. Most forms of the latter are a white powder, composed mostly of a papaya extract called **papain**, an enzyme that breaks down tough meat fibers. The use of this enzyme is nothing new—South American cooks have been using papaya juice to tenderize meat for ages. Powdered meat tenderizer is available at most supermarkets. Most brands contain salt, sugar (in the form of DEXTROSE) and the anti-caking agent calcium stearate.

meat thermometer Cooks use this tool to read the temperature of meat in order to ascertain when it has reached the desired degree of doneness. The dials on meat thermometers not only indicate the temperature, but some also have a scale indicating at what degree each type of meat (beef, lamb, pork, etc.) is done. A thermometer can be inserted at the beginning of the cooking time and left in throughout the duration. There are also **instant thermometers** that take the reading in just a few seconds; these are inserted into the meat toward the end of the cooking time. Meat thermometers come with 1- or 2-inch dials, usually measuring from 0° (sometimes 100°) to 220°F. Look for those with thin probes, which make smaller holes in the meat for the juices to escape from. Always insert a meat thermometer as near to the center of the meat as possible, avoiding bone or gristle areas.

medallion [meh-DAL-yuhn] A small coin-shaped piece of meat, usually beef, veal or pork.

Melba sauce Created by the famous French chef Auguste Escoffier for Australian opera singer Dame Nellie Melba, this sauce is a combination of pureed and strained fresh raspberries, red currant jelly, sugar and cornstarch. It's classically used to adorn the dessert PEACH MELBA but can also top ice cream, fruit, pound cakes and puddings.

Melba toast Also created by Auguste Escoffier for opera singer Dame Nellie Melba (*see* MELBA SAUCE), this toast is exceedingly thin and dry. It's sold packaged in most supermarkets and is used to accompany soups, salads and the like.

melon Hieroglyphics dating back to 2400 B.C. show that Egyptians knew the pleasures of these sweet, perfumy fruits even then. Melons belong to the gourd family, as do squash and pumpkin. There are two broad categories of edible melon, the MUSKMELON and the WATERMELON, each of which has many varieties.

melon baller A small, bowl-shaped tool used to cut round- or oval-shaped pieces of melon. The best melon ballers are rigidly constructed with wood or metal handles and sharp-edged, stainless-steel bowls. They come in several sizes, from about ¼ inch to 1 inch.

melt Using heat to convert food (such as butter or chocolate) from a solid to a liquid or semiliquid.

menudo [meh-NOO-doh; meh-NOO-thoh] Long touted as a hangover cure, menudo is particularly popular in Mexico on New Year's morning. It's a hearty, spicy soup made with TRIPE, CALF'S FEET, green CHILI PEPPERS,

HOMINY and seasonings. It's usually garnished with lime wedges, bowls of chopped chili peppers and onion and served with hot TORTILLAS.

mère de vinaigre *see* MOTHER OF VINEGAR

meringue [muh-RANG] Very simply, a meringue is a mixture of stiffly beaten egg whites and granulated sugar. In order for the sugar to dissolve completely (and therefore produce an absolutely smooth meringue), it must be beaten into the whites a tablespoon at a time. **Soft meringue** is used as a swirled topping for pies, puddings and other desserts such as BAKED ALASKA. It's baked only until the peaks are nicely browned and the valleys golden. **Hard meringues** begin by being piped onto a PARCHMENT-lined baking sheet. They're usually round and may be large or small. They're then baked at a very low temperature (about 200°F) for as long as 2 hours and left in the turned-off oven until completely dry. Hard meringues often have a center depression that is filled with ice cream, custard, whipped cream and fruit, etc. Tiny, one- or two-bite size, mound-shape meringues are called KISSES and are eaten as a confection. Kisses often contain chopped nuts, cherries or coconut. They may be baked until completely dry or just until crisp on the outside and chewy inside. An **Italian meringue** is made by gradually pouring hot SUGAR SYRUP over stiffly beaten egg whites, then beating constantly until the mixture is smooth and satiny. This versatile mixture may be used to create either soft or hard meringues.

Merlot [mer-LOH] A red-wine grape widely grown in France's Pomerol district of Bordeaux and, to a lesser extent, in California and the Pacific Northwest. The wine it produces is similar in flavor to CABERNET SAUVIGNON, but tends to be softer and more mellow. It also matures sooner than CABERNET. Though the Merlot grape has been principally used for blending in the U.S., it's now beginning to be appreciated on its own. The French have long known its value as is indicated by the great Château Petrus of Pomerol, which is over 90 percent Merlot.

mescal [mehs-KAL] Called "the nectar of the (Aztec) gods" by Cortez, mescal is a liquor distilled from AGAVE. It has a bitter-almond flavor and is often sold with an agave worm in the bottle.

mesquite [meh-SKEET] A low-slung hardwood tree that grows wild throughout the southwestern U.S. and northern Mexico. Used in barbecuing and smoking foods, mesquite wood gives off a slightly sweet smoke.

Metaxa [meh-TAK-suh] A sweet, dark Greek BRANDY.

Methuselah [meh-THOO-zuh-luh] *see* WINE BOTTLES

Mettwurst [MEHT-wurst; MEHT-vursht] Also called *Schmierwurst* because it's soft enough to smear or spread, this German pork sausage is bright red, fatty and seasoned with coriander and white pepper. Though it's uncooked, mettwurst is cured, smoked and ready to eat. It's usually spread on bread or crackers. *See also* SAUSAGE.

meunière [muhn-YAIR] French for "miller's wife," referring to a style of cooking whereby a food (usually fish) is seasoned, lightly dusted with flour and sautéed simply in butter. Such a preparation is served with **beurre meuniere**, which is BEURRE NOISETTE flavored with lemon juice and parsley.

Mexican breadfruit *see* MONSTERA

Mexican chocolate Flavored with cinnamon, almonds and vanilla, this sweet chocolate is available in Mexican markets and some supermarkets. Mexican chocolate has a much grainier texture than other chocolates. It's used in the preparation of a Mexican hot chocolate drink and certain Mexican specialties such as *mole poblano*, a CHILI PEPPER-almond sauce usually served with fowl. One ounce semisweet chocolate, ½ teaspoon ground cinnamon and 1 drop almond extract can be substituted for 1 ounce Mexican chocolate.

Mexican green tomato *see* TOMATILLO

Mexican potato *see* JÍCAMA

Mexican wedding cakes A buttery, melt-in-your mouth cookie that's usually ball-shaped and generally contains finely chopped almonds, pecans or hazelnuts. It's usually rolled in confectioners' sugar while still hot, then again after the cookie has cooled. Many countries have their own rendition of this rich cookie. Two versions are **Russian tea cakes** and Spain's **polvorones**.

meze [meh-ZAY] The Greek word for HORS D'OEUVRE or appetizer.

microwave oven A microwave oven cooks with high-frequency radio waves that cause food molecules to vibrate, creating friction that heats and cooks the food. Microwaves travel so fast (and therefore cook food quickly) because they're extremely short. Nonmetal containers are used in these special ovens because microwaves pass through them (unlike metal), thereby cooking the food from all angles (top, bottom and sides) at once. The fact that the waves pass through glass and ceramics means that the containers stay relatively cool while the food they contain becomes quite hot. Because microwaves only penetrate about 1 inch into food, the center of most foods is cooked by heat conduction. Some microwave ovens have turntables for even microwave distribution. Others have revolving antennae for the same purpose. Microwave ovens use relatively little energy and do not heat up the kitchen.

Midori liqueur [mih-DOOR-ee] A Japanese LIQUEUR that has the flavor of honeydew melon.

mignonette [mee-nyohn-EHT] 1. The French term for coarsely ground white pepper. 2. A small, coin-shaped fillet of lamb, also called a MEDALLION.

milanaise [mee-lah-NEHZ] A French cookery term for PASTA tossed with butter and grated cheese and topped with a tomato sauce made with shredded ham, pickled tongue, mushrooms and truffles.

Milanese [mee-lah-NAY-zay] A term meaning "in the style of Milan," referring to food (usually meat) dipped in beaten egg, then into a bread-crumb-Parmesan mixture and fried in butter.

milfoil [MIHL-foyl] *see* YARROW

milk Milk has been used for human consumption for thousands and thousands of years, as proven by cave drawings showing cows being milked. Today cow's milk is still one of the most popular (especially in the U.S.) animal milks consumed by humans. Around the world, people drink the milk from many other animals including camels, goats, llamas, reindeer, sheep and water buffalo. Most milk packs a nutritional punch and contains protein, calcium, phosphorus, vitamins A and D, LACTOSE (milk sugar) and riboflavin. On the minus side, milk's natural sodium content is quite high. Most milk sold in the U.S. today is PASTEURIZED, which means the microorganisms that cause diseases (such as salmonella and hepatitis) and spoilage have been destroyed by heating, then quick-cooling the milk. Pasteurization eliminates the possibility of disease and gives milk a longer shelf life. Most commercial milk products have also been HOMOGENIZED, meaning that the butterfat globules have been broken down mechanically until they are evenly and imperceptibly distributed throughout the milk. The end result is that the cream does not separate from the milk and the liquid is uniformly smooth. Milk is available in many varieties. **Raw milk**, usually only commercially available in health-food stores, has not been pasteurized. Advocates say it's better nutritionally because vitamins and natural enzymes have not been destroyed by heat. The dairies that are certified to sell raw milk have rigid hygiene standards and their herds are inspected regularly. But the milk is still not pasteurized and therefore carries some potential risk of disease. Almost all other pasteurized and homogenized milks are fortified with vitamins A and D. **Whole milk** is the milk just as it came from the cow and contains about 3½ percent butterfat. **Lowfat milk** comes in two basic types: *2 percent*, meaning 98 percent of the fat has been removed; and *1 percent*, which is 99 percent fat-ree. A few lowfat milks contain only ½ percent butterfat but they're not widely available. **Nonfat** or **skim milk** must by law contain less than ½ percent butterfat. Both lowfat and nonfat milk are available with milk solids added, in which case the label states "Protein-fortified." Not only does this boost the protein to 10 grams per cup, but it also adds body and richness. Federal law requires that both lowfat and nonfat milk be fortified with 2,000 International Units (IU) of vitamin A per quart. Though vitamin D fortification is optional, 400 IU per quart is usually also added. **Buttermilk** of times past was the liquid left after butter was churned. Today it is made commercially by adding special bacteria to nonfat or lowfat milk, giving it a slightly thickened texture and tangy flavor. Some manufacturers add flecks of butter to give it an authentic look. **Dry** or **powdered buttermilk** is also available (*see* POWDERED MILK). **Sweet acidophilus milk** (whole, lowfat or nonfat) has had friendly and healthful lactobacillus acidophilus bacteria added to it. It tastes and looks just like regular milk but many scientists believe it has an advantage because the acidophilus culture restores nature's balance to the digestive tract. **Low-sodium milk**, in which 90 percent of the sodium is replaced by potassium, is a special product available in limited supply for those on sodium-restricted diets. **Lactose-reduced lowfat milk** is for people suffering from lactose intolerance. The lactose content in this special lowfat milk has been reduced to only 30 percent. **Ultrapasteurized milk** has been quickly heated to 300°F, then vacuum-packed. It may be stored without refrigeration until opened, after which it must be refrigerated.Though the high heat destroys spoilage-causing microorganisms, it also gives a "cooked" flavor to the milk. **Chocolate milk** is whole milk with sugar and chocolate added to it. **Chocolate dairy drink** (sometimes labeled simply **chocolate drink**) is skim milk with the same flavorings added. In either case, if cocoa is used instead of chocolate, the product is labeled "chocolate-flavored drink." There are several types of **powdered milk** and **canned milk**. *For information on* EVAPORATED MILK, POWDERED MILK *and* SWEETENED CONDENSED MILK, *see those listings. See also listings for milk's most widely distributed byproducts:* BUTTER; CHEESE; CREAM; SOUR CREAM; YOGURT.

milk punch An alcoholic drink made with liquor (typically rum, whiskey or brandy), milk, sugar and sometimes vanilla. The mixture is usually blended with crushed ice and strained into a tall glass.

milk shake This American original consists of a blended combination of milk, ice cream and flavored syrup, fruit or other flavorings. The drink is quickly made with the aid of a BLENDER and is sometimes enriched with an added egg. *See also* MALTED MILK.

milk sugar *see* LACTOSE

milk toast Buttered toast, sometimes sprinkled with cinnamon and sugar, over which hot milk is poured. It was once popular fare for children and the ailing.

mille-feuille [meel-FWEE] French for "a thousand leaves," this classic dessert is made with two large oblong pieces of crisp PUFF PASTRY spread with whipped cream, custard, jam or fruit puree. The pastries are stacked and topped with another pastry layer, which is generally dusted with confectioners' sugar. A serrated knife is used to cut the dessert into individual servings. Savory mille-feuille can be filled with cheese and served as an appetizer.

millet [MIHL-leht] Though America cultivates this cereal grass almost exclusively for fodder and bird seed, millet is a staple for almost ⅓ of the world's population, particularly in disadvantaged regions of Asia and Africa. There are many varieties of millet, most of which are rich in protein. Millet has a bland flavor that lends itself well as a background to other seasonings. It's prepared like rice by boiling it in water and is used to make hot cereal and dishes like PILAF. Ground millet is used as a flour to make puddings, breads and cakes. Millet can be found in oriental markets and health-food stores.

mimosa [mih-MOH-suh] 1. A garnish so named because it resembles the yellow mimosa flower. Consisting of finely chopped, hard-cooked egg yolk, it is sprinkled over salads and vegetables. 2. A COCKTAIL of equal parts champagne and orange juice, served icy cold but not over ice. It's a favorite with brunch.

mince [MIHNS] To cut food into very small pieces. Minced food is in smaller pieces than chopped food. *See also* CHOP.

mincemeat A rich, spicy preserve made of fruit (usually chopped cherries, dried apricots, apples or pears, raisins and candied citrus peel), nuts, beef SUET, various spices and brandy or rum. Old-time mincemeats included minced, cooked lean meat (usually beef)—hence the name. Most modern versions do not use meat. The ingredients are combined, then covered and allowed to mature for a month for the flavors to mingle and mellow. Commercially prepared mincemeat is available in jars in most supermarkets—particularly around Thanksgiving and Christmas. Mincemeat can be used in many dishes including pies, tarts, puddings and cookies.

mineral water   Water containing various minerals and sometimes gases, taken from wells or natural springs. Mineral water is often effervescent and was once drunk almost exclusively for medicinal purposes. It's now also used as a refreshing beverage, either alone or mixed with flavoring.

minestra   [mih-NAYS-truh]   Italian for "soup," *minestra* most often describes a soup of medium thickness, frequently containing meat and vegetables. **Minestrina** ("little soup") is a thin broth, while **minestrone** ("big soup") refers to a thick vegetable soup that generally contains pasta and sometimes peas or beans. It's usually topped liberally with grated Parmesan cheese and is hearty enough to be considered a complete meal.

minestrone   *see* MINESTRA

Ming Dynasty egg   *see* HUNDRED-YEAR EGG

mini muffin pan   *see* GEM PAN

mint   Long a symbol of hospitality, Greek mythology claims that mint was once the nymph Mentha. She angered Pluto's wife Persephone, who turned her into this aromatic herb. There are over 30 species of mint, the two most popular and widely available being peppermint and spearmint. **Peppermint** is the more pungent of the two. It has bright green leaves, purple-tinged stems and a peppery flavor. **Spearmint** leaves are gray-green or true green and have a milder flavor and fragrance. Mint grows wild throughout the world and is cultivated in Europe, the U.S. and the Orient. It's most plentiful during summer months but many markets carry it year-round. Choose leaves that are evenly colored with no sign of wilting. Store a bunch of mint, stems down, in a glass of water with a plastic bag over the leaves. Refrigerate in this manner for up to a week, changing the water every 2 days. Mint is used in both sweet and savory dishes and in drinks such as the famous MINT JULEP. Mint is available fresh, dried, as an EXTRACT, and in the form of **oil of spearmint** or **oil of peppermint**, both highly concentrated flavorings. Most forms can usually be found in supermarkets. *See also* HERBS; Herb and Spice Chart, page 538.

mint julep   One of Kentucky's claims to fame, the mint julep is an alcoholic drink made with fresh mint (sometimes MUDDLED with sugar), bourbon and plenty of crushed ice. It's traditionally served in an iced silver or pewter mug at the running of the famous Kentucky Derby. However, it's a refreshing favorite on any hot day.

minute steak A very thin, boneless beefsteak sometimes scored for tenderizing. It's small (6 to 9 ounces) and therefore usually cooked briefly—1 minute per side—over very high heat. *See also* BEEF; Beef Chart, page 573.

mirabelle [mihr-uh-BEHL; MIHR-uh-behl] 1. Grown in Great Britain (where they're called *cherry plums*) and parts of Europe, the small, round mirabelle plum ranges in color from golden yellow to red. It's sweet, but not acidic enough to make it very interesting when eaten raw. It does, however, make delicious tarts and preserves. 2. A fine EAU DE VIE of the same name made from the mirabelle plum.

mirepoix; mirepois [mihr-PWAH] A mixture of diced carrots, onions, celery and herbs sautéed in butter. Sometimes ham or bacon is added to the mix. Mirepoix is used to season sauces, soups and stews, as well as for a bed on which to braise foods, usually meats or fish.

mirin [MIHR-ihn] A low-alcohol, sweet, golden wine made from glutinous rice. Essential to the Japanese cook, mirin adds sweetness and flavor to a variety of dishes, sauces and glazes. It's available in all Japanese markets and the gourmet section of some supermarkets. Mirin is also referred to simply as *rice wine*.

mirliton [MIHR-lih-ton] *see* CHAYOTE

mise en place [MEEZ ahn plahs] A French term referring to having all the ingredients necessary for a dish prepared and ready to combine up to the point of cooking.

miso [MEE-soh] Also called bean paste, this Japanese culinary mainstay has the consistency of peanut butter and comes in a wide variety of flavors and colors. This fermented soybean paste has three basic categories—barley miso, rice miso and soybean miso—all of which are developed by injecting cooked soybeans with a mold (*koji*) cultivated in either a barley, rice or soybean base. Additionally, the miso's color, flavor and texture are affected by the amounts of soybeans, *koji* and salt used. It's further influenced by the length of time it is aged, which can range from 6 months to 3 years. Miso is a basic flavoring in much of Japanese cooking. The lighter-colored versions are used in more delicate soups and sauces, and the darker colored in heavier dishes. There are also low-salt varieties available. **Shinshu miso** is a golden yellow, all-purpose variety with a mellow flavor and rather high salt content. There are regional favorites such as **sendai miso,** a fragrant, reddish-brown variety found in northern Japan, and the dark brown **hatcho miso,** popular in central Japan. Miso is used in sauces, soups, marinades, dips, main dishes, salad dressings and as a table condiment. It's easily digested and extremely nutritious, having rich amounts of B vitamins and protein. Miso can be found in Japanese markets and health-food stores. It should be refrigerated in an airtight container.

Mission olive *see* OLIVE

misto [MEES-toh]   The Italian word for "mixed" or "mixture." For example, *fritto misto* means "mixed fry" and refers to a dish that includes various pieces of meat, fish, vegetables and cheese, all of which are dipped in batter and fried.

mixed grill   A dish of grilled or broiled meats, which can include lamb chops, beefsteak, liver, kidneys, bacon and sausages and is usually accompanied by grilled or broiled mushrooms, tomatoes and potatoes.

mixer   1. Any of various electric kitchen machines used to beat, mix or whip foods. There are two basic kinds—stationary (or stand) and portable (or hand-held). **Stationary mixers** have more powerful motors and therefore can handle heavier mixing jobs. They also take up more counter space. In addition to the standard beaters, stationary mixers are usually equipped with an assortment of attachments that can include dough hooks, wire whisks and flat, paddle-style beaters. Many have attachments such as citrus juicers, ice crushers, pasta makers, sausage stuffers and meat grinders. **Portable mixers,** as the name implies, can be used anywhere. Their small size is due in part to a small motor, which also limits these machines to smaller tasks. But size also makes the portable mixer easy to store. *See also* ROTARY BEATER. 2. Beverages such as soda water, cola or fruit juice that are combined with liquor to make a COCKTAIL.

mocha [MOH-kah]   1. Originally the word "mocha" referred only to a very fine coffee grown in Arabia and shipped from Yemen's port of Mocha. Today, this strong, slightly bitter coffee is still available but not as popular as it was in the 16th and 17th centuries. 2. A hot coffee-and-chocolate beverage. This flavor combination is also used in desserts, icings, candies and sweet sauces.

mochi [MOH-chee]   A sweet, short-grained, very glutinous rice with a high starch content. Mochi is commonly used to make rice cakes, for which it is pounded in large tubs until it becomes extremely sticky. It is then formed into balls or squares, which can be found in Japanese markets. Mochi is also used in confections and rice dishes, and it is made into a RICE FLOUR called **mochiko**. *See also* RICE.

mochiko [MOH-chee-koh] *see* RICE FLOUR

mock turtle soup This soup has nothing to do with turtles but is made instead from a calf's head cooked in water. After cooking, most recipes call for the head to be taken out of the broth and cooled, after which the meat is removed and cut into small pieces. Just before serving, the meat is returned to the clear, brownish broth, which is often flavored with wine and various spices, and usually thickened. Mock turtle soup is sometimes garnished with calves' BRAINS.

moisten This term is often used in baking recipes to instruct that only enough liquid be added to flour and other dry ingredients to make them damp or moist, but not wet.

molasses [muh-LAS-ihz] During the refining of sugar cane and sugar beets, the juice squeezed from these plants is boiled to a syrupy mixture from which sugar crystals are extracted. The remaining brownish-black liquid is molasses. **Light molasses** comes from the first boiling of the sugar syrup and is lighter in both flavor and color. It's often used as a pancake and waffle syrup. **Dark molasses** comes from a second boiling and is darker, thicker and less sweet than light molasses. It's generally used as a flavoring in American classics such as GINGERBREAD, SHOOFLY PIE, INDIAN PUDDING and BOSTON BAKED BEANS. **Blackstrap molasses** comes from the third boiling and is what amounts to the dregs of the barrel. It's very thick, dark and somewhat bitter. Though it's popular with health-food followers, it's more commonly used as a cattle food. Contrary to what many believe, blackstrap is not a nutritional panacea. In truth, it's only fractionally richer than the other types in iron, calcium and phosphorus and many of its minerals are not assimilable. **Sorghum molasses** is the syrup produced from the cereal grain SORGHUM. Whether or not molasses is **sulphured** or **unsulphured** depends on whether sulphur was used in the processing. In general, unsulphured molasses is lighter and has a cleaner sugar-cane flavor. Light and dark molasses are available in supermarkets; blackstrap is more readily found in health-food stores. *See also* TREACLE.

mold *n.* 1. A container, usually distinctively shaped, into which a food is placed in order to take on the shape of that container. Molds can range in size from tiny, individual candy-size molds to large pudding molds. The food (such as butter, chocolate, ice cream, ASPIC, PÂTÉ or a gelatin-based dessert) is poured or packed into the mold and then customarily refrigerated until it becomes firm enough to hold its shape. 2. The finished dish made in such a container. 3. Any of thousands of varieties of fungi that grow on food items such as bread, cheese, fruit and jam. Molds grow best when the food is acidic and the environment is warm, damp and dark, with some air circulation. Mold reproduces from its spores, which are carried through the air until they find the right food and environment to germinate. Most molds are simply nuisances which spoil food but are not harmful. Among the beneficial molds are those purposely nurtured to create wonderful blue cheeses like ROQUEFORT and STILTON, and that which grows on the rind of CAMEMBERT, providing its distinctive flavor. **mold** *v.* To form food into a distinctive shape either by hand-forming (as with a bread dough) or by pouring (as with ASPIC) into a decorative mold and chilling or freezing until firm.

molded cookie *see* HAND-FORMED COOKIES

mole [MOH-lay] From the Nahuatl *molli,* meaning "concoction," mole is a rich, dark, reddish-brown sauce usually served with poultry. There are many variations of this spicy Mexican specialty, usually depending on what's in the cook's kitchen. Generally, mole is a smooth, cooked blend of onion, garlic, several varieties of CHILI PEPPERS, ground seeds (such as sesame seeds or pumpkin seeds—known as *pepitas*) and a small amount of Mexican chocolate, its best-known ingredient. (Some Americanized mole recipes use bitter chocolate.) The chocolate contributes richness to the sauce without adding overt sweetness.

mollusk [MOL-uhsk] One of the two main classifications of SHELLFISH (the other being CRUSTACEAN), mollusks are invertebrates with soft bodies covered by a shell of one or more pieces. Mollusks are further divided into GASTROPODS (also called *univalves*), such as the ABALONE and SNAIL; BIVALVES, like the CLAM and OYSTER; and CEPHALOPODS, such as the OCTOPUS and SQUID. *For information on specific mollusks, see individual listings.*

Mongolian grill This audience-participation cooking is said to have originated during the time of Genghis Khan when his warriors in the field would sit around grills and enjoy cooking their own food. The basic approach is for each diner to dip thin slices of lamb (or other meat) into a ginger-soy sauce MARINADE before placing them on a hot grill (usually a large HIBACHI) set on the center of the table. Each individual cooks his meat (the Mongolian grill) according to personal preference. The grill is sometimes garnished with chopped scallions, mushrooms or watercress and eaten on plain buns.

Mongolian hot pot   This is a kind of Chinese FONDUE, also known as *Chinese firepot* or *boiling firepot*. A giant communal pot of slowly simmering stock is placed in the center of the table and the participants are provided with a variety of raw, thinly sliced meats (lamb, beef, fish, poultry, etc.) and vegetables. Diners immerse pieces of their food into the simmering stock, cook it to their liking and, if desired, dip the food into one of a selection of CONDIMENTS. After the food is cooked, the rich broth is consumed by any who have room for it.

monkey bread   1. A sweet yeast bread formed by arranging small clumps of dough (which are usually dipped in melted butter) in 3 or 4 overlapping layers in a pan. The pan can be round, oblong or tube-shape. After baking, the clumps cling together to form a solid loaf. Monkey bread can be sweet (flavored with raisins, nuts, cinnamon and sugar) or savory (often made with grated cheese). 2. A gourdlike fruit of the baobab, a thick-trunked tree native to Africa. The extremely high-starch fruit is generally only eaten by monkeys.

monkfish   *see* ANGLER FISH

monosodium glutamate; M.S.G. [mon-uh-SOH-dee-uhm GLOO-tuh-mayt]   Commonly known as *MSG*, this white crystalline powder is derived from glutamic acid, one of the 22 amino acids. This natural amino acid is found in seaweed, vegetables, cereal gluten and the residue of sugar beets. It was first discovered by Japanese scientists in the 1920s. Japan is still today's largest producer of MSG, a popular flavor enhancer in Japanese and Chinese cooking. Even though it has no pronounced flavor of its own, monosodium glutamate has the ability to intensify the flavor of savory foods. Some people have reactions to MSG which cause them to suffer from a variety of maladies including dizziness, headache, flushing and burning sensations. MSG is found in the spice section of supermarkets either as monosodium glutamate, MSG or under brand names such as *Ac'cent*. Many seasoning mixes also contain MSG. Additionally, it's present in many processed foods.

monounsaturated oils; monounsaturates [mon-oh-uhn-SACH-uh-ray-tihd]   *see* FATS AND OILS

monstera   [mon-STAIR-uh]   Also called *ceriman* and *Mexican breadfruit*, this unique tropical-American fruit looks like a narrow, foot-long pine cone. The thick, green skin has hexagonal scales that individually separate and pop off as the fruit begins to ripen. Inside, the ripe, off-white flesh is formed in segments correlating to the skin's pattern. It's creamy-smooth and resembles a very firm custard. The flavor is sweet-tart and reminiscent of pineapple with touches of banana and mango. If underripe, however, the monstera has an off-taste and an irritant that will inflame both mouth and throat. In the United States, the monstera can be found in California, Florida and a few other locales that have produce markets specializing in exotic fruit. The monstera should be ripened at room temperature until the scales pop off and expose the luscious fruit, which is best plucked out and eaten plain with a spoon or fork.

mont blanc [mawh*n* BLAH*N;*] A classic dessert of sweetened, pureed chestnuts subtly flavored with vanilla. The mixture is RICED and mounded into a high, fluffy mountain on a platter. This sweet alp is capped with whipped cream or CRÈME CHANTILLY. Mont Blanc ("white mountain") is a peak in the French Alps near the Italian border.

Monte Cristo sandwich [MON-tee KRIHS-toh] A sandwich consisting of slices of cooked chicken or turkey, cheese (usually Swiss) and sometimes baked ham. The sandwich is dipped into beaten egg and grilled in butter until golden brown.

Monterey Jack cheese So named because it originated in Monterey, California, this versatile cheese can be made from whole, partly skimmed or skimmed cow's milk. It's also called *California Jack* or simply *Jack* cheese. The widely available **unaged version** is buttery-ivory in color, semisoft in texture and has a mild, somewhat bland flavor reminiscent of American Muenster. It has high moisture and good melting properties, making it excellent for sandwiches as well as for cooked dishes. Some versions contain flavorings such as jalapeño pepper, garlic and dill. **Aged** or **dry Monterey Jack** bears a closer resemblance to cheddar, with its yellow color, firmer texture and richer, sharper flavor. Because of its lower moisture content it's often used as a grating cheese. Unaged Monterey Jack is available throughout the U.S., whereas the aged version is usually only found on the West Coast or in specialty cheese shops. **Sonoma Jack cheese**, produced in Sonoma County, California, is very similiar to Monterey Jack and has both semisoft and dry versions. *See also* CHEESE.

Montmorency, à la [mont-muh-REHN-see; maw*n*-moh-rah*n*-SEE] A term meaning "made or served with cherries," applying to various desserts and entrees such as *caneton à la Montmorency*—roast duckling with cherry sauce.

Montmorency cherry [mont-muh-REHN-see] An extremely popular sour cherry and the primary cherry grown to be sold fresh (most sour cherries are used for canning purposes). The skin is a medium red and the extremely juicy flesh a creamy beige. As with most sour cherries, cooking brings out the fresh, tart flavor of the Montmorency. It can be used in cold soups, in entree sauces or in desserts. *See also* CHERRY.

Montrachet cheese [mohn-truh-SHAY; mawn-ruh-SHEH] A white CHEVRE from Burgundy with a soft, moist and creamy texture and a mildly tangy flavor. It's usually sold in logs covered in a gray, salted ash. *Montrachet* is best when quite young and fresh. *See also* CHEESE.

moonshine *see* CORN WHISKEY

moo shu; moo shoo [MOO shoo] A stir-fried Chinese dish containing shredded pork, scallions, TIGER LILY BUDS, WOOD EARS and various seasonings. This mixture is scrambled with eggs, rolled in small thin pancakes (called *moo shu pancakes* or *Peking doilies*) and served hot.

mountain cranberry *see* COWBERRY

Moravian Christmas cookies [moh-RAY-vee-uhn] A spicy ginger-molasses cookie traditionally served at Christmastime in Moravia, a region of Czechoslovakia. The Moravian settlements in the United States—particularly in Old Salem, North Carolina—continue this tradition by making these cookies ultra-thin and cutting them into various festive shapes.

morel [muh-REHL] Belonging to the same fungus species as the truffle, the morel is an edible wild mushroom. Its spongy, honeycombed, cone-shape cap ranges in size from 2 to 4 inches high and in color from a rich tan to an extremely dark brown. The morel is widely applauded by gourmets, who savor its smoky, earthy, nutty flavor. In general, the darker the mushroom the stronger the flavor. Morels usually appear in specialty produce markets in April and the season can last through June. Imported canned morels can be found in gourmet markets year-round. The marvelous flavor of the morel needs little embellishment and the mushroom is best when simply sautéed in butter. *See also* MUSHROOM.

Morello cherry; English Morello cherry [muh-REHL-oh] Seldom found fresh, this sour cherry with dark red skin and flesh is used in a variety of processed products. The blood-red juice is used in making liqueurs and brandies, and the cherries can be found canned, packed in syrup, dried and in preserves. The sharp, sour taste makes the Morello unsuitable for eating raw but perfect for cooking. *See also* CHERRY.

Mornay sauce [mohr-NAY] A BÉCHAMEL SAUCE to which cheese, usually Parmesan and Swiss, has been added. It's sometimes varied by the addition of fish or chicken stock or, for added richness, cream or egg yolks. Mornay sauce is served with eggs, fish, shellfish, vegetables and chicken.

mortadella [mohr-tuh-DEHL-uh] This smoked sausage originated in Bologna, Italy, and is the original from which the slang name "baloney" came. It's made with ground beef and pork, cubes of pork fat and seasonings. The Italian version, which is not imported because it requires additional cooking steps before the U.S. government will approve it, is air-dried and has a smooth, delicate flavor. Canned, cooked versions are imported from Italy but they do not taste like the original. The American mortadella is basically bologna with cubes of pork fat and added garlic flavor. The Germans produce an excellent mortadella that contains pistachio nuts. *See also* SAUSAGE.

mortar and pestle A mortar is a bowl-shaped container and a pestle is a rounded, batlike instrument. As a pair, the mortar and pestle are used for grinding and pulverizing spices, herbs and other foods. The pestle is pressed against the mortar and rotated, grinding the ingredient between them until the desired consistency is obtained. The mortar and pestle are usually made from the same material, generally marble, hardwood, porcelain or stoneware.

Moscow mule Said to have the kick of a mule, this COCKTAIL is made by filling a copper mug (the traditional container) or glass with ice cubes and adding a generous amount of vodka (2 to 3 ounces), a squeeze of lemon or lime juice and topping with GINGER BEER. A Moscow mule is garnished with a lime wedge and a cucumber stick. The drink was developed in the late 1940s as part of a Smirnoff vodka promotion and has been popular ever since.

mostaccioli [mos-tah-chee-OH-lee] Large, 2 inch-long macaroni tubes—"mustaches"—cut on the diagonal. Mostaccioli can have either a ridged or plain surface. *See also* MACARONI; PASTA.

mother of vinegar A slimy, gummy substance made up of various bacteria—specifically *mycoderma aceti*—that cause fermentation in wine and cider and turn them into vinegar. Known as *mère de vinaigre* in French and sometimes simply as "mother" in English, its growth is best fostered in a medium-warm environment (60°–85°F). The mother should be transferred to a new mixture or discarded once the liquid has turned to vinegar.

Mouli grater [MOO-lee] A French rotary grater that is perfect for grating small amounts of foods like cheese, chocolate and nuts. The hand-held unit consists of two sections with hinged handles. The end of one handle contains a food hopper with a grating cylinder and a crank for rotating the cylinder. The other section has a rounded surface which acts as a clamp, pressing the food to be grated into the grating cylinder. The hinged handles are held in one hand and squeezed so that the food presses against the grating cylinder. Meanwhile, the other hand turns the crank, causing the cylinder to rotate and the food to be grated.

mountain oysters Also called *Rocky Mountain oysters* and *prairie oysters*, these are the testicles of an animal such as a calf, sheep or boar. Those from a younger animal are best. Mountain oysters can be special-ordered through most meat markets. They should be used as soon as possible, preferably within a day of purchase. Though they're not terribly popular in the U.S., testicles are considered a delicacy in Italy and France. They can be sautéed, deep-fried, braised and poached.

moussaka; mousaka [MOO-sah-kah] Originally from Greece, moussaka is a popular dish throughout most of the Near East. Its basic form consists of sliced eggplant and ground lamb or beef that are layered, then baked. The variations, however, are endless and the dish is often covered with a BÉCHAMEL SAUCE enriched with eggs and/or cheese. Other variations include the addition of onions, artichokes, tomatoes or potatoes.

mousse [MOOS] A French term meaning "froth" or "foam," mousse is a rich, airy dish which can be either sweet or savory and hot or cold. Cold dessert mousses are usually made with fruit puree or a flavoring such as chocolate. Their fluffiness is due to the addition of whipped cream or beaten egg whites and they're often fortified with gelatin. Savory mousses can be made from meat, fish, shellfish, FOIE GRAS, cheese or even vegetables. Hot mousses usually get their light texture from the addition of beaten egg whites. They're generally baked in a WATER BATH to prevent the mixture from curdling.

mousseline [moos-LEEN] 1. Any sauce to which whipped cream or beaten egg whites have been added just prior to serving to give it a light, airy consistency. **Mousseline sauce** is HOLLANDAISE blended with whipped cream. 2. Various dishes based on meat, fish, shellfish or foie gras (usually pureed) to which whipped cream or, less frequently, beaten egg whites are added to lighten the texture. 3. Any of various baked goods that have a light and delicate texture.

moutarde [moo-TARD] French for "mustard."

mozzarella cheese [maht-suh-REHL-lah; moht-suh-REHL-lah] Though still made from water-buffalo's milk in southern Italy where it originated, around the rest of the world (including most of Italy) mozzarella is now made from cow's milk. Fresh mozzarella is a soft white cheese with a mild, delicate flavor. There's a variation called *manteca* which has the cheese molded around a large lump of butter, and a smoked version called *mozzarella affumicata*. Most American mozzarella is factory-produced and is drier, stringier and not as delicately flavored as the fresh cheese. It's best used for cooking and is popular for pizza because of its excellent melting qualities. Fresh Italian-style mozzarella can be found in Italian markets, cheese shops and some supermarkets. It's excellent simply spread on bread with salt, pepper and a little olive oil. *See also* CHEESE.

MSG *see* MONOSODIUM GLUTAMATE

muddle To mash or crush ingredients with a spoon or a muddler (a rod with a flattened end). Usually identified with the preparation of mixed drinks, such as when mint leaves and sugar are muddled together for a MINT JULEP.

Muenster cheese; Munster cheese [MUHN-stuhr; MOON-ster] This widely imitated cheese varies greatly, from that of the original produced in France's Alsace region to versions made in the United States. The highly prized European Muensters have red or orange rinds and a smooth, yellow interior with small holes. The texture is semi-soft and the flavor ranges from mild when young to quite assertive when aged. The American versions have an orange rind, a lighter yellow interior and a decidedly bland flavor that in no way resembles the more robust European originals. *See also* CHEESE.

muesli [MYOOS-lee] Developed as a health food by Swiss nutritionist Dr. Bircher-Benner near the end of the 19th century, muesli has since become a popular breakfast cereal. The German word *muesli* means "mixture," and this one can include raw or toasted cereals (oats, wheat, millet, barley, etc.), dried fruits (such as raisins, apricots and apples), nuts, bran, wheat germ, sugar and dried-milk solids. It is usually eaten with milk, yogurt or fruit juice. There are a number of commercial variations available in most supermarkets, usually labeled GRANOLA.

muffin A small, cakelike bread that can be made with a variety of flours and often contains fruits and nuts. Most American-style muffins fall into the QUICK BREAD category and are LEAVENED with either baking powder or baking soda. The yeast-raised type, such as the ENGLISH MUFFIN, is generally finer in texture. These small breads are usually made in a muffin pan (also called *muffin tin*), a special baking pan with 6 or 12 cup-shaped depressions that hold the muffin batter. Each standard muffin cup is about 2½ inches in diameter. There are giant muffin pans with 3¼-inch cups and miniature muffin pans (GEM PANS) in which the diameter of each indentation is 1¼ inches. Muffins can be sweet or savory and, though they were once considered breakfast or tea fare, are now also served with lunch and dinner.

muffin pan *see* MUFFIN

mulberry There are three principal varieties of the mulberry—black, red and white. The black (really purplish-black) variety is commonly found in Europe, the red in the eastern and southern United States and the white in Asia. Mulberries look somewhat like blackberries in size and shape. When fully ripe, their flavor is sweet-sour but somewhat bland. Unripe berries are inedibly sour. Mulberries are not commercially grown in the U.S. but grow wild from Massachusetts to the Gulf states and as far west as Nebraska. They can be eaten raw or used for jams, jellies, desserts and mulberry wine.

mull To flavor a beverage by heating it with various ingredients such as herbs, spices, fruit and sugar. The beverages most often infused in this fashion are wine, cider and beer. *See also* MULLED WINE.

mulled wine Red or white wine that is heated with various citrus fruits and spices such as cinnamon, cloves, allspice or nutmeg. Mulled wine is generally sweetened with sugar and often fortified with a spirit, usually BRANDY. Some recipes call for stirring the hot wine mixture into beaten eggs, which adds flavor and body to the beverage.

mullet [MUHL-iht] The appellation "mullet" is used to identify many fish that are not mullets at all—such as the highly prized RED MULLET, which actually belongs to the GOATFISH family. True mullets belong to the gray mullet family and are commercially available in the U.S. as *striped mullet* and *silver mullet*. These silver-gray, moderate- to high-fat fish range in size from ½ to 4 pounds. They have firm white flesh with a mild, nutlike flavor. Mullet can be found year-round in most South Atlantic and Gulf states, less frequently elsewhere. They may be fried, baked, broiled or poached. *See also* FISH.

mulligan stew Said to have originated in hobo camps during the early 1900s, mulligan stew is a sort of catch-all dish of whatever is available. It usually contains meat, potatoes and vegetables in just about any combination. The name indicates that its origins might come from IRISH STEW, but it's also often compared to Kentucky BURGOO. The cook at a hobo camp responsible for putting this tasty concoction together was called a "mulligan-mixer."

mulligatawny soup [muhl-ih-guh-TAW-nee] The name derives from the Tamil, a people inhabiting southern India and the surrounding area, and means "pepper water." This soup is based on a rich meat or vegetable broth highly seasoned with curry and other spices. It usually contains bits of chicken (sometimes other meats), and can also include rice, eggs, coconut shreds and even cream.

mung bean A small dried bean with yellow flesh and a skin that is normally green but sometimes yellow or black. It's most commonly used to grow BEAN SPROUTS. Mung beans are widely used in both China and India. They need no presoaking and when cooked have a tender texture and slightly sweet flavor. Dried mung beans are ground into flour, which is used to make noodles in China and a variety of dishes in India. See also BEANS.

Munster cheese see MUENSTER CHEESE

Muscadet [muhs-kuh-DAY; moos-kuh-DAY] The French produce this light, dry white wine from Muscadet grapes grown in the Loire Valley. Although not as great as other French whites (like BURGUNDY and CHABLIS), Muscadet is quite good, particularly in light of its reasonable price. It should be served chilled and goes nicely with fish, shellfish and poultry.

muscadine grape [MUHS-kuh-dihn] Found in the southeastern United States, this thick-skinned purple grape has a strong, musky flavor. It's a native American grape grown mainly to be eaten although it's also used to make a limited amount of wine. In fact, the muscadine was one of the first varieties from which wine was made in America. One of its varieties—the *scuppernong*—is used to make a sweet wine that is still popular in the South. See also GRAPE.

muscat grape [MUHS-kat; MUHS-kuht] Any of several varieties of white or black grapes. The characteristic trait of the muscat is its sweet, musky flavor. Muscat grapes are grown around the world in temperate climates such as Italy, France, Greece, Spain and California. In addition to being eaten out of hand and made into raisins, the muscat grape is used to make MUSCATEL WINE. See also GRAPE.

muscatel wine [muhs-kuh-TEHL] A rich, sweet dessert wine created from the MUSCAT GRAPE. It's made from both the black and white varieties, so its color can range from golden to amber to pale amber-red. Muscatel's flavor typifies the characteristically musty flavor of the muscat grape.

muscovy duck see DUCK

mush A thick, cooked cereal or porridge made by cooking cornmeal with milk or water. It's served as a breakfast dish by adding either melted butter, milk or maple syrup. Mush is also cooked, poured into a pan and cooled. It's then cut into squares, sautéed until golden brown (much like POLENTA) and served hot, sometimes with gravy, as a side dish.

mushroom Early Greeks and Romans are thought to be among the first cultivators of mushrooms, using them in a wide array of dishes. Today there are literally thousands of varieties of this fleshy fungus. Sizes and shapes vary tremendously and colors can range from white to black with a full gamut of colors in between. The cap's texture can be smooth, pitted, honeycombed or ruffled and flavors range from bland to rich, nutty and earthy. The cultivated mushroom is what's commonly found in most U.S. supermarkets today. However, those that more readily excite the palate are the more exotic wild mushrooms such as CEPE, CHANTERELLE, ENOKITAKE, MOREL, PUFFBALL, SHIITAKE and WOOD EAR. Because so many wild mushrooms are poisonous, it's vitally important to know which species are edible and which are not. Extreme caution should be taken when picking them yourself. The readily available **cultivated mushroom** has a mild, earthy flavor. The cap ranges in size from ½ to 3 inches in diameter and in color from white to pale tan. Those labeled "button mushrooms" are simply the small youngsters of the cultivated variety. These common mushrooms are available year-round but are at their peak in fall and winter. They're sold in bulk and in 8-ounce packages. Look for those that are firm and evenly colored with tightly closed caps. If all the gills are showing, the mushrooms are past their prime. Avoid specimens that are broken, damaged or have soft spots or a dark-tinged surface. If the mushrooms are to be cooked whole, select those of equal size so they will cook evenly. Fresh mushrooms should be stored with cool air circulating around them. Therefore, they should be placed on a tray in a single layer, covered with a damp paper towel and refrigerated. Before use, they should be wiped with a damp paper towel or, if necessary, rinsed with cold water and dried thoroughly. Mushrooms should never be soaked because they absorb water and will become mushy. Trim the stem ends and prepare according to directions. **Canned mushrooms** are available in several forms including whole, chopped, sliced and caps only. **Frozen or freeze-dried mushrooms** are also available. Some mushrooms—usually the imported varieties—are available dried either whole or in slices, bits or pieces. Mushrooms are one of nature's most versatile foods and can be used in hundreds of ways and cooked in almost any way imaginable. *For information on specific mushrooms, see individual listings.*

muskellunge [MUHS-kuh-lunj] *see* PIKE

muskmelon This juicy fruit is one of two broad classes of MELONS, the other being WATERMELON. It's been grown by the Chinese, Greeks, Romans and Egyptians for thousands of years. The two principal varieties of muskmelon are those with netted skins (including CANTALOUPE, PERSIAN MELON and SANTA CLAUS or Christmas MELON), and those with smooth skins (such as CASABA, CRENSHAW and HONEYDEW MELON). The skin can range in color from creamy white to celadon green to jade green, with many variations and shades in between. Flesh colors vary similarly and include beautiful salmon, golden, lime-green and orange shades. All muskmelons have seeds in a fibrous center hollow. Although muskmelons of one variety or another are available throughout most of the year, they're most abundant from late summer to early fall. When ripe, most muskmelons are slightly soft at the blossom end and give off a sweet, perfumy odor. Those picked before they're mature will never reach their delectably sweet and flavorful potential. Unripe melons should be stored at room temperature until they ripen, then kept in a cool place until ready to use. As with all melons, these should be halved and seeded before using. *For information on specific melons, see individual listings. See also* MELON.

mussel [MUHS-uhl] Archaeological findings indicate that this BIVALVE MOLLUSK (*see both listings*) has been used as food for over 20,000 years. Europeans love mussels, which are cultivated on special farms to meet the high demand. Americans, however, have never been as enamored of mussels as they have of oysters and clams, and huge quantities along U.S. coasts go unharvested. There are dozens of mussel species, all of which have an extremely thin, oblong shell that can range in color from indigo blue to bright green to yellowish-brown. Depending on the species, the shell can be from 1½ to 6 inches in length. The creamy-tan meat is tougher than that of either the oyster or clam but it has a delicious, slightly sweet flavor. The most abundant and best-tasting mussel is the **blue** or **common mussel** found along the Mediterranean, Atlantic and Pacific coasts. Its shell is dark blue and 2 to 3 inches in length. Live, fresh mussels are generally available year-round. On the West Coast, however, the mussel season is November through April. This is because microscopic organisms (of "red tide" notoriety) make mussels unsafe to eat during the spring and summer months. Buy mussels with tightly closed shells or those that snap shut when tapped—otherwise they're not alive and fresh. Avoid those with broken shells, that feel heavy (meaning they're full of sand) or that feel light and loose when shaken (signalling that the mussel is dead). Smaller mussels will be more tender than large ones. Fresh mussels should be stored in the refrigerator and used within a day or two. Plain and smoked mussels packed in oil are also available. Mussels may be steamed, fried, baked or used as an ingredient in dishes like BOUILLABAISSE or PAELLA. *See also* SHELLFISH.

must The freshly pressed juice of grapes or other fruit before fermentation occurs.

mustard Any of several species of plant grown for its acrid seeds and leaves, which are called mustard greens. The plant belongs to the same family as broccoli, Brussels sprouts, collards, kale and kohlrabi. Down through the centuries it has been used for culinary as well as medicinal purposes; the most notable example of the latter is mustard's purported efficacy as a curative for the common cold. The name is said to come from a Roman mixture of crushed mustard seed and MUST (unfermented grape juice), which was called *mustum ardens* ("burning wine"). Likewise, the French word *moutarde* ("mustard") comes from a contraction of their *moust* ("must") and a form of *ardent* ("hot" or "fiery"). There are two major species of **mustard seed**— white (or yellow) and brown (or oriental). A third species, the black mustard seed, has been replaced for most purposes by the brown species because the latter can be grown and harvested more economically. White mustard seeds are much larger than the brown variety but a lot less pungent. They're the main ingredient in American-style mustards. White and brown seeds are blended to make ENGLISH MUSTARD. Brown mustard seeds are used for pickling and as a seasoning, and are the main ingredient in European and Chinese mustards. Mustard seeds are sold whole, ground into powder or processed further into prepared mustard. **Powdered mustard** is simply finely ground mustard seed. **Prepared mustard** is generally made from powdered mustard combined with seasonings and a liquid such as water, vinegar, wine, beer or must. *American-style prepared mustard* is a mild mixture made from the less-pungent white seed flavored with sugar, vinegar and turmeric (which makes it yellow). *European* and *Chinese prepared mustards* are made from brown seeds and are much zestier and more flavorful. The French are famous for their tangy DIJON MUSTARD, made with brown seeds. The German prepared mustards can range from very hot to sweet and mild. Chinese mustards are usually the hottest and most pungent of the prepared mustards. White and brown seeds, mustard powders and a multitude of domestic and imported prepared mustards are readily available in supermarkets. Mustard seeds can be stored for up to a year in a dry, dark place and powdered mustard for about 6 months. Once opened, prepared mustards should be refrigerated. Whole seeds are used for pickling, flavoring cooked meats and vegetables, and as a source for freshly ground mustard. Prepared mustards, powdered mustards and freshly ground seeds are used in sauces, as a seasoning in main dishes and as an ingredient in salad dressings. *For information on specific mustards, see individual listings.* See also MUSTARD GREENS; Herb and Spice Chart, page 538.

mustard greens The peppery leaves of the mustard plant are a popular SOUL FOOD ingredient, ranking second only to collard greens. They're both members of the same family along with broccoli, Brussels sprouts, kale and kohlrabi. The leaves are a rich, dark green and have a pungent mustard flavor. Though they can be found year-round in some locales, fresh mustard greens are most abundant from December through early March. They're also available frozen and canned. When choosing fresh greens, look for crisp young leaves with a rich green color. Reject those with yellow, flabby or pitted leaves or thick, fibrous stems. Refrigerate greens, tightly sealed in a plastic bag, for up to a week. Wash them just before using. Mustard greens can be steamed, sautéed or simmered. They are usually served as a side dish, often flavored with onion, garlic, ham, salt pork or bacon. Mustard greens are an excellent source of vitamins A and C, thiamine and riboflavin.

mustard seed *see* MUSTARD

mutton *see* LAMB

muttonfish *see* ABALONE

mysost cheese [MY-sohst] *see* GJETOST

aan; nan [NAHN] An East Indian, white-flour flat bread that is lightly leavened by a natural STARTER developed from airborne yeasts. Naan is traditionally baked in a TANDOOR OVEN. A flattened round of dough is placed on a cloth puff which is used to slap the bread directly onto the side of the special high-heat oven. In less than 60 seconds, the bread puffs slightly, browns on the side touching the oven wall and takes on a light smoky flavor. The bread is speared with a skewer and removed from the oven wall to be served hot.

nacho [NAH-choh] A crisp TORTILLA chip topped with melted cheese (usually CHEDDAR) and chopped CHILI PEPPERS, usually served as an appetizer or snack. Nachos sometimes appear on menus as "Mexican Pizza," in which case they generally have additional toppings such as cooked, ground CHORIZO, onions and sometimes olives.

nam pla [nahm PLAH] Popular in Thailand, nam pla is a salty, fermented fish sauce with an extremely pungent odor. It's used as a condiment, sauce and seasoning ingredient. Nam pla is popular throughout Southeast Asia and is known as *nuoc nam* in Vietnam and as *shottsuru* in Japan. Ancient Romans used a nam pla counterpart called GARUM.

nan *see* NAAN

Nantua sauce [nan-TOO-uh] A BÉCHAMEL-based sauce made with cream and CRAYFISH butter and garnished with crayfish tails. Nantua sauce is served with seafood or egg dishes.

nap To coat food lightly with a sauce so that it completely covers the food with a thin, even layer.

napa cabbage *see* CHINESE CABBAGE

napoleon [nuh-POH-lee-uhn] A delectable dessert made with crisp layers of PUFF PASTRY spread with CRÈME PÂTISSIÈRE and either glazed with a thin icing or dusted with confectioners' sugar. Napoleons are usually made in small rectangular shapes just large enough for an individual serving.

nasi goreng [nahg-SEE goh-REHNG) The Indonesian term for "fried rice," of which there are hundreds of versions throughout Indonesia, Malaysia and the surrounding areas. The rice is cooked with various ingredients including shrimp or other shellfish, meat, chicken, eggs, onions, chilies, garlic, cucumber, peanuts and a wide array of seasonings. If noodles are substituted for rice, the dish is called *bahmi goreng.*

nasturtium [nuh-STER-shuhm] All parts of this beautiful plant are eaten except the roots. Young leaves and stems add a peppery accent to salads and sandwiches, or be can used in dishes as a WATERCRESS substitute. The flower blossoms may be minced and used to flavor butter, cream cheese or vinegar, and the whole flowers are colorful and delicious in salads or as a garnish. Nasturtium seeds and immature flower buds can be pickled and used like capers. *See also* FLOWERS, EDIBLE.

natto [NAH-toh] These steamed, fermented and mashed soybeans have a glutinous texture and strong cheeselike flavor. Natto is particularly popular in Japan, where it's used as a flavoring and table CONDIMENT and is greatly favored served over rice for breakfast. It's often mixed with other ingredients such as mustard, soy sauce and chives.

navel orange Grown in California, Arizona and Florida, the navel is an excellent eating orange. Its name originates from the fact that the blossom end resembles the human navel. This large fruit has a bright-orange skin that's thick and easy to peel. The pulp is sweet, flavorful and seedless. Available from late fall through late spring, the navel orange is sometimes called *Washington, Riverside* or *Bahia navel. See also* ORANGE.

navy bean This small white LEGUME, also known as *Yankee bean*, gets its name from the fact that the U.S. Navy has served it as a staple since the mid-1800s. The navy bean is widely used for commercially canned pork and beans. It also makes wonderful soups and is often used in the preparation of BOSTON BAKED BEANS (though New Englanders prefer using the smaller PEA BEAN for this purpose). Navy beans require lengthy, slow cooking. *See also* BEAN.

Neapolitan ice cream [nee-uh-PAHL-uh-tuhn] Brick-shaped ice cream made up of three differently flavored ice creams (usually vanilla, chocolate and strawberry). It's normally served in slices, each of which displays the tricolored ice cream. Other desserts (or gelatin salads) made in three distinct layers are also labeled "neapolitan."

neat 1. A term referring to liquor that is drunk undiluted by ice, water or MIXERS. 2. An old term used mainly in England for a member of the bovine family such as the ox or cow. Neat's-foot jelly was what today is called CALF'S-FOOT JELLY.

Nebuchadnezzar [nehb-uh-kuhd-NEHZ-uhr] *see* WINE BOTTLES

nectarine [nehk-tah-REEN] The nectarine's flesh is sweet, succulent and firmer than that of its relative, the peach. When ripe, its smooth skin is a brilliant golden yellow with generous blushes of red. Nectarines are

N

available from mid-spring to late September with a peak during July and August. Look for fragrant, brightly colored fruit that gives slightly to the touch. Avoid those with bruises or other blemishes as well as those that are hard or overly green. Slightly underripe nectarines can be left to ripen at room temperature for a couple of days. Ripe fruit should be refrigerated and used within 2 to 3 days. They're wonderful eaten out of hand and can be used in salads, a variety of fresh and cooked desserts and as a garnish for many hot and cold dishes. Nectarines contain a fair amount of vitamins A and C.

Nesselrode [NEHS-uhl-rohd] Count Nesselrode, the 19th-century Russian diplomat, lived and ate lavishly and had a number of rich dishes dedicated to him. The most famous is Nesselrode pudding, developed by his head chef Mouy. It consists of cream-enriched CUSTARD mixed with CHESTNUT puree, candied fruits, currants, raisins and MARASCHINO LIQUEUR. This elegant mixture is often frozen, or made into a pie or dessert sauce. Other dishes named after the Count include a game soup and a braised sweetbread dish, but none gained the same fame as the Nesselrode pudding.

Neufchâtel cheese [noo-shuh-TELL; NOO-shuh-tell] The French original, hailing from the town of Neufchâtel in the region of Normandy, is a soft, white, unripened cheese. When young, its flavor is slightly salty but delicate and mild. After ripening, Neufchâtel becomes more pungent. It's made from cows' milk and the butterfat content varies widely (from 20 to 45 percent). Neufchâtel is available in a variety of shapes—square, rectangular, cylindrical and the special heart-shape variety called *Coeur de Bray*. For information on the American version of Neufchâtel, *see* CREAM CHEESE. *See also* CHEESE.

Newburg An extraordinarily rich dish of chopped cooked shellfish (usually lobster, crab and shrimp) in an elegant sauce composed of butter, cream, egg yolks, SHERRY and seasonings. It's usually served over buttered toast points. The sauce can be used with other foods, in which case the dish is usually given the appellation "newburg".

New England boiled dinner Originally made with salted beef, today this East Coast classic more commonly contains corned beef, ham or SALT PORK. Additional items such as chicken, cabbage, potatoes, parsnips, onions, carrots and seasonings are added at various times and slowly simmered together to create this hearty one-pot meal. New England boiled dinner is traditionally accompanied by horseradish and mustard.

new potato *see* POTATO

Newtown pippin apple This all-purpose apple is great for both eating and cooking. The skin is greenish-yellow to yellow, the flesh crisp and juicy and the flavor slightly tart. Also called simply *pippin* or sometimes *yellow pippin*, this flavorful apple is available mid-winter through mid-spring. *See also* APPLE.

New York steak Also known as *New York strip steak* and *shell steak*, this cut of meat comes from the most tender section of beef, the SHORT LOIN. It's the boneless top loin muscle and is equivalent to a PORTERHOUSE steak minus tenderloin and bone. Depending on the region, it's also marketed as *Delmonico steak, Kansas City (strip) steak* and *strip steak*. This tender cut may be broiled, grilled or sautéed. *See also* BEEF; Beef Chart, page 573.

Niagara grape A North American table grape grown in the eastern United States and, because it doesn't ship well, found only in the areas where it's grown. The large, juicy Niagara is in season from September through October. It's round to oval in shape, pale greenish-white and has a sweet, foxy flavor. A limited number of Niagara grapes are made into wine. *See also* GRAPE.

niçoise, à la [nee-SWAHZ] A French phrase that means "as prepared in Nice," typifying the cuisine found in and around that French Riviera city. This cooking style is identified with hot and cold dishes that include the integral ingredients of tomatoes, black olives, garlic and ANCHOVIES. **Salade niçoise** contains these basic ingredients plus French green beans, onions, tuna, hard-cooked eggs and herbs.

niçoise salad *see* NIÇOISE À LA

no-eyed pea *see* PIGEON PEA

noble rot *see* BOTRYTIS CINEREA

nockerl [NOK-uhrl] There are two basic versions of this Austrian dumpling. The heartier, flour-based, savory rendition is served in soups and stews. The sweet version contains very little flour and is made fluffy by the addition of stiffly beaten egg whites. It's generally used as an addition to fruit soups or served for dessert accompanied by fruit.

nökkelost cheese *see* KUMINOST CHEESE

nog 1. A nickname for EGGNOG. 2. Any beverage made with beaten egg, milk and usually liquor. 3. In certain parts of England the term "nog" refers to strong ALE.

noisette [nwah-ZEHT] 1. The French word for "hazelnut." 2. A small, tender, round slice of meat (usually lamb, beef or veal) taken from the rib or loin. 3. *Pommes noisette* are potatoes that have been cut into tiny, hazelnut-shape balls before being sautéed in butter until well-browned. *See also* BEURRE NOISETTE.

nondairy creamer Though called a "creamer," this product neither contains dairy products nor tastes particularly like cream. Its main function is to lighten the color and dilute the flavor of coffee. Nondairy creamers are made from ingredients such as COCONUT OIL, PALM OIL or HYDRONGENATED OIL, a sweetener, emulsifiers and preservatives. Because they're so high in saturated fat, these pseudo-cream products are not recommended for those on low-cholesterol diets. Nondairy creamers are sold in several forms—powdered, liquid and frozen.

nonpareil [non-puh-REHL] 1. A tiny colored-sugar pellet used to decorate cakes, cupcakes, cookies, candy, etc. 2. A confection consisting of a small chocolate disc covered with these colored candy pellets. 3. A French term meaning "without equal," most often used in reference to small pickled CAPERS from the region of Provence in France.

nonstick finishes These special coatings on cookware and bakeware allow for fat-free cooking, prevent food from sticking and require minimal clean-up. Some nonstick finishes are applied to the surface and can wear off over a period of time. Others are fired right onto the metal, making for a sturdier finish (and a higher cost). Most nonstick finishes are dishwasher-safe but require the use of nonmetal utensils to prevent scratching the surfaces.

noodle The main difference between noodles and MACARONI or SPAGHETTI is that, in addition to flour and water, noodles contain eggs or egg yolks. Noodles can be cut into flat, thick or thin strips of various lengths. They may also be cut into squares. A wide variety of noodles is available in markets, including those enriched with vitamins and minerals, and colored noodles (red tinted with tomato paste or beet juice and green with spinach). Noodles are sold fresh (these should be refrigerated for no more than 3 days) and dried (best stored in a cool, dry place for no more than 6 months). *See also* ASIAN NOODLES.

nopales [noh-PAH-lays] Long popular in Mexico, these fleshy oval leaves (or paddles) of the *nopal* (PRICKLY PEAR) cactus are gaining popularity in the United States. They range in color from pale to dark green and have a delicate, slightly tart green-bean flavor. Though fresh *nopales* are available year-round in Mexican markets and some supermarkets, they're at their most tender and juicy best in the spring. Look for small, firm, pale-green *nopales* with no sign of wrinkling. Refrigerate tightly wrapped for up to a week. Before use, the thorns must be removed; a VEGETABLE PEELER will shave them off quickly. The flesh is generally cut into small pieces or strips, simmered in water until tender and used in a variety of dishes from scrambled eggs to salads. **Nopalitos** (nopales that are diced or cut into strips) are available canned (pickled or packed in water).

nopalitos [noh-pah-LEE-tohs] *see* NOPALES

nori [NOH-ree] These paper-thin sheets of dried seaweed can range in color from dark green to dark purple to black. They have a sweet ocean taste and are popular at Japanese meals. Nori is generally used for wrapping sushi and rice balls. When finely cut it serves as a seasoning or garnish. It can be purchased toasted (labeled *yakinori*); if purchased plain, it is usually lightly toasted before being used. Nori that has been brushed with soy sauce is called *ajisuke-nori*. Japanese markets and some supermarkets carry nori either in plastic packaging or canned. All nori is very rich in protein, vitamins, calcium, iron and other minerals.

normande, à la [nohr-MAHND] A French phrase meaning "in the style of Normandy," referring to dishes based on the cooking of that region. Most commonly, it refers to fish (generally SOLE) garnished with shellfish (such as OYSTERS, SHRIMP and MUSSELS), mushrooms and TRUFFLES. Such a dish is usually served in **normande sauce,** a fish-stock-based VELOUTÉ enriched with butter, cream and egg yolks. Other Normandy-style dishes include those made with regional products such as butter, fresh cream, apples, apple cider and CALVADOS.

Northern Spy apple A large, sweet-tart apple with a red skin marked with yellow streaking. This all-purpose apple is available from October through March. It's also simply called *spy apple. See also* APPLE.

Northwest Greening apple *see* RHODE ISLAND GREENING APPLE

nougat [NOO-guht] Particularly popular in southern Europe, this confection is made with sugar or honey, roasted nuts (such as almonds, walnuts, pistachios or hazelnuts) and sometimes chopped candied fruit. It can be chewy or hard and variously colored. *White nougat* is made with beaten egg white and is therefore softer. *Brown nougat* is made with caramelized sugar and, in addition to being a darker color, is normally firmer in texture.

nouvelle cuisine [noo-vehl kwee-ZEEN] A French term meaning "new cooking," referring to a culinary style, begun in the early 1970s, which moved away from the rich, heavy style of classic French cuisine toward fresher, lighter food served in smaller portions. The sauces are lighter because they're REDUCED instead of being thickened with flour. Nouvelle-cuisine vegetables are quickly cooked and therefore are tender yet slightly crisp.

Nova Scotia salmon *see* SMOKED SALMON

nuoc-nam *see* NAM PLA

noyaux [nwah-YOH] *see* CRÈME DE NOYAUX

nutmeg When Columbus sailed from Spain looking for the East Indies, nutmeg was one of the spices for which he was searching. Native to the Spice Islands, this seed from the nutmeg tree (a tropical evergreen) was extremely popular throughout much of the world from the 15th to the 19th century. When the fruit of the tree is picked, it is split to reveal the nutmeg seed surrounded by a lacy membrane which, when dried and ground, becomes the spice MACE. The hard, egg-shaped nutmeg seed is grayish-brown and about 1 inch long. The flavor and aroma are delicately warm, spicy and sweet. Nutmeg is sold ground or whole. Whole nutmeg freshly ground with a NUTMEG GRATER or GRINDER is superior to that which is commercially ground and packaged. Nutmeg is excellent when used in baked goods, milk- or cream-based preparations like custards, white sauces or eggnog, and on fruits and vegetables—particularly potatoes, spinach and squash. *See also* SPICES; Herb and Spice Chart, page 538.

nutmeg grater; nutmeg grinder Small tools used to turn the whole NUTMEG seed into a coarse powder. A **nutmeg grater** has a fine-rasp, slightly curved surface. The grating is accomplished by rubbing the nutmeg across the grater's surface. Many graters store the whole nutmegs in containers attached to the bottom or back of the unit. A **nutmeg grinder** resembles a pepper grinder, except the cavity is designed specifically to hold a whole nutmeg with a small 4-pronged plate at the end of a central, spring-mounted post. The spring serves to keep downward pressure on the nutmeg, forcing it into a sharp blade that, when the crank is rotated, grates the nutmeg.

nut mill A utensil that attaches to the top of a countertop by means of a clamp-and-screw housing. Shelled nuts are placed in a top opening. When a hand crank is rotated, the nuts are pressed against a grating drum, which pulverizes them without releasing their natural oil. Nut mills are usually made of enameled cast iron.

nuts Any of various dry fruits which generally consist of an edible kernel enclosed in a shell that can range from medium-hard, thin and brittle to woody and tough. Botanically speaking, some foods we know as nuts are actually seeds (such as the BRAZIL NUT) or LEGUMES (like the PEANUT). Among the more popular of the other "nuts" are ALMONDS, CASHEWS, CHESTNUTS, MACADAMIAS, PECANS, PISTACHIOS, PINE NUTS and WALNUTS. Most nuts are sold both shelled and unshelled. Shelled nuts come in many forms including blanched or not, whole, halved, chopped, sliced or minced. Additionally, shelled nuts come raw, dry-roasted, oil-roasted, with or without salt, smoked, candied and with various flavorings such as jalapeño and garlic. They're sold in plastic bags and boxes, and vacuum-packed in cans and jars. When buying unshelled nuts in bulk, choose those that are heavy for their size, with solid shells sans cracks or holes. Except for the peanut, the nut's kernel should not be loose enough to rattle when shaken. Shelled nuts should be plump, crisp and uniform in color and size. In general, nuts should be purchased as fresh as possible. Rancid nutmeats will ruin whatever food they flavor. To be sure that nuts are fresh —whether shelled or unshelled—buy them from a supplier with rapid turnover. Because of their high fat content, rancidity is always a hazard with nuts. For that reason they should be stored airtight in a cool place. Shelled nuts can be refrigerated in this manner up to 4 months, frozen up to 6 months. As a general rule (and depending on their freshness at the time of storage), unshelled nuts will keep about twice as long as shelled. Popular nut byproducts include meal or flour (usually found in health-food stores), nut butter and oils (the most popular being almond, hazelnut, peanut and walnut oils). Nuts are wonderful simply eaten out of hand as well as used in a wide variety of sweet and savory dishes for meals from breakfast to dinner. The flavor of most nuts benefits from a light toasting, either on stovetop or in the oven. In general, nuts are a good source of protein and contain fair amounts of iron, phosphorus and thiamine. *For details on specific nuts, see individual listings.*

at bran *see* OATS

oat flour *see* OATS

oatmeal *see* OATS

oats According to a definition in Samuel Johnson's 1755 *Dictionary of the English Language,* oats were "a grain which in England is generally given to horses, but which in Scotland supports the people." Since oats are by far the most nutritious of the cereal grasses, it would appear that the Scots were ahead of the rest of us. Today, whole oats are still used as animal fodder. Humans don't usually consume them until after the oats have been cleaned, toasted, hulled and cleaned again, after which time they become **oat groats** (which still contain most of the original nutrients). Oat groats can be cooked and served as cereal, or prepared in the same manner as rice and used as a side dish or in a dish such as a salad or stuffing. When steamed and flattened with huge rollers, oat groats become regular **rolled oats** (also called *old-fashioned oats*). They take about 15 minutes to cook. **Quick-cooking rolled oats** are groats that have been cut into several pieces before being steamed and rolled into thinner flakes. Though they cook in about 5 minutes, many think the flavor and texture are never quite as satisfying as with regular rolled oats. Old-fashioned oats and quick-cooking oats can usually be interchanged in recipes. **Instant oats**, however, are not interchangeable because they're made with cut groats that have been precooked and dried before being rolled. This precooking process so softens the oat pieces that, after being combined with a liquid, the mixture can turn baked goods such as muffins or cookies into gooey lumps. Most instant oatmeal is packaged with salt, sugar and other flavorings. **Scotch oats** or **steel-cut oats** or **Irish oatmeal** are all names for groats that have been cut in 2 to 3 pieces and not rolled. They take considerably longer to cook than rolled oats and have a decidedly chewy texture. **Oat flour** is made from groats that have been ground into powder. It contains no gluten, however, so—for baked goods that need to rise, like yeast breads—must be combined with a flour that does. **Oat bran** is the outer casing of the oat and is particularly high in soluble fiber, thought to be a leading contender in the fight against high cholesterol. Oat bran, groats, flour and Scotch oats are more likely to be found in health-food stores than supermarkets. Oats are high in vitamin B-1 and contain a good amount of vitamins B-2 and E.

O'Brien potatoes Although the origin of the name is vague, it seems to come from the longtime association between the Irish and potatoes. The dish consists of diced potatoes (sometimes precooked) that are fried with chopped onions and PIMIENTOS until the potatoes are crisp and brown. Some variations use sweet red or green peppers instead of pimientos.

octopus [OK-tuh-puhs] Though there are some 50-foot specimens—and despite the fact that it's also called *devilfish*—this monster of the deep is not particularly fearful and seldom reaches the size seen in the movies. In fact, the majority reach only 1 to 2 feet (tentacles extended) and weigh about 3 pounds. As a member of the CEPHALOPOD class in the MOLLUSK family, the octopus is related to the SQUID and CUTTLEFISH. Its rich diet of clams and scallops gives it a highly flavorful meat that, though rubbery, is extremely popular in Japan and the Mediterranean countries. Predressed fresh and frozen octopus is available in many supermarkets and specialty fish markets. As with most species, those that are younger and smaller are more tender. The 8 tentacles and the body to which they're attached are edible, but the eyes, mouth area and viscera are discarded. The ink sac contains a black liquid that can be used to color and flavor foods such as pasta, soups and stews. Smoked and canned octopus are also available. Octopus can be eaten in a variety of ways including raw, boiled and pickled, sautéed, deep-fried or for more mature specimens, simmered or boiled for several hours. *See also* SHELLFISH.

oenology [ee-NOL-uh-jee] The science of growing grapes and making wines.

oeuf [OUF] The French word for "egg."

oeufs à la neige [OUF ah lah nehzh] *see* FLOATING ISLANDS

offal [OH-fuhl; OFF-uhl] *see* VARIETY MEATS

oil *see* FATS AND OILS

oilstone *see* WHETSTONE

oke [OH-kee] *see* OKOLEHAO

okolehao [oh-koh-leh-HAH-oh] An 80 PROOF Hawaiian liquor made from a mash of the TI plant. It's often substituted for rum and, like rum, comes in white (colorless) and golden versions. Okolehao is known on the islands as *oke*.

okra [OH-kruh] Ethiopian slaves brought the okra plant to America's South, where it's still popular today. The green okra pods have a ridged skin and a tapered, oblong shape. Although available fresh year-round in the South, the season for the rest of the country is from about May through October. When buying fresh okra look for firm, brightly colored pods under 4 inches long. Larger pods may be tough and fibrous. Avoid those that are dull in color, limp or blemished. Refrigerate okra in a plastic bag for up to 3 days. Canned and frozen okra is also available. These green pods can be prepared in a variety of ways including braising, baking and frying. When cooked, okra gives off a rather viscous substance that serves to thicken any liquid in which it is cooked. Throughout the South, it's a favorite ingredient in many dishes, the best known being GUMBO, where it's used both for thickening and for flavor. Fresh okra contains fair amounts of vitamins A and C.

olallieberry; olallie berry [AHL-uh-lee] Grown mainly on the West Coast, this cross between a YOUNGBERRY and a LOGANBERRY has a distinctive, sweet flavor and resembles a large, elongated BLACKBERRY. It's delicious both fresh and cooked and makes excellent jams and jellies.

old fashioned cocktail Said to have been made initially with a brand of Kentucky bourbon called "Old 1776" in the late 1800s, this drink is made by combining WHISKEY (usually BOURBON or RYE), a small amount of water, a dash of BITTERS and a sugar cube (or the equivalent amount of sugar syrup). It's served over ice in a squat glass—commonly called an old-fashioned glass—and garnished with an orange slice and a maraschino cherry.

olive The olive branch has long been a symbol of peace, and the silvery-leaved olive tree has been considered sacred at least as far back as the 17th century B.C. Native to the Mediterranean area, the olive is a small, oily fruit that contains a pit. It's grown both for its fruit and its oil in subtropical zones including the U.S. (Arizona, California and New Mexico), Latin America and throughout the Mediterranean. Olive varieties number in the dozens and vary in size and flavor. All fresh olives are bitter and the final flavor of the fruit greatly depends on how ripe it is when picked and the processing it receives. Underripe olives are always green, whereas ripe olives may be either green or black. **Spanish olives** are picked young, soaked in lye, then fermented in brine for 6 to 12 months. When bottled, they're packed in a weak brine and sold in a variety of forms including pitted, unpitted or stuffed with foods such as PIMIENTOS, almonds, onions, JALAPEÑOS, etc. Olives picked in a riper state contain more oil and are a deeper green color. The common **black olive** or **Mission olive** is a ripe green olive that obtains its characteristic color and flavor from lye curing and oxygenization. Olives that are tree-ripened turn dark brown or black naturally. The majority of these olives are used for oil but the rest are brine- or salt-cured and are usually packed in olive oil or a vinegar solution. The Greek *kalamata* and the French *niçoise* olives are two of the more popular imported ripe olives. The purple-black **kalamata olive** is often slit to allow the wine-vinegar marinade in which it's soaked to penetrate the flesh. Kalamatas are packed in either olive oil or vinegar. The tiny, dark-brown **niçoise olive** is brine-cured before being packed in olive oil. **Dry-cured olives** have been packed in salt, which removes most of their moisture and creates dry, wrinkled fruit. These olives are sometimes rubbed with olive oil or packed with herbs. Both domestic and imported olives are available bottled, canned and in bulk year-round in a variety of forms including whole (pitted, unpitted and stuffed), sliced and chopped. Unopened olives can be stored at room temperature for up to 2 years. Once opened they can be refrigerated in their own liquid (in a nonmetal container) for several weeks. *See also* OLIVE OIL.

olive oil   Pressing tree-ripened olives extracts a flavorful, MONOUNSATURATED OIL which is prized throughout the world both for cooking (particularly in Mediterranean countries) and for salads. Today's marketplace provides a wide selection of domestic olive oil (most of which comes from California) and imported oils from France, Italy and Spain. All olive oils are graded in accordance with the degree of acidity they contain. The best are **cold-pressed**, which produces a natural level of low acidity. **Extra virgin olive oil**, the cold-pressed result of the first pressing of the olives, is only 1 percent acid. It's considered the finest and fruitiest of the olive oils and is therefore also the most expensive. Extra virgin olive oil can range from a crystalline champagne color to greenish-golden to bright green. In general, the deeper the color, the more intense the olive flavor. After extra virgin, olive oils are classified in order of ascending acidity as **superfine, fine** and **pure** (or **virgin**). The latter is extracted with the aid of solvents and is paler in both color and flavor. The new **light olive oil** contains the same amount of beneficial monounsaturated fat as regular olive oil . . . and it also has exactly the same number of calories. What the term "light" refers to is that—because of an extremely fine filtration process—this olive oil is lighter in both color and fragrance, and has little of the classic olive-oil flavor. It's this rather nondescript flavor that makes "light" olive oil perfect for baking and cooking where regular olive oil's obvious essence might be undesirable. The filtration process for this light-style oil also gives it a higher SMOKE POINT than regular olive oil. Light olive oils can therefore be used for high-heat frying, whereas regular olive oil is better suited for low- to medium-heat cooking, as well as for many uncooked foods such as salad dressings and MARINADES. The International Olive Oil Institute recommends using pure olive oil for frying, since the flavor of extra virgin olive oil tends to break down at frying temperatures, making the added expense a waste. Olive oil should be stored in a cool, dark place for up to 6 months. It can be refrigerated, in which case it will last up to a year. Chilled olive oil becomes cloudy and too thick to pour.

However, it will clear and become liquid again when brought to room temperature. *See also* FATS AND OILS.

oloroso [oh-loh-ROH-soh] A sweet, full-flavored SHERRY that has a dark, rich color. Olorosos are usually aged longer than most sherries and are therefore also more expensive. They're often labeled *cream* or *golden* sherry.

Olympia oyster [oh-LIHM-pee-uh] Native to the Pacific Coast, the Olympia oyster is found primarily in the Pacific Northwest around Washington's Puget Sound. It's very small, seldom exceeding 1½ inches. The Olympia has an excellent flavor and is a favorite for eating ON THE HALF SHELL. Because they are so small, it takes a fair number to satisfy most oyster aficionados. *See also* OYSTER.

Omega-3 oils *see* FATS AND OILS

omelet; omelette [AHM-leht] A mixture of eggs, seasonings and sometimes water or milk, cooked in butter until firm and filled or topped with various fillings such as cheese, ham, mushrooms, onions, peppers, sausage and herbs. Sweet omelets can be filled with jelly, custard or fruit, sprinkled with confectioners' sugar or flamed with various LIQUORS or LIQUEURS. For fluffy omelets, the whites and yolks can be beaten separately and folded together. They can also be served flat or folded. *See also* FRITTATA.

omelet pan A pan with shallow sloping sides, a flat bottom and a long handle. It's designed for easy movement, turning and removal of an OMELET or other egg mixtures. Omelet pans range from 6 to 10 inches in diameter and can be made of aluminum, plain or enameled cast iron or stainless steel. Many of today's omelet pans have NON-STICK FINISHES.

onion Related to the lily, this underground bulb is prized around the world for the magic it makes in a multitude of dishes with its pungent flavor and odor. There are two main classifications of onion—**green onions** (also called SCALLIONS) and **dry onions**, which are simply mature onions with a juicy flesh covered with dry, papery skin. Dry onions come in a wide range of sizes, shapes and flavors. Among those that are mild-flavored are the white or yellow **Bermuda onion**, available March through June; the larger, more spherical **Spanish onion**, which is usually yellow-skinned and in season from August to May; and the **red** or **Italian onion**, which is available year-round. The stronger-flavored **globe onions** can have yellow, red or white skins. They can range from 1 to 4 inches in diameter and in flavor from mildly pungent to quite sharp. Among the special onion varieties are three exceedingly juicy specimens. The **Maui onion,**

hailing—as its name implies—from the Hawaiian island of the same name, is sweet, mild and crisply moist. It can range in color from white to pale yellow and is usually shaped like a slightly flattened sphere. The Maui onion's season is from April to July. **Vidalia onions** are the namesake of Vidalia, Georgia, where they thrive. At their best, these large, pale yellow onions are exceedingly sweet and juicy. They're usually available from May through June only in the regions where grown or by mail order. The state of Washington is the source of **Walla Walla onions,** named after the city of the same name. Large, round and golden, they're in season from June to September but are usually available outside their growing area only by mail order. Tiny **pearl onions** are mild-flavored and about the size of a small marble. They can be cooked (and are often creamed) and served as a side dish or pickled and used as a CONDIMENT or garnish (as in the GIBSON cocktail). **Boiling onions** are about 1 inch in diameter and mildly flavored. They're cooked as a side dish, used in stews and pickled. When buying onions, choose those that are heavy for their size with dry, papery skins with no signs of spotting or moistness. Avoid onions with soft spots. Store in a cool, dry place with good air circulation for up to 3 months (depending on their condition when purchased). Humidity breeds spoilage in dry onions. Once cut, an onion should be tightly wrapped, refrigerated and used within 4 days. Dried or freeze-dried onion byproducts include **onion powder** (ground dehydrated onion), **onion salt** (onion powder and salt), **onion flakes** and **onion flavoring cubes**. Onions are also sold canned or pickled (usually pearl onions) and frozen (whole or chopped). Onions contain a fair amount of vitamin C with traces of other vitamins and minerals. *See also* CHIVE; LEEK; SCALLION; SHALLOT.

onion powder *see* ONION

onion salt *see* ONION

ono [OH-noh] *see* WAHOO

on the half shell A phrase commonly used to describe raw oysters served on the bottom shell only, usually on a plate of crushed ice or, in the case of cooked dishes such as OYSTERS ROCKEFELLER, on a bed of rock salt. Some oyster lovers eat these fresh oysters without any CONDIMENTS, sipping the oyster liquor from its bottom shell. Others adorn theirs with lemon juice, horseradish, tabasco sauce, cocktail sauce, ketchup or vinegar.

on the rocks When a beverage (usually liquor) is served over ice without added water or other MIXER, it's usually referred to as "on the rocks."

oolong tea [OO-long] *see* TEA

open-faced A descriptor used culinarily for a "sandwich" consisting of one slice of bread topped with various ingredients such as sliced meat, cheese, pickles, etc. Open-faced sandwiches are very popular in Scandinavia, where they've become an art form with elaborately arranged and decorated combinations. For the most part, open-faced sandwiches are cold, but there are also hot ones, which usually consist of bread topped with meat slices and gravy.

orange Contrary to what most of us think, this fruit was not named for its color. Instead, the word *orange* comes from a transliteration of the sanskrit *naranga* . . . which comes from the Tamil *naru* . . . which means "fragrant." It's thought that the reason oranges have long been associated with fertility (and therefore, weddings) is because this lush evergreen tree can simultaneously produce flowers, fruit and foliage. Though oranges originated in Southeast Asia, they now also thrive around the world in warm-climate areas including Portugal, Spain, North Africa and, in the U.S. (the world's largest producer), Arizona, California, Florida and Texas. There are three basic types of orange—sweet, loose-skinned and bitter. **Sweet oranges** are prized both for eating and for their juice. They're generally large and have skins that are more difficult to remove than their loose-skinned relatives. They may have seeds or be seedless. Among the more popular sweet oranges are the seedless NAVEL, the juicy, coarse-grained VALENCIA and the thin-skinned, red-fleshed BLOOD ORANGE. Sweet oranges are better eaten fresh than cooked. **Loose-skinned oranges** are so named because their skins easily slip off the fruit. Their segments are also loose and divide with ease. Members of the MANDARIN ORANGE family are all loose-skinned; they vary in flavor from sweet to tart-sweet. **Bitter oranges**, the most well-known of which are the SEVILLE and the BERGAMOT, are—as their name implies—too sour and astringent to eat raw. Instead, they're cooked in preparations such as MARMALADE and BIGARADE SAUCE. Bitter oranges are also greatly valued for their peel, which is candied, and their essential oils, which are used to flavor foods as well as some LIQUEURS, such as CURAÇAO. Most of the bitter orange supply comes from Spain. USDA grading of oranges is voluntary and not considered necessary by most growers. The two grades used are **U.S. Fancy** (best) and **U.S. No. 1.** Fresh oranges are available year-round at different times, depending on the variety. Choose fruit that is firm and heavy for its size, with no mold or spongy spots. Unfortunately, because oranges are sometimes dyed with food coloring, a bright color isn't necessarily an indicator of quality. Regreening sometimes occurs in fully ripe oranges, particularly with Valencias. A rough, brownish area (russeting) on the skin doesn't affect flavor or quality either. Oranges can be stored at cool room temperature for a day or so, but should then be refrigerated and can be kept there for up to 2 weeks. Oranges are an excellent source of vitamin C and contain some vitamin A. Once cut or squeezed, however, the vitamin C quickly begins to dissipate. After only 8 hours at room temperature or 24 hours in the refrigerator, there's a 20-percent vitamin C loss. Canned, bottled and frozen-concentrate orange juices have a greatly decreased vitamin C content. *For information on specific oranges, see individual listings.*

orange-flower water A perfumy distillation of bitter orange flowers. Orange flower water is used as a flavoring in baked goods, various sweet and savory dishes and a variety of drinks, such as the Ramos GIN FIZZ cocktail.

orange pekoe tea *see* PEKOE

orange roughy [RUHF-ee] This New Zealand fish (also known as *slimehead*) is fast becoming popular in the United States. It's low in fat, has firm white flesh and a mild flavor. Orange roughy is available in specialty fish markets and some supermarkets. It can be poached, baked, broiled or fried. *See also* FISH.

oregano [oh-REHG-uh-noh] Greek for "joy of the mountain," oregano was almost unheard of in the U.S. until soldiers came back from Italian World War II assignments raving about it. This herb, sometimes called *wild marjoram*, belongs to the mint family and is related to both marjoram and THYME. Oregano is similar to marjoram but is not as sweet and has a stronger, more pungent flavor and aroma. Because of its pungency, it requires a bit more caution in its use. Mediterranean oregano is milder than the Mexican variety, which is generally used in highly spiced dishes. Fresh Mediterranean or European oregano is sometimes available in gourmet produce sections of supermarkets and in Italian or Greek markets. Choose bright-green, fresh-looking bunches with no sign of wilting or yellowing. Refrigerate in a plastic bag for up to 3 days. Dried Mediterranean oregano is readily available in any supermarket in both crumbled and powdered forms. The stronger-flavored Mexican oregano can generally be found in its dried form in Latin markets. As with all dried herbs, oregano should be stored in a cool, dark place for no more than 6 months. Oregano goes extremely well with tomato-based dishes and is a familiar pizza herb. *See also* HERBS; Herb and Spice Chart, page 538.

organic food Food which is cultivated and/or processed without the use of chemicals of any sort including fertilizers, insecticides, artificial coloring or flavoring and additives. The term applies mainly to produce.

orgeat syrup [OHR-zhat] The original version of this sweet syrup was made with a barley-almond blend. Today, however, it's made with almonds, sugar and ROSE WATER or ORANGE-FLOWER WATER. Orgeat syrup has a pronounced almond taste and is used to flavor many cocktails including the MAI TAI and SCORPION.

oriental radish *see* DAIKON

ormer [OHR-muhr] *see* ABALONE

orzo [OHR-zoh] In Italian this means "barley," but it's actually a tiny, rice-shaped PASTA, slightly smaller than a PINE NUT. It's ideal for soups and wonderful when served as a substitute for rice.

osso buco; ossobuco [AW-soh BOO-koh; OH-soh BOO-koh] An Italian dish made of veal shanks braised with olive oil, white wine, stock, onions, tomatoes, garlic, anchovies, carrots, celery and lemon peel. Traditionally, osso buco is garnished with GREMOLADA and served accompanied by RISOTTO.

ostrich fern *see* FIDDLEHEAD FERN

ouzo [OO-zoh] From Greece, this clear, sweet anise–flavored LIQUEUR is usually served as an APÉRITIF. It's generally mixed with water, which turns it whitish and opaque.

oven thermometer A thermometer designed to read oven temperatures, which are often inaccurately indicated by the oven dial. Erroneous oven temperatures can create all kinds of culinary havoc, from gooey centers in baked goods to burning or drying of a wide range of foods. Oven thermometers can vary in quality and, consequently, price. The spring-style thermometer available in most supermarkets can become unreliable with a small jolt or with continual use. Mercury oven thermometers, available in gourmet supply shops, are more accurate and reliable.

oxalic acid [ok-SAL-ihk] This acid occurs in many plants and is poisonous in excessive amounts. Some of the plants that contain a measurable amount of oxalic acid are SORREL, SPINACH and RHUBARB. Because it forms insoluble compounds with calcium and iron, inhibiting their absorption by the human body, oxalic acid greatly diminishes the purported nutritional punch of spinach.

oxtail The oxtail was once really from an ox but nowadays the term generally refers to beef or veal tail. Though it's quite bony, this cut of meat is very flavorful. Because it can be extremely tough (depending on the age of the animal), oxtail requires long, slow braising. It's often used for stews or soups such as the hearty English classic oxtail soup, which includes vegetables, barley and herbs and is often flavored with SHERRY or MADEIRA.

oyster Though 18th-century satirist Jonathan Swift once wrote, "He was a bold man that first ate an oyster," this BIVALVE has been a culinary favorite for thousands of years. The hard, rough, gray shell contains a meat which can vary in color from creamy beige to pale gray, in flavor from salty to bland and in texture from tender to firm. There are both natural and cultivated oyster beds throughout the world. In the United States, there are three primary species of oysters that are commercially harvested—Pacific (or Japanese), Eastern (or Atlantic) and the Olympia. Each species is sold under different names depending on where they're harvested. **Olympia oysters** are rarely larger than 1½ inches and hail from Washington's Puget Sound. The **Pacific oyster** or **Japanese oyster** is found along the Pacific seaboard and can reach up to a foot long. Considered culinarily superior to the Pacific oysters are **Atlantic oysters** or **Eastern oysters**, the most well-known of which is the BLUEPOINT. Others from the Atlantic seaboard—named for their place of origin—include *Apalachicola, Cape Cod, Chincoteague, Indian River, Kent Island, Malpeque* and *Wellfleet*. In Europe, the French are famous for their **belon oysters** (which are now also being farmed in the U.S.) and their green-tinged **Marennes oysters**; the English have their **Colchester, Helford** and **Whitstable oysters**; and the Irish have **Galway oysters**. Fresh oysters are available year-round. Today's widespread refrigeration keeps them cool during hot weather, debunking the old myth of not eating them during months spelled without an "r". However, oysters are at their best—particularly for serving raw ON THE HALF SHELL during fall and winter because they spawn during the summer months and become soft and fatty. Shipping costs generally prohibit movement of oysters far from their beds, limiting the abundant supply to local varieties. Live oysters are best as fresh as possible and therefore should be purchased from a store with good turnover. Reject those that do not have tightly closed shells or that don't snap shut when tapped. The smaller the oyster is (for its species) the younger and more tender it will be. Fresh, SCHUCKED oysters are also available and should be plump, uniform in size, have good color, smell fresh and be packaged in clear, not cloudy oyster LIQUOR. Live oysters should be covered with a damp towel and refrigerated (larger shell down) up to 3 days. The sooner they're used the better they'll taste. Refrigerate shucked oysters in their liquor and use within 2 days. Oysters are also available canned in water or their own liquor, frozen and smoked. Oysters in the shell can be served raw, baked, steamed, grilled or in specialty dishes such as OYSTERS ROCKEFELLER. Shucked oysters can be batter-fried, sautéed, grilled, used in soups or stews or in special preparations such as dressings, poultry stuffings or appetizers like ANGELS ON HORSEBACK. Oysters are high in calcium, niacin and iron, as well a good source of protein. *See also* SHELLFISH.

oyster crab A diminutive (less than 1 inch wide) soft-shell crab that makes its home inside an oyster and lives off the food its host eats. Oyster crabs are certainly not found in all oysters, and most oyster processing plants don't bother to collect them during shucking so the supply is very limited. They're best prepared simply sautéed in butter. Gourmets consider these pale-pink CRUSTACEANS a delicacy. *See also* CRAB.

oyster mushroom This fan-shaped mushroom grows both wild and cultivated in close clusters, often on rotting tree trunks. They're also called *oyster caps, tree mushrooms, tree oyster mushrooms* and *summer oyster mushrooms.* The cap varies in color from pale gray to dark brownish-gray. The stems are grayish-white. The flavor of raw oyster mushrooms is fairly robust and slightly peppery but becomes much milder when cooked. They're available in some areas year-round, particularly in specialty produce and Asian markets. Young oyster mushrooms (1½ inches in diameter and under) are considered the best. Also available are canned oyster mushrooms, which should be rinsed before using. *See also* MUSHROOM.

oyster plant *see* SALSIFY

oyster sauce A dark-brown sauce consisting of oysters, brine and soy sauce cooked until thick and concentrated. It's a popular oriental seasoning used to prepare a multitude of dishes (particularly STIR-FRIES) and as a table CONDIMENT. Oyster sauce imparts a richness to dishes without overpowering their natural flavor. It's available in many supermarkets and all oriental markets.

oysters Rockefeller Created at Antoine's restaurant in New Orleans in the late 1890s, this popular dish was reportedly named for John D. Rockefeller because it's so rich. Today there are many versions of this classic, the most common being oysters ON THE HALF SHELL topped with a mixture of chopped spinach, butter, breadcrumbs and seasonings and either baked or broiled. The shells are usually placed on a bed of rock salt, which keeps them from toppling and spilling the ingredients. The original oysters Rockefeller is said to have been made with watercress, not spinach.

acific littleneck clam *see* LITTLENECK CLAM

Pacific oyster Also called the *Japanese oyster*, this species has an elongated fragile shell that can reach up to a foot across. It's found along the Pacific seaboard. Because of its size, the Pacific oyster is generally cut up and used in soups, stews and other cooked dishes. *See also* OYSTER.

Pacific pompano *see* BUTTERFISH

paella [py-AY-yuh; py-AYL-uh] A Spanish dish of SAFFRON-flavored rice combined with a variety of meats and shellfish (such as shrimp, lobster, clams, chicken, pork, ham and CHORIZO), garlic, onions, peas, artichoke hearts and tomatoes. It's named after the special two-handled pan—also called *paella*—in which it's prepared and served. The pan is wide, shallow and 13 to 14 inches in diameter.

pain [PAN] The French word for "bread" or "loaf of bread."

pain perdu [pahn pehr-DOO] *see* FRENCH TOAST

palacsinta A thin Hungarian pancake or CRÊPE, referred to by the Austrians as *palatschinke*. They are usually assembled in a stack of 6 or 7, layered with a filling. The savory rendition is often filled with chopped ham, lobster, pork, veal, mushrooms or other vegetables combined with a cream sauce or sour cream. The dessert version is made with slightly sweeter batter and spread with a sweet filling such as jam. Before serving, the stack is cut into wedges.

palmier [pahlm-YAY] Also called *palm leaves*, this crispy delicacy is PUFF PASTRY dough that is sprinkled with granulated sugar, folded and rolled several times, then cut into thin strips. After baking, these golden brown, caramelized pastries are served with coffee or tea or as a dessert accompaniment.

palm oil The reddish-orange oil extracted from the pulp of the fruit of the African palm. It's extremely high in saturated fat (78 percent) and has a distinctive flavor that is popular in West African and Brazilian cooking. **Palm-kernel oil,** though also high in saturated fat, is a different oil extracted from the nut or kernel of palms. It's a yellowish-white color and has a pleasantly mild flavor. Palm-kernel oil is used in the manufacture of margarine and cosmetics. It's usually listed on labels simply as "palm oil." *See also* FATS AND OILS.

palm sugar *see* JAGGERY

panada; panade [puh-NAH-duh (Sp.); puh-NAHD (Fr)] **1.** A thick paste made by mixing breadcrumbs, flour, rice, etc. with water, milk, stock, butter or sometimes egg yolks. It's used to bind meatballs, fish cakes, FORCEMEATS and QUENELLES. **2.** A sweet or savory soup made with breadcrumbs and various other ingredients. It may be strained before serving.

pan-broil To cook meats or fish quickly in a heavy, ungreased (or lightly greased) frying pan over high heat. Drippings are poured off as they form.

pancake As one of man's oldest forms of bread, the versatile pancake has hundreds of variations and is served for breakfast, lunch and dinner and as appetizers, entrees and desserts. Pancakes begin as a batter that is poured into rounds, either on a griddle or in a skillet, and cooked over high heat. These round cakes vary in thickness from the wafer-thin French CRÊPE to the much thicker American breakfast pancake (also called *hotcake*, *griddlecake* and *flapjack*). Many countries have specialty pancakes such as Hungarian PALACSINTA and Russian BLINI.

pancake turner *see* TURNERS

pancetta [pan-CHEH-tuh] An Italian bacon that is cured with salt and spices but not smoked. Flavorful, slightly salty pancetta comes in a sausagelike roll. It's used in Italian cooking to flavor sauces, pasta dishes, FORCEMEATS, vegetables and meats. Pancetta can be tightly wrapped and refrigerated for up to 3 weeks, or frozen up to 6 months.

pandowdy Also called *apple pandowdy*, this DEEP-DISH dessert is made of sliced apples, butter, spices, brown sugar or molasses, all topped with a biscuit batter that becomes crisp and crumbly after baking. It can be served hot or at room temperature and is often accompanied by cream or ice cream. The origin of the name is unclear, although some seem to think it comes from the dessert's dowdy (plain and old-fashioned) appearance.

pan drippings *see* DRIPPINGS

panettone [pan-uh-TOH-nee] A sweet yeast bread made with raisins, CITRON, PINE NUTS and ANISE and baked in a tall cylindrical shape. It originated in Milan, Italy, and is traditionally served at Christmastime, but also for celebrations such as weddings and christenings. Panettone can be served as a bread, coffeecake or dessert.

panforte [pan-FOHR-tay; pan-FOHRT] Because this confection is a specialty of Siena, Italy, it's also called *Siena cake*. This dense, flat cake is rich with honey, hazelnuts, almonds, candied CITRON, citrus peel, cocoa and spices. It contains only a tiny amount of flour—just enough to hold the fruits and nuts together. After baking, *panforte* becomes hard and chewy.

pan-fry *see* FRY

papain [puh-PAY-ihn] An enzyme extracted from PAPAYA and employed as a meat tenderizer, and as an agent used to CLARIFY liquids (especially beer). *See also* MEAT TENDERIZERS.

papaw [PA-paw] Both the PAPAYA and the papaw are sometimes referred to as *pawpaw*, which is thoroughly confusing because they're entirely different fruits. The papaw is a North American native that's a member of the CUSTARD APPLE family. It can range from 2 to 6 inches long and looks like a fat, dark-brown banana. The aromatic flesh is pale yellow and peppered with a profusion of seeds. It has a custardlike texture and a sweet flavor reminiscent of bananas and pears. Papaws are seldom cultivated and are rarely found in markets.

papaya [puh-PY-yuh; puh-PAH-yuh] Like the PAPAW, the papaya is also native to North America (and in some regions, also called *pawpaw*). But with those two comparisons the similarities end. The papaya tree is a horticultural wonder, growing from seed to a 20-foot, fruit-bearing tree in less than 18 months. Papayas are cultivated in semitropical zones around the world and can range in size from 1 to 20 pounds. The papaya variety found most often in the U.S. is the **Solo**, grown in Hawaii and Florida. It's large (about 6 inches long and 1 to 2 pounds in weight) and pear-shaped; when ripe, it has a vivid golden-yellow skin. The similarly colored flesh is juicy and silky-smooth, with an exotic sweet-tart flavor. The rather large center cavity is packed with shiny, greyish-black seeds. Though the peppery seeds are edible (and make a delicious salad dressing), they're generaly discarded. Look for richly colored papayas that give slightly to palm pressure. Slightly green papayas will ripen quickly at room temperature, especially if placed in a paper bag. Refrigerate completely ripe fruit and use as soon as possible. Ripe papaya is best eaten raw, whereas slightly green fruit can be cooked as a vegetable. Papaya juice (or nectar) is available in many supermarkets and health-food stores. The fruit contains PAPAIN, a digestive enzyme that is used chiefly in MEAT TENDERIZERS. Papaya is a very good source of vitamins A and C.

papillote [pah-pee-YOHT; PAH-peh-loht] 1. The French word for a paper frill used to decorate the tips of rib bones, such as those on CROWN ROASTS. 2. *En papillote* refers to food baked inside a wrapping of greased PARCHMENT PAPER. As the food bakes and lets off steam, the parchment puffs up into a dome shape. At the table, the paper is slit and peeled back to reveal the food.

pappadam; poppadum [PAH-pah-duhm] A wafer-thin East Indian bread made with LENTIL flour. This TORTILLAlike bread can be unseasoned (as preferred in southern India) or variously flavored with red or black pepper, garlic or other seasonings, as in northern India. *Pappadams* are available in Indian markets in various sizes and flavors. Deep-fried *pappadams* puff up to almost double their original size. Grilling them over an open flame will give them a smoky flavor.

paprika [pa-PREE-kuh; PAP-ree-kuh] Used as a seasoning and garnish for a plethora of savory dishes, paprika is a powder made by grinding certain sweet red pepper pods. The pods are quite tough, so several grindings are necessary to produce the proper texture. The flavor of paprika can range from mild to pungent and hot, the color from bright orange-red to deep blood-red. Most commercial paprika comes from Spain, South America, California and Hungary, with the Hungarian variety considered by many to be superior. Indeed, Hungarian cuisine has long used paprika as a mainstay flavoring rather than simply as a garnish. All supermarkets carry mild paprikas, while ethnic markets must be searched out for the more pungent varieties. As with all herbs and spices, paprika should be stored in a cool, dark place for no more than 6 months. *See also* SPICES; Herb and Spice Chart, page 538.

paprikás csirke [PAH-pree-kash CHEER-kah] Also called *chicken paprikash*, this Hungarian dish consists of chicken and onions browned in bacon drippings, then braised with chicken stock, paprika and other seasonings. A sauce is made from the braising liquid mixed with sour cream. Although chicken is traditionally used, versions of this dish are also made with meat and fish.

paratha [pah-RAH-tah] This flaky East Indian bread is made with whole-wheat flour and fried on a griddle. Parathas range from the simple to the exotic. The basic version simply has GHEE (clarified butter) brushed between multiple layers of dough that are then folded and rolled out again. This technique creates a flaky bread resembling puff pastry. More exotic versions of paratha are stuffed with various vegetables, fruits, herbs or spices.

parboil, To partially cook food by boiling it briefly in water. This time-saving technique is used in particular for dense foods such as carrots. If parboiled, they can be added at the last minute with quick-cooking ingredients (such as bean sprouts and celery) in preparations such as STIR-FRIES. The parboiling insures that all the ingredients will complete cooking at the same time. *See also* BLANCH.

parboiled rice *see* RICE

parchment paper A heavy, grease- and moisture-resistant paper with a number of culinary uses including lining baking pans, wrapping foods that are to be baked en PAPILLOTE and to make disposable PASTRY BAGS. Parchment paper is available in gourmet kitchenware stores and many supermarkets.

pare To remove the thin outer layer of foods like fruits and vegetables with a small, short-bladed knife (called a PARING KNIFE) or with a VEGETABLE PEELER.

pareve; parve [PAHR-uh-vuh; PAHR-vuh] A Jewish term describing food made without animal or dairy ingredients. According to KOSHER dietary laws, animal food cannot be consumed at the same meal with dairy food, but a pareve food may be combined or eaten with either. In order to be pareve, breads and cakes must be made with vegetable oils and not with butter or other animal fat.

parfait [pahr-FAY] 1. In the United States, this dessert consists of ice cream layered with flavored syrup or fruit and whipped cream. It's often topped with whipped cream, nuts and sometimes a MARASCHINO CHERRY. 2. A French parfait is a frozen custard dessert made with egg yolks, sugar, whipped cream and a flavoring such as fruit puree. In French, *parfait* means "perfect," which is how many view this dessert. Both American and French parfaits are served in tall, narrow, footed "parfait glasses."

paring knife *see* KNIFE

Paris-Brest [pair-ihs-BREHST] A delightful French dessert said to have been created by a pastry chef in honor of a bicycle race between Paris and Brest. It consists of a baked almond-topped CHOUX PASTRY ring (patterned after a bicycle tire) that is split and filled with a praline-flavored BUTTERCREAM.

parisienne sauce [puh-ree-zee-EHN] 1. A creamy sauce, classically used to top cold asparagus, made by blending cream cheese, oil, lemon juice, CHERVIL and sometimes PAPRIKA. 2. Another name for ALLEMANDE SAUCE.

Parker House roll; Parkerhouse A yeast roll that became famous during the late 19th century at the Parker House, a Boston hotel. It gets its special shape when an off-center crease is made in a round piece of dough before it's folded in half. The result after baking is a light, puffy bun.

Parma ham [PAHR-muh] The true PROSCIUTTO, this superior Italian ham hails from northern Italy's province of Parma, the same area famous for Parmesan cheese. The special diet of chestnuts and WHEY (from the cheese-making process) that Parma pigs enjoy results in an excellent quality of meat. Parma hams are seasoned, salt-cured and air-dried but not smoked. They have a rosy-brown flesh that is firm and dense. The best of these special hams come from the little village of Langhirano, just south of the city of Parma. Parma hams are usually thinly sliced and eaten raw as an appetizer (often with melon) but they can be used in cooking as well. Italians use the rind to flavor soups. *See also* HAM.

Parmesan cheese [PAHR-muh-zahn] This hard, dry cheese is made from skimmed or partially skimmed cow's milk. It has a hard, pale-golden rind and a straw-colored interior with a rich, sharp flavor. There are Parmesan cheeses made in Argentina, Australia and the United States, but none compares with Italy's preeminent **Parmigiano-Reggiano**, with its granular texture that melts in the mouth. Whereas the U.S. renditions are aged 14 months, Parmigiano-Reggianos are more often aged 2 years. Those labeled stravecchio have been aged 3 years, while stravecchiones are 4 years old. Their complex flavor and extremely granular texture are a result of the long aging. The words Parmigiano-Reggiano stenciled on the rind mean that the cheese was produced in the areas of Bologna, Mantua, Modena or Parma (from which the name of this cheese originated). Parmesans are primarily used for grating and in Italy are termed GRANA, meaning "grain" and referring to their granular textures. Pre-grated Parmesan is available but doesn't compare with freshly grated. Both domestic and imported Parmesans are available in specialty cheese stores, Italian markets and many supermarkets. *See also* CHEESE.

parmigiana, à la [pahr-muh-ZHAH-nuh] A term describing food that is made or cooked with PARMESAN CHEESE. For instance, VEAL PARMIGIANA is a pounded veal cutlet dipped in an egg-milk solution and then into a mixture of breadcrumbs, grated Paremesan cheese and seasonings. The cutlet is then sautéed and covered with a tomato sauce. **Eggplant parmigiana** consists of eggplant slices prepared in the same manner. Slices of MOZZARELLA CHEESE are sometimes melted on top of the food prior to adding the tomato sauce.

Parmigiano-Reggiano [pahr-muh-ZHAH-noh-reh-zhee-AH-noh] *see* PARMESAN CHEESE

parsley In ancient times parsley wreaths were used to ward off drunkenness—though proof of their efficacy in that capacity is scarce. Today, this slightly peppery, fresh-flavored herb is more commonly used as a flavoring and garnish. Though there are more than 30 varieties of this herb, the most popular are **curly-leaf parsley** and the more strongly flavored **Italian** or **flat-leaf parsley.** Fresh curly leaf parsley is widely available year-round, while Italian parsley must sometimes be searched out in gourmet produce markets. Parsley is sold in bunches and should be chosen for its bright-green leaves that show no sign of wilting. Wash fresh parsley, shaking off excess moisture, and wrap first in paper towels, then in a plastic bag. Refrigerate for up to a week. **Dried parsley** is available in the spice section of most supermarkets but bears little resemblance to the flavor of fresh. Parsley is an excellent source of vitamins A and C. *See also* HERBS; Herb and Spice Chart, page 538.

P

parsley root Also called *Hamburg parsley* and *turnip-rooted parsley*, this parsley subspecies is grown for its beige, carrotlike root, which tastes like a carrot-celery cross. It's used in parts of Europe in soups, stews and simply as a vegetable. Parsley root is rarely found in U.S. markets. When available, choose firm roots with feathery, bright-green leaves. Refrigerate in a plastic bag for up to a week. Remove leaves just before using roots. Parsley-root leaves may be used in the same manner as regular parsley.

parsnip Europeans brought the parsnip to the United States in the early 1600s but this creamy-white root has never become an American favorite. The first frost of the year converts the parsnip's starch to sugar and gives it a pleasantly sweet flavor. Fresh parsnips are available year-round with the peak period during fall and winter. Look for small to medium, well-shaped roots. They can be refrigerated in a plastic bag for up to a month. Parsnips are suitable for almost any method of cooking including baking, boiling, sautéing and steaming. They're often boiled, then mashed like potatoes. Parsnips contain small amounts of iron and vitamin C.

parson's nose *see* POPE'S NOSE

partridge Strictly speaking, there are two main varieties of this GAME BIRD—the **gray partridge** and the **red-legged partridge**—neither of which is a North American native. In various regions of the United States, the name "partridge" is erroneously applied to other birds including the ruffed grouse, QUAIL and bobwhite. All of these birds are plump and have white, tender, slightly gamey flesh. Frozen partridges are available at some specialty meat and poultry markets. They usually weigh 12 to 14 ounces. Partridges can be cooked in a variety of ways including roasting, broiling and braising. The meat also makes a tasty addition to soups and stews.

pasilla chili pepper [pah-SEE-yah] In its fresh form this CHILI PEPPER is called a *chilaca*. It's generally 6 to 8 inches long and 1 to 1½ inches in diameter. The mature *chilaca* turns from dark green to dark brown. After it's dried (becoming the *pasilla*), its hue changes to a blackish-brown. Both fresh and dried versions of this pepper have a rich, hot flavor. In its fresh form it's usually toasted, skinned and shredded for use in various dishes. The dried chili pepper is generally ground and used for sauces.

paskha [PAHS-khuh] A Russian dessert traditionally served at Easter. It consists of a combination of sweetened POT CHEESE (or cottage cheese), nuts (usually almonds) and candied or dried fruit. Classically, this mixture is molded into the shape of a four-sided pyramid. The paskha is decorated with nuts or candy to form the letters *XB*, which stands for "Christ is risen." Paskha is the traditional accompaniment for the sweet yeast bread KULICH.

passion fruit This tropical fruit is said to be named not for the passionate propensity it promotes but because various parts of the plant's flowers resemble different symbols of Christ's crucifixion, such as the the the crown of thorns. Though native to Brazil, passion fruit (also called *granadilla*) is now also grown in Australia, California, Florida, Hawaii and New Zealand. The most common variety marketed in the U.S. is egg-shaped and about 3 inches long. When ripe, it has a dimpled, deep- purple skin and a soft, golden flesh generously punctuated with tiny, edible black seeds. The flavor is seductively sweet-tart and the fragrance tropical and perfumy. Fresh passion fruit is available from March through September in Latin markets and some supermarkets. Choose large, heavy, firm fruit with a deep-purple color. Store ripe passion fruit in the refrigerator for up to 5 days. It can be served plain as a dessert or used to flavor a variety of foods like sauces, ice creams and beverages. Canned passion-fruit nectar is available in many supermarkets. Passion fruit contains a small amount of vitamins A and C.

pasta [PAH-stuh] Though many pundits claim that Marco Polo brought the idea of noodles back with him to Italy from China, the truth is that this food form existed in both places independently long before Polo's expeditions. Almost every country has a form of pasta. The Germans enjoy SPAETZLE, Poles have their PIEROGI and throughout the Orient there are dozens of noodles, usually made with rice or soy flour rather than wheat flour (see ASIAN NOODLES). In Italian, the word *pasta* means "paste," and refers to the dough made by combining durum wheat flour called SEMOLINA with a liquid, usually water or milk. The term "pasta" is used broadly and generically to describe a wide variety of noodles made from this type of dough. Some doughs have a little egg added, though doughs made with only flour and eggs are generally referred to as NOODLES. There are hundreds of shapes, sizes, thicknesses and colors of pasta. MACARONI and SPAGHETTI are probably the most popular, though each of those categories has many size and shape varieties. Additionally, there are dozens of fancy shapes such as CONCHIGLIE (shells), FRAFALLE (bows) and ROTELLE (little corkscrews). Other pastas, such as RAVIOLI and TORTELLINI, have fillings. Some pastas are colored, often with spinach (green), beet juice or tomato paste (red) and squid ink (charcoal gray). Pasta also comes in both dried and fresh forms. As a general rule, imported **dried pasta** is superior to American factory-made products, mainly because the imported pasta is only made with semolina, which doesn't absorb too much water and is pleasantly firm when cooked AL DENTE. A good selection of dried pastas can be found in most supermarkets, and an even broader variety is available in Italian markets. It should be stored airtight in a cool, dry place and can be kept almost indefinitely. **Fresh pasta** is often made with eggs instead of water; it can increasingly be found in many supermarkets and is always available in Italian markets. Because it's highly perishable, it must be refrigerated airtight and can be stored in this manner for about 4 days. It can also be frozen for up to a month. Fresh pastas cook in a fraction of the time necessary for dried pastas. When it comes to saucing pasta, a general rule is to use light sauces for delicate pastas like CAPELLI D'ANGELO and chunky, heavy sauces for sturdy pastas such as FUSILLI. *For information on specific pasta shapes, see individual listings.*

pasta machines There are two basic types of machines that can be used to make homemade pasta—the roller type and the extruder type. **Roller-type pasta machines** come in hand-cranked and electric versions. Both come with several attachments—usually one pair of smooth rollers for rolling out the sheets of dough, and two notched pairs (one narrow and one wide) used to cut noodles. With this type of machine, the dough is run between the smooth rollers at increasingly thinner settings until it reaches the desired thickness. The sheets of dough are then fed through either pair of the notched rollers, which cut them into noodles. Some machines have additional attachments, such as crinkle-edge cutters for making lasagne noodles. **Extruder pasta machines** mix the dough inside the unit, then force it out through special plates with variously shaped perforations. Depending on the perforations, solid or hollow-shaped pastas can be produced. Both types of pasta machines are generally available in gourmet kitchenware stores and the small- appliance section of many department stores.

pasta filata [PAH-stuh fih-LAH-tuh] *see* CHEESE

pasta primavera *see* PRIMAVERA

pasteurize [PAS-chuh-ryz; PAS-tuh-ryz] To kill bacteria by heating milk or other liquids to moderately high temperatures for a short period of time.

Milk must be heated to at least 145°F for not less than 30 minutes or at least 161°F for 15 seconds, and then rapidly cooled to 40°F or lower. The process was discovered by the famous French scientist Louis Pasteur while he was researching the cause of beer and wine spoilage. Although pasteurization is used in beer processing and for some wines and fruit juices, the major beneficiary is milk. Pasteurization kills the bacteria in milk that were once responsible for transmitting diseases such as typhoid fever, tuberculosis, scarlet fever, polio and dysentery. LACTIC ACID bacteria, which cause milk to sour, are not destroyed by pasteurization. Neither is the food value of milk greatly diminished by the process. *See also* HOMOGENIZE.

pastilla [pah-STEE-yuh] *see* B'STEEYA

pastille [pas-TEEL] A small, round, hard confection made of sugar, water and various flavorings. In the U.S. pastilles are usually referred to as drops, as in lemon drops.

pastis [pas-TEES] 1. Similar to PERNOD, this clear, strong (90 PROOF), licorice-flavored APÉRITIF is very popular in the south of France. It's usually mixed with water, which turns it whitish and cloudy. 2. Any of various yeast-leavened pastries of southwestern France such as *pastis Beranais*, which is flavored with brandy and ORANGE-FLOWER WATER.

pastrami [puh-STRAH-mee] A highly seasoned beef made from a cut of PLATE, BRISKET or ROUND. After the fat is trimmed, the meat's surface is rubbed with salt and a seasoning paste that can include garlic, ground peppercorns, cinnamon, red pepper, cloves, allspice and coriander seeds. The meat is dry-cured, smoked and cooked. Pastrami can be served hot or cold, usually as a sandwich on rye bread. It's widely available in chunks or pre-sliced in most supermarkets.

pastry bag A cone-shaped bag with two open ends. The small end can be fitted with decorative tips of different sizes and designs, while doughs, whipped cream, fillings, etc. are spooned into the large end. When the bag is squeezed, the contents are forced through the tip. Pastry bags have a multitude of uses including decorating cakes, forming pastries or cookies and piping decorative borders. They come in various sizes and can be made of a variety of materials, the most popular being nylon and plastic-lined cotton or canvas. Pastry bags can be found in gourmet shops, some supermarkets and the kitchenware section of most department stores.

pastry blender A kitchen implement consisting of 5 or 6 U-shaped, sturdy steel wires, both ends of which are attached to a wooden handle. It's used in making pastry dough to cut cold fat (usually butter) into a flour mixture, evenly distributing the tiny pieces of fat without warming them.

pastry brush A small brush used for applying glazes to breads, pastries, cookies, etc. either before or after baking. The best all-purpose size has a width of 1 to 1½ inches. Pastry brushes can be made of nylon bristles, sterilized natural bristles or goose feathers. Natural-bristle brushes are considered best because they're softer and hold more liquid. Goose feathers are excellent for egg glazes because they leave a thin, even coating. The harder nylon bristles will last longer but may melt if accidentally touched to a hot surface. Softer bristles are especially desirable for delicate unbaked pastries where harder bristles might leave unwanted marks.

pastry cloth A large canvas cloth on which pastry dough can be rolled out. Rubbing flour down into the fibers makes the pastry cloth an excellent nonstick surface. After use, the cloth must be thoroughly cleaned before storing. Otherwise, any fat residue in the cloth will turn rancid and affect the flavor of future doughs.

pastry cream *see* CREME PATISSIERE

pastry flour *see* FLOUR

pastry jagger *see* PASTRY WHEE

pastry wheel A small utensil consisting of a sharp cutting wheel attached to a handle. Small pastry wheels with plain cutting edges are used to mark and cut rolled-out pastry or cookie dough. Larger, plain-edged wheels are used to cut pizza. **Jagging wheels** or **pastry jaggers** have fluted cutting edges that make a decorative design in pastry doughs.

pasty [PAS-tee] *see* CORNISH PASTRY

pâte [PAHT] This *pâte* (without an accent over the "e") is the French word for "dough," "paste," "batter" or "pastry." PÂTE BRISÉE is pie dough or short pastry; PÂTE SUCRÉE is sweet pastry. PASTA is translated as *pâte alimentaire*, ALMOND PASTE as *pâte d'amandes* and TOMATO PASTE as *pâte de tomates*.

pâté [pah-TAY; pa-TAY] French for "pie," this word—with accent over the "e"—is generally used to refer to various elegant, well-seasoned ground-meat preparations. A pâté can be satiny-smooth and spreadable or, like country pâté, coarsely textured. It can be made from a finely ground or chunky mixture of meats (such as pork, veal, liver or ham), fish, poultry, game, vegetables, etc. Seasonings and usually fat are also included in the mixture, which can be combined before or after cooking. Pâtés may be cooked in a crust, in which case they're referred to as pâté en croûte. They may also be cooked in a pork fat- lined container called a TERRINE (or any other similarly sized mold). Traditional parlance says that when such a mixture is cooked and served in a terrine, the dish is also called a terrine, and when unmolded it becomes a pâté. Today, however, the two terms are often used interchangeably. Pâtés may be hot or cold and are usually served as a first course or appetizer.

pâte à choux [paht uh SHOO] *see* CHOUX PASTRY

pâté brisée [paht bree-ZAY] A French term for "short pastry," a rich flaky dough used for sweet and savory crusts for dishes such as pies, tarts, QUICHES and BARQUETTES.

pâté de fois gras *see* FOIE GRAS

pâté feuilletée [paht fuh-yuh-TAY] The French term for "PUFF PASTRY." *See also* FEUILLETAGE.

pâte sucrée [paht soo-CRAY] A French term for a rich, sweetened short pastry used for desserts such as pies, tarts and filled cookies.

pâtisserie [puh-TIHS-uh-ree; pah-tees-REE] This French word has three different meanings: 1. The general category of sweet baked goods including cakes, cookies, cream puffs, etc. 2. The art of pastrymaking. 3. A shop where pastries are made and sold.

pâtissier [pah-tees-SYAY] The French word for "pastry cook" or "pastry chef."

patty 1. A small, thin round of ground or finely chopped food such as meat (as with a hamburger patty), fish or vegetables. 2. A round, flat piece of candy, one of the most popular being the **peppermint patty**.

pattypan squash A round, flattish SUMMER SQUASH with a scalloped edge. Tender young pattypans can be identified by their pale-green skin (which turns white as the squash matures) and small size (3 to 4 inches in diameter). The thin skin, which can be smooth to slightly bumpy, is usually not removed. Pattypan squash can be cooked in the same manner as other summer squash. *See also* SQUASH.

patty shell Usually made of PUFF PASTRY, this small cup-shaped shell is used to hold creamed dishes of meat, poultry, fish or vegetables. Fresh patty shells are available in bakeries, while frozen unbaked shells can usually be found in supermarkets.

paua [pah-OO-ah] *see* ABALONE

paupiette [poh-PYEHT] A thin slice of meat—usually veal or beef—rolled around a filling of finely ground meat or vegetables. The paupiette can be fried, baked or braised in wine or stock. It's sometimes wrapped in bacon before being cooked. Paupiettes are also called ROULADES.

pavé [pah-VAY] French for a square or rectangular "paving stone" or "cobblestone." In culinary usage the word refers to: 1. A square or rectangular dessert consisting of several layers of sponge cake filled with BUTTERCREAM or other filling and coated with FROSTING. 2. A square-shaped, aspic-coated mousse made of meat, fish or poultry, usually served cold. It can also be made with a sweet mousse.

Pavlova [pav-LOH-vuh] Hailing from Australia, this famous dessert is named after the Russian ballerina Anna Pavlova. It consists of a crisp MERINGUE base topped with whipped cream and fruit such as strawberries, PASSION FRUIT and KIWI. A pavlova is usually served with fruit sauce or additional whipped cream.

pawpaw [PAW-paw] Another name for both PAPAYA and PAPAW.

pea There are many varieties of pea, all members of the LEGUME family. Some—like the ENGLISH PEA (the common garden pea)—are grown to be eaten fresh, removed from their pods. Others—like the FIELD PEA—are grown specifically to be used dried. Still other varieties are eaten pod and all, namely the SNOW PEA and SUGAR SNAP PEA. *See also* BLACK-EYED PEA; CHICKPEA.

pea bean The smallest of the dried white beans, the others being NAVY, GREAT NORTHERN and MARROW BEANS (in order of ascending size). Pea beans are very popular in the Northeast and are the first choice for BOSTON BAKED BEANS. Some producers and packagers do not differentiate between pea beans and navy beans, so packages identified as white beans may contain both. Pea beans are also used in soups. They require long, slow cooking. *See also* BEANS.

peach Native to China, this fruit came to Europe (and subsequently to the New World) via Persia, hence its ancient appellation *Persian apple*. Throughout its evolution, the peach has propagated hundreds of varieties that vary greatly in color and flavor. In general, a peach falls into one of two classifications—**freestone**, in which case the stone or pit falls easily away from the flesh, and **clingstone**, where the fruit adheres stubbornly to the pit. It's the freestones that are more commonly found in markets, while the firmer-textured clingstones are widely used for commercial purposes. The peach's velvety skin can range from pink-blushed creamy-white to red-blushed yellow and its flesh from pinkish-white to yellow-gold. Peaches are available from May to October in most regions of the U.S.

Southern hemisphere imports are frequently found in coastal cities during the winter. Look for intensely fragrant fruit that gives slightly to palm pressure. Because peaches bruise easily they should be thoroughly perused for soft spots. Avoid those with signs of greening. Refrigerate ripe peaches in a plastic bag for up to 5 days. Bring to room temperature before eating. Because of their fuzzy skins, peaches are often peeled before eating. This can be done easily by BLANCHING the peach in boiling water for about 30 seconds, then plunging it into icy-cold water. Canned peaches are available, sliced or in halves, packed either in sugar syrup or water. Frozen peach slices are also available, as are dried peach halves. Peaches contain both vitamins A and C.

peach Melba A dessert created in the late 1800s by the famous French chef Escoffier for Dame Nellie Melba, a popular Australian opera singer. It's made with two peach halves that have been poached in syrup and cooled. Each peach half is placed hollow side down on top of a scoop of vanilla ice cream, then topped with MELBA SAUCE (a raspberry sauce) and sometimes with whipped cream and sliced almonds.

peanut Though today peanuts are considered a rather common nut, ancient Peruvians held them in such high esteem that they buried pots of peanuts with their mummified dead to nourish them during their long journey to the hereafter. Peanuts are widely grown throughout the southern U.S. and about half the national crop is used to make PEANUT BUTTER. At one stage of its growth, the peanut plant looks very much like the common garden pea plant . . . which is not at all illogical, since the peanut is actually a LEGUME, not a NUT. The nuts (or seeds) have a papery brown skin and are contained in a thin, netted, tan-colored pod. Peanuts are also called *groundnuts* (as well as *earth nuts* and, in the South, GOOBERS or *goober peas*) because, after flowering, the plant bends down to the earth and buries its pods in the ground. Though there are several varieties of peanut, the two most popular are the Virginia and the Spanish peanut. The **Virginia peanut** is larger and more oval in shape than the smaller, rounder **Spanish peanut.** Peanuts are sold unshelled and shelled. The former should have clean, unbroken shells and should not rattle when shaken. Shelled peanuts, often available in vacuum-sealed jars or cans, are usually roasted and sometimes salted. Refrigerate unshelled peanuts tightly wrapped for up to 6 months. Vacuum-packed shelled peanuts can be stored unopened at room temperature for up to a year. Once opened, shelled peanuts should be refrigerated airtight and used within 3 months. Peanuts are high in fat and rich in protein. The two most popular peanut byproducts are Peanut butter and PEANUT OIL.

peanut butter Developed in 1890 and promoted as a health food at the 1904 St. Louis World's fair, peanut butter is a blend of ground shelled peanuts, vegetable oil (often HYDROGENATED) and usually a small amount of salt. Some contain sugar and additives to improve creaminess and prevent the oil from separating. **Natural peanut butter** uses only peanuts and oil, usually PEANUT OIL. Peanut butter is sold in two forms—smooth or chunky, which contains bits of peanut. It can be easily made at home in a blender or food processor. Natural peanut butter must be refrigerated after opening and can be stored in this manner up to 6 months. Most other commercial peanut butters can be stored at room temperature for up to 6 months. Peanut butter is high in fat and contains fair amounts of iron, niacin and protein. *See also* PEANUT.

peanut oil A clear oil pressed from peanuts; it is used for salads and, because it has a high SMOKE POINT, especially prized for frying. Most American peanut oils are mild-flavored, whereas Chinese peanut oils have a distinctive peanut flavor. Peanut oil is about 50 percent monounsaturated and 30 percent polyunsaturated. If stored in a cool, dark place it will keep indefinitely. *See also* FATS AND OILS.

pear There are over 5,000 varieties of pears grown throughout the world in temperate climates. France is known for its superior pears and in the U.S. most of the crop comes from California, Oregon and Washington. Mother nature protected the easily bruised pear by making it better when picked while still hard. Unlike most fruit, it improves in both texture and flavor after it's picked. Pears range in shape from spherical to bell-shaped and in color from celadon green to golden yellow to tawny red. Ripe pears are juicy and, depending on the variety, can range in flavor from spicy to sweet to tart-sweet. Pears are in season from late July to early spring, depending on the variety. Choose those that are fragrant and free of blemishes and soft spots. Store at room temperature until ripe; refrigerate ripe fruit. It's not necessary to peel pears before using, but if they are peeled, they should be dipped in ACIDULATED WATER to prevent the flesh from browning. For cooking, choose fruit that is still quite firm. Pears are also available dried as well as canned in either water, SUGAR SYRUP or their natural juice They contain small amounts of phosphorus and vitamins A. *For information on specific pear varieties, see individual listings.*

pearl barley *see* BARLEY

pearl onion *see* ONION

pecan [pih-KAHN; pih-KAN; PEE-kan] This native American nut is a member of the hickory family. It has a fat content of over 70 percent . . .

more than any other nut. Pecan trees prefer temperate climates and are widely grown in Georgia, Oklahoma and Texas, and as far north as Virginia. The nut's smooth, tan shell averages about 1 inch in length and, though hard, is relatively thin. The buttery-rich kernel is golden-brown on the outside and beige inside. Chopped or halved shelled pecans are available year-round in cellophane packages, cans and jars. Though unshelled pecans are also available throughout the year, their peak season is during the autumn months. Choose unshelled pecans by their clean, unblemished, uncracked shells. When shaken, the kernel should not rattle. Store tightly wrapped in a cool, dry place for up to 6 months. Refrigerate shelled pecans in an airtight container for up to 3 months, or freeze up to 6 months. Care must be taken when storing pecans because their high fat content invites rancidity. Pecans are favorites for eating out of hand, as well as for using in a variety of sweet and savory dishes. Probably the most well-known pecan dessert is the deliciously rich Southern pecan pie, usually dolloped generously with whipped cream. *See also* NUTS.

pecorino cheese [peh-kuh-REE-noh] In Italy, cheese made from sheep's milk is known as *pecorino*. Most of these cheeses are aged and classified as GRANA (hard, granular and sharply flavored); however, the young, unaged **Ricotta pecorino** is soft, white and mild in flavor. Aged pecorinos range in color from white to pale yellow and have a sharp, pungent flavor. The best known of this genre is **Pecorino Romano**, which comes in large cylinders with a hard yellow rind and yellowish-white interior. Other notable pecorinos are **Sardo, Siciliano** and **Toscano**. These hard, dry cheeses are good for grating and are used mainly in cooking. They can be used in any recipe that calls for PARMESAN CHEESE, especially if a sharper flavor is desired. *See also* CHEESE.

pectin [PEHK-tihn] Present in various ripe fruits and vegetables, this natural, water-soluble substance is used for its thickening properties in the preparation of jams, jellies and preserves. The gelatinlike pectin is added to fruits that don't have enough natural pectin to JELL by themselves. If pectin isn't used, the alternative is to continue cooking the mixture until it's reduced to the desired consistency. Pectin only works properly when mixed with the correct balance of sugar and acid. It's available in two forms—liquid (usually made from apples) and dry (from citrus fruits or apples).

peel *n.* 1. The rind or skin of a fruit or vegetable, such as a tomato or potato peel. 2. A flat, smooth, shovellike tool used to slide pizzas and yeast breads onto a BAKING STONE or BAKING SHEET in an oven. Also called a *baker's peel*, this implement is made of hardwood and can usually be found in gourmet specialty shops. **peel** *v.* To use a knife or VEGETABLE PEELER to remove the rind or skin from a fruit or vegetable, e.g. to peel a potato.

Peking duck [PEE-king; PAY-king] An elaborately prepared Chinese dish that starts with air being pumped between a duck's skin and flesh. The duck is then coated with a honey mixture and hung until the skin is dry and hard. After the duck is roasted the skin becomes golden and intensely crisp. While hot, it's cut into small squares and served with thin pancakes (called Peking doilies) or steamed buns, accompanied by scallions and HOISIN SAUCE. The meat is considered a secondary attraction and is usually served after the skin. This specialty is also sometimes called *Beijing* [BAY-jeeng] *duck*.

Peking sauce *see* HOISIN SAUCE

pekoe tea [PEE-koh] Because similar-sized tea leaves brew at the same speed (larger, coarser leaves take longer), tea leaves are graded and sorted by size. **Orange pekoe** is the grade for the smallest leaves, which are picked from the top of the plant. "Pekoe" describes medium-size, slightly coarser tea leaves.

penne [PEN-nay] Large, straight tubes of MACARONI cut on the diagonal. *See also* PASTA.

penuche; panocha; penuchi [puh-NOO-chee] A creamy, fudgelike candy made with brown sugar, butter, milk or cream and vanilla. Chopped nuts are sometimes added. The mixture is heated to the SOFT-BALL STAGE, whipped until thick and either dropped onto a cookie sheet or poured into a pan and allowed to set. The name is derived from the Mexican word for "raw sugar" or "brown sugar."

peperonata [pehp-uh-roh-NAH-tah] An Italian mixture of sweet peppers, tomatoes, onions and garlic cooked in olive oil. It's served hot as a CONDIMENT with meats or cold as an ANITPASTO.

pepino [puh-PEE-noh] Also called *pepino melon*, this fragrant fruit has its origins in Peru, though it's now grown in New Zealand, California and other subtropical and temperate climates. The exotic-looking pepino has a smooth, glossy, golden skin streaked with violet. It can range in size anywhere from that of a plum to that of a large papaya. The perfumy yellow-gold flesh is juicy and lightly sweet. Pepinos are available from late fall to mid-spring in specialty produce markets and some supermarkets that carry exotic produce. Choose those that are fragrant and give slightly to palm pressure. They can be ripened at room temperature, if necessary.

Judge the ripeness by the deep-golden background color. Pepinos should be peeled before using for out-of-hand eating, in fruit salads or as an accompaniment or garnish to meats or vegetables.

pepitas [puh-PEE-tahs] These edible *pumpkin seeds* are a popular ingredient in Mexican cooking. With their white hull removed, they are a medium-dark green and have a deliciously delicate flavor, which is even better when the seeds are roasted and salted. Pepitas are sold salted, roasted and raw, and with or without hulls. They're available in health-food stores, Mexican markets and many supermarkets.

pepper, black and white *see* PEPPERCORN

pepper, chili *see* CHILI PEPPER

pepper, hot *see* CHILI PEPPER

pepper, sweet green or red *see* SWEET PEPPER

peppercorn Most cooks today don't appreciate the plentiful and inexpensive supply of a spice that was once so valuable and rare it was sometimes used as currency. Its merit was so high that many of the European sailing expeditions during the 15th century were undertaken with the main purpose of finding alternate trade routes to the Far East, the primary source of the prized peppercorn and other spices. Pepper in one form or other is used around the world to enhance the flavor of both savory and sweet dishes. Because it stimulates gastric juices, it delivers a digestive bonus as well. The world's most popular spice is a berry that grows in grapelike clusters on the pepper plant (*Piper nigrum*), a climbing vine native to India and Indonesia. The berry is processed to produce three basic types of peppercorn—black, white and green. The most common is the **black peppercorn,** which is picked when the berry is not quite ripe, then dried until it shrivels and the skin turns dark brown to black. It's the strongest flavored of the three—slightly hot with a hint of sweetness. Among the best black peppers are the **Tellicherry** and the **Lampong**. The less pungent **white peppercorn** has been allowed to ripen, after which the skin is removed and the berry is dried. The result is a smaller, smoother-skinned, light-tan berry with a milder flavor. White pepper is used to a great extent for appearance, usually in light-colored sauces or foods where dark specks of black pepper would stand out. The **green peppercorn** is the soft, underripe berry that's usually preserved in brine. It has a fresh flavor that's less pungent than the berry in its other forms. Black and white peppercorns are available whole, cracked, coarsely or finely ground. Whole peppercorns freshly ground with a pepper mill deliver more flavor than does pre-ground pepper, which loses its flavor fairly quickly. Whole dried peppercorns can be stored in a cool, dark place for about a year. Green peppercorns packed in brine are available in jars and cans. They should be refrigerated once opened and can be kept for several weeks. Water-packed green peppercorns must also be refrigerated but will only keep for about a week. Freeze-dried green peppercorns are also available and can be stored in a cool, dark place for up to 6 months. *See also* PINK PEPPERCORN; SZECHWAN PEPPER.

pepper mill   A hand-held grinder designed for crushing dry peppercorns. Pepper mills are made from a variety of materials including plastic, wood and ceramic. The internal grinding mechanism is generally made of stainless steel. Good pepper mills can be adjusted to produce fine or coarse grinds. Freshly ground pepper has a sharper, more lively flavor than the pre-ground variety.

peppermint   *see* MINT

peppermint schnapps   *see* SCHNAPPS

pepperoni; peperoni   [pehp-puh-ROH-nee] An Italian SALAMI made of pork and beef highly seasoned with black and red pepper. This slender, firm, air-dried sausage is ready to eat, often sliced very thin and used as an appetizer. It can also be used to add flavor to many cooked dishes, as those who love pepperoni pizza will attest. *See also* SAUSAGE.

pepper pot; pepperpot   1. A thick soup of TRIPE, meat, vegetables, pepper and other seasonings. It's also called *Philadelphia pepper pot*. The soup is said to have been created during the desperate winter of 1777–1778, when Washington's army was down to tripe, peppercorns and various scraps of other food. The cook devised this tasty dish and named it in honor of his hometown, Philadelphia. 2. A West Indian stew containing CASSAREEP, meat or seafood, vegetables, chili peppers, cayenne pepper and other seasonings.

pepper steak   1. A beefsteak generously sprinkled with coarsely ground black pepper, sautéed in butter and served with a sauce made from pan drippings, stock, wine and cream. Pepper steak is sometimes flamed with BRANDY or COGNAC. In French it's called *steak au poivre*. 2. A Chinese STIR-FRY dish consisting of strips of steak, green pepper and onion cooked with soy sauce and other seasonings.

perch   Any of various spiny-finned freshwater fish found in North America and Europe. In the United States the best known is the **yellow perch,** found mainly in the East and Midwest. In France, the **common** or **river perch** is highly favored. These similar-looking fish have olive-green backs blending to yellow on the sides, dark vertical bands and reddish-orange fins. They have a mild, delicate flavor and firm flesh with a low fat content. Related to the true perch are the **pike perch** (so called because their bodies resemble the PIKE), the best known of which are the **walleyed pike** and the **sauger** or **sand pike**. There are several saltwater fish that are incorrectly called perch including the **white perch** (really a member of the BASS family) and the **ocean perch** (a member of the ROCKFISH family). Perch range in size from ½ to 3 pounds. They're available fresh and frozen, whole and filleted. Small perch are usually best broiled or sautéed larger ones can be prepared in a variety of ways including poaching, steaming, baking and in soups and stews. *See also* FISH.

périgourdine, à la [pay-ree-goor-DEEN] French for "as prepared in the style of Périgord," referring to dishes garnished or flavored with TRUFFLES. The term is named for France's Périgord region, which is famous for its black truffles.

Périgueux sauce [pay-ree-GOUH] A rich brown sauce flavored with MADEIRA and TRUFFLES. The sauce, which goes with a variety of dishes including meat, game, poultry and eggs, is named after Périgueux, a city in the Périgord region of Southwest France that is noted for its truffles. Dishes using the sauce are often labeled *à la périgourdine* or simply *Périgueux*.

periwinkle [PEHR-ih-wing-kuhl] There are over 300 species of this conical, spiral-shelled UNIVALVE MOLLUSK (*see both listings*), but few are edible. Periwinkles, also called *sea snails* or *winkles*, are found attached to rocks, wharves, pilings, etc. in both fresh and sea water. The most common edible periwinkle is found along the Atlantic coasts of Europe and North America. It grows to about 1 inch in size and is gray to dark olive with reddish-brown bands. Periwinkles are popular in Europe but rarely found in the U.S. They're usually boiled in their shells, then extracted with a small pick.

Pernod [pair-NOH] A yellowish, licorice-flavored LIQUEUR similar to ABSINTHE. Pernod is very popular in France and is usually mixed with water, which turns it whitish and cloudy.

Persian apple *see* PEACH

Persian melon A large green MUSKMELON with a delicate netting on the rind and a rich salmon-colored flesh. Persian melons weigh around 5 pounds (larger than a CANTALOUPE) and have a delicious, sweet flavor. They're available from July through October, with a peak in the late summer. Choose and use a Persian melon in the same manner as cantaloupe. *See also* MELON.

Persian walnut *see* ENGLISH WALNUT

persillade [pair-see-YAHD] *Persil* is the French word for "parsley" and persillade is a mixture of chopped parsley and garlic. It's usually added as a flavoring or garnish to dishes just before cooking is complete. A dish finished in this fashion is often described as a *persillé*. For example, lamb *persillé* is a lamb dish topped with persillade mixed with breadcrumbs.

persimmon [puhr-SIHM-uhn] The most widely available persimmon in the U.S. is the **Hachiya,** also called *Japanese persimmon*. It's large (up to 3 inches in diameter) and round, with a slightly elongated, pointed base. The **Fuyu** persimmon is smaller and more tomato-shaped. When ripe, both have a red-orange skin and flesh. The Hachiya is quite soft when completely ripe and has a smooth, creamy texture and a tangy-sweet flavor. If eaten even slightly underripe, it will pucker the mouth with an incredible astringency. The Fuyu, however, is still firm when ripe and is not at all astringent. Persimmons are available from October to February. Choose fruit that is plump and soft but not mushy (the Fuyu should be quite firm). The skin should be smooth, glossy and brightly colored. Persimmons that are not quite ripe can be ripened at room temperature. Store ripe fruit in the refrigerator for up to 3 days. Persimmons can be used in baked goods, puddings and other desserts, as well as eaten out of hand. They contain a good amount of vitamin A and some vitamin C.

pestle [PEHS-tl; PEHS-uhl] *see* MORTAR AND PESTLE

pesto [PEH-stoh] An uncooked sauce made with fresh basil, garlic, PINE NUTS, PARMESAN or PECORINO CHEESE and olive oil. The ingredients can either be crushed with mortar and pestle or finely chopped with a food processor. This wonderful, fresh-tasting sauce originated in Genoa, Italy, and although used on a variety of dishes, it is a favorite with pasta.

petit déjeuner [puh-TEE day-zhoo-NAY] French for "breakfast."

petit four [PEH-tee fohr; puh-tee FOOR] 1. Any of various bite-size iced and elaborately decorated cakes. *Petits fours* can be made with any flavor cake, though white and chocolate are the most common. 2. The French also use this term to describe small, fancy cookies.

petit-gris [peh-tee-GREE] *see* SNAIL

petits pois [peh-tee PWAH] The French term for "small young green peas." *See also* ENGLISH PEA.

Petit Suisse [peh-tee SWEES] A rich, soft French cheese which, because it contains between 60 and 75 percent butterfat, ranks between a DOUBLE- and TRIPLE-CREAM CHEESE. It's the consistency of very soft CREAM CHEESE and has a delicate, sweetly tangy flavor. Petit Suisse is usually sold in small cylinders or flat squares. It's wonderful served as an appetizer with crackers or after dinner with fruit. The most popular brand of Petit Suisse is GERVAIS, named after the well-known French cheesemaker Jules Gervais. *See also* CHEESE.

Petite Syrah [peh-TEET sih-RAH] Grown mainly in California, this red wine grape produces a big, robust and peppery wine. Although not as popular as California's CABERNET SAUVIGNON, PINOT NOIR or ZINFANDEL, Petite Syrah has a following among those who like big, full-bodied wines. The Petite Syrah grape is also used as a blending grape to give a little more zest and complexity to other red wines. This varietal is also spelled *Petit Syrah, Petite Sirah* and *Petit Sirah*.

petrale sole [peh-TRAH-lee SOHL] Not a true SOLE, but rather a FLOUNDER that is found in the Pacific Ocean from Alaska to Mexico. It's highly prized for its excellent flavor and fine-textured, lowfat flesh. Those found in the market generally weigh from 1 to 5 pounds. They can be purchased fresh and frozen, whole or in fillets. Petrale sole can be prepared in almost any manner including sautéing, broiling, grilling and poaching. *See also* FISH; FLATFISH.

pfeffernuesse [FEHF-uhr-noos] Traditionally served at Christmastime, *pfeffernuesse* (German for "peppernuts") are very popular in many European countries. Scandinavians call the cookies *pepperkaker* in Norway, *pepparnotter* in Sweden and *pebernodder* in Denmark. These tiny ball-shaped cookies are full of spices such as cinnamon, cardamom, ginger and the ingredient for which they're named—black pepper.

pheasant [FEH-suhnt] A medium-sized GAME BIRD, originally from Asia but now found in Europe and North America. As with many birds, the male has a more brilliant plumage than the female and is larger, weighing 2½ to 5 pounds compared to the female's 3-pound average. The female's flesh is plumper, juicier and more tender. Very young cocks and hens may be roasted as is but older pheasants should be BARDED or cooked with moist heat because their flesh is lean and dry. Farm-raised pheasants do not have the same flavor as the wild birds. Pheasants are sometimes found dressed and frozen in specialty meat markets, usually by special order.

Philadelphia cheese steak *see* CHEESE STEAK

Philadelphia pepper pot *see* PEPPER POT

phyllo [FEE-loh] Literally translated, the Greek word *phyllo* means "leaf." Culinarily, it refers to tissue-thin layers of pastry dough used in various Greek and Near Eastern sweet and savory preparations, the best known being BAKLAVA and SPANAKOPITA. Packaged fresh and frozen phyllo dough is readily available—the former in Greek markets, the latter in supermarkets. Phyllo (also spelled *filo*) is very similar to STRUDEL dough.

picadillo [pee-kah-DEE-yoh] This dish, a favorite in many Spanish-speaking countries, consists of ground pork and beef or veal plus tomatoes, garlic, onions and whatever else the regional version dictates. In Cuba it's served with rice and black beans. In Mexico, picadillo is used as a stuffing for various dishes.

piccalilli [PIHK-uh-lih-lee] A highly seasoned pickled vegetable relish. The vegetables used vary from recipe to recipe and can include tomatoes, sweet peppers, onions, zucchini, cucumber, cauliflower, beans, etc.

piccata [pih-CAH-tuh] *see* VEAL PICCATA

pickerel [PIHK-uh-ruhl] *see* PIKE

pickle *n.* Food that has been preserved in a seasoned brine or vinegar mixture. Among the more popular foods used for pickling are cucumbers, pearl onions, cauliflower, baby corn, watermelon rind, pig's feet and herring. Pickles can be sour, sweet, hot or variously flavored, such as with DILL for the popular dill pickle. **pickle** *v.* To preserve food in a vinegar mixture or brine.

pickled cucumber *see* TEA MELON

pickled herring *see* HERRING

pickling spices A spice blend used in mixtures to PICKLE various foods, as well as to season certain dishes. The blend can differ greatly according to the manufacturer, and the ingredients (usually whole or in coarse pieces) can include allspice, bay leaves, cardamom, coriander, cinnamon, cloves, ginger, mustard seeds and peppercorns. Prepackaged pickling spice mixes are sold in most supermarkets.

picnic ham Not really a true ham (which comes from the pig's back leg), the picnic ham is taken from the upper part of the foreleg and includes a portion of the shoulder. This cut is also more accurately referred to as the *picnic shoulder* or *pork shoulder*. The picnic ham is smoked, which gives it a very hamlike flavor. It often has the bone removed. Though it's slightly tougher (requiring longer cooking) and has more waste because of the bone structure, picnic ham is a good, inexpensive substitute for regular ham. *See also* HAM.

picnic shoulder *see* PICNIC HAM

pie A sweet or savory dish made with a crust and filling (such as fruit, pudding, meat or vegetable). Pies can have bottom crusts only, or top and bottom crusts or, as with DEEP-DISH pies, only a top crust. Sweet pies are generally served as dessert and savory pies as the main course or appetizer. Crusts can be made of a variety of mixtures including SHORT CRUST pastry, PUFF PASTRY, cookie crumbs, MERINGUE and even, as with SHEPHERD'S PIE, mashed potatoes. *See also* TART.

pierogi [peer-OH-gee] A Polish specialty, pierogi are half-moon-shaped noodle dumplings filled with a minced mixture, the most common being pork, onions, cottage cheese and seasonings. Mushrooms, cabbage, potatoes and rice are also used as filling ingredients. After the pierogi are cooked in boiling water, they're sometimes sautéed briefly in butter and topped with toasted breadcrumbs. They can be served as a first course or side dish.

pie weights Small pelletlike metal or ceramic weights used when baking an unfilled pie or tart crust. Pie weights can be found in gourmet specialty shops. *See also* BAKE BLIND.

pigeon pea Native to Africa, this tiny LEGUME is also called *Congo pea* and *no-eyed pea*. In the U.S., it's particularly popular in southern states where it grows in long, twisted fuzzy pods. The peas are about the size of the standard garden pea and are usually a grayish-yellow color. Pigeon peas can be eaten raw but are most often dried and split. They're available dried in many supermarkets and can often be found fresh, frozen and canned in the regions where they're grown, as well as Latin American and Indian markets. Pigeon peas are cooked like dried beans. *See also* BEANS.

pignoli; pignolia [peen-YOH-lee (uh)] *see* PINE NUT

pig's feet Called *trotters* by the British, these are the feet and ankles of pigs. Because they're bony and sinewy, pig's feet require long, slow cooking. They're quite flavorful and full of natural gelatin. Pig's feet are available pickled, fresh and smoked—the latter two are particularly good in soups, stews and sauces. *See also* PORK.

pigs in blankets A term that is generally used to describe a sausage with an outside covering (blanket). The most common example is a small cocktail sausage wrapped in pie dough and baked, then served as an appetizer. Pigs in blankets can also refer to breakfast sausages wrapped in pancakes or any other similar style of food.

pike [PYK] A family of freshwater fish that includes the pike, pickerel and muskellunge. They all have long bodies, large mouths and ferocious-looking teeth. **Pickerel** are the smallest—generally weighing 2 to 3 pounds. **Pike** range from 4 to 10 pounds and the **muskellunge** (or *muskie*) averages from 10 to 30 pounds but can reach up to 60 pounds and 6 feet in length. The **walleye pike** is not a pike but rather a PERCH. The pike family of fish is known for its lean, firm, low-fat (but bony) flesh. Although fished mainly for sport in the United States, they are imported from Canada and available fresh and frozen, either whole, filleted or in steaks. Pike can be cooked in almost any manner available. It's the fish traditionally used in France's fish QUENELLES, as well as the Jewish GEFILTE FISH. *See also* FISH.

pilaf [PEE-lahf; PIH-lahf] This rice- or BULGHUR-based dish (also called *pilau*) originated in the Near East and always begins by first browning the rice in butter or oil before cooking it in stock. Pilafs can be variously seasoned and usually contain other ingredients such as chopped cooked vegetables, meats, seafood or poultry. In India they're highly spiced with CURRY. Pilaf can be served as a side dish or main dish.

pilau [pih-LOW] *see* PILAF

pilchard [PIHL-chuhrd] A small, high-fat saltwater fish found in abundance off the European Atlantic coast from Scandinavia to Portugal. Though Europeans can buy fresh pilchard from July to December, it's usually canned in oil or tomato sauce like SARDINES. *See also* FISH.

Pilsner; Pilsener [PIHLZ-nuhr] 1. Originally this term referred to a very fine beer brewed in Pilsen, Czechoslovakia. Today, however, it more commonly refers to any pale, light LAGER beer. 2. A "pilsner glass" is a footed, tall glass that tapers from the mouth to the base. It's generally used to serve beer.

pimiento; pimento [pih-MYEHN-toh] 1. A large, red, heart-shaped SWEET PEPPER. 2. *Pimento* is the name of the tree from which ALLSPICE comes.

piña colada [PEEN-yuh koh-LAH-duh] Literally translated, this Spanish phrase means "strained pineapple." A piña colada is a tropically flavored drink made with coconut cream, pineapple juice and rum served over ice and usually garnished with a pineapple chunk. The piña-colada (pineapple-coconut) flavor has also become a popular favorite for many foods such as ice cream, candy, cakes, etc.

pinch A measuring term referring to the amount of a dry ingredient (such as salt or pepper) that can be held between the tips of the thumb and forefinger. It's equivalent to approximately 1/16 teaspoon. *See also* DASH.

pineapple This tropical beauty received its appellation from the English because of its resemblance to the pine cone. Most other Europeans call it *ananas*, derived from the Paraguayan *nana* meaning "excellent (or exquisite) fruit." The pineapple is native to Central and South America, where symbolic representations of its form were found in pre-Incan ruins. Hawaii, now this fruit's leading producer, didn't see its first pineapple until the late 1700s. For centuries the pineapple (in the form of carved wood, stone sculptures and the like) has been used to symbolize hospitality. The two major varieties found commercially in the U.S. are the Cayenne (from Hawaii) and the Red Spanish (mainly from Florida and Puerto Rico). The **Cayenne,** the longer and more cylindrical of the two, has a golden-yellow skin and long, swordlike leaves sprouting from a single tuft. The **Red Spanish** is squatter in shape, has a reddish golden-brown skin and leaves that radiate from several tufts. Mexico grows a third variety called the **Sugar Loaf,** a large, exquisitely flavored specimen whose skin is still green when ripe. All varieties have bumpy diamond-patterned skins. Because it doesn't ship well, the Sugar Loaf is rarely imported into the U.S. Pineapples can weigh up to 20 pounds, though the average size marketed ranges between 2 and 5 pounds. Though there are slight flavor variations depending on the variety, all ripe pineapple is exceedingly juicy and has a tangy sweet-tart flavor. Fresh pineapple is available year-round with a peak season from March to July. This is one fruit that must be picked ripe because the starch will not convert to sugar once it's off the plant. Choose pineapples that are slightly soft to the touch with a full, strong color (depending on the variety) and no sign of greening. The leaves should be crisp and green with no yellow or brown tips. Overripe pineapples show their advanced state with soft or dark areas on the skin. Refrigerate fresh pineapple tightly wrapped for up to 3 days. If it's slightly underripe, keeping it at room temperature for several days will reduce its acidity (though it won't increase its sweetness). Pineapple is available canned (in its own juice or in sugar syrup), crushed or in chunks, slices or tidbits. It can also be found frozen and candied. Pineapple can be used in a variety of dishes including fresh fruit desserts and salads, and as a garnish for vegetables and meats. It's also delicious cooked—either simply sautéed or broiled, or in a dish like the famous pineapple UPSIDE-DOWN CAKE. Fresh and frozen pineapple cannot be used in gelatin mixtures because of a natural enzyme that prevents them from setting (canned pineapple doesn't cause a problem). Pineapples are a fair source of vitamins C and A.

pineapple guava *see* FEIJOA

pine nut Also called *Indian nut, piñon, pignoli* and *pignolia*, this high-fat nut comes from several varieties of pine trees. The nuts are actually inside the pine cone, which generally must be heated to facilitate their removal. This labor-intensive process is what makes these nuts so expensive. Pine nuts grow in China, Italy, Mexico, North Africa and the southwest United States. There are two main varieties. Both have a thin shell with an ivory-colored nutmeat that averages about ½ inch in length. The **Mediterranean** or **Italian pine nut** is from the stone pine. It's torpedo-shaped, has a light, delicate flavor and is the more expensive of the two. The stronger-flavored **Chinese pine nut** is shaped like a squat triangle. Its pungent pine flavor can easily overpower some foods. Pine nuts can be found in bulk in nut shops and health-food stores, and packaged in many supermarkets. The Chinese variety will more likely be available in oriental markets. Because of their high fat content, pine nuts turn rancid quickly. They should be stored airtight in the refrigerator for up to 3 months, frozen for up to 9 months. Pine nuts can be used in a variety of sweet and savory dishes and are well known for their flavorful addition to the classic Italian PESTO. *See also* NUTS.

pink bean A smooth, reddish-brown dried bean that is very popular in the western U.S. It's interchangeable with the PINTO BEAN in any dish. Pink beans are used to make REFRIED BEANS and CHILI CON CARNE. They're available in dried form year-round in most supermarkets. *See also* BEANS.

pink lady A COCKTAIL consisting of gin, lemon or lime juice, GRENADINE, egg white and cream. It's shaken with ice, then strained into a shallow, stemmed cocktail glass.

pink peppercorn Pink peppercorns are not true peppercorns but actually the dried berries from the *Baies* rose plant. They're cultivated in Madagascar and imported via France, hence their exorbitant price. These rose-hued berries are pungent and slightly sweet. Pink peppercorns can be found in gourmet stores either freeze-dried or packed in brine or water. Once opened, refrigerate water-packed berries for about a week, those packed in brine for 3 to 4 weeks. Freeze-dried pink peppercorns can be stored in a cool, dark place for about 6 months. Pink peppercorns are used as colorful, flavorful additions to a variety of sauces and meat and fish dishes. Though there was once widespread controversy regarding their safety, pink peppercorns have now been approved by the Food and Drug Administration. They should not, however, be confused with pink berries (also referred to as peppercorns) from an ornamental plant in Florida and California that can cause severe allergic reactions if eaten. *See also* PEPPERCORN.

pink salmon *see* SALMON

piñon nut [PIHN-yuhn] *see* PINE NUT

Pinot Blanc [PEE-noh BLAH*N*; PEE-noh BLAH*N*GK] A variety of white grape that is used in some white BURGUNDY WINES and bottled as a varietal by a few California wineries. Pinot Blanc wine is crisp and dry but has less intensity and flavor than its relative, CHARDONNAY. Its price is also considerably lower. Pinot Blanc goes well with chicken and seafood.

Pinot Chardonnay [PEE-noh shahr-duh-NAY] Another name used by some wineries for their CHARDONNAY wines.

Pinot Noir [PEE-noh NWAHR] The red grape that produces the spicy, rich, complex French red BURGUNDIES as well as Pinot Noirs from California, Oregon and Washington. It's also important in making French CHAMPAGNES and American sparkling wines. French Burgundy wines like Romanée-Conti and Chambertin are world renowned for being elegant, soft and smooth. They also command tremendous prices. The American Pinot Noirs are less expensive and some—particularly those from California—are rapidly gaining in excellence and popularity. Pinot Noirs go well with almost any food.

pinto bean The pinto (Spanish for "painted") bean has streaks of reddish-brown on a background of pale pink. The beans are grown in the U. S. Southwest and are common in most Spanish-speaking countries, where they're often served with rice or used in soups and stews. The pinto can be used interchangeably with the PINK BEAN, which is lighter in color prior to cooking but looks the same afterwards. Both the pinto and pink bean are commonly used in the preparation of REFRIED BEANS and CHILI CON CARNE. Pinto beans are available in dried form year round. They are also called *red Mexican beans. See also* BEANS.

pipérade [pee-pay-RAHD] This dish from the Basque region of France has many versions but is always based on tomatoes and sweet green peppers cooked in olive oil. Additions can include onions, garlic, ham, bacon or other vegetables and quite often lightly beaten egg. Depending on how hearty it is, pipérade can be served as a side dish or main dish.

pippin apple *see* NEWTON PIPPIN APPLE

piquante sauce [pee-KAHNT] A spicy brown sauce made with shallots, white wine, vinegar, GHERKINS, parsley and various herbs and seasonings. It's served with sliced meats such as pork, tongue and beef.

piroshki [pih-ROSH-kee] A small Russian TURNOVER consisting of a pastry wrapping and various fillings such as meat, seafood, cheese and mushrooms. Piroshki can be served as an HORS D'OEUVRE or as an accompaniment to soups or salads.

pisco [PIHS-koh; PEE-skoh] A potent (90 PROOF) Peruvian grape BRANDY that's aged in paraffin-lined containers rather than oak to prevent it from absorbing either color of flavor from the wood.

pismo clam [PIHS-moh] This Pacific hard-shell clam is considered one of the choicest of its genre. Unfortunately, it's also becoming one of the scarcest. Pismos are tender, sweet and large—usually with a minimum shell diameter of 5 inches. The adductor muscle (which hinges the two shells) is so tender that it can be served ON THE HALF SHELL. The body meat can be steamed, fried or used in chowder. *See also* CLAM.

pissaladière [pee-sah-lah-DYAIR] A flaky pizzalike tart topped with onions, anchovies, black olives and sometimes tomatoes. Pissaladière is a specialty of Nice, in southern France.

pistachio nut [pih-STASH-ee-oh; pih-STAH-shee-oh] Cultivated in California, Italy, Turkey and Iran, the pistachio has a hard, tan shell that encloses a pale- green nut. The shells of some pistachios are colored red (with vegetable dye), while others have been blanched until white. The California Pistachio Commission states that these nuts are dyed for two reasons: because many people find that form familiar; and so they're easier to spot in a bowl of mixed nuts. Pistachios are available year-round shelled and unshelled, either raw or roasted and salted or not. When buying unshelled pistachios make sure the shells are partially open—not only because it's a great help in getting the nutmeat out, but because closed shells mean the nutmeat is immature. Pistachio nuts have a delicate, subtle flavor that is wonderful either for eating out of hand or for flavoring both sweet and savory dishes. Pistachio nuts are rich in calcium, thiamin, phosphorus, iron, and Vitamin A. *See also* NUTS.

pisto [PEES-toh] A Spanish vegetable dish originally from La Mancha, south of Madrid. Pisto can include chopped tomatoes, sweet red or green peppers, onions, garlic, mushrooms, eggplant and sundry other vegetables all cooked together. Sometimes ham or other meat is added. This Spanish favorite can be eaten hot or cold, served as a main course, side dish or appetizer.

pistou [pees-TOO] 1. A mixture of crushed basil, garlic and olive oil used as a CONDIMENT or sauce. It's the French version of Italy's PESTO. 2. A French vegetable soup that usually includes green beans, white beans, onions, potatoes, tomatoes and VERMICELLI; it is seasoned with the basil-garlic condiment in definition 1. The soup is similiar to an Italian MINESTRONE.

pit *n.* The stone or seed of a fruit such as a cherry, peach, apricot or plum.
pit *v.* To remove the stone or seed of a fruit. This is most often done by using a sharp knife to cut it loose or a specialized utensil (known as a PITTER) to push it out.

pita [PEE-tah] Also called *pocket bread*, this Middle Eastern FLAT BREAD can be made of white or whole-wheat flour. Each pita round splits horizontally to form a pocket into which a wide variety of ingredients can be stuffed to make a sandwich. Throughout the Middle East, pitas are served with meals or cut into wedges and used as dippers for dishes such as BABA GHANOUSH and HUMMUS. Pita bread is available in Middle Eastern markets and in most supermarkets.

pitter, olive or cherry A fairly simple tool consisting of two attached hinged handles, one with a ring at the end, the other with a blunt prong. The olive or cherry is placed in the ring and the handles are squeezed together, forcing the prong through the fruit and pushing the pit out through the hole in the ring. Pitters (also called *stoners*) come in various designs and sizes. They can be found in gourmet shops and in the kitchenware section of many department stores.

pizza [PEET-suh] Made popular in the U.S. by soldiers who brought the idea back from Italy at the end of World War II, pizza is thought to have evolved from early Egyptian flat bread. Literally translated, the word means "pie," but it has come to represent a round savory tart made with a crisp yeast dough covered with tomato sauce, MOZZARELLA CHEESE and other ingredients such as peppers, onions, Italian sausage, mushrooms, anchovies and PEPPERONI. Varations such as deep-dish pizza, with its thick breadlike crust, have been popular over the years. More recently, some menus now feature pizzas sans tomato sauce and mozzarella cheese. They're topped instead with ingredients such as sun-dried tomatoes, duck sausage, fresh basil, smoked salmon, goat cheese or wild mushrooms.

pizza pan A round metal sheet with a shallow, rounded raised rim, used for baking pizza. Some pans are perforated with hundreds of small holes that allow moisture to escape, which helps the dough brown evenly. Pizza pans can be found in gourmet shops and in the kitchenware section of many department stores.

plaice [PLAYC] The **American plaice,** also called *Canadian plaice* and *dab,* is a member of the FLOUNDER family, which is found on both sides of the Atlantic. The fish can be various shades of reddish- to gray-brown and has a lowfat, fine-textured flesh with a mild, sweet flavor. The American plaice can get as large as 12 pounds but is usually marketed in the 2- to 3-pound range. It's available fresh and frozen, either whole or filleted. The **European plaice,** a similar fish but with different coloring, is found in the North Sea and is widely popular in Europe. Both the American and European plaice are suitable for almost any cooking method. *See also* FISH; FLATFISH.

plank A cooking method handed down by American Indians whereby meat or fish is cooked—usually by baking or broiling—on a wooden board. This method of cookery imparts a soupçon of the wood's flavor to the food. Food referred to as "planked" has been cooked in this manner.

plantain [PLAN-tihn] *see* BANANA

plastic wrap The ability of this versatile food wrap to cling to both food and containers makes it superior for forming an airtight seal. There are many varieties of plastic wrap, some of which are thicker, cling better and have better moisture-vapor retention than others. Most plastic wraps are made of *polyethylene*, whose components are not absorbed by foods to any degree. The wrap that is considered to have the best cling and moisture retention is made of *polyvinylidene chloride*; another leading brand is made of *polyvinyl chloride* (*PVC*). For added flexibility, both require the addition of plasticizers which, if in direct extended contact with food, can be absorbed. However, the USDA has approved their use with food and, though little is known of the effects of human ingestion of plasticizers over a prolonged period of time, there is no current evidence that they are harmful. There is some concern, however, that wraps containing plasticizers can transfer their components to food during lengthy heating in a microwave oven.

plover [PLUH-vuhr; PLOH-vuhr] A small GAME BIRD which cannot be hunted legally in the U.S. Plovers are now farm-raised, however, and are also imported from Europe. They're available on a limited basis in specialty produce markets. The **golden plover** is considered superior and has a delicate and delicious meat. Plover is usually roasted.

plum There are hundreds of plum varieties cultivated throughout the world. All grow in clusters, have smooth, deeply colored skin and a center pit. Plums can range in shape from oval to round and in size from 1 to 3 inches in diameter. Their color can be yellow, green, red, purple, indigo blue and almost anything in between. Fresh plums are available from May to late October. Choose firm plums that give slightly to palm pressure. Avoid those with skin blemishes such as cracks, soft spots or brown discolorations, the latter indicating sunburn. Very firm plums may be stored at room temperature until slightly soft. Refrigerate ripe plums in a plastic bag for up to 4 days. Some plums are grown specifically to be dried as PRUNES. The majority, however, are enjoyed fresh for out-of-hand eating or for use in a wide variety of sweet and savory preparations. Also available are canned plums, packed in either water or sugar syrup. Plums contain a fair amount of vitamin A and potassium.

plum pudding The name of this specialty comes from the fact that it originally contained plums, which it no longer does. Instead, this traditional Christmas dessert is made with SUET, dried currants, raisins, almonds and spices. It's either steamed or boiled and is often served warm, flamed with brandy or rum, and accompanied by HARD SAUCE.

plum sauce *see* DUCK SAUCE

plum tomato *see* TOMATO

poach To cook food gently in liquid at or just below the boiling point. The amount and temperature of the liquid used depends on the food being poached. Meats and poultry are usually simmered in stock, fish in COURT-BOUILLON and eggs in lightly salted water, often with a little vinegar added. Fruit is often poached in a light SUGAR SYRUP.

poblano chili pepper [poh-BLAH-noh] A dark (sometimes almost black) green CHILI PEPPER with a rich flavor that varies from mild to snappy. The darkest poblanos have the richest flavor. This chili pepper is about 2½ to 3 inches wide and 4 to 5 inches long, tapering from top to bottom in a triangular shape. The very best poblanos are found in central Mexico, though they are now also grown in the U.S. Southwest. Fresh poblanos can be found in Mexican markets and in many supermarkets. Their peak season is summer and early fall. They're also available canned. In their dried state they're known as ANCHO chili peppers. Poblanos can be used in a variety of dishes, but are perhaps best known as the chili of choice for CHILES RELLENOS.

pocket bread *see* PITA

poi [POY; POH-ee] This native Hawaiian dish is definitely an acquired taste. It's made from cooked TARO ROOT that is pounded to a smooth paste, then mixed with water, the amount depending on how the poi is to be served. Since poi is eaten with the fingers, its consistency is measured accordingly and ranges from "one-finger" (the thickest) to "three-finger" (the thinnest). Poi is generally fermented for several days, which gives it a sour, acidic taste. It can be eaten by itself, mixed with milk to make a porridge or served as a CONDIMENT for meat and fish. Poi is available in cans in Hawaii and in some specialty stores on the mainland.

poire [PWAHR] The French word for "pear."

poire Hélène [pwahr ay-LEN] A dessert consisting of a pear that has been poached in a vanilla-flavored SUGAR SYRUP, chilled, then placed on a scoop of vanilla ice cream and topped with warm chocolate sauce.

Poire William [pwahr WEEL-yahm] A clear pear EAU DE VIE from Switzerland. Some bottles of Poire William have a whole pear inside, a feat accomplished by placing a bottle over the budding fruit and allowing it to grow inside.

pois [PWAH] The French word for "pea" or "peas." *Petits pois* are small green peas.

poisson [pwah-SOHN] The French word for "fish."

poivre [PWAHV-r] The French word for "pepper." *Poivre blanc* is white pepper and *poivre gris* or *poivre noir* is black pepper.

polenta [poh-LEHN-tah] A staple of northern Italy, polenta is a MUSH made from cornmeal. It can be eaten hot with a little butter or cooled until firm, cut into squares and fried. For added flavor, polenta is sometimes mixed with cheese such as PARMESAN or GORGONZOLA. It can be served as a first course or side dish and makes hearty breakfast fare.

Polish sausage *see* KIELBASA

pollock; pollack [POL uhk] This member of the COD family is found in the North Atlantic. The low- to moderate-fat flesh is white, firm and has a delicate, slightly sweet flavor. The pollock can reach about 35 pounds but is normally found in markets between 4 and 10 pounds. It's available fresh, frozen and smoked, either whole or in fillets or steaks. Pollock may be prepared in any way suitable for cod. It's often used to make the imitation crab that's now commonly available. *See also* FISH.

polonaise, à la [poh-loh-NEHZ] French for "in the manner of Poland," generally referring to cooked vegetables (most often cauliflower or asparagus) that are sprinkled with chopped hard-cooked egg, breadcrumbs, parsley and melted butter.

polvorones [pohl-voh-ROHN-ay] *see* MEXICAN WEDDING CAKES

polyunsaturated oil; polyunsaturates [pol-ee-uhn-SACH-uh-ray-tehd] *see* FATS AND OILS

pomegranate [POM-uh-gran-uht] Nature's most labor-intensive fruit is about the size of a large orange and has a thin, leathery skin which can range in color from red to pink-blushed yellow. Inside are hundreds of seeds packed in compartments that are separated by bitter, cream-colored membranes. Each tiny, edible seed is surrounded by a translucent, brilliant-red pulp that has a sparkling sweet-tart flavor. Pomegranates are grown throughout Asia, the Mediterranean countries and in California. In the U.S., they're available in October and November. Choose those that are heavy for their size and have a bright, fresh color and blemish-free skin. Refrigerate for up to 2 months or store in a cool, dark place for up to a month. To use, cut the pomegranate in half and pry out the pulp-encased seeds, removing any of the light-colored membrane that may adhere. Pomegranates can be eaten as fruit, used as a garnish on sweet and savory dishes or pressed to extract the juice. They're rich in potassium and contain a fair amount of vitamin C.

pomelo; pommelo; pummelo [pom-EH-loh] This giant citrus fruit is native to Malaysia (where it still grows abundantly) and thought to be ancestor to the grapefruit. Like grapefruits, pomelos vary greatly in color, size and shape. They range from cantaloupe-size to as large as a 25-pound watermelon and have very thick, soft rind that can vary in color from yellow to pale yellowish-brown to pink. The light yellow to coral-pink flesh can vary from juicy to slightly dry and from seductively spicy-sweet to tangy and tart. The pomelo is also called *shaddock*, after an English sea captain who introduced the seed to the West Indies. Choose fruit that is heavy for its size, blemish-free and sweetly fragrant. Store in the refrigerator for up to a week. Pomelos may be used in any way suitable for GRAPEFRUIT. They're high in vitamin C and potassium.

pomfret [POM-friht] *see* BUTTERFISH

pomme [POM] The French word for "apple."

pomme de terre [pom duh TAIR] A French phrase that literally means "apple of the earth," but which refers to the potato. The phrase is usually shortened to simply *pommes*, as in *pommes frites* (FRENCH FRIES).

pommelo *see* POMELO

pommes Anna [pom ANNA] Translated as "Anna potatoes," this classic French dish is a simple preparation of thinly sliced potatoes baked in a shallow dish or pie plate. Layers of potatoes are buttered and sprinkled with salt and pepper. The dish is then tightly covered with foil and the top weighted. After baking, the dish is inverted onto a serving plate and the potatoes turned out. The resulting potato "pie" is brown and crisp on the outside and soft and buttery on the inside. It's cut into wedges to serve.

pommes frites [pom FREET] *see* FRENCH FRIES

pommes soufflées [pom soo-FLAY] Also known as *soufflé potatoes*, these crisp potato puffs are the result of deep-frying thinly sliced potatoes twice. The first time the potatoes are fried in 300°F oil. After cooling, they're fried in 375°F oil until they inflate and turn golden brown.

pompano [PAHM-puh-noh] 1. A member of the jack family, this saltwater fish is found in waters off South Atlantic and Gulf states. Its succulent, fine-textured, moderately fat flesh has a mild, delicate flavor. Pompano is considered by many to be America's finest fish—one reason, no doubt, that it's so expensive. It's marketed whole and in fillets, both fresh and frozen. Pompano may be prepared by almost any cooking method. The most famous dish made from this fish is **pompano en papillote**, where it's baked in PARCHMENT PAPER with mushrooms and a VELOUTÉ SAUCE. 2. **Pacific pompano** is a variety of BUTTERFISH. *See also* FISH.

Pont l'Évêque cheese [pon lay-VEHK] This uncooked, ripened cheese was well known as far back as the 13th century. It's made from whole or partially skimmed cow's milk and has a butterfat content of about 50 percent. The square-shape cheese has a golden or golden-orange rind. The interior is pale yellow with a creamy, softly oozing texture and a fresh, sweet-tart flavor. A well-ripened Pont l'Eveque will smell strong but not stinky. Avoid those that are gummy or bitter tasting. *See also* CHEESE.

pony 1. A small (about 1 ounce) bar measure, which is sometimes also used to serve LIQUEURS. 2. The term also refers to the amount of liquid such a glass holds, usually 1 ounce.

poorboy; po' boy *see* HERO SANDWICH

poori; puri [POOR-ee] This deep-fried bread is round, flat and unleavened. It's made with whole-wheat flour, water and GHEE or other fat—the dough is almost identical to that for CHAPATI. Poori is very popular in northern India as well as in neighboring Pakistan.

popadam; poppadum *see* PAPPADUM

pope's nose Also known as a *parson's nose*, this is the stubby tail protuberance of a dressed fowl. It seems to have originated as a derogatory term meant to demean the Catholics in England during the late 17th century.

popover A puffy, muffin-size bread with a crisp brown crust and a somewhat hollow, moist interior. Basic popovers begin with a simple batter of eggs, milk, butter and flour. The high proportion of liquid in the batter creates steam that LEAVENS the bread. Popovers may be baked in muffin tins or special popover pans, which have extra-deep cups. The name is said to come from the fact that as the batter bakes and expands, it "pops over" the sides of the cup-shaped indentations. Popovers can be plain or variously flavored with items such as cheese, spices or herbs.

poppy seed; poppyseed These small, dried, bluish-gray seeds of the poppy plant measure less than ¹⁄₁₆ inch in diameter—it takes about 900,000 of them to equal a pound. Poppy seeds have a crunchy texture and a nutty flavor. They're used as a filling in various cakes, pastries and coffeecakes, as a topping for a myriad of baked goods, in salad dressings and in a variety of cooked dishes—particularly those originating in central Europe, the Middle East and India. Poppy seeds can be purchased whole or ground in most supermarkets. *See also* SPICES; Herb and Spice Chart, page 538.

porcini [pohr-CHEE-nee] *see* CÈPE

porgy [POHR-gee] Widely known as *sea bream,* there are many different varieties of this fish family in the U.S. and around the world. The most popular U.S. porgy is the **scup,** which is found in Atlantic waters. Porgies have a firm, low-fat flesh with a delicate, mild flavor. Although some grow to 20 pounds, most fall into the ½- to 3-pound range. They're available fresh and frozen, and are generally sold whole. The porgy is suitable for almost any method of cooking, including baking, grilling and frying. *See also* FISH.

pork The tried-but-true saying that everything but the pig's squeal can be used is accurate indeed. Though pigs are bred primarily for their meat (commonly referred to as pork) and fat, the trimmings and lesser cuts (feet, jowl, tail, etc.) are used for SAUSAGE, the bristles for brushes, the hair for furniture and the skin for leather. The majority of pork in the marketplace today is CURED—like BACON and HAM—while the remainder is termed "fresh." Slaughterhouses can (but usually don't) request and pay for their pork to be graded by the U.S. Department of Agriculture (USDA). The grades are USDA 1, 2, 3, 4 and utility—from the best downwards—based on the proportion of lean to fat. Whether graded or not, all pork used for intrastate commerce is subjected to state or Federal inspection for wholesomeness, insuring that the slaughter and processing of the animal was done under sanitary conditions. Pork shipped interstate must be federally inspected. Today's pork is leaner (about ⅓ fewer calories) and higher in protein than that consumed just 10 years ago. Thanks to improved feeding techniques, trichinosis in pork is now also rarely an issue. Normal precautions should still be taken, however, such as washing anything (hands, knives, cutting boards, etc.) that comes in contact with raw pork and never tasting uncooked pork. Cooking it to an internal temperature of 137°F will kill any trichinae. However, allowing for a safety margin for thermometer inaccuracy, most experts recommend an internal temperature of from 150 to 165°F, which will still produce a juicy, tender result. The 170° to 185°F temperature recommended in many cookbooks produces overcooked meat. Though pork generally refers to young swine under a year old, most pork today is slaughtered at between 6 to 9 months, producing a leaner, more tender meat. Though available year-round, fresh pork is more plentiful (and the prices lower) from October to February. Look for pork that is pale pink with a small amount of marbling and white (not yellow) fat. The darker pink the flesh, the older the animal. Fresh pork that will be used within 6 hours of purchase may be left in its store packaging. Otherwise, remove the packaging and store loosely wrapped with waxed paper in the coldest part of the refrigerator for up to 2 days. Wrapped airtight, pork can be frozen from 3 to 6 months, with the larger cuts having longer storage capabilities than ground meat or chops. Some of the more popular fresh pork cuts are **pork chops, pork loin** and **pork ribs**. The most popular cured pork products include ham, bacon, CANADIAN BACON and SALT PORK. *See also* Pork Chart, page 571. *For information on specific pork cuts, see individual listings.*

pork sausage, fresh A general category for uncooked sausage made with fresh ground pork and pork fat, usually mildly seasoned with pepper and sage. Under Federal law, fresh pork sausage cannot contain more than 50 percent fat or 3 percent added moisture. It comes in link, patty and bulk form and is available in most supermarkets. *See also* SAUSAGE.

pork shoulder *see* PICNIC HAM

porridge [POR-ihj] A thick, puddinglike dish made of cereal or grain (usually oatmeal) cooked in water or milk. Porridge is usually eaten hot for breakfast with sugar and milk or cream.

port; Porto A sweet FORTIFIED WINE most often served after a meal. BRANDY is added to the wine partway through fermentation, stopping the process at a point where the wine has plenty of sweetness and alcohol (18 to 20 percent). Port wines originated in the Douro Valley in northern Portugal; the best ports still come from that area. The name is derived from the fact that these wines are shipped out of the Portugese city of Oporto and, in fact, such wines are labeled "Porto," rather than "port." There are many types of port and the various labels can be confusing. The best and most expensive are **Vintage Ports,** which are made from grapes of a single vintage, bottled within 2 years. The very best of these can age 50 years or more. **Late-bottled Vintage Ports** and **Single Vintage Ports** are also made from grapes of a single vintage (though the grapes are not of as high a quality as those for vintage Ports). Late-bottled Vintage Ports are aged in wood for up to 6 years, while Single Vintage Ports have been wood-aged at least 7 years. Both are ready to drink when bottled and do not have the aging potential of Vintage Ports. **Tawny Ports** are a blend of grapes from several different years and can be aged in wood for as long as 30 years. They're tawny in color and ready to drink when bottled. **Vintage Character Ports** are essentially high-quality **Ruby Ports,** which are considered the lowest grade of port. They're blended from several vintages and wood-aged, but not nearly as long as Tawnies. They're the lightest and fruitiest in flavor and are ready to drink when bottled. American wineries have been bottling vintage ports since the early 1970s.

porter A heavy, dark-brown, strongly flavored beer. The dark color and strong flavor come from the addition of roasted MALT. Porters are usually higher in alcohol than regular LAGER beers. *See also* BEER.

porterhouse steak A steak cut from the large end of the SHORT LOIN containing meat from both the TENDERLOIN (the most tender cut of meat) and the top loin muscle. This is one of the best and most expensive steaks. *See also* BEEF; Beef Chart, page 573.

Port-Salut cheese [por suh-LOO] This semisoft cheese was first made by 19th-century Trappist monks at the Monastery of Port-du-Salut in the Brittany region of France. Made from cow's milk, Port-Salut comes in thick cylinders (about 9 inches in diameter) with an orange rind and pale-yellow interior. It has a mild, savory flavor and smooth, satiny texture. It's a perfect partner for fruit. *See also* CHEESE.

posole; pozole [poh-SOH-leh] A thick, hearty soup usually eaten as a main course. It consists of pork (sometimes chicken) meat and broth, HOMINY, onion, garlic, dried CHILI PEPPERS and CILANTRO. It's usually served with chopped lettuce, radishes, onions, cheese and cilantro, which diners can add to the soup as they please. Posole originated in Jalisco, in the middle of Mexico's Pacific Coast region, and is traditionally served at Christmastime.

posset [POS-iht] In the Middle Ages this hearty hot drink was considered a remedy for colds. It consists of hot milk, wine or ale, sugar and spices. Some versions add beaten egg, making it even richer.

pot *n*. A round, deep cooking container that usually has two handles and a lid. Pots can range from small to large. Except for SKILLETS, most cooking

containers can be called pots. **pot** *v.* An older method of preserving food
by cooking it in plenty of fat and a small amount of water. After cooking,
the food is placed in small pots or jars and covered with a layer of fat. As
the fat cools and hardens it forms an airtight seal, protecting the food from
airborne bacteria. Refrigeration and other modern food-packaging
methods have limited the necessity for potting foods, but some traditional
dishes like French CONFITS are still potted and enjoyed today.

potable *adj.* [POH-tuh-bl] A word used to describe a liquid suitable for
drinking, such as *potable* water. **potable** *n.* Any beverage, particularly
those containing alcohol.

potage [poh-TAHZH] The French have three separate words for soup.
CONSOMMÉ is a clear, thin broth. *Soupe* refers to a thick, hearty melange with
chunks of food. Potage falls somewhere between the first two in texture
and thickness. A potage is usually pureed and is often thickened slightly
with cream or egg yolks. Today, the words *soupe* and *potage* are often used
interchangeably.

potato The ancient Incas were cultivating this humble tuber thousands
of years ago. The potato was not readily accepted in Europe, however,
because it was known to be a member of the nightshade family (as are the
tomato and eggplant) and therefore thought to be poisonous. In the 16th
century, Sir Walter Raleigh was instrumental in debunking the poisonous
potato superstition when he planted them on property he owned in
Ireland. The Irish knew a good thing when they saw it and a hundred years
later were growing and consuming the potato in great quantities. Today,
hundreds of varieties of this popular vegetable are grown around the
world. In America, the potato can be divided into four basic categories:
russet, long white, round white and round red. The **russet Burbank
potato** (also simply called *russet* and *Idaho*) is long, slightly rounded and
has a brown, rough skin and numerous eyes. Its low moisture and high
starch content not only give it superior baking qualities but also make it
excellent for FRENCH FRIES. The russet Burbank was named for its developer,
horticulturalist Luther Burbank of Idaho. Although grown throughout the
Midwest, the russet is also commonly called IDAHO POTATO (whether or not
it's grown there). **Long white potatoes** have a similar shape as the russet
but they have thin, pale gray-brown skins with almost imperceptible eyes.
They're sometimes called *white rose* or *California long whites*, after the
state in which they were developed. Long whites can be baked, boiled or
roasted. The medium-size **round white** and **round red potatoes** are also
commonly referred to as *boiling potatoes*. They're almost identical except
that the round white has a freckled brown skin and the round red a reddish-
brown coat. They both have a waxy flesh that contains less starch and more

moisture than the russet and long white. This makes them better suited for boiling (they're both commonly used to make mashed potatoes) than for baking. They're also good for roasting and frying. The round white is grown mainly in the Northeast where it's sometimes referred to by one of its variety names, *Katahdin*. The round red is cultivated mainly in the Northwest. **New potatoes** are simply young potatoes (any variety). They haven't had time to convert their sugar fully into starch and consequently have a crisp, waxy texture and thin, undeveloped wispy skins. New potatoes are small enough to cook whole and are excellent boiled or pan-roasted. Because they retain their shape after being cooked and cut, new potatoes are particularly suited for use in potato salad. The season for new potatoes is spring to early summer. Potatoes of one variety or another are available year-round. Choose potatoes that are suitable for the desired method of cooking. All potatoes should be firm, well-shaped (for their type) and blemish-free. New potatoes may be missing some of their feathery skin but other types should not have any bald spots. Avoid potatoes that are wrinkled, sprouted or cracked. A green tinge—indicative of prolonged light exposure—is caused by the alkaloid solanin, which can be toxic if eaten in quantity. This bitter green portion can be cut or scraped off and the potato used in the normal fashion. Store potatoes in a cool, dark, well-ventilated place for up to 2 weeks. New potatoes should be used within 3 days of purchase. Refrigerating potatoes causes them to become quite sweet and to turn dark when cooked. Warm temperatures encourage sprouting and shriveling. Potatoes are probably the most versatile vegetable in the world and can be cooked in any way imaginable. They're available in a wide selection of commercial products including POTATO CHIPS, instant mashed potatoes (dehydrated cooked potatoes), canned new potatoes and a plethora of frozen products including HASH BROWNS, FRENCH FRIES and stuffed baked potatoes. Potatoes are not at all hard on the waistline (a 6-ounce potato contains only about 120 calories) and pack a nutritional punch. They're low in sodium, high in potassium and an important source of complex carbohydrates and vitamins C and B-6, as well as a storehouse of minerals. Neither SWEET POTATOES nor YAMS are botanically related to the potato.

potato chips   Because these deep-fried, thinly sliced potatoes were invented by the chef of a Saratoga Springs, New York, hotel at the behest of a mid-19th-century guest, they're also called *Saratoga chips*. Now these all-American favorites come commercially in a wide selection of sizes, cuts (ripple and flat), thicknesses, and flavors such as chive, barbecue and NACHO. Most commercial potato chips contain preservatives; those labeled "natural" usually do not. Some are salted while others are labeled "low-salt"; though most potato chips are skinless, others do include the flavorful skin. There are even chips made from mashed potatoes formed into perfect rounds and packed into crushproof cardboard cylinders. All potato chips should be stored in an airtight container in a cool, dark place. The storage time depends on whether or not they contain preservatives and how old they were when purchased. Some chips have a freshness date stamped on the package.

potato flour Also called *potato starch*, this gluten-free flour is made from cooked, dried and ground potatoes. It's used as a thickener and, because it produces a moist crumb, in some baked goods.

potato ricer *see* RICER

potato salad A salad of cooked, diced or cubed potatoes mixed with other ingredients such as chopped onion, green peppers, celery, hard-cooked eggs, seasonings and a mayonnaise- or sour cream-based dressing. German potato salad, often served hot, is bound with a vinegar-bacon fat dressing.

potato starch *see* POTATO FLOUR

pot-au-feu [poh-toh-FEUH] "Pot on fire" is the literal translation of this French phrase. Culinarily it refers to a French dish of meat and vegetables slowly cooked in water. The resulting rich broth is served with croutons as a first course, followed by an entree of the meat and vegetables. Any combination of meat and vegetables can be used and the mix varies according to the region. If the meat has MARROW-filled bones, the marrow can be served on toast as another course preceding the entree.

pot cheese A soft, fresh cheese that is basically COTTAGE CHEESE that is drained longer and therefore has a slightly drier texture. *See also* CHEESE.

pot liquor; potlikker The vitamin-rich liquid left after cooking greens, vegetables, meat, etc. This broth is particularly popular in the southern U.S. and is traditionally served separately with cornbread or CORN PONE.

pot marjoram *see* MARJORAM

pot roast *n.* Usually an inexpensive, less tender cut of beef that is first browned, then braised very slowly in a covered pot with a little liquid. The result is a flavorful, tender piece of meat. CHUCK or ROUND cuts are the most popular for this dish. The dish is called **Yankee pot roast** when vegetables are added to the pot partway through the cooking process. **pot roast** *v.* To cook meat by browning, then braising in a covered pot either on top of the stove or in the oven.

pots de crème; pot-au-crème [poh duh KREHM; poht-oh-KREHM]
1. Small, lidded cups used to hold custards, mousses, etc. The lids keep a
surface skin from forming on cooked custards. 2. The creamy custard
baked and served in these small containers.

pot stickers Small dumplings made of WON TON SKINS filled with ground
meat or shellfish, chopped water chestnuts, scallions and seasonings. The
pot stickers are browned on one side, then turned and simmered in broth.
Pot stickers are usually served as appetizers, accompanied with various
dipping sauces.

potted shrimp Finely diced or pureed cooked shrimp mixed with
seasoned butter, then placed in small pots covered with additional melted
butter and refrigerated. Potted shrimp is usually spread on toast and served
as an HORS D'OEUVRE. *See also* POT *v.*

poularde [poo-LAHRD] The French term referring to a fat chicken or
hen suitable for roasting.

poulet [poo-LAY] The French word for a young, tender spring chicken.

poultry Any domesticated bird used as food. Centuries ago the Chinese
began raising a variety of birds which were gradually brought to the West
via Asia, Greece and Rome. Today there are many domesticated varieties
of poultry including CHICKEN, TURKEY, DUCK, GOOSE, ROCK CORNISH HEN,
GUINEA FOWL and PHEASANT. All poultry ranks high nutritionally. It's
classified as a complete protein, is a good source of calcium, phosphorus
and iron and contains riboflavin, thiamine and niacine. *See* CHICKEN *for
information regarding purchasing, storing and preparing poultry.*

poultry shears A scissorlike implement designed to cut up poultry. A
good pair of poultry shears has slip-proof handles and slightly curved
blades, one with a serrated and notched edge for gripping the flesh and
cutting bones. Poultry shears make easy work of cutting up a duck,
snipping out the backbone of a chicken or cutting up a stewing hen to be
used for stock. They also perform additional useful tasks such as trimming
artichokes and other vegetables.

pound cake Originally this fine-textured loaf cake was made with one
pound each of flour, butter, sugar and eggs, plus a flavoring like vanilla
or lemon. A myriad of variations have evolved throughout the years, with
additions such as leavening (baking powder or baking soda) and
flavorings such as coconut, nuts, raisins and dried fruit.

pousse-café [poos ka-FAY] 1. This French term literally means "push
the coffee," and in France refers in general to cordials, brandies, etc. that

might be served after dinner with coffee. 2. In the U.S., it refers to a very elaborate, multi-colored after-dinner drink made by layering various LIQUEURS on top of one another without disturbing the layer below. A slender liqueur glass is used and the heaviest (usually the sweetest) liqueurs are poured in first.

poussin [poo-SAHN] French for a very young, small chicken, sometimes also called *petit poussin.*

powdered milk Milk from which almost all the moisture has been removed. Powdered milk is less expensive and easier to store than fresh milk but has a disadvantage in that it never tastes quite like the real thing. It comes in three basic forms—whole milk, nonfat milk and buttermilk. Because of its butterfat content, **powdered whole milk** must be refrigerated—both in its dry form and after it's reconstituted. **Nonfat dry milk** has had most of the butterfat removed. It's available in regular and instant forms; the former tastes slightly better, while the latter mixes more easily. **Powdered buttermilk** is simply desiccated buttermilk and is generally used for baking. Until opened, powdered nonfat milk and buttermilk can be kept in a cool, dry place for up to 6 months. Refrigerating opened packages will help retain their freshness. A USDA "U.S. Extra Grade" shield on the label signifies that the product meets exacting government quality standards. Powdered milks may or may not be fortified with vitamins A and D.

powdered sugar *see* CONFECTIONERS' SUGAR

prairie oyster *see* MOUNTAIN OYSTERS

praline [PRAH-leen; prah-LEEN; PRAY-leen] 1. A brittle confection made of almonds and CARAMELIZED sugar. It may be eaten as candy, ground and used as a filling or dessert ingredient, or sprinkled atop desserts as a garnish. 2. A special patty-shaped candy from Louisiana made with pecans and brown sugar.

prawn There is a great deal of confusion about this term because it's used to describe several different SHELLFISH. 1. The first definition refers to a species that's part of the lobster family and includes those CRUSTACEANS variously called *Dublin Bay prawn, Danish lobster, Italian scampi, langoustine* (French), *langostino* (Spanish), *Caribbean lobsterette* and *Florida lobsterette.* These "prawns" have bodies shaped like tiny Maine LOBSTERS including minuscule claws. The meat has a sweet, delicate flavor that some claim is better than either lobster or shrimp. These "prawns" are 6 to 8 inches in length and have pale-red bodies deepening to dark-red tails. 2. A second definition applies to the freshwater prawn (identified by the Latin name *Macrobrachium*); the term distinguishes SHRIMP as living in salt water and prawns as freshwater creatures. In truth, these prawns migrate (much like salmon) from salt water to fresh water to spawn. They look like a cross between a shrimp and a lobster, with their bodies having narrower abdomens and longer legs than shrimp. 3. The term "prawn" is also loosely used to describe any large shrimp, especially those that come 15 (or fewer) to the pound (also called "jumbo shrimp").

preserve To prepare foods so that they can be kept for long periods of time without spoiling or deteriorating. Depending on the food and the length of time it's to be stored, preserving can be accomplished in a number of different ways including refrigeration, freezing, canning, salting, smoking, freeze-drying, dehydrating and pickling.

preserves Fruit cooked with sugar and usually PECTIN, used as a spread for bread. Preserves differ from JAM in that the chunks of fruit are medium to large rather than the texture of thick puree. *See also* JELLY.

pressed cookie Fancy cookies that are formed by pressing dough through a COOKIE PRESS or PASTRY BAG fitted with a decorative tip. *See also* COOKIE.

pressed duck 1. A French specialty in which the breast and legs are removed from a cooked duck. The remainder of the bird is compressed in a special implement called a DUCK PRESS, which extracts all the juices. The extracted juice is mixed with reduced red wine, cognac and butter to produce a delicious sauce that is served with the sliced breast and legs. 2. A Chinese dish in which the duck is steamed, boned and flattened, then steamed and flattened again. The duck is then cut into quarters and deep-fried to a golden brown. Before serving, it's cut into squares and served on a bed of shredded lettuce, garnished with toasted almonds and accompanied with a pungent sauce.

pressure cooker A special cooking pot with a locking, airtight lid and a valve system to regulate internal pressure. Pressure cookers operate on a principle whereby the steam that builds up inside the pressurized pot cooks food at a very high temperature. This reduces the cooking time by as much as 50 percent without destroying the food's nutritional value. Most pressure cookers are equipped with detachable pressure regulators that can adjust the pressure for low (5 pounds), medium (10 pounds) or high (15 pounds). The more pounds of pressure, the higher the internal temperature and the quicker the food cooks. Pressure cookers have a safety valve, which will automatically vent the steam should there be a malfunction. There are many styles of pressure cooker on the market today, most of which are made for stove-top cooking. But there are also small pressure cookers that can be used in a microwave oven. Some of the newer pressure cookers have built-in pressure regulators. Pressure cookers are useful for foods that would normally be cooked with moist heat such as soups, stews, steamed puddings, tough cuts of meat, artichokes, etc. They can also be used for canning, and there are special **pressure canners** made specifically for this purpose.

pretzel [PREHT-zuhl] The pretzel can be traced back to the Romans, although the twisted loose knot shape is thought to have been introduced in the early part of the 7th century. The first U.S. commercial pretzel factory was established in 1861 in Lititz, Pennsylvania. There are two main types of pretzel—hard and crisp or soft and chewy (the older of the two forms). The latter is often sold hot with mustard by street vendors from their pretzel carts. Pretzels can be sprinkled with coarse salt or not, and shaped in the form of knots, sticks or rings. Crisp pretzels are available in many sizes, shapes and even flavors (such as rye) in supermarkets.

prick To make small holes in the surface of food. The best example is an unfilled pie dough that is pricked all over with the tines of a fork so it bakes without blistering or rising (*see* BAKE BLIND).

prickly pear Named for its pearlike shape and size, this fruit comes from any of several varieties of cactus. Its prickly skin can range in color from green to purplish-red; its soft, porous flesh (scattered with black seeds) from light yellow-green to deep golden. Also called *cactus pear*, the prickly pear has a melonlike aroma and a sweet but rather bland flavor. It's extremely popular in Mexico, Central and South America, the Mediterranean countries and southern Africa, and is slowly gaining favor in the U.S. Prickly pears are available in Mexican markets and some specialty produce markets from fall through spring. Choose fruit that gives slightly to palm pressure. It should have a deep, even color. Ripen firm prickly pears at room temperature until soft. Store ripe fruit in the refrigerator for up to a week. Prickly pears are usually served cold, peeled and sectioned with the seeds removed.

primavera, alla [pree-muh-VAIR-uh] This Italian phrase means "spring style" and culinarily refers to the use of fresh vegetables (raw or blanched) as a garnish to various dishes. One of the most popular dishes prepared in this manner is **pasta primavera**.

prime rib The term "prime rib" is often incorrectly used as a label for what is actually a RIB ROAST. Culinarily, the term "prime" actually refers to the highest USDA beef grade. It's only given to the finest beef, hallmarked by even marbling and a creamy layer of fat. Very little prime beef makes it past the better hotels and restaurants or prestige butchers. The best grade of beef generally found in supermarkets is USDA Choice. Therefore, although "prime rib" is how rib roast is often labeled, chances are that it's USDA Choice beef. *See* BEEF; Beef Chart, page 573.

primost cheese   *see* GJETOST CHEESE

prix fixe [PREE FIHKS; PREE FEEKS] A French phrase meaning "fixed price," referring to a complete meal served by a restaurant or hotel for a preset price. Sometimes a menu offers several choices for each course for this set price. *See also* À LA CARTE; TABLE D'HÔTE

processed cheese   *see* AMERICAN CHEESE, PROCESSED

profiterole [pruh-FIHT-uh-rohl] A miniature CREAM PUFF filled with either a sweet or savory mixture. Savory profiteroles are usually served as appetizers. One of the most famous desserts made with these tiny pastries is the elaborate CROQUEMBOUCHE.

proof *n.* A term used to indicate the amount of alcohol in liquor. In the U.S., proof is exactly twice the percentage of alcohol. Therefore, a bottle of liquor labeled "86 Proof" contains 43 percent alcohol. **proof** *v.* To dissolve YEAST in a warm liquid (sometimes with a small amount of sugar) and set it aside in a warm place for 5 to 10 minutes until it swells and becomes bubbly. This technique proves that the yeast is alive and active and therefore capable of LEAVENING a bread or other baked good.

prosciutto [proh-SHOO-toh] The Italian word for "ham," prosciutto is a term broadly used to describe a ham that has been seasoned, salt-cured (but not smoked) and air-dried. The meat is pressed, which produces a firm, dense texture. Italy's PARMA HAM is the true prosciutto, although others are also now made in the U.S. Italian prosciuttos are designated **prosciutto cotto**, which is cooked, and **prosciutto crudo**, which is raw (though, because of its curing, ready to eat). This type of Italian ham is also labeled according to its city or region of origin, for example **prosciutto di Parma** and **prosciutto di San Daniele**. Prosciutto is available in gourmet and Italian markets and some supermarkets. It's usually sold in transparently thin slices. Prosciutto is best eaten as is and is a classic first course when served with melon or figs. It can also be added at the last minute to cooked foods such as pastas or vegetables. Prolonged cooking will toughen it.

provençal [proh-vahn-SAHL] A term referring to dishes prepared in the style of Provence, a region in southeastern France. Garlic, tomatoes and olive oil are the major trademark of provençal cooking. Onions, olives, mushrooms, anchovies and eggplant also play a prominent part in many of these dishes.

provolone cheese [proh-voh-LOH-nee] This southern Italian cow's-milk cheese has a firm texture and a mild, smoky flavor. It has a golden-brown rind and comes in various forms, though the squat pear shape is most recognizable. Most provolone is aged for 2 to 3 months and has a pale-yellow color. However, some are aged 6 months to a year or more. As the cheese ripens, the color becomes a richer yellow and the flavor more pronounced. It is an excellent cooking cheese and aged provolones can be used for grating. Provolone is packaged in various sizes from little pear-shaped packages to giant sausage-shaped 200-pounders. Provolone is also now manufactured in the United States. *See also* CHEESE.

prune 1. A dried plum. Prunes can be traced back to Roman times and have long been a popular northern European winter fruit because they could be stored without problem. Although any plum can be made into a prune, those with the greatest flavor, sweetness and firmness are best suited for that use. Commercial dehydration has replaced sun-drying as the primary method of producing prunes. Though the best prunes are found in the fall, they're available year-round. Prunes come in various sizes and are usually labeled small, medium, large, extra large and jumbo. When purchasing prunes look for those that are slightly soft and somewhat flexible. They should have a bluish-black skin and be blemish-free. Store them airtight in a cool, dry place (or refrigerate) for up to 6 months. Prunes can be eaten out of hand or used in a variety of sweet and savory dishes. 2. A variety of Italian plum. 3. In French, the word *prune* means "plum," while *pruneau* means "prune."

prunelle [proo-NEHL] A sweet, pale-green, BRANDY-based LIQUEUR flavored with SLOES (wild plums).

puffball mushroom A firm, round, white mushroom that can range in size from 4 ounces to a giant 50-pounder. It has a mild, nutty flavor that complements many foods. Puffball mushrooms are available sporadically in specialty produce markets. They can be cut into thick or thin slices, breaded and sautéed, or chopped and used in a variety of dishes. *See also* MUSHROOM.

puff pastry The French call this rich, delicate, multi-layered pastry PÂTE FEUILLETÉE. It's made by placing pats of chilled fat (usually butter) between layers of pastry dough, then rolling it out, folding it in thirds and letting it rest. This process, which is repeated 6 to 8 times, produces a pastry comprising hundreds of layers of dough and butter. When baked, the moisture in the butter creates steam, causing the dough to puff and separate into hundreds of flaky layers. Puff pastry is used to make a variety of crisp creations including CROISSANTS, NAPOLEONS, PALMIERS and ALLUMETTES. It's also used as a wrapping for various foods such as meats, cheese and fruit.

pullet [POOL-iht] A young hen, less than 1 year old. *See also* CHICKEN.

pulque [POOL-keh] The unofficial national drink of Mexico, pulque is the fermented sap of the AGAVE. It's white, thick and quite sweet.

pulse The dried seed of any of several LEGUMES including BEANS, PEAS and LENTILS.

pulverize To reduce to powder or dust, usually by crushing, pounding or grinding.

pummelo *see* POMELO

pumpernickel [PUHM-puhr-nihk-uhl] A coarse dark bread with a slightly sour taste. Pumpernickel is usually made of a high proportion of rye flour and a small amount of wheat flour. Molasses is often used to add both color and flavor.

pumpkin When the colonists landed in North America they found the Indians growing and using pumpkins. This large, ungainly fruit was enthusiastically embraced by the new Americans and subsequently pumpkin pie became a national Thanksgiving tradition. It was so loved that one early Connecticut colony delayed Thanksgiving because the molasses needed to make this popular pie wasn't readily available. Large, round and orange, the pumpkin is a member of the gourd family, which also includes MUSKMELON, WATERMELON and SQUASH. Its orange flesh has a mild, sweet flavor and the seeds—husked and roasted—are delicately nutty. Pumpkin seeds are commonly known as PEPITAS. Fresh pumpkins are available in the fall and winter and some specimens have weighed in at well over 100 pounds. In general, however, the flesh from smaller sizes will be more tender and succulent. Choose pumpkins that are free from blemishes and heavy for their size. Store whole pumpkins at room temperature up to a month or refrigerate up to 3 months. Pureed pumpkin is also available canned. Pumpkin may be prepared in almost any way suitable for winter squash. It's a good source of vitamin A.

pumpkin seeds *see* PEPITAS

pupu; pu pu [POO-poo] The Hawaiian term for any hot or cold appetizer, which can include a wide range of items such as macadamia nuts, WON TONS, chunks of fresh pineapple or coconut and barbecued meats.

puree *n.* Any food (usually a fruit or vegetable) that is finely mashed to a smooth, thick consistency. Purees can be used as a garnish, served as a side dish or added as a thickener to sauces or soups. **puree** *v.* To grind or mash food until it's completely smooth. This can be accomplished by one of several methods including using a food processor or blender or by forcing the food through a sieve.

puri *see* POORI.

purple laver *see* LAVER

pyramide cheese [pih-rah-MEED] A truncated pyramid is the shape of this small French CHEVRE that's often coated with an edible dark-gray vegetable ash. It's produced around the central Loire valley area of France. Pyramide can range in texture from soft to slightly crumbly and, depending on age, in flavor from mild to sharp. It's wonderful served with crackers or bread and fruit. *See also* CHEESE.

uahog [KWAH-hog] The American Indian name for the East Coast hard-shell clam. The term "quahog" is also sometimes used to describe the largest of these hard-shell clams (also known as CHOWDER or large CLAM).

quail [KWAYL] The American quail is not related to the European quail, a migratory GAME BIRD belonging to the partridge family. But when colonists discovered birds that resembled the European version they called then by the same name. American quail are known by various names depending on the region—*bobwhite* in the East, *partridge* in the South, *quail* in North and *blue quail* in the Southwest. Other notable members of this family are **California quail, mountain quail** and **Montezuma quail**. American quail nest on the ground and are not migratory—in fact, they'd rather walk than fly. They're very social and travel in small groups called coveys. The meat of the American quail is white and delicately flavored. In general, they should be cooked like other game birds—young birds can be roasted, broiled or fried and older fowl should be cooked with moist heat. Most of the quail marketed today are raised on game bird farms. Fresh quail can be ordered through specialty butchers, who might also carry frozen quail.

quatre épices [KAH-tr ay-PEES] A French phrase meaning "four spices," referring to any of several finely ground spice mixtures. Though there's no standard mixture for quatre épices, the blend is usually mixed from the following selection: pepper (usually white), nutmeg, ginger, cinnamon or cloves. Quatre épices is used to flavor soups, stews and vegetables. *See also* SPICES.

quenelle [kuh-NEHL] A light, delicate dumpling made of seasoned, minced or ground fish, chicken, veal or game bound with eggs or PANADA. This mixture is formed into small ovals and gently poached in stock. Quenelles are usually served with a rich sauce and can be used as a first course, main course or garnish.

quesadilla [keh-sah-DEE-yah] A flour TORTILLA filled with a savory mixture, then folded in half to form a turnover shape. The filling can include shredded cheese, cooked meat, REFRIED BEANS or a combination of items. After the tortilla is filled and folded, it's toasted under a broiler or fried. Quesadillas are usually cut into strips before being served, often as an appetizer.

queso [KEH-soh] The Spanish word for "cheese."

quiche [KEESH] This dish originated in northeastern France in the region of Alsace-Lorraine. It consists of a pastry shell filled with a savory custard made of eggs, cream, seasonings and various other ingredients such as onions, mushrooms, ham, shellfish or herbs. The most notable of these savory pies is the **quiche Lorraine**, which has crisp bacon bits (and sometimes GRUYÈRE cheese) added to the custard filling. Quiches can be served as a lunch or dinner entree, or as a first course or HORS D'OEUVRE.

quick bread Bread that is quick to make because it doesn't require kneading or rising time. That's because the LEAVENER in such a bread is usually baking powder or baking soda which, when combined with moisture, starts the rising process immediately. In the case of double-acting baking powder, oven heat causes a second burst of rising power. Eggs can also be used to leaven quick breads. This genre includes most BISCUITS, MUFFINS, POPOVERS and a wide variety of sweet and savory loaf breads.

quince [KWIHNC] Ancient Romans used the flowers and fruit of the quince tree for everything from perfume to honey. It was also considered a symbol of love and given to one's intended as a sign of commitment. Though the quince has been around for over 4,000 years throughout Asia and the Mediterranean countries, it's not particularly popular with Americans. This yellow-skinned fruit looks and tastes like a cross between an apple and a pear. The hard, yellowish-white flesh is quite dry and has an astringent, tart flavor. Its texture and flavor make it better cooked than raw, and because of its high pectin content it's particularly popular for use in jams, jellies and preserves. Quinces are available in supermarkets from October through December. Select those that are large, firm and yellow with little or no sign of green. Wrap quinces in a plastic bag and refrigerate for up to 2 months. Peel before using in jams, preserves, desserts and savory dishes.

quinine water [KWY-nyn] *see* TONIC WATER

quinoa [KEEN-wah] Although quinoa is new to the American market, it was a staple of the ancient Incas, who called it "the mother grain." To this day it's an important food in South American cuisine. Hailed as the "supergrain of the future," quinoa contains more protein than any other grain. It's considered a *complete protein* because it contains all eight essential amino acids. Quinoa is also higher in unsaturated fats and lower in carbohydrates than most grains, and it provides a rich and balanced source of vital nutrients. Tiny and bead-shaped, the ivory-colored quinoa cooks like rice (taking half the time of regular rice) and expands to four times its original volume. Its flavor is delicate, almost bland, and has been compared to that of COUSCOUS. Quinoa is lighter than but can be used in any way suitable for rice—as part of a main dish, a side dish, in soups, in salads and even in puddings. It's available packaged as a grain, ground into flour and in several forms of pasta. Quinoa can be found in most health-food stores and some supermarkets.

abbit The domesticated members of the rabbit family (a rodent relation) have fine-textured flesh that is almost totally white meat. They're plumper and less strongly flavored than their wild counterparts. A mature rabbit averages between 3 and 5 pounds, much smaller than its relative the hare (which usually weighs in at between 6 and 12 pounds). Fresh and frozen rabbit is available dressed either whole or cut into pieces. The best will be young and weigh between 2 and 2½ pounds, and should have light-colored flesh. These are the most tender and mild-flavored and can be prepared in any manner suitable for young chicken (such as frying, grilling or roasting). Older or wild rabbits benefit from moist-heat cooking such as braising. *See also* GAME ANIMALS.

rack of lamb A portion of the rib section of a lamb, usually containing eight ribs. A rack of lamb can be cut into chops or served in one piece—either as a rack or formed into a CROWN ROAST. *See also* Lamb Chart, page 570; LAMB.

raclette cheese [rah-KLEHT; ra-KLEHT] 1. A cow's-milk cheese from Switzerland that's similar to GRUYÈRE in both texture (semifirm and dotted with small holes) and flavor (mellow and nutty). It can be found in specialty cheese stores and many supermarkets. 2. A dish by the same name consisting of a chunk of raclette cheese that is exposed to heat (traditionally an open fire) and scraped off as it melts. The word *raclette* comes from *racler*, French for "to scrape." It's served as a meal with boiled potatoes, dark bread and CORNICHONS or other pickled vegetables.

radicchio [rah-DEE-kee-oh] This red-leafed Italian CHICORY is most often used as a salad green. There are several varieties of radicchio, but the two most widely available in the U.S. are *Verona* and *Treviso*. The **radicchio di Verona** has burgundy-red leaves with white ribs. It grows in a small, loose head similar to BUTTERHEAD LETTUCE. The leaves of **radicchio di Treviso** are narrow and pointed and form tighter, more tapered heads. They also have white ribs but can range in color from pink to dark red. Other radicchio varieties have variegated or speckled leaves in beautiful shades of pink, red and green. All radicchios have tender but firm leaves with a slightly bitter flavor. Radicchio is available year-round, with a peak season from mid-winter to early spring. Choose heads that have crisp, full-colored leaves with no sign of browning. Store in a plastic bag in the refrigerator for up to a week. Besides being used in salads, radicchio may also be cooked by grilling, sautéing or baking.

radish From the Latin *radix*, meaning "root," the radish is in fact the root of a plant in the mustard family. Its skin can vary in color from white to red to purple to black (and many shades in between). In shape and size, the radish can be round, oval or elongated and can run the gamut from globes ½ inch in diameter to carrotlike giants (such as the DAIKON) 1½ feet in length. The most common variety found in American markets is the globular or oval-shaped red-skinned radish, which ranges in size from that of a small cherry to that of a tiny orange. The flavor can be mild to peppery, depending on factors such as variety and age. Available year-round, radishes are sold both trimmed (in plastic bags) and with their greens and roots attached. Choose those that feel firm when gently squeezed. If the radish gives to pressure, the interior will likely be pithy instead of crisp. Any attached leaves should be green and crisp. Remove and discard leaves and refrigerate radishes in a plastic bag for up to 5 days. Wash and trim root ends just before using. For added crispness, soak radishes in icewater for a couple of hours. Though radishes are most often used raw in salads, as garnishes and for CRUDITÉS, they can also be cooked. **Radish sprouts** can be used as a peppery accent to salads and as a garnish for a variety of cold and hot dishes. They can be found in specialty produce markets, health-food stores and some supermarkets.

ragoût [ra-GOO] A derivative of the French verb *ragoûter*, meaning "to stimulate the appetite," ragout is a thick, rich, well-seasoned stew of meat, poultry or fish that can be made with or without vegetables.

rainbow trout *see* TROUT

raisin [RAY-sihn] In the most basic terms, a raisin is simply a dried grape. About half of the world's raisin supply comes from California. The most common grapes used for raisins are THOMPSON SEEDLESS, ZANTE and MUSCAT. Grapes are either sun-dried or dehydrated mechanically. Both dark and golden seedless raisins can be made from Thompson seedless grapes. The difference is that the dark raisins are sun-dried for several weeks, thereby producing their shriveled appearance and dark color. Golden raisins have been treated with sulphur dioxide (to prevent their color from darkening) and dried with artificial heat, thereby producing a moister, plumper product. The tiny seedless Zante grapes produce dried currants, and muscat grapes (which usually have their seeds removed before processing) create a dark, perfumy and intensely sweet raisin. All raisins can be stored tightly wrapped at room temperature for several months. For prolonged storage (up to a year), they should be refrigerated in a tightly sealed plastic bag. Raisins can be eaten out of hand, as well as used in a variety of baked goods and in cooked and raw dishes. They have a high natural sugar content, contain a variety of vitamins and minerals and are especially rich in iron.

ramekin; ramequin [RAM-ih-kihn] 1. An individual baking dish (3 to 4 inches in diameter) that resembles a miniature soufflé dish. Ramekins are usually made of porcelain or earthenware and can be used for both sweet and savory dishes—either baked or chilled. 2. A tiny baked pastry filled with a creamy cheese custard.

ramen [RAH-mehn] 1. Japanese instant-style deep-fried noodles that are usually sold in cellophane packages, sometimes with bits of dehydrated vegetables and broth mix. 2. A Japanese dish of noodles, small pieces of meat and vegetables and broth.

Ramos gin fizz; Ramos fizz [RAY-mohs] *see* GIN FIZZ

R

ramp This wild onion grows from Canada to the Carolinas and resembles a SCALLION with broad leaves. Also known as *wild leek*, ramp has an assertive, garlicky-onion flavor. It can be found—usually only in specialty produce markets—from March to June. Choose those that are firm with bright-colored greenery. Wrap tightly in a plastic bag and refrigerate for up to a week. Trim the root ends just before using. Though the flavor of a ramp is slightly stronger than the LEEK, SCALLION or ONION, it can be used—raw or cooked—in many dishes as a substitute for any of those three.

range chicken *see* CHICKEN

rape [RAYP] 1. A vegetable related to both the cabbage and turnip family, the leafy green rape has 6- to 9-inch stalks and scattered clusters of tiny broccolilike buds. It's also called *broccoli raab*, *brocoletti di rape* and *rapini*. The greens have a pungent, bitter flavor that is not particularly popular in America where, more often than not, they're used as animal fodder. Italians are particularly fond of rape, however, and cook it in a variety of ways including frying, steaming and braising. It can also be used in soups or salads. Rape can be found from fall to spring in markets with specialty produce sections. It should be wrapped in a plastic bag and refrigerated for no more than 5 days. **Rapeseed oil,** expressed from rape seeds, is commonly marketed under the name CANOLA OIL. Once used only in parts of Europe and the Middle East, rapeseed oil has been discovered to have more cholesterol-balancing MONOUNSATURATED FAT than any other oil except OLIVE OIL. 2. The residue of grape stalks, stems and skins after the juice has been extracted for winemaking.

rapeseed oil *see* CANOLA OIL; RAPE

rapini [rah-PEE-nee] *see* RAPE

rarebit *see* WELSH RAREBIT

rasher 1. A strip or slice of meat such as bacon or ham. 2. A serving of two to three thin pieces of such meat.

raspberry [RAZ-behr-ee] Considered by many the most intensely flavored member of the berry family, the raspberry is composed of many connecting drupelets (individual sections of fruit, each with its own seed) surrounding a central core. There are three main varieties—black, golden and red, the latter being the most widely available. Depending on the region, raspberries are available from May through November. Choose brightly colored, plump berries sans hull. If the hulls are still attached, the berries were picked too early and will undoubtedly be tart. Avoid soft, shriveled or moldy berries. Store (preferably in a single layer) in a moistureproof container in the refrigerator for 2 to 3 days. If necessary, rinse lightly just before serving. Raspberries are very fragile and are at their best served fresh with just a kiss of cream. They also make excellent jam. Seedless raspberry jam is available commercially. The berries contain a fair amount of iron, potassium and vitamins A and C.

ratafia [rat-uh-FEE-uh] *see* LIQUEUR

ratatouille [ra-tuh-TOO-ee; ra-tuh-TWEE] A popular dish from Provence that combines eggplant, tomatoes, onions, bell peppers, zucchini, garlic and herbs—all simmered in olive oil. The vegetables can vary according to the cook. They can be cooked together, or cooked separately and then combined and heated briefly together. Ratatouille can be served hot, cold or at room temperature, either as a side dish or as an appetizer with bread or crackers.

ravioli [rav-ee-OH-lee; ra-VYOH-lee] An Italian specialty of little square or round pillows of noodle dough filled with any of various mixtures such as cheese, meat or vegetables. Ravioli are boiled, then usually baked with a cream, cheese or tomato sauce. Chinese-style ravioli are called WON TONS; Jewish-style are known as KREPLACH. *See also* PASTA.

raw milk *see* MILK

raw sugar *see* SUGAR

ray *see* SKATE

razor clam The most famous West Coast SOFT-SHELL CLAM, the razor clam is so-named because its shell resembles a folded, old-fashioned straight razor. It's best when steamed. *See also* CLAM.

reamer [REE-muhr] *see* JUICER

Reblochon cheese [reh-bluh-SHOHN] This uncooked French cows' milk cheese has a creamy-soft texture and a delicate flavor when perfectly ripe. It becomes bitter, however, when overripe. Reblochon has a dark golden rind and is sold in small discs. It's available in most specialty cheese shops and is good both for snacks and with fruit. *See also* CHEESE.

reconstitute [ree-CON-stih-toot; ree-CON-stih-tyoot] Culinarily, the term means to return a dehydrated food (such as dried milk) to its original consistency by adding a liquid, usually water.

red beans Popular in Mexico and the southwestern U.S., this dark red, medium-size bean is a favorite for making CHILI CON CARNE (with beans) and REFRIED BEANS (*refritos*). Red beans are available dried in most supermarkets. *See also* BEANS.

red bell pepper *see* SWEET PEPPERS

red cabbage *see* CABBAGE

red caviar *see* CAVIAR

red cooking A Chinese cooking method whereby food (such as chicken) is browned in SOY SAUCE, thereby changing the color to a deep, dark red.

red date *see* CHINESE DATE

Red Delicious apple This large, brilliant red (sometimes streaked with green) apple has an elongated shape with five distinctive knobs at its base. It's juicy and sweet but lacks any distinguishing tartness. The red Delicious is in season from September through April. It's good for eating out of hand but does not cook well. *See also* APPLE; GOLDEN DELICIOUS APPLE.

red drum *see* DRUM

redeye gravy A traditional southern gravy made by combining the drippings from fried ham (purists insist on COUNTRY-CURED HAM *only*) with water and hot coffee—the latter being optional. The mixture is cooked until thickened. It's served with the ham and spooned atop biscuits, cornbread . . . and whatever else the diner fancies.

redfish *see* DRUM

red flannel hash A New England specialty made by frying chopped cooked beets, potatoes, onions and crisp bacon together until crusty and brown. Traditional recipes state that about 85 percent of the volume should be beets. Red flannel hash is usually served with cornbread.

red Mexican bean *see* PINTO BEAN

red mullet This reddish-pink marine fish is not really a true MULLET but a Mediterranean member of the GOATFISH family. The red mullet ranges in size from ½ to 2 pounds and has very firm, lean flesh. It's found on menus all over Europe but is rarely available in the U.S. *See also* FISH.

red pepper A generic term applied to any of several varieties of hot, red CHILI PEPPERS. The most commonly available forms are ground red pepper and red pepper flakes. *See also* Herb and Spice Chart, page 538.

red snapper *see* SNAPPER

reduce Culinarily, to boil a liquid (usually stock, wine or a sauce mixture) rapidly until the volume is reduced by evaporation, thereby thickening the consistency and intensifying the flavor. Such a mixture is sometimes referred to as a *reduction*.

reduction *see* REDUCE

refried beans; frijoles refritos; refritos [free-HOH-lehs reh-FREE-tohs] This popular Mexican specialty consists of cooked RED BEANS or PINTO BEANS that are mashed, then fried, often in melted lard. Refried beans are sold canned in most supermarkets. The term *frijoles refritos* translates as "well-fried beans."

refrigerator cookie Also called *icebox cookie*, this style of cookie is made by forming the dough into a log, wrapping in plastic wrap or waxed paper and chilling until firm. The dough is then sliced into rounds and baked. *See also* COOKIE.

refritos [reh-FREE-tohs] *see* REFRIED BEANS

Reggiano Parmigiano cheese [rej-JYAH-noh pahr-muh-ZHAH-nah] *see* PARMESAN CHEESE

Rehoboam [ree-uh-BOH-uhm] *see* WINE BOTTLES

reindeer [RAYN-deer] *see* GAME ANIMALS

rémoulade [ray-muh-LAHD] This classic French sauce is made by combining MAYONNAISE (usually homemade) with mustard, CAPERS and chopped GHERKINS, herbs and ANCHOVIES. It's served chilled as an accompaniment to cold meat, fish and shellfish.

render To melt animal fat over low heat so that it separates from any connective pieces of tissue which, during rendering, turn brown and crisp and are generally referred to as CRACKLINGS. The resulting clear fat is then strained through a paper filter or fine CHEESECLOTH to remove any dark particles. The term *try out* is used synonymously with *render*.

rennet [REN-iht] A coagulating enzyme obtained from a young animal's (usually a calf's) stomach, rennet is used to curdle milk in foods such as cheese and JUNKET. It's available in most supermarkets in tablet or powdered form.

retsina [reht-SEE-nah] Made for more than 3,000 years, this traditional Greek wine has been resinated—treated with pine-tree resin. The resin gives the wine a distinctively sappy, turpentinelike flavor which, according to most non-Greeks, is an acquired taste. Retsinas are either white or rosé and should be served very cold.

Reuben sandwich [ROO-behn] Reportedly originally named for its creator, Arthur Reuben (owner of New York's once-famous and now-defunct Reuben's delicatessen), this sandwich is made with generous layers of corned beef, Swiss cheese and sauerkraut on sourdough rye bread. Reuben is said to have created the original version (which was reportedly made with ham) for Annette Seelos, the leading lady in a Charlie Chaplin film being shot in 1914. Another version of this famous sandwich's origin is that an Omaha wholesale grocer (Reuben Kay) invented it during a poker game in 1955. It gained national prominence when one of his poker partner's employees entered the recipe in a national sandwich contest the following year . . . and won. The Reuben sandwich can be served either cold or grilled.

Rhode Island Greening apple This medium-size, green to yellow-green apple has a sweet-tart flavor that seems to intensify when cooked. Because both texture and flavor hold up to heat, most of the Rhode Island greening crop is sold for commercial processing (applesauce, pies, etc.). It's also good for out-of-hand eating and is available from October to April, mainly in the eastern and central U.S. A variant grown in the western half of the country is called **Northwest Greening**. *See also* APPLE.

Rhône wine *see* CÔTES DU RHÔNE

rhubarb [ROO-bahrb] The thick, celerylike stalks of this buckwheat-family member can reach up to 2 feet long. They're the only edible portion of the plant—the leaves contain OXALIC ACID and can therefore be toxic. Though rhubarb is generally eaten as a fruit, it's botanically a vegetable. There are many varieties of this extremely tart food, most of which fall into two basic types—hothouse- and field-grown. Hothouse rhubarb is distinguished by its pink to pale red stalks and yellow-green leaves, whereas field-grown plants (which are more pronounced in flavor) have cherry red stalks and green leaves. Hothouse rhubarb is available in some regions almost year-round. The field-grown plant can usually be found from late winter to early summer, with a peak from April to June. Choose crisp stalks that are brightly hued. The leaves should be fresh-looking and blemish-free. Highly perishable, fresh rhubarb should be refrigerated, tightly wrapped in a plastic bag, for up to 3 days. Wash and remove leaves just before using. Because of its intense tartness, rhubarb is usually combined with a considerable amount of sugar. It makes delicious sauces, jams and desserts and in some regions is also known as *pieplant* because of its popularity for that purpose. In America, a traditional flavor combination is rhubarb and strawberries; in Britain, rhubarb and ginger. Rhubarb contains a fair amount of vitamin A.

rhubarb chard *see* CHARD

rib 1. The meat cut (beef, lamb or veal) from between the SHORT LOIN and the CHUCK. Chops, steaks and roasts (depending on the animal) are cut from the rib section, which is very tender. *See also* RIB ROAST; RIB STEAK. 2. A single stalk of a celery bunch, though some cooks refer to the entire bunch as a rib. In general, the words *rib* and *stalk* describe the same thing.

ribbon A cooking term describing the texture of an egg-and-sugar mixture that has been beaten until pale and extremely thick. When the beater or whisk is lifted, the batter falls slowly back onto the surface of the mixture, forming a ribbonlike pattern which, after a few seconds, sinks back into the batter.

rib-eye steak *see* RIB STEAK

Ribier grape [RIHB-yuhr] One of America's bestselling grapes, the Ribier is large, round and has a tough blue-black skin. The flesh is juicy, sweet and contains a few seeds. Ribier grapes are in season from July to February. *See also* GRAPE.

rib roast A beef roast from the rib section between the SHORT LOIN and the CHUCK. The three most popular styles are standing rib roast, rolled rib roast and rib-eye roast. The **standing rib roast** usually includes at least three ribs (less than that is really just a very thick steak). It's roasted standing upright, resting on its rack of ribs, thereby allowing the top layer of fat to melt and self-baste the meat. A **rolled rib roast** has had the bones removed before being rolled and tied into a cylinder. Removing the bones also slightly diminishes the flavor of this roast. The boneless **rib-eye roast** is the center, most desirable and tender portion of the rib section. Therefore, it's also the most expensive. Many rib roasts are often inappropriately labeled PRIME RIB. In fact, they can't be called prime rib unless the cut actually comes from USDA Prime beef—rarely found in meat markets today. *See also* BEEF; Beef Chart, page 573.

rib steak This tender, flavorful beef steak is a boneless cut from the rib section (between the SHORT LOIN and the CHUCK). If the bones are removed the result is the extremely tender *rib-eye steak*. Both should be quickly cooked by grilling, broiling or frying. *See also* BEEF; RIB ROAST; Beef Chart, page 573.

rice *n.* This ancient and venerable grain has been cultivated since at least 5000 B.C., and archaeological explorations in China have uncovered sealed pots of rice that are almost 8,000 years old. Today, rice is a staple for almost half the world's population—particularly in parts of China, India, Indonesia, Japan and Southeast Asia. The 7,000-plus varieties of rice are grown in one of two ways. *Aquatic rice* (paddy-grown) is cultivated in flooded fields. The lower-yielding, lower-quality *hill-grown rice* can be grown on almost any tropical or subtropical terrain. The major rice-growing states in the U.S. are Arkansas, California, Louisiana, Mississippi, Missouri and Texas. Rice is commercially classified by its size—long-, medium- or short-grain. The length of **long-grain rice** is four to five times that of its width. There are both white and brown varieties of long-grain rice which, when cooked, produce light, dry grains that separate easily. One of the more exotic varieties in the long-grain category is the perfumy East Indian BASMATI RICE. **Short-grain rice** has fat, almost round grains that have a higher starch content than either the long- or medium-grain varieties. When cooked, it tends to be quite moist and viscous, causing the grains to stick together. This variety (also called *pearl rice* and *glutinous rice*, though it's gluten-free) is preferred in the Orient because it's easy to handle with chopsticks. Italian ARBORIO RICE—used to make creamy RISOTTOS—and the Japanese MOCHI are also varieties of short-grain rice. **Medium-grain rice**, as could be expected from its name, has a size and character between the other two. It's shorter and moister than long-grain and generally not as starchy as short-grain. Though fairly fluffy right after being cooked, medium-grain rice begins to clump once it starts to cool. Rice can be further divided into two other broad categories—brown and white. **Brown rice** is the entire grain with only the inedible outer husk removed. The nutritious, high-fiber bran coating gives it a light tan color, nutlike flavor and chewy texture. The presence of the bran means that brown rice is subject to rancidity, which limits its shelf life to only about 6 months. It also takes slightly longer to cook (about 30 minutes total) than regular white long-grain rice. There is a *quick brown rice* (which has been partially cooked, then dehydrated) that cooks in only about 15 minutes. **White rice** has had the husk, bran and germ removed. Regular white rice is sometimes referred to as *polished rice*. For *converted* or *parboiled white rice*, the unhulled grain has been soaked, pressure-steamed and dried before milling. This treatment gelatinizes the starch in the grain (for fluffy, separated cooked rice) and infuses some of the nutrients of the bran and germ into the kernel's heart. Converted rice has a pale beige cast and takes slightly longer to cook than regular white rice. *Talc-coated rice* is white rice that has a coating of talc and glucose, which gives it a glossy appearance. The coating acts as a preservative and the practice was once widely used to protect exported rice during long sea voyages. Today coated rice (which is clearly labeled as such) is available only in a few ethnic markets, usually those specializing in South American foods. It must be thoroughly rinsed before being cooked, as there is a chance that the talc can be contaminated with asbestos. **Instant** or **quick white rice** has been fully or partially cooked before being dehydrated and packaged. It takes only a few minutes to prepare but delivers lackluster results in both flavor and texture. **Rice bran,** the grain's outer layer, is high in soluble fiber and research indicates that, like oat bran, it's effective in lowering cholesterol. Rice should be stored in an airtight container in a cool, dark, dry place. White rice can be stored this way almost indefinitely, brown rice up to 6 months. The life of the latter can be extended considerably by refrigeration. Rice can be prepared in a multitude of ways, the method greatly depending on the type of rice. Consult a general cookbook for cooking directions. Rice, which is cholesterol- and gluten-free, is low in sodium, contains only a trace of fat and is an excellent source of complex carbohydrates. Enriched or converted rice contains calcium, iron and many B-complex vitamins, with brown rice being slightly richer in all the nutrients. *See also* RICE FLOUR; WILD RICE. **rice** *v.* To push cooked food through a perforated kitchen utensil called a RICER. The result is food that looks vaguely ricelike.

rice bran *see* RICE

rice flour   Regular rice flour is a fine, powdery flour made from regular white rice. It's used mainly for baked goods. **Glutinous** or **sweet rice flour** (such as the Japanese MOCHI) is made from high-starch short-grain rice. It's widely used in Asian cooking to thicken sauces and for some desserts.

rice-flour noodles   These extremely thin Chinese noodles resemble long, translucent white hairs. When deep-fried, they explode dramatically into a tangle of airy, crunchy strands that are a traditional ingredient in Chinese chicken salad. Rice-flour noodles can also be presoaked and used in soups and STIR FRIES. The term *rice sticks* is generally applied to rice-flour noodles that are about ¼-inch wide. Rice-flour noodles can be found in Asian markets and some supermarkets. They're usually sold in coiled nests packaged in cellophane. *See also* ASIAN NOODLES.

rice paper An edible, translucent paper made from a dough of water combined with the pith of an Asian shrub called, appropriately enough, the rice-paper plant (or rice-paper tree). RICE FLOUR is sometimes also used. The paper comes in various sizes—small to large, round or square. Rice paper can be used to wrap foods to be eaten as is or deep-fried. It's also useful as a baking-sheet liner on which delicate cookies are baked. After baking, the cookies may be removed from the sheet without damage and the flavorless rice paper (which sticks to the cookies' bottom) eaten along with the confection. Rice paper can be found in oriental markets and some supermarkets.

ricer Also called a *potato ricer*, this kitchen utensil resembles a large garlic press. Cooked food such as potatoes, carrots or turnips is placed in the container. A lever-operated plunger is pushed down into the food, forcing it out through numerous tiny holes in the bottom of the container. The result is food that (vaguely) resembles grains of rice. Ricers come in a variety of shapes, the most common being a 3- to 4-inch round basket or a V-shaped bucket. They're generally made of chromed steel or cast aluminum and can be found in specialty cookware shops.

rice sticks *see* RICE-FLOUR NOODLES

rice vinegar There are Japanese as well as Chinese rice vinegars, both made from fermented rice, and both slightly milder than most Western vinegars. Chinese rice vinegar comes in three types: white (clear or pale amber), used mainly in SWEET-AND-SOUR dishes; red, a popular accompaniment for boiled or steamed crab; and black, used mainly as a table CONDIMENT. The almost colorless Japanese rice vinegar is used in a variety of Japanese preparations, including SUSHI rice and *sunomono* (vinegared salads). Rice vinegar can be found in Asian markets and some supermarkets.

rice wine *see* MIRIN

rickey [RIHK-ee] A drink made with lime (sometimes lemon) juice, soda water and liquor, usually gin or whiskey. If sugar is added, the drink becomes a Tom COLLINS. A non-alcoholic rickey always has sugar or sugar syrup added to it.

ricotta cheese [rih-KAHT-uh] This rich fresh cheese is slightly grainy but smoother than cottage cheese. It's white, moist and has a slightly sweet flavor. Most Italian ricottas are made from the WHEY drained off while making cheeses such as MOZZARELLA and PROVOLONE. Technically, this type of ricotta is not really cheese because it's made from a cheese by-product. In the U.S., ricottas are usually made with a combination of whey and whole or skim milk. The word *ricotta* means "recooked," and is derived from the fact that the cheese is made by heating the whey from another cooked cheese. Ricotta is a popular ingredient in many Italian savory preparations like LASAGNA and MANICOTTI, as well as desserts like CASSATA and CHEESECAKE. *See also* CHEESE.

Riesling   *see* JOHANNISBERG RIESLING

rigatoni   [rihg-ah-TOH-nee] Short, grooved tubes of MACARONI. *See also* PASTA.

rijsttafel   [RRY-stah-fuhl; RIHS-tah-fuhl] Dutch for "rice table," rijsttafel is the Dutch version of an Indonesian meal consisting of hot rice accompanied by a profusion of small, well-seasoned side dishes such as steamed or fried seafoods and meats, vegetables, fruits, sauces, CONDIMENTS, etc. The Dutch adopted this style of dining during their occupation of Indonesia in the 18th and 19th centuries.

rillettes   [rih-LEHTS; ree-YEHT] Meat, usually pork but also rabbit, goose, poultry, fish, etc., that is slowly cooked in seasoned fat and then pounded or pulverized (along with some of the fat) into a paste. This mixture is then packed in small pots, RAMEKINS or other containers and covered with a thin layer of fat. Rillettes can be stored for several weeks in the refrigerator providing the fatty seal is not broken. This mixture, resembling a smooth PÂTÉ, is served cold, usually as an appetizer spread on toast or bread.

ripe olive   *see* OLIVE

ris   [REE] French for "SWEETBREADS." *Ris de veau* are from a calf, *ris d'agneau* from a lamb.

risotto   [rih-SAW-toh; ree-ZAW-toh] An Italian rice specialty made by stirring hot stock into a mixture of rice (and often chopped onions) that has been sautéed in butter. The stock is added ½ cup at a time and the mixture is stirred continually while it cooks until all the liquid is absorbed before more stock is added. This labor-intensive technique results in rice that is delectably creamy while the grains remain separate and firm. Risottos can be flavored variously with ingredients such as chicken, shellfish, sausage, vegetables, cheese, white wine and herbs. The famous

risotto Milanese is scented with SAFFRON. The use of Italian ARBORIO RICE is traditional in the preparation of risotto.

rissole *n.* [rih-SOHL; ree-SOHL] 1. Sweet- or savory-filled pastry (often shaped like a turnover) that is fried or baked and served as an appetizer, side dish or dessert (depending on the size and filling). 2. Small, partially cooked potato balls that are browned in butter until crisp. **rissolé** *adj.* [RIHS-uh-lee; rihs-uh-LAY; ree-saw-LAY] Food that has been fried until crisp and brown.

riz à l'impératrice [REE ahl-ahn-pair-ah-TREES] 1. French for "rice as the empress likes it," *riz à l'impératrice* is a very rich rice pudding made with vanilla custard, whipped cream and crystallized fruit (which is often soaked in KIRSCH). 2. The term *à l'impératrice* is used to describe a variety of rich sweet or savory dishes.

roast *n.* 1. A piece of meat—such as a RIB ROAST—that's large enough to serve more than one person. Such a meat cut is usually cooked by the roasting method. 2. Food, usually meat, that has been prepared by roasting. **roast** *v.* To oven-cook food in an uncovered pan, a method that usually produces a well-browned exterior and ideally a moist interior. Roasting requires reasonably tender pieces of meat or poultry. Tougher pieces of meat need moist cooking methods such as braising.

roaster *see* CHICKEN

roasting rack A slightly raised rack—usually made of chrome or stainless steel—that elevates meat above the pan in which it's roasting. This prevents the meat from cooking in any drippings and allows adequate air circulation for even cooking and browning. Roasting racks can be flat, V-shaped or adjustable so they can be used either way.

Rob Roy A COCKTAIL made with SCOTCH, sweet VERMOUTH and BITTERS. It's sometimes called a *Scotch Manhattan* because it substitutes scotch for the bourbon used in the standard MANHATTAN recipe.

rocambole [ROK-uhm-bohl] Also called *sand leek* and *giant garlic*, rocambole has LEEKlike bulbs that taste like mild garlic. It grows wild (and is sometimes cultivated) throughout Europe and may be used in any way suitable for garlic. Rocambole is rarely commercially available in the U.S.

rock and rye An American rye whiskey–based LIQUEUR flavored with lemon or orange essence and distinguished by a chunk of ROCK CANDY in the bottom of each bottle.

rock bass *see* SUNFISH

rock bun Also called *rock cake*, this spicy British cross between a cookie and a small cake is full of coarsely chopped dried fruit. It's baked in small mounds which, after baking, take on a rocklike appearance.

rock candy A simple hard candy made by allowing a concentrated SUGAR SYRUP to evaporate slowly (sometimes for up to a week), during which time it crystallizes into chunks. The crystals can be formed around strings or small sticks (the latter can be used as stir sticks for sweet drinks). Small rock-candy crystals can be used as a fancy sweetener for tea or coffee. ROCK AND RYE liqueur has a large chunk of rock candy in the bottom of the bottle. Rock candy can be made at home or purchased in candy shops.

Rock Cornish hen; Rock Cornish game hen *see* CHICKEN

rocket *see* ARUGULA

rockfish 1. With over 50 varieties, this is the largest of the Pacific Coast fish families. The low-fat rockfish can be broken down into two broad categories—deep-bodied and elongated. The flesh of the deep-bodied varieties (such as **yellowtail, blue rockfish** and **goldeneye**) is firmer and more full-flavored than the softer, milder flesh of the elongated species (like **bocaccio, chilipepper** and **shortbelly**). Rockfish range widely in color from reddish-pink with black-tipped fins to orange-mottled brown to dark olive green with bright yellow fins. They average from 5 to 15 pounds and are sold whole or in fillets. The firm-fleshed rockfish is suitable for virtually any cooking method, whereas the softer flesh of the elongated varieties must be handled gently—preferrably baked or poached. Some rockfish are marketed as "Pacific snapper" or "Pacific red snapper," but they are not related to the true Atlantic RED SNAPPER. 2. STRIPED BASS is also referred to as "rockfish."

rock lobster *see* LOBSTER

rock salt *see* SALT

rock sugar Not as sweet as regular granulated sugar, rock sugar comes in the form of amber-colored crystals, the result of sugar cooked until it begins to color. It's used to sweeten certain Chinese teas and meat glazes. *See also* SUGAR.

rocky road A bumpy-textured candy that's a mixture of miniature marshmallows, nuts and sometimes small chunks of dark, white or milk chocolate. The candy is so named because it resembles a "rocky road" in appearance. This favorite flavor combination is also used for a number of desserts from ice cream to pies.

Rocky Mountain Oyster *see* MOUNTAIN OYSTER

roe [ROH] This delicacy falls into two categories—hard roe and soft roe. **Hard roe** is female fish eggs, while **soft roe** (also called *white roe*) is the milt of male fish. The eggs of some CRUSTACEANS (such as lobster) are referred to as CORAL. Roe can range in size from 1 to 2 ounces to over 3 pounds. If the fish is small, the roe is cooked inside the whole fish. The roe of medium and large fish is usually removed and cooked separately. Most fish roe is edible but others (including that of the great barracuda and some members of the puffer and trunkfish families) are toxic. The choicest roe comes from carp, herring, mackerel and shad, but those from cod, flounder, haddock, lumpfish, mullet, perch, pike, salmon, sturgeon and whitefish also have their fans. Salting roe transforms it into CAVIAR. Roe is marketed fresh, frozen and canned. Fresh roe is available in the spring. It should have a clean smell and look moist and firm. The extremely fragile membrane that holds the eggs or milt must be gently washed before preparation. Roe can be sautéed, poached or, providing it's medium-size or larger, broiled. It can also be used in sauces.

roll out A baking term that describes the technique of using a ROLLING PIN to flatten a dough (such as for a pie crust or cookies) into a thin, even layer.

rolled cookie A cookie that begins by rolling a rather firm dough into an even, thick to thin layer. A COOKIE CUTTER is then used to cut the rolled-out dough into various shapes before baking. *See also* COOKIE.

rolled oats *see* OATS

rolled roast *see* RIB ROAST

rolling boil *see* BOIL

rolling cookie cutter *see* COOKIE CUTTER

rolling pin Though this kitchen tool is used mainly to roll out dough, it's also handy for a number of other culinary tasks including crushing crackers and breadcrumbs, shaping cookies like TUILES and flattening meats such as chicken breasts. Rolling pins can be made of almost any material including brass, ceramic, copper, glass, marble, plastic and porcelain. The favored material, however, is hardwood. The heavier pins deliver the best results because their weight and balance produce smoother doughs with less effort. There are many rolling pin styles but by far the most popular and easiest for most people to use are the **bakers' rolling pins**. Those of higher quality are characterized by sturdy handles anchored with a steel rod running through the center of the pin and fitted with ball bearings. Many professional cooks prefer the **straight French rolling pin** (a solid piece of hardwood sans handles) because they get the "feel" of the dough under their palms. The **tapered rolling pin** is larger in the center and tapers to both ends, which allows it to be rotated during the rolling process—a feature particularly useful for rolling circles of dough. There are also "cool" rolling pins made of ceramic, marble, glass or plastic, some of which are hollow and can be filled with ice or iced water. These special-purpose pins are designed to work with delicate pastry doughs that become difficult as they warm.

rollmops   *see* HERRING

romaine lettuce [roh-MAYN] Because it's said to have originated on the Aegean island of Cos, romaine is also called *Cos lettuce*. Romaine's elongated head has dark green outer leaves that lighten to pale celadon in the center. The leaves are crisp and slightly bitter and the crunchy midrib is particularly succulent. Romaine adds crunch and flavor to mixed green salads and is the lettuce of choice for CAESAR SALADS. *See also* LETTUCE.

Romano cheese [roh-MAH-noh] There are several different styles of Romano cheese, all of which take their name from the city of Rome. Probably the best known is the sharp, tangy **pecorino Romano,** made with sheep's milk. **Caprino Romano** is an extremely sharp goat's-milk version, **vacchino Romano** a very mild cow's-milk cheese. Most U.S. Romanos are made of cow's milk or a combination of cow's milk and goat's or sheep's milk. In general, the pale yellow Romano is very firm and mostly used for grating. *See also* CHEESE; PECORINO CHEESE.

Rome Beauty apple In season from November through May, the Rome Beauty apple has a deep red skin with some yellow speckling. The off-white flesh ranges from tender to mealy, its flavor from mildly tart to sweet and bland. It holds it shape well when cooked and for that reason is often the fruit of choice for baked apples or for other cooked dishes. *See also* APPLE.

root beer Created in the mid-1800s by Philadelphia pharmacist Charles Hires, the original root beer was a (very) low-alcohol, naturally effervescent beverage made by fermenting a blend of sugar and yeast with various roots, herbs and barks such as SASAPARILLA, SASSAFRAS, wild cherry, WINTERGREEN and GINGER. Today's commercial root beer is completely non-alcoholic and generally contains sugar, caramel coloring, a combination of artificial and natural flavorings (including some of those originally used) and carbonated water for sparkle.

Roquefort cheese [ROHK-fuhrt] If not the "king of cheeses" as many proclaim, Roquefort is at least one of the oldest and best known in the world. This blue cheese has been enjoyed since Roman times and was a favorite of Charlemagne. It is made from sheep's milk that is exposed to a mold known as *Penicillium roqueforti* and aged for 3 months or more in the limestone caverns of Mount Combalou near the village of Roquefort in southwestern France. This is the only place true Roquefort can be aged. Roquefort has a creamy-rich texture and pungent, piquant, somewhat salty flavor. It has a creamy white interior with blue veins and a snowy white rind. It's sold in squat foil-wrapped cylinders. True Roquefort can be authenticated by a red sheep on the wrapper's emblem. The name "Roquefort" is protected by law from imitators of this remarkable cheese. For example, salad dressings made from blue cheese other than Roquefort cannot be labeled "Roquefort dressing." In addition to salad dressings, Roquefort can be used in a wide variety of preparations from savory breads to CANAPE spreads. Aficionados love Roquefort at the end of a meal served only with a fine SAUTERNES, PORT or other DESSERT WINE.

rose hip Though too tart to eat raw, the ripe reddish-orange fruit of the rose (especially the wild or dog rose) is often used to make jellies and jams, syrup, tea and even wine. Because they're an excellent source of vitamin C, rose hips are also dried and ground into powder (and sometimes compressed into tablets) and sold in health-food stores.

rosemary Used since 500 B.C., rosemary is native to the Mediterranean area (where it grows wild) but is now cultivated throughout Europe and the U.S. Early on, this mint-family member was used to cure ailments of the nervous system. Rosemary's silver-green, needle-shaped leaves are highly aromatic and their flavor hints of both lemon and pine. This herb is available in whole-leaf form (fresh and dried) as well as powdered. Rosemary ESSENCE is used both to flavor food and to scent cosmetics. Rosemary can be used as a seasoning in a variety of dishes including fruit salads, soups, vegetables, meat (particularly lamb), fish and egg dishes, stuffings and dressings. *See also* HERBS; Herb and Spice Chart, page 538.

rosette; rosette iron [roh-ZEHT] A small fried pastry made by dipping a rosette iron first into a thin, sweet batter, then into hot deep fat. When the mixture turns crisp and golden brown, the rosette is removed from the iron and drained on paper towels. While warm, these pastries are usually sprinkled with cinnamon-sugar. A nonsweetened batter may be used to make savory rosettes, which can be sprinkled with salt and served as an appetizer. A **rosette iron** has a long metal rod with a heatproof handle at one end and various decorative shapes (such as a butterfly, heart, star or flower) that can be attached to the other end.

rose water A distillation of rose petals that has the intensely perfumy flavor and fragrance of its source. Rose water has been a popular flavoring for centuries in the cuisines of the Middle East, India and China. In addition to culinary uses, rose water is also used in religious ceremonies and as a fragrance in some cosmetics.

rosé wines [roh-ZAY] Rosé wines are usually made from red grapes but—contrary to the normal process of making red wine—the skins and stems are removed almost immediately, usually within 2 to 3 days. This brief contact with the skins and stems gives the wine its light pink (or rose) color. It also, however, is the reason that rosés lack the body and character of most red or white wines. In general, rosé wines are very light-bodied and slightly sweet. They should be served chilled and can accompany a variety of lightly flavored foods. In the U.S., the term BLUSH WINE has all but replaced that of "rosé."

Rossini [roh-SEE-nee] Dishes that include FOIE GRAS, TRUFFLES and a DEMI-GLACE sauce—either as an integral part or as a garnish—are tagged with this appellation. TOURNEDOS Rossini and eggs Rossini are two popular examples. Such dishes were named after 19th-century Italian composer Gioacchino Rossini because of his passionate love of food.

rösti [RAW-stee; ROOSH-tee] In Switzerland *rösti* means "crisp and golden." The term refers to foods (today, usually shredded potatoes) sautéed on both sides until crisp and browned. **Rösti potatoes** are pressed into a flattened pancake shape while browning.

rotary beater A hand-powered kitchen utensil with two beaters connected to a gear-driven wheel with a handle—all of which is attached to a housing topped with a handle-grip. The rotary beater requires two hands to operate—one to hold the unit, the other to turn the wheel. As the gear-driven wheel is turned, the two beaters rotate, providing aeration that can whip cream, eggs, batters, etc. The best roatary beaters have rounded, stainless-steel hoops and nylon gears. Others are made of cast aluminum, chromed steel or plastic.

rotelle [roh-TELL-ay] Small round PASTA that resembles a wheel with spokes.

rotini [roh-TEE-nee] Short (about 1½ inches) spaghetti spirals. *See also* PASTA.

rotisserie [roh-TIHS-uh-ree] 1. A unit that cooks food while it slowly rotates. A rotisserie contains a spit fitted with a pair of prongs that slide along its length. Food (usually meat) is impaled on the spit and the prongs (which are inserted on each side of the food) are screwed tightly into place to hold the food securely. Modern rotisseries have a motor that automatically turns the shaft, while their predecessors relied on manpower. Many ovens and outdoor barbecue units have built-in electric rotisseries. This type of cooking allows heat to circulate evenly around the food while it self-bastes with its own juices. 2. A restaurant or meat shop that specializes in roasted meats. 3. The area where roasting is done (usually in a large restaurant kitchen), often by specially trained chefs (*rôtisseurs*).

rouille [roo-EE; roo-YUH] Literally French for "rust," culinarily rouille is a fiery-flavored, rust-colored sauce of hot chilies, garlic, fresh breadcrumbs and olive oil pounded into a paste and often mixed with fish stock. It's served as a garnish with fish and fish stews such as BOUILLABAISSE.

roulade [roo-LAHD] The French term for a thin slice of meat rolled around a filling such as mushrooms, breadcrumbs, cheese or a mixture of vegetables and cheese or meat. The rolled package is usually secured with string or a wooden pick. A roulade is browned before being baked or braised in wine or stock. Also referred to as *paupiette, bird* and, in Italy, *braciola.*

round This section of the hind leg of beef extends from the rump to the ankle. Since the leg has been toughened by exercise, the round is less tender than some cuts. There are six major sections into which the round can be divided: the rump; the four main muscles (top round, sirloin tip, bottom round and eye of round); and the heel. The **rump** is a triangular cut taken from the upper part of the round. This flavorful section is generally cut into *rump steaks* or two or three roasts that, when boned and rolled, are referred to as *rump roasts.* Those with the bone in are called *standing rump roasts.* Pieces from the rump section are best cooked by moist-heat methods. The **top round,** which lies on the inside of the leg, is the most tender of the four muscles in the round. Thick top-round cuts are often called *butterball steak* or *London broil,* whereas thin cuts are referred to simply as *top round steak.* The boneless **sirloin tip** is also called *top sirloin, triangle* and *loin tip.* The better grades can be oven-roasted; otherwise moist-heat methods should be used. The **bottom round** can vary greatly in tenderness from one end of the cut to the other. It's usually cut into steaks (which are often CUBED) or the *bottom round roast.* The well-flavored **eye of the round** is the least tender muscle, although many mistakenly think otherwise because it looks like the TENDERLOIN. Both steaks and roasts from this cut require slow, moist-heat cooking. A cut that includes all four of these muscles is usually called *round steak* and those cut from the top (and which are of the best grades) can be cooked with dry heat. Near the bottom of the round is the toughest cut, the **heel of the round**. It's generally used for ground meat but can sometimes be found as a roast. *See also* BEEF; Beef Chart, page 573.

roux [ROO] A mixture of flour and fat that, after being slowly cooked over low heat, is used to thicken mixtures such as soups and sauces. There are three classic roux—white, blond and brown. The color and flavor is determined by the length of time the mixture is cooked. Both **white roux** and **blond roux** are made with butter. The former is cooked just until it begins to turn beige and the latter until pale golden. Both are used to thicken cream and white sauces and light soups. The fuller-flavored **brown roux** can be made with butter, drippings or pork or beef fat. It's cooked to a deep golden brown and used for rich, dark soups and sauces. CAJUN and CREOLE dishes use a lard-based roux, which is cooked (sometimes for almost an hour) until a beautiful mahogany brown. This dark nutty-flavored base is indispensable for specialties like GUMBO.

Royal Ann cherry Big and heart-shaped, this firm and juicy sweet cherry has a golden-pink skin and flesh. The Royal Ann (also called *Napoleon*) is used mainly for commercial canning and to make MARASCHINO CHERRIES. It's delicious for out-of-hand eating as well. *See also* CHERRY.

royal icing An icing made of confectioners' sugar, egg whites and a few drops of lemon juice. It hardens when dry, making it a favorite for durable decorations (such as flowers and leaves) and ornamental writing. Royal icing is often tinted with FOOD COLORING.

ruby port; ruby Porto *see* PORT

rucola; rugala *see* ARUGULA

rugalach [RUHG-uh-luhkh] A Hanukkah tradition, rugalach are bite-size crescent-shaped cookies that can have any of several fillings including raisins (or other fruit) and nuts, poppy-seed paste or jam. They're generally made with a rich cream-cheese dough.

rum A LIQUOR distilled from fermented sugar-cane juice or MOLASSES. Most of the world's rum comes from the Caribbean. Puerto Rico's **white** or **silver rum** is clear and light in body and flavor. The Puerto Rican **golden** and **amber rums** have a deeper color and a flavor to match. Dark, rich and full-bodied best describes Jamaican and Cuban rums. The sugar cane that grows along Guyana's Demerara River produces the darkest, strongest and richest of all, **Demerara rum**. This slightly sweet liquor is used in a variety of cocktails including the CUBRA LIBRE, MAI TAI, DAIQUIRI and PIÑA COLADA.

rumaki [ruh-MAH-kee] A hot HORS D'OEUVRE consisting of a strip of bacon wrapped around a slice of WATER CHESTNUT and a bite-size piece of chicken liver that has been marinated overnight in a soy sauce-ginger-garlic mixture. Sometimes the water chestnut slice is inserted into a slit made in the chicken liver. This combination is skewered with a toothpick before being grilled or broiled until the bacon is crisp.

rump roast; rump steak *see* ROUND

runner bean This climbing plant—one of Britain's favorite green beans—was brought to the British Isles in the 17th century for decorative use because of its beautiful flowers. The scarlet runner bean has a long, green bean–type pod that holds red-streaked beige, medium-size seeds. Young runners may be prepared in any way suitable for GREEN BEANS. In U.S. markets consumers are more likely to find the shelled dried beans, which can be cooked like PINTO or PINK BEANS and used in dishes such as soups and stews.

rusk [RUHSK] Known in France as *biscotte* and in Germany as ZWIEBACK, a rusk is a slice of yeast bread (thick or thin) that is baked until dry, crisp and golden brown. Some breads used for this purpose are slightly sweetened. Rusks, plain or flavored, are available in most supermarkets.

russet Burbank potato *see* POTATO

Russian dressing Actually American in origin, this salad dressing includes mayonnaise, pimiento, chili sauce (or ketchup), chives and various herbs. Some think that the "Russian" title comes from the fact that earlier versions of this dressing contained CAVIAR.

Russian tea cakes *see* MEXICAN WEDDING CAKES

rusty nail A COCKTAIL made with equal parts of SCOTCH and DRAMBUIE and served over ice.

rutabaga [ROO-tuh-bay-guh] This cabbage-family root vegetable resembles a large (3 to 5 inches in diameter) TURNIP and, in fact, is thought to be a cross between cabbage and turnip. The name comes from the Swedish *rotabagge*, which is why this vegetable is also called a *Swede* or *Swedish turnip*. Rutabagas have a thin, pale yellow skin and a slightly sweet, firm flesh of the same color. There is also a white variety but it is not generally commercially available. This root vegetable is available year-round with a peak season of July through April. Choose those that are smooth, firm and heavy for their size. Rutabagas can be refrigerated in a plastic bag for up to a month. They may be prepared in any way suitable for turnips. Nutritionally, rutabagas contain small amounts of vitamins A and C.

rye flour Milled from a hardy cereal grass, rye flour contains less GLUTEN (protein) than all-purpose or whole-wheat flour. For that reason, it won't produce a well-risen loaf of bread without the addition of some higher-protein flour. Rye flour is also heavier and darker in color than most other flours, which is why it produces dark, dense loaves. There are several different types of rye flour, the most common of which is **medium rye flour**, available in most supermarkets. **Light** or **dark rye flours**, as well as **pumpernickel flour** (which is dark and coarsely ground), are available in health-food stores and some supermarkets. *See also* FLOUR.

rye whiskey Though wheat and barley are often used in the MASH, law requires that this American WHISKEY be made with a minimum of 51 percent rye. Rye has a flavor that is similar to a smooth, rich BOURBON. **Straight ryes** are those from a single distiller, while **blended ryes** are a combination of several straight ryes. *See also* LIQUOR.

abayon [sah-bah-YAW*N*] *see* ZABAGLIONE

sablé [SAH-blay] This classic French cookie is said to hail from Caen, in the province of Normandy. The French word *sable* means "sand," and the cookies are so named because of their delicate, crumbly texture. Sablés can be variously flavored with additions such as almonds or lemon or orange zest. They can also be dipped in chocolate or two cookies may be sandwiched together with jam.

sablefish [SAY-bl-fihsh] Also known as *Alaska cod, black cod* and *butterfish*, the sablefish is actually neither a COD nor a BUTTERFISH. It ranges in size from 1 to 10 pounds and is found in deep waters off the Pacific Northwest coast. The white flesh of the sablefish is soft-textured and mild-flavored. Its high fat content makes it an excellent fish for smoking and it's commonly marketed as *smoked black cod*. Sablefish is available year-round whole, as well as in fillets and steaks. It can be prepared in a variety of ways including baking, broiling or frying. *See also* FISH.

Sabra liqueur [SAH-bruh] A chocolate-orange-flavored LIQUEUR made in Israel.

saccharin [SAK-uh-rihn] Containing only ⅛ calorie per teaspoon, this sugar substitute is said to be 300 to 500 times sweeter than sugar. Saccharin was discovered by accident in the late 1800s by scientists at Johns Hopkins University. Though it's widely used to sweeten a multitude of commercial foods and beverages—as well in the home—some find that it has a decidedly bitter aftertaste. This unpleasant effect is particularly noticeable when a food sweetened with saccharin is heated. Saccharin is available in both powdered and liquid forms in supermarkets. It has been the center of controversy during the last few decades because of its reported possible carcinogenic effects. Because the issue is still being researched, the FDA requires that saccharin products carry a warning label to that effect. *See also* ASPARTAME.

Sachertorte; Sacher torte [SAH-kuhr-tohrt] An extremely rich Viennese classic made with layers (usually three) of chocolate cake filled with apricot jam and enrobed in a creamy-rich chocolate glaze. Sachertorte is traditionally served with billows of whipped cream. It was created in 1832 by Franz Sacher, of the famous family of Viennese hoteliers and restaurateurs.

saddle A cut of meat (most often lamb, mutton, veal or venison) that is the unseparated LOIN (from rib to leg) from both sides of the animal. The saddle is a very tender cut and makes an elegant (but expensive) roast.

safflower oil This flavorless, colorless oil is expressed from the seeds of the safflower, also called *saffron thistle* or *bastard saffron*. It contains more POLYUNSATURATES than any other oil, has a high SMOKE POINT (which makes it good for deep-frying) and is favored for salad dressings because it doesn't solidify when chilled. Safflower oil isn't as nutritionally beneficial as some of the other oils, however, because it lacks vitamin E. *See also* FATS AND OILS.

saffron [SAF-ruhn] It's no wonder that saffron—the yellow-orange stigmas from a small purple crocus (*Crocus sativus*)—is the world's most expensive spice. Each flower provides only three stigmas, which must be carefully hand-picked and then dried—an extremely labor-intensive process. It takes over 14,000 of these tiny stigmas for each ounce of saffron. Thousands of years ago saffron was used not only to flavor food and beverages but to make medicines and to dye cloth and body oils a deep yellow. Today this pungent, aromatic spice is primarily used to flavor and tint food. Fortunately (because it's so pricey), a little saffron goes a long way. It's integral to hundreds of dishes like BOUILLABAISSE, RISOTTO Milanese and PAELLA, and flavors many European baked goods. Saffron is marketed in both powdered form and in threads (the whole stigmas). Powdered saffron loses its flavor more readily and can be easily adulterated with imitations. The threads should be crushed just before using. Store saffron airtight in a cool, dark place for up to 6 months. *See also* SPICES; Herb and Spice Chart, page 538.

saganaki [sah-gah-NAH-kee] A popular Greek appetizer in which ½-inch-thick slices of KASSERI CHEESE are fried in butter or olive oil. Saganaki is sprinkled with lemon juice (and sometimes fresh oregano) and served with PITA BREAD. Some Greek restaurants have a dramatic form of presentation: the cheese is first soaked in alcohol (such as BRANDY), then flambéed before being doused with lemon juice. Saganaki is generally served as an appetizer or first course.

sage [SAYJ] This native Mediterranean herb has been enjoyed for centuries for both its culinary and medicinal uses. The name comes from a derivative of the Latin *salvus*, meaning "safe," a reference to the herb's believed healing powers. The narrow, oval, gray-green leaves of this pungent herb are slightly bitter and have a musty mint taste and aroma. Small bunches of fresh sage are available year-round in many supermarkets. Choose sage by its fresh color and aroma. Refrigerate wrapped in a paper towel and sealed in a plastic bag for up to 4 days. Dried sage comes whole, rubbed (crumbled) and ground. It should be stored in a cool, dark place for no more than 6 months. Sage is commonly used in dishes containing pork, cheese and beans, and in poultry and game stuffings. Sausage makers also frequently use it to flavor their products. *See also* HERBS; Herb and Spice Chart, page 538.

sago [SAY-goh] A starch extracted from the sago (and other tropical) palms that is processed into flour, meal and pearl sago, which is similar to tapioca. South Pacific cooks frequently use sago for baking and for thickening soups, puddings and other desserts. In the Orient and in India it's used as a flour and in the U.S. it's occasionally used as a thickener.

Saint-Germain [san-zhehr-MAHN] A French term describing various dishes garnished or made with fresh green peas or pea puree. **Potage Saint-Germain** is a thick pea soup enriched with butter.

Saint-Honoré; gâteau Saint-Honoré [san-toh-naw-RAY] A traditional French cake named for Saint Honoré, the patron saint of pastry bakers. It consists of a base of PÂTÉ BRISÉE topped with a ring of CREAM PUFFS which are dipped in caramel prior to being positioned on the base. This caramel coating "glues" the puffs together. The center of the ring is then filled with Saint-Honoré cream—CRÈME PÂTISSIÈRE lightened with beaten egg whites or whipped cream.

Saint John's bread *see* CAROB

sake [SAH-kee] This Japanese wine, the national alcoholic drink of Japan, is traditionally served warm in small porcelain cups. The yellowish, slightly sweet sake is made from fermented rice and doesn't require aging. It has a relatively low alcohol content of 12 to 15 percent. Sake is used in Japanese cooking, particularly in sauces and marinades. Once opened, it will keep tightly sealed in the refrigerator for at least 3 weeks.

salad dressing *see* MAYONNAISE

salad spinner A kitchen utensil that uses centrifugal force to dry freshly washed salad greens, herbs, etc. Wet ingredients are placed in an inner basket. The basket is set into an outer container fitted with a lid with a gear-operated handle or pull-cord. As the handle is turned (or cord pulled), the perforated inner container spins rapidly, forcing moisture off the food out through the perforations and into the outer container.

salamander [SAL-uh-man-duhr] 1. A kitchen tool used to brown the top of foods. It consists of a long iron rod with a cast-iron disc at one end and a wooden handle at the other. The disc is heated over a burner until red-hot before being passed closely over food. In addition to quickly browning foods, salamanders are used for dishes (such as CRÈME BRÛLÉE) which require that a surface layer of sugar be caramelized quickly so that the custard below remains cold. They can be purchased in cookware shops and the kitchenware section of most department stores. 2. A small broiler unit in a professional oven that quickly browns the tops of dishes.

salami [suh-LAH-mee] The name applied to a family of sausages similar to CERVELATS. Both styles are uncooked but safe to eat without heating because they've been preserved by curing. Salamis, however, tend to be more boldly seasoned (particularly with garlic), coarser, drier and, unlike cervelats, rarely smoked. Salamis are usually air-dried and vary in size, shape, seasoning and curing process. Though they're usually made from a mixture of beef and pork, the KOSHER versions are strictly beef. Among the best-known Italian salamis are **Genoa** (rich, fatty and studded with white peppercorns) and **cotto** (studded with black peppercorns). The non-pork **kosher salamis** are cooked and semi-soft. Italian-American favorites include Alesandri and Alpino. FRIZZES and PEPPERONI are also salami-type sausages. With the casing uncut, whole dry salamis will keep for several years. Once cut, they should be tightly wrapped and refrigerated for up to 2 weeks. Salami is best served at room temperature and can be eaten as a snack or as part of an ANTIPASTO platter, or chopped and used in dishes such as soups and salads. *For information on specific salamis, see individual listings. See also* SAUSAGE.

salicornia *see* SAMPHIRE

Salisbury steak [SAWLZ-beh-ree] Essentially a ground-beef patty that has been flavored with minced onion and seasonings before being fried or broiled. It was named after a 19th-century English physician, Dr. J. H. Salisbury, who recommended that his patients eat plenty of beef for all manner of ailments. Salisbury steak is often served with gravy made from pan drippings.

Sally Lunn This rich, slightly sweet yeast bread was brought to the Colonies from England and subsequently became a favorite in the South. There are several tales as to its origin, the most popular being that Sally Lunn, an 18th-century lass from Bath, England, created this delicate cakelike bread in her tiny bakery for her prominent patrons' tea parties. Those original Sally Lunns were baked as large buns, split horizontally and slathered with thick CLOTTED CREAM.

salmon [SAM-uhn] Salmon was an important food to many early American Indians whose superstitions prevented certain tribe members from handling or eating the fish lest they anger its spirit and cause it to leave their waters forever. Salmon are anadromous, meaning that they migrate from their saltwater habitat to spawn in fresh water. Over the years, some salmon have become landlocked in freshwater lakes. In general, the flesh of those salmon is less flavorful than that of their sea-running relatives. There are several varieties of North American salmon. All but one are found off the Pacific coast, and about 90 percent come from Alaskan waters. Among the best Pacific salmon is the superior **Chinook** or **king salmon**, which can reach up to 120 pounds. The color of its high-fat, soft-textured flesh ranges from off-white to bright red. Other high-fat salmon include the **coho** or **silver salmon,** with its firm-textured, pink to red-orange flesh, and the **sockeye** or **red salmon** (highly prized for canning) with its firm, deep red flesh. Not as fatty as the preceding species are the **pink** or **humpback salmon**—the smallest, most delicately flavored of the Pacific varieties—and the **chum** or **dog salmon**, which is distinguished by having the lightest color and lowest fat content. Pacific salmon are in season from spring through fall. The population of the once-abundant **Atlantic salmon** has diminished greatly over the years because of industrial pollution of both North American and European tributaries. The Atlantic salmon has a high-fat flesh that's pink and succulent. Canada provides most of the Atlantic salmon, which is in season from summer to early winter. Depending on the variety, salmon is sold whole or in fillets or steaks. It's also available canned and as SMOKED SALMON, which comes in a variety of styles. The increasingly popular bright red salmon roe (see CAVIAR) is readily available in most supermarkets. Fresh salmon is integral to some of the world's most famous dishes, including GRAVLAX and COULIBIAC. It can be served as a main course, in salads, as a spread or dip . . . its uses are myriad. All salmon are high in protein as well as a rich source of vitamin A, the B-group vitamins and OMEGA-3 OILS. *See also* FISH.

salmonella [sal-muh-NEHL-uh] A strain of bacteria that can enter the human system through contaminated water or food such as meat or poultry, and eggs with cracked shells. Other foods can be contaminated by touching salmonella-carrying foods or unwashed surfaces (like wooden cutting boards) that have had contact with them. The presence of salmonella is difficult to detect because it gives no obvious warnings (such as an off smell or taste). The bacteria can cause stomach pain, nausea, vomiting, diarrhea, headache, fever and chills. It can attack in as little time as 6 to 7 hours or take as long as 3 days. It seldom causes death and can be cured with antibiotics.

salpicon [sal-pee-KOM] A French term describing cooked, diced ingredients bound with a sauce (for savory ingredients), or syrup or cream (for fruit mixtures) and used for fillings or garnishes. Fish, meat, poultry, mushrooms, truffles and vegetables are often included in savory salpicons, which are used to make CANAPÉS, to fill BARQUETTES or CROUSTADES, to make CROQUETTES, as a garnish, etc.

salsa [SAHL-sah] The Mexican word for "sauce," which can signify cooked or fresh mixtures.

salsify [SAL-sih-fee] This root vegetable is also known as *oyster plant* because its taste resembles a delicately flavored oyster. The parsnip-shaped salsify can reach up to 12 inches in length and 2½ inches in diameter. The most commonly found salsify has a white-fleshed root with grayish skin, though there are varieties with a pale golden skin, as well as one with a black skin (also called *scorzonera*). Though salsify is more popular in Europe than in the U.S., it can be found here from June through February, usually in Spanish, Italian and Greek markets. Choose well-formed roots that are heavy for their size and not too gnarled. Refrigerate, wrapped in a plastic bag, up to a week. Salsify is generally eaten plain as a vegetable, or used in savory pies and soups.

salt Today salt is inexpensive and universally available, but that wasn't always the case. Because of its importance in food preservation and the fact that the human body requires it (for the regulation of fluid balance), salt has been an extremely valuable commodity throughout the ages. It was even once used as a method of exchange—Roman soldiers received a salt allowance as part of their pay. Salt was valued by the ancient Hebrews and Greeks, throughout the Middle Ages and well into the 19th century when it began to become more plentiful and therefore reasonable in price. Salt (sodium chloride) comes either from salt mines or from the sea. Most of today's salt is mined and comes from large deposits left by dried salt lakes throughout the world. **Table salt,** a fine-grained refined salt with additives that make it free-flowing, is mainly used in cooking and as a table condiment. **Iodized salt** is table salt with added iodine (sodium iodide)—particularly important in areas that lack natural iodine, an important preventative for hypothyroidism. **Kosher salt** is an additive-free coarse-grained salt. It's used in the preparation of meat by religious Jews, as well as by gourmet cooks who prefer its texture and flavor. **Sea salt** is the type used down through the ages and is the result of the evaporation of sea water—the more costly of the two processes. It comes in fine-grained or larger crystals. **Rock salt** has a grayish cast because it's not as refined as other salts, which means it retains more minerals and harmless impurities. It comes in chunky crystals and is used predominantly as a bed on which to serve baked oysters and clams and to combine with ice to make ice cream in crank-style ice-cream makers. **Pickling salt** is a fine-grained salt used to make brines for pickles, sauerkraut, etc. It contains no additives, which would cloud the brine. **Seasoned salt** is regular salt combined with other flavoring ingredients, examples being onion salt, garlic salt and celery salt. **Salt substitutes,** frequently used by those on low-salt diets, are products containing little or no sodium.

salt cod *see* COD

saltimbocca [sahl-tihm-BOH-kuh] Literally translated, this Italian term means "jump mouth." It refers to a Roman specialty made of finely sliced veal sprinkled with sage and topped with a thin slice of PROSCIUTTO. It's sautéed in butter, then braised in white wine. Sometimes the meat layers are rolled and secured with picks before being cooked.

salt pork So named because it is salt-cured, this is a layer of fat (usually with some streaks of lean) that is cut from the pig's belly and sides. Salt pork is often confused with FATBACK, which is unsalted. It varies in degree of saltiness and often must be BLANCHED to extract excess salt before being used. It's similar to bacon but much fattier and unsmoked. Salt pork can be refrigerated tightly wrapped for up to a month. It's used primarily as a flavoring and is an important ingredient in many dishes throughout New England and the South.

salt-rising bread A bread popular in the 1800s, before yeast LEAVENING was readily available. It relies on a FERMENTED mixture of warm milk or water, flour, cornmeal, sugar and salt to give it rising power. Salt-rising bread has a very smooth texture with a tangy flavor and aroma.

sambal [SAHM-bahl] Popular throughout Indonesia, Malaysia and southern India, sambal is a multi-purpose CONDIMENT. In its most basic form it's known as *sambal bajak* (or *badjak*) and is simply a paste of hot CHILI PEPPERS, various spices and lime juice. It has a multitude of variations, however, depending on the ingredients added, which can include coconut, meat, seafood or vegetables. Sambals are usually served as an accompaniment to rice and curried dishes, either as a condiment or as a side dish. Sambal bajak, as well as some variations, can be found in Indonesian and some Chinese markets.

sambuca [sam-BOO-kuh] An anise-flavored, not-too-sweet Italian LIQUEUR which is usually served with 2 or 3 dark-roasted coffee beans floating on top.

samosa [sah-MOH-sah] In India, street pushcarts and roadside vendors sell their delicious samosas to passersby who enjoy immediate gratification from these satisfying snacks. Samosas are fried, triangular pastries that may be filled with vegetables or meat or a combination of both. In the United

States, these delicious packages are most often served as appetizers in East Indian restaurants.

samp Broken or coarsely ground HOMINY.

samphire [SAM-fy-uhr] There are two edible, very similar plants known as samphire. The first is *Crithmum maritimum* (commonly referred to as *rock samphire*), which grows along the coasts of Great Britain and northwestern Europe and is available only through costly import in the U.S. What we have in the U.S. is the second type of samphire known as *salicornia*, (also called *glasswort, marsh samphire, sea bean* and *sea pickle*). It's abundant along both the Pacific and Atlantic coasts and has spiky green leaves that are so arranged as to make the plant look somewhat like a spindly, miniature cactus, sans needles. Both the leaves and stem are crisp, aromatic and taste of a salty sea breeze. They're often pickled and can sometimes be found in jars in gourmet markets. Fresh salicornia can be found from summer through fall, though it's at its most tender during summer months. Choose crisp, brightly colored sprigs with no sign of softness. Refrigerate tightly wrapped for up to 2 weeks—though the sooner salicornia is used the better the flavor. It's best used fresh, either in salads or as a garnish. When cooked, salicornia tends to taste quite salty and fishy.

Samsoe cheese Named for the island where it originated, this national cheese of Denmark is made from cow's milk and contains about 45 percent butterfat. It's a Swiss-style cheese with a yellow interior accented with small irregular holes. Samsoe has a distinctive, mild, nutlike flavor that's suitable for almost any use from cooked dishes to salads and sandwiches. *See also* CHEESE.

sand dab A small FLATFISH found in Pacific waters from Southern California to Alaska. It has a sweet, delicately moist flesh that's quite low in fat. Sand dabs are marketed whole and usually range from 4 to 12-ounces. They can be prepared by almost any cooking method including baking, broiling, poaching and sautéing. *See also* DAB; FISH.

sangría [san-GREE-uh] The blood-red color of this beverage inspired its name, which is Spanish for "bleeding." Sangría is made with red wine, fruit juices, soda water, fruit and sometimes LIQUEURS and BRANDY or COGNAC. Sangría *blanco* (white sangría) is made with white wine. Both are served cold over ice and make a refreshing cooler on a hot summer day.

Santa Claus melon From the outside a Santa Claus melon, with its long oval shape and splotchy green-and-yellow skin, looks like a small WATERMELON. Inside, however, its yellowish-green flesh looks and tastes more like HONEYDEW MELON. This member of the MUSKMELON family grows to about a foot in length, with some specimens weighing as much as 10 pounds. Santa Claus melon, also called *Christmas melon*, was so named because its peak season is in December. Choose a melon that is slightly soft at the blossom end, heavy for its size and has a yellowish cast to the rind. Avoid those with soft spots or with damaged skin. *See also* MELON.

Santa Fe Grande chili pepper   These small, tapered, conical peppers are generally marketed when yellow, though if allowed to mature longer, they turn orange or red. Santa Fe Grandes have a slightly sweet taste and are medium-hot to hot in spiciness. They may be used in both cooked and raw dishes. *See also* CHILI PEPPERS.

sapsago cheese [sap-SAY-goh]   Also known as *Schbzieger*, sapsago is a hard cone-shaped cheese from Switzerland. It's made from skimmed cows' milk and contains less than 10 percent fat. It has a light green color and pungent herbal flavor that come from the addition of blue melilot, a special variety of clover. Sapsago is used primarily for grating and adds interest to everything from salads to pasta. *See also* CHEESE.

Saratoga chips   *see* POTATO CHIPS

sardine [sahr-DEEN]   A generic term applied broadly to any of various small, soft-boned, saltwater fish such as SPRAT and young PILCHARD and HERRING. These tiny fish are iridescent and silvery and swim in huge schools, usually near the water's surface. Fresh sardines are available on a limited basis during the summer months, usually only along the coast where they're caught. In general, their fatty flesh is best when grilled, broiled or fried. In the U.S., sardines are more commonly found salted, smoked or canned, either in oil, tomato sauce or mustard sauce. Some are packed as is, while others are skinned, boned and sold as fillets. The name is thought to have come from the young pilchards caught off the coast of Sardinia, which were one of the first fish packed in oil. *See also* FISH.

sarsaparilla [sas-puh-RIHL-uh]   Originally derived from the dried roots of tropical smilax vines, this flavor is usually associated with a carbonated drink popular in the mid-1800s. Today's sarsaparilla products—including the no-longer-popular soft drink—use artificial flavorings.

sashimi [sah-SHEE-mee]   Sliced raw fish that is served with CONDIMENTS such as shredded DAIKON radish or GINGER ROOT, WASABI and SOY SAUCE. Because it's served raw, only the freshest and highest-quality fish should be used for sashimi. Some Japanese restaurants keep the fish alive in water until just before preparing it. Special sashimi chefs are trained in slicing the fish in a particular way—depending on the variety—for the best presentation and eating enjoyment. Sashimi is usually the first course in the

Japanese meal and sashimi bars abound in the U.S. for Westerners with Eastern tastes. *See also* SUSHI.

sassafras [SAS-uh-fras] The leaves of the native North American sassafras (*albidum* or *variifolium*) tree, which are dried and used to make FILÉ POWDER and sassafras tea. The root bark is used as a flavoring agent in ROOT BEER.

saté; satay *see* SATÉ

saté; satay [sah-TAY] An Indonesian favorite consisting of small marinated cubes of meat, fish or poultry threaded on skewers and grilled or broiled. Saté is usually served with a spicy peanut sauce. It's a favorite snack food but is also often served for an appetizer and sometimes as a main dish.

satsuma orange [sat-SOO-muh] *see* MANDARIN ORANGE

saturated fat [SACH-uh-ray-tihd] *see* FATS AND OILS

sauce *n*. In the most basic terms, a sauce is a thickened, flavored liquid designed to accompany food in order to enhance and bring out its flavor. In the days before refrigeration, however, sauces were more often used to smother the taste of foods that had begun to go bad. The French are credited with refining the sophisticated art of sauce making. It was the 19th-century French chef Antonin Carême who evolved an intricate methodology by which hundreds of sauces were classified under one of five "mother sauces." Those are: ESPAGNOLE (brown stock-based), VELOUTÉ (light stock-based), BÉCHAMEL (basic white sauce), HOLLANDAISE and MAYONNAISE (EMULSIFIED sauces) and VINAIGRETTE (oil-and-vinegar combinations). *For information on specific sauces, see individual listings.* **sauce** *v*. To cover or mix a food with a sauce.

sauce boat; sauceboat *see* GRAVY BOAT

saucepan A round cooking utensil with a relatively long handle and (usually) a tight-fitting cover. The sides can be straight or flared and deep (the standard shape) or as shallow as 3 inches. Depending on the style, the versatile saucepan has a multitude of uses including making soups and sauces, boiling vegetables and other foods, braising and even sautéing (in the low-sided models). Saucepans come in sizes ranging from 1 pint to 4 quarts. They are made from various materials including aluminum, anodized aluminum, ceramic, copper, enameled (cast iron or steel), glass and stainless steel. Choose saucepans that are well balanced, with handles that allow the pan to be easily lifted.

sauce piquante *see* PIQUANTE SAUCE

saucisse [soh-SEES] French for "small sausage." *Saucisson* is a large, smoke-cured sausage. *See also* SAUSAGE.

sauerbraten [SOW-uhr-brah-tihn; ZOW-uhr-brah-tihn] German for "sour roast," sauerbraten is a German specialty made by marinating a beef roast in a SOUR-SWEET MARINADE for 2 to 3 days before browning it, then simmering the meat in the marinade for several hours. The result is an extremely tender roast and a delicious sauce. Sauerbraten is traditionally served with dumplings, boiled potatoes or noodles.

sauerkraut [SOW-uhr-krowt] Although sauerkraut—German for "sour cabbage"—is thought of as a German invention, Chinese laborers building the Great Wall of China over 2,000 years ago ate it as standard fare. Chinese sauerkraut, made from shredded cabbage fermented in RICE WINE, eventually found its way to Europe, where the Germans and Alsatians adopted it as a favorite. Today's sauerkraut is made by combining shredded cabbage, salt and sometimes spices, and allowing the mixture to ferment. It can be purchased in jars and cans in supermarkets. Fresh sauerkraut is sold in delicatessens and in plastic bags in a supermarket's refrigerated section. It should be rinsed before being used in casseroles, as a side dish and even on sandwiches like the famous REUBEN SANDWICH. Sauerkraut is an excellent source of vitamin C as well as of some of the B vitamins.

sausage [SAW-sihj] What started out simply as a means of using and preserving all of the animal trimmings has turned into the art of sausage making. Simply put, sausage is ground meat mixed with fat, salt and other seasonings, preservatives and sometimes fillers. Such a mixture is usually packed into a casing. Sausages can differ dramatically depending on their ingredients, additives, shape, curing technique, level of dryness and whether fresh or cooked. Most sausages are made with pork or pork combined with other meat, but there are also those made almost entirely from beef, veal, lamb, chicken or game animals. All contain varying amounts of fat. Seasonings can run the gamut from garlic to nutmeg. Some sausages are hot and spicy and others so mild they border on bland. Many sausages today contain additives to help preserve, thicken or color the mixture. Some sausages use fillers (such as various cereals, soybean flour and dried-milk solids) to stretch the meat. The most common shape for sausage is link, which varies in size and shape depending on the type of sausage. Other sausage (fresh) is sold in bulk, which can then be used to mix with other meats or made into patties or balls. Sausage can be fresh or CURED with salt or smoke (or both). Curing extends storage life. Some sausages are also dried; the drying times can vary from a few days to as much as 6 months. The sausage becomes firmer the longer it's dried.

Sausage can be fully cooked (ready to eat), partially cooked (enough to kill any trichinae) and uncooked, which may or may not require cooking depending on how or whether it's been cured. All these factors produce an almost endless number of sausages that can be used in a variety of ways and which appeal to a multitude of tastes. *For information on specific sausages, see individual listings.*

sauté [saw-TAY; soh-TAY] To cook food quickly in a small amount of oil in a skillet or sauté pan over direct heat. *See also* FRY.

sauté pan A wide pan with straight or slightly curved sides that are generally a little higher than those of a frying pan. It has a long handle on one side; heavy sauté pans usually have a loop handle on the other side so the pan can be easily lifted. Sauté pans are most often made of stainless steel, enameled cast iron, aluminum, anodized aluminum or copper. As the name suggests, a sauté pan efficiently browns and cooks meats and a variety of other foods.

Sauternes [soh-TERN] An elegant sweet wine from the Sauternes region of western France. It's made from SAUVIGNON BLANC or SEMILLON grapes that have been infected by a beneficial mold called BOTRYTIS CINEREA, which causes the grapes to shrivel, leaving a sugary fruit with concentrated flavors. The best Sauternes come from vines that have been hand-picked (as many as 12 separate times) to ensure that the grapes are not removed from the vines before reaching the perfect degree of ripeness required for these wines. Sauternes are most notable as DESSERT WINES but, because of their high acidity, they also make excellent partners for rich dishes like PÂTÉ, CAVIAR and FOIE GRAS. "Sauterne" without the ending "s" usually refers to an inexpensive semisweet California wine.

Sauvignon Blanc [SOH-vihn-yohn BLAH*N*GK; SOH-vee-nyaw*n* BLAH*N*GK] Widely cultivated in France and California (and also grown in Italy, Australia, New Zealand and Chile), the Sauvignon Blanc grape imparts a grassy, herbaceous flavor to wine. It's one of the main grapes used to produce the elegant dry wines from Bordeaux (**Graves**) and the Loire Valley (**Pouilly-Fumé**), as well as the seductively sweet SAUTERNES. Many wineries—particularly in California—use this grape to produce wonderful wines that are bottled under the varietal name, Sauvignon Blanc (sometimes labeled Fumé Blanc).

savarin [SAV-uh-rihn; sa-va-RA*N*] This variation on the BABA is made without raisins and baked in a large ring mold. Named after Brillat-Savarin, a famous 18th-century food writer, this rich yeast cake is soaked with rum-flavored syrup and filled with PASTRY CREAM, crème CHANTILLY or fresh fruit.

savory *n.* [SAY-vuh-ree] An herb of which there are two types, summer and winter, both closely related to the mint family. Savory has an aroma and flavor reminiscent of a cross between thyme and mint. Summer savory is slightly milder than the winter variety but both are strongly flavored and should be used with discretion. Dried savory is available year-round; fresh savory can be found in specialty produce markets. Savory adds a piquant flavor to many foods including PÂTÉS, soups, meat, fish and bean dishes. *See also* HERB; Herb and Spice Chart page 538. **savory** *adj.* A term describing food that is not sweet but rather piquant and full-flavored.

savoury [SAY-vuh-ree] A British term initially used to describe dishes that were served after dessert to cleanse and refresh the palate. Today it more often refers to tidbits served as appetizers, as well as to more substantial dishes that can be served for lunch, HIGH TEA or light supper.

savoy cabbage This mellow-flavored cabbage is considered by many to be one of the best of its genre for cooking. Savoy has a loose, full head of crinkled leaves varying from dark to pale green. *See also* CABBAGE.

Sazerac [SAZ-uh-rak] A COCKTAIL consisting of whiskey, SUGAR SYRUP and a dash each of BITTERS and PERNOD. Its name comes from the fact that it was originally served at the Sazerac Coffee House in New Orleans. The first of these potent drinks is said to have been made with Sazerac-du-Forge, a French brandy.

Sbrinz cheese [ZBRIHNZ] A hard grating cheese that originated in the central mountains of Switzerland. It's made from whole cow's milk and contains 45 to 50 percent butterfat. Aged from 2 to 3 years, Sbrinz has a dark yellow interior with a brownish-yellow rind. If aged less than this, it is called *Spalen*. The rich mellow flavor of Sbrinz makes it ideal for both cooking and as a table cheese. *See also* CHEESE.

scald *n.* [SKAWLD] A dry, tan- or brown-colored area on the skin of a fruit, such as an apple. It's usually caused by overexposure to sunlight and rarely affects the fruit quality. **scald,** *v.* 1. A cooking technique—often used to retard the souring of milk—whereby a liquid is heated to just below the boiling point. 2. To plunge food such as tomatoes or peaches into boiling water (or to pour boiling water over them), in order to loosen their skin and facilitate peeling. Also referred to as BLANCH.

scale *v.* A technique by which the scales are removed from the skin of a fish, generally using a dull knife or a special kitchen tool called a fish scaler.

scale, kitchen A kitchen device used to accurately record the weight of ingredients. Kitchen scales are particularly important for consistent baking results and for weighing meats in order to estimate cooking time. Though there are many styles of kitchen scales, there are two basic types—spring and balance scales. **Spring scales** register weight when an item is placed in the weighing pan, which then depresses a spring attached to a recording dial. A *bowl scale* is a type of spring scale which uses a bowl container rather than a shallow-sided pan. As spring scales get older the spring may weaken, thereby reducing the scale's accuracy. The more accurate **balance scales** usually have a pan for ingredients on one side and a platform for weights on the other. The ingredient's weight is determined when it balances with the weights on the other side. The main disadvantage of a balance scale is that it usually takes up more room than a spring scale. The less popular **beam balance scales** use weights that slide along two bars. The correct weight of the ingredients registers when the bars balance.

scallion [SKAL-yuhn] The name "scallion" is applied to several members of the onion family including a distinct variety called scallion, immature onions (also marketed as green or spring onions), young leeks, and sometimes the tops of young shallots. In each case the vegetable has a white base that has not fully developed into a bulb and green leaves that are long and straight. Both parts are edible. True scallions are generally identified by the fact that the sides of the base are straight, whereas the others are usually slightly curved, showing the beginnings of a bulb. All can be used interchangeably although true scallions have a milder flavor than immature onions. Scallions are available year-round but are at their peak during spring and summer. Choose those with crisp, bright green tops and a firm white base. Mid-sized scallions with long white stems are the best. Store, wrapped in a plastic bag, in the vegetable crisper section of the refrigerator for up to 3 days. Scallions can be cooked whole as a vegetable much as you would a LEEK. They can also be chopped and used in salads, soups and a multitude of other dishes for flavor.

scallop *n.* [SKAHL-uhp; SKAL-uhp] 1. This popular BIVALVE MOLLUSK (*see both listings*) has two beautiful fan-shaped shells that are often used as containers in which to serve dishes such as COQUILLES ST. JACQUES. Though the entire scallop including the ROE is edible (and relished by many Europeans), the portion most commonly found in U.S. markets is the adductor muscle that hinges the two shells. There are many scallop species but in general they're classified into two broad groups—bay scallop and sea scallop. **Bay scallops**, generally found only on the East Coast, are very tiny (the muscle is about ½ inch in diameter). They average about 100 per pound and their meat is sweeter and more succulent than that of the sea scallop. They're also more expensive because they're less plentiful. The small *calico scallops*—though they're deep-sea creatures—are often sold as bay scallops on the West Coast. They're found in the Gulf of Mexico and along the east coast of Florida. The muscle of the larger, more widely available **sea scallop** averages 1½ inches in diameter (about 30 to the pound) and is not as tender as the smaller varieties. Though slightly chewier, the meat is still sweet and moist. The color of scallops ranges from pale beige to creamy pink. If scallops are stark white, it's a sign that they've been soaked in water—a marketing ploy to increase the weight. Fresh bay scallops are available on the East Coast in the fall, whereas the peak season for fresh sea scallops is mid-fall to mid-spring. Because scallops perish quickly out of water, they're usually sold shucked. All fresh scallops should have a sweet smell and a fresh, moist sheen. They should be refrigerated immediately after purchase and used within a day or two. Frozen scallops are generally available year-round, either breaded or plain. Scallops benefit from brief cooking and are suitable for a variety of preparation methods including sautéing, grilling, broiling and poaching. They're also used in soups, stews and salads. *See also* MOLLUSK; SHELLFISH. **2.** A thin, boneless, round- or oval-shaped slice of meat or fish that is usually lightly breaded and quickly sautéed. Known as *escalope* in French. **scallop** *v.* **1.** To prepare a food (most notably potatoes) by layering slices of it with cream or a creamy sauce in a casserole. Scalloped foods are often topped with bread or cracker crumbs before being baked. **2.** To form a decorative edge in the raised rim of pie dough. Also referred to as CRIMP and FLUTE.

scaloppine [skah-luh-PEE-nee; ska-luh-PEE-nee] A term in Italian cookery describing a thin SCALLOP of meat (most often veal), usually prepared by dredging the meat in flour before sautéing it. Scaloppine dishes are generally served with a sauce based on wine or tomatoes.

scamorze cheese; scamorza; scamorzo [ska-MOHRT-zuh; ska-MOHRT-zoh] Though today this Italian cheese is usually made from whole cow's milk (sometimes mixed with sheep's or goat's milk), scamorze was originally made only from buffalo milk. It's a PASTA FILATA type of cheese that resembles a very firm, slightly salty MOZZARELLA. Scamorze, which contains about 44 percent butterfat, has a creamy white color and a mild, nutty flavor. It's sold in small ovals or gourd shapes and can sometimes be found smoked. Scamorze can be used in much the same way as mozzarella, generally as a table cheese or in cooking. *See also* CHEESE.

scampi [SKAM-pee] **1.** The Italian name for the tail portion of any of several varieties of lobsterettes, the most well known being the Dublin Bay

PRAWN. *Scampo* is the singular form of the word. 2. On U.S. restaurant menus, the term is often used to describe large SHRIMP that are split, brushed with garlic oil or butter and broiled.

schaum torte; schaumtorten [SHOWM tohrt] This classic dessert from Austria consists of baked MERINGUE layers filled with fruit and topped with whipped cream.

Schbzieger cheese [SHB-zee-guhr] *see* SAPSAGO CHEESE

schlag [SHLAHG] A German word (used mainly in Austria) for "whipped cream." *Mit schlag* means "with whipped cream," which is how Austrians love to top many foods and beverages including fruit, desserts and coffee.

schmaltz herring [SHMAHL-tz] *see* HERRING

S

schmaltz [SHMAHL-tz; SHMOHL-tz] A rendered chicken fat (sometimes flavored with onions, apples and seasonings) that is strained and used in many dishes of Middle-European Jewish origin much like butter—both in cooking and as a spread for bread.

Schmierwurst [SHMEER-wurst] *see* METTWURST

schnapps; schnaps [SHNAHPS; SHNAPS] Any of several strong, colorless alcoholic beverages made from grains or potatoes and flavored variously. **Peppermint schnapps** is one of the best known of this genre.

schnitz and knepp [SHNIHTS and NEHP] A Pennslyvania Dutch dish consisting of dried apples that are soaked in water before being cooked in that liquid with ham. At the end of the cooking time, spoonfuls of batter are added to the cooking liquid to make dumplings.

schnitzel [SHNIHT-suhl] The German word for "CUTLET," usually describing meat that is dipped in egg, breaded and fried. **Wiener Schnitzel** is a veal cutlet prepared in this manner.

scone [SKOHN; SKON] This Scottish QUICK BREAD is said to have taken its name from the Stone of Destiny (or Scone), the place where Scottish kings were once crowned. The original triangular-shaped scone was made with oats and griddle-baked. Today's versions are more often flour-based and baked in the oven. They come in various shapes including triangles, rounds, squares and diamonds. Scones can be savory or sweet and are usually eaten for breakfast or tea.

score To make shallow cuts (usually in a diamond pattern) in the surface of certain foods, such as meat or fish. This is done for several reasons: as a decoration on some foods (breads and meats); as a means of assisting flavor absorption (as with MARINATED foods); to tenderize less tender cuts of meat; and to allow excess fat to drain during cooking.

scorpion [SKOR-pee-uhn] A potent COCKTAIL consisting of light rum, brandy, orange juice, lemon juice and ORGEAT SYRUP, served over ice.

Scotch barley *see* BARLEY

Scotch broth A Scottish soup made with lamb or mutton, barley and various vegetables. Also known as *barley broth*.

Scotch egg A hard-cooked egg that is coated with sausage, dipped into beaten egg, rolled in breadcrumbs and deep-fried. Scotch eggs are halved or quartered lengthwise and may be served hot or cold, usually as an appetizer.

Scotch whisky; Scotch Made only in Scotland, this distinctive liquor uses barley for flavoring instead of the corn that's used for most American whiskies. The characteristic smoky flavor of Scotch comes from the fact that the sprouted malted barley is dried over peat fires. There are two main types of this liquor available—**blended Scotches,** which are a combination of 50 to 80 percent grain (unmalted) whisky and 20 to 50 percent MALT whisky; and **single-malt Scotches,** which are made exclusively from malt, produced by a single distillery and have a richer smoky flavor. Though blended Scotch is generally preferred in the U.S., single-malts are rapidly gaining favor. Traditionally, whiskies made in Scotland are spelled without the "e." *See also* LIQUOR; WHISKEY.

Scotch woodcock A British specialty consisting of toast spread with anchovy paste and topped with a softly scrambled mixture of eggs and cream. It can be served as a first course or entree.

scrapple The name of this Pennslvania Dutch dish is derived from the finely chopped "scraps" of cooked pork that are mixed with fine-ground cornmeal, pork broth and seasonings before being cooked into a MUSH. The mush is packed into loaf pans and cooled. Slices of the scrapple are then cut from the loaves, fried in butter and served hot, usually for breakfast or brunch.

screwdriver A mixed drink of orange juice and vodka served over ice. Its origins are unknown but the most popular tale is that it was named in the 1950s by American oil-rig workers stationed in the Middle East who opened and stirred cans of this mixture with their screwdrivers.

scrod [SKRAHD] *see* COD

scungilli [skuhn-GEE-lee] *see* WHELK

scuppernong grape [SKUHP-uhr-nawng] *see* MUSCADINE GRAPE

sea anemone [uh-NIHM-uh-nee] Any of many varieties of flowerlike marine animals of which two—the **oplet** and the **beadlet**—are used as food in France. The body cavity is cut into pieces and usually either batter-fried or used in soups.

sea bass A term used to describe any of various saltwater fish, most of which aren't members of the BASS family. BLACK SEA BASS is a true bass (as is STRIPED BASS), but **white sea bass,** which is generally marketed simply as "sea bass," is actually a member of the DRUM family. The **giant sea bass** is related to the GROUPER family and can weigh as much as 550 pounds. It's sometimes mistakenly called both *black sea bass* and *jewfish.* Sea bass can be found whole and in steaks or fillets. In general, the flesh is lean to moderately fat and is suitable for almost any method of cooking including baking, broiling, poaching and sautéing. *See also* FISH.

sea bean *see* SAMPHIRE

sea cucumber This marine animal's name comes from the fact that it has a cucumberlike shape with short tentacles at one end. It's also known as *sea slug.* Though it is seldom found fresh in the U.S., it's sold dried (usually marketed as *trepang, iriko* or *bêche-de-mer*) in oriental markets. It must be soaked in water for at least 24 hours, during which time it doubles in size and takes on a gelatinous quality. Its texture is rather rubbery and it's therefore most often used in soups.

sea devil *see* ANGLER

seafoam *see* DIVINITY

seafood Any edible fish or shellfish that comes from the sea. *For information on specific fish or shellfish, see individual listings.*

sear To brown meat quickly by subjecting it to very high heat either in a skillet, under a broiler or in a very hot oven. The object of searing is to seal in the meat's juices, which is why British cooks often use the word "seal" to mean the same thing.

sea salt *see* SALT

sea slug *see* SEA CUCUMBER

season 1. To flavor foods in order to improve their taste. *See also* SEASONING. 2. To age meat, which helps both to tenderize it and to improve its flavor. 3. To smooth out the microscopic roughness of new pots and pans, particularly cast-iron, which might cause foods to stick to the cooking surface. This is normally done by coating the cooking surface with vegetable oil, then heating the pan in a 350°F oven for about an hour. Continued use and gentle cleaning will improve the seasoning.

seasoned salt *see* SALT

seasoning Ingredients added to food to intensify or improve its flavor. Some of the most commonly used seasonings include herbs (such as oregano, rosemary and basil), spices (like cinnamon, nutmeg, cloves and allspice), condiments (such as Worcestershire sauce, soy sauce and mustard), a variety of vinegars and—the most common of all—salt and pepper. *For information on specific seasonings, see individual listings.*

sea urchin Rarely found on U.S. menus, this marine animal is considered a delicacy throughout Japan and many Mediterranean countries. There are many varieties (ranging in diameter from 1 to 10 inches) but all have a hard shell covered by prickly spines that make it look like a pincushion. Though it can be briefly cooked, sea urchin ROE is more often scooped out of the shell with a spoon and consumed raw. A popular method of serving sea urchin roe is to heap it atop a slice of French bread and sprinkle it with lemon juice.

seaweed An important food source in many oriental cultures, seaweed is a primitive sea plant belonging to the algae family with origins dating back millions of years. Japanese cuisine employs different varieties (such as KOMBU, LAVER and NORI) for many uses including soups, vegetables, tea, SUSHI and as a general seasoning. The Irish are partial to the seaweed known as CARRAGEEN, and AGAR is widely used throughout Asia. Seaweed is a rich source of iodine, an important nutrient. Many seaweeds also provide alginic acid, a jellylike substance that's used as a stabilizer and thickener in a wide variety of commercially processed foods such as ice creams, puddings, flavored milk drinks, pie fillings, soups and syrups.

sec [SEHK] This French word literally means "dry" and when used to describe still (non-bubbly) wines, indicates that the wine has little if any residual sugar left after fermentation, meaning the wine is dry (not sweet). In sparkling wines such as CHAMPAGNE, however, the word takes on quite another meaning: "sec" indicates a relatively sweet wine (DEMI-SEC even sweeter), while the driest sparkling wines are referred to as BRUT.

Seckel pear [SEHK-uhl] An 18th-century Pennsylvania farmer (for whom it was named) is credited with introducing the Seckel pear. It's a small, russet-colored fruit with a sweet, spicy flavor. The Seckel's firm flesh makes it excellent for both cooking and canning but some people find it too crisp for out-of-hand eating. It's available late August through December. *See also* PEAR.

sediment The grainy deposit sometimes found in wine bottles, most often with older wines. Sediment is not a bad sign but in fact may indicate a superior wine. It should be allowed to settle completely before the wine is DECANTED into another container so that when the wine is served none of the sediment will transfer to the glass.

seed *v.* To remove the seeds from foods, such as fruits or vegetables.

seed sprouts When given the right conditions (usually a container, water and a warm environment), seeds will begin to sprout (grow). Edible sprouts can be produced from many seeds, the most popular being ALFALFA seeds, LENTILS, MUNG BEANS, PEAS and SOYBEANS. Fresh sprouts can be found in health-food stores and many supermarkets. Canned mung-bean sprouts are also available. Sprouts have long been popular in oriental cuisine. They can be eaten raw (in salads or sandwiches) or cooked by briefly sautéing or steaming. Seed sprouts are low in calories and rich in protein, minerals and vitamins, particularly vitamin C.

self-rising flour *see* FLOUR

seltzer water [SELT-suhr] A flavorless, naturally effervescent water that takes its name from the town of Nieder Selters in the Weisbaden region of Germany. Man-made "seltzer," also referred to as *soda water*, was introduced in the latter half of the 18th century when carbon dioxide was injected into water. It was the forerunner to soda pops, which came into being in the 1840s when flavors were added to seltzer water. *See also* SODA WATER.

Sémillon [say-mee-YOHM] A white grape grown in France and, to a lesser extent, in California, Australia, Chile and Argentina. Semillon is bottled on a limited basis as both a DRY and semisweet VARIETAL. It's also sometimes blended with SAUVIGNON BLANC. Its greatest claim to fame, however, is its susceptibility to BOTRYTIS CINEREA, making it one of the grapes most often used for DESSERT WINES such as the French SAUTERNES and some U.S. LATE-HARVEST wines.

semolina [seh-muh-LEE-nuh] 1. Durum wheat that is more coarsely ground than normal wheat flours, a result that is often obtained by sifting out the finer flour. Most good PASTA is made from semolina. It is also used to make GNOCCHI, puddings, soups and in various confections. *See also* WHEAT. 2. Similarly ground grains are sometimes referred to as "semolina" but with the grain's name attached—corn semolina, rice semolina, etc.

serrano chili pepper [seh-RRAH-noh] A small (about 1½ inches long), slightly pointed CHILI PEPPER that has a very hot, savory flavor. As it matures, its smooth, bright green skin turns orange, then yellow. Fresh serranos can be found in Mexican markets and some supermarkets. They are also available canned, pickled or packed in oil, sometimes with carrots, onions or other vegetables. Serranos can be used fresh or cooked in various dishes and sauces such as GUACAMOLE and SALSA.

sesame oil [SEHS-uh-mee] Expressed from SESAME SEED, sesame oil comes in two basic types. One is light in color and flavor and has a deliciously nutty nuance. It's excellent for everything from salad dressings to sautéing. The darker, oriental sesame oil has a much stronger flavor and fragrance and is used a flavor accent flavor for some oriental dishes. Sesame oil is high in POLYUNSATURATED fats ranking fourth behind safflower, soybean and corn oil. Its average SMOKE POINT is 420°F, making it excellent for frying. Sesame oil is particularly popular in India as well as in the Orient. *See also* FATS AND OILS.

sesame seed [SEHS-uh-mee] History tells us that sesame seed is the first recorded seasoning, dating back to 3000-B.C. Assyria. It grows widely in India and throughout the Orient. The seeds were brought to America by African slaves, who called it *benné* (pronounced BEHN-nee) *seed*, and it subsequently became very popular in Southern cooking. These tiny, flat seeds come in shades of brown, red and black, but those most commonly found are a pale grayish-ivory. Sesame seed has a nutty, slightly sweet flavor that makes it versatile enough for use in baked goods such as breads, pastries, cakes and cookies, in confections like the Middle Eastern HALVAH, and in salads and other savory dishes. The seed is available packaged in supermarkets and can be found in bulk in Middle Eastern markets and health-food stores. Because of a high oil content, sesame seed turns rancid quickly. It can be stored airtight in a cool, dark place for up to 3 months, refrigerated up to 6 months or frozen up to a year. *See also* Herb and Spice Chart, page 538.

seven-minute frosting A fluffy, meringue-type frosting consisting of egg whites, sugar, cream of tartar, water and vanilla. The mixture is beaten constantly in the top of a double boiler over hot water. When stiff peaks form (a process which, as the name suggests, takes about 7 minutes), the frosting is done.

seviche [seh-VEE-chee; seh-VEE-cheh; seh-VEESH] An appetizer popular in Latin America consisting of raw fish marinated in citrus (usually lime) juice. The action of the acid in the lime juice "cooks" the fish, thereby firming the flesh and turning it opaque. Onions, tomatoes and green peppers are often added to the marinade. Only very fresh fish should be used for this dish. POMPANO, RED SNAPPER and SOLE are the fish most often selected for seviche (which is also spelled *ceviche* and *cebiche*).

Seville orange [seh-VIHL] A popular bitter orange grown in the Mediterranean region. It has a thick, rough skin and an extremely tart, bitter flesh full of seeds. Because of its high acid content, the Seville is not an eating orange but (because of that same acidity) is extremely popular for making marmalades as well as LIQUEURS such as COINTREAU, CURAÇAO, GRAND MARNIER and TRIPLE SEC. The Seville orange also finds its way into sauces and relishes, and is a particular favorite with duck because its acidity helps counteract the fatty flavor. The dried peel is often used for seasoning. *See also* ORANGE.

sevruga caviar [sehv-ROO-guh] *see* CAVIAR

shad *see* HERRING

shad roe *see* HERRING; ROE

shaddock [SHAD-uhk] *see* POMELO

shallot [SHAL-uht; shuh-LOT] The name of this onion-family member (*Allium ascalonicum*) comes from Ascalon, an ancient Palestinian city where the shallot is thought to have originated. Shallots are formed more like garlic than onions, with a head composed of multiple cloves, each covered with a thin, papery skin. The skin color can vary from pale brown to pale gray to rose, and the off-white flesh is usually barely tinged with green or purple. The two main types of shallots are the **Jersey** or **"false" shallot** (the larger of the two) and the more subtly flavored **"true" shallot**. Fresh green shallots are available in the spring, but as with garlic and onions, dry shallots (i.e., with dry skins and moist flesh) are available year-round. Refrigerate fresh shallots for up to a week. Store dry shallots in a cool, dry, well-ventilated place for up to a month. Freeze-dried and dehydrated forms are also available. Shallots are favored for their mild onion flavor and can be used in the same manner as onions.

shank The front leg of beef, veal, lamb or pork. Though very flavorful, it's full of connective tissue and is some of the toughest meat on the animal. It therefore requires a long, slow cooking method such as braising. Beef shank is used for ground beef; a popular veal shank preparation is OSSO BUCO.

shark Though the United States has only recently begun to appreciate the merits of this fish, other cultures have eaten shark for eons. Some of the more popular shark species are *leopard, mako, spiny dogfish, soupfin* and *thresher*. Sharks marketed for food range in size from 15 to 120 pounds. Though some of the smaller ones are sold whole, fillets, steaks or chunks are the more common market forms. The shark's flavorful, lowfat flesh is dense and meatlike. Because of its metabolism, however, it has a tendency to smell of ammonia. This offputting odor can easily be eliminated by soaking the fish in milk or ACIDULATED WATER. Shark can be prepared in a variety of ways including broiling, grilling, baking, poaching and frying. It's also delicious in soups, and cold, cooked shark can be used in salads. *See also* FISH; SHARK'S FIN.

shark's fin Reputed to be an aphrodisiac, this expensive delicacy is actually the cartilage of the shark's dorsal fin, pectoral fin and the lower portion of the tail fin. Though the fins of many shark species can be used, the soupfin shark is the one most broadly utilized for this purpose. Dried shark's fin can be found in oriental markets and is sold either whole or in shreds (sans skin and bones). The latter is more expensive because the labor-intensive work of removing the cartilage from the fin's framework is already done. Shark's fin cartilage provides a protein-rich gelatin that is used in Chinese cooking mainly to thicken soups—most notably, shark's fin soup.

sharpening steel Long and pointed, this thin round rod (also called a *butcher's steel*) is made of extremely hard, high-carbon steel (some of diamond steel or ceramic) and is used to keep a fine edge on sharp knives. The rod is attached to a handle, which usually has a guard to protect the user's hand from the knife blade. Sharpening steels come in a variety of sizes, the ideal being about 12 inches long. Knives are sharpened by drawing them (while applying slight pressure) across the steel at a 20- to 30-degree angle. Doing this 5 to 6 times on both sides of the blade prior to each use keeps the blade razor-sharp. Dull blades will not be helped by a sharpening steel; they need to be re-sharpened on a WHETSTONE and then fine-honed on a steel. For maximum efficiency, choose a sharpening steel that is longer than the knife to be sharpened. To prevent metal filings from building up, occasionally clean the steel according to manufacturer's directions.

shashlik [shahsh-LIHK; SHAHSH-lihk] *see* SHISH KEBAB

she-crab soup This creamy South Carolina specialty is made with crab meat and ROE and flavored with sherry and WORCESTERSHIRE SAUCE. Since fresh crab roe is available only in the spring, she-crab soup is seasonal.

shell *n. see* HULL. **shell** *v.* To remove the shell or tough outer covering of a food such as nuts, eggs, garden peas, etc. *See also* SCHUCK.

shell bean *see* CRANBERRY BEAN

shell steak Depending on the locale, shell steak is another name for either a boneless CLUB STEAK or a NEW YORK STEAK. In either case a shell steak should be tender, since both the club and the New York are cut from the SHORT LOIN, the most tender section of BEEF. *See also* BEEF; Beef Chart, page 573.

shellfish A broad term for all aquatic animals that have a shell of some kind. Shellfish are separated into two basic categories—CRUSTACEANS and MOLLUSKS. **Crustaceans** include CRABS, CRAYFISH, LOBSTER and SHRIMP. **Mollusks** are divided into three groups—GASTROPODS (also called *univalves*) such as the ABALONE and SNAIL; BIVALVES like the CLAM and OYSTER; and CEPHALOPODS such as the OCTOPUS and SQUID. *For information on specific shellfish, see individual listings.*

shepherd's pie A dish of cooked ground or diced meat (traditionally lamb or mutton) mixed with gravy (and sometimes vegetables) and topped with mashed potatoes. The pie is then baked until the mixture is hot and the potato "crust" browns. Shepherd's pie was originally created as an economical way to use leftovers from the ubiquitous "Sunday roast."

sherbet [SHER-biht] The origins of sherbet can be traced to a popular Middle Eastern drink (*charbet*) made of sweetened fruit juice and water. Today the term *sherbet* commonly refers to a frozen mixture of sweetened fruit juice (or other liquid such as wine) and water. It can also contain milk, egg whites and/or gelatin. Sherbet is lighter than ICE CREAM but richer than an ICE. *See also* SORBET.

sherry A FORTIFIED WINE originally made in and around the town of Jerez in the Andalusia region of southern Spain. It's now also made in the United States and other parts of the world such as Australia and South Africa. As with many wines, sherries range from connoisseur quality to inexpensive mass-produced versions. The Spanish are the acknowledged experts, using the *solera* system of topping off older wines with the more recently made sherry. Thus there are no vintage sherries and the quality is consistent year after year. Sherries range in color, flavor and sweetness. FINOS are dry and light, while MANZANILLAS are very dry, delicate finos with a hint of saltiness. Considered a medium sherry, the nutty-flavored AMONTILLADOS are sweeter, softer and darker in color than finos. They're sometimes labeled *milk sherry*. The sweet OLOROSOS are fuller-flavored and darker than dry or medium sherries. They are usually aged longer and are also more expensive. Olorosos are often labeled *cream* or *golden* sherries.

Sherries can be drunk as an APÉRITIF or after dinner. Dry sherries are usually drunk chilled, sweet sherries at room temperature.

shiitake [shee-TAH-kay] Though originally from Japan and Korea, the delicious shiitake mushroom is now being cultivated in the U.S. (where it's often called *golden oak*) in a number of states including California, Pennsylvania, Vermont, Washington and Virginia. The cap of the shiitake is dark brown, sometimes with tan striations, and can be as large as 8 to 10 inches across. The average size, however, is 3 to 6 inches in diameter. The meaty flesh has a full-bodied (some say steaklike), bosky flavor. Though both fresh and dried shiitakes are now available almost year-round in many supermarkets, they're very expensive. Spring and autumn are the seasons when fresh shiitakes are most plentiful. Choose plump mushrooms with edges that curl under. Avoid any with broken or shriveled caps. The versatile shiitake is suitable for almost any cooking method including sautéing, broiling and baking. *See also* MUSHROOM.

Shirley Temple A nonalcoholic drink made with GRENADINE syrup and ginger ale and garnished with a MARASCHINO CHERRY. It's popular with children who want to have a "cocktail" with the adults and was named after the 1930s child star.

shirred eggs [SHERD] Eggs baked in a small dish with a covering of cream or milk and often topped with buttered breadcrumbs. The whites of the finished dish are firm while the yolks are usually still soft.

shish kebab [SHIHSH kuh-bob] Chunks of marinated meat (sometimes fish) and vegetables that are threaded on a skewer and grilled or broiled. Also called *shashlik*.

shoofly pie Thought to be of Pennsylvania Dutch origin, the extremely sweet filling of a shoofly pie is a mixture of molasses, brown sugar, water and butter. There are several different stories concerning the origin of the pie's name. One is that it's so sweet that one must shoo away the flies; another declares that the pie was originally made to attract flies away from other foods.

short Culinarily, this term is used to describe a non-yeast pastry or cookie dough that contains a high proportion of fat to flour. The baked goods made from short doughs are tender, rich, crumbly and crisp.

shortbread Though it's now a year-round favorite, this tender-crisp, butter-rich cookie was once associated mainly with Christmas and Hogmanay (Scottish New Year's Eve). The traditional round shape comes from the ancient Yule BANNOCK, which was notched around the edges to signify the sun's rays. The classic way of making shortbread is to press the dough into a shallow earthenware mold that is decoratively carved. After baking, the large round cookie is turned out of the mold and cut into wedges. Today, more often than not, shortbread cookies are formed into simple squares or rounds.

shortcake Though it's most commonly a rich biscuit, shortcake can also refer simply to cake. The classic American shortcake is a large, sweet biscuit that is split in half, then filled and topped with sliced or chopped fruit (traditionally strawberries) and softly whipped cream. Shortcake is most often thought of as a dessert but savory versions can be made by filling and topping the biscuit with creamed chicken or other food.

shortening *see* VEGETABLE SHORTENING

short loin Of the major wholesale cuts of beef, this is the most tender. It lies in the middle of the back between the sirloin and the rib, and the muscles in this section do little that could toughen them. The two main muscles in the short loin are the tenderloin and the top loin. The elongated **tenderloin** muscle (when separated from the bone and the rest of the short loin) can be sold as *tenderloin roasts* (often labeled *chateaubriands*), or cut into *tournedos* or *filet mignon steaks*. The **top loin** muscle with the bone attached is called a *club steak*. When removed from the bone, the same muscle is marketed as *New York* (or *Kansas City*) *strip steak* or *Delmonico steak*. When the bone is left in and portions of both the tenderloin and top loin muscles are included, the short loin is the source of *porterhouse steaks* and *T-bone steaks*. *See also* BEEF; Beef Chart, page 573. *For information on specific meat cuts, see individual listings.*

short ribs Rectangles of beef about 2 inches by 3 inches, usually taken from the CHUCK cut. Short ribs consist of layers of fat and meat and contain pieces of the rib bone. Short ribs are very tough and require long, slow, moist-heat cooking. *See also* BEEF; Beef Chart, page 573.

shot; shot glass *see* JIGGER

shoyu [SHOH-yoo] Japanese for SOY SAUCE.

shred To cut food into narrow strips, either by hand or by using a grater or a food processor fitted with a shredding disc. Cooked meat can be separated into shreds by pulling it apart with two forks.

shrimp This delicious CRUSTACEAN is America's favorite SHELLFISH. Most of the shrimp in the U.S. comes from bordering waters, notably the Atlantic and Pacific Oceans and the Gulf Coast. There are hundreds of shrimp species, most of which can be divided into two broad classifications—warm-water shrimp and cold-water shrimp. As a broad and general rule, the colder the water, the smaller and more succulent the shrimp. Shrimp come in all manner of colors including reddish- to light brown, pink, deep red, grayish-white, yellow, gray-green and dark green. Some have color striations or mottling on their shells. Because of a heat-caused chemical change, most shrimp shells change color (such as from pale pink to bright red or from red to black) when cooked. Shrimp are marketed according to size (number per pound), but market terms vary greatly from region to region and from fish market to fish market. Keeping that variance in mind, the general size categories into which shrimp fall are: **colossal** (10 or less per pound), **jumbo** (11–15), **extra-large** (16–20), **large** (21–30), **medium** (31–35), **small** (36 to 45) and **miniature** (about 100). In the U.S., jumbo and colossal shrimp are commonly called "prawns," though the PRAWN is, in fact, a different species. Though there are slight differences in texture and flavor, the different sizes (except the miniatures) can usually be substituted for each other. As a rule, the larger the shrimp, the larger the price. In general, 1 pound of whole, raw shrimp yields ½ to ¾ pound of cooked meat. Shrimp are available year-round and are usually sold sans head and sometimes legs. When raw and unshelled, they're referred to as "green shrimp." Many forms of shrimp are found in the marketplace—shelled or unshelled, raw or cooked, and fresh or frozen. There are also processed shrimp products such as breaded or stuffed, frozen shrimp, shrimp spread, dried shrimp and shrimp paste (the last two found in oriental markets). Raw shrimp should smell of the sea with no hint of ammonia. If it smells strongly of iodine, it simply reflects the type of food on which the shrimp has fed. Cooked, shelled shrimp should look plump and succulent. Whether or not to DEVEIN shrimp is a matter of personal preference. In general, small and medium shrimp do not need deveining except for cosmetic purposes. However, because the intestinal vein of larger shrimp contains grit, it should be removed. Shrimp can be prepared in a variety of ways including boiling, frying and grilling.

shrimp boil *see* CRAB BOIL

shrub Colonial-day shrubs were spiked with liquor (usually brandy or rum) but today these fruit juice, sugar and vinegar drinks are usually nonalcoholic. Shrubs are served over ice, with or without soda water.

shuck To remove the shell from SHELLFISH such as oysters or clams. Also, to peel the husk from an ear of corn.

sidecar The appellation of this COCKTAIL is said to have come from its originator, who always traveled in a motorcycle sidecar. It consists of BRANDY, orange-flavored LIQUEUR (such as COINTREAU or TRIPLE SEC) and lemon juice, shaken with ice and strained into a cocktail glass.

Siena cake [see-EH-nuh] *see* PANFORTE

sieve *n*. [SIHV] *see* STRAINER **sieve** *v*. To strain liquid or particles of food through the mesh or perforated holes of a sieve or STRAINER.

sift To pass dry ingredients through a fine-mesh SIFTER so any large pieces can be removed. Sifting also incorporates air to make ingredients (such as confectioners' sugar or flour) lighter.

sifter A mesh-bottomed kitchen utensil used to sift ingredients such as flour or confectioners's sugar. Sifters are usually made of stainless steel or heavy-weight plastic. There are versions with rotary cranks as well as those that are battery-operated.

silver fizz *see* GIN FIZZ

simmer To cook food gently in liquid at a temperature (about 185°F) low enough that tiny bubbles just begin to break the surface.

simple syrup *see* SUGAR SYRUP

Singapore sling Said to have originated at Singapore's Raffles Hotel, this COCKTAIL consists of gin, cherry brandy and lemon juice shaken with ice and strained into a tall glass. The drink is finished by topping it off with soda water.

sirloin This cut of beef lies between the very tender SHORT LOIN and the much tougher ROUND. As would be expected, the meat cuts from the portion near the short loin are more tender than those closer to the round. Sirloin is usually cut into steaks or roasts. Bone removed, the cuts are referred to by the names of the three main muscles. **Top sirloin** is a continuation of the tender top loin muscle of the short loin. The **tenderloin** is part of the tenderest muscle (which also continues from the short loin) and the **bottom sirloin,** which is part of the same (less tender) sirloin tip muscle found in the ROUND. The best-known bone-in sirloin steaks (in order of tenderness) are **pinbone, flat bone, round bone** and **wedge bone.** *See also* BEEF; Beef Chart, page 573.

sizzling rice soup A Chinese specialty consisting of broth combined with chicken or pork (and sometimes shrimp) and various vegetables. Deep-fried rice squares are placed in each soup bowl; when the soup is ladled over the squares, the rice sizzles and pops.

skate This odd-looking, kite-shaped fish is also called a *ray*. The names are used interchangeably, though in some quarters the term "skate" is applied to the members of this species that are used for eating, while "ray" generally refers to those (like the electric ray and giant manta ray) that are fished for sport. Skates have winglike pectoral fins that undulate as the fish meanders along the ocean floor (there are also freshwater rays). The fins are the edible part of a skate. Their delicious flesh is firm, white and sweet—not unlike that of the SCALLOP. Depending on the region, skate is available year-round. Like SHARK meat, skate must be soaked in ACIDULATED WATER to remove its natural ammonia odor. Skate can be prepared in a variety of ways including poaching, baking and frying. *See also* FISH.

skewer *n.* [SKYOO-uhr] A long, thin, pointed rod that comes in various sizes. Skewers are made of metal or wood; the former often has a ring at one end. They're most often used to hold meat in place during cooking, as well as to skewer meat and vegetables to be grilled for SHISH KEBAB. The best skewers are square or flat—shapes that hold food securely when moved. **skewer** *v.* To impale small pieces of food on skewers.

skillet *see* FRYING PAN

skim To remove the top layer from a liquid, such as cream from milk or foam and fat from stock, soups, sauces, etc.

skimmer A metal kitchen utensil consisting of a handle attached to either a perforated disc or a shallow bowl-shaped wire mesh. Skimmers are used to lift foods out of hot liquids or to remove unwanted surface fat and foamy residue from soups, etc.

skim milk *see* MILK

skin *v.* To remove the skin of food before or after cooking. Skinning is done for a variety of reasons including appearance, taste and diet. Foods that are often skinned include poultry, fish and game.

skirt steak Cut from the beef flank, the skirt steak is the diaphragm muscle (which lies between the abdomen and chest cavity). It's a long, flat piece of meat that's flavorful but rather tough. Properly cooked, skirt steak can be quite tender and delicious. It can either be quickly grilled, or stuffed, rolled and braised. Recently, skirt steak has become quite fashionable because of the delicious Southwestern dish, FAJITAS. *See also* BEEF; Beef Chart, page 573.

sliver *n.* A long, thin piece of food such as meat or cheese, or a thin wedge of pie, etc. **sliver** *v.* To cut food into thin strips.

slivovitz [SLIHV-uh-vihts; SLIHV-uh-wihts; SCHLIHV-uh-vihts] A dry, slightly bitter plum BRANDY made in Hungary, Yugoslavia and the Balkans.

sloe [SLOH] This wild European plum is the fruit of the blackthorn (*Prunus spinosa*), which also bears showy white flowers. The purple-skinned sloe has an extremely tart yellow flesh. Though too sour for out-of-hand eating, sloes are used for jams, jellies and to flavor LIQUEURS such as PRUNELLE and SLOE GIN. They're not generally available fresh in the U.S.

sloe gin [sloh JIHN] A liqueur made by steeping pricked or crushed SLOES in gin.

slumgullion [sluhm-GUHL-yuhn] This slang term originated during the California Gold Rush and described dishes (usually stews) made from leftovers.

slump An old-fashioned New England dessert of fruit, usually berries, topped with biscuit dough and stewed until the biscuit topping is cooked through. Also called *grunt*.

smallage; smellage [SMAW-lihj] *see* LOVAGE

smelt The smelt is anadromous, meaning that it migrates from its North American saltwater habitat to spawn in fresh water. It's a small (average 4 to 7 inches long) fish with a translucent silver-green back shading into shimmering silver sides and belly. Its delicate flesh is rich, oily and mild-flavored. There are many varieties of this fish, the most widely distributed being the **rainbow smelt**, found along the Atlantic coast. Two popular Pacific Coast varieties are **whitebait** and **eulachon**. The latter is also called **candlefish**, a nickname that came about because Indians would dry these high-fat fish, run a wick through the flesh and use them for candles. Fresh smelts are best from September through May. Because they're very perishable, many are now flash-frozen immediately after being caught. They are also available canned. Smelts are marketed whole and are usually eaten that way—head, viscera and bones. Though they can be cooked in a variety of ways, they're generally simply coated with flour and fried. *See also* FISH.

Smithfield ham Considered by many to be the premier COUNTRY-CURED HAM, the Smithfield is said to have been so loved by Queen Victoria that she had six sent to her household every week. These special hams are produced from hogs raised on a privileged diet of acorns, hickory nuts and peanuts. To be accorded the appellation of "Smithfield," the hams must be cured and processed in the area of Smithfield, Virginia. The elaborate processing includes dry-curing, seasoning, lengthy hickory smoking and aging of 6 to 12 months (sometimes up to 2 years). The result is a lean, dark-colored ham with a flavor that's rich, salty and dry. Smithfield ham can be purchased through mail order or from gourmet butcher shops or food stores. It may be served raw like PROSCIUTTO, but it's usually baked or boiled. Before being cooked, Smithfields must be soaked 12 to 24 hours to remove excess saltiness. *See also* HAM.

smoke curing *see* CURE

smoked salmon Fresh salmon that has undergone a smoking process, usually by one of two methods—hot-smoking or cold-smoking. **Hot-smoking** is a process by which the fish is smoked from 6 to 12 hours at temperatures ranging from 120° to 180°F. The time and temperature depend on the size of the fish, how close it is to the source of smoke and the degree of flavor desired. In **cold-smoking**, a temperature of 70° to 90°F is maintained and the fish might remain in the smokehouse for anywhere from 1 day to 3 weeks. There are many types of smoked salmon. **Indian-cure salmon** is brined fish that has been cold-smoked for up to 2 weeks, which results in a form of salmon JERKY. **Kippered salmon**—U.S. style—is a chunk, steak or fillet that has been soaked in a mild brine and hot-smoked. It's usually made from chinook salmon that has been dyed red. European kippered salmon differs in that it's a whole salmon that has been split before being brined and cold-smoked. **Lox** is brine-cured cold-smoked salmon, much of which is slightly saltier than other smoked salmon. Some lox, however, has had sugar added to the brine, which produces a less salty product. Lox is a favorite in American-Jewish cuisine, particularly when served with BAGELS and cream cheese. **Nova** or **Nova Scotia salmon** is an idiom used in the eastern U.S. that broadly describes cold-smoked salmon. **Scotch-smoked**, **Danish-smoked** and **Irish-smoked salmon** are all geographical references to cold-smoked *Atlantic* salmon (whereas the Pacific species—usually coho or chinook—treated in this manner is generally simply labeled *smoked salmon*). **Squaw candy** consists of thin strips of salmon that has been cured in a salt-sugar brine before being hot-smoked. Other fish such as trout and haddock can also be smoked. *See also* SALMON.

smoke point The stage at which heated fat begins to emit smoke and acrid odors, and impart an unpleasant flavor to foods. The higher the smoke point, the better suited a fat is for frying. Because both reusing fat and exposing it to air reduces its smoke point, it should be discarded after being used a maximum of three times. Though processing affects an individual fat's smoke point slightly, the ranges for some of the more common fats are: butter (350°F); lard (361° to 401°F); vegetable shortenings (356° to 370°F); vegetable oils (441° to 450°F)—corn, grapeseed, peanut and safflower oils all have high smoke points, while that of olive oil is relatively low (about 375°F). *See also* FATS AND OILS. *For information on specific fats and oils, see individual listings.*

smorgasbord [SMOHR-guhs-bohrd; SCHMOHR-guhs-bohrd] Swedish for "bread and butter table," smorgasbord has come to refer to a buffet consisting of a variety of foods such as various HORS D'OEUVRE, OPEN-FACED SANDWICHES, salads, cooked vegetables (which may be served hot or cold), pickled or marinated fish, sliced meats, cheeses and desserts. A smorgasbord may be simple or elaborate and can consist entirely of appetizers or make up the entire meal.

smorrebrod [SMUHR-uh-bruth] Danish OPEN-FACED SANDWICHES.

snail Prehistoric sites have uncovered piles of this GASTROPOD MOLLUSK'S spiral shell, indicating that snails were popular early on. They were greatly favored by ancient Romans, who cultivated special vineyards on which the snails could feed and fatten. The best-known varieties today are the vineyard or Burgundy snail and the *petit-gris*. The **vineyard snail** has a diet of grape leaves and, though it grows slowly and is somewhat difficult to raise, is considered the best eating. It grows to about 1¾ inches, has a streaked, dull, yellowish brown shell and mottled flesh. The smaller (about 1 inch) French **petit-gris** is now being cultivated in the United States and has a brownish-gray shell and flesh. Other varieties are cultivated in Algeria, Turkey, China, Indonesia and Africa but are not as highly esteemed as the vineyard snail and petit-gris. Live snails are available year-round and can be found in specialty markets. Fresh American-cultivated snails do not require the purification period that European snails do but should be used the same day they're purchased. Snails are usually boiled before being baked or broiled in the shell with a seasoned butter. Canned snails and packaged snail shells are available in gourmet markets and many supermarkets. *See also* SNAIL PLATE; SNAIL TONGS; SHELLFISH.

snail plate Special ovenproof plates with six small indentations, designed to hold snails served in their shell in place so they don't roll around while being cooked or eaten.

snail tongs Small, spring-operated tongs used to hold hot snail shells while extracting the snail. Unlike most tongs, these open by squeezing the handles. When the pressure is released, the tongs snap securely around the snail shell.

snap bean *see* GREEN BEAN

snapper There are about 250 species of this saltwater fish, 15 of which can be found in U.S. waters from the Gulf of Mexico to the coastal waters of North Carolina. Some of the better-known species include the **gray snapper, mutton snapper, schoolmaster snapper** and **yellowtail snapper**. By far the best known and most popular, however, is the **red snapper**, so named because of its reddish-pink skin and red eyes. Its flesh is firm-textured and contains very little fat. Red snapper grows to 35 pounds but is most commonly marketed in the 2- to 8-pound range. The smaller sizes are often sold whole, while larger snappers can be purchased in steaks and fillets. Snapper is available fresh all year with the peak season in the summer months. It's suitable for virtually any cooking method. Though some varieties of ROCKFISH are marketed under the names "Pacific snapper" and "red snapper," and a variety of TILEFISH is called "yellow snapper," none of these are true snapper. *See also* FISH.

snickerdoodle [SNIHK-uhr-doo-dl] Originating in 19th-century New England, this whimsically named cookie has a characteristically crackly surface and can be either crisp or soft. The dough sometimes contains nutmeg and cinnamon as well as raisins and nuts. Traditionally, snickerdoodles are sprinkled with cinnamon sugar before being baked. The name appears to have no particular meaning or purpose . . . other than fun.

snifter A short-stemmed, pear-shape glass that's larger at the bottom than it is at the top. Snifters are recommended for drinking fine BRANDY. When the brandy-filled snifter is cradled in the hands, the liquid—warmed by body heat—releases its delightful aroma.

snow A light, frothy dessert made by chilling a mixture of stiffly beaten egg whites, sugar, gelatin and various flavorings. Adding lemon juice, for example, creates lemon snow.

snow pea The fact that this LEGUME is entirely edible—including the pod—accounts for its French name, *mange-tout*, or "eat it all." Its almost translucent, bright green pod is thin and crisp. The tiny seeds inside are tender and sweet. Snow peas are available year-round with peak seasons in the spring and fall. Choose crisp, brightly colored pods with small seeds. Refrigerate in a plastic bag for up to 3 days. Both tips of a snow pea should be pinched off just before using. They're an essential vegetable in Chinese cooking and may also be used raw in salads. Snow peas are also called *Chinese snow peas* and *sugar peas*. *See also* PEA.

soba [SOH-buh] A Japanese noodle made from buckwheat flour, which gives it a dark brownish-gray color. **Chasoba** is a variation of the noodle made with green tea. *See also* ASIAN NOODLES.

sockeye salmon *see* SALMON

soda 1. Another name for BAKING SODA. 2. A generic term for any flavored SOFT DRINK. 3. Any of many SODA WATERS. 4. A fountain drink of one or more scoops of ice cream topped with a flavored SOFT DRINK or SODA WATER and flavored syrup.

soda bread A QUICK BREAD that is LEAVENED with baking soda combined with an acid ingredient, usually buttermilk. IRISH SODA BREAD is the best known of this genre.

soda water Water that has been highly charged with carbon dioxide, which gives it effervescence. Soda water, also called *club soda* or *seltzer water*, contains a small amount of sodium bicarbonate which, because it's alkaline, can help neutralize an acidic stomach. Soda water is combined with sweeteners and various flavorings to produce a wide variety of SOFT DRINKS. Many COCKTAILS also use soda water as an ingredient. *See also* SELTZER WATER.

sofrito *(Sp.);* **soffrito** *(It.)* [soh-FREE-toh] 1. The Spanish *sofrito* is a sauce made by sautéing ANNATTO SEEDS in rendered pork fat. The seeds are removed before chopped onions, green peppers, garlic, pork and various herbs are cooked in the flavored, now-red oil until the ingredients are tender and the mixture is thick. The sauce is used in recipes as needed. 2. The Italian *soffrito* is a similar mixture (usually chopped celery, green peppers, onions, garlic and herbs) sautéed in olive oil and used to flavor soups, sauces and meat dishes.

soft-ball stage A test for SUGAR SYRUP describing the point at which a drop of boiling syrup immersed in cold water forms a soft ball that flattens of its own accord when removed. On a CANDY THERMOMETER, the soft-ball stage is between 234° and 240°F. *See also* Candy-making Temperatures and Cold-water Tests Chart, page 537.

soft-crack stage A test for SUGAR SYRUP describing the point at which a drop of boiling syrup immersed in cold water separates into hard though pliable threads. On a CANDY THERMOMETER, the soft-crack stage is between 270° and 290°F. *See also* Candymaking Temperatures and Cold-water Tests Chart, page 537.

soft drinks A generic term applied to beverages that do not contain alcohol. Soft drinks are most often thought of as carbonated, though effervescence is not a requisite.

soft-shell clam; soft clam This variety of clam actually has a thin, brittle shell. The soft-shell clam can't completely close its shell because of a long neck (or siphon) that extends beyond its edge. This long extension is why the soft-shell is also referred to as a *long-neck clam*. There are several types of soft-shells but the most prevalent are the STEAMER, RAZOR and GEODUCK CLAM. *For information on specific soft-shell clams, see individual listings. See also* CLAM.

soft-shell crab A term describing a growth state of the crab, during which time it casts off its shell in order to grow one that's larger. Soon after the crab sheds its shell, its skin hardens into a new one. During those few days before the new shell hardens, these CRUSTACEANS are referred to as "soft-shell" crabs. In the U.S., the **blue crab** (found along the Atlantic and Gulf Coasts) is the species most commonly eaten in its soft-shell state. *See also* CRAB.

soft wheat *see* WHEAT

sole The popularity of sole dates back at least to the ancient Romans, who called it *solea Jovi* (Jupiter's sandal), undoubtedly because of the elongated-oval shape of this FLATFISH. Though a number of FLOUNDER family members (such as Petrale sole, lemon sole, rex sole and butter sole) are incorrectly called sole in the U.S., the highly prized **true sole** is found only in European waters. The best-known of these is the **Dover sole** (also called *Channel sole*), which is found in coastal waters from Denmark to the Mediterranean Sea. The body of the Dover sole averages about a foot long and ranges in color from pale gray to dark brown on the top side, with the underside a pale beige. Its delicately flavored flesh has a fine, firm texture. True Dover sole is imported frozen to the U.S. from several of the northern European countries and is available in better fish markets. Other true sole include the **thickback** and the **sand** (or *partridge*) **sole,** both smaller and less flavorful than the Dover. Much of what is sold as Dover sole in the U.S. is actually flounder. Sole can be prepared in a variety of ways including poaching, steaming, baking, broiling and sautéing. It's ideally suited for combining with other foods and sauces. *See also* FISH.

sole Véronique *see* VÉRONIQUE

sommelier [suhm-uhl-YAY; saw-muh-LYAY] The French term for a steward or waiter in charge of wine. For hundreds of years, sommeliers were responsible for the cellaring and serving of wines for royalty. Eventually the tradition of the sommelier spread to restaurants, where such an individual is expected to have extensive knowledge of wines and their suitability with various dishes.

sopa seca [SOH-pah SEH-kuh] Literally translated as "dry soup," sopa seca is really not a soup at all. It is, in fact, a dish usually based on rice, VERMICELLI or dry TORTILLA strips combined with tomatoes, onions and garlic and cooked in a broth. It's assumed that the name comes from the fact that, although the mixture begins "soupy," it is cooked until the liquid is entirely absorbed—thereby becoming a "dry soup." The Mexicans usually serve sopa seca as a luncheon dish or as a separate course, much as Italians serve a pasta course.

sopaipilla [soh-py-PEE-yuh] This crisp, puffy, deep-fried pastry resembles an air-filled pillow. The sopaipilla is thought to have originated in Albuquerque, New Mexico, more than 200 years ago. It's a favorite Southwestern U.S. dessert, usually served with honey or syrup flavored with anise or cinnamon. Sopaipillas are also sometimes filled with savory ingredients like REFRIED BEANS.

sorbet [sor-BAY] The French word for "sherbet," which Italians call *sorbetto*. Sorbet is sometimes distinguished from sherbet by the fact that it never contains milk. It's also often a softer consistency than sherbet. Savory or lightly sweetened sorbets are customarily served either as a palate refresher between courses or as dessert. They're sometimes also referred to as ICES or GRANITÀS, though both of these mixtures are generally more granular in texture than a sorbet. *See also* SHERBERT.

sorbitol [SOR-bih-tawl] A sugar substitute found naturally in some fruits and seaweeds. Besides being used as a sweetener, sorbitol is employed as a thickener and stabilizer in candies, gums and numerous other food products.

sorghum [SOR-guhm] This cereal grass has broad, cornlike leaves and huge clusters of cereal grain at the end of tall, pithy stalks. Sorghum is a powerhouse of nutrition but, though it's the third leading cereal crop in the U.S., almost all of it is used for animal fodder. Around the world, however, it's the third largest food grain. A few U.S. mills do sell it by mail order. One sorghum byproduct the United States does use for human consumption is the sweet juice extracted from the stalks which, like that from the sugar cane, is boiled down to produce a thick syrup called **sorghum molasses**

(also *sorghum syrup* or simply *sorghum*). It's often used as a table syrup and to sweeten and flavor baked goods.

sorrel [SOR-uhl] Any of several varieties of a hardy perennial herb belonging to the buckwheat family, all with some degree of acidity and sourness resulting from the presence of OXALIC ACID. Sorrel has grown wild for centuries throughout Asia, Europe and North America. The most strongly flavored of the sorrels is the **garden** or **belleville sorrel**, also called *sour dock* and *sour grass*. The mildest variety is **dock sorrel**, also called *spinach dock* and *herb patience dock*. As all sorrel matures it becomes more acidic. Sorrel leaves are shaped much like those of spinach and range from pale to dark green in color and from 2 to 12 inches in length. Fresh sorrel is available in limited supply year-round with a peak season in the spring. It should be chosen for its bright green, crisp leaves. Sorrel with woody-looking stems or leaves that are yellow or wilted should be avoided. Refrigerate fresh sorrel in a plastic bag for up to 3 days. Gourmet food stores sometimes carry cooked sorrel in jars and cans. The more acidic sorrels are used to flavor cream soups, pureed as accompaniments for meats and vegetables or used in omelets and breads. In the spring, when at its youngest and mildest, sorrel is used in salads or cooked as a vegetable. It's high in vitamin A and contains some calcium, phosphorus, potassium, magnesium and vitamin C.

soubise [soo-BEEZ] 1. A rich, velvety sauce made by combining BÉCHAMEL (white sauce) with pureed cooked onions and sometimes a small amount of cream. 2. A meat accompaniment of pureed cooked onions and rice. 3. A term applied to dishes (such as **eggs à la soubise**) topped with or accompanied by a creamy onion sauce.

soufflé [soo-FLAY] A light, airy mixture that usually begins with a thick egg yolk–based sauce or puree that is lightened by stiffly beaten egg whites. Souffles may be savory or sweet, hot or cold. Baked souffles are much more fragile than those which are chilled or frozen because the hot air entrapped in the soufflé begins to escape (causing the mixture to deflate) as soon as the dish is removed from the oven. Savory soufflés are usually served as a main dish, are almost always hot and can be made with a variety of ingredients including cheese, meat, fish or vegetables. Dessert soufflés may be baked, chilled or frozen and are most often flavored with fruit purees, chocolate, lemon or LIQUEURS. Both sweet and savory soufflés are often accompanied by a complementary sauce. Soufflés are customarily baked in a classic **soufflé dish**, which is round and has straight sides to facilitate the soufflé's rising. These special dishes are ovenproof and come in a variety of sizes ranging from 3½-ounce (individual) to 2-

quart. They're available in kitchenware shops and the housewares section of most department stores. Foil or parchment "collars" are sometimes wrapped around the outside of a soufflé dish so that the top of the foil or paper rises about 2 inches above the rim of the dish. Such collars are used for cold dessert soufflés so that the sides of the frozen or molded mixture are supported until they set. Once the collar is removed, the souffle stands tall and appears to "rise" out of the dish.

soufflé dish *see* SOUFFLÉ

soufflé potatoes *see* POMMES SOUFFLÉES

soul food Though this traditional African-American fare has long been popular in the South, the term itself is relatively new (circa 1960). The expression "soul food" is thought to have derived from the cultural spirit and soul-satisfying flavors of Black-American food. Some of the dishes commonly thought of as soul food include HAM HOCKS, GRITS, CHITTERLINGS, BLACK-EYED PEAS and COLLARD GREENS.

soup Theoretically, a soup can be any combination of vegetables, meat or fish cooked in a liquid. It may be thick (like GUMBO), thin (such as a CONSOMMÉ), smooth (like a BISQUE) or chunky (CHOWDER or BOUILLABAISSE). Though most soups are hot, some like VICHYSSOISE and many FRUIT SOUPS are served cold. Soups are often garnished with flavor enhancers such as CROUTONS, grated or cubed cheese or sour cream. They can be served as a first course or as a meal, in which case they're often accompanied by a sandwich or salad. *For information on specific soups, see individual listings.*

soupe [SOOP] *see* POTAGE

sour *n.* A COCKTAIL made by combining liquor with lemon juice and a little sugar. It's usually shaken with crushed ice and can be strained and served ON THE ROCKS or STRAIGHT UP. Sours are often garnished with an orange slice and a MARASCHINO CHERRY. Though the **whiskey sour** is probably the most famous of these cocktails, they can be made with many other liquors including bourbon, gin and rum. **sour** *adj.* Having a sharp, tart taste, usually from an acidic ingredient such as lemon juice or vinegar.

sour cream *see* CREAM

sourdough; sourdough bread This delicious bread has a slightly sour, tangy flavor created by using a special YEAST STARTER as the LEAVENER. San Francisco is known for its superior sourdough bread and many food stores in the area sell packages of dry SOURDOUGH STARTER for home bread bakers. Though most sourdoughs are made from all-purpose flour, there are many delicious variations including those made from whole-wheat or rye flour.

sourdough starter *see* YEAST STARTER

sour grass *see* SORREL

sour mash *see* BOURBON

sour salt *see* CITRIC ACID

sous-vide [soo-VEED] A food-packaging technique pioneered in Europe whereby fresh ingredients are combined into various dishes, vacuum-packed in individual-portion pouches, cooked under a vacuum, then chilled. *Sous-vide* food is used most often by hotels, restaurants and caterers, though it's expected to become increasingly available in supermarkets.

Southern Comfort Produced in St. Louis, Missouri, this traditional American LIQUEUR is made from bourbon and peaches. Southern Comfort is potent at 100 PROOF (50% alcohol).

souvlaki; souvlakia [soo-VLAH-kee; soo-VLAH-kee-uh] This Greek specialty consists of lamb chunks that have been MARIANTED in a mixture of oil, lemon juice, oregano and seasonings before being skewered and grilled. Some souvlakia skewers also include chunks of vegetables such as green pepper or onion.

soybean It's thought that the first written record of soybeans is dated 2838 B.C., and the Chinese have been cultivating them for thousands of years. So important are soybeans to the Chinese that they're considered one of the five sacred grains along with rice, wheat, barley and millet. Soybeans didn't find their way to Japan until the 6th century and to Europe until the 17th century. Their extraordinary nutritive value was not scientifically confirmed until the 20th century. Although the United States didn't really become interested in soybeans until the 1920s, it now supplies one-third of the world's total production. There are over 1,000 varieties of this nutritious LEGUME, ranging in size from as small as a pea to as large as a cherry. Soybean pods, which are covered with a fine tawny to gray fuzz, range in color from tan to black. The beans themselves come in various combinations of red, yellow, green, brown and black. Their flavor is generally quite bland, which may explain why they weren't embraced by Western cultures until their nutritive value was discovered. Unlike other legumes, the soybean is low in carbohydrates and high in protein and desirable oil. Because they're inexpensive and nutrition-packed, soybeans are used to produce a wide variety of products including TOFU (soybean curd), SOYBEAN OIL, SOY FLOUR, SOY MILK, SOY SAUCE, MISO and TAMARI. Soybeans can be cooked (after being presoaked) like any other dried bean to be used in soups, stews, casseroles, etc. They can also be sprouted (*see* BEAN SPROUTS) and used in salads or as a cooked vegetable. Additionally, soybean byproducts are used in making margarines, as emulsifiers in many processed foods and in non-food items such as soaps and plastics. Fresh soybeans are not generally available except in oriental markets or specialty produce markets in late summer and early fall. Dried soybeans, beans for sprouting and a huge variety of soybean products are available in supermarkets and health-food stores. The soybean is also called *soya bean, soy pea, soja* and *soi. See also* BEAN.

soybean curd *see* TOFU

soybean oil Extracted from soybeans, this light yellowish oil is high in both polyunsaturated fats (58 percent) and monounsaturated fats (23 percent), and low in saturated fats (15 percent). It's used extensively in the United States in the manufacture of MARGARINE and SHORTENING. Soybean oil has always been popular as a cooking oil in Chinese cuisine and is gaining favor in the U.S. because it is inexpensive, healthful and has a high SMOKE POINT. *See also* FATS AND OILS.

soy flour This finely ground flour is made from soybeans and, unlike many flours, is very high in protein (twice that of wheat flour) and low in carbohydrates. Soy flour is ordinarily mixed with other flours rather than being used alone. It has a wide variety of uses including in baking and to bind sauces. In Japan, it's very popular for making confections. Soy flour is sold in health-food stores—sometimes under the name *kinako*—and in some supermarkets.

soy milk Higher in protein than cow's milk, this milky, iron-rich liquid is a non-dairy product made by pressing ground, cooked SOYBEANS. Soy milk is cholesterol-free and low in calcium, fat and sodium. It makes an excellent milk substitute for anyone with a milk allergy; such milk substitutes are often fortified with calcium. There are also soy-based formulas for infants with milk allergies. Soy milk has a tendency to curdle when mixed with acidic ingredients such as lemon juice and wine; it's intentionally curdled in the making of TOFU.

soy sauce This extremely important ingredient in oriental cooking is a dark, salty sauce made by fermenting boiled soybeans and roasted wheat or barley. Although there is essentially one main type of soy sauce widely made in the U.S., China and Japan produce a number of varieties ranging in color from light to dark and in texture from thin to very thick. There are also several low-sodium soy sauces available on the market. Soy sauce is used to flavor soups, sauces, marinades, meat, fish and vegetables.

spaetzle [SHPEHT-sluh; SHPEHT-sehl; SHPEHT-slee]   Literally translated from German as "little sparrow," spaetzle is a dish of tiny noodles or dumplings made with flour, eggs, water or milk, salt and sometimes nutmeg. The spaetzle dough can be firm enough to be rolled and cut into slivers or soft enough to be forced through a SIEVE or COLANDER with large holes. The small pieces of dough are usually boiled before being tossed with butter or added to soups or other dishes. In Germany, spaetzle is served as a side dish much like potatoes or rice, and is often accompanied by a sauce or gravy.

spaghetti [spuh-GEHT-ee] Like its cousin MACARONI, spaghetti is made from SEMOLINA and water. Sometimes eggs are added. The name of this PASTA comes from the Italian word for "strings" and in general spaghetti is in the form of long, thin strands that are round and solid. **Spaghettini** is very thin spaghetti (but thicker than VERMICELLI). Some spaghettis—like FETTUCCINE and LINGUINE—are flat rather than round. On the other hand, FUSILLI is a spiral shape, rather than being straight. *For information on specific types of spaghetti, see individual listings.*

spaghettini *see* SPAGHETTI

spaghetti squash Also called *vegetable spaghetti*, this creamy-yellow, watermelon-shaped squash was so named because of its flesh which, when cooked, separates into yellow-gold spaghettilike strands. Averaging from 4 to 8 pounds, spaghetti squash are available year-round with a peak season from early fall through winter. Choose squash that are hard and smooth with an even pale yellow color. Avoid greenish squash (a sign of immaturity) and those with bruised or damaged spots. Store uncut spaghetti squash at room temperature for up to 3 weeks. After the whole squash is baked, the rather bland-tasting strands can be removed from the shell and served with sauce, like pasta. They can also be served as part of a casserole or cold as a salad ingredient. *See also* SQUASH.

spanakopita [span-uh-KOH-pih-tuh] Of Greek origin, this savory pie consists of top and bottom PHYLLO-dough crusts with a filling of sautéed spinach and onions mixed with FETA CHEESE, eggs and seasonings.

Spanish melon This MUSKMELON family member is large and egg-shaped, with a ribbed green skin and a pale green flesh. Its flavor is succulent and sweet, much like that of a CRENSHAW MELON. Spanish melons are available from early July to November. *See also* MELON.

Spanish olive *see* OLIVE

Spanish onion *see* ONION

spareribs A long, narrow cut of meat taken from the lower portion of the ribs and breastbone of a hog. Spareribs are quite fatty, which contributes to their delicious flavor. Barbecuing spareribs (usually after they've been MARINATED) is the most popular method of preparation. *See also* PORK; Pork Chart, page 571.

Spätlese [SHPAYT-lay-zuh] German for "late picking," this wine term refers to grapes that are picked after the regular harvest. Because such fruit is riper, it contains more sugar and produces wines that are rich and sweet. The selective picking process also makes them quite expensive. *See also* AUSLESE; BEERENAUSLESE; TROCKENBEERENAUSLESE.,

spatula [SPACH-oo-luh] A flattish, rather narrow kitchen utensil that comes in a variety of shapes and sizes. Depending on the material from which it's made (which includes wood, metal, rubber and plastic), spatulas can be used for a plethora of kitchen tasks. Rigid wood spatulas are good for scraping the sides of pots and turning foods, whereas softer plastic or rubber spatulas are better for stirring ingredients in a curved bowl and folding mixtures together. Flexible metal spatulas—both long and short— are perfect for spreading frosting on cakes. *See also* TURNER.

spätzle *see* SPAETZLE

spearmint *see* MINT

spices Pungent or aromatic seasonings obtained from the bark, buds, fruit, roots, seeds or stems of various plants and trees (whereas HERBS usually come from the leafy part of a plant). Spices were prized long before recorded history. Though they've always been used to flavor food and drink, throughout the eons spices have also been favored for a plethora of other uses including crowning emperors, making medicines and perfumes, religious ceremonies and as burial accoutrements for the wealthy. Over 3,000 years ago the Arabs monopolized the spice trade, bringing their rare cargo back from India and the Orient by arduous camel caravans. During the Middle Ages the demand for spices was so high that they became rich commodities—a pound of mace could buy three sheep and the same amount of peppercorns could buy freedom for a serf. By that time Venice had a tight hold on Western commerce and controlled the incredibly lucrative European spice trade. That Venetian monopoly was an important catalyst for the expeditions that resulted in the discovery of the New World. Today, the United States is the world's major spice buyer. Among the more popular spices are ALLSPICE, CARDAMOM, CINNAMON, CLOVES, GINGER, MACE, NUTMEG, PAPRIKA, PEPPER, SAFFRON and TUMERIC. Spices are also sold in blends, such as CURRY POWDER and SPICE PARISIENNE. Many spices are available in both whole and ground forms. Ground spices quickly lose their aroma and flavor, so it's wise to buy them in small quantities. Whole spices can be ground as needed. Store spices in airtight containers in a cool, dark place for no more than 6 months. Spices are used to enhance a wide variety of food, both sweet and savory. They should be used sparingly so they don't overpower the foods being seasoned. *For information on specific spices, see individual listings. See also* Herb and Spice Chart, page 538.

Spice Parisienne [pa-ree-ZYEHN] The market name for a complex spice and herb blend, also called EPICES FINES. French cooks usually make their own blends, which can vary greatly depending on the individual. In general, Spice Parisienne includes WHITE PEPPER, ALLSPICE, MACE, NUTMEG, CLOVES, CINNAMON, BAY LEAVES, SAGE, MARJORAM and ROSEMARY. As with all spices, this blend should be stored in a cool, dark place for no more than 6 months. *For information on specific spices, see individual listings. See also* SPICES.

spinach [SPIHN-ihch] Originating in the Middle East, spinach was being grown in Spain during the 8th century, and the Spaniards are the ones who eventually brought it to the U.S. Popeye's addiction to this "power-packed" vegetable comes from the fact that it's a rich source of iron as well as of vitamins A and C. But because spinach contains OXALIC ACID—which inhibits the body's absorption of calcium and iron—the truth is that its nutritional value is somewhat diminished. It's this same oxalic acid that gives spinach its slightly bitter taste, which is prized by some while others find it offputting. Spinach has dark green leaves that, depending on the variety, may be either curled or smooth. The smaller **New Zealand spinach** has flat, spade-shape leaves that are often covered with a fine fuzz. Fresh spinach is available year-round. Choose leaves that are crisp and dark green with a nice fresh fragrance. Avoid those that are limp, damaged or which have yellow spots. Refrigerate in a plastic bag for up to 3 days. Spinach, which is usually very gritty, must be thoroughly rinsed. Frozen and canned spinach is also available. Spinach may be used raw in salads, or cooked (usually by boiling or sautéing) and used as a vegetable or as part of a dish. Many dishes that use spinach as an integral ingredient are appended with the phrase À LA FLORENTINE.

spiny lobster *see* LOBSTER

split *see* WINE BOTTLES

split pea *see* FIELD PEA

sponge [SPUHNJ] 1. A frothy, GELATIN-based dessert that has been lightened by the addition of beaten egg whites. Sometimes whipped cream is added, though it makes the dessert richer and not as airy. Sponges may be variously flavored, usually with fruit purees. 2. A light bread-dough mixture made by combining the yeast with some of the flour and liquid called for in a recipe. The thick, batterlike mixture is covered and set aside until it bubbles and becomes foamy which, depending on the combination of ingredients, can take up to 8 hours. During this time, the sponge develops a tangy flavor. The remaining ingredients are added to this sponge and the bread is kneaded and baked as usual. Using a sponge also makes the final loaf slightly denser.

sponge cake; spongecake This light, airy cake gets its ethereal texture from beaten egg whites, which are folded into a fluffy mixture of beaten egg yolks and sugar. They get their leavening power entirely from eggs. Sponge cakes are further characterized by the fact that they do not contain shortening of any kind. The cakes can be variously flavored with anything from lemon ZEST to ground almonds.

spoom A frothy type of SHERBERT made with a light SUGAR SYRUP mixed with a liquid such as fruit juice, CHAMPAGNE or SAUTERNES. Halfway through the freezing process, the mixture is combined with uncooked MERINGUE, which gives spoom its airy texture. The Italians call this frozen specialty *spuma*, which means "foam" or "froth."

spoon bread; spoonbread A puddinglike bread usually based on cornmeal and baked in a casserole dish. Spoon bread is generally served as a side dish and, in fact, is soft enough that it must be eaten with a spoon or fork.

sprat A close relative of the HERRING, the sprat is a small (about 6 inches in length) fish that can be found off the European Atlantic coast. Because of its high fat content, sprats are perfect for broiling or grilling. They're also available either salted or smoked. The smallest sprats are packed in oil, in which case they're usually called **brisling** or **brisling sardines**. *See also* FISH.

springerle [SPRING-uhr-lee; SHPRING-uhr-luh] One of Germany's most famous Christmas sweets, the anise-flavored springerle are beautiful embossed cookies that originated centuries ago in the German duchy of

Swabia. The embossed designs on the cookie's surface are formed with a special carved wooden rolling pin which, when rolled over the dough, imprints it decoratively. Alternatively, the dough can be pressed into a carved cookie mold. Once the dough is imprinted with the design, the cookies are allowed to sit out at room temperature overnight. This allows the dough's surface to dry so the design will remain as the cookie bakes.

springform pan A round pan with high, straight sides (2½ to 3 inches) that expand with the aid of a spring or clamp. The separate bottom of the pan can be removed from the sides when the clamp is released. This allows cakes, tortes or cheesecakes which might otherwise be difficult to remove from the pan to be extricated easily by simply removing the pan's sides.

spring roll *see* EGG ROLL

spritz *n.* [SPRIHTS; SHPRIHTS] Pretty Scandinavian cookies formed into a variety of fanciful shapes when the dough is forced through a COOKIE PRESS. Spritz are rich and buttery. The name comes from *spritzen*, which is German for "to squirt or spray." **spritz** *v.* To quickly spray or squirt, as in adding a "spritz" of soda to a mixed drink .

spritzer [SPRIHT-suhr] A tall, chilled drink, customarily made with wine and SODA WATER.

sprouts *see* SEED SPROUTS

spuma [SPOO-muh] *see* SPOOM

spumante [spoo-MAHN-tay] The Italian word for "sparkling," as in wine. *See also* ASTI SPUMANTE.

spumone; spumoni [spuh-MOH-nee] This frozen molded Italian dessert consists of two layers of ice cream (such as chocolate and vanilla) between which is sandwiched a layer of sweetened whipped cream that has been flavored with rum and mixed with toasted nuts and candied fruit. Sometimes the ice cream is lightened with whipped cream before being spooned into the mold. Spumone is cut into slices and sometimes served with a sweet sauce that complements the ice cream flavors.

spun sugar Fine strands of hardened boiled sugar that are used to decorate various desserts. Spun sugar begins by cooking sugar, water and CREAM OF TARTAR to the HARD-CRACK STAGE. A fork or whisk is then used to dip into the sugar syrup and draw out fine threads. These hairlike strands can be placed directly on a dessert or on a waxed paper–lined surface, then transferred later to the dish. Once the spun sugar hardens, it may also be gathered and sprinkled or arranged on top of a dessert.

squab [SKWAHB] A young (about 4 weeks old) domesticated pigeon that has never flown and is therefore extremely tender. It was a popular special-occasion dish in Victorian England. Squabs usually weigh 1 pound or less and have delicately flavored dark meat. Fresh squab is available throughout the summer months (year-round in some regions) in gourmet markets. Frozen squab is marketed year-round. Choose fresh birds by their plump, firm appearance. Store as for CHICKEN. Likewise, squab can be prepared in any manner suitable for chicken. A classic method is to stuff and roast it.

squab chicken *see* CHICKEN

squash [SKWAHSH] The fruit of various members of the gourd family native to the Western Hemisphere. There is evidence of squash being eaten in Mexico as far back as 5500 B.C., and in South America over 2,000 years ago. Squash varies widely in size, shape and color. Generally, they're divided into two categories—*summer squash* and *winter squash*. **Summer squash** have thin, edible skins and soft seeds. The tender flesh has a high water content, a mild flavor and doesn't require long cooking. The most widely available varieties of summer squash are CROOKNECK, PATTYPAN and ZUCCHINI. Summer squash is best from early through late summer, although some varieties are available year-round in certain regions. Select the smaller specimens with bright-colored skin free of spots and bruises. Summer squash is very perishable and should be refrigerated in a plastic bag for no more than 5 days. It can be prepared by a variety of methods including steaming, baking, sautéing and deep-frying. Summer squash are high in vitamins A and C as well as niacin. **Winter squash** have hard, thick skins and seeds. The deep yellow to orange flesh is firmer than that of summer squash and therefore requires longer cooking. Winter squash varieties include ACORN, BUTTERCUP, BUTTERNUT, HUBBARD, PUMPKIN, SPAGHETTI and TURBAN. Though most varieties are available year-round, winter squash is best from early fall through the winter. Choose squash that are heavy for their size and have a hard, deep-colored rind free of blemishes or moldy spots. The hard skin of a winter squash protects the flesh and allows it to be stored longer than summer squash. It does not require refrigeration and can be kept in a cool, dark place for a month or more, depending on the variety. Once the seeds are removed, winter squash can be baked, steamed or simmered. They're a good source of iron, riboflavin and vitamins A (more than summer squash) and C. *For information on specific squash varieties, see individual listings. See also* SQUASH BLOSSOMS.

squash blossoms The flowers from either summer or winter squash are edible and delicious. Squash blossoms come in varying shades of yellow and orange, with flavors that hint of the squash itself. They can be found from late spring through early fall in specialty produce markets as well as Italian, Latin and Filipino markets. Squash blossoms are naturally soft and somewhat limp, but choose those that look fresh, with closed buds. They're extremely perishable and should be stored in the refrigerator for no more than a day. Squash blossoms may be used as a garnish (whole or slivered) for almost everything from soups to main dishes. They also add color and flavor to salads. The most common method of cooking them is sautéing, often after coating the blossoms with a light batter. Squash blossoms are sometimes stuffed with ingredients such as soft cheese before being baked or batter-dipped and fried. They contain vitamins A and C, as well as iron and calcium. *See also* FLOWERS, EDIBLE.

squid [SKWIHD] As a 10-armed member of the CEPHALOPOD class in the MOLLUSK family, squid is related to both the OCTOPUS and CUTTLEFISH. Squid meat has a firm, chewy texture and mild, somewhat sweet flavor. Also called *calamari*, squid can range in size from 1 inch to the seldom seen 80-foot behemoth of the deep. Smaller squid are marketed in fresh, frozen, canned, sun-dried and pickled forms. They are very popular in oriental and Mediterranean cuisines and can be found in ethnic markets and some supermarkets. When buying fresh squid choose those that are small and whole with clear eyes and an ocean-fresh fragrance. They should be refrigerated, airtight, for no more than a day or two. Squid can be panfried, baked, boiled, stir-fried or coated with batter and deep-fried. The cooking time should always be short, since the texture of squid becomes rubbery when overcooked. Squid is used raw by the Japanese in SUSHI dishes. The ink can be extracted from the ink sacs and used to color preparations like PASTA or to flavor dishes such as *calamares en su tinta* ("squid in its ink"), a popular Spanish dish. Squid are rich in protein and phosphorus. *See also* SHELLFISH.

stainless steel cookware Stainless steel cookware has many advantages: it doesn't react (as does aluminum) with acidic or alkaline foods, it is corrosion-resistant, strong and easy to clean, and it doesn't scratch, pit or dent easily. The main disadvantage of stainless steel is its poor heat conductivity, a problem somewhat reduced in heavy, well-made pans. The best of all possible worlds is achieved by "sandwiched" cookware, with a layer of either aluminum or copper (both excellent at conducting heat) between two thin sheets of stainless steel.

standing rib roast *see* RIB ROAST

star anise A star-shaped, dark brown pod that contains a pea-sized seed in each of its eight segments. Native to China, star anise comes from a small evergreen tree. Although the flavor of its seeds is derived from anethol (the same oil that gives ANISE SEED its pronounced flavor), star anise has a different heritage—the magnolia family. Its flavor is slightly more bitter than that of regular anise seed. In oriental cuisine, star anise is a commonly used spice and tea flavoring. It's also widely used to flavor LIQUEURS and baked goods in Western cultures. It can be found whole in oriental markets and some supermarkets, and as a ground ingredient in Chinese FIVE-SPICE POWDER.

star fruit *see* CARAMBOLA

starter *see* YEAST STARTER

Stayman apple A striped, dull red apple with an off-white flesh that's juicy, crisp and tart. The Stayman apple is good both raw and cooked. It's available from late October to April. *See also* APPLE.

steak and kidney pie A traditional British dish consisting of a cooked mixture of chopped beef, kidneys, mushrooms, onions and beef stock. This mixture is placed in a pie or casserole dish, covered with a pastry crust and baked until crisp and brown. Sometimes potatoes, hard-cooked eggs or oysters are also added to the dish.

steak au poivre [oh PWAHV-rh] Steak that is covered with coarsely ground pepper before being sautéed or broiled. Steak au poivre is usually finished either by topping it with a chunk of sweet butter or by making a simple sauce from the pan drippings. Elaborate presentations often call for flaming (*see* FLAMBÉ) the steak with BRANDY.

steak fries *see* FRENCH FRIES

steak tartare *see* BEEF TARTARE

steam A method of cooking whereby food is placed on a rack or in a special steamer basket over boiling or simmering water in a covered pan. Steaming does a better job than boiling or poaching of retaining a food's flavor, shape, texture and many of the vitamins and minerals.

steamed bread BOSTON BROWN BREAD is probably the most famous steamed bread in the U.S. This type of bread is made by placing a batter in a covered container on a rack set over gently boiling water in a large pot. The pot is covered and the bread steamed for about 3 hours. It can also be made in a pressure cooker in about half the time. The bread doesn't require a special container in which to be steamed—a 12-ounce coffee can covered with aluminum foil works nicely. The characteristic texture of steamed breads is moist and tender.

steamed pudding A sweet or savory pudding that is cooked (usually in a special STEAMED-PUDDING MOLD) on a rack over boiling water in a covered pot. The pudding mold is usually decorative so that when the finished pudding (which is firm) is unmolded it retains its decorative shape. Steamed puddings can take up to 3 hours to cook on stovetop, half that time in a pressure cooker. They're customarily served with a sauce. The traditional Christmas PLUM PUDDING, for instance, is customarily accompanied with HARD SAUCE.

steamed-pudding mold Although STEAMED PUDDING can be cooked in a variety of containers, there are special steamed-pudding molds with decorative sides and bottom, as well as a lid that clamps tightly shut. Many molds also have a central tube (like an angel-food cake pan) that provides more even heat distribution, thereby cooking the pudding more evenly.

steamer clam These East Coast soft-shell clams have a thin, brittle shell that doesn't close entirely due to the long, rubbery neck (siphon) extending from the body. Steamers are the smallest of the Atlantic soft-shell variety. They are, as their name indicates, delicious steamed. They're also suitable for batter-dipping and frying. *See also* CLAM.

steel *see* SHARPENING STEEL

steep To soak dry ingredients such as tea leaves, ground coffee, herbs, spices, etc. in liquid (usually hot) until the flavor is infused into the liquid. *See also* INFUSION.

stew *n.* Any dish that is prepared by stewing. The term is most often applied to dishes that contain meat, vegetables and a thick souplike broth resulting from a combination of the stewing liquid and the natural juices of the food being stewed. **stew** *v.* A method of cooking by which food is barely covered with liquid and simmered slowly for a long period of time in a tightly covered pot. Stewing not only tenderizes tough pieces of meat but also allows the flavors of the ingredients to blend deliciously.

stewing chicken *see* CHICKEN

Stilton cheese [STIHL-tn] This marvelous blue cheese is the English contender for "King of Cheeses." Although it is made in parts of Leicestershire, Derbyshire and Nottinghamshire, it received its name in the 18th century because it was first sold in the small village of Stilton in Huntingdonshire. Stilton is made from whole cow's milk and allowed to ripen for 4 to 6 months, during which time it is skewered numerous times to encourage the growth of *Pencillium roqueforti* mold (also present in ROQUEFORT CHEESE). This process creates a pale yellow interior with blue-green veins. The texture is rich and creamy (45 percent fat) but slightly crumbly. The flavor has a mellow CHEDDARlike quality with the pungency of blue cheese. Stilton is sold in tall cylinders with a crusty brownish rind. In addition to this better-known mature version, there is also a young **white Stilton** that is marketed before the colored veins develop. It has a mild and slightly sour flavor. Stilton is at its best eaten by itself with a glass of PORT or a full-bodied dry red wine. *See also* CHEESE.

stinger A COCKTAIL classically made with equal parts BRANDY or COGNAC and white CRÈME DE MENTHE. Other stinger versions can be made substituting another spirit or LIQUEUR for the brandy or cognac, but the white crème de menthe is intrinsic to the drink.

stir-fry *n.* Any dish of food that has been prepared by the stir-fry method. **stir-fry** *v.* To quickly fry small pieces of food in a large pan over very high heat while constantly and briskly stirring the food. This cooking technique, which is associated with oriental cooking and the WOK, requires a minimum amount of fat and results in food that is crisply tender.

stock In the most basic terms, stock is the strained liquid that is the result of cooking vegetables, meat or fish and other seasoning ingredients in water. A **brown stock** is made by browning bones, vegetables and other ingredients before they're cooked in the liquid. Most soups begin with a stock of some kind, and many sauces are based on REDUCED stocks.

stollen [STOH-luhn; SHTOH-luhn] Germany's traditional Christmas yeast bread, stollen is a rich, dried fruit–filled loaf that's often topped with a confectioners' sugar icing and decorated with candied cherries. It's shaped like a folded oval and somewhat resembles a giant PARKER HOUSE ROLL.

stone crab Found along America's coast from North Carolina to Texas, the stone crab is most prolific in Florida waters. Its name comes from the rocklike, oval-shape shell of this crab, of which only the claw meat is eaten. Because of that fact, fishermen usually simply twist off the claws and throw the crab back to grow new ones. This regeneration process can take up to 2 years of the stone crab's 10-year lifespan. It in no way inhibits the crab's feeding capabilities, as the claws are used for defensive purposes only. Stone crabmeat has a firm texture and a sweet, succulent flavor. It's marketed precooked (usually frozen) because the meat has a tendency to adhere to the shell if frozen raw. *See also* CRAB.

stone-ground flour *see* FLOUR

stoneware Strong, hard pottery that is fired at very high temperatures (around 2,200°F) and that is usually fully glazed. Stoneware is generally nonporous, chip-resistant and safe to use in both microwave and standard ovens. It's ideal for baking and slow cooking.

stout [STOWT] A strong, dark beer that originated in the British Isles. Stout is more redolent of HOPS than regular beer and is made with dark-roasted BARLEY, which gives it a deep, dark color and bittersweet flavor. *See also* BEER.

straight up This term is used to describe COCKTAILS that are served without ice.

strain 1. To pour liquid through a SIEVE, STRAINER or CHEESECLOTH to remove undesirable particles. 2. To press soft food through the holes of a sieve, which results in a pureed texture. Food for infants or those on special diets is sometimes processed this way.

strainer A kitchen utensil with a perforated or mesh bottom used to strain liquids or semiliquids, or to sift dry ingredients such as flour or confectioners' sugar. Strainers, also called *sieves*, come in a variety of sizes, shapes and mesh densities. There are flat-bottomed, drum-shaped strainers with interchangeable meshes of different coarseness, as well as those that are bowl-shaped and some that are conical. Strainers are made of various materials including stainless steel, tinned steel and aluminum. The better ones have strong handles and frames and contain hooks for resting the strainer on top of pots or bowls.

straw potatoes Potatoes cut into very thin, long sticks and then deep-fried.

strawberries Romanoff This deliciously decadent dessert is made by soaking strawberries in orange juice and CURAÇAO or COINTREAU, then serving them topped with whipped cream. It's one of many dishes named after the Russian royal family by French chefs.

strawberry Sixteenth-century author William Butler wrote this tribute to the strawberry: "Doubtless God could have made a better berry, but doubtless God never did." Red, juicy and conically shaped, the strawberry is a member of the rose family and has grown wild for centuries in both the Americas and Europe. The Romans valued the fruit for its reputed therapeutic powers for everything from loose teeth to gastritis. However, it wasn't until the late 13th century that the plant was first cultivated. The most common American variety is the result of several centuries of crossbreeding of the wild Virginia strawberry (North America's main native strawberry) and a Chilean variety. It's probably today's most hardy berry and is able to withstand both shipping and storage. More flavorful, however, are European Alpine strawberries—the tiny, exquisitely sweet wild strawberries of France known as *fraises des bois* ("strawberry of the woods"). They're considered by many to be the "queen of strawberries." Stawberries vary in size, shape and color (some are off-white or yellowish). In general, the flavor of the smaller berries is better than that of the larger varieties since the latter are often watery. Fresh strawberries are available year-round in many regions of the country, with the peak season from April to June. Choose brightly colored, plump berries that still have their green caps attached and which are uniform in size. Avoid soft, shriveled or moldy berries. Do not wash until ready to use, and store (preferably in a single layer on paper towel) in a moistureproof container in the refrigerator for 2 to 3 days. Fresh strawberries are wonderful eaten with cream, macerated in wine or LIQUEUR or used in various desserts. Canned and frozen strawberries are also available. Commercial strawberry products include preserves, jams, jellies, syrups and various desserts. Strawberries are an excellent source of vitamin C and also provide some potassium and iron.

strawberry shortcake *see* SHORTCAKE

Strega [STRAY-guh] A golden-colored Italian LIQUEUR made from herbs and flowers, Strega has a sweet, mildy flowery flavor.

streusel [STROO-zuhl; SHTROY-zuhl] A crumbly topping consisting of flour, sugar, butter and various spices that is sprinkled on coffeecakes, breads, muffins and cakes. The word *streusel* is German for "sprinkle" or "strew."

string bean *see* GREEN BEAN

strip steak A beef steak cut from the top loin muscle in the SHORT LOIN. Coming as it does from the tenderest region of the animal, the strip steak is expensive. It's usually sold boneless and is equivalent to a PORTERHOUSE steak minus bone and TENDERLOIN. A strip steak has many different names across the country including *New York strip, Kansas City strip, shell steak* and *sirloin club steak. See also* BEEF; Beef Chart, page 573.

striped bass From the Atlantic coast, this true BASS is also called *striper* and, in the Chesapeake Bay region, *rockfish* (not to be confused with the species ROCKFISH). The striped bass is anadromous, meaning that it migrates from a saltwater habitat to spawn in fresh water. It can range in size from 2 to 70 pounds, though market weight is usually between 2 and 15 pounds.

The striped bass is olive green fading to silver, and has 6 to 8 longitudinal black stripes. It has a moderately fat, firm-textured flesh with a mild, sweet flavor. Striped bass can be prepared in a variety of ways including broiling, grilling, poaching and steaming. Both **white bass** and **yellow bass** are freshwater members of the striped bass family. *See also* FISH.

stroganoff [STRAW-guh-noff; STROH-guh-noff] Named after 19th-century Russian diplomat, Count Paul Stroganov, this dish consists of thin slices of tender beef (usually TENDERLOIN or TOP LOIN), onions and sliced mushrooms, all quickly sautéed in butter and combined with a sour-cream sauce. Stroganoff is usually accompanied by RICE PILAF.

strudel [STROOD-l; SHTROO-duh] German for "whirlpool" or "eddy," *strudel* is a type of pastry made up of many layers of very thin dough spread with a filling, then rolled and baked until crisp and golden brown. It's particularly popular in Germany, Austria and much of central Europe. The paper-thin *strudel* dough resembles PHYLLO and is equally difficult to handle. Apple strudel is probably the most famous of this genre, but the filling variations are limitless and can be savory or sweet.

stud *v.* Culinarily, "stud" means to insert flavor-enhancing or decorative edible items (such as whole cloves, slivered almonds or garlic slivers) partway into the surface of a food so that they protrude slightly. For example, hams are often studded with cloves.

stuffing *see* DRESSING

sturgeon [STER-juhn] A large migratory fish known for its delicious flesh, excellent ROE (the true CAVIAR) and ISINGLASS. This prized fish was so favored by England's King Edward II that he gave it royal status, which meant that all sturgeon caught had to be offered to the king. Sturgeon are anadromous, meaning that they migrate from their saltwater habitat to spawn in fresh water. Their average weight is 60 pounds but gargantuan specimens can reach over 3,000 pounds. The sturgeon's long, thin body is pale gray and has large scales. Its rich, high-fat flesh has a fresh, delicate flavor and is so firm that it's almost meatlike. Sturgeon are fished in the Black and Caspian Seas and in the U.S., mainly in the Pacific Northwest and along the Southern Atlantic. The best U.S. variety is the **white sturgeon**, and the smaller specimens are considered the best eating. Fresh sturgeon comes whole (up to about 8 pounds), in steaks or in chunks. It can be braised, grilled, broiled, sautéed or baked. The supply of this fish in its fresh form, however, is limited and most of that caught in U.S. waters is smoked. Frozen and canned (pickled or smoked) forms are also available. *See also* FISH.

submarine sandwich *see* HERO SANDWICH

succotash [SUHK-uh-tash] This southern U.S. favorite is a cooked dish of lima beans, corn kernels and sometimes chopped red and green sweet peppers. The name is taken from the Naragansett Indian word *msickquatash*, "boiled whole kernels of corn."

sucrose [SOO-krohs] A crystalline, water-soluble sugar obtained from sugar cane, sugar beets and SORGHUM. Sucrose also forms the greater part of MAPLE SUGAR. It's sweeter than GLUCOSE but not as sweet as FRUCTOSE. *See also* SUGAR.

suet [SOO-iht] Found in beef, sheep and other animals, suet is the solid white fat found around the kidneys and loins. Many British recipes call for it to lend richness to pastries, puddings, stuffings and MINCEMEATS. Suet was once widely used to make tallow candles.

sugar Once a luxury only the extremely affluent could afford, sugar was called "white gold" because it was so scarce and expensive. Although Persia and ancient Arabia were cultivating sugar in the 4th century B.C., the Western World didn't know of it until the 9th century when the Moors conquered the Iberian peninsula. Early sugar wasn't the granulated, alabaster substance most of us know today. Instead, it came in the form of large, solid loaves or blocks ranging in color from off-white to light brown. Chunks of this rock-hard substance had to be chiseled off and ground to a powder with a MORTAR AND PESTLE. Modern-day sugar is no longer scarce or expensive and comes in myriad forms from many origins. Sugar cane and sugar beets are the sources of most of today's sugar, also known as SUCROSE (which also comes from maple sap—*see* MAPLE SUGAR— and SORGHUM). Other common forms of sugar are DEXTROSE (grape or corn sugar), FRUCTOSE (levulose), LACTOSE (milk sugar) and MALTOSE (malt sugar). The uses for sugar are countless. Besides its sweetening value, sugar adds tenderness to doughs, stability to mixtures such as beaten egg whites for MERINGUE, golden-brown surfaces to baked goods and, in sufficient quantity, it contributes to the preservation of some foods. **Granulated** or **white sugar** is highly refined cane or beet sugar. This free-flowing sweetener is the most common form both for table use and for cooking. Granulated sugar is also available in cubes or tablets of various sizes, as well as a variety of textures. **Superfine sugar,** known in Britain as **castor** (or *caster*) **sugar,** is more finely granulated. Because it dissolves almost instantly, superfine sugar is perfect for making meringues and sweetening cold liquids. It can be substituted for regular granulated sugar cup for cup. **Confectioners'** or **powdered sugar** is granulated sugar that has been crushed into a fine powder. To prevent clumping, a small amount (about 3 percent) of CORNSTARCH is added. Confectioners' sugar labeled XXXX is slightly finer than that labeled XXX but they can be used interchangeably and both may need to be sifted before using. Because it dissolves so readily, confectioners' sugar is often used to make icings and candy. It's also used decoratively, as a fine dusting on desserts. One and three-quarters (packed) cups confectioners' sugar equals 1 cup granulated sugar. Confectioners' sugar is called *icing sugar* in Britain and *sucre glace* in France. **Decorating** or **coarse sugar** (also called *sugar crystals*) has granules about four times larger than those of regular granulated sugar. It's used for decorating baked goods and can be found in cake-decorating supply shops and gourmet markets. ROCK CANDY is an even larger form of sugar crystals. **Colored sugar,** also used for decorating, is tinted granulated sugar and can be found in several crystal sizes. **Flavored sugar** is granulated sugar that's been combined or scented with various ingredients such as cinnamon or vanilla (*see* VANILLA SUGAR). *All granulated sugar can be stored indefinitely if tightly sealed and kept in a cool, dry place.* Today's **brown sugar** is white sugar combined with MOLASSES, which gives it a soft texture. The two most commonly marketed styles of brown sugar are *light* and *dark,* with some manufacturers providing variations in between. In general, the lighter the brown sugar, the more delicate the flavor. The very dark or "old-fashioned" style has a more intense molasses flavor. Brown sugar is usually sold in 1-pound boxes or plastic bags—the latter help the sugar retain its moisture and keep it soft. Hardened brown sugar can be resoftened by placing it with an apple wedge in a plastic bag and sealing tightly for 1 to 2 days. A firmly packed cup of brown sugar may be substituted for 1 cup granulated sugar. Both granulated and liquid brown sugar are also now available. Neither of these forms should be substituted for regular brown sugar in recipes. Though similar in color, brown sugar should not be confused with **raw sugar**, the residue left after sugar cane has been processed to remove the molasses and refine the sugar crystals. The flavor of raw sugar is akin to that of brown sugar. In this raw state, however, sugar may contain contaminants such as molds and fibers. Raw sugar marketed in the U.S. has been purified, negating much of what is thought to be its superior nutritive value. Two popular types of raw sugar are the coarse-textured dry **Demerara sugar** from the Demerara area of Guyana, and the moist, fine-textured **Barbados sugar. Turbinado sugar** is raw sugar that has been steam-cleaned. The coarse turbinado crystals are blond-colored and have a delicate molasses flavor. Other sources of sugar include maple sap, palm sap and sorghum. Almost 100 percent of sugar is carbohydrate. Granulated white sugar contains about 770 calories per cup, as does the same weight (which equals about 2 cups) of confectioners' sugar. A cup of brown sugar is slightly higher at 820 calories. It also contains 187 milligrams of calcium, 56 of phosporus, 4.8 of iron, 757 of potassium and 97 of sodium, compared to only scant traces of those nutrients found in granulated sugar. Artificial sweeteners such as ASPARTAME and SACCHARIN are essentially calorie-free and are used as a sugar substitute both commercially and by the home cook. Sugar also comes in syrup form, the most common being CORN SYRUP, GOLDEN SYRUP, HONEY, MAPLE SYRUP, MOLASSES, SORGHUM and TREACLE. *See also* GLUCOSE; JAGGERY; ROCK SUGAR; SPUN SUGAR.

sugar pea *see* SUGAR SNAP PEA

sugarplum A small confection, often consisting of fruit such as a candied cherry or dried apricot surrounded by FONDANT.

sugar snap pea Also called *sugar pea*, this delightfully sweet pea is a cross between the ENGLISH PEA and the SNOW PEA. It's entirely edible—pod and all. Sugar snap peas are available during spring and fall. Choose plump, crisp pods with a bright green color. Refrigerate in a plastic bag for up to 3 days. Sugar snap peas should be served raw or only briefly cooked in order to retain their crisp texture. *See also* PEA.

sugar syrup Also called *simple syrup*, sugar syrup is a solution of sugar and water that is cooked over low heat until clear, then boiled for a minute or so. Sugar syrup can be made in various densities—thin (3 parts water to 1 part sugar), medium (2 parts water to 1 part sugar) and heavy (equal parts water and sugar). Depending on the thickness, simple sugar syrups have various uses including soaking cakes (such as BABAS), glazing baked goods, poaching or preserving fruit, adding to frostings, etc. They can be flavored with a variety of EXTRACTS, juices, LIQUEURS, etc. Sugar syrup is the foundation for most candies, the concentration of the mixture depending upon its temperature, which can either be checked by a CANDY THERMOMETER or by a series of cold-water tests. The tests and appropriate thermometer readings are as follows: **thread stage**—the point at which a spoon coated with boiling syrup forms a 2-inch thread when immersed in cold water (230° to 234°F); **soft-ball stage**—a drop of boiling syrup immersed in cold water forms a soft ball that flattens of its own accord when removed (234° to 240°F); **firm-ball stage**—a drop of boiling syrup immersed in cold water forms a firm but pliable ball (244° to 248°F); **hard-ball stage**—a drop of boiling syrup immersed in cold water forms a rigid ball that is still somewhat pliable (250° to 265°F); **soft-crack stage**—a drop of boiling syrup immersed in cold water separates into hard though pliable threads (270° to 290°F); **hard-crack stage**—a drop of boiling syrup immersed in cold water separates into hard, brittle threads (300° to 310°F). *See also* CARAMEL.

sukiyaki [soo-kee-YAH-kee; skee-YAH-kee] Known in Japan as the "friendship dish" because it appeals to foreigners, sukiyaki consists of STIR-FRIED bite-sized pieces of meat, vegetables and sometimes noodles and TOFU. It's flavored with soy sauce, spices and sometimes SAKE and is often prepared at the table.

sultana [suhl-TAN-uh] Originating in Smyrna, Turkey, this small, pale golden-green grape was once used to make wine. Today, however, it's cultivated primarily for raisins. Its offspring in the United States is known as the Thompson seedless grape. *See also* RAISIN.

summer coating *see* CONFECTIONERY COATING

summer pudding This classic English dessert consists of sweetened fresh berries and often red CURRANTS that are briefly cooked, then cooled before being placed in a bread-lined casserole dish. The fruit is topped with additional slices of bread, covered with a plate and weighted overnight in the refrigerator. The cold dessert is unmolded and served with whipped cream.

sun-dried tomatoes *see* TOMATO

sunchoke *see* JERUSALEM ARTICHOKE

sundae One to three scoops of ice cream, topped with one or more sweet sauces and various other ingredients including fruit, nuts and whipped cream. The sundae is said to have originated in the late 19th century because moralists decried the consumption of carbonated soda on Sunday . . . even in the popular weekend treat, ice-cream sodas. The non-corruptive "dry" version of that treat was ice cream topped with syrup and named after the day on which soda was banned. The spelling of this frozen confection was changed to "sundae" so as not to be sacrilegious.

sunfish Any of a large variety of North American freshwater fish noted for their interesting shapes and bright colors. Members of this family include largemouth, smallmouth, redeye, rock and spotted BASS, and both the white and black CRAPPIE. *See also* FISH.

sunflower seeds The showy sunflower, with its bright yellow petals radiating from a dark hub of seeds, can reach up to 12 inches in diameter. This tall, rangy plant is thought to be so named because its flowers resemble the sun, and because they twist on their stems to follow the sun throughout the day. Sunflowers were cultivated by the Indians of the Americas long before Europeans discovered them. Today, the Russians are one of the largest sunflower seed producers in the world. Though it's the state flower of Kansas, the largest U.S. sunflower producers are California, Minnesota and North Dakota. The seeds have a hard black-and-white striped shell that must be removed. Sunflower seeds can be dried or roasted (either in or out of the shell), and are sold either plain or salted. They can be eaten as a snack, used in salads or sandwiches or added to a variety of cooked dishes or baked goods. The iron-rich sunflower seeds are, by weight, 47 percent fat and 24 percent protein. The pale yellow, delicately-flavored **sunflower-seed oil** extracted from the seeds is very high in polyunsaturated fat and low in saturated fat. Though it has a relatively low SMOKE POINT, sunflower-seed oil is used in cooking as well as for salad dressings. *See also* FATS AND OILS.

sunflower-seed oil *see* SUNFLOWER SEEDS

superfine sugar *see* SUGAR

sushi [SOO-shee] A Japanese specialty based on boiled rice flavored with a sweetened RICE VINEGAR mixture. Once cooled, the rice has a glossy sheen and separates easily. There is a wide variety of sushi including **nigiri sushi** (thin slices of raw fish seasoned with WASABI and wrapped around or layered with this rice), **hosomaki** (thin sushi rolls) and **futomaki** (thick sushi rolls). To make these rolls, various chopped vegetables, raw fish, pickles, TOFU, etc. are enclosed in sushi rice and wrapped in thin sheets of NORI (seaweed). The rolls are then cut into slices. Sushi are designed to be finger food and can be served as appetizers, snacks or a full meal. Soy sauce is often served with sushi for dipping. *See also* SASHIMI.

Swedish limpa bread *see* LIMPA BREAD

Swedish meat balls A blend of ground meat (often a combination of beef, pork or veal), sautéed onions, milk-soaked breadcrumbs, beaten egg and seasonings. This mixture is formed into small (½-inch) balls before being sautéed until brown. Swedish meatballs are served in a pale brown cream sauce made by combining the pan drippings with cream or milk. They're a popular buffet item or hot appetizer and are seen on most Swedish SMORGASBORDS.

sweet acidophilus milk [ass-ih-DOFF-uh-luhs] *see* MILK

sweet-and-sour This term is used to describe dishes that have a flavor balanced between sweet and pungent, usually accomplished by combining sugar and vinegar. The flavor is often incorporated into a sauce or dressing that can be served with meat, fish or vegetables. The Chinese are famous for their sweet-and-sour specialties and the Germans are noted for their delicious sweet-and-sour cabbage dishes.

sweet basil *see* BASIL

sweetbreads Prized by gourmets throughout the world, sweetbreads are the thymus glands of veal, young beef, lamb and pork. There are two glands—an elongated lobe in the throat and a larger, rounder gland near the heart. These glands are connected by a tube, which is often removed before sweetbreads are marketed. The heart sweetbread is considered the more delectable (and is therefore more expensive) of the two because of its delicate flavor and firmer, creamy-smooth texture. Sweetbreads from milk-fed veal or young calves are considered the best. Those from young lamb are quite good, but beef sweetbreads are tougher and pork sweetbreads (unless from a piglet) have a rather strong flavor. Veal, young calf and beef sweetbreads are available year-round in specialty meat markets, whereas those from lamb and pork must usually be special-ordered. Choose sweetbreads that are white (they become redder as the animal ages), plump and firm. They're very perishable and should be prepared within 24 hours of purchase. Before being cooked, sweetbreads must be soaked in several changes of ACIDULATED WATER and their outer membrane removed. Some recipes call for the glands to be blanched to firm them, and refrigerated until ready for use. Sweetbreads can be prepared in a variety of ways including poaching, sautéing and braising. They are also sometimes used in PÂTÉS and SOUFFLÉS.

sweet cider *see* CIDER

sweet cucumber *see* TEA MELON

sweetened condensed milk A mixture of cow's milk and sugar, 40 to 45 percent of which is sugar. This mixture is heated until about 60 percent of the water evaporates. The resulting condensed mixture is extremely sticky and sweet. Unsweetened condensed milk is referred to as EVAPORATED MILK.

sweet marjoram *see* MARJORAM

sweetmeat A small piece of something sweet such as a PETIT FOUR, candied fruit, nut or candy.

sweet peppers In the U.S., the term "sweet pepper" encompasses a wide variety of mild peppers which, like the CHILI PEPPER, belong to the *Capsicum* family. Both sweet and hot peppers are native to tropical areas of the Western Hemisphere and were brought back by Christopher Columbus to his homeland where they quickly found their way into Spanish cuisine. Sweet peppers can range in color from pale to dark green, from yellow to orange to red, and from purple to black. Their color can be solid or variegated. Their usually juicy flesh can be thick or thin and the flavors can range from bland to sweet to bittersweet. The best known sweet peppers are the **bell peppers,** so-named for their rather bell-like shape. They have a mild, sweet flavor and crisp, exceedingly juicy flesh. When young, the majority of bell peppers are a rich, bright green, but there are also yellow, orange, purple, red and brown bell peppers. The red bells are simply vine-ripened green bell peppers which, because they've ripened longer, are very sweet. Bell peppers vary from 3½ to 5½ inches long and from 2½ to 4 inches wide. Green bell peppers are available all year long, while the red, orange, yellow, purple and brown varieties are found sporadically throughout the year. With their tops cut off and seeds removed, bell peppers are excellent for stuffing with a variety of fillings. The large, red, heart-shaped **pimiento** is another popular sweet pepper. Fresh pimientos are available in some specialty produce markets from late summer to fall. Canned or bottled pimientos are marketed year-round in halves, strips and small pieces. Pimientos are the familiar red stuffing found in green olives. Other sweet pepper varieties include the thin, curved, green **bull's horn;** the long, tapered **Cubanelle,** which can range in color from yellow to red; and the **sweet banana pepper,** which is long, yellow and banana-shaped. Most sweet peppers are available year-round with a peak from July through September. Choose peppers that are firm, have a richly colored, shiny skin and which are heavy for their size. Avoid those that are limp, shriveled or which have soft or bruised spots. Sweet peppers are used raw in salads and as part of a vegetable platter served with various dips. In cooking, they find their way into a variety of dishes and can be sautéed, baked, grilled, braised and steamed. Sweet peppers are an excellent source of vitamin C and contain fair amounts of vitamin A and small amounts of calcium, phosphorus, iron, thiamin, riboflavin and niacin.

sweet potato This large edible root belongs to the morning-glory family and is native to tropical areas of the Americas. There are many varieties of sweet potato but the two that are widely grown commercially are a pale sweet potato and the darker-skinned variety Americans erroneously call "yam" (the true YAM is not related to the sweet potato). The pale sweet potato has a thin, light yellow skin and a pale yellow flesh. Its flavor is not sweet and after being cooked, the pale sweet potato is dry and crumbly, much like a white baking potato. The darker variety has a thicker, dark orange skin and a vivid orange, sweet flesh that cooks to a much moister texture. Fresh sweet potatoes are available sporadically throughout the year, though not as readily during the summer months. Canned and frozen sweet potatoes are available year-round and are sometimes labeled as yams. When buying fresh sweet potatoes choose those that are small-to medium-sized with smooth, unbruised skins. Sweet potatoes don't store well unless the environment is just right, which is dry, dark and around 55°F. Under perfect conditions they can be stored for 3 to 4 weeks. Otherwise, store in a cool, dark place and use within a week of purchase. Do not refrigerate. Sweet potatoes—particularly the pale variety—can be substituted for regular potatoes in most recipes. They can be prepared in a variety of ways including baking, boiling and sautéing. Sweet-potato chips can now be found on some restaurant menus. Sweet potatoes are high in vitamins C and A. *See also* POTATO.

sweet potato squash *see* DELICATA SQUASH

sweetsop Also called *sugar apple*, the sweetsop is the egg-shaped fruit of a small tropical-American tree. It has a thick, coarse yellow-green (sometimes purple-tinged) skin and yellow flesh with dark seeds. The very sweet, custardlike flesh is divided into segments like a citrus fruit. The sweetsop is often mistaken for the CHERIMOYA (or custard apple), to which it is related. It's grown in Florida and California and is usually available from mid-summer to mid-winter only in the locales where it's grown. After the skin and seeds are removed, sweetsops are usually eaten raw. They're often used in desserts.

Swiss chard *see* CHARD

Swiss cheese A generic term for cheeses that have a pale yellow, slightly nutty-flavored flesh with large holes. American Swiss cheeses were patterned after Switzerland's world-famous EMMENTALER and GRUYÈRE cheeses. These Swiss-style cheeses are good for sandwiches and salads and have excellent melting properties. *See also* CHEESE.

Swiss fondue *see* FONDUE

Swiss steak Called smothered steak in England, this dish begins with a thick cut of beef—usually ROUND or CHUCK—that has been tenderized by pounding, coated with flour and browned on both sides. The meat is then smothered with chopped tomatoes, onions, carrots, celery, beef broth and various seasonings before being covered and braised, baked or simmered for about 2 hours.

swordfish This large food and sport fish is found in temperate waters throughout the world. Swordfish average between 200 to 600 pounds, though some specimens caught weigh over 1,000 pounds. They have a distinctive saillike dorsal fin and a striking swordlike projection extending from the upper jaw. Their mild-flavored, moderately fat flesh is firm, dense and meatlike, making swordfish one of the most popular fish in the U.S. Fresh swordfish is available from late spring to early fall, whereas it's available frozen year-round. Both forms are sold in steaks and chunks. Because it's so firm, swordfish can be prepared in almost any manner including sautéing, grilling, broiling, baking and poaching. *See also* FISH.

syllabub [SIHL-uh-buhb] This thick, frothy drink or dessert originated in old England. It's traditionally made by beating milk with wine or ale, sugar, spices and sometimes beaten egg whites. A richer version made with cream can be used as a topping for cakes, cookies, fruit, etc. It's thought that the name of this concoction originated during Elizabethan times and is a combination of the words *Sille* (a French wine that was used in the mixture) and *bub* (Old-English slang for "bubbling drink").

Sylvaner [sihl-VAH-nuhr] Long popular in Germany and surrounding areas of Europe, this white wine grape is now being grown in other parts of the world such as the United States and Chile. Though the wine produced from Sylvaner grapes is light and pleasant, it's not as flavorful or fruity as Germany's JOHANNISBERG RIESLING.

syrniki [sihr-NEE-kee] Russian in origin, syrniki is a dish of fried cheese cakes that can be served sweet—sprinkled with confectioners' sugar and sour cream—or savory, topped with sour cream and herbs such as dill. Syrniki are made with a mixture of POT CHEESE or FARMER'S CHEESE, flour and beaten eggs, which is formed into cakes before being sautéed on both sides until brown.

Szechuan pepper; Szechwan [SEHCH-wahn; SEHCH-oo-ahn] Native to the Szechuan province of China, this mildly hot spice—also called *Chinese pepper*— comes from the prickly ash tree. Though not related to the PEPPERCORN family, Szechuan berries resemble black peppercorns but contain a tiny seed. Szechuan pepper has a distinctive flavor and fragrance. It can be found in oriental markets and specialty stores in whole or powdered form. Whole berries are often heated before being ground to bring out their tantalizing flavor and aroma.

abasco pepper; Tabasco Sauce [tuh-BAS-koh] A very hot, small red pepper originally from the Mexican state of Tabasco. The word itself means "damp earth." Though these peppers are now grown in parts of Louisiana, they're not commercially available. Instead, they're used specifically to make Tabasco Sauce, a trademarked name held by the McIlhenny family since the mid-1800s. Produced since Civil War times, this fiery sauce is made from tabasco peppers, vinegar and salt. The peppers are fermented in barrels for 3 years before being processed into the sauce. Tabasco Sauce adds zest to numerous dishes as well as being integral to the famous BLOODY MARY cocktail.

tabbouleh [tuh-BOO-luh] A Middle Eastern dish of BULGHUR WHEAT mixed with chopped tomatoes, onions, parsley, mint, olive oil and lemon juice. It's served cold, often with a crisp bread such as LAVOSH.

table d'hôte [tah-buhl DOHT] This French term literally means "the table of the host." On restaurant menus, however, *table d'hôte* refers to a complete meal of several courses for the price of the entree. *See also* À LA CARTE; PRIX FIXE.

taco [tah-COH] A Mexican-style "sandwich" consisting of a folded corn TORTILLA filled with various ingredients such as beef, pork, chicken, CHORIZO sausage, tomatoes, lettuce, cheese, onion, GUACAMOLE, REFRIED BEANS and SALSA. Most tacos in the U.S. are made with crisp (fried) tortilla shells, but there are also "soft" (pliable) versions. The latter are more likely to be found in the Southwest and California. Tacos may be eaten as an entree or snack.

taffy [TAF-ee] Soft and chewy, taffy is a candy made with sugar, butter and various flavorings. Its delectable, supple consistency is achieved by twisting and pulling the candy as it cools into long, pliable strands, which are then usually cut into bite-size chunks. The famous **saltwater taffy**, made popular in the late 1800s in Atlantic City, was so named because it used a small amount of salt water in the mixture. Today's saltwater taffy doesn't necessarily follow tradition. The British version of taffy, called TOFFEE or toffy, is harder than America's version.

tagliatelle [tahl-yuh-TEHL-ee] Long, thin, flat strips of PASTA about ¼ inch wide. "Tagliatelle" is the name used in northern Italy for FETTUCCINE.

tahini [tuh-HEE-nee] Used in Middle Eastern cooking, tahini is a thick paste made of ground SESAME SEED. It's used to flavor various dishes such as HUMMUS and BABA GHANOUSH.

Taleggio cheese [tahl-EH-zhee-oh] Hailing from Italy's Lombardy region, this rich (48 percent fat), semisoft cheese is made from whole cow's milk. Its flavor can range from mild to pungent, depending on its age. When young, Taleggio's color is pale yellow and its texture semisoft. As it ages it darkens to deep yellow and becomes rather runny. Taleggio is sold in flat blocks or cylinders and is covered either with a wax coating or a thin mold. It's excellent with salad greens or served with fruit for dessert. *See also* CHEESE.

tamale [tuh-MAH-lee] From the *Nahuatl* word (*tamalii*), the tamale is a popular Mexican dish that consists of various fillings (such as finely chopped meat and vegetables) coated with a MASA dough and wrapped in a softened corn husk. This package is then tied and steamed until the dough is cooked through. The corn husk is peeled back before the tamale is eaten. Although savory tamales are the most popular in the U.S., many cooks in Mexico also serve sweet tamales, usually filled with fruit.

tamari [tuh-MAH-ree] Similar to but thicker than SOY SAUCE, tamari is also a dark sauce made from SOYBEANS. It has a distinctively mellow flavor and is used primarily as a table CONDIMENT, as a dipping sauce or for basting.

tamarillo [tam-uh-RIHL-oh; tam-uh-REE-oh] Native to South America, this egg-shaped fruit is also known as a *tree tomato*. Although not yet widely accepted in the U.S., the tamarillo is very popular in South and Central America, the Caribbean, and parts of Asia, New Zealand (from where most of the fruit in the U.S. is imported) and Australia. The tamarillo has a tough, bitter skin that can be various glossy shades of red, purple, amber or yellow. The tart but very flavorful golden pink flesh is purple-tinged around the seeds. Tamarillos are available from May through October in specialty produce stores and some supermarkets. Choose firm, blemish-free fruit that's heavy for its size. When ripe, tamarillos should be fragrant and should yield slightly to palm pressure. They can be ripened at room temperature. Once ripe, they should be refrigerated, tightly wrapped in a plastic bag, up to 10 days. Tamarillos can be eaten fresh or cooked, and are used for both sweet and savory dishes. One requisite, however, is sugar, which reduces the fruit's natural tartness and enhances its flavor. Tamarillos are a good source of vitamins A and C.

tamarind [TAM-uh-rihnd] Also known as *Indian date*, the tamarind is the fruit of a tall shade tree native to Asia and northern Africa and widely grown in India. The large (about 5-inch-long) pods contain small seeds and a sour-sweet pulp which, when dried, becomes extremely sour. Tamarind pulp is popular as a flavoring in East Indian and Middle Eastern cuisines much like lemon juice is in Western culture. It's used to season full-flavored foods such as CHUTNEYS, CURRY dishes and pickled fish. Additionally, tamarind is used to make a sweet syrup flavoring soft drinks. It's also an integral ingredient in Worcestershire sauce. Tamarind can be found in East Indian and some oriental markets in various forms: jars of concentrated pulp with seeds; canned paste; whole pods dried into "bricks" or ground into powder. Tamarind syrup can be found in Dutch, Indonesian and East Indian markets.

tamis [TAM-ee; tam-EE; TAM-ihs] Also called *tammycloth*, a tamis is a worsted-cloth STRAINER used to strain liquid mixtures such as sauces.

tandoor oven; tandoori [tahn-DOOR; tahn-DOOR-ee] Used throughout India (and found in Indian restaurants throughout the world), the traditional rounded-top tandoor oven is made of brick and clay. It's used to bake foods over direct heat produced from a smoky fire. The dough for the delicious Indian bread NAAN is slapped directly onto the oven's clay walls and left to bake until puffy and lightly browned. Meats cooked in the tall, rather cylindrical tandoor are usually skewered and thrust into the oven's heat, which is so intense (usually over 500°F) that it cooks a chicken half in less than 5 minutes. Chicken and other meats cooked with this method are identified as *tandoori chicken*, etc.

tangelo [tan-JEHL-oh] A juicy, sweetly tart citrus fruit with few seeds that takes its name from the fact that it's a cross between the TANGERINE and the POMELO. There are many hybrids of this loose-skinned fruit, ranging in size from that of a tiny orange to that of a small grapefruit. The skins, which can be rough to smooth, range in color from yellow-orange to deep orange. The most common variety of tangelo available in the U.S. is the **Minneola**, which is easily recognized by its nipple-shaped stem end. Tangelos are in season from November through March. *See also* MANDARIN ORANGE; ORANGE.

tangerine [tan-juh-REEN] *see* MANDARIN ORANGE

tannin [TAN-ihn] An astringent substance found in the seeds and stems of grapes, the bark of some trees and in tea. Tannin is important in the making of good red wines, aiding them in long and graceful aging. When such wines are young, the tannin often gives them a noticeable astringency—a quality that diminishes as the wine ages, mellows and develops character.

tapas [TAH-pahs] Popular throughout Spain in bars and restaurants, *tapas* are appetizers that usually accompany SHERRY or other APERITIFS or COCKTAILS. They can also form an entire meal and can range from simple items such as olives or cubes of ham and cheese to more elaborate preparations like cold omelets, snails in a spicy sauce, stuffed peppers and miniature sandwiches.

tapenade [TA-puh-nahd; ta-pen-AHD] Hailing from France's Provence region, tapenade is a thick paste made from capers, anchovies, ripe olives, olive oil, lemon juice, seasonings and sometimes small pieces of tuna. It's used as a CONDIMENT and served with CRUDITÉS, fish, meat, etc.

tapioca; tapioca flour [tap-ee-OH-kuh] A starchy substance extracted from the root of the CASSAVA plant. It's available in several forms including granules, flakes, pellets (called *pearl tapioca*) and flour or starch. The most widely available forms are *tapioca flour* (also called *cassava flour*) and pearl tapioca. The flour is used as a thickening agent for soups, fruit fillings, glazes, etc., much like CORNSTARCH. Pearl tapioca is used mainly to make pudding and comes in several sizes, regular or instant forms, and in a variety of prepackaged flavors. Pearl tapioca is available in most supermarkets, whereas the other forms are more commonly found in health-food stores and Asian markets. If stored in a cool, dark place, all types of tapioca will keep indefinitely.

taramasalata [tah-rah-mah-sah-LAH-tah] This Greek specialty is a thick, creamy mixture made with *tarama* (pale orange carp ROE), lemon juice, milk-soaked breadcrumbs, olive oil and seasonings. *Taramasalata* is usually served with bread or crackers as an HORS D'OEUVRE. It may also be used as a dip for CRUDITÉS.

taro root [TAHR-oh; TAIR-oh] A starchy, potatolike tuber with a brown, fibrous skin and gray-white (sometimes purple-tinged) flesh. Taro is grown in tropical areas and is an important starchy food in West Africa, the Caribbean and Polynesian islands. A variety of taro grown in the southern U.S. since the early 1900s is called **dasheen**. Taro roots range in length from about 5 inches to a foot or more, and can be several inches wide. Though acrid-tasting in its raw state, the root has a somewhat nutlike flavor when cooked. It's also extremely easy to digest. It should be noted, however, that some varieties are highly toxic unless thoroughly cooked. The taro root has large edible leaves (called *callaloo* in the Caribbean) which can be prepared and eaten like mustard or turnip greens. Taro root can be found in ethnic markets and some specialty produce stores. Choose roots that are firm and smooth and refrigerate up to 4 days. Much like the potato, the taro root may be prepared in a variety of ways including boiling, frying and baking. In Hawaii, it's used to make the famous (or infamous) POI.

tarragon [TAIR-uh-gon; TAIR-uh-guhn] Narrow, pointed, dark green leaves distinguish this perennial aromatic herb known for its distinctive aniselike flavor. Tarragon is widely used in classic French cooking for a variety of dishes including chicken, fish and vegetables, as well as many sauces, the best-known being BÉARNAISE. It's also an integral ingredient in various herbal combinations such as FINES HERBES. Tarragon is available fresh in the summer and early fall and year-round in dried and powdered forms. Care should be taken when using tarragon since its assertiveness can easily dominate other flavors. Tarragon vinegar is a popular item in gourmet markets. *See also* HERBS; Herb and Spice Chart, page 538.

tart *n.* Very simply, a tart is a pastry crust with shallow sides, a filling and no top crust. The filling can be sweet (such as fruit or sweet custard) or savory (like meat, cheese or savory custard). Depending on the type of tart, the pastry shell can be baked and then filled, or filled and then baked. Tarts can be bite-sized (often served as HORS D'OEUVRE), individual-sized (sometimes called *tartlets*) or full-sized. They can be used as appetizers, entrees or desserts. *See also* TARTE TATIN. **tart** *adj.* Sharp, acidic or sour.

T

tartare steak *see* BEEF TARTARE

tartare, beef *see* BEEF TARTARE

Tartarian cherry; black Tartarian cherry [tar-TAIR-ee-uhn] Large and heart-shaped, the Tartarian cherry has a dark purple, almost black skin and flesh. Inside the thin skin the flesh is sweet, juicy and extremely flavorful. The Tartarian cherry is available from May to September. *See also* CHERRY.

tartaric acid [tahr-TAR-ihk; tahr-TAHR-ihk] A natural crystalline compound found in plants, especially those with tart characteristics such as TAMARIND and unripe grapes. The principal acid in wine, tartaric acid is the component that promotes graceful aging and crispness of flavor. One of the byproducts of tartaric acid is CREAM OF TARTAR, which is used in baking and candy-making.

tartar sauce; tartare sauce [TAHR-tuhr] Based on MAYONNAISE, tartar sauce is a mixture of minced capers, dill pickles, onions or shallots, olives, lemon juice or vinegar and seasonings. It's traditionally served with fried fish, but can also be used with vegetables.

tarte Tatin [tart tah-TAN] A famous French upside-down apple TART made by covering the bottom of a shallow baking dish with butter and sugar, then apples and finally a pastry crust. While baking, the sugar and butter create a delicious CARAMEL that becomes the topping when the tart is inverted onto a serving plate. The tart was created by two French sisters who lived in the Loire Valley and earned their living making it. The French call this dessert *tarte des demoiselles Tatin*, "the tart of two unmarried women named Tatin."

tasso [TAH-soh; TA-soh] Much to the dissappointment of anyone who's tasted it, this Cajun specialty is very hard to find outside Louisiana. Tasso is a lean chunk of cured pork (usually shoulder) or beef that's been richly seasoned with ingredients such as red pepper, garlic, FILÉ POWDER and any of several other herbs or spices, depending on the manufacturer. It's then smoked for about (again, depending on the cook) 2 days. The result is a firm, smoky and flavorfully tangy meat that is principally used for seasoning. Outside of Cajun country, tasso is available in some specialty gourmet shops and by mail order. It can be refrigerated, tightly wrapped, for up to a week. Though it's sometimes referred to as *tasso ham* and is most often finely chopped and used (like ham, PROSCIUTTO, PANCETTA or SALT PORK) to flavor foods such as beans, eggs and pastas, the spicy-hot tasso most definitely isn't ham.

tawny port [TAW-nee] *see* PORT

T-bone steak Cut from the center of the SHORT LOIN, this steak has a T-shaped bone that separates the small tenderloin section from the larger top loin. The porterhouse steak differs from the T-bone in that it contains a larger portion of the tenderloin. *See also* BEEF; Beef Chart, page 573.

tea Tea is native to China, where it grew wild until the Chinese determined that the leaves helped flavor the flat taste of the water they boiled to prevent getting sick. Tea plant cultivation in China began about 4,000 years ago but it wasn't until the 8th century A.D. that outsiders (the Japanese) discovered it. Europeans were finally introduced to tea during the 17th century and the British (who were the true tea lovers) spread its use by implementing new growing areas such as India. In fact, the English so enjoy their tea that they developed a meal around it, HIGH TEA. Tea also played an important role in the development of the U.S.—its taxation led to the Boston Tea Party, one of the issues that triggered the War of Independence. Americans further influenced tea use both by inventing tea bags and by starting the practice of drinking iced tea at the St. Louis World's Fair in 1904. The word "tea" can refer to the beverage, the leaves used to make the beverage and the magnolia-related evergreen shrub from which the leaves come. All tea plants belong to the same species but varying climates, soils, etc. combine in different ways to create a plethora of distinctive leaves. The processing of those leaves is responsible for the individual characteristics of each tea. Leaves are sorted by size—those which are young and tender are superior to older, coarser leaves. Black, green and oolong *tea* are the main types produced during processing. **Black tea** comes from leaves that have been fermented before being heated and dried. Such leaves produce a dark reddish-brown brew. Black teas are graded according to the size of the leaf; *orange pekoe* describes leaves that are smaller than the medium-size coarser PEKOE leaves. Although black tea flavors vary, most are more assertive than those of green or oolong teas. Among the more well-known black teas are *Darjeeling, English Breakfast* and *Lapsang Souchong*. **Green tea,** favored among Orientals, is produced from leaves that are steamed and dried but *not* fermented. Such leaves produce a greenish-yellow tea and a flavor that's slightly bitter and closer to the taste of the fresh leaf. Two of the more well-known green teas are *Basket Fried* and *Gunpowder*. **Oolong tea** is produced from leaves that are partially fermented, a process which creates teas with a flavor, color and aroma that falls between black tea and green tea. The best known oolong is *Formosa oolong*, from Taiwan. In addition to these three main types of tea there are **specialty teas.** Such teas are flavored with various floral or spice additions such as jasmine or chrysanthemum blossoms, or orange or lemon peel. **Instant tea,** which dissolves quickly in cold or hot water, consists of brewed tea that is dehydrated and granulated. It often contains sugar or sugar substitutes and other flavorings such as cinnamon or lemon. **Herb tea** (*see* TISANE) is not a true tea based on tea-shrub leaves, but rather an infusion of various herbs, flowers and spices. Both black teas (in leaf and tea-bag form) and instant teas are readily available in most supermarkets. Other teas can be found in great variety in health-food stores, ethnic markets and stores specializing in tea and coffee. *For information on specific types of tea, see individual listings.*

tea egg A Chinese specialty prepared by hard-cooking eggs, crushing (but not peeling) the shells, then simmering the eggs in strong tea for about an hour. The tea seeps through the cracked shell, thereby flavoring the egg and giving it a marbleized appearance. Tea eggs are usually served as an appetizer.

tea melon Also called *sweet cucumber*, the yellow-colored tea melon is a tiny (2-inch-long) fruit that's shaped like a cucumber. It has a sweet, mild flavor and a delightfully crisp texture. This mini melon is most often preserved, usually in honey and spices but sometimes in soy sauce. Tea melon is not sold fresh in the U.S. but can be found in preserved form in oriental markets. Once preserved, it goes by many names including *Chinese pickle, preserved sweet melon, sweet tea pickle* and *pickled* *cucumber.* Tea melon is usually served as a CONDIMENT or pickle and is also used to flavor various oriental dishes.

Teleme cheese [TEHL-uh-may] Available mainly in northern California, Teleme cheese is similar in texture to domestic BRIE. It contains about 50 percent butterfat and has a pronounced tangy flavor. When young, Teleme's texture is soft and creamy. As it ages, it becomes runnier and stronger in flavor. *See also* CHEESE.

temple orange This loose-skinned orange is somewhat oval in shape and has a rough, thick, deep orange skin. Thought to be a cross between a TANGERINE and an orange, the temple has a sweetly tart flesh and a goodly number of seeds. It's in season from December to March. *See also* ORANGE.

tempura [tehm-POOR-uh] A Japanese specialty of batter-dipped, deep-fried pieces of fish or vegetables. Tempura, which is usually accompanied by soy sauce, can be served an HORS D'OEUVRE, first course or entree.

tenderizer *see* MEAT TENDERIZERS

tenderloin *see* SHORT LOIN

tequila [tuh-KEE-luh] A colorless or pale straw-colored liquor made by fermenting and distilling the sweet sap of the AGAVE plant. It originated in Tequila, Mexico, hence the name. Most tequilas imported to the United States range from 80 to 86 PROOF, although some versions are over 100 proof. Tequila is the base liquor in the popular MARGARITA cocktail.

teriyaki *n.* [tehr-uh-YAH-kee; tehr-ee-YAK-kee] 1. A Japanese dish consisting of food, such as beef or chicken, that has been marinated in a mixture of soy sauce, SAKE (or SHERRY), sugar, ginger and seasonings before being grilled, broiled or fried. The sugar in the marinade gives the cooked food a slight glaze. 2. A homemade or commercially prepared sauce made with the above ingredients. **teriyaki** *adj.* A phrase describing food cooked in this manner, as in "chicken teriyaki."

terrapin [TEHR-uh-pihn] *see* TURTLE

terrine [teh-REEN] *see* PÂTÉ

Tetrazzini [teh-trah-ZEE-nee] *see* CHICKEN TETRAZZINI

Tex-Mex [TEHKS-MEHKS] A term given to food (as well as music, etc.) based on the combined cultures of Texas and Mexico. Tex-Mex food encompasses a wide variety of dishes including BURRITOS, NACHOS and TACOS.

Thermidor [THER-mih-dohr] *see* LOBSTER THERMIDOR

thimbleberry [THIHM-buhl-bair-ee] Any of several thimble-shaped American raspberries, especially the black raspberry. *See also* RASPBERRY.

thin *v.* To dilute mixtures such as soups, sauces, batters, etc. by adding more liquid.

Thompson seedless grape The best-selling grape in the U.S., the Thompson seedless is medium-sized with a thin, pale green skin. It contains no seeds and has a sweet, rather bland flavor. Its peak season is from June to November. *See also* GRAPE

Thousand Island dressing A MAYONNAISE-based salad dressing made with CHILI SAUCE and finely chopped ingredients such as stuffed green olives, green peppers, pickles, onions and hard-cooked egg. Thousand Island dressing is also sometimes used as a sandwich spread.

thousand-year egg *see* HUNDRED-YEAR EGG

thread stage A test for SUGAR SYRUP in which a drop of boiling syrup forms a soft 2-inch thread when immersed in cold water. On a CANDY THERMOMETER, the thread stage is between 230° and 234°F. *See also* Candy-making Temperature and Cold-water Tests, page 537.

Thuringer sausage [THOOR-ihn-juhr; TOOR-ihn-juhr] Any of several fresh and smoked sausages named for the former German region of Thuringia. Thuringers include some CERVELATS and BLOOD SAUSAGES. The spice CORIANDER is integral to many of these sausages. *See also* SAUSAGE.

thyme [TYM] There are several varieties of this mint-family member, a perennial herb native to southern Europe and the Mediterranean. **Garden thyme,** the most often used variety, is a bush with gray-green leaves giving off a pungent minty, light-lemon aroma. Subvarieties include the narrow-leafed *French thyme* and broad-leafed *English thyme*. The most well-known subvariety of **wild thyme**—a thick ground cover—is *lemon thyme*, an herb with a more pronounced lemon aroma than garden thyme. Whatever the variety, thyme is widely used in cooking to add flavor to vegetables, meat, poultry and fish dishes, soups and cream sauces. It's a basic herb of French cuisine and integral to BOUQUET GARNI. Fresh thyme is available in some specialty produce shops and supermarkets during the summer months. Dried thyme—both leaf and powder form—is available year-round. As with all herbs, thyme should be stored in a cool, dark place for no more than 6 months. *See also* HERBS; Herb and Spice Chart, page 538.

ti leaves [TEE] The leaves of a member of the AGAVE family, used in Polynesia to wrap foods to be cooked. The leaves are removed before the food is eaten. Dried ti leaves, which can be found in some ethnic markets, must be soaked to soften before using. A Hawaiian liquor called OKOLEHAO is made from a mash of the ti plant.

Tía Maria [tee-uh muh-REE-uh] Based on RUM, this dark brown Jamaican LIQUEUR has a strong coffee flavor.

tiger lily buds Also called *golden needles* and simply *lily buds*, the dried golden buds of the tiger lily are 2 to 3 inches long and have a delicate, musky-sweet flavor. They're used both as vegetable and garnish in various STIR-FRIED dishes. The delicate tiger lily buds are available in 4- to 8-ounce cellophane bags in oriental markets. They must be soaked in water prior to using.

tilefish A diet of crab and other CRUSTACEANS gives the tilefish a marvelously delicate flavor. This Atlantic-based fish is multicolored and dotted with distinctive yellow spots. Its low-fat flesh is very firm yet tender. The tilefish ranges from 2 to over 50 pounds. Atlantic tilefish is available fresh and frozen in whole (smaller ones), steak and fillet forms. It's suitable for almost any method of cooking. *See also* FISH.

Tillamook cheese [TIHL-uh-mook] A yellow CHEDDAR produced in and around the area of Tillamook, Oregon. It is made from raw milk and ranges from mild to sharp in flavor. Aged Tillamook cheese is highly prized but seldom seen anywhere but the West Coast. *See also* CHEESE.

Tilsit cheese [TIHL-ziht] A cheese said to have orginated in Tilsit, East Prussia (now part of the Soviet Union), when Dutch immigrants accidentally created it while attempting to make GOUDA. Tilsit has a medium-firm texture with irregular eyes or cracks. Commercially produced Tilsit is made from pasteurized milk, ranges from 30 to 50 percent butterfat and has a pale yellow interior surrounded by a dark yellow rind. Its flavor is mild but becomes more pungent with age. A very strong version, called **Farmhouse Tilsit**, is made from raw milk and is aged for about 5 months, which creates a cheese approaching LIMBURGER in aroma. Tilsit is used to flavor foods such as sauces and vegetable dishes. *See also* CHEESE.

timbale [TIHM-buhl; tihm-BAHL] 1. A mold, generally high-sided, drum-shaped and slightly tapered at one end, used to bake various dishes. 2. A dish—usually based on custard, FORCEMEAT or RISOTTO combined with meat, fish, vegetables, cheese, etc.—baked in such a mold. The dish is unmolded and often served as an entree (and sometimes as a first course) with a sauce such as BÉCHAMEL. 3. A pastry shell made by dipping a timbale iron first into a batter, then into deep, hot fat. When the crisp pastry is pushed off the iron and cooled, it can be filled with a sweet or savory mixture. **Timbale irons** come in various sizes and shapes such as hearts, stars and butterflies. They're available in specialty cookware stores.

tipsy parson; tipsy pudding   Similar to TRIFLE, this old-fashioned English dessert consists of several layers of SPONGE CAKE soaked with wine or BRANDY, sprinkled with almonds and layered with whipped cream or custard. It was thought that too much of this would make one tipsy.

tisane [tih-ZAN; tih-ZAHN]   Commonly called *herb tea*, a tisane is a tealike drink made by steeping any of various herbs, flowers, spices, etc. in boiling water. Such brews have long been used for their calming and rejuvenating qualities. Some of the herbs more commonly used for tisane blends are balm, camomile, hyssop, mint and tansy. Tisanes can be found in health-food stores, often under the label "herb tea."

toad-in-the-hole   This comically named British dish consists of a YORKSHIRE PUDDING batter to which small cooked link sausages are added. The dish is baked until the batter puffs up around the sausages (making them the "toads in the hole") and becomes golden brown. It's most often served for lunch or dinner.

toddy [TOD-ee]   An alcoholic drink—usually hot—made with whiskey, rum or brandy, very hot water, sugar, spices and lemon. This drink seems to have evolved from *tari*, the Hindu word used for the sap or juice of a palm tree. In Asia, this sap was often fermented to create an alcoholic beverage. British sailors picked up on the idea, which eventually evolved into the toddy.

toffee; toffy [TAWF-ee]   A hard but chewy candy made by cooking sugar, water (or cream) and usually butter. Depending on the recipe, a toffee mixture may be cooked to anywhere from 260° to 310°F. Other ingredients such as nuts or chocolate are sometimes added.

tofu [TOH-foo]   Also known as *soybean curd* and *bean curd*, custardlike white tofu is made from curdled SOY MILK, an iron-rich liquid extracted from ground, cooked SOYBEANS. The resulting curds are drained and pressed in a fashion similar to cheesemaking. The firmness of the resulting tofu cake depends on how much WHEY has been pressed out. Tofu is popular throughout the Orient, particularly in Japan. It has a bland, slightly nutty flavor that gives it a chameleonlike capability to take on the flavor of the food with which it's cooked. Tofu's texture is smooth and creamy yet it's firm enough to slice. It's available in health-food stores, oriental markets and many supermarkets. The cakes are sold in a variety of forms including packaged in water, vacuum-packed and in bulk (usually in large crocks or jars of water). Tofu, which is sometimes fortified with calcium, is very perishable and should be refrigerated for no more than a week. If it's packaged in water, drain it and cover with fresh water. All tofu should be stored covered with water, which should be changed daily. Tofu can be frozen up to 3 months. Freezing will change its texture, making it slightly chewier. The versatile tofu can be sliced, diced or mashed and used in a variety of dishes including soups, SITR-FRIES, casseroles, salads, sandwiches, salad dressings and sauces. It's easy to digest, low in calories, calcium and sodium, high in protein and cholesterol-free—all of which makes it one of today's most healthful foods.

Tokay grape [toh-KAY] 1. A large, oval California table grape (also called *Flame Tokay*) with a thick red skin and bland-tasting flesh with seeds. Tokays are available from August through December. They're also sometimes used to make wine of the same name. 2. A fine white grape from Hungary (also called *Furmint*), used to make both dry and sweet wines. Grapes from the better vintages that are infected with BOTRYTIS CINEREA produce marvelous DESSERT WINES which rival the best from France and Germany. *See also* GRAPE.

Toll House cookie This—the original chocolate-chip cookie—was created in the 1930s by Ruth Wakefield, who ran the Toll House Restaurant outside of Whitman, Massachusetts. Mrs. Wakefield, in a moment of brilliant inspiration, cut up bars of chocolate to add to a basic butter-cookie dough. History was made. Today, the chocolate-chip cookie is the most popular in the U.S.

tomalley [TOM-al-ee; toh-MAL-ee] Considered a delicacy, tomalley is the green-colored liver of a lobster. It may be eaten alone but is often also added to sauces. *See also* LOBSTER.

Tom and Jerry Favored by skiers and cold-weather captives, the Tom and Jerry is a hot drink made with beaten eggs, hot milk or water, liquor (such as brandy, bourbon or rum), sugar and spices. It's served in a large mug and usually sprinkled with grated nutmeg. The drink takes its name from the principal characters in the early 19th-century novel, *Life in London*.

tomatillo [tohm-ah-TEE-oh] This fruit belongs to the same nightshade family as the tomato, and in fact resembles a small green tomato in size, shape and appearance except for the fact that it has a thin parchmentlike covering. The papery husk is a clue to the fact that the tomatillo is also related to the CAPE GOOSEBERRY. Although tomatillos can ripen to yellow, they are generally used while still green and quite firm. Their flavor has hints of lemon, apple and herbs. Tomatillos are available sporadically year-round in specialty produce stores, Latin-American markets and some supermarkets. Choose firm fruit with dry, tight-fitting husks. Store in a paper bag in the refrigerator for up to a month. Remove husk and wash fruit before using. Cooking enhances the tomatillo's flavor and softens its thick skin. Tomatillos are popular in Mexican and Southwest cooking for use in a variety of dishes including GUACAMOLE and many sauces. They can be used raw in salads and SALSAS for a more acidic taste. Canned tomatillos are available in ethnic markets. Tomatillos are rich in vitamin A and contain a good amount of vitamin C. They're also called *Mexican green tomato.*

tomato [tuh-MAY-toh; tuh-MAH-toh] Like the potato and eggplant, the tomato is a member of the nightshade family. It's the fruit of a vine native to South America. By the time European explorers arrived in the New World, the tomato had made its way up into Central America and Mexico. The Spanish carried plants back home from Mexico, but it took some time for tomatoes to be accepted in Spain because it was thought that—like various other members of the nightshade family—they were poisonous. Some tomato advocates, however, claimed the fruit had aphrodisiac powers and, in fact, the French called them *pommes d'amour,* "love apples." It wasn't until the 1900s that the tomato gained some measure of popularity in the U.S. Today this fruit is one of America's favorite "vegetables," a classification the government gave the tomato for trade purposes in 1893. Dozens of tomato varieties are available today—ranging widely in size, shape and color. Among the most commonly marketed is the **beefsteak tomato,** which is delicious both raw and cooked. It's large, bright red and slightly elliptical in shape. **Globe tomatoes** are medium-sized, firm and juicy. Like the beefsteak, they're good both raw and cooked. Another variety is the **plum tomato** (also called *Italian plum*), a flavorful egg-shaped tomato that comes in red and yellow versions. The medium-sized **green tomato** has a piquant flavor, which makes it excellent for frying, broiling and adding to relishes. The small **cherry tomato** is about 1 inch in diameter and can be red or yellow-gold in color. It's very popular—both for eating and as a garnish—because of its bright color and excellent flavor. The yellow cherry tomato is slightly less acidic than the red and therefore somewhat blander in flavor. Though it's long been popular raw in salads, the cherry tomato is gaining favor as a cooked side dish, quickly sautéed with herbs. The **yellow pear tomato** is slightly smaller than the cherry tomato and resembles a tiny pear. It's used in the same manner as the cherry tomato. Fresh tomatoes are available year-round, with the peak season from June through September. The most succulent, flavorful tomatoes are those which are "vine-ripened," usually only available in specialty produce markets. Unfortunately, such tomatoes are very perishable, which is why supermarkets almost always carry tomatoes that have been picked green and ripened with ethylene gas or in special warming rooms. Such tomatoes will never have the texture, aroma and taste of the vine-ripened fruit. Choose firm, well-shaped tomatoes that are noticeably fragrant and richly colored (for their variety). They should be free from blemishes, heavy for their size and give slightly to palm pressure. Ripe tomatoes should be stored at room temperature and used within a few days. They should never be refrigerated—cold temperatures make the flesh pulpy and kills the flavor. Unripe fruit can be ripened by placing it in a pierced paper bag with an apple for several days at room temperature (65° to 75°F). Do not refrigerate or set in the sun. Tomato skins can be removed by BLANCHING. **Sun-dried tomatoes** are, as the name indicates, dried in the sun (or by other artificial methods). The result is a chewy, intensely flavored, sweet, dark red tomato. Sun-dried tomatoes are usually either packed in oil or dry-packed in cellophane. The dry-pack type benefits from soaking in oil or other liquid before use. Sun-dried tomatoes add their rich flavor to sauces, soups, sandwiches, salads and a myriad of other dishes. **Canned tomatoes** are available in various forms including peeled whole, crushed, and those with herbs such as oregano and/or basil added. **Tomato paste,** which is available in cans and tubes, consists of tomatoes that have been cooked for several hours, strained and reduced to a deep red, richly flavored concentrate. Canned **tomato puree** consists of tomatoes that have been cooked briefly and strained, resulting in a thick liquid. **Tomato sauce** is a slightly thinner tomato puree, often with seasonings and other flavorings added so that it is ready to use in various dishes or as a base for other sauces. Tomatoes are rich in vitamin C and contain appreciable amounts of vitamins A and B, potassium, iron and phosphorus. A medium tomato has about as much fiber as a slice of whole-wheat bread and only about 35 calories. *See also* TOMATILLO.

tomato paste *see* TOMATO

tomato puree *see* TOMATO

tomato sauce *see* TOMATO

Tom Collins *see* COLLINS

tongue [TUHNG] Tongues of beef, veal, lamb and pork are nutritious and appetizing VARIETY MEATS. They can be found fresh, pickled, smoked and CORNED and can be prepared in a variety of ways to be served hot or cold. All tongue is tough and requires long, slow cooking to make it tender. Beef tongues weigh from 2 to 5 pounds, veal tongues from ½ to 2 pounds, pork tongues about 1 pound and lamb tongues around ¼ pound. Fresh tongue should be refrigerated for no more than a day before cooking. It must be scrubbed thoroughly before using.

tongue sausage   Available in large or small links, tongue sausage is made from TONGUE and various other meats. It often contains PISTACHIO NUTS. *See also* SAUSAGE.

tonic water   [TAHN-ik]   Also called *quinine water*, tonic is water charged with carbon dioxide and flavored with fruit EXTRACTS, sugar and usually a tiny amount of quinine (a bitter alkaloid). It's especially popular as a mixer, such as with gin to create the gin and tonic COCKTAIL.

top loin   *see* SHORT LOIN

top round   *see* ROUND

top sirloin   *see* SIRLOIN

torta   [TOHR-tuh]   1. The Italian word for "tart," "pie" or "cake." 2. The Spanish word for "cake," "loaf" or "sandwich."

torte   [TOHRT]   A rich cake, often made with little or no flour but instead with ground nuts or breadcrumbs, eggs, sugar and flavorings. Tortes are often multi-layered and filled with BUTTERCREAM, jams, etc. The word is also applied to some tartlike preparations.

tortellini   [tohr-tl-EE-nee]   Small PASTA stuffed with various fillings, folded over and then shaped into a ring or hat shape.

tortilla   [tohr-TEE-yuh]   1. Mexico's everyday bread, the unleavened tortilla is round and flat—it resembles a very thin pancake. The hand-shaped tortilla can be made from corn flour (MASA) or wheat flour, but is always baked on a griddle. It can be eaten plain or wrapped around various fillings. Tortillas are the base for BURRITOS, TACOS and a multitude of other dishes. Both corn and flour tortillas are sold prepackaged in the refrigerator section of most supermarkets. 2. In Spain, the word *tortilla* refers to a thin OMELET.

tortoise   [TOHR-tuhs]   *see* TURTLE

tortoni   [tohr-TOH-nee]   Hailing from Italy, this rich frozen dessert consists of sweetened whipped cream (sometimes ice cream) flavored with spirits such as SHERRY or RUM and combined or topped with chopped almonds or MACAROON crumbs. This dessert is often called *biscuit tortoni*, especially when served in small paper cups.

toss To turn pieces of food over multiple times, thereby mixing the ingredients together. The term is most often applied to salad, where various ingredients and the salad dressing are tossed together, mixing the ingredients and coating them with the dressing.

tostada [toh-STAH-duh] A crisp-fried TORTILLA (corn or flour) topped with various ingredients such as REFRIED BEANS, shredded chicken or beef, shredded lettuce, diced tomatoes, grated cheese, sour cream or GUACAMOLE. Tostadas can be large or small and served as an appetizer or entree.

Toulouse sausage [too-LOOZ] A small French sausage made of coarsely diced pork flavored with wine, garlic and seasonings. Toulouse sausage is usually braised or fried and makes a good addition to many dishes such as CASSOULET. *See also* SAUSAGE.

tourage [too-RAHJ] A French term for the technique of making PUFF PASTRY whereby the dough is repeatedly folded into thirds, rolled out and folded into thirds again. This process creates hundreds of flaky pastry layers.

tournedo [TOOR-nih-doh; toor-nih-DOH] A beef steak cut from the TENDERLOIN, measuring ¾ to 1 inch thick and 2 to 2½ inches in diameter. Since tournedos are very lean, they're sometimes wrapped in pork fat or bacon prior to grilling or broiling. Classically, they're served on fried bread rounds and topped with a sauce, such as mushroom sauce.

treacle [TREE-kuhl] A term used mainly in Great Britain for the syrupy byproduct created during sugar refining. There are two types: **dark treacle**—which is very much like MOLASSES and which has a somewhat bitter taste, and **light treacle**, which contains fewer impurities than the dark variety, has a lighter flavor and is also called GOLDEN SYRUP.

tree ear *see* WOOD EAR

tree tomato *see* TAMARILLO

trifle [TRY-fuhl] Originally from England, this dessert consists of SPONGE CAKE or LADYFINGERS doused with spirits (usually SHERRY), covered with jam and custard, topped with whipped cream and garnished with candied or fresh fruit, nuts or grated chocolate.

tripe [TRYP] The tripe found in most markets today is the lining of beef stomach, though that from pork and sheep also fall under the definition. There are two beef stomach chambers and three kinds of tripe, all of which are tough and require long cooking. The best tripe, from the second stomach chamber, is called **honeycomb tripe** because the inner side has a pattern similiar to a honeycomb. It's the most tender and subtly flavored. **Pocket tripe** is cut from the end of the second stomach chamber. It's shaped like a pocket with the inside also being honeycombed. The least desirable **plain or smooth tripe** (with a smooth texture on both sides) comes from the first stomach. Tripe is available fresh (which is actually partially cooked by the packer) in most supermarkets. Choose tripe with a pale off-white color and store for up to a day in the refrigerator. Tripe is also available pickled and canned. The most famous French dish using this VARIETY MEAT is the Norman dish called *tripes à la mode de Caen*—tripe braised with carrots, onions and cider. In Spanish-speaking countries, *menudo* (tripe soup) is a well-known favorite.

Triple Sec [TRIH-pl-sehk] A strong, clear orange-flavored liqueur very similiar to CURAÇAO. Triple Sec is used to make the mixed drink, MARGARITA.

triple-cream cheeses; triple-creme *see* DOUBLE-CREAM CHEESES

triticale [triht-ih-KAY-lee] This modern, extremely nutritious hybrid of wheat (*Triticum*) and rye (*Secale*) contains more protein and less gluten than wheat and has a nutty-sweet flavor. It comes in several forms including whole berry, flakes and flour and can be found in health-food stores. Triticale flour is also available in some supermarkets. Whole triticale can be cooked and used in a variety of dishes including cereals, casseroles, PILAF-style dishes, etc. Because triticale flour is low in gluten, bread made from it alone is quite heavy. For that reason, it's usually combined half-and-half with wheat flour.

trivet [TRIHV-iht] A short-legged (or otherwise raised) stand used to support hot dishes and protect the surface of a table.

Trockenbeerenauslese [trok-uhn-bair-uhn-OWS-lay-zuh] Germany's highest classification for very sweet wines made from grapes left on the vine until nearly dry. Because these grapes, picked one by one at fullest maturity, are very concentrated in flavor and sugar, they produce extremely rich, nectarous wines. *Trockenbeerenausleses* are very rare and therefore even more expensive than *Beerenausleses*. See also AUSLESE; SPÄTLESE.

trotters *see* PIG'S FEET

trout [TROWT] A large group of fishes belonging to the same family as SALMON and WHITEFISH. Though most trout are freshwater fish, some live in marine waters. When the first European settlers arrived in North America, trout were very abundant. By the late 1860s, however, a number of factors including overfishing and pollution caused the trout population to diminish drastically. By the end of the 19th century trout hatcheries—along with other prevention and regenerative measures taken to forestall the extinction of this delicious fish—were in existence. Today trout are plentiful and vary widely in appearance and size. In general, their flesh is firm-textured with medium to high fat content. Probably the best known of the freshwater species is the **rainbow trout** which, though native to California, has been transplanted to many different countries and is now one of the most popular varieties in the world. Rainbow trout can grow to up to 50 pounds, but most commercially raised fish average around 8 ounces. **Brook** or **speckled trout** are small (6 to 8 inches long) but considered by many as the best eating. Other popular species include **steelhead** or **salmon trout** (a large—up to 35 pounds—subspecies of the rainbow trout), **cutthroat trout, Dolly Varden, lake trout** and **brown trout.** Saltwater trout or sea trout species, which are generally available only on the East Coast, include **gray trout, silver trout, spotted trout** and **white trout.** Trout are available whole—fresh and frozen—and in fillets. They're most often fried but can also be poached, baked, steamed, grilled and broiled. Whole trout is often stuffed before being cooked. In addition to fresh and frozen, trout can also be found canned, smoked and kippered. *See also* FISH.

truffle [TRUHF-uhl; TROO-fuhl] It's hard to believe that one of the rarest and most expensive foods in the world is located by pigs and dogs. This exceptional fungus grows 3 to 12 inches underground near the roots of trees (usually oak but also chestnut, hazel and beech), never beyond the range of the branches. The difficult-to-find truffle is routed out by animals that have been specially trained for several years. Pigs have keener noses, but dogs are less inclined to gobble up the prize. Once the truffle is found, the farmer (*trufficulteur*) scrapes back the earth, being careful not to touch the truffle with his hands (which will cause the fungus to rot). If the truffle isn't ripe, it's carefully reburied for future harvesting. This methodically slow and labor-intensive harvesting method is what makes truffles so extremely expensive. Truffles have been prized by gourmets for centuries and were credited by the ancient Greeks and Romans with both therapeutic and aphrodisiac powers. A truffle has a rather unappealing appearance—round and irregularly shaped with a thick, rough, wrinkled skin that varies in color from almost black to off-white. Of the almost 70 known varieties, the most desirable is the black truffle, also known as *black diamond*, of France's Périgord and Quercy regions and the Umbria region of Italy. Its extremely pungent flesh is black (really very dark brown) with white striations. The next most popular is the white (actually off-white or beige) truffle of Italy's Piedmont region, with its earthy, garlicky aroma and flavor. Fresh imported truffles are available from late fall to mid-winter in specialty markets. Choose firm, well-shaped truffles with no sign of blemishes. Truffles should be used as soon as possible after purchase but can be stored up to 3 days in the refrigerator. To take full advantage of their perfumy fragrance, bury them in a container of rice or whole eggs and cover tightly before refrigerating. The truffle fragrance will permeate the ingredients they're stored with, giving the cook a double-flavor bonus. Brush any surface dust off the truffle and peel the dark species (saving the peelings for soups). White truffles need not be peeled. Canned truffles, truffle paste in a tube and, to a limited extent, frozen truffles are also found in specialty stores. Dark truffles are generally used to flavor cooked foods such as omelets, POLENTAS, RISOTTOS and sauces, like the famous PÉRIGUEUX. The more mildly flavored white truffles are usually served raw by grating them over foods such as pasta or cheese dishes. They're also added at the last minute to cooked dishes. A special implement called a TRUFFLE SLICER can be used to shave off paper-thin slivers and slices of truffle. Dishes flavored or garnished with truffles are often referred to as À LA PÉRIGOURDINE. *See also* TRUFFLE, CHOCOLATE.

truffle, chocolate [TRUHF-uhl; TROO-fuhl] A rich confection made with a mélange of melted chocolate, butter or cream, sugar and various flavorings such as liquors, liqueurs, spices, vanilla, coffee and nuts. After the mixture is cooled, it's rolled into balls and coated with various coverings such as unsweetened cocoa powder (the classic coating), chocolate sprinkles, shaved chocolate or sugar. Some truffles are dipped in melted white or dark chocolate which, after cooling, becomes a hard coating. These confections were so named because the original, cocoa-coated and rather misshapen truffle resembled the famous and rare fungus of the same name.

truffle slicer A small kitchen device consisting of an adjustable blade mounted on a stainless-steel frame. The slicer's blade is held at a 45-degree angle and the TRUFFLE is pressed down and across it, allowing the blade to shave off small slivers and slices.

truss [TRUHS] To secure poultry or other food (usually meat) with string, pins or skewers so the food maintains a compact shape during cooking.

trussing needle Long stainless-steel needles threaded with twine and used to TRUSS food. They vary in size, usually somewhere from 4 to 10 inches in length.

try out *see* RENDER

tube pan A round pan with deep sides and a hollow center tube used for baking cake, especially ANGEL FOOD or SPONGE CAKE. The tube promotes even baking for the center of the cake. *See also* BUNDT PAN.

tuile [TWEEL] French for "tile," a tuile is a thin, crisp cookie that is placed over a rounded object (like a rolling pin) while still hot from the oven. Once cooled and stiff, the cookie resembles a curved roof tile. The classic tuile is made with crushed almonds but the cookie can also be flavored with orange, lemon, vanilla or other nuts.

tulipe [too-LEEP] The French word for "tulip," culinarily referring to a thin cookie that is gathered into a ruffled-flower shape while still warm. The ruffled cookie is usually placed into a cup mold (such as a muffin tin) until cool. It can also be draped over an inverted water glass. The crisp cookie cup is used as an edible container for berries, MOUSSE or ice cream.

tuna [TOO-nuh] Found in temperate marine waters throughout the world, tuna is a member of the MACKEREL family. It's probably the most popular fish used for canning today. There are numerous varieties of tuna, the best known being albacore, bluefin, yellowfin and bonito. All tunas have a distinctively rich-flavored flesh that is moderate to high in fat, firmly textured, flaky and tender. The high-fat **albacore** weighs in the 10- to 60-pound range, has the lightest flesh (white with a hint of pink) and is the only tuna that can be called "white." Its mild flavor and prized white flesh make it the most expensive canned tuna. **Yellowfin tunas** are usually larger than albacores, reaching up to 300 pounds. Their flesh is pale pink (it must be called "light"), with a flavor slightly stronger than that of the albacore. Among the largest tunas are the **bluefin,** which can weigh over 1,000 pounds. Young bluefins have a lighter flesh and are less strongly flavored, but as they grow into adulthood, their flesh turns dark red and their flavor becomes more pronounced. The small **bonitos** rarely exceed 25 pounds. They range from moderate- to high-fat and are the most strongly flavored of the tunas. Many Japanese dishes use dried bonito, called DASHI. Depending on the variety, fresh tuna is available seasonally— generally starting in late spring and continuing into early fall. Frozen tuna is available year-round and is sold in both steaks and fillets. It may be cooked by almost any method including baking, broiling, grilling and frying. **Canned tuna** is precooked and is sold as albacore (or white meat) and light meat. It comes in three grades, the best being *solid* or *fancy* (large pieces), followed by *chunk* (smaller pieces) and *flaked* or *grated* (bits and pieces). Canned tuna is packed in either water or oil—the latter containing far more calories. *See also* FISH.

turban squash This family of winter squashes all have hard bumpy shells and turbanlike formations at the blossom end. BUTTERCUP SQUASH is one of the more popular varieties. Turban squashes come in a variety of sizes ranging from 2 to 15 inches in diameter at the base. Because they're quite colorful, with varying bright hues of orange, green and yellow, turban squashes are often used for decoration rather than eating. They can be baked, steamed or simmered. *See also* SQUASH.

turbinado sugar [tur-bih-NAH-doh] *see* SUGAR

turbot [TUR-buht; TUR-boh] 1. Found in European waters from Iceland to the Mediterranean, this highly prized FLATFISH has firm, lean, white flesh with a deliciously mild flavor. Many Europeans rate turbot in the same category as the highly regarded Dover SOLE. Turbot can reach 30 pounds but are generally marketed at weights closer to 3 to 6 pounds. They're usually imported frozen to the U.S. They may be poached, steamed, baked, broiled or fried. 2. The market name used for several types of FLOUNDER found in the Pacific. *See also* FISH.

tureen [too-REEN; tyoo-REEN] Any of various deep, lidded dishes used for the table service of soups, stews and the like.

turkey For most families, Thanksgiving dinner would be unthinkable without this large native-American bird on the table. Long before the arrival of European settlers, wild turkeys populated the U.S., Mexico and Central America and the Aztecs were busily domesticating them. The *conquistadores* took some of these domesticated birds back to Spain, and before long Europeans were breeding them into a much plumper version. Interestingly enough, European settlers brought some of these domesticated birds back to the New World in the 1600s and eventually began crossing them with America's wild turkeys. Most U.S. turkeys raised today are from the White Holland variety, which has been bred to produce a maximum of white meat (a U.S. favorite). Although male (*tom*) turkeys can reach 70 pounds, those over 20 pounds are becoming less and less available. The female (*hen*) turkey usually weighs from 8 to 16 pounds. Gaining in popularity is a smaller version of both sexes (sometimes called a *fryer-roaster*), which weighs in at between 5 and 8 pounds. The trend toward these compact turkeys is the result of both smaller families and the desire of turkey producers to make turkey everyday rather than exclusively holiday fare. Turkeys are available fresh and frozen year-round. They're sold both whole and as separate parts—such as breasts or drumsticks. Some whole turkeys have a built-in plastic thermometer that pops up when the turkey is done. **Self-basting turkeys** have been injected with butter or vegetable oil. Smoked turkey—whole or breast—is also available, as is canned boned turkey. Turkey is very similar to chicken in many regards, including USDA grading. *See* CHICKEN *for information regarding purchasing, storing and preparing turkey.*

Turkish coffee Very strong coffee made by bringing finely ground coffee, sugar and water to a boil three times, allowing it to cool very briefly between boilings. Turkish coffee is made in a special pot called a *jezve* or *ibrik* and served in tiny cups immediately after the third boil. *See also* COFFEE.

Turkish delight Called *rahat loukoum* ("rest for the throat") in Turkey, this rubbery-textured candy is extremely popular throughout the Middle East. It's made from CORNSTARCH or GELATIN, sugar, honey and fruit juice or jelly, and is often tinted pink or green. Chopped almonds, pistachio nuts, pine nuts or hazelnuts are frequently added. Once the candy becomes firm, it is cut into small squares and coated with confectioners' sugar. Turkish delight is available commercially in candy shops and some supermarkets.

turmeric [TUR-muh-rihk] Used in cooking since 600 B.C., turmeric is the root of a tropical plant related to GINGER. Though native to the Orient, this spice is now also cultivated in India and the Caribbean. It has a bitter, pungent flavor and an intense yellow-orange color. In Biblical times, turmeric was often used to make perfume, a comment on its rather exotic fragrance. Today it's used mainly to add both flavor and color to food. Turmeric is very popular in East Indian cooking and is almost always used in CURRY preparations. It's also a primary ingredient in MUSTARD and is what gives American-style prepared mustard its bright yellow color. Powdered turmeric is widely available in supermarkets. As with all spices, it should be stored in a cool, dark place for no more than 6 months. *See also* SPICES; Herb and Spice Chart, page 538.

turner A utensil for lifting or removing food from a pan or baking sheet, or for turning food that's being cooked so the second side can brown. Such foods include pancakes, bacon, ham, hamburgers, fish, potatoes, eggs and cookies. Turners come in a variety of shapes and designs in order to conveniently meet different cooking tasks. Some turners have holes or slots to allow liquids or fats to drain off the item being lifted. Others are shaped for special uses—like the Chinese turner, which has curved edges to fit WOK contours. Turners are usually made of nylon (so as not to scratch NON-STICK FINISHES) or stainless steel. *See also* SPATULA.

turnip Not only is this root vegetable easy to grow, but it keeps well, too. Because of this, turnips have long been popular in Great Britain and northern Europe. The white-fleshed turnip has a white skin with a purple-tinged top. The so-called **yellow turnip** is actually a turnip relative, the RUTABAGA. Small, young turnips have a delicate, slightly sweet taste. As they age, however, their taste becomes stronger and their texture coarser, sometimes almost woody. Fresh turnips are available year-round, with the peak season from October through February. Choose heavy-for-their-size small turnips, as they are the youngsters and will be more delicately flavored and textured. The roots should be firm and the greens (if attached) bright-colored and fresh-looking. Though turnips can be refrigerated, tightly wrapped, for up to a month, they do best in a cool (55°F), well-ventilated area such as a root cellar. Before using, they should be washed, trimmed and peeled. Turnips may be boiled or steamed, then mashed or pureed. They can also be stir-fried, cubed and tossed with butter, or used raw in salads. Turnips are a fair source of vitamin C. *See also* TURNIP GREENS.

turnip greens Long a popular SOUL FOOD, turnip greens are slightly sweet when young but, as with aging TURNIPS, can become quite tough and strong-tasting as they age. Fresh greens are available year-round, with the peak season from October through February. Choose those that are crisp-looking with a good even color. Avoid greens that are wilted or off-colored. Refrigerate in a plastic bag for up to 3 days. Thoroughly wash and remove any thick ribs before preparing. Turnip greens may be cooked in a variety of ways including boiling, sautéing, steaming and stir-frying. They can be served alone as a vegetable or cooked and served with other greens. Canned and frozen turnip greens are also available in some regions. Turnip greens are an excellent source of vitamins A and C and a good source of riboflavin, calcium and iron.

turnip-rooted parsley *see* PARSLEY ROOT

turnover Pastry-dough circles or squares that are covered with a sweet or savory filling, then folded in half to create a pastry in the shape of a triangle or semicircle. The edges are usually pinched or crimped to prevent the filling from leaking. Turnovers may be baked or deep-fried. They can range from bite-size to about 6 inches across and can be served as appetizers, luncheon entrees or desserts.

turtle [TUR-tl] Any of several varieties of reptiles which can live in fresh water, salt water or on land and have a hard shell covering their bodies. Some turtles can grow quite large, weighing over 1,000 pounds. For culinary purposes the **sea** or **green turtle**—found in temperate marine waters—is best known. It has a smooth olive green shell and green to whitish flesh; the green flesh is considered superior. These turtles are often made into a thick turtle soup which usually includes MADEIRA or SHERRY as an ingredient. **Terrapin,** a small (7- to 8- inch) turtle species that inhabits fresh or brackish water, is considered by many to have the best meat. Terrapin meat is sometimes pounded and served like steak. **Tortoises** live on land and are considered less desirable than terrapin or sea turtles. Regardless of the species, the meat of the female is much more tender than that of the male. Conservation measures have limited the availability of this reptile, but some turtle meat can be found in East Coast markets, along the Gulf Coast and in Chinese markets in various regions. Canned and frozen turtle meat can sometimes be found in specialty food stores. *See also* MOCK TURTLE SOUP.

turtle bean *see* BLACK BEAN

tutti-frutti [TOO-tee FROO-tee] 1. An Italian term meaning "all fruits" that refers to a preserve made with various diced fruits mixed with sugar and brandy. It's since been used to describe ice cream or other desserts that contain a variety of minced, candied fruits. 2. A synthetic, fruity flavoring used in various gums and candies.

Tybo cheese [TY-boh] Similar to a mild-flavored SAMSOE, the Danish, loaf-shaped Tybo is made from cows' milk. Its yellow rind encloses a cream-colored interior dotted with holes. Its mild taste makes it good for sandwiches, salads, sauces and a variety of cooked dishes. Some tybos are flavored with caraway seeds. *See also* CHEESE.

tzimmes [TSIHM-ihs] Traditionally served on Rosh Hashana, this sweet Jewish dish consists of various combinations of fruits, meat and vegetables. Tzimmes may include brisket of beef, sweet potatoes, potatoes, FARFEL, prunes and other dried fruit, carrots or apples—all flavored with honey and often cinnamon. This casserole-style dish is cooked at very low heat so the flavors have a chance to blend.

gli fruit [UHG-lee] Its origins are vague, but the native Jamaican ugli fruit is believed to be a TANGERINE-GRAPEFRUIT hybrid (though the POMELO may also have been involved). It ranges in size between that of a NAVEL ORANGE and a giant grapefruit. Its acid-sweet flavor suggests grapefruit with hints of orange. The extremely thick, yellow-green skin fits rather loosely over the large, juicy, yellow-orange pulp sections. Ugli fruit is available on a limited basis around the country from winter to spring. Choose fruit that's heavy for its size and that gives slightly to palm pressure. Store at room temperature and use within 5 days or refrigerate up to 3 weeks. Ugli fruit may be prepared and eaten in any way suitable for grapefruit. It's an excellent source of vitamin C.

univalve [YOO-nuh-valv] *see* GASTROPOD

unmold To remove molded food from the container (usually a decorative MOLD) in which it was made. The process generally requires inverting the container over a serving plate.

unsalted butter *see* BUTTER

upside-down cake Of this genre, the most popular is undoubtedly the traditional pineapple upside-down cake. Any fruit can be used, however, and this dessert is made by covering the bottom of a cake pan with butter and sugar topped with decoratively arranged fruit, then cake batter. During the baking process, the sugar, butter and fruit juices combine to create a CARAMELIZED glaze. Before serving, the cake is inverted onto a serving plate so the glazed fruit becomes the top of the cake.

acherin [vash-RAN] A dessert consisting of several crisp MERINGUE rings stacked on top of each other and placed on a meringue or pastry base. Alternatively, the rings may be made with almond paste. This "container" may be filled with ice cream or CREME CHANTILLY and/or various fruits.

vacherin cheeses [VASH-ra*n*] Any of several rich and creamy cow's-milk cheeses from France or Switzerland, characteristically containing 45 to 50 percent butterfat. **Vacherin Fribourgeois** from the Swiss canton of Fribourg has a grayish-yellow rind and a pale yellow, semisoft interior. Its mildly acidic, resiny flavor is reminiscent of GRUYÈRE. **Vacherin Mont d'Or,** which is made both in France and Switzerland, has a rich, slightly sweet flavor. The ripest of these cheeses are often so runny that they're eaten with a spoon. **Vacherin d'Abondance** and **Vacherin des Dauges** are French varieties that are soft and sweet-tasting. *See also* CHEESE.

Valencia orange [vuh-LEHN-she-uh; vuh-LEHN-shuh; vuh-LEHN-see-uh] Grown in Arizona, California, Florida and Texas, the Valencia orange has a thin, deep golden skin that's difficult to peel. Its flesh is sweet, juicy and contains few seeds. The Valencia is good both as a juice fruit and for eating out of hand. It's in season from January to November. *See also* ORANGE.

Valpolicella [val-poh-lih-CHEHL-uh; vahl-paw-lee-CHEHL-ah] Produced in northern Italy, this dry red wine is light-bodied and has a fragrant bouquet and fruity flavor. It's best served young and is sometimes viewed as Italy's version of a French BEAUJOLAIS.

vanilla [vuh-NIHL-uh; vuh-NEHL-uh] Dictionaries describe the term "plain-vanilla" as something "simple, plain or ordinary." Few statements could be further from the truth—for there is definitely nothing ordinary about the seductively aromatic vanilla bean. This long, thin pod is the fruit of a luminous celadon-colored orchid (*vanilla planifolia*) which, of over 20,000 orchid varieties, is the only one that bears anything edible. Native to tropical America, the vanilla bean was cultivated and processed by the Aztecs, who used it to flavor their cocoa-based drink, *xocolatl*, later transliterated to *chocolatl*. That basic flavoring wisdom is still true today . . . vanilla deliciously heightens chocolate's flavor. The vanilla bean was once considered an aphrodisiac, and was so rare that it was reserved for royalty. Because of the extremely labor-intensive, time-consuming process by which it's obtained, pure vanilla is still relatively expensive today. The saga begins with the orchid blossoms, which open only one day a year (and then only for a few hours). Because this particular orchid has only one natural pollinator (the Melipona bee), which cannot possibly handle the task in such a small period of time, the flower must be hand-pollinated. Otherwise, no vanilla bean. After pollination, pods take 6 weeks to reach full size (6 to 10 inches long), and 8 to 9 months after that to mature. The mature pods, which must be hand-picked, are green and have none of the familiar vanilla flavor or fragrance. For that they need curing, a 3- to 6-month process that begins with a 20-second boiling-water bath followed by sun heating. Once the beans are hot, they're wrapped in blankets and allowed to sweat. Over a period of months of drying in the sun by day and sweating in blankets at night, the beans ferment, shrinking by 400 percent and turning their characteristic dark brown. The better grades of beans become thinly coated with a white, powdery coating called *vanillin* (which is also produced synthetically). Although the best vanilla once came from its homeland in Mexico, most areas where the orchid thrives are now dedicated to oil fields and orange groves. Additionally, some Mexican vanilla products—though considerably cheaper than their U.S. supermarket counterparts—are suspect because they contain coumarin (banned by the FDA), a potentially toxic substance that can cause liver and kidney damage. Unfortunately, there's no way for the consumer to tell which Mexican vanilla products contain this toxin. Today, the Madagascar area produces about 75 percent of the world's vanilla-bean supply and most U.S. vanilla comes from that area. The bold-flavored Tahitian vanilla, however, is now also being imported to the United States. **Vanilla extract** is the most common form used today. It's made by MACERATING chopped beans in an alcohol-water solution in order to extract the flavor. To meet FDA standards, **pure vanilla extract** must contain 13.35 ounces of vanilla beans per gallon during extraction and 35 percent alcohol. The resulting brown liquid is clear and richly fragrant. You can count on products labeled "natural vanilla flavor" containing only pure vanilla extract. **Imitation vanilla** is composed entirely of artifical flavorings (most of which are paper-industry byproducts treated with chemicals). It often has a harsh quality that leaves a bitter aftertaste. Pure vanilla extract is about twice as expensive as its imitation counterpart, but there's no real comparison in flavor intensity and quality, and only about half the amount is needed. Vanilla descriptions on labels can be confusing. *Natural vanillin* is a substance intrinsic to the vanilla bean, whereas *artificial vanillin* is made from wood-pulp byproducts. *Vanilla flavoring* describes a blend of pure and imitation vanilla. In the U.S., a label that reads *vanilla ice cream* may only be made with pure vanilla extract and/or vanilla beans, whereas *vanilla-flavored ice cream* may contain up to 42 percent artificial flavorings and *artificial-flavored ice cream* contains *only* imitation flavorings. Vanilla extracts are readily available and vanilla beans can be found in many supermarkets and most specialty food stores. Extracts can be stored indefinitely if sealed airtight and kept in a cool, dark place. Vanilla beans should be wrapped tightly in plastic wrap, placed in an airtight jar and refrigerated. They can be stored in this manner for about 6 months. In order for its flavor not to dissipate, vanilla extract should be added to cooked mixtures after they've been briefly cooled. To use vanilla beans, slit them lengthwise down the center and scrape out the thousands of diminutive seeds. These seeds can be added directly to foods such as ice-cream mixtures, shortening to be used for pastry dough, sauces, etc. Homemade vanilla extract can be made by placing a split bean in a jar containing ¾ cup vodka, sealing and letting it stand for 6 months. Vanilla beans may also be used to make deliciously fragrant VANILLA SUGAR. Whole beans that have been used to flavor sauces or other mixtures may be rinsed, dried and stored for reuse. Vanilla adds flavor magic to a multitude of sweet and some savory dishes.

vanilla sugar Wonderfully fragrant and flavorful sugar made by burying vanilla beans in granulated or confectioners' sugar—usually in the proportion of two beans for each pound of sugar. The mixture is stored in an airtight container for about a week before the vanilla bean is removed. The result is a delicious and perfumy sugar that can be used as an ingredient or decoration for baked goods, fruit and other desserts. Vanilla beans may be reused in this fashion for up to 6 months.

varietal wine [vuh-RY-ih-tl] A wine term describing wines made chiefly from one variety of grape. Such wines portray the dominant characteristics of the primary grape used. Among the more popular varietals are CABERNET SAUVIGNON, CHARDONNAY, CHENIN BLANC, GEÜRZTRAMINER, PETITE SIRAH, PINOT NOIR, SAUVIGNON BLANC and ZINFANDEL.

variety meats Called *offal* in Great Britain, variety meats are animal innards and extremities that can be used in cooking. They include BRAINS, feet and ankles (*see* PIG'S FEET), HEART, KIDNEYS, LIVER, SWEETBREADS, TONGUE and TRIPE. Some of the more obscure variety-meat trimmings are used for SAUSAGE.

veal Though there are no precise age standards for veal, the term is generally used to describe a young calf from 1 to 3 months old. **Milk-fed veal** comes from calves up to 12 weeks old who have not been weaned from their mother's milk. Their delicately textured flesh is firm and creamy white with a pale grayish-pink tinge. **Formula-fed veal** can come from calves up to about 4 months old, fed a special diet of milk solids, fats, various nutrients and water. The meat from formula-fed veal is not as rich or delicate as milk-fed veal because of the diet's missing butterfat. The term **Bob veal** applies to calves younger than 1 month old. Their pale, shell-pink flesh is quite bland and the texture is soft. In all true veal, the animals haven't been allowed to eat grains or grasses, either of which would cause the flesh to darken. Calves between 6 and 12 months old are called **baby beef,** and have flesh that's coarser, stronger-flavored and from pink to light red in color. True veal is usually plentiful in the spring and late winter. At other times of the year, calves over 3 months old are often sold as veal. The USDA grades veal in six different categories; from highest to lowest they are Prime, Choice, Good, Standard, Utility and Cull. The last three grades are rarely sold in retail outlets. When choosing veal, let color be your guide. The flesh should be creamy white—barely tinged with grayish-pink—and the fat white. Meat that's pink turning red means the so-called "veal" is older than it should be. Veal's texture should be firm, finely grained and smooth. *For storage information, see listing for* BEEF. Veal is often cooked by moist-heat methods to compensate for its lack of natural fat. It is easy to overcook and dry out, so careful attention must be paid during preparation. The delicate flavor and fine texture of veal have appealed to diners for centuries. Among the numerous dishes created to highlight this meat are veal CORDON BLEU, veal MARENGO, VEAL ORLOFF, VEAL OSCAR, OSSO BUCO, veal PARMIGIANA, VEAL PICCATA and veal SCALOPPINE. *See also* Veal Chart, page 572.

veal cordon bleu *see* CORDON BLEU

veal Marengo *see* MARENGO

veal Orloff [OR-lawf] This classic presentation begins with a braised loin of veal carved into even horizontal slices. Each slice is spread with a thin layer of pureed sautéed mushrooms and onions. The coated slices are stacked back in place and tied together to reform the loin. Then the layered loin is smothered with additional mushroom-onion puree, topped with BÉCHAMEL SAUCE and grated Parmesan cheese and oven-browned for about 10 minutes.

veal Oscar; veal Oskar [OS-kuhr] Said to have been named in honor of Sweden's King Oscar II, who was especially partial to its ingredients, this dish consists of sautéed veal cutlets topped with crab or CRAYFISH meat and BÉARNAISE SAUCE. Veal Oscar is finished with a garnish of asparagus spears.

veal parmigiana; veal Parmesan *see* PARMIGIANA, À LA

veal piccata [pih-CAH-tuh] Hailing from Italy, this classic dish consists of a seasoned and floured veal ESCALOPE that is quickly sautéed and served with a sauce made from the pan drippings, lemon juice and chopped parsley. Chicken is also sometimes prepared in this manner.

veau [VOH] French for "veal."

vegetable oil *see* FATS AND OILS

vegetable marrow Cultivated in England, this green, oval summer squash can grow to the size of a watermelon. It's closely related to the ZUCCHINI and can be cooked in any manner suitable for that vegetable. Because of its bland flavor, vegetable marrow (also called *marrow squash*) is often stuffed with a meat mixture. It's available in limited supplies in some specialty produce markets during the summer months. *See also* SQUASH.

vegetable peeler A kitchen utensil designed to peel away the outer skin of vegetables. Vegetable peelers come in many designs and are made from a variety of materials. The better ones have a swivel-action blade that conforms to the contour of the vegetable being peeled, thereby cutting away a minimum of skin.

vegetable squash *see* SPAGHETTI SQUASH

velouté sauce [veh-loo-TAY] One of the five "mother sauces," velouté is a STOCK-based white sauce. It can be made from chicken or veal stock or fish FUMET thickened with white ROUX. Enrichments such as egg yolks or cream are sometimes also added. Velouté sauce is the base for a number of other sauces. *See also* SAUCE.

velvet hammer A rich, creamy COCKTAIL made with COINTREAU or TRIPLE SEC, TÍA MARÍA, heavy cream and sometimes BRANDY. The mixture is shaken with ice and strained into a cocktail glass. The result is smooth but potent.

venison [VEHN-uh-suhn; VEHN-uh-zuhn] *see* GAME ANIMALS

verbena [ver-BEE-nuh] *see* LEMON VERBENA

vermicelli [ver-mih-CHEHL-ee] Italian for "little worms," culinarily the term refers to PASTA shaped into very thin strands. Vermicelli is much thinner than regular SPAGHETTI.

vermouth [ver-MOOTH] White wine that has been fortified and flavored with various herbs and spices. The name "vermouth" comes from the German *wermut* ("WORMWOOD") which, before it was declared poisonous, was once the principal flavoring ingredient. There are several types of this wine, the most popular being **white dry vermouth**, commonly thought of as French (although it's made in other countries including the U.S.). It's drunk as an APÉRITIF and used in non-sweet COCKTAILS like the MARTINI.

Sweet vermouth is reddish brown (colored with CARAMEL) and is also used as an apéritif as well as in slightly sweet cocktails such as the MANHATTAN. A third style—not as popular as the other two—is white and slightly sweet. It's called *Bianco* by Italians.

Véronique [vay-roh-NEEK] A term describing dishes garnished with seedless white grapes. One of the most popular of these dishes is **sole Véronique**—fillet of SOLE poached in white wine, covered with a white sauce and garnished with white grapes.

viande [vee-YAWND] The French word for "meat."

vichyssoise [vihsh-ee-SWAHZ; VEE-she-swahz] A rich, creamy potato-and-leek soup that's served cold, garnished with chopped chives. In this country it's often mispronouced "vinsch-ee-SWAH."

Viennese coffee [vee-uh-NEEZ] Strong hot coffee, sweetened to taste, served in a tall glass and crowned with whipped cream. *See also* COFFEE.

vin [VAM] French for "wine."

vinaigrette [vihn-uh-GREHT] One of the five "mother sauces," vinaigrette is a basic oil-and-vinegar combination, generally used to dress salad greens and other cold vegetable, meat or fish dishes. In its simplest form, vinaigrette consists of oil, vinegar (usually 3 parts oil to 1 part vinegar), salt and pepper. More elaborate variations can include any of various ingredients such as spices, herbs, shallots, onions, mustard, etc. *See also* SAUCE.

vine leaves *see* GRAPE LEAVES

vinegar [VIHN-ih-ger] Derived from the French *vin aigre*, "sour wine," vinegar is made by bacterial activity which converts fermented liquids such as wine, beer or cider into a weak solution of ACETIC ACID (the constituent that makes it sour). Vinegar has been used for centuries for everything from beverages (like SHRUBS), to an odor-diminisher for strong foods such as cabbage and onions, to a hair rinse and softener. There are a multitude of vinegar varieties available today. In the U.S., the most popular styles are the fruity **apple cider vinegar,** made from fermented apple cider, and the rather harsh-tasting **distilled white vinegar,** made from a grain-alcohol mixture. The French prefer pleasantly pungent **wine vinegars,** which can be made from either red or white wine. In Britain the favorite is mild **malt vinegar,** obtained from malted barley. The exquisite Italian **balsamic vinegar,** made from white Trebbiano grape juice, gets its dark color and pungent sweetness from aging in barrels of various woods and graduating sizes over a period of years. **Herb vinegars** are made by steeping fresh herbs such as dill and tarragon in vinegar. Popular **fruit vinegars** include those made with raspberries and blueberries. Mild and slightly sweet **rice vinegar,** made from fermented rice, is widely used in Japanese and Chinese cooking. It's a key element in dishes such as SUSHI. Vinegar is essential in making pickles, mustards and VINAIGRETTES. It adds a jolt of flavor to numerous sauces, MARINADES and dressings, and to preparations such as SAUERBRATEN, SWEET-AND-SOUR dishes and marinated HERRING. It's also widely used as a table CONDIMENT for dishes such as England's FISH AND CHIPS. Vinegar should be stored airtight in a cool, dark place. Unopened, it will keep indefinitely; once opened it can be stored for about 6 months. *See also* MOTHER OF VINEGAR.

vintage [VIHN-tihj] This wine term describes a grape harvest of a specific year. A vintage wine is one made totally from those grapes. Wines made from grapes harvested from several years are called "non-vintage."

violet, crystallized *see* CRYSTALLIZED FLOWERS

Virginia ham *see* SMITHFIELD HAM

viticulture [VIHT-ih-kuhl-cher] The science or study of growing grapes for wine.

vodka [VOD-kuh] A clear, colorless, unaged liquor originally made in Russia from potatoes. Today's vodka, which is almost odorless and tasteless, may be made from other ingredients such as corn, wheat or rye. Vodka is integral to many COCKTAILS such as the SCREWDRIVER, BLOODY MARY and vodka MARTINI. If served STRAIGHT, it should always be icy-cold. Flavored vodkas have become popular in the U.S. and may be flavored with anything from fruits to hot peppers. Some flavored vodkas are even sweetened slightly.

vol-au-vent [vawl-oh-VAHM] Said to have been created by the famous French chef Carême, a *vol-au-vent* is a PUFF PASTRY shell that resembles a pot with a lid. It can be small (individual-size) or large (6 to 8 inches in diameter). The pastry is classically filled with a cream sauce-based mixture, usually of chicken, fish, meat or vegetables. The puff-pastry lid is set on top of the filling. This dish may be served as an appetizer or an entree. The term *vol-au-vent*, "flying in the wind," refers to the pastry's incredible lightness.

Vouvray [voo-VRAY] Any of various white wines made in and around the French village of Vouvray in the Loire Valley, usually from CHENIN BLANC grapes. These wines can vary greatly, with a broad range including dry, semisweet, sweet, slightly sparkling or fully sparkling. Vouvrays can range from average to excellent, depending on the vintner.

V.S.; V.S.O.P.; V.V.S.O.P. *see* COGNAC

affle [WAHF-uhl] The honeycombed surface of this crisp, light bread is perfect for holding pockets of syrup. Waffles are made by pouring a light batter onto one side of a waffle iron, a special hinged cooking utensil with two honeycomb-patterned griddles. The second side is closed over the batter and the waffle is cooked until browned and crisp. **Waffle irons** can be electric or designed for stovetop cooking. Electric waffle irons have heating elements in both sides, thereby cooking the two sides of the bread at once. Irons heated on top of a stove must be turned over once during cooking to finish the second side. There are a number of waffle-iron shapes available including square, rectangular, round and even heart-shape. **Belgian waffles,** which are often heaped with fresh strawberries and whipped cream, are made on special waffle makers with particularly large, deep grids. Most modern waffle irons have nonstick surfaces. Waffles are popular not only for breakfast, but for desserts as well. Savory waffles can be topped with creamed meat or vegetable mixtures.

waffle iron *see* WAFFLE

wahoo [wah-HOO; WAH-hoo] With a flavor often compared to that of ALBACORE, the wahoo's moderate- to high-fat flesh is fine, white (with a little red) and slightly sweet. In fact, Hawaiians call this fish *ono,* which means "sweet." Wahoo are normally caught in the 20- to 40-pound range although they can get much larger. Those that reach the market are usually in the form of chunks or in fillet pieces. Wahoo may be baked, broiled or grilled. *See also* FISH.

 Waldorf salad [WAWL-dorf] Created at New York's Waldorf-Astoria Hotel in the 1890s, the original version of this salad contained only apples, celery and mayonnaise. Chopped walnuts later became an integral part of the dish. Waldorf salad is usually served on top of a bed of lettuce.

walleyed pike *see* PERCH

walnuts The fruit of the walnut tree, which grows in temperate zones throughout the world. The two most popular varieties of walnut are the ENGLISH (also called *Persian*) WALNUT and the BLACK WALNUT. A close relative is the BUTTERNUT, also referred to as *white walnut.* English walnuts are the most widely available and come in many varieties—some with moderately thick shells, others with shells so thin a tiny bird can crack them open. They're available year-round and come in three main sizes: large, medium and babies. When buying walnuts in the shell, choose those free of cracks or holes. Shelled walnuts should be plump, meaty and crisp; shriveled nutmeats are past their prime. Walnuts in the shell can be stored in a cool, dry place up to 3 months. Shelled nutmeats should be refrigerated, tightly covered, up to 6 months. They can be frozen up to a year. Walnuts are delicious in a variety of sweet and savory dishes and baked goods. They're also used to make a fragrant, flavorful oil (*see* WALNUT OIL). *See also* NUTS.

walnut oil Its distinctively nutty flavor and fragrance make it obvious that this oil is extracted from walnut meats. Walnut oil is expensive and can be found in some supermarkets and most gourmet food stores. A blander, less expensive variety can be found in health-food stores. Store walnut oil in a cool, dark place for up to 3 months. To prevent rancidity, refrigeration is best. Walnut oil is frequently used in salad dressings, often combined with less flavorful oils. It can also be used in sauces, main dishes and baked goods, and for sautéing. *See also* FATS AND OILS.

wasabi; wasabe [WAH-suh-bee] This Japanese version of HORSERADISH comes from the root of an Asian plant. It's used to make into a green-colored CONDIMENT that has a sharp, pungent, fiery flavor. Wasabi is available in specialty and oriental markets in both paste and powder form. The latter is mixed with water much like dry mustard. Some specialty produce markets carry fresh wasabi, which may be grated like horseradish. In Japan, SUSHI and SASHIMI are served with a condiment of wasabi mixed with soy sauce.

wassail [WAHS-uhl; WAHS-ayl] *Ves heill*, Norse for "be in good health," is an old toast and the origin of this word. Wassail is a drink consisting of ALE or wine sweetened with sugar and flavored with spices. This brew is traditionally served in a large "wassail bowl," garnished with small roasted apples and ladled into serving cups.

water bath The French call this cooking technique *bain marie*. It consists of placing a container (pan, bowl, soufflé dish, etc.) of food in a large, shallow pan of warm water, which surrounds the food with gentle heat. The food may be cooked in this manner either in an oven or on top of a range. This technique is designed to cook delicate dishes such as custards, sauces and savory mousses without breaking or curdling them. It can also be used to keep cooked foods warm.

water biscuit A bland, crisp cracker that's often served with cheese and wine. The fact that the cracker is almost flavorless makes it a perfect foil for most foods because it allows their natural flavor to be appreciated.

water chestnut The edible tuber of a water plant indigenous to Southeast Asia. The water chestnut's brownish-black skin resembles that of a true chestnut, but its flesh is white, crunchy and juicy. The flavor is bland with a hint of sweetness. Water chestnuts are very popular in oriental cooking, especially in STIR-FRIED dishes where their crunchy texture is a standout. Water chestnuts are available fresh in most Chinese markets. Choose those that are firm with no sign of shriveling. Refrigerate, tightly wrapped in a plastic bag, for up to a week. Peel before using raw or in cooked preparations. Water chestnuts are also available canned—either whole or sliced—in most supermarkets, but the fresh are far superior. *See also* WATER CHESTNUT POWDER.

water chestnut powder   Also called *water chestnut flour*, this powdered starch is ground from dried water chestnuts. It's used as a thickener in oriental cooking. Like CORNSTARCH, it's mixed with a small amount of water before being added to the hot mixture to be thickened. It can also be used to DREDGE foods before frying. Water chestnut powder is available in Asian markets and in some health-food stores.

watercress   Cool running water is the growing ground for this member of the mustard family, which can often be found wild in and around streams and brooks. Watercress has small, crisp, dark green leaves. Its pungent flavor is slightly bitter and has a peppery snap. Watercress is available year-round and is customarily sold in small bouquets. Choose crisp leaves with deep, vibrant color. There should be no sign of yellowing or wilting. Refrigerate in a plastic bag (or stems-down in a glass of water covered with a plastic bag) for up to 5 days. Wash and shake dry just before using. Watercress may be used in salads, sandwiches, soups and a variety of cooked dishes. It's also a popular garnish, fast replacing the ubiquitous parsley.

watermelon   Native to Africa, the watermelon is one of two broad categories of melon, the other being MUSKMELON. It's considered the less sophisticated of the two because it lacks flavor complexity and has a watery texture. But there are those who wouldn't trade a slice of watermelon on a hot summer day for anything. There are an untold number of watermelon varieties but America's most popular is the large, elongated-oval shape with a variegated or striped, two-tone green or gray-green rind. It averages 15 to 35 pounds but may be much smaller or larger, depending on the variety. There are even relatively tiny varieties about the size of a medium cantaloupe. An abundance of shiny, black seeds dot the sweet, red, refreshingly moist flesh. Other watermelon varieties have flesh that ranges in color from white to yellow to pink. The seeds may be speckled or solid and variously colored—black, brown, green, red or white. **Seedless watermelons** actually do, more often than not, have a few scattered seeds. What seeds there are, however, are small, soft and edible. All parts of the watermelon can be used. Asians love the roasted seeds, and the pickled rind is a favorite in many parts of the world. Watermelons are available May to September, though they're at their peak from mid-June to late August. They're sold whole as well as in halves, quarters or by the slice. Look for symmetrical melons without any flat sides. Depending on the variety, the shape can be round or an oblong oval. Slap the side of the watermelon— if it resounds with a hollow thump, it's a good indicator that the melon is ripe. The rind should just barely yield to pressure. Never take home a melon with soft spots, gashes or other blemishes on the rind. Cut watermelons should display a brightly colored flesh. An abundance of small, white seeds means the melon is immature. Avoid cut melons with a grainy or dry-looking flesh. Store whole watermelon in the refrigerator if at all possible and keep no more than a week. If it's too large for your unit, keep in a cool, dark place. Cut watermelon should always be tightly wrapped, refrigerated and used within a day or so. It should be served cold, either in wedges or made into balls and served as part of a fruit cup or salad. Watermelon contains a fair amount of vitamins A and C. *See also* MELON.

waterzooi [VAH-tuhr-zoh-ee] This classic Belgian dish is a creamy-rich fish stew that can be made with either fresh- or saltwater fish. A chicken rendition is also popular. All versions include a variety of vegetables and herbs, and are enriched with egg yolks, cream and butter.

wax bean *see* GREEN BEAN

wax paper; waxed paper Semitransparent paper with a thin coating of wax on both sides. Because of its moistureproof and nonstick characteristics, wax paper used to play a major role in the kitchen for duties such as covering food and lining baking pans. In recent years, however, wax paper has been replaced in many of its roles by aluminum foil or plastic wrap.

weisswurst [VYC-voorst; vyc-vurscht] German for "white sausage," weisswurst is a delicate sausage made with veal, cream and eggs. It's traditionally served during Oktoberfest with sweet mustard, rye bread and beer. *See also* SAUSAGE.

well-and-tree platter A platter with troughs formed into the bottom to resemble bare tree branches attached to a central trunk, at one end of which is a shallow well. Such a configuration allows the juices of meats being cut on the platter to drain.

Wellington, beef *see* BEEF WELLINGTON

Welsh rabbit; Welsh rarebit This popular British dish consists of a melted mixture of CHEDDAR CHEESE, beer (sometimes ALE or milk) and seasonings served over toast. The cheese mixture can also be toasted on the bread. Welsh rabbit is usually served as a main course or for HIGH TEA, often accompanied with tomatoes. Welsh rabbit becomes a *golden buck* when topped with a poached egg.

Western sandwich *see* DENVER SANDWICH

Westphalian ham [wehst-FAYL-yuhn] Extremely fine ham produced from pigs raised on acorns in Germany's Westphalia forest. Westphalian ham is cured before being slowly smoked over beechwood mixed with juniper branches. The combination of the gourmet diet, curing and smoking results in a dark brown, very dense ham with a distinctive, light smoky flavor. Connoisseurs consider these hams among the best. *See also* HAM.

wheat Thought to have been growing since Paleolithic times and cultivated for at least 6,000 years, wheat is the world's largest CEREAL-grass crop. Its status as a staple is second only to rice. One reason for its popularity is that—unlike other cereals—wheat contains a relatively high amount of GLUTEN, the protein that provides the elasticity necessary for excellent breadmaking. Though there are over 30,000 varieties of wheat, the three major types are hard wheat, soft wheat and durum wheat. **Hard wheat** is high in protein (10 to 13 percent) and yields a flour rich in gluten, making it particularly suitable for YEAST BREADS. The low-protein (6 to 10 percent) **soft wheat** yields a flour lower in gluten and therefore better suited for tender baked goods such as biscuits and cakes. **Durum wheat,** although high in gluten, is not good for baking. Instead, it's most often ground into SEMOLINA, the basis for excellent pasta. In the U.S., wheat is also classified according to the time of year it is sown—namely, **spring wheat** and **winter wheat** (which is actually sown in the fall). The unprocessed wheat kernel, commonly known as a *wheat berry*, is made up of three major portions—BRAN, germ and endosperm. **Wheat bran,** the rough outer covering, has very little nutritional value but plenty of fiber. During milling, the bran is removed from the kernel. It's sold separately and used to add flavor and fiber to baked goods. **Wheat germ,** essentially the embryo of the berry, is a concentrated source of vitamins, minerals and protein. It has a nutty flavor and is very oily, which causes it to turn rancid quickly. Wheat germ is sold in both toasted and natural forms and is used to add nutrition to a variety of foods. *Wheat germ oil*, an extraction of the germ, is strongly flavored and expensive. The **wheat endosperm,** which makes up the majority of the kernel, is full of starch, protein, niacin and iron. It's the primary source of many wheat flours. In addition to flour, wheat is available in several other forms including wheat berries, cracked wheat and BULGHUR WHEAT. **Wheat berries** are whole, unprocessed kernels, whereas **cracked wheat** is the whole berry broken into coarse, medium and fine fragments. Both are sold in health-food stores and may be cooked as cereal, or in PILAFS, breads or other dishes. *See also* KAMUT.

whelk [HWEHLK;WEHLK] This member of the GASTROPOD branch of the MOLLUSK family is a large marine snail. It has a beautiful spiraled shell and a rather tough but flavorful footlike muscle. Although the **waved whelk** is found along America's northern Atlantic coast, it has never gained wide popularity in the U.S. **Knobbed whelks** and **channeled whelks** are also marketed in the States. Fresh whelks are generally available in the spring and fall. They're also available cooked, preserved in vinegar and canned. Because of their lack of popularity, whelks may be difficult to find except in Chinese or Italian markets or specialty food stores. Whelk is naturally tough and must usually be tenderized by pounding. It benefits from brief, gentle cooking. The Italians refer to whelk as *scungilli*, and the famous *scungilli marinara* is a garlicky dish of whelk cooked in a tomato sauce flavored with basil, oregano and hot pepper seeds.

whetstone [HWEHT-stohn; WEHT-stohn] Whetstones, also called *oilstones*, are rectangular blocks made of the extremely hard carborundum (a composition of silicon carbide). They are fine-grained, often with one side slightly coarser than the other. Knives should periodically be honed on whetstones to keep them really sharp. This is done by first lubricating the stone with oil or water, then drawing the knife blade with slight pressure across the whetstone at about a 20-degree angle. Doing this 5 to 6 times on each side of the knife is adequate. If the whetstone's two sides are of differing textures, this activity should be performed first on the coarser side and finished on the finer-grained side. This will give the knife an even sharper edge. The sharpness of a knife's blade can be maintained by using a SHARPENING STEEL prior to each use.

whey [HWAY; WAY] The watery liquid that separates from the solids (CURDS) in cheesemaking. Whey is sometimes further processed into **whey cheese** (*see* CHEESE). It can be separated another step, with butter being made from the fattier share. Whey is also used in processed foods such as crackers. Primarily, however, whey is more often used as livestock feed than it is in the human diet.

whip *n.* 1. A gelatin-based dessert that's airy and light because of the addition of either whipped cream or stiffly beaten egg whites. Such desserts are usually made with fruit puree but can also be flavored with other ingredients such as chocolate or coffee. 2. Another name for a WHISK.

whip *v.* To beat ingredients, such as egg whites, cream, etc., thereby incorporating air into them and increasing their volume until they are light and fluffy.

whipping cream *see* CREAM

whisk [HWIHSK;WIHSK] Also called a *whip*, this kitchen utensil consists of a series of looped wires forming a three-dimensional teardrop shape. The wires are joined and held together with a long handle. Whisks are used for whipping ingredients (such as cream, eggs, sauces, etc.), thereby incorporating air into them. They come in different sizes for different tasks and are most often made of stainless steel or tinned steel.

whiskey; whisky [HWIHSK-ee; WIHSK-ee] An alcoholic distillate obtained from a fermented mash of grains such as barley, rye or corn. There are many varieties of whiskey—or *whisky*, as it's spelled in Scotland and Canada. The final result is affected by many factors including the water, type of grain, how the grain is treated and processed, and the aging. Among the more popular whiskies are BOURBON, CANADIAN WHIKSY, IRISH WHISKEY, RYE and SCOTCH.

whiskey sour *see* SOUR

whitebait *see* SMELT

white bean This rather generic term is applied to several dried beans falling into the four categories of MARROW BEANS, GREAT NORTHERN BEANS, NAVY BEANS and PEA BEANS.

white chocolate *see* CHOCOLATE

whitefish Found in lakes and streams throughout North America, the whitefish is a member of the SALMON family. Its high-fat, mild-flavored flesh is firm and white. Fresh whitefish can be found year-round and are generally marketed whole (from 2 to 6 pounds) or in fillets. They're also available frozen and smoked. Whitefish can be poached, baked, broiled or grilled. The ROE can be used for CAVIAR or cooked. *See also* FISH.

white lightning *see* CORN WHISKEY

white mustard cabbage *see* BOK CHOY

white pepper; white peppercorn *see* PEPPERCORN

White Riesling *see* JOHANNISBERG REISLING

White Russian A COCKTAIL made with VODKA, coffee-flavored LIQUEUR (such as KAHLÚA) and cream. *See also* BLACK RUSSIAN.

white sauce *see* BÉCHAMEL SAUCE

white seabass *see* DRUM

white walnut *see* BUTTERNUT

whiting Small gray and silver fish related to both COD and HAKE. They're sometimes called *silver hake*. The whiting's low-fat flesh is white, firm-textured and delicately flavored. The fish weighs between 1 and 5 pounds and is marketed (fresh and frozen) both whole and in fillets. Whiting is also available salted and smoked. It can be poached, steamed, broiled, panfried or baked. *See also* FISH.

whole-wheat flour *see* FLOUR

whortleberry [HWUHR-tl-bair-ee] *see* BILBERRY

wiener [WEE-nuhr] *see* FRANKFURTER

Wiener schnitzel; Wienerschnitzel [VEE-nuhr SHNIHT-suhl] German for "Viennese cutlet," this famous Viennese dish actually originated in France. It's a veal SCALLOP that is dipped in flour, beaten egg and breadcrumbs before being sautéed. *Wiener schnitzel* is usually garnished with lemon slices and sometimes hard-cooked egg, anchovies or capers.

wild leek *see* RAMP

wild rice Known for its luxurious nutty flavor and chewy texture, wild rice isn't really rice at all. Instead, it's a long-grain marsh grass native to the northern Great Lakes area, where it's harvested by the local Indians. There's also now commercial wild rice production in California, as well as several Midwest states. It's important to clean wild rice thoroughly before cooking it. The best method is to place the rice in a medium bowl and fill it with cold water. Give it a couple of stirs and set aside for a few minutes. Any debris will float to the surface and the water can then be poured off. Depending on the method used, wild rice can take up to an hour to cook; overcooking will produce starchy results. Admittedly, wild rice is expensive, but both pleasure and budget are extended by combining it with brown rice or BULGHUR WHEAT. *See also* RICE.

wine Unless otherwise specified, wine refers to the naturally fermented juice of grapes. More broadly, the term can include alcoholic beverages created from other fruits and even vegetables. Wine has a rich history that has evolved along with that of man. Its historical roots reach back almost 12,000 years. As various cultures spread out into new parts of the world, so did the grapevine and the art of winemaking. Today there are vineyards throughout the world with good wine being produced in far-ranging locations from the U.S. to South Africa to Australia to South America to Europe. Wine is broadly classified in the following categories: 1. **natural still** (non-sparkling) **wines**—including red, white and rosé—which can be DRY (non-sweet), semisweet and sweet; 2. **sparkling wines**, including French CHAMPAGNES as well as effervescent wines from other parts of the world; 3. FORTIFIED WINES (such as SHERRY and PORT), which have been augmented with a dose of BRANDY or other spirit; and 4. *aromatic wines*, such as VERMOUTH, which have been flavored with ingredients like herbs or spices. *For information on specific wines, see individual listings. See also* COOKING WINE.

wine bottles The **standard wine bottle** is 750 ml (milliliters), which is almost exactly equivalent to an American fifth (⅘ of a quart or 25.6 ounces). Other bottle sizes used to contain wine include: **split** (¼ of a standard wine bottle or 6.4 ounces); **half-bottle** (½ of a standard wine bottle or 12.8 ounces); **magnum** (1.5 liters, equivalent to 2 standard bottles); **Jeroboam** (4 bottles in one); **gallon** (5 in one); **Rehoboam** (6 in one); **Methuselah** (8 in one); **Salmanazar** (12 in one); **Balthazar** (16 in one); and **Nebuchadnezzar** (20 in one).

Winesap apple Juicy and tart, the Winesap apple has a crisp, yellowish flesh covered with a deep red skin. This all-purpose apple has good keeping qualities and is available November through May. *See also* APPLE.

winged bean Also called *goa bean*, this tropical LEGUME is rapidly becoming a staple throughout the poorer regions of the world where it grows. The reasons are basic: it grows quickly, is disease resistant and is high in protein. The winged bean is also valued because it's entirely edible, including the shoots, flowers, roots, leaves, pods and seeds. The pods, which can be green, purple or various shades of red, are four-sided and flare from the center into ruffled ridges or "wings." These beans have a flavor similar to that of a CRANBERRY BEAN with a hint of GREEN BEAN. The texture is like that of a starchy green bean. Winged beans may be found in specialty produce markets and some supermarkets. Choose small beans with no sign of discoloration. Refrigerate, tightly wrapped in a plastic bag, for up to 3 days. Wash and trim before using. Winged beans may be prepared in any way suitable for green beans. *See also* BEAN.

wintergreen The name of this evergreen plant, which is native to eastern North America, comes from the fact that it retains foliage all winter long. In addition to its rich green leaves, wintergreen bears white flowers and bright red berries. The leaves produce a pungent oil that's used to flavor a variety of products including candy, gum, medicine, etc. Wintergreen is also known as *checkerberry*.

winter melon This large, frost-green MUSKMELON can weigh up to 30 pounds and resembles a huge HONEYDEW. The porous flesh is snowy white and has a flavor reminiscent of ZUCCHINI. Winter melon is available year-round in Chinese markets and specialty produce stores. It should be cooked briefly and is popular in STIR-FRY dishes as well as various oriental soups, especially winter melon soup, which is classically served in a scooped-out winter-melon shell. *See also* MELON.

witloof [WIHT-lohf] *see* ENDIVE

wok [WAHK] A round-bottomed cooking utensil popular in oriental cooking, where its uses include stir-frying, steaming, braising, stewing and even deep-frying. Woks are traditionally made of rolled steel, which provides excellent heat control, but they can also be made of sheet iron, anodized aluminum and stainless steel. They come in various sizes, usually have two handles and are generally accompanied by a ring-shaped stand for use on a gas stovetop. Special flat-bottom woks are also available for use on electric stoves. Electric woks (usually with a NONSTICK FINISH) are also available.

won ton; wonton [WAHN-tahn] A Chinese specialty similar to an Italian RAVIOLI. These bite-size dumplings consist of paper-thin dough pillows filled with a minced mixture of meat, seafood and/or vegetables. The dough comes prepackaged as WON TON SKINS. Won tons may be boiled, steamed or deep-fried and served as an appetizer, snack or side dish, usually with several sauces. They are, of course, intrinsic to WON TON SOUP.

won ton skins; egg roll skins Paper-thin sheets of dough made from flour, eggs and salt, and used to make WON TON, EGG ROLLS and similar preparations. Won ton skins can be purchased prepackaged in some supermarkets and in most Chinese markets. The wrappers usually come in both squares and circles and are available in various thicknesses.

won ton soup A Chinese favorite consisting of WON TONS cooked in and served in a clear broth flavored variously with ingredients like scallions, celery and soy sauce. The soup is often garnished with JULIENNED strips of chicken, pork, vegetables, etc. The broth's flavor as well as the garnishes are prepared to correspond to the won ton filling.

wood ear A variety of mushroom also known as *cloud ear, tree ear* (the larger, thicker specimens) or *silver ear* (albinos). They have a slightly crunchy texture and delicate, almost bland flavor that more often than not absorbs the taste of the more strongly flavored ingredients with which they are cooked. Oriental markets sell dried wood ears which, except for the albino varieties, look like brownish-black, dried chips. Upon reconstituting they increase 5 to 6 times in size and resemble the shape of an ear. Wood ears are popular in STIR-FRIES and soups and are often combined with TIGER LILY BUDS. *See also* MUSHROOM.

woodruff Often described as having the smell of freshly cut hay, woodruff is the leaf of a ground cover native to Europe. Its most famous use is as a flavoring in MAY WINE, a white-wine punch popular in Germany. In Germany and Austria, woodruff is also used to season sausages, candies and many cooked dishes. Live plants are available through many nurseries, and the dried herb is available in gourmet stores and through mail-order. Also called *sweet woodruff.*

Worcestershire sauce [WOOS-tuhr-shuhr; WOOS-tuhr-sheer] Though this CONDIMENT was originally developed in India by the English, it takes its name from the fact that it was first bottled in Worcester, England. It's a thin, dark, rather piquant sauce used to season meats, gravies, soups and vegetable juices, and as a table condiment. It's also an essential ingredient in the popular BLOODY MARY cocktail. Worcestershire's formula usually includes garlic, soy sauce, tamarind, onions, molasses, lime, anchovies, vinegar and various seasonings. It's widely available in supermarkets.

wormwood A bitter, aromatic herb used in flavoring ABSINTHE, some wines such as VERMOUTH, and occasionally (but not in the U.S.) in cooking. In the past, wormwood was popular as a medicinal herb for colds, stomach problems and rheumatism. Because the flavoring oil extracted from this herb is potentially poisonous, the U.S. has banned preparations (such as absinthe) made with an excessive amount of it. *See also* HERB.

wurst [WUHRST; WOORST; vurscht] The German word for "sausage."

anthan gum [ZAN-thuhn] Produced from the fermentation of corn sugar, xanthan gum is used as a thickener, emulsifier and stabilizer in foods such as dairy products and salad dressings. *See also* Additives Directory, page 515.

XXX; XXXX Label symbols used for CONFECTIONERS' SUGAR.

akinori [yah-kee-NOH-ree] *see* NORI

yakitori [yah-kih-TOH-ree] A Japanese term meaning "grilled" (*yaki*) "fowl" (*tori*), usually referring to small pieces of marinated chicken that are skewered and grilled.

yam This thick, tropical-vine tuber is popular in South and Central America, the West Indies and parts of Asia and Africa. Although sweet potatoes and yams are similar in many ways and therefore often confused with one another, they are from different plant species. In the southern U.S., sweet potatoes are often called yams and to add to the confusion, canned sweet potatoes are frequently labeled yams. True yams, however, are not widely marketed and are seldom grown in the U.S. Though they can be similar in size and shape to sweet potatoes, yams contain more natural sugar and have a higher moisture content. On the downside, they're not as rich in vitamins A and C as sweet potatoes. There are over 150 species of yam grown throughout the world. They can range in size from that of a small potato to behemoths over 7½ feet long and 120 pounds. Depending on the variety, a yam's flesh may be various shades of off-white, yellow, purple or pink, and the skin from off-white to dark brown. The texture of this vegetable can range from moist and tender to coarse, dry and mealy. Yams can be found in most Latin-American markets, often in chunks, sold by weight. When buying yams, select unblemished specimens with tight, unwrinkled skins. Yams may be substituted for sweet potatoes in most recipes. *See* SWEET POTATO *for information regarding storing and cooking yams.*

Yankee bean *see* NAVY BEAN

Yankee pot roast *see* POT ROAST

yard-long bean A pencil-thin LEGUME that resembles a GREEN BEAN except that it can grow up to about 3 feet long (though it's usually picked at 18 inches or less). Yard-long beans belong to the same plant family as the BLACK-EYED PEA. In fact, in parts of China the bean is allowed to mature until full-fledged peas are produced in the pod. Yard-longs have a flavor similar to but not as sweet as that of a green bean, with hints of its black-eyed-pea lineage. The texture of the pod is more pliable and not as crisp as that of a green bean. This legume, also called *long bean* or *asparagus bean*, can be found year-round (with peak season in the fall) in most oriental markets and some supermarkets with specialty produce sections. Select those that are small (which equates to younger) and very flexible; the peas should not have matured. Refrigerate in a plastic bag for up to 5 days. Yard-long beans are most often cut into 2-inch lengths and sautéed or STIR-FRIED. Overcooking will make them mushy. These beans are rich in vitamin A and contain a fair amount of vitamin C.

yarrow [YAR-oh; YAIR-oh] Any of several very pungent, aromatic herbs found in Europe and North America. Known as *milfoil* in Europe, yarrow has a very strong aroma and flavor and is therefore used sparingly to flavor salads, soups and occasionally egg dishes. It may also be used to brew a TISANE (herb tea).

yeast [YEEST] Yeast is a living, microscopic, single-cell organism which, as it grows, converts its food (through a process known as fermentation) into alcohol and carbon dioxide. This trait is what endears yeast to winemakers, brewmasters and breadbakers. In the making of wine and beer, the yeast's manufacture of alcohol is desired and necessary for the final product; and carbon dioxide is what makes BEER and CHAMPAGNE effervescent. The art of breadmaking needs the carbon dioxide produced by yeast in order for certain doughs to rise. To multiply and grow, all yeast needs is the right environment, which includes moisture, food (in the form of sugar or starch) and a warm, nurturing temperature (70° to 85°F is best). Wild yeast spores are constantly floating in the air and landing on uncovered foods and liquids. No one's sure when these wild spores first interacted with foods but it's known that the Egyptians used yeast as a LEAVENING agent more than 5,000 years ago. Wine and other fermented beverages were made for millennia before that. Today, scientists have been able to isolate and identify the various yeasts that are best for winemaking, beermaking and baking. The two types commercially available are baker's yeast and brewer's yeast. **Baker's yeast,** as the name implies, is used as a leavener. It's catagorized into three basic types—active dry yeast, compressed fresh yeast and YEAST STARTERS. **Active dry yeast** is in the form of tiny, dehydrated granules. The yeast cells are alive but dormant because of the lack of moisture. When mixed with a warm liquid (105° to 115°F), the cells once again become active. Active dry yeast is available in two forms, *regular* and *quick-rising*, of which the latter takes about half as long to leaven bread. They may be used interchangeably (with adjustments in rising time) and both are available in ¼-ounce envelopes. Regular active dry yeast may also be purchased in 4-ounce jars or in bulk in some health-food stores. It should be stored in a cool, dry place, but can also be refrigerated or frozen. It should always be at room temperature before being dissolved in liquid. Properly stored, it's reliable when used by the expiration date, which should be stamped on the envelope or jar label. One package of dry yeast is equal to 1 scant tablespoon dry yeast or 1 cake of compressed fresh yeast. **Compressed fresh yeast,** which comes in tiny (.06-ounce), square cakes, is moist and extremely perishable. It must be refrigerated and used within a week or two, or by the date indicated on the package. It can be frozen, but should be defrosted at room temperature and used immediately. One cake of fresh yeast can be substituted for one envelope of dry yeast. The use of compressed fresh yeast has been primarily replaced by the more convenient active dry yeast. All baker's yeast should be given a test called PROOFING to make sure it's still alive. To proof yeast, dissolve it in warm water and add a pinch of sugar. Set the mixture aside in a warm place for 5 to 10 minutes. If it begins to swell and foam, the yeast is alive, active and capable of leavening bread. **Brewer's yeasts** are special non-leavening yeasts used in beermaking. Because it's a rich source of B vitamins, brewer's yeast is also used as a food supplement. It's available in health-food stores. Brewer's yeasts are also marketed in specialty beermaking equipment shops, with different strains used for different beers.

yeast bread Any bread that uses YEAST as the LEAVENING agent. As the yeast ferments, it converts the flour's starchy nutrients into alcohol and carbon dioxide gas. The gas bubbles trapped in the elastic GLUTEN mesh of the dough are what make it rise. Oven heat kills the yeast and evaporates the alcohol. The gas expands in a final burst of energy and causes the bread to rise. Among the more well-known yeast breads are BRIOCHE, CROISSANTS, FRENCH BREAD and SOURDOUGH BREAD.

yeast starter Prior to the evolution of commercially available baking powders and yeasts during the 19th century, yeast starters were the LEAVENERS used in breadmaking. Such starters are a simple mixture of flour, water, sugar and YEAST. (At one time, airborne yeast was the only source used, but today convenient commercially packaged baker's yeast is more common.) This batter is set aside in a warm place until the yeast ferments and the mixture is foamy. A portion of the starter—usually about 2 cups—is removed and used as the base and leavener for some bread recipes. Once fermented, yeast starters—the most famous of which is *sourdough starter*—can be kept going in the right environment for years simply by adding equal parts flour and water. Starter should be refrigerated and can be stored this way indefinitely as long as it's replenished every 2 weeks. Before using or replenishing, it should be brought to room temperature. If a starter turns orange or pink and develops an unpleasantly acrid odor, undesirable bacteria have invaded it and the mixture must be discarded. Two cups of the foamy starter mixture can be substituted for each package of yeast called for in a recipe.

yellow-eyed pea *see* BLACK-EYED-PEA

yellowfin tuna *see* TUNA

yellowtail 1. This large (up to 100 pounds) game fish is found off the coast of Southern California and further south into Mexican waters. It's a member of the jack family—related to POMPANO—with a flavor and texture similar to TUNA. Yellowtail is only occasionally available commercially. It may be prepared in any way suitable for tuna. 2. A variety of SNAPPER. *See also* FISH.

yogurt; yoghurt [YOH-gert] A dairy product that's the result of milk that has fermented and coagulated because it's been invaded by friendly bacteria. This can be accomplished naturally by keeping the milk at about 110°F for several hours. The end result is a creamy-textured yogurt with an astringent, slightly tart taste. Yogurt-making is thought to have been originated by nomadic Balkan tribes thousands of years ago, probably first by accident and then as a means of preserving milk. Today, yogurt is made commercially in carefully controlled environments and the requisite bacteria (usually *Lactobacillus bulgaricus and Streptococcus thermophilus*) are added to the milk. Though yogurt can be made from the milk of many animals, cow's milk is the most commonly used. There are a variety of commercial yogurts now produced. **Plain yogurt** is made from whole milk, low-fat or nonfat milk without additional flavoring ingredients. **Flavored yogurt** has sugar and either artificial flavorings or natural fruit (or both) added. Some flavored yogurts contain gelatin or stabilizers for a thicker texture. Fruit-flavored yogurts can either have the fruit on the bottom (to be mixed in by the consumer) or be already stirred—in which case they're referred to as *Swiss-style*. Recently, **frozen yogurt**—which resembles soft-serve ice cream in texture—has become very popular and competes head-to-head in some markets with ice cream. The health benefits of yogurt have long been touted. It is certainly a good source of B vitamins, protein and calcium and is much more digestible than fresh milk. It's also said to keep the intestinal system populated with good bacteria and therefore in healthy condition. These benefits, however, are thought to be lost when yogurt is frozen, which destroys most of the beneficial bacteria.

yokan [YOH-kahn] This Japanese confection is made with AGAR (the jelling agent), sugar and ADZUKI-BEAN paste. Other flavorings such as persimmons or chestnuts are also sometimes used. Yokan, which is sold in oriental markets, will keep indefinitely in the refrigerator.

York Imperial apple A medium to large apple with firm flesh that's tartly sweet. The York Imperial's skin is red with yellowish streaks and the flesh is off-white. It's an excellent cooking apple and is a favorite for baked apples because it keeps its shape during cooking. This apple is available October through April. *See also* APPLE.

Yorkshire pudding [YORK-sheer; YORK-shuhr] British roast beef wouldn't be complete without Yorkshire pudding, which is like a cross between a POPOVER and a SOUFFLÉ and not at all like a pudding. It's made with a batter of eggs, milk and flour, baked in beef drippings until puffy, crisp and golden brown. It may be prepared in a shallow baking dish, muffin tins or other small containers, or in the same pan as the roast. Like a hot soufflé, Yorkshire pudding will deflate shortly after it's removed from the oven. This specialty takes its name from England's northern county of Yorkshire.

youngberry A hybrid BLACKBERRY variety with dark red color and sweet, juicy flesh.

yuca [YUHK-uh] *see* CASSAVA

yule log [YOOL] *see* BÛCHE DE NOËL

Y

abaglione [zah-bahl-YOH-nay] One of Italy's great gifts to the rest of the world, zabaglione is an ethereal dessert made by whisking together egg yolks, wine (traditionally MARSALA) and sugar. This beating is done over simmering water so that the egg yolks cook as they thicken into a light, foamy custard. Traditional zabaglione must be made just before serving. (There is also a frozen version.) The warm froth can be served either as a dessert by itself or as a sauce over cake, fruit, ice cream or pastry. In France it's called *sabayon* or *sabayon sauce*.

Zante grape [ZAN-tee] In the United States, where California is the major grower, this tiny (⅛ to ¼ inch in diameter) purple grape is predominantly used to make the dried CURRANT. The seedless, very sweet Zante grape also still flourishes in Greece, where it originated. Fresh Zantes can sometimes be found from late summer to late fall in specialty produce markets. Trendy restaurants often use tiny clusters of them as a garnish. They're available year-round as dried currants. *See also* GRAPE; RAISIN.

zest [ZEHST] The perfumy outermost skin layer of citrus fruit (usually oranges or lemons), which is removed with the aid of a CITRUS ZESTER, paring knife or VEGETABLE PEELER. Only the colored portion of the skin (and not the white pith) is considered the zest. The aromatic oils in citrus zest are what add so much flavor to food. Zest can be used to flavor raw or cooked and sweet or savory dishes.

zester *see* CITRUS ZESTER

zinfandel [ZIHN-fuhn-dehl] A red wine grape originally thought to be indigenous to California. Recently, however, experts have concluded that the Zinfandel grape was brought to the U.S. from Italy's Puglia region, and is a descendant of the *primitivo grape* grown there. Regardless, the zinfandel grape—with its spicy, raspberry flavors—makes marvelous, fruity red wines ranging from lighter styles to big, rich bottlings that can almost rival CABERNET SAUVIGNON. In the 1980s, **white Zinfandel** (a BLUSH WINE) also gained considerable popularity. Occasionally, late-picked grapes full of concentrated sugar are made into **late-harvest zinfandels** and served as DESSERT WINE or in place of PORT.

zingara, à la [zihn-GAH-rah] This French phrase translates to "gypsy style" and refers to a garnish consisting of chopped ham, tongue, mushrooms and TRUFFLES combined with tomato sauce, tarragon and sometimes MADEIRA. This garnish is served with meat, poultry and sometimes eggs.

ziti [ZEE-tee] Long, thin tubes of MACARONI. *See also* PASTA.

zombie [ZAHM-bee] Extraordinarily potent, this COCKTAIL is made with at least two types each of rum and LIQUEUR plus two or three fruit juices such as pineapple, orange and lime. It's usually served in a large goblet over crushed ice, garnished with slices of pineapple and orange and a MARASCHINO CHERRY. The origin of the name is unknown, but it's been said that one or two of these drinks can make one feel numb . . . rather like a zombie.

zucchini [zoo-KEE-nee] This popular summer squash is shaped like a slightly curved cylinder, a bit smaller at the top than the bottom. A zucchini's skin color can vary from dark to light green, sometimes with yellow markings that give it a mottled or striped look. The off-white flesh has a very pale green cast and the flavor is light and delicate. Common market length is 4 to 8 inches long and 2 to 3 inches thick. However, some specimens are as tiny as a finger while others—usually those that are home-grown—can reach a mammoth 2 feet long by 6 inches in diameter (or more). Fresh zucchini is available year-round in most supermarkets, with a peak period during late spring. Select small zucchini, which will be younger and therefore more tender and have thinner skins. The skins should be free of blemishes and have a vibrant color. Zucchini can be cooked by a variety of methods including steaming, grilling, sautéing, deep-frying and baking. *See also* SQUASH.

zuccotto [zoo-COHT-oh] Thought to have been inspired by the cupola of Florence, Italy's, Duomo (the city's main cathedral), this dome-shaped dessert begins with a bowl lined with LIQUEUR-moistened cake (usually pound cake) slices. The bowl is then filled with a mixture of sweetened whipped cream, chopped or grated chocolate and various chopped nuts before being topped with additional cake slices. The zuccotto is refrigerated at least a day so the filling can set. It's inverted onto a plate before being served.

zungenwurst [ZUHNG-uhn-voorst; zuhng-uhn-vurscht] A variety of German BLOOD SAUSAGE that contains chunks of pickled TONGUE. This dried sausage can be eaten raw, although it's more commonly sliced and browned in butter or bacon fat. *See also* SAUSAGE.

zuppa [ZOO-puh] The Italian word for "soup."

zuppa inglese [ZOO-puh ihn-GLAY-zay] Literally translated as "English soup," this Italian dish is, in fact, a refrigerated dessert similar to the British favorite, TRIFLE. It's made with rum-sprinkled slices of sponge cake layered with a rich custard or whipped cream (or both) and candied fruit or toasted almonds (or both).

zwieback [ZWY-bak; ZWY-bahk; SWY-bak; SWY-bahk] This German word translates to "twice baked" and refers to bread that is baked, cut into slices and then returned to the oven until very crisp and dry. Zwieback, which has a hint of sweetness to it, is popular for its digestibility and is often served to younger children or to people who have digestive problems. It is commercially available in most stores. *See also* RUSK.

Z

APPENDIX

ADDITIVES DIRECTORY

Food additives are substances intentionally added to food either directly or indirectly with one or more of the following purposes: 1. to maintain or improve nutritional quality; 2. to maintain product quality and freshness; 3. to aid in the processing or preparation of food; and 4. to make food more appealing. The following chart lists substances commonly added to foods and the reasons for their use. The explanatory key to definitions is below. *See also* ADDITIVES.

Key To Definitions

◆ **Maintain or Improve Nutritional Quality**
Nutrients: enrich (replace vitamins and minerals lost in processing) or fortify (add nutrients that may be lacking in the diet).

● **Maintain Product Quality and/or freshness**
Preservatives (antimicrobials): prevent food spoilage from bacteria, molds, fungi and yeast; extend shelf life; protect natural color or flavor.

■ **Aid in Processing or Preparation**
Emulsifiers: help to evenly distribute tiny particles of one liquid into another; improve homogeneity, consistency, stability or texture.
Stabilizers, Thickening Texturizers: impart body; improve consistency or texture; stabilize emulsions; affect "mouth feel" of food.
Leavening Agents: affect cooking results—texture and volume.
pH Control Agents: change/maintain acidity or alkalinity.
Humectants: cause moisture retention.
Maturing and Bleaching Agents, Dough Conditioners: accelerate the aging process; improve baking qualities.
Anticaking Agents: prevent caking, lumping or clustering of a finely powdered or crystalline substance.

▲ **Make Food More Appealing**
Flavor Enhancers: supplement, magnify or modify the original taste and/or aroma of food without imparting a characteristic flavor of their own.
Flavors: heighten natural flavor; restore flavors lost in processing.
Colors: give desired, appetizing or characteristic color of food.
Sweeteners: make the aroma or taste of food more agreeable or pleasurable.

Substances Commonly Added to Some Foods

Acetic acid	■ pH control agent
Acetone peroxide	■ maturing and bleaching agent, dough conditioner
Ammonium alginate	■ pH control agent
Annatto extract	▲ color
Arabingalactan	■ stabilizer, thickening texturizer
Benzoic acid	● preservative
Beta carotene	▲ nutrient
	● color
BHA (butylated hydroxyanisole)	● antioxidant
BHT (butylated hydroxytoluene)	● antioxidant
Butylparaben	● preservative
Calcium bromate	■ maturing and bleaching agent, dough conditioner
Calcium phosphate	■ leavening agent
Calcium propionate	● preservative
Canthaxanthin	▲ color
Carob bean gum	■ stabilizer, thickening texturizer
Cellulose	■ stabilizer, thickening texturizer
Dextrose	▲ sweetener
Diglycerides	■ emulsifier
Disodium guanylate	▲ flavor enhancer
Dried algae meal	▲ color
EDTA (ethylenediaminetetra-acetic acid)	● antioxidant
FD&C Colors	
Blue No. 1	▲ color
Red No. 2	▲ color
Red No. 40	▲ color
Yellow No. 5	▲ color
Fructose	▲ sweetener
Glycerine	■ humectant
Grape-skin extract	▲ color
Guar gum	■ stabilizer, thickening texturizer
Gum arabic	■ stabilizer, thickening texturizer
Heptylparaben	● preservative
Hydrogen peroxide	■ maturing and bleaching agent, dough conditioner

Reprinted from *FDA Consumer* by permission of U.S. Department of Health Education, and Welfare Publication No. (FDA) 79-2115.

Invert sugar	▲ sweetener
Iodine	◆ nutrient
Iron-ammonium citrate	■ anticaking agent
Iron oxide	▲ color
Lactic acid	■ pH control agent preservative
Locust bean gum	■ stabilizer, thickening texturizer
Mannitol	▲ sweetener
	■ anticaking agent; stabilizer, thickening
	■ texturizer
Methylparaben	● preservative
Modified food starch	■ stabilizer, thickening texturizer
Niacinamide	◆ nutrient
Phosphoric acid	■ pH control agent
Polysorbates	■ emulsifier
Potassium bromate	■ maturing and bleaching agent, dough
	conditioner
Potassium propionate	● preservative
Propylene glycol	■ stabilizer, thickening texturizer;
	humectant
Riboflavin	◆ nutrient
	▲ color
Saffron	▲ color
Silicon dioxide	■ anticaking agent
Sodium benzoate	● preservative
Sodium citrate	■ pH control agent
Sodium nitrate	● preservative
Sodium propionate	● preservative
Sodium stearyl	■ maturing and bleaching agent, dough
fumarate	▲ conditioner
Sorbitan mono	■ emulsifier stearate
Tagetes (Aztec marigold)	▲ color
Tartaric acid	■ pH control agent
TBHQ (tertiary butyl	● antioxidant
hydroquinone)	
Titanium dioxide	▲ color
Tocopherols (vitamin. E)	◆ nutrient
	● antioxidant
Tragacanth gum	■ stabilizer, thickening texturizer
Ultramarine blue	▲ color
Vanilla	▲ flavor
Vitamin A	◆ nutrient
Vitamin C	◆ nutrient
	● preservative
	● antioxidant

INGREDIENT BUYING GUIDE & EQUIVALENTS

Food	Weight or Amount	Approximate Equivalent
Almonds (shelled, blanched)	1 lb	3 cups; 4 cups slivered
Apples (fresh)	1 lb	3 medium; 2¾ cups chopped or sliced
Apples (dried)	1 lb	4⅓ cups; 8 cups cooked
Apricots (fresh)	1 lb	8 to 12; 2½ cups sliced or halved
Apricots (dried)	1 lb	2¾ cups; 5½ cups cooked
Asparagus spears (fresh)	1 lb	16 to 20 spears
Asparagus spears (canned)	14½ to 16 oz	12 to 18 spears
Asparagus (frozen, cut)	10 oz	2 cups
Avocados	1 lb	2½ cups sliced, diced or chopped
Bananas (fresh)	1 lb	3 to 4; 2 cups sliced; 1⅓ cups mashed
Bananas (dried)	1 lb	4½ cups slices
Beans, green (fresh)	1 lb	3 cups
Beans, green (frozen)	9 oz	1½ cups
Beans, green (canned)	15½ oz	1¾ cups
Beans, kidney (canned)	16 to 17 oz	2 cups
Beans, kidney (dried)	1 lb	2½ cups; 5½ cups cooked
Beans, navy (dried)	1 lb	2⅓ cups; 5½ cups cooked
Beans, soy (dried)	1 lb	2 cups
Beets (fresh, without tops)	1 lb	2 cups chopped
Beets (canned)	16 to 17 oz	2 cups
Blueberries (fresh)	1 pint	2 cups
Blueberries (frozen)	10 oz	1½ cups
Blueberries (canned)	14 oz	1½ cups
Bread	1 slice fresh	½ cup soft crumbs
Bread	1 slice dry	⅓ cup dry crumbs
Broccoli (fresh)	1 lb	2 cups chopped
Broccoli (frozen)	10 oz	1½ cups chopped
Brussels sprouts (fresh)	1 lb	4 cups
Brussels sprouts (frozen)	10 oz	18 to 24 sprouts
Bulghur	1 lb	2¾ cups; 3¾ cups cooked

Food	Weight or Amount	Approximate Equivalent
Butter and margarine (regular)	1 lb	2 cups
Butter and margarine (regular)	¼-lb stick	½ cup; 8 Tbsp
Butter and margarine (whipped)	1 lb	3 cups
Cabbage	1 lb	3½ to 4½ cups shredded; 2 cups cooked
Carrots (fresh without tops)	1 lb	3 cups chopped or sliced; 2½ cups shredded
Carrots (frozen)	1 lb	2½ to 3 cups sliced
Carrots (canned)	16 oz	2 cups sliced
Catsup	16 oz	1⅔ cups
Cauliflower (fresh)	1 lb	1½ cups chopped or sliced
Cauliflower (frozen)	10 oz	2 cups chopped or sliced
Celery	1 medium stalk	½ cup chopped or sliced
Cheese (Cheddar-style; processed)	1 lb	4 cups grated
Cheese (cottage)	16 oz	2 cups
Cheese (cream)	8 oz/3 oz	1 cup/6 tablespoons
Cherries (fresh)	1 lb	1¾ cups unpitted; 2⅓ cups pitted
Cherries (frozen)	10 oz	1 cup
Cherries (canned)	1 lb	1½ cups
Chocolate wafers	18 wafers	1 cup crumbs
Chocolate (chips)	6 oz	1 cup
Chocolate (squares)	8 oz	8 squares (1 ounce each)
Coconut, shredded	1 lb	5⅔ cups
Coffee (ground)	1 lb	80 Tbsp
Corn syrup (light or dark)	16 fl oz	2 cups
Corn (fresh)	2 medium ears	1 cup kernels
Corn (frozen)	10 oz	1¾ cups kernels
Corn (canned, cream style)	16 to 17 oz	2 cups
Corn (canned, whole kernel)	12 oz	1½ cups
Cornmeal	1 lb	3 cups
Cornmeal	1 cup	4 cups cooked
Cornstarch	1 lb	3 cups
Crackers (see Graham Crackers; Soda Crackers)		

Food	Weight or Amount	Approximate Equivalent
Cranberries (fresh)	12 oz bag	3 cups
Cranberries (canned, sauce)	1 lb	1⅔ cups
Cream (light, half & half and sour)	½ pt	1 cup
Cream (heavy, whipping)	½ pt	1 cup; 2 cups whipped
Currants (dried)	1 lb	3¼ cups
Dates	1 lb	2 cups unpitted; 2¾ cups pitted and chopped
Eggplant	1 lb	2½ cups diced
Eggs, whole (extra large)	1 doz	3 cups
Eggs, whole (large)	1 doz	2⅓ cups
Eggs, whole (medium)	1 doz	2 cups
Eggs, whole (small)	1 doz	1¾ cups
Egg whites (extra large)	1 doz	1¾ cups
Egg whites (large)	1 doz	1½ cups
Egg whites (medium)	1 doz	1⅓ cups
Egg whites (small)	1 doz	1¼ cups
Egg yolks (extra large)	1 doz	1 cup
Egg yolks (large)	1 doz	⅞ cup
Egg yolks (medium)	1 doz	¾ cup
Egg yolks (small)	1 doz	⅔ cup
Figs (fresh)	1 lb	12 medium
Figs (canned)	1 lb	12 to 16
Figs (dried)	1 lb	3 cups chopped
Filberts (*see* Hazelnuts)		
Flour, gluten	1 lb	3 cups sifted
Flour, rice	1 lb	3½ cups sifted
Flour, rye (light/dark)	1 lb	5 cups; 3½ cups sifted
Flour, (all-purpose, bread, self-rising)	1 lb	3 cups sifted
Flour, (cake, pastry)	1 lb	4½ to 5 cups sifted
Flour, (whole-wheat)	1 lb	3½ cups unsifted
Gelatin, unflavored	1 oz	¼ cup; 4 Tbsp granulated
Graham crackers	15	1 cup crumbs
Grapefruit (fresh)	1 lb	1 medium; 1½ cups segments
Grapefruit (frozen)	13½ oz	1½ cups sections
Grapefruit (canned)	16 oz	2 cups sections
Grapes (seeded)	1 lb	2½ to 3 cups

Food	Weight or Amount	Approximate Equivalent
Greens (fresh)	1 lb	3 cups cooked
Greens (frozen)	10 oz	1½ to 2 cups
Grits	1 lb	3 cups
Grits	1 cup	3⅓ cups cooked
Hazelnuts (shelled, whole)	1 lb	3½ cups
Hominy (whole)	1 lb	2½ cups
Hominy (whole)	1 cup	6⅔ cups cooked
Honey	1 lb	1⅓ cups
Ice Cream, ice milk and sherbet	1 qt	4 cups
Lemons	1 lb	4 to 6 medium; 1 cup juice
Lemons	1 medium	3 Tbsp juice; 2 to 3 tsp zest
Lentils (dried)	1 lb	2¼ cups; 5 cups cooked
Lettuce	1 lb	6 cups pieces
Limes	1 lb	6 to 8 medium; ½ cup juice
Limes	1 medium	1 to 2 Tbsp juice; 1 tsp zest
Macaroni, 1-inch pieces	1 lb	3¾ cups; 9 cups cooked
Maple syrup	16 fl oz	2 cups
Margarine (*see* Butter)		
Marshmallows (large)	1 cup	11 marshmallows
Marshmallows (miniature)	1 cup	110 marshmallows
Milk (whole, skim or buttermilk)	1 qt	4 cups
Milk (sweetened condensed)	15 oz	1⅓ cups
Milk (evaporated, whole or skim)	14½ oz	1⅔ cups; 3⅓ cups reconstituted
Milk (dry)	1 lb	3⅔ cups; 14 cups reconstituted
Mixed vegetables (frozen)	10 oz	2 cups, cut
Mixed vegetables (canned)	16 to 17 oz	2 cups, cut
Molasses	16 fl oz	2 cups
Mushrooms (fresh)	1 lb	5 to 6 cups sliced
Mushrooms (canned)	4 oz	⅔ cup sliced or chopped
Noodles, 1-inch pieces	1 lb	6 to 8 cups; 8 cups cooked
Oats, rolled	1 lb	5 cups
Oats, rolled	1 cup	1¾ cups cooked
Oil (corn, olive, peanut, safflower, etc.)	1 qt	4 cups
Okra (fresh)	1 lb	2¼ cups chopped
Okra (frozen)	10 oz	1¼ cups chopped
Okra (canned)	15½ oz	1¾ cups chopped

Food	Weight or Amount	Approximate Equivalent
Onions, green (fresh)	9 onions with tops	1 cup sliced
Onions, white (fresh)	1 lb	4 medium onions; 2 to 2½ cups chopped
Onions, white (frozen)	12 oz	3 cups chopped
Oranges (fresh)	1 lb	3 medium; 1 cup juice
Oranges (fresh)	1 medium	⅓ cup juice; 3 Tbsp zest
Oranges (canned mandarin, fruit and juice)	11 oz	1¼ cups
Parsnips	1 lb	4 medium; 2 cups chopped
Pasta (*see* Macaroni; Noodles; Spaghetti)		
Peaches (fresh)	1 lb	4 medium; 2½ cups sliced
Peaches (frozen)	10 oz	1⅛ cups slices and juice
Peaches (canned)	1 lb	6 to 10 halves; 2 cups slices
Peaches (dried)	1 lb	2¾ cups; 5½ cups cooked
Peanuts	1 lb	3 cups
Pears (fresh)	1 lb	4 medium; 2 cups sliced
Pears (dried)	1 lb	2¾ cups; 5½ cups cooked
Peas, black-eyed (fresh)	1 lb	2⅓ cups
Peas, black-eyed (frozen, cooked)	10 oz	1½ cups
Peas, black-eyed (canned)	16 to 17 oz	2 cups
Peas, green (fresh, in pod)	1 lb	1 cup shelled
Peas, green (frozen)	10 oz	2 cups
Peas, green (canned)	1 lb	2 cups
Peas, green (dried, split)	1 lb	2¼ cups; 5 cups cooked
Pecans	1 lb	4 cups halves; 3¾ cups chopped
Pistachios	1 lb	3¼ to 4 cups
Plums (fresh)	1 lb	8 to 20 plums; 2 cups pitted and quartered
Plums (canned, whole)	1 lb	10 to 14 plums
Potatoes, sweet (fresh)	1 lb	3 medium; 3½ to 4 cups chopped or sliced
Potatoes, sweet (canned)	16 to 17 oz	1¾ to 2 cups
Potatoes, white	1 lb	3 medium; 3½ to 4 cups chopped or sliced; 1¾ cups cooked and mashed

Food	Weight or Amount	Approximate Equivalent
Prunes (dried, with pits)	1 lb	2½ cups; 4 to 4½ cups cooked
Prunes (dried, pitted)	1 lb	2¼ cups; 4 cups cooked
Prunes (canned)	1 lb	10 to 14 prunes
Pumpkin (fresh)	1 lb	1 cup cooked and mashed
Pumpkin (canned)	16 to 17 oz	2 cups mashed
Radishes	½ lb	1⅔ cups sliced
Raisins (seeded)	1 lb	2½ cups
Raisins (seedless)	1 lb	3 cups
Rhubarb (fresh)	1 lb	2 cups chopped and cooked
Rhubarb (frozen)	12 oz	1½ cups chopped and sliced
Rice (regular)	1 lb	2¼ cups; 6¾ cups cooked
Rice (converted)	14 ounces	2 cups; 8 cups cooked
Rice (quick-cooking)	14 ounces	4 cups; 8 cups cooked
Rice (brown)	12 ounces	2 cups; 8 cups cooked
Rice (wild)	1 lb	3 cups; 11 to 12 cups cooked
Rutabaga	1 lb	2½ cups cubed
Shortening, vegetable	1 lb	2 cups
Soda crackers (saltines)	28	1 cup crumbs
Spaghetti (12 inch pieces)	1 lb	about 7 cups cooked
Spinach (fresh)	1 lb	10 to 12 cups pieces; 1½ to 2 cups cooked
Spinach (frozen)	10 oz	1½ cups
Spinach (canned)	15 oz	2 cups
Split green peas (see Peas, green (dried, split)		
Squash, summer (fresh)	1 lb	3 medium; 2½ cups sliced
Squash, summer (frozen)	10 oz	1½ cups sliced
Squash, winter (fresh)	1 lb	1 cup cooked and mashed
Squash, winter (frozen)	12 oz	1½ cups
Strawberries (fresh)	1 pint	1½ to 2 cups sliced
Strawberries (frozen, sliced or halved)	10 oz	1 cup
Strawberries (frozen, whole)	1 lb	1⅓ cups
Sugar, brown (light or dark)	1 lb	2¼ cups packed
Sugar, granulated	1 lb	2 cups
Sugar, confectioners'	1 lb	3½ to 4 cups unsifted; 4½ cups sifted
Tomatoes (fresh)	1 lb	3 medium; 1½ cups chopped

Food	Weight or Amount	Approximate Equivalent
Tomatoes (canned)	16 oz	2 cups
Turnips	1 lb	3 medium
Vanilla wafers	22 wafers	1 cup crumbs
Vegetables, mixed (*see* Mixed vegetables)		
Walnuts	1 lb	3¾ cups halves; 3½ cups chopped
Wheat germ	1 lb	4 cups
Yogurt	½ pt	1 cup

EMERGENCY SUBSTITUTIONS OF INGREDIENTS

At one time or another, most cooks find themselves without an ingredient needed to complete a recipe. No need to panic. The following ingredient substitutions can be made with satisfactory results in most recipes. The exception would be baked goods for which—if at all possible—it's safer not to use substitutions.

If The Recipe Calls For:		Substitute
ARROWROOT — 1⅓ tablespoons (1 tablespoon + 1 teaspoon)	=	2 tablespoons all-purpose flour *OR* 1 tablespoon cornstarch, potato starch or rice starch
BAKING POWDER, DOUBLE ACTING — 1 teapsoon	=	¼ teaspoon baking soda plus ⅝ teaspoon cream of tartar *OR* ¼ teaspoon baking soda plus ½ cup buttermilk or sour milk (reduce liquid in recipe by ½ cup) *OR* ¼ teaspoon baking soda plus ⅜ cup molasses (reduce liquid in recipe by ¼ cup; adjust sweetener) *OR* 1½ teaspoons phosphate or tartrate baking powder
BEEF BROTH (*see* BROTH)		
BREADCRUMBS, DRY — 1 cup	=	¾ cup cracker crumbs
BROTH, CHICKEN OR BEEF — 1 cup	=	1 bouillon cube or 1 teaspoon granules mixed with 1 cup boiling water
BUTTER — 1 cup (2 sticks; 16 tablespoons)	=	1 cup margarine *OR* ⅞ cup vegetable oil, lard or vegetable shortening *OR* ⅘ cup strained bacon fat *OR* ¾ cup strained chicken fat
BUTTERMILK OR SOUR MILK — 1 cup	=	1 cup plain yogurt *OR* 1 tablespoon vinegar or lemon juice plus enough milk to equal 1 cup (let stand 5 minutes) *OR* 1¾ teaspoons cream of tartar plus 1 cup milk

If The Recipe Calls For:		**Substitute**
CHICKEN BROTH (*see* BROTH)		
CHOCOLATE, SEMISWEET —1 ounce	=	½ ounce unsweetened chocolate plus 1 tablespoon granulated sugar
CHOCOLATE, SEMISWEET — 6 ounces chips	=	½ cup + 1 tablespoon unsweetened cocoa, plus ¼ cup + 3 tablespoons granulated sugar, plus 3 tablespoons butter or margarine
CHOCOLATE, UNSWEETENED — 1 ounce	=	3 tablespoons unsweetened cocoa plus 1 tablespoon butter or margarine *OR* 3 tablespoons carob powder plus 2 tablespoons water
CHOCOLATE, UNSWEETENED — 1 ounce plus 4 teaspoons granulated sugar	=	1⅔ ounce semisweet chocolate
COCONUT, GRATED — 1 cup	=	1⅓ cups flaked coconut
COCONUT MILK, FRESH — 1 cup	=	3 tablespoons canned cream of coconut plus ⅞ cup hot water or lowfat milk
CORNSTARCH — 1 tablespoon	=	2 tablespoons all-purpose flour *OR* 2 teaspoons arrowroot
CORN SYRUP, DARK — 1 cup	=	¾ light corn syrup plus ¼ cup light molasses
CORN SYRUP, LIGHT OR DARK — 1 cup	=	1¼ cups granulated or packed brown sugar plus ¼ cup liquid*
CREAM, HALF-AND-HALF — 1 cup	=	⅞ cup whole milk plus 1½ tablespoons butter *OR* ½ cup light cream plus ½ cup whole milk
CREAM, LIGHT (20% fat) — 1 cup	=	⅞ cup whole milk plus 3 tablespoons butter
CREAM, SOUR — 1 cup	=	1 cup plain yogurt *OR* ¾ cup sour milk, buttermilk or plain yogurt plus ⅓ cup butter *OR* 1 tablespoon lemon juice plus evaporated whole milk to equal 1 cup

If The Recipe Calls For:		**Substitute**
CREAM, WHIPPING (36–40% fat) — 1 cup	=	¾ cup whole milk plus ⅓ cup butter
EGG, WHOLE — 1 egg	=	2 egg yolks plus 1 tablespoon cold water OR 3½ tablespoons thawed frozen egg or egg substitute OR 2½ tablespoons powdered whole egg plus an equal amount of water
EGG WHITE — 1 white	=	2 tablespoons thawed frozen egg white OR 1 tablespoon powdered egg white plus 2 tablespoons water
EGG YOLK — 2 yolks	=	1 whole egg (for thickening sauces, etc.)
1 large yolk	=	3½ teaspoons thawed frozen yolk OR 2 tablespoons powdered yolk plus 2 teaspoons water (for baking)
FLOUR (for thickening) — 2 tablespoons all-purpose	=	1 tablespoon cornstarch, potato starch or rice starch OR 4 teaspoons arrowroot OR 2 tablespoons quick-cooking tapioca
FLOUR — 1 cup sifted all-purpose	=	1 cup minus 2 tablespoons unsifted all-purpose flour
FLOUR — 1 cup sifted cake	=	1 cup minus 2 tablespoons sifted all-purpose flour
FLOUR — 1 cup sifted self-rising	=	1 cup sifted all-purpose flour plus 1½ teaspoons baking powder and ⅛ teaspoon salt
GARLIC — 1 small clove	=	⅛ teaspoon garlic powder
GINGER, FRESH — 1 tablespoon finely chopped	=	⅛ teaspoon powdered ginger
HALF-AND-HALF (see CREAM, HALF-AND-HALF)		
HONEY — 1 cup	=	1¼ cups granulated sugar plus ¼ cup liquid*

If The Recipe Calls For:		**Substitute**
LEMON JUICE — 1 teaspoon	=	½ teaspoon vinegar
MILK, NONFAT (SKIM) — 1 cup	=	⅓ cup powdered plus ¾ cup water
MILK, SOUR — 1 cup	=	1 tablespoon lemon juice or white vinegar plus milk to equal 1 cup (let stand 5 minutes)
MILK, WHOLE — 1 cup	=	1 cup nonfat (skim) milk plus 2 tablespoons butter or margarine *OR* ½ cup evaporated whole milk plus ½ cup water *OR* ⅞ cup water plus ¼ cup powdered whole milk *OR* ⅞ cup water plus ¼ cup powdered skim milk plus 2½ teaspoons butter or margarine *OR* 1 cup soy milk
MUSTARD, PREPARED — 1 tablespoon	=	1 teaspoon powdered mustard
SOUR CREAM (*see* CREAM, SOUR)		
SUGAR, CONFECTIONERS' — 1 cup	=	½ cup plus 1 tablespoon granulated sugar
SUGAR, LIGHT BROWN — 1 cup	=	½ cup dark brown sugar plus ½ cup granulated sugar
SUGAR, GRANULATED — 1 cup	=	1¾ cups confectioners' sugar *OR* 1 cup packed light brown sugar *OR* 1 cup superfine sugar
TOMATO JUICE — 1 cup	=	½ cup tomato sauce plus ½ cup water
TOMATO SAUCE — 1 cup	=	⅜ cup tomato paste plus ½ cup water
VINEGAR — 1 teaspoon	=	2 teaspoons lemon juice
YEAST, ACTIVE DRY — ¼-ounce envelope	=	1 scant tablespoon active dry yeast *OR* 1 (.06-ounce) cake compressed fresh yeast

* Use whatever liquid the recipe calls for.

NOTE: Asterisked substitutions for honey and corn syrup are based on how the ingredients interact in the recipe and not on the flavor or amount of sweetness.

COMMON MEASUREMENTS AND EQUIVALENTS

½ teaspoon	=	30 drops
1 teaspoon	=	⅓ tablespoon or 60 drops
3 teaspoons	=	1 tablespoon
½ tablespoon	=	1½ teaspoons
1 tablespoon	=	3 teaspoons or ½ fluid ounce
2 tablespoons	=	1 fluid ounce
3 tablespoons	=	1½ fluid ounces or 1 jigger
4 tablespoons	=	¼ cup or 2 fluid ounces
5⅓ tablespoons	=	⅓ cup or 5 tablespoons + 1 teaspoon
8 tablespoons	=	½ cup or 4 fluid ounces
10⅔ tablespoons	=	⅔ cup or 10 tablespoons + 2 teaspoons
12 tablespoons	=	¾ cup or 6 fluid ounces
16 tablespoons	=	1 cup or 8 fluid ounces or ½ pint
⅛ cup	=	2 tablespoons or 1 fluid ounce
¼ cup	=	4 tablespoons or 2 fluid ounces
⅓ cup	=	5 tablespoons + 1 teaspoon
⅜ cup	=	¼ cup + 2 tablespoons
½ cup	=	8 tablespoons or 4 fluid ounces
⅝ cup	=	½ cup + 2 tablespoons
¾ cup	=	12 tablespoons or 6 fluid ounces
⅞ cup	=	¾ cup + 2 tablespoons
1 cup	=	16 tablespoons or ½ pint or 8 fluid ounces
2 cups	=	1 pint or 16 fluid ounces
1 pint	=	2 cups or 16 fluid ounces
1 quart	=	2 pints or 4 cups or 32 fluid ounces
1 gallon	=	4 quarts or 8 pints or 16 cups or 128 fluid ounces

APPROXIMATE METRIC EQUIVALENTS

¼ teaspoon	=	1.23 milliliters
½ teaspoon	=	2.46 milliliters
¾ teaspoon	=	3.7 milliliters
1 teaspoon	=	4.93 milliliters
1¼ teaspoons	=	6.16 milliliters
1½ teaspoons	=	7.39 milliliters
1¾ teaspoons	=	8.63 milliliters
2 teaspoons	=	9.86 milliliters
1 tablespoon	=	14.79 milliliters
2 tablespoons	=	29.57 milliliters
¼ cup	=	59.15 milliliters
½ cup	=	118.3 milliliters
1 cup	=	236.59 milliliters
2 cups or 1 pint	=	473.18 milliliters
3 cups	=	709.77 milliliters
4 cups or 1 quart	=	946.36 milliliters
4 quarts or 1 gallon	=	3.785 liters

CONVERTING TO METRIC

When converting to or from metric, be sure to convert *all* measurements. Otherwise, the proportions of the ingredients could be critically imbalanced.

When This Is Known	Multiply It By	To Get
teaspoons	4.93	milliliters
tablespoons	14.79	milliliters
fluid ounces	29.57	milliliters
cups	236.59	milliliters
cups	.236	liters
pints	473.18	milliliters
pints	.473	liters
quarts	946.36	milliliters
quarts	.946	liters
gallons	3.785	liters
ounces	28.35	grams
pounds	.454	kilograms
inches	2.54	centimeters
Fahrenheit	subtract 32 multiply by 5 divide by 9	Celsius (Centigrade)

CONVERTING FROM METRIC

When This Is Known	Divide It By	To Get
milliliters	4.93	teaspoons
milliliters	14.79	tablespoons
milliliters	29.57	fluid ounces
milliliters	236.59	cups
liters	.236	cups
milliliters	473.18	pints
liters	.473	pints
milliliters	946.36	quarts
liters	.946	quarts
liters	3.785	gallons
grams	28.35	ounces
kilograms	.454	pounds
centimeters	2.54	inches
Celsius (Centigrade)	Multiply by 9 divide by 5 add 32	Fahrenheit

TEMPERATURE EQUIVALENTS (FAHRENHEIT/CELSIUS SCALE)

	Fahrenheit	Celsius
Water Freezes	32°F	0° C
	40°	4.4°
	50°	10°
	60°	15.6°
	70°	21.1°
	80°	26.7°
	90°	32.2°
	100°	37.8°
	110°	43.3°
	120°	48.9°
	130°	54.4°
	140°	60°
	150°	65.6°
	160°	71.1°
	170°	76.7°
	180°	82.2°
	190°	87.8°
	200°	93.3°
Water Boils	212°	100°
	250°	121°
	300°	149°
	350°	177°
	400°	205°
	450°	233°
	500°	260°

OVEN TEMPERATURE TERMINOLOGY

Description	Fahrenheit	Celsius
Very slow	250°–300°	121°–149°
Slow	300°–325°	149°–163°
Moderate	350°–375°	177°–190°
Very hot	450°–475°	233°–246°
Extremely hot	500°–525°	.260°–274°

CONVERSION TIME FOR VARIOUS-WATTAGE MICROWAVE OVENS

Most microwave cookbooks are written for 700-watt ovens. Convert the cooking time to a lower-wattage oven by:

- adding 10 seconds (or less) for each minute stated in the recipe — 650-WATT OVEN

- adding 20 seconds for each minute stated in the recipe — 600-WATT OVEN

- adding 40 seconds for each minute stated in the recipe — 500-WATT OVEN

HIGH-ALTITUDE ADJUSTMENTS FOR BAKING

| | Altitude | | |
Ingredient	3,000 Feet	5,000 Feet	7,000 Feet
Reduce baking powder For each teaspoon, decrease	⅛ tsp	⅛ to ¼ tsp	¼ tsp
Reduce sugar For each cup, decrease	0 to 1 Tbsp	0 to 2 Tbsp	1 to 3 Tbsp
Increase liquid For each cup, add	1 to 2 Tbsp	2 to 4 Tbsp	3 to 4 Tbsp

APPROXIMATE BOILING TEMPERATURE OF WATER AT VARIOUS ALTITUDES

Altitude	Boiling Point of Water	
Sea level	212.0°F	100.0°C
2,000 feet	208.4°F	98.4°C
5,000 feet	203.0°F	95.0°C
7,500 feet	198.4°F	92.4°C
10,000 feet	194.0°F	90.0°C

COMPARATIVE BAKING PAN SIZES

The following table will help determine substitutions of pans of similar sizes. It's important to note that adjustments in baking times will be necessary when pan sizes are changed.

Common Pan Size	Approximate Volume
Square and Rectangular Pans	
8" × 8" × 1½" square	6 cups
8" × 8" × 2" square	8 cups
9" × 9" × 1½" square	8 cups
9" × 9" × 2" square	10 cups
11" × 7" × 2" rectangular	6 cups
13" × 9" × 2" rectangular	15 cups
8" × 4" × 2½" loaf	4 cups
8½" × 4½ × 2½ " loaf	6 cups
9" × 5" × 3" loaf	8 cups
Round Pans	
1¾" × ¾" mini muffin cup	⅛ cup
2¾" × 1⅛" muffin cup	¼ cup
2¾" × 1⅜" muffin cup	scant ½ cup
3" × 1¼" giant muffin cup	⅝ cup
8" × 1¼" pie plate	3 cups
9" × 1½" pie plate	4 oups
9" × 2" pie plate (deep dish)	6 cups
8" × 1½" cake	4 cups
8" × 2" cake	7 cups
9" × 1½" cake	6 cups
9" × 2" cake	8½ cups
10" × 2" cake	10 ¾ cups
9" × 3" Bundt	9 cups
10" × 3½" Bundt	12 cups
8" × 3" tube	9 cups
9" × 3" tube	10 cups
10" × 4" tube	16 cups
9½" × 2½" springform	10 cups
10" × 2½" springform	12 cups

CANDYMAKING TEMPERATURES AND COLD-WATER TESTS

Stage of Hardness	Temperature	When a small amount of sugar syrup is dropped into very cold water it:
Thread	230° to 234°F (110° to 112°C)	Forms a soft 2-inch thread
Soft ball	234° to 240°F (112° to 116°C)	Forms a soft ball that flattens of its own accord when removed
Firm ball	244° to 248°F (118° to 120°C)	Forms a firm but pliable ball
Hard ball	250° to 265°F (121° to 129°C)	Forms a rigid ball that is still somewhat pliable
Soft crack	270° to 290°F (132° to 143°C)	Separates into hard but pliable threads
Hard crack	300° to 310°F (149° to 154°C)	Separates into hard, brittle threads

HERB AND SPICE CHART

With today's increasing health consciousness, more people are looking for ways to reduce sodium, and herbs and spices are a natural salt substitute. Following are suggestions on ways to use some of the more popular herbs and spices as seasonings in various foods.

	Appetizers	Breads	Soups & Stews
ALLSPICE (spice)	Fruit Meat Pâtés	Coffeecakes Sweet breads and rolls	Chicken Consommé Fish Potato Tomato Turtle Vegetable
ANISE SEED (spice)	Cheese Fruit Shellfish	Coffeecakes Savory breads Sweet breads and rolls	Fruit Cabbage Cauliflower Rutabaga Turnips
BASIL (herb)	Cheese Italian Seafood	Savory breads	Beef; Chicken Fish Minestrone Pea Potato Spinach Tomato Turtle Vegetable
BAY LEAF (herb)	Poaching liquid for shellfish		Bean Bouillabaisse Chicken Consommé Corn Fish Meat Vegetable

Salads	Cheese and Egg Dishes	Fish and Shellfish	Poultry and Game Birds

Cabbage
Chicken
Tomato
Salad dressings
	Cottage cheese
	  and other
	  mild cheeses
		Poached fish	Chicken
			Duck
			Goose
			Turkey

Apple
Beet
Cabbage
Cucumber
Fruit
Salad dressings
	Cottage cheese
	  and other
	  mild cheeses
			Chicken
			Duck

Aspics Chicken Cucumber Fruit Mixed green Seafood Tomato Vegetable Salad dressings	Cream cheese Deviled eggs Omelets Sandwich spreads Scrambled eggs Soufflés	Crab Halibut Lobster Mackerel Salmon Shrimp Tuna	Chicken Lamb Duck Turkey
Aspics Marinade for beef salads Potato Salad Dressings		Poached fish	Chicken Duck

	Meats and Game Animals	Vegetables	Pasta, Grains and Rice
ALLSPICE (spice)	Beef Ham Lamb Rabbit Sausages Veal Venison	Beets Carrots Parsnips Spinach Squash, winter Sweet potatoes Turnips	Bulghur Couscous Polenta Rice
ANISE SEED (spice)	Beef Veal	Beets Carrots Sauerkraut Turnips	Noodles
BASIL (herb)	Beef Lamb Liver Pork Rabbit Sausages Veal Venison	Asparagus; Beans; Beets; Broccoli; Cabbage; Carrots; Celery; Cucumber; Eggplant; Onions; Peas; Potatoes; Spinach; Squash	Couscous Pasta Polenta Rice
BAY LEAF (herb)	Beef Lamb Rabbit Tongue Veal Venison	Artichokes Beets Carrots Potatoes Tomatoes	

Sauces	Miscellaneous	Desserts	Beverages
Chili Dessert Meat Tomato	Chutneys Preserves Relishes	Cakes Chocolate desserts Cookies Gingerbreads Mincemeats Pies Puddings Pumpkin	Cranberry juice Spice wine Tomato juice
Fruit sauces	Candies Pickles Stuffings	Cakes Cookies	Fruit juices Liqueurs
Butter Cheese Spaghetti Tomato	Herb butters Pizza Stuffings Vinegars	Fruit compotes	Tomato juice Vegetable juices
Barbecue Meat Spaghetti Tomato	Marinades Pickles Poultry stuffings		Tomato juice Vegetable juices

	Appetizers	Breads	Soups & Stews
CARAWAY SEED (spice)	Cheese spreads and dips	Onion bread Irish soda bread Rye bread Topping for breads and rolls	Cabbage Potato
CARDAMOM (spice)	Fruit, especially melon (except watermelon)	Coffeecakes Danish pastry Sweet breads and rolls	Pea Bean
CELERY SEED (spice)	Cheese spreads and dips Fish Shellfish	Cheese breads Herb breads	Beef stew Celery Meat Vegetable
CHERVIL (herb)	Avocado Cheese spreads and dips Chicken Fish Meat	Herb bread	Beef Chicken Potato Sorrel Spinach Vegetable
CHILI POWDER (spice)	Guacamole Mexican appetizers	Cheese breads Cornbreads	Bean Beef Chili Pea Tomato

Salads	Cheese and Egg Dishes	Fish and Shellfish	Poultry and Game Birds
Beet Cucumber Potato Slaw Tomato Salad dressings	Cheese spreads Cheddar cheese Cottage cheese Deviled eggs Omelets		Goose
Orange Salad dressings		Curried fish dishes	Curried Poultry dishes
Aspics Potato Seafood Slaw Salad dressings	Cheese spreads Omelets Soufflés	Fish croquettes	Chicken Turkey
Beet Chicken Cucumber Egg Fruit Mixed greens Potato Tomato Salad dressings	Cottage cheese Cream cheese Deviled eggs Omelets Soufflés	Court bouillon All fish and shellfish	Chicken Duck Turkey
Bean Egg Mixed vegetable Potato Salad dressings	Cottage cheese Deviled eggs Dips and spreads Fondue Omelets	Most fish and shellfish	Chicken Turkey

	Meats and Game Animals	Vegetables	Pasta, Grains and Rice
CARAWAY SEED (spice)	Beef Pork Sauerbraten	Cabbage Carrots Celery Cucumbers Onions Potatoes Turnips	Noodles
CARDAMOM (spice)	Curried meat dishes Sausages	Carrots Pumpkin Squash Sweet potatoes	
CELERY SEED (spice)	Beef	Beets Cabbage Cauliflower Tomatoes	Noodles
CHERVIL (herb)	Beef Game Lamb Pork Sausages Veal	Asparagus Beets Carrots Eggplant Peas Squash, summer and winter Tomatoes	Bulghur Couscous Pasta Rice
CHILI POWDER (spice)	Beef Pork	Beans, dried Corn Eggplant Lima beans Onions Tomatoes	Rice

Sauces	Miscellaneous	Desserts	Beverages
Cucumber Sour cream	Stuffings	Pound cakes Spice cakes and cookies	Tomato juice Liqueurs
Dessert Orange		Fruit	
Celery Tomato	Stuffings		Tomato juice Vegetable juices
Savory sauces -almost all	Garnish Herb butters Stuffings		Buttermilk Tomato juice Vegetable juices
Barbecue Cheese Chili Tomato	Tomato juice Mexican dishes		

	Appetizers	Breads	Soups & Stews
CINNAMON (spice)	Fruit	Biscuits Cinnamon toast Coffeecakes Pumpkin bread Sweet breads and rolls	Beef stews Fruit soups

CLOVES (spice)		Coffeecakes
		Sweet breads
		  and rolls
			Beef stew
			Chicken and
			  meat stocks
			Onion

CORIANDER (SEEDS, WHOLE AND GROUND) (spice)		Danish pastries Sweet breads and rolls	Fruit Pea Stocks
CUMIN (spice)	Cheese spreads	Savory breads	Bean Carrot Chicken Chili Pea
CURRY POWDER (spice blend)			Beef Chicken Consommé Pea Tomato Turtle Vegetable

Salads	Cheese and Egg Dishes	Fish and Shellfish	Poultry and Game Birds
Fruit			B'steeya Chicken
Fruit			
Mixed green Fruit Salad dressings	Cheddar Cream cheese Curried dishes Omelets Sandwich spreads		Curried poultry dishes
Salad dressings	Cheese spreads Cheddar Curried dishes Deviled eggs Edam	Most fish and shellfish	Curried poultry dishes
Chicken Fruit Meat Seafood Salad dressings	Cottage cheese Cream cheese Curried eggs Deviled eggs Fondue Sandwich spreads	Most fish and shellfish	Chicken Turkey

	Meats and Game Animals	Vegetables	Pasta, Grains and Rice
CINNAMON (spice)	Beef stew Ham Pork Sauerbraten	Beets Carrots Onions Pumpkin Squash, winter Sweet potatoes Tomatoes	Noodles Rice
CLOVES (spice)	Ham Lamb Pork Tongue	Beets Carrots Green beans Onions Pumpkin Squash, winter Sweet potatoes	
CORIANDER (SEEDS, WHOLE AND GROUND) (spice)	Beef Curried meat dishes Lamb Pork Sausages	Cauliflower Onions Spinach Tomatoes Sauerkraut	
CUMIN (spice)	Beef Curried meat dishes Lamb Pork		
CURRY POWDER (spice blend)	Beef Lamb Pork	Beets Carrots Parsnips Squash, winter Sweet potatoes Turnips	Noodles Rice

Sauces	Miscellaneous	Desserts	Beverages

Dessert
Meat
	Applesauce
	Candies
	Chutneys
	Jams
	Pickles
		Chocolate
		  desserts
		Cakes
		  and cookies
		Fruit
		Gingerbread
		Ice cream
		Pies
		Puddings
			Cocoa
			Coffees (special)
			Fruit juices
			Spiced wines

Chili Dessert Tomato	Applesauce Chutneys Pickles Stuffings	Cakes and cookies Gingerbread Pies Puddings	Cranberry juice Spiced wines Tomato juice
	Chutneys Stuffings	Cakes and cookies Fruit Gingerbread	
Chili Curry	Pickles Stuffings	Cakes and cookies	
Cheese Curry	Stuffings		

	Appetizers	Breads	Soups & Stews
DILL (herb)	Avocado Dips and spreads Fish Shellfish	Herb breads Rye breads	Bean Borscht Chicken Fish Lamb Pea Tomato
FENNEL (spice)		Italian breads Savory breads Sweet rolls and breads Topping for breads and rolls	Borscht Cabbage Fish Meat stews Minestrone
GINGER (spice)	Beef Chicken Melon	Spice breads Sweet breads and rolls	Beef Chicken Fish Fruit Tomato
MACE (spice)		Sweet breads and rolls	Fish Fruit Vegetable
MARJORAM (herb)	Cheese dips and spreads Mushrooms Pâtés	Herb breads	Beef Chicken Onion Oyster Potato Spinach Tomato

Salads	Cheese and Egg Dishes	Fish and Shellfish	Poultry and Game Birds
Avocado Cucumber Potato Seafood Slaw Tomato Salad dressings	Cottage cheese Cream cheese Deviled eggs Omelets Sandwich spreads	Most fish and shellfish	Chicken Turkey
Seafood Mixed green Pasta	Omeletes Soufflés	Almost all fish and shellfish	Chicken Duck Goose
Fruit Rice Salad dressings	Cheese dishes	Sweet-and-sour fish and meat dishes	Chicken Duck
Bean Fruit Pasta	Cheese dishes	Shellfish	Chicken Duck
Chicken Egg Fish and shellfish Fruit Mixed green Vegetable Salad dressings	Cheese spreads Omelets Soufflés	Shellfish Most fish, especially halibut, salmon and tuna	Chicken Duck Goose Turkey

	Meats and Game Animals	Vegetables	Pasta, Grains and Rice
DILL (herb)	Beef Lamb Pork Sweetbreads Veal	Beets; Cabbage; Carrots; Cauliflower; Celery; Green beans; Parsnips; Peas, Potatoes	Noodles Rice
FENNEL (spice)	Beef Lamb Pork Sausages (esp. Italian)	Beans, dried Beet Cabbage Celery Cucumbers Onions Sauerkraut Squash, summer	Pilafs Rice
GINGER (spice)	Beef Lamb Pork Venison	Cabbage Carrots Squash, summer and winter Sweet potatoes	Rice
MACE (spice)	Beef Rabbit Sausages Veal Venison	Broccoli Brussels sprouts Cabbage Green beans Pumpkin Squash, winter	
MARJORAM (herb)	Beef Lamb Pork Rabbit Veal Venison	Brussels sprouts; Carrots; Celery; Corn; Eggplant; Greens; Onions; Peas; Potatoes; Spinach; Squash, summer	Bulghur Noodles Rice

Sauces	Miscellaneous	Desserts	Beverages
Butter Cream Fish Tartar	Pickles Stuffings Vinegars		Tomato juice Buttermilk
Dessert Fish Italian Meat	Garnish Pickles	Cakes Cookies	
Dessert Meat	Chutneys Conserves Marinades Pickles Relishes	Cakes Cookies Fruit Gingerbread Ice creams Puddings	Apple juice Spiced wines
Fish Sweet	Chutneys Conserves Pickles Relishes	Cakes and cookies Chocolate desserts Puddings	Fruit juices Spiced wines
Cream Fish Meat Tomato	Herb butters Stuffings		Tomato juice Vegetable juices

	Appetizers	Breads	Soups & Stews
MINT (herb)	Fruit Melon		Bean Pea Tomato
MUSTARD (spice)	Cheese Shrimp	Cheese breads	Potato Sorrel
NUTMEG (spice)	Fruit Melon	Sweet breads and rolls	Beef Black bean Fruit Pea Potato Squash, summer and winter Tomato
OREGANO (herb)	Cheese spreads Guacamole Italian Mexican Mushroom	Herb breads	Bean Beef Chili Minestrone Mushroom Onion Tomato Vegetable
PAPRIKA (spice)	Cheese spread and dips	Cheese breads Cornbread Herb breads	Bean Meat Pea

Salads	Cheese and Egg Dishes	Fish and Shellfish	Poultry and Game Birds
Cucumber Fruit Mixed green Slaw Tomato Waldorf	Cottage cheese Cream cheese	Garnish for broiled shrimp and prawns Salmon	Chicken
Egg salad Ham and other meat salads Mixed green Slaw Salad dressings	Most cheese dishes Deviled eggs Sandwich spreads	Deviled crab Most fish and shellfish	Chicken Turkey
Fruit	Most cheese dishes Soufflés		Chicken Duck Turkey
Avocado Bean Egg Potato Shellfish Vegetable Salad dressings	Cheese soufflé Cheese spreads Deviled eggs Omelets	Most fish and shellfish	Chicken Duck Pheasant Turkey
Salad dressings	Most cheese and egg dishes		Chicken Hungarian poultry dishes

	Meats and Game Animals	Vegetables	Pasta, Grains and Rice
MINT (herb)	Ham Lamb	Cabbage Carrots Celery Green beans Peas Potatoes Tomatoes	Bulghur Rice
MUSTARD (spice)	Beef Ham Lamb Pork	Beets Cabbage Cucumbers	
NUTMEG (spice)	Beef Ham Pork Sausages	Beans, dried; Corn; Eggplant; Mushrooms; Onions; Potatoes; Pumpkin; Spinach; Squash, winter; Tomatoes	Rice
OREGANO (herb)	Beef Lamb Liver Sausages Veal Venison	Broccoli Cabbage Dried beans Eggplant Mushrooms Onions Potatoes Tomatoes	Pasta Polenta Rice
PAPRIKA (spice)	Beef Hungarian meat dishes Veal	Cauliflower Corn Potatoes	Rice

Sauces	Miscellaneous	Desserts	Beverages
Sauce for Lamb	Garnish Jelly Vinegars	Fruit Frozen soufflés Ice creams Ices and Sherbets	Cranberry juice Fruit punch Juleps Most fruit juices Teas
Cheese Meat	Condiments Pickles Relishes Seeds as a garnish	Gingerbread	
Fruit sauces Meat sauces Sweet sauces	Chutneys Conserves Pickles	Cakes Cookies Fruit Fruit pies Puddings	Cocoa Eggnog Spiced wines
Barbecue Cheese Mexican Spaghetti Tomato	Herb butters Marinades Pizza Stuffings		Tomato juice Vegetable juices
Barbecue Cheese Cream Meat	Garnish for most savory foods Stuffings		

	Appetizers	Breads	Soups & Stews
PARSLEY (herb)	Aspics Cheese dips and spreads Guacamole	Herb breads	Bean Court bouillon Meat Vegetable
PEPPER (spice)	Cheese spreads and dips Fish and shellfish Pâtés	Savory breads Spice breads	Fish Fruit Meat Vegetable
POPPY SEED (spice)	Corn crisps Cheese spreads and dips	Coffeecakes Savory breads Sweet breads Topping for baked goods	
RED PEPPER (CAYENNE) (spice)	Cheese dips Guacamole Mexican Meat	Cheese breads Cornbread	Bean Chili Meat Mexican Vegetable
ROSEMARY (herb)	Fruit Pâtés	Herb breads	Chicken Fish Meat Pea Potato Spinach Turtle Tomato

Salads	Cheese and Egg Dishes	Fish and Shellfish	Poultry and Game Birds
Aspics Chicken Egg Fish and shellfish Mixed green Potato Vegetable	Cottage cheese Cream cheese Deviled eggs Omelets Soufflés	Most fish and shellfish	Chicken Duck Turkey
Egg Fish and shellfish Vegetable	All savory cheese dishes All savory egg dishes	All fish and shellfish dishes	All poultry dishes
Vegetable Salad dressings	Cheese spreads		
Cheese Egg Macaroni Seafood Bean	Deviled eggs Fondue Omelets Soufflés	Fish Shellfish	Chicken Curried poultry dishes Turkey
Beef Chicken Fish and shellfish Fruit Lamb Salad dressings	Scrambled eggs Soufflés Omelets	Most fish, especially halibut, salmon and tuna Shellfish	Chicken Duck Turkey

	Meats and Game Animals	Vegetables	Pasta, Grains and Rice
PARSLEY (herb)	Beef Lamb Liver Pork Veal Venison	Beets; Cabbage; Carrots; Cauliflower; Celery; Eggplant; Onions; Potatoes; Tomatoes; Turnips	All grains, pasta and rice
PEPPER (spice)	All meat dishes	All vegetables	All grains, pasta and rice
POPPY SEED (spice)		Cabbage Carrots Green beans Onions Potatotes Spinach Squash, winter	Noodles

RED PEPPER (CAYENNE) (spice)	Beef
	Curried meat
	  dishes
	Ham
	Mexican meat
	  dishes
	Pork
		Cabbage
		Green beans
		Greens
		Lima beans
			Macaroni and
			  cheese
			Mexican rice
			Pasta
			Polenta
			Rice

ROSEMARY (herb)	Beef Lamb Liver Pork Rabbit Veal	Beans, dried Cauliflower Cucumbers Mushrooms Peas Potatoes Turnips	Rice

Sauces	Miscellaneous	Desserts	Beverages

Cheese
Most savory
  sauces
Spaghetti
Tartar
	Garnish for
	  savory foods
	Herb butters
	Stuffings		

Barbecue
Butter
Cheese
Cream
Meat
	Chutneys
	Compound
	  butters
	Garnishes
	Marinades
	Pickles
	Relishes
	Stuffings
		Fruit
		Gingerbread
		Spice cakes
		  and cookies
			Tomato juice
			Vegetable juices

Butter Fish	Garnish	Cakes and cookies	
Barbecue Cheese Cream Curry Tomato	Marinades Pickles Pizzas		Tomato juice Vegetable juices
Barbecue Butter Cheese Cream Tomato	Herb butters Marinades Pickles Stuffings Vinegar		Tomato juice Vegetable juices

	Appetizers	Breads	Soups & Stews
SAFFRON (spice)		Sweet and savory rolls and breads	Bouillabaisse Chicken Tomato Turkey
SAGE (herb)	Cheese dips spreads Chicken Pâtés	Cheese breads Cornbreads Savory breads	Chicken Fish Minestrone Pea Potato Tomato Vegetable
SAVORY (herb)	Cheese spreads Pâtés	Herb breads	Bean Chicken Consommé Cucumber Lentil Pea Potato Tomato Vegetable
SESAME SEED (spice)	Dips Spreads	Savory breads Sweet breads Topping for breads	
TARRAGON (herb)	Cheese spreads Pâtés Seafood	Herb breads	Bean Chicken Consommé Meat Mushroom Pea Tomato

Salads	Cheese and Egg Dishes	Fish and Shellfish	Poultry and Game Birds
Chicken Seafood	Cream cheese Scrambled eggs	Most fish Shellfish	Chicken Curried poultry dishes Duck Turkey
Bean Chicken Salad dressings	Cottage cheese Cheese spreads Fondues Omelets Soufflés	Fish such as halibut and sole	Chicken Duck Goose Turkey
Bean Mixed green Potato Tomato Vegetables Salad dressings	Cream cheese Deviled eggs Omelets Scrambled eggs Soufflés	Most fish and shellfish	Chicken Duck Pheasant Turkey
Chicken Fruit Potato Tomato Salad dressings	Cheese spreads Fondues Omelets	Most fish and shellfish	Chicken Duck
Aspics; Bean; Chicken; Egg; Fruit; Mixed greens; Potato; Seafood; Slaw; Tomato Salad dressing	Most egg dishes Cottage cheese	Most fish and shellfish	Chicken Duck Goose Pheasant Turkey

	Meats and Game Animals	Vegetables	Pasta, Grains and Rice
SAFFRON (spice)	Beef Lamb Spanish meat dishes Veal	Squash, winter	Couscous Pilafs Rice
SAGE (herb)	Beef Lamb Pork Rabbit Sausages Veal Veal	Beets Brussles sprouts Carrots Celery Eggplant Onions Peas Squash, winter Tomatoes	Bulghur Rice
SAVORY (herb)	Beef Lamb Pork Veal Venison	Artichokes Asparagus Beets Cabbage Green beans Peas	Most rice, pastas and grains
SESAME SEED (spice)	Beef Lamb Pork	Corn Green beans Squash, summer and winter	Noodles
TARRAGON (herb)	Beef Lamb Pork Veal	Asparagus Beets Carrots Green beans Mushrooms Onions Potatoes Squash, summer and winter	Most rice, pasta and grains

Sauces	Miscellaneous	Desserts	Beverages
Butter Cream Curry Fish	Compound butters Stuffings	Cakes and and cookies Pies Puddings	Tea
Butter Cheese Cream	Herb butters Stuffings		Tomato juice Vegetable juices
Barbecue Butter Fish Horseradish	Garnish Stuffings		Tomato juice Vegetable juices
Butter	Candies Garnish Stffings	Cakes and cookies	
Butter Cream Mustard Tartar	Marinades Mayonnaise Mustard Pickles Vinegars		Tomato juice Vegetable juices

	Appetizers	Breads	Soups & Stews
THYME (herb)	Pâtés Seafood	Cornbread Herb breads	Borscht Chicken Fish Gumbo Pea Tomato Vegetable
TURMERIC (spice)	Curried appetizers		Chicken Fish Pumpkin

Salads	Cheese and Egg Dishes	Fish and Shellfish	Poultry and Game Birds
Aspics Beet Chicken Egg Ham Slaw Tomato Tuna	Cottage cheese Deviled eggs Scrambled eggs Omelets Soufflés	Most fish and shellfish	Chicken Duck Pheasant Turkey
Chicken Egg Potato Salad dressings	Deviled eggs Sandwich spreads	Curried dishes Seafood pilafs	Chicken Curried poultry dishes Duck Turkey

	Meats and Game Animals	Vegetables	Pasta, Grains and Rice
THYME (herb)	Beef Lamb Pork Veal Venison	Asparagus Beans Beets Carrots Onions Potatoes Squash	
TURMERIC (spice)	Curried meat dishes Lamb	Squash, winter	Couscous Rice

Sauces	Miscellaneous	Desserts	Beverages
Fish Mustard Tomato			Tomato juice Vegetable juice
	Chutneys Mustards Pickles Relishes		

Lamb

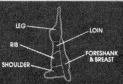

· RETAIL CUTS ·
WHERE THEY COME FROM
HOW TO COOK THEM

LEG · LOIN · RIB · FORESHANK & BREAST · SHOULDER

Whole Leg

Short Cut Leg, Sirloin Off

Shank Portion Roast

Center Leg Roast

Center Slice

American-Style Roast

Frenched-Style Roast

Boneless Leg Roast

Hind Shank

Sirloin Chop

Boneless Sirloin Roast

LEG

Loin Roast

Loin Chop

Double Loin Chop

LOIN

Shank

Spareribs

Boneless Rolled Breast

Riblets

FORESHANK & BREAST

THIS CHART APPROVED BY
NATIONAL LIVE STOCK & MEAT BOARD

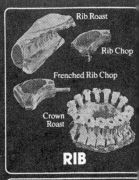

Rib Roast

Rib Chop

Frenched Rib Chop

Crown Roast

RIB

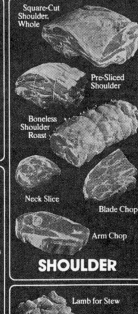

Square-Cut Shoulder, Whole

Pre-Sliced Shoulder

Boneless Shoulder Roast

Neck Slice

Blade Chop

Arm Chop

SHOULDER

Lamb for Stew

Cubes for Kabobs

Ground Lamb

OTHER CUTS

Pork

· RETAIL CUTS ·
WHERE THEY COME FROM
HOW TO COOK THEM

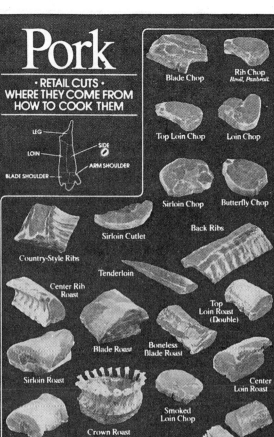

LEG

LOIN

SIDE

ARM SHOULDER

BLADE SHOULDER

LEG/HAM

Leg Cutlet

Top Leg (Inside) Roast

Smoked Ham

Smoked Ham Shank Portion

Smoked Ham Center Slice

Smoked Ham Rump Portion

Canned Ham

Sliced Ham

Boneless Smoked Ham

SHOULDER

Blade Roast

Blade Steak

Boneless Blade Roast

Smoked Shoulder Roll

Boneless Arm Picnic Roast

Smoked Hocks

Smoked Picnic

LOIN

Blade Chop

Rib Chop
Broil, Panbroil.

Top Loin Chop

Loin Chop

Sirloin Chop

Butterfly Chop

Sirloin Cutlet

Back Ribs

Country-Style Ribs

Tenderloin

Center Rib Roast

Top Loin Roast (Double)

Blade Roast

Boneless Blade Roast

Sirloin Roast

Crown Roast

Boneless Sirloin Roast

Smoked Loin Chop

Center Loin Roast

Canadian-Style Bacon

SIDE

Spareribs

Sliced Bacon

OTHER CUTS

Cubed Steak

Pork Pieces

Cubes for Kabobs

Ground Pork

Sausage Links

THIS CHART APPROVED BY
NATIONAL LIVE STOCK & MEAT BOARD

1185250   0·-407

Veal

· RETAIL CUTS ·
WHERE THEY COME FROM
HOW TO COOK THEM

LEG (ROUND)
SIRLOIN
LOIN
RIB
SHOULDER
FORESHANK & BREAST

RIB

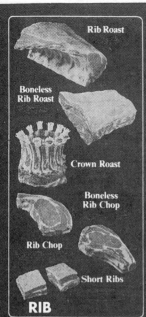

Rib Roast

Boneless Rib Roast

Crown Roast

Boneless Rib Chop

Rib Chop

Short Ribs

SHOULDER

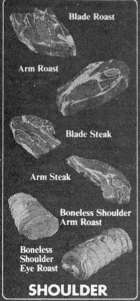

Blade Roast

Arm Roast

Blade Steak

Arm Steak

Boneless Shoulder Arm Roast

Boneless Shoulder Eye Roast

LEG (ROUND)

Boneless Rump Roast

Round Steak

Top Round Steak

Leg Cutlet

FORESHANK & BREAST

Breast

Boneless Breast Roast

Cross Cut Shank

Riblet

Shank

THIS CHART APPROVED BY
NATIONAL LIVE STOCK & MEAT BOARD

LOIN

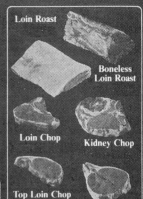

Loin Roast

Boneless Loin Roast

Loin Chop

Kidney Chop

Top Loin Chop

Butterfly Chop

SIRLOIN

Sirloin Roast

Boneless Sirloin Roast

Sirloin Steak

Top Sirloin Steak

OTHER CUTS

Veal for Stew

Ground Veal

Cubes for Kabobs

Cubed Steak

Beef

· RETAIL CUTS ·
WHERE THEY COME FROM
HOW TO COOK THEM

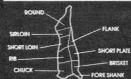

ROUND
SIRLOIN
SHORT LOIN
RIB
CHUCK
FLANK
SHORT PLATE
BRISKET
FORE SHANK

ROUND

Round Steak

Top Round Roast

Top Round Steak

Boneless Rump Roast

Bottom Round Roast

Tip Roast, Cap Off

Eye Round Roast

Tip Steak

SIRLOIN

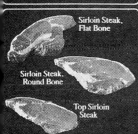

Sirloin Steak, Flat Bone

Sirloin Steak, Round Bone

Top Sirloin Steak

FORE SHANK & BRISKET

Shank Cross Cut

Brisket, Whole

Corned Brisket, Point Half

Brisket, Flat Half

CHUCK

Chuck Eye Roast

Boneless Top Blade Steak

Arm Pot Roast

Boneless Shoulder Pot Roast

Cross Rib Pot Roast

Mock Tender

Under Blade Pot Roast

Blade Roast

Short Ribs

7-Bone Pot Roast

Flanken-Style Ribs

SHORT LOIN

Boneless Top Loin Steak

T-Bone Steak

Porterhouse Steak

Tenderloin Roast

Tenderloin Steak

RIB

Rib Roast, Large End

Rib Roast, Small End

Rib Steak, Small End

Rib Eye Roast

Rib Eye Steak

Back Ribs

FLANK & SHORT PLATE

Flank Steak

Flank Steak Rolls

Skirt Steak

OTHER CUTS

Ground Beef

Cubed Steak

Beef for Stew

Cubes for Kabobs

THIS CHART APPROVED BY
NATIONAL LIVE STOCK & MEAT BOARD

BIBLIOGRAPHY

Adventure in Mexican Cooking, Ortho Books, 1978

All About Apples, Alice A. Martin, Houghton Mifflin Company, 1976

All-Colour South African Cookbook, Sannie Smit, Central News Agency Ltd., 1982

American Food, Evan Jones, Vintage Books, 1981

American Indian Food and Lore, Carolyn Neithammer, Collier Books, 1974

American Table, The, Ronald Johnson, William Morrow, 1984

American Taste, James Villas, Arbor House, 1982

Art of Eating, The, M. F. K. Fisher, Macmillan Publishing Company, 1954

Art of Good Cooking, The, Paula Peck, Simon & Schuster, Inc., 1966

Art of Making Sausage, Pâtés, and Other Charcuterie, Jane Grigson, Knopf, 1976

Art of Turkish Cooking, The, Neset Eren, Doubleday, 1969

Beard on Food, James Beard, Alfred A. Knopf, 1974

Bert Greene's Kitchen Bouquets, Bert Greene, Simon & Schuster, Inc., 1979

Best of German Cooking, Edda Meyer-Berkhout, HPBooks, 1984

Best of Russian Cooking, The, Alexandra Kropotkin, Charles Scribner, 1964

Better Homes and Gardens Barbecue Book, Bantam Books, 1972

Betty Crocker's Cookbook, General Mills, Inc., Bantam Books, Inc., 1969

Betty Crocker's Kitchen Secrets, General Mills, Inc., Random House, 1983

Blessings of Bread, The, Adrian Bailey, Paddington Press, 1975

Book of Coffee and Tea, Joel, David & Karl Schapira, St. Martin's Press, 1975

Book of Tofu, The, William Shurtleff and Akiko Aoyagi, Ten Speed Press, 1975

Book of Whole Foods: Nutrition & Cuisine, Karen MacNeil, Vintage Books, 1981

Book of World Cuisines, The, Howard Hillman, Penguin Books, 1979

Bowl of Red, A, Frank X. Tolbert, Doubleday, 1972

Breads, Sharon Tyler Herbst, HPBooks, 1983

Breads of France, The, Bernard Clayton, Jr., Bobbs-Merrill, 1978

Breads of the World, Mariana Honig, Chelsea House, 1977

British Cookery, Lizzie Boyd, Overlook Press, 1979

Cajun - Creole Cooking, Terry Thompson, HPBooks, 1986

California Seafood Cookbook, Isaac Cronin, Jay Harlow & Paul Johnson, Aris, 1983

California Wine Label Album, Terry Robards, Workman Publishing, 1981

Canning, Sue & Bill Deeming, HPBooks, 1983

Caviar, Susan R. Friedland, Charles Scribner's Sons, 1986

Caviar! Caviar! Caviar!, Gerald M. Stein, Lyle Stuart, 1982

Cheese Book, Vivienne Marquis & Patricia Haskell, Simon and Schuster, 1965

Cheese Cookery, Doris McFerran Townsend, HPBooks, 1980

Cheese Handbook, The, T.A. Layton, Dover, 1973

Cheese of the World, The U.S. Department of Agriculture, Dover, 1972

Cheeses & Wines of England & France, The, John Ehle, Harper & Row, 1972

Chef Paul Prudhomme's Louisiana Kitchen, Paul Prudhomme, Morrow, 1984

Chinese Cooking, Rose Cheng and Michele Morris, HPBooks, 1981

Classic Indian Cooking, Julie Sahni, William Morrow, 1980

Classic Italian Cook Book, The, Marcella Hazan, Alfred A. Knopf, 1973

Cocktail Book, The, Michael Walker, HPBooks, 1980

Coffee, Charles and Violet Schafer, Yerba Buena Press, 1976

Coffee Book, The, John Svicarovich et al., Prentice Hall, 1976

Coffee Cookery, Ceil Dyer, HPBooks, 1978

Commonplace Book of Cookery, A, Robert Grabhorn, Northpoint Press, 1985

Complete Book of Breads, The, Bernard Clayton, Jr., Simon & Schuster, Inc., 1973

Complete Book of Caribbean Cooking, Elisabeth Lambert Ortiz, M. Evans, 1973

Complete Book of Egg Cooking in Color, The, Paul Hamlyn, 1972

Complete Book of Fruits and Vegetables, The, F. Bianchini and F. Corbetta, Crown Publishers, Inc., 1975

Complete Book of High-Protein Baking, The, Martha Ellen Katz, Ballantine, 1975

Complete Book of Meat, The, Phyllis C. Reynolds, William Morrow, 1963

Complete Book of Mexican Cooking, Elisabeth Lambert Ortiz, M. Evans, 1965

Complete Book of Outdoor Cookery, The, James Beard and Helen Evans Brown, Royal Books, 1971

Complete Book of Pasta, The, Jack Denton Scott, Bantam Books, 1970

Complete Book of Pastry, The, Bernard Clayton, Jr., Simon & Schuster, Inc., 1981

Complete International Jewish Cookbook, Evelyn Rose, St. Martin's Press, 1976

Complete Rice Cookbook, The, Carlson Wade, Pyramid Books, 1973

Complete Round-the-World Cookbook, Myra Waldo, Greenwich House, 1973

Complete Seafood Cookbook, The, Arthur Hawkins, Bonanza Books, 1970

Complete Yogurt Cookbook, The, Karen Cross Whyte, Troubador Press, 1970

Concise Encyclopedia of Gastronomy, André L. Simon, Overlook Press, 1952

Condiments, Kathy Gunst, G. P. Putnam & Sons, 1984

Cooking of Germany, The, Nika Standen Hazelton, Time-Life Books, 1969

Cooking With Berries, Margaret Woolfolk, Clarkson N. Potter, Inc., 1979

Cooking with Honey, Hazel Berto, Gramercy Publishing Company, 1972

Cooking with Michael Field, edited by Joan Scobey, Holt, Rinehart & Winston, 1978

Cooking with Smoke & Fire, Phillip Stephen Schulz, Simon & Schuster, Inc., 1986

Cooking with Spices and Herbs, the editors of Sunset Books and Sunset Magazine, Lane Books, 1974

Cook's Almanac, The, Jacqueline Heriteau, World Almanac Publications, 1983

Cook's and Diner's Dictionary, Funk and Wagnalls, 1968

Cook's Book, The, Howard Hillman, Avon Books, 1981

Cook's Companion, Doris McFerran Townsend, Crown Publishers, Inc., 1978

Cook's Companion, The, Frieda Arkin, Doubleday & Company, Inc., 1968

Cook's Encyclopedia, Tom Stobart, Harper & Row, 1980

Cook's Handbook, The, Prue Leith, A & W Publishers, Inc., 1981

Cook's Quotation Book, The, Maria Polushkin Robbins, The Pushcart Press, 1983

Cook's Tools, Susan Campbell, Bantam Books, 1980

Couscous and Other Good Food from Morocco, Paula Wolfert, Harper & Row, 1973

Creole Gumbo and All That Jazz, Howard Mitcham, Addison-Wesley Publishing Company, 1978

Cuisine For All Seasons, Helen Hecht, Atheneum, 1983

Cuisines of Mexico, The, Diana Kennedy, Harper & Row, 1986

Culinary Arts Institute Encyclopedic Cookbook, edited by Ruth Berolzheimer, Culinary Arts Institute, 1972

Culinary Craft, The, Judy Gorman, Yankee Publishing Incorporated, 1984

Culinary Crafting, Doris McFerran Townsend, Rutledge Books, 1976

Culture and Cuisine, Jean-Francois Revel, Doubleday & Company, Inc., 1982

Cutting-up in the Kitchen, Merle Ellis, Chronicle Books, 1975

Dairy Cookbook, The, Olga Nickles, Celestial Arts, 1976

Delicious World of Raw Food, The, Mary Louise Lau, Rawson Associates, 1977

Delights and Prejudices, James Beard, Atheneum, 1964

Dictionary of American Food and Drink, John Mariani, Ticknor & Fields, 1983

Dictionary of Food Supplements, A, Lee Fryer and Annette Dickinson, Mason/Charter, 1975

Dictionary of Gastronomy, André Simon & Robin Howe, Overlook Press, 1978

Dictionary of Health Foods, The, Jeffrey Blish, Galahad Books, 1972

Dictionary of International Food & Cooking Terms, Myra Waldo, Macmillan, 1967

Diet for a Small Planet, Frances Moore Lappé, Ballantine Books, 1975

Doubleday Cookbook, The, Jean Anderson and Elaine Hanna, Doubleday, 1975

Egg Book, The, Gayle and Robert Fletcher Allen, Celestial Arts, 1975

Eggcyclopedia, American Egg Board, 1981

Eggs and Cheese, Time-Life Books, Inc., 1980

Encyclopedia of Cooking, The, Exeter Books, 1964

Encyclopedia of Fish Cookery, The, A. J. McClane, Holt, Rinehart and Winston, 1977

Encyclopedia of Food & Cookery, Margaret Fulton, Gallery Books, 1984

English Bread and Yeast Cookery, Elizabeth David, Viking Press, 1977

Exotic Food, Rupert Croft-Cooke, Herder and Herder, 1971

Extraordinary Origins of Everyday Things, Charles Panati, Harper & Row, 1987

Fine Art of Food, The, Reay Tannahill, A. S. Barnes, 1968

Fine Art of Italian Cooking, The, Giuliano Bugialli, Times Books, 1977

Fish & Shellfish, Charlotte Walker, HPBooks, 1984

Flower Cookery, Mary MacNicol, Fleet Press, 1967

Food, Waverley Root, Simon & Schuster, Inc., 1980

Food and Drink in America, Richard J. Hooker, Bobbs-Merrill , 1981

Food for Thought, Robert Farrar Capon, Harcourt Brace Jovanovich, 1978

Food Is Your Best Medicine, Henry G. Bieler, M.D., Random House, 1965

Food of the Western World, The, Theodora FitzGibbon, Quadrangle, 1976

Foods and Wines of Spain, The, Penelope Casas, Alfred A. Knopf, 1982

Forgotten Art of Flower Cookery, Leona W. Smith, Harper & Row, 1973

French Cheese, Food and Wines From France, 1980

French Provincial Cooking, Elizabeth David, Harper & Row, 1960

Funk and Wagnalls New Comprehensive International Dictionary of the English Language, The Publishers Guild Press, 1978

Future Food, Barbara Ford, William Morrow, 1978

Glorious Oyster, The, Hector Bolitho, Horizon Press, 1960

Good Egg, The, Loretta White, Paperback Library, 1967

Gourmet's Book of Beasts, A, Faith Medlin, Paul S. Erikson, 1975

Grains Cookbook, The, Bert Greene, Workman Publishing, 1988

Grand Diplôme Cooking Course, Volumes 1–20, Danbury Press, 1972

Great Dessert Book, Christian Teubner & Sybil Schonfeldt, Hearst, 1983

Great Peasant Dishes of the World, Howard Hillman, Houghton Mifflin, 1983

Greene on Greens, Bert Greene, Workman Publishing, 1984

Greengrocer Cookbook, The, Joe Carcione, Celestial Arts, 1975

Grossman's Guide to Wines, Spirits and Beers, Harold J. Grossman and revised by Harriet Lembec, Charles Scribner's Sons, 1977

Guide to Organic Foods Shopping and Organic Living, edited by Jerome Goldstein and M. C. Goldman, Rodale Press, 1970

Handbook of Food Preparation, American Home Economics Association, 1980

Handbook of the Nutritional Contents of Foods, Bernice K. Watt and Annabel L. Merrill - USDA, Dover Publications, Inc., 1975

Herbs, Spices & Flavorings, Doris McFerran Townsend, HPBooks, 1982

Herbs, Spices and Flavorings, Tom Stobart, The Overlook Press, 1982

Heritage Cook Book, The, edited by Marlin E. Foose, Donning Company, 1979

Home Style Italian Cookery, Pauline Barrese, HPBooks, 1977

Homemade Sausage Cookbook, The, Bertie Mayone Selinger and Bernadine Sellers Rechner, Contemporary Books, Inc., 1982

Honest American Fare, Bert Greene, Contemporary Books, Inc., 1981

How Cooking Works, Sylvia Rosenthal & Fran Shinagel, Macmillan, 1983

Ice Cream & Frozen Desserts, Lonnie Gandara, The California Culinary Academy - Ortho Information Services, 1988

Indonesian Kitchen, The, Copeland Marks and Mintari Soeharjo, Atheneum, 1981

Innards and Other Variety Meats, Jana Allen & Margaret Gin, 101 Productions, 1974

Introductory Foods, Osee Hughes, The Macmillan Company, 1962

Invitation to Indian Cooking, An, Madhur Jaffrey, Alfred A. Knopf, 1973

Irish Countryhouse Cooking, Rosie Tinne, Weathervane Books, 1974

Irish Traditional Food, Theodora FitzGibbon, St. Martin's Press, 1983

Italian Food, Elizabeth David, Alfred A. Knopf, 1958

Italian Regional Cooking, Ada Boni, Bonanza Books, 1969

James Beard's American Cookery, James Beard, Little, Brown & Co., 1972

James Beard's New Fish Cookery, James Beard, Little Brown & Co., 1976

James Beard's Theory & Practice of Good Cooking, Alfred A. Knopf, 1977

Jane Brody's Good Food Book, Jane Brody, Bantam Books, 1985

Jane Grigson's Vegetable Book, Jane Grigson, Atheneum, 1979

Japanese Cooking, Susan Fuller Slack, HPBooks, 1985

Japanese Cooking, A Simple Art, Shizuo Tsuji, Kodansha, 1980

Jewish Holiday Kitchen, The, Joan Nathan, Schocken Books, 1979

Joy of Cookies, The, Sharon Tyler Herbst, Barron's Educational Series, Inc., 1987

Joy of Cooking, Irma S. Rombauer & Marion Rombauer Becker, Bobbs-Merrill, 1975

Joys of Yiddish, The , Leo Rosten, McGraw-Hill, 1968

Key to Greek Cooking, The Assumption Guild, Greek Orthodox Church of the Assumption, Seattle, Washington 1960

Kitchen Science, Howard Hillman, Houghton Mifflin, 1981

Kitchen Tools, Patricia Gentry, 101 Productions, 1985

Knife Knowledge, Chicago Cutlery Consumer Products, Inc., 1978

La Méthode, Jacques Pépin, Times Books, 1979

Lang's Compendium of Culinary Nonsense and Trivia, George Lang, Clarkson N. Potter, Inc., 1980

Larousse Book of Cocktails, The, Holt, Rinehart and Winston, 1983

Larousse Dictionary of Wines of the World, Gérard Debuigne, Larousse, 1970

Larousse Gastronomique, Prosper Montagné, Crown Publishers, Inc., 1961

La Technique, Jacques Pépin, Times Books, 1976

Le Guide Culinaire, Auguste Escoffier, Mayflower Books, 1921

Lord Krishna's Cuisine–The Art of Indian Vegetarian Cooking, Yamuna Devi, E. P. Dutton, 1987

Los Angeles Times Natural Foods Cookbook, The , Jeanne Voltz, New American Library, 1973

Madam Chu's Cooking School, Grace Zia Chu, Simon & Schuster, Inc., 1975

Making of a Cook, The, Madeleine Kamman, Atheneum, 1975

Maple Harvest Cookbook, The, Diane Lewis, Stein and Day, 1977

Maple Sugar Book, The, Helen and Scott Nearing, Schocken Books, 1971

McCall's Cook Book, the food editors of McCall's, Random House, 1963

Meat Board Meat Book, The, Barbara Bloch, McGraw-Hill, 1977

Mediterranean Cookbook, The, Betty Wason, Henry Regnery Company, 1973

Menu Mystique, Norman Odya Krohn, Jonathan David Publishers, Inc., 1983

Mexican Cook Book, the editors of Sunset Books, Lane Books, 1969

Michael Field's Cooking School, Michael Field, M. Barrows, 1965

Michele Evans's All Poultry Cookbook, Michele Evans, Dell, 1974

Middle Eastern Cooking, Rose Dosti, HPBooks, 1982

More Classic Italian Cooking, Marcella Hazan, Alfred A, Knopf, 1978

Mushrooms of North America, Orson K. Miller, Jr., E. P. Dutton, 1977

Mustard Cookbook, The, Sally and Martin Stone, Avon Books, 1981

M. F. K. Fisher's Translation of Brillat-Savarin's The Physiology of Taste, M. F. K. Fisher, Harcourt Brace Jovanovich, 1949

New Orleans Cookbook, The, Rima and Richard Collin, Alfred A. Knopf, 1975

New York Times Bread & Soup Cookbook, Yvonne Young Tarr, Ballantine, 1972

North Atlantic Seafood, Alan Davidson, Viking Press, 1979

Northern Italian Cooking, Biba Caggiano, HPBooks, 1981

Nutrition Almanac, Nutrition Search, Inc., McGraw-Hill, 1979

Nutrition Cookbook, The, Stephen N. and Susan L. Kreitzman, Harcourt Brace Jovanovich, 1977

Nutritive Value of Foods, Susan E. Gebhardt and Ruth H. Matthews, USDA, 1960

Old Mr. Boston DeLuxe Official Bartender's Guide, Leo Cotton, Mr. Boston Distiller Inc., 1965

On Food and Cooking, Harold McGee, Charles Scribner's Sons, 1984

Onion Cookbook, The, Jean Bothwell, Dover Publications, 1976

Pasta Cookery, Sophie Kay, HPBooks, 1979

Playboy's New Bar Guide, Thomas Mario, Jove Books, 1972

Pleasures of Seafood, Rima & Richard Collin, Holt, Rinehart & Winston, 1976

Pleasures of the Table, The, Theodora FitzGibbon, Oxford University Press, 1981

Pocket Guide to Cheese, The, Barbara Ensrud, G. P. Putnam's Sons, 1981

Pocket Guide to French Food and Wine, The, Tessa Youell and George Kimball, Simon & Schuster, Inc., 1985

Potato Book, The, Myrna Davis, William Morrow, 1973

Random House Dictionary of the English Language—Second Edition, Random House, 1987

Recipes from Scotland, F. Marian McNeill, The Albyn Press, 1972

Rodale Cookbook, The, Nancy Albright, Rodale Press, 1973

Roots & Other Edible Tubers!, Jeffrey Feinman, Zebra Brooks, 1978

Sausage Book, The, Richard Gehman, Weathervane Books, 1969

Scandinavian Cooking, Beatrice Ojakangas, HPBooks, 1983

Seafood Book, The, Shirley Ross, McGraw-Hill, 1978

Seafood Cook Book, the editors of Sunset Magazine, Lane Books, 1972

Sheryl and Mel London's Creative Cooking With Grains & Pasta, Sheryl and Mel London, Rodale Press, 1982

Signet Book of Cheese, The, Peter Quimme, New American Library, 1976

Signet Book of Sausage, The, Richard Gehman, New American Library, 1969

Signet Encyclopedia of Wine, The, E. Frank Henriques, Signet, 1984

Simple Art of Perfect Baking, Flo Braker, Morrow and Company, Inc., 1985

Simply Sensational Desserts, Sharon Tyler Herbst, HPBooks, 1986

Spice Cookbook, Avanelle Day & Lillie Stuckey, David White Company, 1964

Stalking the Wild Asparagus, Euell Gibbons, David McKay, 1973

Step-by-Step Japanese Cooking, Lesley Downer & Minoru Yoneda, Barron's, 1986

Substituting Ingredients, Becky Sue Epstein and Hilary Dole Klein, The Globe Pequot Press, 1986

Sunset Barbecue Cook Book, the editors of Sunset Books, Lane Books, 1973

Taste of France, The, Fay Sharman, Houghton Mifflin Company, 1982

Taste of the Sea, A, Theodora FitzGibbon, A.S. Barnes, 1977

Taster's Guide to Beer, The, Michael A. Weiner, Collier Books, 1977

Tea, Milane Christiansen, Ventures International, 1972

Tea Lover's Treasury, The, James Norwood Pratt, 101 Productions, 1982

Time-Life Food of the World Series, Time-Life Books, 1969

Time-Life The Good Cook/Techniques and Recipes Series, Time-Life Books, 1982

Unabridged Vegetable Cookbook, Nika Hazelton, M. Evans and Company, 1976

Uncommon Fruits & Vegetables, Elizabeth Schneider, Harper & Row, 1986

Unusual Vegetables, the editors of Organic Gardening and Farming, Rodale Press, 1978

Vanilla Cookbook, Patricia Rain, Celestial Arts, 1986

Veal Cookery, Craig Claiborne/Pierre Franey, Harper & Row, 1978

Vegetarian Alternative, The, Vic S. Sussman, Rodale Press, 1978

Vermont Maple Syrup Cook Book, edited by Reginald L. Muir, Phoenix, 1974

Von Welanetz Guide to Ethnic Ingredients, The, Diana & Paul Von Welanetz, J. P. Tarcher, Inc., 1982

What You Need To Know About Food & Cooking For Health, Lawrence E. Lamb, M.D., Viking Press, 1973

Whole Grain Baking, Diana Scesny Greene, The Crossing Press, 1984

Why The Cake Won't Rise, Kathleen Thorne-Thomsen and Linda Brownridge, A & W Publishers, 1979

Williams-Sonoma Cookbook and Guide to Kitchen Ware, The, Chuck Williams, Random House, 1986

Woman's Day Encyclopedia of Cookery, Volumes 1–12, Fawcett, 1966

Wonderful World of Cooking Volumes, The, Volumes 1–4, edited by William I. Kaufman, Dell Publishing Co, 1964

Word Origins and Their Romantic Stories, Wilfred Funk, Bell, 1950

World Atlas of Cheese, The, Nancy Eekhof-Stork, Paddington Press, 1976

World Atlas of Food, The, Exeter Books, 1984

World Atlas of Food, The, Simon & Schuster, Inc., 1974

ABOUT THE AUTHOR

Sharon Tyler Herbst is a Tastemaker Award–winning author of three cookbooks—*The Joy of Cookies, Breads* and *Simply Sensational Desserts*. She is President of the International Association of Culinary Professionals (IACP) and has served on the IACP Board since 1982. Besides being a food writer, Sharon is a consultant to major food and drink companies and makes regular appearances on television and radio. She lives in the San Francisco Bay area with her husband Ron.